Women and society in Greek and Roman Egypt
A sourcebook

A wealth of evidence for the lives of ordinary men and women – from texts (including personal letters) written on papyrus and other materials to objects of everyday use and funerary portraits – has survived from the Graeco-Roman period of Egyptian history. But much of this unparalleled resource has been available only to specialists because of the difficulty of reading and interpreting it. Now eleven leading scholars in this field have collaborated to make available to students and other non-specialists a selection of over three hundred texts translated from Greek, Latin and Egyptian, as well as more than fifty illustrations, documenting the lives of women within this society, from queens to priestesses, property-owners to slave-girls, from birth through motherhood to death. Each item is accompanied by full explanatory notes and bibliographical references.

Jane Rowlandson is Lecturer in Ancient History at King's College London and the author of *Landowners and Tenants in Roman Egypt: The Social Relations of Agriculture in the Oxyrhynchite Nome* (1996).

Mummy portrait of Eirene

Women and society in Greek and Roman Egypt

A sourcebook

Edited by
JANE ROWLANDSON

with the collaboration of
Roger Bagnall, Alan Bowman, Willy Clarysse,
Ann Ellis Hanson, Deborah Hobson, James Keenan,
Peter van Minnen, Dominic Rathbone,
Dorothy J. Thompson, and Terry Wilfong

CAMBRIDGE
UNIVERSITY PRESS

CAMBRIDGE UNIVERSITY PRESS
Cambridge, New York, Melbourne, Madrid, Cape Town, Singapore, São Paulo, Delhi

Cambridge University Press
The Edinburgh Building, Cambridge CB2 8RU, UK

Published in the United States of America by Cambridge University Press, New York

www.cambridge.org
Information on this title: www.cambridge.org/9780521588157

First published 1998

A catalogue record for this publication is available from the British Library

ISBN 978-0-521-58212-4 hardback
ISBN 978-0-521-58815-7 paperback

Transferred to digital printing 2009

Contents

Maps

Figures

Plates

Frontispiece: Mummy portrait of Eirene

Portrait of a young woman, dressed in a vermilion mantle over a green tunic, wearing hooped earrings decorated with pearls and crowned with a wreath of gold leaves and berries. Her hairstyle, with close curls and curled tresses behind her ears, suggests a date in the mid-first century A D, although the earrings and dress may point to the reign of Trajan (see Walker and Bierbrier, 1997, cat. 111). The strongly Greek style of portraiture contrasts with the inscription in Egyptian Demotic script across her neck, which appears to read: 'Eirene, daughter of Silvanus, whose mother is Senpnoutis. May her soul rise before Osiris-Sokar, the great god, lord of Abydos, for ever' (cf. **6.279(b)**). The subject's name is rendered in Demotic 'Hrn', which possibly represents Greek 'Helene' rather than 'Eirene'. Her father's name, if correctly read as 'Silvanus' (Slwns), is Roman, supporting the later of the possible dates. Traces of bitumen imprinted with linen cloth show where the portrait on its wooden panel was inserted into the mummy wrappings. See also Borg (1996), 30, 151.

Preface

This sourcebook originated from an idea of Deborah Hobson to make available to non-specialists some of the extraordinary range of evidence for women's lives in Graeco-Roman Egypt. In the making, it has grown in length and complexity. The editorial material and bibliographical references may, it is hoped, be of use to readers capable of reading Greek sources in the original, as well as to those completely dependent on the translations.

All eleven contributors have collaborated closely on its construction, criticising one another's work at every stage. Deborah Hobson coordinated the earlier stages of assembly until administrative responsibilities obliged her to withdraw from her editorial role. Each main chapter was initially compiled by a pair of contributors: Chapter 2, Dominic Rathbone and Dorothy Thompson; Chapters 3 and 6, Ann Hanson and Peter van Minnen; Chapter 4, Roger Bagnall and Jim Keenan; and Chapter 5, Alan Bowman and myself; I also drafted Chapter 1. The texts in Egyptian were provided by Willy Clarysse (Demotic) and Terry Wilfong (Coptic), with additional contributions by John Baines and W. John Tait. For most of the completed text, it would be impossible to identify a single author, but each chapter retains a distinctive 'flavour' imparted by the initial compilers, despite the later additions, alterations and rearrangements of material.

We have also received assistance or advice from many other colleagues, including Antti Arjava, Sally-Ann Ashton, Jean Bingen, Euphrosyne Doxiadis, Bernard Gredley, Michael Sharp, Michael Trapp, and Susan Walker. To these, and to John Baines and John Tait for their help with the Egyptian texts, we are immensely grateful. Girton College Publications Fund generously contributed towards the cost of illustrations for chapter 2. Finally, I must add my personal thanks to the other contributors, whose expertise, on which I have frequently drawn during my editorial work, has enriched my own understanding of Graeco-Roman Egypt. The book's remaining shortcomings are my responsibility.

Jane Rowlandson

Acknowledgements

Acknowledgement is made to the following for permission to reproduce illustrations:

Kelsey Museum, Ann Arbor   Plates 11, 16–23, 38, 45, 46
University of Michigan Library, Ann Arbor   Plates 30, 41
Benaki Museum, Athens   Plate 39
Ägyptisches Museum und Papyrussammlung, Staatliche Museen zu Berlin   Plates 10, 14, 47
Musées Royaux d'Arts et d'Histoire, Brussels   Plates 9, 44
The Egyptian Museum, Cairo   Plates 33(a), 36
The Syndics, Fitzwilliam Museum, Cambridge   Plates 1, 6, 8
The Mistress and Fellows, Girton College, Cambridge   Plate 34
The Syndics of Cambridge University Library   Plate 15
Ny Carlsberg Glyptotek, Copenhagen   Plate 7
Royal Museum of Scotland, Edinburgh   Plate 42
Biblioteca Medicea Laurenziana, Florence   Plate 40
Rijksmuseum van Oudheden, Leiden   Plate 35
Papyrologisch Instituut, Leiden   Plate 48
Trustees of the British Museum, London   Plates 28, 33(b)
Département des antiquités égyptiennes, Musée du Louvre, Paris   Plates 4, 13
Württembergisches Landesmuseum, Stuttgart   Frontispiece
Österreichische Nationalbibliothek, Vienna   Plate 27

Acknowledgement is made to the following for providing photographs:

Sally-Ann Ashton   Plates 2 and 5
Margarete Büsing   Plate 10
Revel Coles   Plate 15
Euphrosyne Doxiadis   Plate 39
Machteld Mellink   Plate 3

Abbreviations

Full details of works cited by author and date may be found in the Bibliography. Most ancient texts are cited by their standard abbreviations: for papyri and related works, see J. F. Oates et al., *Checklist of Editions of Greek and Latin Papyri, Ostraca and Tablets*, fourth edn (*BASP* Supp. 7, 1992), available on the internet: http://scriptorium.lib.duke.edu/papyrus/texts/clist.html. The *Checklist* also lists (pp. 88–9) the full details of the Proceedings of the International Congresses of Papyrology. Abbreviations used for periodicals may also be found in the *Checklist* (76–8), or in *L'Année Philologique* (Paris, 1927–). For editions of Greek inscriptions, see *Supplementum Epigraphicum Graecum* (Leiden, 1923–), or e.g. Austin (1981).

In addition, the following abbreviations are used:

Äg.Abh.   Ägyptologische Abhandlungen.
CEML   F. Baratte and B. Boyaval, 'Catalogue des étiquettes de momies du Musée du Louvre', *CRIPEL* 2 (1974), 155–264 (nos. 1–259); 3 (1975), 151–261 (nos. 260–688); 4 (1976), 173–254 (nos. 689–999); 5 (1977), 237–339 (nos. 1000–1209).
Ep   W. E. Crum and H. G. Evelyn White (eds.), *The Monastery of Epiphanius at Thebes, Part II: Coptic Ostraca and Papyri; Greek Ostraca and Papyri* (New York, 1926).
Heitsch   E. Heitsch, *Die griechischen Dichterfragmente der römischen Kaiserzeit* vol. I (2nd. edn, Göttingen, 1963).
I.Alex.   F. Kayser, *Recueil des inscriptions grecques et latines (non funéraires) d'Alexandrie impériale (Ier–IIIe s. apr. J.-C.)* (Cairo, 1994).
I.Fay.   E. Bernand, *Recueil des inscriptions grecques du Fayoum* vols. I–III (Leiden–Cairo, 1975–81).
IGA v   G. Lefebvre (ed.), *Inscriptiones Graecae Aegypti* v. *Inscriptiones Christianae Aegypti* (Cairo, 1907; repr. Chicago, 1978).
I.Memnon A. and E. Bernand, *Les inscriptions grecques et latines du colosse de Memnon* (IFAO: Bibliothèque d'Etude 31; Cairo, 1960).
I.Métr.   E. Bernand, *Inscriptions métriques de l'Egypte gréco-romaine* (Annales littéraires de l'Université de Besançon 98; Paris, 1969).
I.Port.   A. Bernand, *Les portes du désert: Recueil des inscriptions grecques d'Antinooupolis, Tentyris, Koptos, Apollonopolis Parva et Apollonopolis Magna* (Paris, 1984).
KRU   W. E. Crum and G. Steindorff (eds.), *Koptische Rechtsurkunden des achten Jahrhunderts aus Djême (Theben)* (Leipzig, 1912).

Mertens-Pack[3]	M.-H. Marganne and P. Mertens, 'Medici et Medica, 2° édition', in I. Andorlini (ed.), 'Specimina' *per il Corpus dei Papiri Greci di Medicina* (Florence, 1997).
New Primer	P. W. Pestman, *The New Papyrological Primer* (2nd edn, revised, Leiden, 1994).
OMH	E. Stefanski and M. Lichtheim, *Coptic Ostraca from Medinet Habu* (Oriental Institute Publications 71; Chicago, 1952).
Pack[2]	*The Greek and Latin Literary Texts from Greco-Roman Egypt* (2nd edn, Ann Arbor, 1965).
P.Cairo dem.	see Spiegelberg (1906–8).
P.Count.	W. Clarysse and D. J. Thompson, *Counting the People* (forthcoming).
PDM	Demotic Magical Papyri, as translated in Betz (1992).
PGM	K. Preisendanz (ed.), *Papyri Graecae Magicae*, 2 vols. (revised by A. Heinrichs; Stuttgart, 1973–4).
P.Kellis	K. A. Worp et al. (eds.), *Greek Papyri from Kellis I (P.Kell.G.)* (Oxbow Monograph 54; Oxford, 1995).
P.Lond.dem. IV	C. A. R. Andrews, *Catalogue of Demotic Papyri in the British Museum* vol. IV, *Legal texts from the Theban area* (London, 1990).
P.Lond.Lit.	H. J. M. Milne (ed.), *Catalogue of Literary Papyri in the British Museum* (London, 1927).
P.Oxf. Griffith	E. Bresciani, *L'Archivio demotico del tempio di Soknopaiu Nesos nel Griffith Institute Oxford*, I (Testi e documenti per lo Studio dell'Antichità 49; Milan, 1975).
P.Tor.Botti	G. Botti, *L'Archivio demotico da Deir el-Medineh* (Florence, 1967).
Pros.Ptol.	E. Peremans, E. Van't Dack et al., *Prosopographia Ptolemaica* vols. I–IX (Louvain, 1950–81).
Rec.dém.biling.	P. W. Pestman, J. Quaegebeur and R. L. Vos, *Recueil de textes démotiques et bilingues* (Leiden, 1977).
SAK	*Studien zur altägyptischen Kultur* (Hamburg, 1974–).
Tab.Vindol. II	A. K. Bowman and J. D. Thomas, *The Vindolanda Writing Tablets (Tabulae Vindolandenses II)* (London, 1994).

Notes for the reader

Transliteration of words and names

This book is intended primarily for readers who do not know ancient Greek (or Egyptian); Greek words are quoted in transliteration except in a few cases where the significance of a passage depends on the use of the Greek alphabet, and in titles of works cited in the Bibliography (readers should be warned that many works listed in the Bibliography do assume a knowledge of Greek). A few Egyptian words are also quoted in the standard transliteration.

To achieve complete consistency in the spelling of proper names, which might be Egyptian, Greek, Roman, or a combination of these, is a doomed task. In general, we have rendered names as closely as possible to their Greek form (using 'k' not 'c' for κ, etc.), except for Roman names, which are Latinised (so 'Aurelius', not 'Aurelios'), and when it would seem pedantic not to use the Latinised or anglicised form by which the individual is commonly known (so 'Ptolemy' for the kings, but 'Ptolemaios' for other individuals of that name).

A note on the presentation of the translated sources

Brackets occurring within the passages from the sources are of three kinds. Round brackets (thus) enclose matter additional to the original text, supplied for explanation (*when italicised, thus*), expansion or connection. Brackets <thus> indicate text which the editors think has been accidentally omitted by the scribe. Square brackets [thus] indicate text 'restored' by modern scholars where the document itself is fragmentary or illegible; it should be noted, however, that restorations are indicated only where the translator regards them as substantial or doubtful. 'NN' (=No Name) represents a name which is lost or illegible.

Egyptian dating systems

Various different calendars and methods of dating were employed in Egypt during the period covered by this book. The Egyptian year consisted of twelve months of thirty days, followed by five intercalary ('epagomenal') days. From the reign of Augustus, a sixth intercalary day was added every fourth year to preserve the correct relationship with the astronomical solar year, fixing the first day of the Egyptian year (1 Thoth) at 29 August. The Macedonian calendar, also used in the early Ptolemaic period, was progressively assimilated to the Egyptian year, so that after the third century BC, the Macedonian months became equivalent to Egyptian months. In the Roman period, some months acquired honorific names connected with the Imperial house; the most common are given in the table below:

Date by Julian calendar	Egyptian date	Macedonian month name	Roman honorific month name
August 29	Thoth 1	Dios	Sebastos
September 28	Phaophi 1	Apellaios	
October 28	Hathyr 1	Audnaios	Neos Sebastos
November 27	Choiak 1	Peritios	
December 22	Tybi 1	Dystros	
January 26	Mecheir 1	Xandikos	
February 25	Phamenoth 1	Artemisios	
March 27	Pharmouthi 1	Daisios	
April 26	Pachon 1	Panemos	
May 26	Pauni 1	Loios	
June 25	Epeiph 1	Gorpiaios	
July 25	Mesore 1	Hyperberetaios	Kaisareios
August 24–28	Intercalary days		

The year is expressed most commonly as the regnal year of the current ruler (whether Ptolemaic monarch or Roman emperor); a new ruler's first year lasted only from accession to the end of the current Egyptian year, the next 1 Thoth beginning his second year. Latin documents employ the Roman system of dating, by 'consular' years (i.e. by the names of the current consuls at Rome); see **4.139** for an example of both consular and regnal year dating. Latin documents express days by counting backwards from the Kalends, Nones or Ides of the month (1st, 5th and 13th; except that in March, May, July, and October, the Nones are the 7th, and the Ides the 15th); also see **4.139**.

From the reign of Diocletian (AD 284–305), consular dating became normal for all official documents (or post-consular dating, by the names of the previous year's consuls, if the current names were not yet known), and other ways of dating years also appear. Indiction dates identify a year of the current indiction cycle (a series of fifteen-year tax cycles starting from AD 312); without further information, they do not supply an absolute date (e.g. **5.178**). For the so-called 'era of Oxyrhynchos' also used in dating, see **2.61**.

Money, weights and measures

In Ptolemaic and Roman Egypt, the standard coin was the tetradrachm (4-drachma piece, or *stater*). In the Ptolemaic period, this was a silver coin weighing *c.* 14 g, and remained relatively pure. From the late third century BC, however, monetary values are normally expressed in the papyri in the token bronze money, which underwent successive depreciations in relation to the silver. In Egyptian texts, the *deben* and the *kite* were employed: 1 deben = 10 kite = 20 drachmas.

By the early Roman period, the 'silver' tetradrachm had become a billon coin, consisting of an alloy of silver and base metal which became increasingly debased; by the mid-third century AD, it was almost completely bronze. The tetradrachm was treated as equivalent to the Roman *denarius* (which did not circulate in Egypt), although it contained less silver.

> 1 talent = 60 minas = 1,500 staters (tetradrachms) = 6,000 drachmas
> 1 drachma = 6 or 7 obols

After Diocletian's reforms of the imperial currency (between *c.* 295/6 and 300), the coinage of Egypt was assimilated to that elsewhere in the Roman empire. The gold solidus (4 g) was divided into 24 carats. Payments also continued to be made in the debased billon currency, expressed as multiples of the denarius (i.e. the tetradrachm): talents and myriads (1 myriad = 10,000 denarii); see **2.61**.

The drachma and its multiples and subdivisions were units of weight as well as of money.

Most dry and liquid measures varied in capacity according to the size of the container used to measure them. The main dry measure was the artaba. The government artaba of the Roman period was *c.* 40 litres, containing 40 choinikes, but artabas of other sizes were also used.

Glossary

agoranomos	A municipal official responsible for the marketplace, who also in Ptolemaic and early Roman Egypt functioned as a notary in a wide variety of transactions.
annona	A requisition or tax in kind.
apomoira	A tax on vineyards and orchards.
archidikastes	A judicial official.
aroura	The standard unit of area; equivalent to 0.68 acre or 0.275 hectare.
athlophoros	The title of the priestess of Queen Berenike II; 'prize-bearer', referring to her Olympic victory.
chiton	Greek tunic, worn by both men and women.
choinix	Sub-division ($\frac{1}{40}$ or $\frac{1}{48}$) of the artaba; approx. 1 litre in capacity.
chora	The hinterland of Egypt (including the *metropoleis*), as opposed to the city of Alexandria.
deben	An Egyptian monetary unit, equivalent to 20 drachmas.
deme	A sub-division of the citizen body in a Greek polis.
dorea	Revocable gift-estate granted by the Ptolemies to their high officials.
epistates	A local superintendent in the Ptolemaic period.
epistrategos	In the Ptolemaic period, regional governor of the Thebaid. In the Roman period, four epistrategoi provided a tier of administration between the nome officials and those of the province.
epoikion	Farmstead, or 'tied' estate village.
exegetes	A municipal official.
gymnasiarch	The chief official of a gymnasium.
himation	Greek cloak or mantle, worn over the tunic by either sex.
indiction	Year in the series of tax cycles of fifteen years beginning in AD 312.
iuridicus	A Roman official of equestrian status, concerned with legal matters.
kanephoros	The title of the priestess of Queen Arsinoe II; 'basket-bearer'.
katoikic land	The category of land assigned in the Ptolemaic period to high-status kleruchs (cavalrymen). In the Roman period, it became a category of private property, taxed at one artaba per aroura.
kite	An Egyptian monetary unit; 1 kite was equivalent to 2 drachmas.
kleros	A parcel of land assigned to military settlers during the Ptolemaic period. In the Roman period, the term was often simply a topographical description ('in the kleros of so-and-so').
kleruch	A military settler in the Ptolemaic period, assigned a kleros of land.
kleruchic land	The category of land assigned to kleruchs in the Ptolemaic period.

komarch	A village official.
kosmetes	A municipal official.
kyrios	The male guardian required for women in Greek legal contexts.
logistes	The main nome official from the fourth century.
metropolis	The chief town of a nome, granted full civic status by Septimius Severus in AD 200.
mina	A unit of currency (= 100 drachmas), and of weight.
nome	One of the approximately forty districts into which Egypt was divided for the purposes of regional government.
obol	A subdivision (⅙ or ⅐) of the drachma.
pagarch	A local government official.
pastophoros	A low grade of Egyptian priest.
Persian (of the *epigone*)	The exact origin and significance of the term is disputed. In the early Ptolemaic period, 'Persian' seems to designate persons with some sort of privileged status without a claim to a more specific ethnic designation; for the meaning of '*epigone*', see **5.183** note 4. In the late Ptolemaic and Roman periods, the term refers to the legal status of an indebted party who had relinquished certain personal rights in order to secure the collection of the debt.
polis	A Greek city, normally possessing the institutions of political self-government: citizen assembly, council and magistrates.
procurator	A Roman financial administrator.
prytanis	The 'president' of a city council.
quarter	A weight, 1/16 of a mina, ¼ of a 'gold piece' (*chrysos*).
sestertius	Roman coin: 4 sestertii were worth 1 denarius.
sistrum	A rattle used by worshippers in the cult of Isis.
solidus	A gold coin in the period after Diocletian's currency reforms between *c.* 295/6 and 300.
stater	A weight of approximately 14 g. Also a denomination of money (4 drachmas).
strategos	The chief administrative official of a nome.
subscription	The 'signature' normally appended at the bottom of a document.

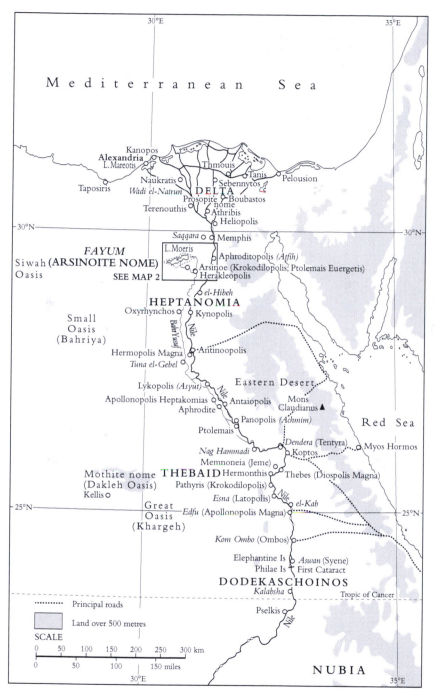

Map 1   Egypt in the Graeco–Roman period

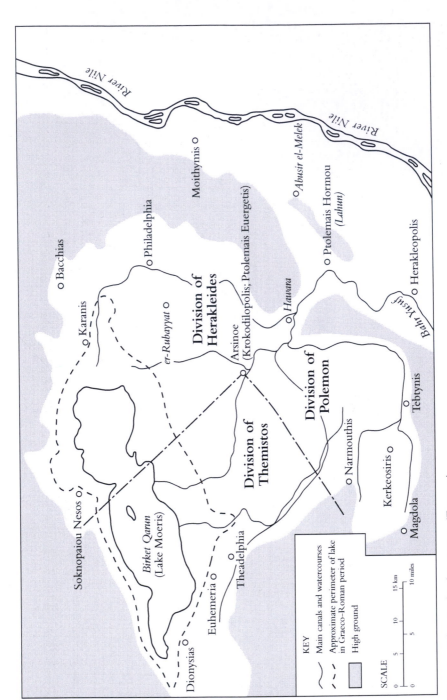

Map 2　The Arsinoite nome (Fayum)

River Nile

River Nile

Moithynis ○

Abusir el-Melek ○

Ptolemais Hormou
(Lahun) ○

Bacchias ○

Philadelphia ○

Division of
Herakleides

Arsinoe
(Krokodilopolis; Ptolemais Euergetis)

Hawara ○

Herakleopolis ○

Bahr Yusuf

Karanis ○

er-Rubayyat ○

Division of
Themistos

Division of
Polemon

Narmouthis ○

Tebtynis ○

Soknopaiou Nesos ○

Birket Qarun
(Lake Moeris)

Kerkeosiris ○

Euhemeria ○

Theadelphia ○

Magdola ○

Dionysias ○

KEY

⌇　Main canals and watercourses

⌇　Approximate perimeter of lake
　　in Graeco-Roman period

▨　High ground

SCALE

0　　　5　　　10　　　15 km

0　　　　5　　　　10 miles

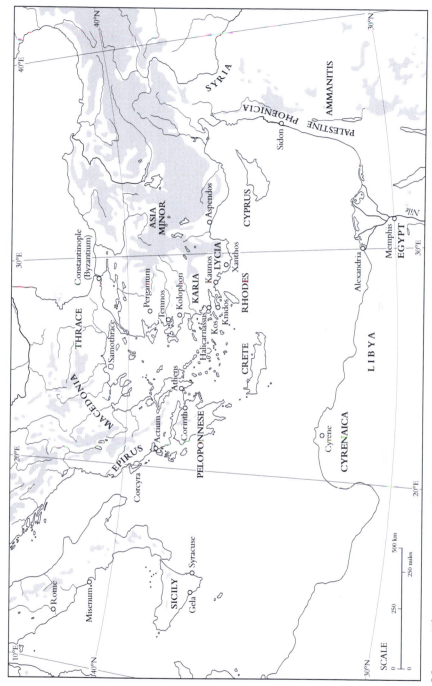

Map 3   The Eastern Mediterranean

1 Introduction

1. The purpose of this book

Ancient Egyptian civilisation is striking for the wealth of the material remains it has left for posterity: the pyramids, temples and other monuments, statues and painting, written texts, even the bodies of both humans and animals preserved through mummification. Thus many people are familiar with the names, not only of many of its male rulers, but also of royal women, such as Hatshepsut, Nefertiti, and Kleopatra, the last queen of the Ptolemaic dynasty. It is this late period of ancient Egyptian history (332 BC–AD 641), when Egypt was subject first to the Macedonian dynasty of the Ptolemies, and subsequently incorporated into the Roman and later the Byzantine empire, with which this book is primarily concerned. This period has left a copious range of documentation about the lives of ordinary people in the country towns and villages, consisting of both written texts and archaeological and other material evidence (discussed further below in section 3). This evidence depicts a culturally heterogeneous society formed by the interaction of the traditional Egyptian civilisation, which had been subject both to Near Eastern and African influence and to classical Greek and Roman culture.

The material collected in this sourcebook, documenting the lives of women in Ptolemaic and Roman Egypt,[1] reflects the complexity of this cultural interaction, and thus provides a body of evidence of great interest for students of ancient history (whether Greek, Roman or Near Eastern); social, cultural and gender history; and for anyone interested generally in the history of women or of ancient society. This introductory chapter, and the introductions and notes in subsequent chapters, are intended to make the

---

[1] Although not all the texts derive from Egypt (the texts of most Greek authors cited were preserved through the manuscript tradition, not through papyri from Egypt, and **6.238** is taken from a school book probably from the western Roman empire), they do all in some way bear on the lives of women in Egypt. Papyri or similar texts relating to women in other parts of the ancient world are not included; for examples which offer good parallels to the material collected here, see *P.Babatha* (legal texts relating to a Jewish woman from Maoza at the south of the Dead Sea in Israel), the similar archive of Salome (Cotton, 1995), and *Tab.Vindol.* II 291–2 (a birthday invitation and letter from Claudia Severa to Sulpicia Lepidina from Vindolanda in Northumberland, England).

book accessible to readers who have no previous knowledge of Ptolemaic or Roman Egypt.

All the sources collected in this book relate in some way to women. But is it right to concentrate on women as opposed to the other half of humanity? That women have traditionally been largely excluded from political and military history (distinctively 'male' spheres of action) is no justification for an exclusive concentration on women's behaviour in those spheres of society and economy in which both sexes participated and interacted. It has been argued, with much plausibility, that we can appreciate what it means to be female only in conjunction with an understanding of what it means to be male; that 'male' and 'female', 'men' and 'women' are relational terms, which can be defined only in contradistinction to one another. For this reason, it is preferable to write the history of 'gender', in which women's and men's behaviour is explored in relation to one another.[2]

In fact, one of the strengths of the sources collected in this book is that throughout women are shown not in isolation, but interacting with others, male and female, in contexts ranging from the immediate family to society at large. This material enables us both to identify cases in which women's behaviour was not sharply differentiated from men's (for instance, in the procedures for borrowing grain, or in casting a magical spell), and to see what was genuinely distinctive in women's experience.

Thus the texts, although chosen to illustrate aspects of women's experience, incidentally also throw light both on men's activities and on broader aspects of Egyptian society in this period, from demography to literacy, governmental structures to religious practices. The editorial material draws attention where appropriate to such matters, as well as to whether a particular text is typical of the overall range of evidence from Ptolemaic and Roman Egypt, or whether it is unusual or even unique. Although one purpose of a sourcebook is to allow the sources to 'speak for themselves', to enable readers to draw whatever conclusions they find appropriate from the material included, it is also incumbent upon the editors to provide, for a readership which may have little or no background knowledge, sufficient context for each item to ensure that its significance is not fundamentally misinterpreted.

The editorial material in this book is arranged in the following way. The rest of this chapter provides general background information on Ptolemaic and Roman Egypt: a brief survey of its history and of the changing structures of its government and administration and the rhythms of everyday life; and finally some general information on the kinds of source material used in the book. The sources are then grouped into five thematic chapters, each with an introduction explaining its arrangement and general issues relevant to the source material within it. Within chapters, the sources are grouped by

---

[2] See for instance Scott (1986).

topic into sections. The precise arrangement of material, however, and particularly the extent to which arrangement is chronological, varies between the chapters to suit the nature of their subject matter. Naturally, many individual texts are relevant to several different themes, and may indeed be relevant to more than one chapter; cross-references[3] in the introductions to the chapters or the sources themselves draw attention to the relevance of passages elsewhere in the book, while the index provides another way of following up themes illustrated by material arranged in disparate places.

2.   Greek and Roman Egypt: historical background

In the mid-fifth century BC, the Greek historian Herodotus visited Egypt. At this time Egypt was part of the Persian empire, and had been since its conquest by Kambyses in 525 BC. Thereafter, except for periods of rebellion when native pharaohs temporarily re-established control, it remained subject to rule by a succession of foreign powers. In his account of the conflict between Greece and Persia, Herodotus included a lengthy discussion of Egypt's history and social customs, one important theme of which is the 'otherness' of Egypt in comparison with the practices of the Greek world. The reversal of gender roles forms a prominent aspect of this comparison:

Not only is the climate different from that of the rest of the world, and the rivers unlike any other rivers, but the people also in most of their manners and customs exactly reverse the common practice of mankind. The women manage the marketplace and the shops, while the men weave indoors; and although other people push the woof upwards when they weave, Egyptians push it down. The men carry their burdens on top of their heads, but the women carry them on their shoulders. The women urinate standing up, but the men squat down. They do their eating outside in the streets, but defecate inside their houses; on the grounds that what is shameful yet necessary should be carried out secretly, while what is not shameful should be done in the open. A woman cannot serve in the priestly office of any deity, whether male or female, but men serve as priests to all, gods and goddesses. Sons need not take care of their parents unless they choose, but daughters must do so, even if they are unwilling.

While there is clearly more to this theme of reversal than mere literal description, some of the points of contrast reflect real differences of gender roles between traditional Egyptian and Greek society.[4]

---

[3] References to texts in the same chapter simply give the number of the text (e.g. **236**); those to texts in other chapters cite both chapter and text (e.g. **6.236**). References to chapter 3 may be to an archive (see below) rather than a single text (e.g. **Ch.3 Arch. H**).

[4] Herodotus, *Histories*, II.35; on the accuracy or otherwise of Herodotus' description, see Lloyd (1976), 146–52. For women in Pharaonic Egyptian society, see Lesko (1989) parts I and II, Robins (1993), Tyldesley (1994), Capel and Markoe (1996).

The climate and ecology would indeed also appear strange to a visitor from the Mediterranean. Since prehistoric times, rainfall in Egypt has been negligible; instead the country was totally dependent for water on the river Nile and its annual flood, which inundated the entire valley for a month or two in summer, leaving towns and villages raised on mounds like islands. As the water receded, depositing a layer of fertile silt on the fields, farmers sowed their seed in the damp earth for crops to be harvested the following spring. Thus the Egyptians divided the year into three, not four, seasons: *akhet*, the flood, *peret*, the sowing, and *shemu*, the harvest. The religious calendar of ritual and festivals also followed the rhythm of the Nile, reflecting anxieties that the flood might be insufficient or excessive.

The Nile, too, dictates the regional structure of Egypt, which has a long, narrow strip of cultivable land over 600 miles along the valley, fanning out in the north where the Nile splits into a broad delta. Despite the ease of transport and communication provided by the river, Egypt was perceived as the union of two distinct areas: Upper (southern) Egypt, focussed on the great religious centre of Thebes (modern Luxor), and Lower (northern) Egypt with its most important city, Memphis, just south of the apex of the Delta. To east and west, the boundary between valley and desert is remarkably sharp; immediately the ground rises, it turns from fertile green to barren rock or sand. Some towns and villages, as well as many tombs and necropoleis for the dead, lay just beyond the cultivated area on the desert edge. A little further out the monks of late antiquity sited their hermits' cells. Routes radiated from the valley across the desert: to the Red Sea (important for trade with the east), and the stone quarries in the mountains of the eastern desert, exploited by rulers from native pharaohs to Roman emperors; and to the oases of the western desert.

At the time of Herodotus' visit, there were already Greeks living in Egypt: since the seventh century BC, they had been attracted to the country as traders and mercenaries. Indeed, a Greek city called Naukratis had been founded in the Delta as a port of trade; from here, according to Herodotus (II.134–5), came a famous *hetaira* (courtesan) Rhodopis who was bought by the poet Sappho's brother. The city of Memphis, a major economic as well as religious centre, included many Greeks in its cosmopolitan population.

Persian rule seems to have been bitterly resented by the Egyptians, and Alexander the Great was welcomed as a liberator when he took control of Egypt in the winter of 332/1 BC during his conquest of the Persian empire. Alexander conciliated the Egyptians by sacrificing to the native gods, held games at Memphis, which would have pleased the Greeks living there, and found time to journey through the desert to the Siwah oasis, to consult the oracle of Ammon, from which (according to later accounts) he learnt that he was the son of Zeus. But for Egypt, the most substantial legacy of his visit was his foundation of Alexandria on the Mediterranean coast, destined to become for the next six centuries the largest city of the Greek world, a major political, cultural and economic centre. In spring 331, Alexander departed, to further conquests and a sudden and premature death at Babylon in Mesopotamia in June 323 BC.

Alexander's death precipitated a prolonged struggle among his generals for control of his empire. The initial allocation of governorships gave Egypt to Ptolemy son of Lagos, who immediately took physical control of the country, defending and consolidating his position throughout the bitter 'Wars of the Successors' against his rivals. At first, like the other generals, he ruled his territories in the name of kings Philip III, Alexander the Great's half-brother, and Alexander IV, Alexander's infant son, who succeeded him as Macedonian kings; but these two soon fell victim to the ambitions of the rival generals, and from November 305 Ptolemy himself took the royal title, as Pharaoh to the Egyptians and *basileus* ('king') to his Greek and Macedonian subjects.[5]

From the start, Ptolemy I was eager to attract immigrants to Egypt from the Greek world, both to Alexandria and to the Egyptian countryside, known in Greek as the *chora*. Alexandria was rapidly developed both as an economic centre, its three excellent harbours providing a link between the Nile valley and the Mediterranean sea, and as a cultural centre rivalling the prestige of Athens. Ptolemy was assisted by Demetrius of Phaleron, a pupil of Aristotle, in founding the famous Museum and Library within the area of the royal palace, which dominated the eastern quarter of the city.[6] In order to maintain the loyalty of his troops in a period of volatile allegiances, as well as to develop a hellenised population in the chora, Ptolemy provided his soldiers with *kleroi*, allotments of land, in many parts of Egypt. This policy, continued by his successors, had a profound impact on Egyptian rural society, as the military settlers (kleruchs) and their families came into contact with the local Egyptian population, and often intermarried with them. Unfortunately we do not know exactly how many settlers came in total, even less how many women accompanied the kleruchs, but a rough estimate would suggest perhaps 100,000 kleruchs and active soldiers, in addition to many thousands of male civilians, settling in the chora, accompanied by probably rather fewer women.[7] Kleruchs were settled throughout the Delta and Nile valley, although because of the survival of the papyri (see

[5] The title 'Soter' (Saviour), by which Ptolemy I was known to later generations, was not used as an official title in Egypt during his lifetime. Hazzard (1992) argues against the common view that it was first granted to Ptolemy in 304 BC by the people of Rhodes in gratitude for his help during a siege.

[6] The best description of the topography and organisation of Ptolemaic Alexandria is by Strabo (XVII.1.6–10), who himself visited Egypt shortly after the Roman takeover, during the 20s BC.

[7] On settlement numbers in the chora, see Rathbone (1990), 113; also *P.Count.* (forthcoming). In addition, there must have been over 100,000 male immigrants to Alexandria, with perhaps a not greatly inferior number of women; we should expect some attempt to maintain the hellenic identity of its citizen population, although now evidence has come to light of a second generation Alexandrian citizen, Monimos son of Kleandros, who married an Egyptian woman, Esoeris (Clarysse, 1992).

below, pp. 19–20), our knowledge of it is concentrated on two areas: the northern part of the Nile valley from Memphis south to around Hermopolis, and the Fayum, a fertile area adjacent to the Nile valley to the south-west of Memphis. Ptolemy I also founded a Greek city (*polis*), Ptolemais, in Upper Egypt, perhaps as a counterweight to the enormous regional influence of the priests of Amun in the old Pharaonic capital of Thebes.

Ptolemy's son, Ptolemy II (Philadelphos), who had been associated as joint ruler for the last three years of his father's reign, did much to consolidate and enhance the profile of the dynasty, as well as to develop the political and economic strength of his kingdom, which encompassed numerous overseas territories in addition to Egypt. In these policies, he is sometimes regarded as having been influenced by his second wife, his sister Arsinoe (see **2.2**), and certainly the public image of Arsinoe, and of their parents, Ptolemy I and Berenike, was very important in legitimating Ptolemaic rule, both in Egypt and overseas, through the institution of festivals and of cults, both of the dynasty as a whole and of its individual female members.[8] The practices of brother–sister marriage and of using cult to enhance the dynasty's image continued under subsequent generations of the family.

The reigns of Ptolemy II (285–246) and Ptolemy III (Euergetes: 246–221) have often been regarded as the apogee of Ptolemaic prosperity and power:

In Egypt, there is everything that exists anywhere in the world: wealth, gymnasia, power, peace, fame, sights, philosophers, gold, young men, the shrine of the Sibling Gods, a good king, the Museum, wine – all the good things one could want. And women – more of them, I swear by the daughters of Hades than heaven boasts stars – and their looks; like the goddesses who once induced Paris to judge their beauty![9]

The praise of poets working under Ptolemaic patronage should not, of course, be taken literally, and recent assessments have in particular suggested that economic problems arose towards the end of Ptolemy II's reign, as the result of imperialistic over-extension.[10] But the papyri written in Greek, which survive in large numbers from about 260 BC onwards, suggest a spate of activity by officials and other immigrants devoted to consolidating the economic and administrative organisation of Egypt, in the common interest of the royal revenues and the individuals themselves.

Over its long history, Pharaonic Egypt had developed a relatively complex and sophisticated administrative structure. The collection and distribution of revenues by officials were recorded meticulously by the scribes, who occupied a highly regarded position in Egyptian society. These procedures

---

[8] See further **2.3–6**. It is notable that several queens seem to have achieved some genuine popularity as goddesses, whereas cults were not established to individual male members of the dynasty. The cult of Ptolemy I and Berenike (the 'Theoi Soteres') was originally distinct from the main dynastic cult, but was joined to it under Ptolemy IV.

[9] Herodas, *Mimes* 1, lines 26–35; cf. Theokritos, *Idyll* 17 for an encomium of Ptolemaic power. On Herodas, see **6.289**; on Theokritos, **6.262**.   [10] Turner (1984).

were facilitated by the division of the country into some forty administrative districts, called *nomes*. Like the Persians before them, the Ptolemies did not entirely replace this traditional bureaucratic structure, preferring to modify it to suit their needs. The nome remained the basic administrative area, while the traditional scribal and revenue-collecting functions were preserved in officials operating at the level of the nome or of its subdivisions, the toparchy and village; such as the *basilikogrammateus* (royal scribe), *komogrammateus* (village scribe) and komarch.[11] The names of these officials may suggest to the modern bureaucratic mind a clear demarcation both of function and of physical scope of competence, but the documents show that in practice the competence of officials was much more fluid than this implies, with several officials often co-operating in a particular task. At nome-level, new officials were also introduced: the *oikonomos* (steward), whose Greek title reminds us that from one perspective the Ptolemies could regard Egypt as their personal *oikos* (family estate); and the *strategos* (commander), whose role initially concerned only the military settlers, but gradually expanded to become the main nome official. The assessment and collection of royal revenues were a concern of all these officials to some degree, and also of the checking-clerks (*antigrapheis*); one basic principle of this multiplicity of officials was that they should keep a check on one another's honesty and competence. Like other Hellenistic monarchs, the Ptolemies were absolute rulers, unchecked by any council or other elected body, and assisted by only their own appointees: the 'friends' (*philoi*), who were advisers, and various high officials based in Alexandria, such as the *dioiketes*, responsible for financial administration.

Under the early Ptolemies, the concern to maximise royal revenue and to create a kingdom which was at least partially hellenised led to significant economic developments. Major irrigation works in the Fayum (renamed the Arsinoite nome about 257 BC, after Ptolemy II's sister–wife Arsinoe) greatly expanded the cultivable area, providing land for development by settlers from the Greek world, assisted by a workforce attracted from other parts of Egypt (and abroad: Syrians and other Semites). The scale of this new development may have helped to minimise, although it certainly did not wholly prevent, resentment by the Egyptian population of their new neighbours and overlords. Two crop changes of major importance reflected Greek dietary preferences – for *puros* (durum wheat) as opposed to *olyra*, the traditional Egyptian grain (probably *triticum dicoccum*, emmer wheat), and for wine alongside the traditional barley beer. The tax revenue of ⅙ (the *apomoira*) on the vast new areas of vineyard was devoted exclusively to funding the cult of Arsinoe.[12] On oil, however, the Greeks may have had to compromise their cultural preferences; although the cultivation of olives was

---

[11]   Cf. Falivene (1991).
[12]   Only the *apomoira* from non-temple land was devoted to the cult of Arsinoe; that from temple land continued to be paid to the Egyptian temples for the gods in general, as in pre-Ptolemaic times; Clarysse and Vandorpe (1998).

apparently expanded, particularly in the Fayum (cf. **5.169**), Egypt is not ideally suited to olive-growing, and it is clear from the surviving regulations concerning the monopoly of oil production that most oil in Egypt came not from olive trees, but from various field-crops.[13]

Perhaps the most important economic change was the monetisation of sectors of the economy; hitherto Egypt had issued no coinage for internal use, operating a 'natural' economy.[14] Under the Ptolemies (and the Romans later) taxes on most grain production continued to be collected in kind, but money taxes were introduced on some agricultural produce (notably that from pasture), trades and manufactured goods, and for a bewildering variety of small personal taxes. Thus no one in Egypt, Greek or Egyptian, male or female, could have remained unaffected by these changes. The Ptolemies initially issued gold, silver and bronze coins, but ordinary monetary transactions attested in our documents refer only to silver and bronze: drachmas and their sub-divisions, obols and chalkoi. From the late third century onward, transactions were conducted only with reference to the bronze currency.[15] The currency was a 'closed' system: Ptolemaic coins did not circulate outside Egypt and the Ptolemaic overseas possessions, while foreign currency was forbidden to circulate within Ptolemaic territory, and had to be exchanged (at a cost) for Ptolemaic coin.

By the late third century, new immigration seems to have tailed off; families who had been settled in the Egyptian chora for two generations or more would mostly have lost their links with their ancestral Greek cities, and some would have intermarried with local Egyptian families. From now until the end of the Ptolemaic period, it becomes increasingly difficult for the historian to establish an individual's ethnicity; certainly nomenclature is a poor guide, since one individual could have both an Egyptian and a Greek name, used in different contexts.[16] Even persons described explicitly as 'Greek' might be of predominantly Egyptian ancestry. Ethnic identity had clearly become partly a matter of self-definition within the officially defined categories, reflecting one's social aspirations as well as cultural preferences. The ambiguities and tensions arising from such choices, which the historian can barely grasp, must have been much more immediate for the individuals themselves.

In 207 BC a major rebellion broke out in the Thebaid. For some twenty years two rebel pharaohs, Haronnophris and Chaonnophris, controlled parts of Upper Egypt. Egyptian documents from this area are dated by their reigns

---

[13] E.g. sesame oil for food, castor oil for lights (called kiki or kroton; see **3.79, 86**). See the 'Revenue Laws of Ptolemy Philadelphos' (*P.Rev.*), partly translated in Austin (1981), nos. 236 (*apomoira*), and 235 (oil-crops); and Sandy (1989).

[14] However, the deben and kite were used as accounting units; see Glossary.

[15] While the gold and silver coins remained relatively pure, the bronze was a token currency, whose value dropped considerably against the silver and gold in the course of the third and second centuries.   [16] Clarysse (1985).

(see **5.163**), and work temporarily ceased on the great temple of Horos at Edfu, begun in 238 by Ptolemy III as an act of royal patronage.[17] Worse, Ptolemy V Epiphanes was a young child when he succeeded to the throne on the premature death of his father (Ptolemy IV Philopator, 221–204 BC), and two aggressive rival kings, Philip V of Macedon and the Seleucid Antiochos III, seized the chance to dismember much of the Ptolemaic overseas empire. By an astute policy of alliance with the priesthood of Memphis, royal authority was gradually reasserted over the whole of Egypt.[18] But a marriage link with Kleopatra I, daughter of Antiochos, failed to regain the crucial territory of Syria–Phoenicia, despite claims that it had constituted her dowry.

The dynastic problems worsened: Epiphanes also died young (in 180 BC), and his two sons on reaching adulthood spent much of their energies disputing the monarchy with one another, both seeking the support of Rome which from the early second century was an increasingly dominant factor in the politics of the Hellenistic East. But Rome showed little interest in Ptolemaic affairs apart from one celebrated occasion in 168 when the proconsul Popillius Laenas obliged the Seleucid king Antiochos IV to withdraw from an attempted takeover of Egypt.[19] After the death of the elder brother (Ptolemy VI Philometor, 180–145), and of his son (Ptolemy VII, rapidly disposed of in 145), Ptolemy VIII, along with his second wife, his niece Kleopatra III, became embroiled in a civil war against his first wife, Kleopatra II (mother of Kleopatra III). The deleterious effect of this war on the whole country is reflected in the amnesty decree issued jointly by the three rulers after their reconciliation in 118 BC.[20] Kleopatra III remained a powerful figure after Ptolemy VIII's death (in 116 BC), ruling jointly with first her elder son, then her younger son, who eventually murdered her in 101 BC.[21]

In the first century, Egypt's fate became closely bound up with that of Rome. The Roman general Sulla's choice of Ptolemy XI as ruler in 80 BC failed to secure the approval of the increasingly vociferous Alexandrian populace. But the longer reign of his successor Ptolemy XII 'Auletes' (80–51 BC) was dogged by the need to resort to bribery to secure Roman support, firstly for recognition by Rome in the face of the plans of some politicians

---

[17] Pestman (1995b).

[18] D. J. Thompson (1988), ch. 4, esp. 118–21. The famous Rosetta stone contains a priestly decree of 196 thanking Epiphanes for restoring order in the country; several other similar decrees followed in the 180s.

[19] Polybius, XXIX.27; cf. Livy, XLV.12. The recent discovery at Saqqara of a group of ostraka written by an Egyptian priest called Hor, who claimed to have foreseen Antiochos' withdrawal in a dream, has confirmed our knowledge of these events, and added details: Ray (1976), texts 1–7; cf. pp. 124–30.

[20] *P. Tebt.* 1 5, translated in *Sel. Pap.* II 210 and Austin (1981), no. 231.

[21] Ptolemies IX and X; see **2.8**, for Pausanias' account of these events.

(notably Crassus and Caesar) for a takeover of Egypt, and secondly for restoration to his throne from which the Alexandrians had expelled him (58–55 BC). A Roman, Rabirius Postumus, was brought in as Auletes' financial minister (*dioiketes*) to help him in his financial straits, and the troops of Gabinius, the Roman governor of Syria, who had assisted in the restoration remained to support him. Egypt had become a Roman protectorate.

However, the final and most famous Ptolemaic ruler managed to seize the opportunity provided by civil war in Rome to restore a brief semblance of Ptolemaic greatness. Although the 'myth' of Kleopatra VII may be now easier to grasp than the historical realities, it does seem that an initial phase of insecurity culminated in her accompanying Caesar to Rome. On her return to Egypt after his murder in 44 BC, Kleopatra began consciously to devise policies and to project an image of herself designed to enhance her popularity in Egypt. In particular, she was able to influence Marcus Antonius (Mark Antony), who as triumvir and governor of the eastern half of the Roman empire had the power to delegate authority to 'client rulers', and hence to grant her control of significant parts of the former Ptolemaic overseas empire.[22] In 34 BC a massive public relations exercise, the so-called 'donations of Alexandria', was staged to divide the eastern territories (including some which Rome did not in fact control) among Kleopatra herself, her son (allegedly by Caesar) Ptolemy XV Caesarion, and her sons and daughter by Antony, Alexander Helios (Sun), Kleopatra Selene (Moon), and Ptolemy Philadelphos. But such displays merely made it easier for Antony's rival Octavian (Caesar's adopted son, the future emperor Augustus) to consolidate Roman public opinion behind him in a concerted campaign of vilification against Antony's liaison with the 'Eastern queen'. Octavian's victory in the war which followed owed almost as much to the effectiveness of this propaganda as to the military victories of his generals; at Actium in September 31 BC, Kleopatra and Antony managed to escape the enemy blockade with part of their fleet, to hold out in Egypt until their final defeat and death nearly a year later (August 30 BC) (see **2.14**). Caesarion (whose paternity made him a severe threat to Octavian) was rapidly eliminated, and Kleopatra Selene married off to a 'client king', Juba of Mauretania (the other two sons disappear from the historical record). Egypt, much too dangerous to remain a client kingdom, was made into a Roman province.

Roman Egypt was undoubtedly a 'province of the Roman people', and not (as some older views claim) a personal possession of the Roman emperor; nevertheless there were some anomalies in its administration.[23] Presumably because of its perceived threat to Roman stability (we must remember that Alexandria remained a great and cosmopolitan city,

---

[22] See further **2.13**, and the works cited in its introduction. For a general narrative of this period, see Pelling (1996).

[23] See Bowman, Champlin and Lintott (1996), 676–702 for a general survey of early Roman Egypt.

second only to Rome), its governors and other leading officials[24] were taken not from the senatorial class as were the governors of all other major provinces, but from the second, equestrian, rank. Moreover, neither senators nor prominent equestrians were allowed to visit the country without explicit imperial permission; when the emperor Tiberius' popular nephew Germanicus did so in AD 19, it was a politically sensitive moment.[25] Augustus (as Octavian was known from 27 BC onwards) and his successors did, however, allow favoured relatives and friends to hold estates in Egypt (see **2.17**). The Romans also retained a monetary system for Egypt separate from that in the rest of the empire, although the two were brought quite closely into line.[26]

In contrast to the early Ptolemies, the Romans did not encourage immigration into Egypt. In the Augustan period we find a number of distinctively Roman names in Egypt,[27] of persons who had either accompanied the military dynasts of the mid-first century (often their freedmen), or were locals granted citizenship for some service. Later nearly all the Roman citizens, apart from officials, mentioned in our documents were natives of the province who had acquired citizen status, often through military service. Normally only Egyptians who already possessed citizenship of Alexandria (and could therefore be regarded as suitably 'hellenised') were granted Roman citizenship (Pliny, *Ep.* x.6); nevertheless Roman citizenship gradually extended among at least the upper echelons of society (women as well as men) until in AD 212 the emperor Caracalla granted Roman citizenship to the entire population of the empire (see **Ch. 4 Sect. III**).

From the Augustan period, a hierarchy of status encompassed the entire population of Egypt.[28] Apart from the Roman citizens, the citizens of Alexandria and the other Greek poleis (Naukratis, Ptolemais, and from its foundation in AD 130, Antinoopolis; each with its own laws), the whole population was classed as *Aiguptioi*, Egyptians, presumably reflecting how thoroughly, by the end of the Ptolemaic period, the descendants of the original Greek immigrants into the chora had merged with the local inhabitants.[29] However, within this class of 'Egyptians' a sharp distinction was drawn between the masses and the more hellenised élite, who lived in the *metropoleis*, the chief town of each nome. Admittance to metropolite status

---

[24] I.e. the Prefect (governor), *iuridicus* (legal official), *idios logos* (in charge of the imperial 'private account'), procurators (financial officials), *epistrategoi* (four regional governors), and commanders of the legions (three; later two).

[25] Tacitus, *Annals* II.59ff.; see Weingärtner (1969).

[26] The Alexandrian *tetradrachm* (4–drachma piece) was deemed equivalent to the Roman *denarius*.

[27] The '*tria nomina*', possessed only by Roman citizens; for an explanation of Roman nomenclature, see **Ch. 4 Sect. III** introduction.

[28] See further Bowman and Rathbone (1992).

[29] See further **Ch. 4**, especially on how law applied to the different groups.

gave a reduced rate of poll tax (payable by males between the ages of four-teen and sixty-two, but not by women);[30] but even more privileged was the strictly hereditary group (by both paternal and maternal descent) of 'those from the gymnasium', or in the Arsinoite nome, the '6475 Greek men in the Arsinoite' (**3.69**). Even though women could not obtain these statuses directly (paralleling women's lack of full civic status in a Greek *polis*), they were integrated into the hierarchy through their fathers and husbands, and by passing on their father's status to their own sons.

Over the next centuries, the *metropoleis* gradually acquired the physical and institutional features characteristic of Greek cities throughout the eastern empire: civic buildings, baths, gymnasia, colonnaded streets, the-atres, and temples in the 'classical' style juxtaposed with the older Egyptian temples.[31] The emperor Septimius Severus' grant of town councils to the *metropoleis* in AD 200 completed their institutional transformation into full Greek *poleis*; but even before that, offices like the gymnasiarchy (head of the gymnasium) provided a focus for the aspirations of the metropolitan élite.[32]

The larger *metropoleis* were sizeable communities: Hermopolis had per-haps as many as 40,000 inhabitants, Oxyrhynchos maybe around 25,000. The villages, although generally lacking the amenities of a hellenised urban existence, varied tremendously in size, from simple farming hamlets of a few hundred inhabitants to communities like Karanis or Tebtynis, whose sub-stantial remains are testimony, both to a large population (several thousand inhabitants each), and to some imposing buildings. Impressive stone temples were a repository of wealth and traditional Egyptian culture.[33] Although we know of no village gymnasia in the Roman period, some villages possessed baths, patronised by women as well as men.[34] Private houses, in both vil-lages and *metropoleis*, were closely packed on narrow and often crooked streets, and were constructed of unbaked mud brick; but this material is well suited to the dry Egyptian climate, and can support buildings several storeys high, with cool underground vaults for storage (**Plates 20–2**).

One respect in which Egypt remained different from most other provinces of the empire was in the continuation from the Ptolemaic period of the nome-based system of regional administration. The titles of many officials were retained under Roman rule, although their functions were often modified: thus the strategos was the main (civil) official, assisted by the

---

[30] See Bagnall and Frier (1994), 27.
[31] See Bagnall (1993a), ch. 2, for a description of the town-centres' appearance.
[32] See Lewis (1983), ch. 3. Women may occasionally have served as gymnasiarchs: e.g. *P.Amh.* II 64.6, *SB* XVI 12235; see Casarico (1982), and cf. van Bremen (1996), 68–73 on other eastern provinces.
[33] Village size: Rathbone (1990), 124–37. Remains at Karanis: Husselman (1979); Tebtynis: Gallazzi (1994), Gallazzi and Hadji-Minaglou (1989). Compare the wealth of the temple at Pela in the Oxyrhynchite nome: *P.Oxy.* XLIX 3473.
[34] **6.254**; cf. **4.130** and **Plate 25**.

royal scribe. An important concern of these officials continued to be the assessment and collection of the land taxes in kind, in conjunction with the village officials and the men in charge of the village granaries, the *sitologoi*. As in the Ptolemaic period, the strategos had responsibility for settling disputes at nome level in response to the large numbers of petitions of complaint. He would attempt to resolve the problem by ordering the appropriate action, if necessary summoning the parties involved to a formal court hearing. More important cases might be considered by the *epistrategos*, or by the prefect himself at his annual assize.[35] The strategoi and royal scribes were drawn from the Alexandrian or metropolitan élites, and would normally be substantial landowners. They held office in nomes away from their homes and estates, to minimise potential conflicts of interest.[36]

Under Roman rule the bureaucratic tradition reached a peak of systematisation. Everybody and everything were counted and recorded: the human population through the house-to-house census (used as the basis for the poll tax) and declarations of birth and death, their property through declarations to the *bibliophylakes* (property-record keepers) and various kinds of land register, their animals through declarations of livestock. Even if the ultimate stimulus was the government's desire to get its taxes, there were some pay-offs for private individuals (as there are for the historian!), who gained a more secure title to their property through the plethora of documentation. Copies and records of legal contracts were assiduously kept (if not eaten by worms) in village record-offices, *grapheia*, or in the various record-offices of the *metropoleis* or in the central archives at Alexandria.[37]

All documents relating to the civil administration were written in Greek; Latin was used only within the army, and for wills and some other documents relating to Roman citizens.[38] The Egyptian Demotic script was still used for some private legal contracts at the beginning of the Roman period, but its use apparently shrank rapidly, continuing a trend towards the dominance of Greek which had begun even in the Ptolemaic period. The Egyptian temples themselves, with which were associated the schools for teaching Egyptian writing, seem to have suffered a progressive withdrawal of imperial (and local) patronage through the first and second centuries A D. This was probably not a deliberate policy aimed at suppressing local culture but a natural consequence of the removal of the centre of decision-making from Egypt itself to the imperial court at Rome. Although a significant number of literary and medical papyri in Egyptian were produced by the temples of Tebtynis and Soknopaiou Nesos during the first and second cen-

---

[35] See especially **3.91**, **4.138**; for the Ptolemaic period, **2.5** etc. For the administration of justice in general, see Lewis (1983), ch. 9; specifically on the handling of petitions, Haensch (1994).

[36] See **Ch.3 Arch. E** for the correspondence between the strategos Apollonios and his family.   [37] See Burkhalter (1990a) with further references, and Haensch (1992).

[38] **3.70**, cf. **71**; **4.136**, **140**; **6.270**.

turies A D, this has been seen as a kind of 'Indian summer' for the priests, keen to preserve Egyptian writings in face of threatened extinction of the traditional culture.[39] By the end of the third century, a new form of written Egyptian had been devised, using a modified version of the Greek alphabet; but this Coptic script was initially confined to Biblical texts and private letters mostly from monastic or ecclesiastical contexts; only centuries later was its use extended to legal documents.

Literacy in Greek was, as the documents in this collection make clear, an accomplishment possessed by some (particularly upper-class) women, although one to be boasted about, rather than taken for granted.[40] Even among men, the ability to write clearly tails off rapidly as we look down the social scale: tenant farmers, for instance, were often unable to sign their names at the bottom of their leases. It is important to remember that the different contexts in which writing was employed made different demands on the writers' competence: from the scholars of the Alexandrian Museum, whose annotations on literary works were preserved on the rubbish-heaps of Oxyrhynchos, to the 'slow writers' who with difficulty appended clumsy signatures to documents whose official or legal jargon they may or may not have comprehended. It was normal for even fluent writers to use a scribe to draw up the body of documents, and even letters, adding their 'subscription' (authentication and signature) at the end. It is perhaps surprising that even men or women who could not read might apparently use written communication on a regular basis.

The third century A D, often labelled a period of 'crisis' and decline in the Roman empire, in Egypt paradoxically appears to mark the full development of the *metropoleis* as prosperous, hellenised cities, their upper classes competing for prestige with conspicuous generosity, the 'euergetism' which in cities of the other eastern provinces reached its apogee somewhat earlier. For example, the wealthy landowner Aurelius Horion gained permission from Septimius Severus to provide a benefaction funding annual gymnastic contests for young men in Oxyrhynchos, and to support the impoverished villages of the nome, where he and his sons owned estates. Some fifty years later, his granddaughter Calpurnia Herakleia alias Eudamia was herself an extremely wealthy landowner; but the texts which mention her hint both at wider economic problems and administrative efforts to relieve them.[41]

Papyri from the mid-third century show several attempts at administrative change, with the eclipse of some older procedures and officials, and the introduction of new ones, such as the replacement of *sitologoi* by *dekaprotoi* to oversee the grain collection. But throughout the half-century from the

---

[39] See further on Egyptian language and the temples, Bagnall (1993a), 235ff., 261ff., with further references, especially to Zauzich (1983) and Tait (1992); see also Lewis (1993).

[40] More detail in **Ch.6 Sect. II** introduction.

[41] A grain shortage, and inadequate inundation: **5.174**. Horion's benefactions: *P. Oxy.* IV 705; cf. Bowman (1992). On third-century Egypt generally, see Johnson (1950).

death of Severus Alexander in 235 to the accession of Diocletian in 284, the rapid turn-over of emperors, the appearance of rivals controlling parts of the empire, and threats from external enemies, especially Sassanid Persia, gravely undermined all efforts to improve administrative efficiency and continuity. From 270, Egypt was briefly in the sphere of the Palmyrene dynasts Zenobia and her son Vaballathus, until recovered by Aurelian in 272. The frequent changes of ruler occasionally posed difficulties for scribes, who dated documents by the regnal year of the reigning emperor, but everyday life in Egypt was not severely affected. Like the earlier Roman civil wars (AD 68–9, 193–4) the political upheavals of the third century caused less disruption for the population of Egypt than the domestic conflicts of the Ptolemaic royal house had done.

Similarly, for most Egyptians, the economic effects of currency depreciation and price rises appear to have been less drastic than a modern reader might expect, since much wealth was held in land or grain stocks rather than deposits of money (cf. **5.175**). A sharp rise in prices occurred around 274/5, after a progressive depreciation of the silver coinage since the Severan period which left the currency with virtually no silver content at all. This primarily affected the government, which responded by adding requisitions in kind to supplement its money taxes. Despite attempts at currency reform by both Aurelian and Diocletian, price inflation in the debased coin grew more severe through the fourth century, although Diocletian succeeded in introducing a stable (because quite pure) gold currency, based on the *aureus* or *solidus*.[42] Diocletian also carried out an empire-wide reorganisation of tax assessment. In Egypt the complex system of land 'categories' which had previously formed the basis for the taxation of land (see **Ch.5 Sect. I** introduction) was replaced by a simpler categorisation of land into 'private' or 'public' (both now in fact in private ownership; the 'public' land merely paid a higher rate of tax), 'productive' and 'unproductive'.

Diocletian successfully restored political stability to the empire, although his particular solution for a 'tetrarchy', consisting of two senior emperors (Augusti) assisted by two juniors (Caesars), did not long outlast him. His retirement in 305 precipitated a struggle among his successors from which Constantine ultimately emerged with sole power.

The reigns of Diocletian and Constantine undoubtedly mark a major watershed in the history of both Egypt and the empire more generally, not only transforming the administrative structures and tying Egypt more closely to the centres of imperial power (especially following the foundation of Constantinople), but also having a fundamental impact on the religious life of the country. Administratively, Diocletian initiated a series of experiments in sub-dividing Egypt into two (later more) provinces.[43] Local

[42] Rathbone (1996); Bagnall (1993a), 330f.
[43] Bagnall (1993a), 63f. summarises the details.

administration was also transformed: each nome was now governed by its main city (the old *metropolis*), under the *logistes* (*curator civitatis* in Latin) assisted by the *exactor* (replacing the old strategos) and other officials, all drawn from the local curial class, the city councillors, rather than from outside the nome as before. From 307, the toparchies into which nomes had been divided were replaced by smaller *pagi*, each under a *praepositus pagi*, also drawn from the curial class, answerable to the *logistes*.[44]

The Christianisation of Egypt involved more than a profound change of mentality; it created a new system of institutions and power structures in place of the traditional temples and priesthood, whose role was already much diminished from that in the Ptolemaic period and earlier. The changed mentality was in fact not confined to Christians, but embraced both pagan and Christian in an intellectual transformation which introduced personal belief alongside ritual activity as the defining features of religious adherence. The difficulty of estimating the extent and spread of Christianity in Egypt arises not only because the intermittent persecutions (under Decius,[45] Valerian, and especially the Great Persecution of Diocletian from 303) did not encourage Christians to publicise their faith, but also because in the second and third centuries both personal names and expressions (particularly reference to 'god' in the singular) which we might regard as distinctively Christian were shared, not only with Jews, but even with pagans (see **Ch.3 Arch. K**).

Imperial persecution of Christians ceased in 311, and Constantine (in the 'Edict of Milan', 313) restored property rights and status to the Church, later giving positive encouragement to Church building and privileges to the clergy. Thus the institutional structures of the Church, which had already achieved considerable sophistication over three centuries, were further enhanced, forming an organisation parallel to that of the civil authorities. Indeed, the power of the Bishop (later Patriarch) of Alexandria was both more extensive and more concentrated than that of a contemporary provincial governor, with almost one hundred bishops and an increasing number of village clergy (presbyters and deacons) directly dependent on him.[46]

The rapid spread of Christianity in the fourth century opened up new activities and opportunities for both men and women in Egypt, as well as new ways of talking about gender roles, sexuality and the body. Christian hagiographical works provide exemplars of female continence, both sexual and dietary; control of the body through fasting offered women an opportunity for extreme renunciation, equivalent to that of the male hermits in their desert cells.[47] Such texts, while undoubtedly valuable as a supplement to what little the papyri offer on attitudes to the body, must be read care-

---

[44] See further Bagnall (1993a), 54–62.   [45] See **2.52–3**.
[46] Bagnall (1993a), 283–7; Bowman (1986), 48.
[47] See Brown (1988), ch. 13; cf. chs. 11–12.

fully, as constituting a discourse with its own conventions and limitations. While Christianity unquestionably did have a general impact on attitudes to marriage (see especially **4.152–5, 157–8**), renunciation, whether of sex, food, or possessions, was clearly not an aspiration widespread among the population at large. Many of the growing number of coenobitic monks and nuns (i.e. those living in monastic communities) retained close links with their families and villages, where they even continued to own property and to be involved in property transactions. Although monastic life to some degree provided an alternative focus to family loyalties, monasteries were not isolated institutions, set far into the desert, but were often perched beside towns and villages on the desert edge, fully integrated into the life of their locality.[48]

On the death of Theodosius I in 395, the link between Egypt and Rome was definitively broken, with the division of the empire between Arcadius, ruling the east from Constantinople, and Honorius, who ruled the west. Egypt's relationship with Constantinople was somewhat ambivalent: on the one hand, Constantinople had displaced Alexandria as the greatest city of the eastern Mediterranean, but it did give prominent Egyptians the opportunity (as Rome had scarcely done) to pursue political careers at the centre of imperial power. The Apions, a great landowning family from sixth-century Oxyrhynchos, are a notable example. Doctrinal disputes within the Church provided a focus for Egypt to assert its identity against central authority, first over the Nestorian controversy, and then over the monophysite doctrine (the belief that Christ had a single, composite, nature, both divine and human). Despite condemnation at the Council of Chalcedon in 451, the Coptic Church remained steadfastly monophysite, and became involved in a prolonged struggle with the Chalcedonians for control over the Patriarchy of Alexandria.

Landed wealth in Egypt seems to have become progressively more polarised throughout the Roman period and late antiquity. But our evidence for this is complicated by the fact that, certainly by the sixth century, the great 'Houses' (*oikoi* in Greek) whether imperial, ecclesiastical or private, held responsibility, not only for the tax payments of their own tenants and workers, but more generally for tax collection and similar areas of 'public administration'.[49] Thus evidence for the 'private' economic activities of these Houses is difficult to distinguish from their public duties. Nevertheless, their enormous wealth, and influence over whole localities, seem undeniable. At the same time, small and medium-sized properties certainly continued to exist, well-documented for instance in Aphrodite in the Antaiopolite nome (e.g. **3.116, 5.197**), a village which had been granted the right to pay its own taxes direct to the imperial government.

---

[48] On monasticism, see further Rousseau (1985).
[49] Gascou (1985), briefly summarised by Bagnall (1993a), 159f.

In 619, the Persians under Chosroes II invaded Egypt, and held it until expelled by the emperor Heraclius in 628. Even more momentous events followed. Within a decade of the prophet Mohammed's death in 632, the Arabs had destroyed the Sassanid Persian empire and taken control of both Syria and Egypt from the Byzantines. The Arab conquest was undoubtedly a major turning-point in Egypt's political and religious history, making it a province of the Caliphate. But the treaty of surrender, signed in November 641, and departure of the last Byzantine troops the following year, did not bring an immediate transformation to many aspects of life. Christians remained free to practise their faith, and continued to use Coptic (or some-times Greek) for their documents, the last examples of a hybrid legal tradi-tion now over a millennium old. The wealth of seventh- and eighth-century Coptic documents from Jeme, opposite Thebes, provides the latest evidence included in this volume. The sources available for exploring the lives of women in Egypt through later centuries are written in Arabic, and reflect the increasing influence of Islam.[50]

3.   The nature of the source material

Ancient Egypt owes the richness of its material remains to a combination of two factors: a dry climate which has preserved in excellent condition all forms of organic material lying above the water table of the valley, and a cultural preoccupation with both physical preservation and record-keeping. The survival of the written and other material on which this book draws is thus only in part a random process, and if we are to draw legitimate histor-ical conclusions from it, we must be aware of the reasons for, and contexts of, its survival. The rest of the chapter therefore comprises a brief survey of the characteristics of the various types of evidence, starting with the written evidence on papyrus and other materials. It deserves emphasis here that, although much of this was written by men, referring to women or on their behalf, some of these texts were actually written by women themselves; rarely can historians gain similarly unmediated access to women in the ancient world. This chapter concludes with a look at the material evidence from funerary and other contexts.

Our main perspective on the social history of Greek and Roman Egypt comes from the papyrus documents which have survived in literally hun-dreds of thousands. The papyrus plant, *cyperus papyrus*, although not confined to Egypt, grew in particular abundance there, thriving in the marshes of the Delta and the Arsinoite nome. The writing material was made from the triangular stems, growing up to ten feet tall and topped with a tuft of grass-like leaves. The stems were sliced vertically into strips and laid

---

[50] See for example Keddie and Baron (1991), and Walther (1981).

alongside each other, a second layer of strips was placed crosswise on top of the first, and the two layers subjected to pressure, so that the plant's natural sap bound them together into sheets. The resulting paper, which was originally quite white in colour, flexible, and durable, was sold in rolls made by glueing together about twenty sheets; individual users would then cut off portions to suit their needs, or could glue rolls together to make longer ones.[51]

Books were written on papyrus rolls throughout the Greek and Roman world until superseded by the codex (of papyrus or parchment) in late antiquity. In Egypt papyrus was also extensively used, because of its ready availability, for many kinds of text, long or short, important or ephemeral, including legal contracts, administrative records, and even private letters. But it was not so cheap that there was no incentive to re-use sheets. Some of our most important discoveries of Greek literary works come from copies made on the backs of long rolls of obsolete tax lists taken home as 'waste paper' by high officials after their terms of office expired.[52] Papyrus was also re-used to make mummy-cases from cartonnage, a sort of papier mâché.

Because papyrus is organic matter, it can survive only where conditions are completely dry, or have allowed its preservation in other ways. Thus scarcely any papyri have been found in the Delta, except for some texts carbonised by fire at Tanis, Thmouis and Boubastos. This places a very severe limitation on our knowledge of Greek and Roman Egypt, since the Delta was clearly an extremely fertile and populous region. From Alexandria, we possess only a few documents preserved after being carried to other parts of Egypt, such as the group of legal documents found at Abusir el-Melek near the entrance to the Fayum (e.g. **4.127**). There is simply no basis for studying in detail the society and economy of Alexandria and its hinterland.

Even in the Nile valley, papyri have been recovered only in specific circumstances. The valley floor itself is too damp, and the continuous cultivation has in any case tended to destroy ancient sites. The debris of ancient settlement sites created raised mounds (*koms*), which in some cases have yielded significant numbers of papyri,[53] but our evidence comes mostly from the fringe of the desert, either from the ruins or rubbish dumps of ancient towns (notably Oxyrhynchos), or from the mummy cartonnage found in desert cemeteries. Ptolemaic papyri in particular are likely to come from mummy cartonnage, since even a site like Oxyrhynchos, now in the desert, has a water table too high to preserve any material from before the first century BC. Similar considerations apply in the Fayum, where papyri (and other organic remains) survive primarily from the ring of village and

---

[51] On the plant and its use, see further Lewis (1974). On the form and survival of papyrus texts, Turner (1980).   [52] Turner (1980), 90; see **4.138** introd.
[53] E.g. Hermopolis and Herakleopolis; also Arsinoe in the Fayum.

burial sites around the periphery which were abandoned to the desert in late antiquity and the early Islamic period, as the irrigation system which the early Ptolemies built to extend the cultivated area fell into disrepair.

Another important factor in the survival of papyri is the circumstance of their rediscovery. Egyptian papyri began to reach Europe in the eighteenth and early nineteenth centuries, as part of the general market in antiquities, but from the 1880s there was a sudden explosion of interest, led specifically by the hope of discovering new classical and Biblical texts. Instead of relying for acquisition on what was brought to the antiquities market by the enterprise of local Egyptian peasants, European scholars began systematically to excavate sites known to be rich in papyri, with massive rewards: from their first season at Oxyrhynchos in 1897, Grenfell and Hunt returned to England with over 280 boxes of papyri, containing by their estimate about 300 literary items, 3000 documents in Greek, and a few in Latin, Coptic and Arabic.[54] To their credit, Grenfell and Hunt and their contemporaries energetically set about the scholarly publication of both the documentary and literary texts (although perhaps half the Greek documentary papyri recovered, and the vast majority of Demotic Egyptian papyri, still remain unpublished), and the new discipline of papyrology was invented, devoted to the technicalities of reading and interpreting these texts.

The early excavators (with the partial exception of Flinders Petrie) were not, however, so assiduous in keeping and publishing detailed records of their excavations, nor did they show great interest in the other archaeological material from their sites. They worked under great pressure of time, not least because the *sebakh* formed from ancient organic waste, in which the papyri were found, was being carted off in large quantities by local farmers as fertiliser. Even the ancient mud-bricks were taken for re-use, and the limestone inscriptions and facings of public buildings were rendered down for lime. When Petrie visited Oxyrhynchos in 1922, he found that a railway, originally intended to reach the Bahriya Oasis, was being used by the locals to denude the site of 100–150 tons of material every day. The unfortunate result is that we cannot now recover the detailed context from which many of the papyri were found, losing invaluable information about which particular texts were found together, and about any other objects found with them. The much more thorough and 'scientific' exacavations of Soknopaiou Nesos and especially Karanis by the University of Michigan in the 1920s and 1930s shows what can be learnt from associating texts with their exact place of discovery (see **Ch.3 Arch. G** and **H**), although until very recently historians have been slow to exploit these advantages. Collections of documents relating to a single individual or family can be much more informative than single texts, but often these 'archives' were dispersed after excavation,

---

[54] Turner (1980) and (1982), both based on Grenfell and Hunt's own excavation reports.

and papyrologists have had to reconstitute them laboriously. This book contains selections from a range of archives, particularly in Chapter 3, the introduction to which provides further explanation of their advantages and problems.

Papyrus was not the only writing material used in Greek and Roman Egypt. Ostraka (fragments of pottery), because of their cheapness and ready availability, were widely used for short ephemeral texts, such as tax receipts and letters, particularly in Upper Egypt, and in desert contexts such as the quarries of Mons Claudianus in the Eastern desert. Waxed wooden tablets are also occasionally found (**3.70–1**), while wooden identifying labels were often attached to mummies (**6.279**). Although Egypt is not as abundant in inscriptions as some areas of the Greek east, inscriptions are an important complement to the papyri in offering alternative perspectives. In particular, Greek inscriptions have survived from Alexandria and other places lacking in papyri, and they differ in nature and content from papyrus texts, often being intended for public display. They preserve some elaborate epitaphs (**6.273–4**; cf. **275–6, 2.26**), as well as decrees and dedications. Egyptian hieroglyphs continued in use until the fourth century A D for inscriptions on the walls of temples and tombs.

Three extended accounts of Egypt have survived in the works of Greek authors; Herodotus (see above, p. 3), and Diodorus and Strabo (both first century B C). Although these accounts, and other allusions to Egyptian customs and religion in classical authors, tend to show a preoccupation with Egypt's strangeness in relation to their own world (a notable cultural phenomenon in itself), they do provide us with useful information on Egyptian culture and history. Allusions to Ptolemaic history are found not only in the historian Polybius (second century B C; **2.7**), but also in Pausanias' 'Guidebook' to Greece from the second century A D (**2.8**); while the voluminous writer Plutarch (early second century A D) provides a famous account of Kleopatra (**2.13–14**; cf. **2.1**) as well as an essay on Egyptian religion. Philo, an Alexandrian Jew (first century A D), is highly informative on contemporary relations between Greeks and Jews in Alexandria, and Roman policy towards them, while the Christian bishop Clement of Alexandria provides useful material on Alexandria in the late second century. Passages relevant to women's lives in Egypt can be derived from many other classical sources, from poetry to science; for, despite the assertions of 'otherness', Egypt was through the Alexandrian Museum and Library very much in the mainstream of classical intellectual culture, a mainstream reflected in the curriculum which schools thoughout the chora zealously imparted to the youthful hellenised élites (see **Ch.6 Sect. II**). From the fourth century A D, a significant new source appears, the writings of the Desert Fathers, and Lives of holy men and women (the latter drawing on an earlier pagan tradition of martyr texts). All written sources, documentary as much as literary or sub-literary texts, need to be read carefully, with sensitivity to their genre and context, but they permit a range of insights into the mental attitudes as well as the social circumstances of those for whom they were written.

The archaeological evidence can be surveyed more briefly, since some of the problems of early excavation in Egypt have already been mentioned. The dry conditions in which papyri survive preserve other organic matter equally well, including items of domestic and personal use like tools, combs, baskets or shoes. Petrie was one of the earliest archaeologists to appreciate the significance of such humble objects, and even Grenfell and Hunt did not entirely overlook them.[55] But only from Karanis (and recent excavations, like the Belgian excavations at El-Kab) do we have substantial numbers of household objects with the precise context of each one recorded.

Several of the best-preserved temples of Upper Egypt are constructions of the Ptolemaic and early Roman periods, including the temple of Isis at Philae, but we are less lucky with urban sites. Hermopolis is the only *metropolis* to have been effectively excavated, yielding significant insights into the hellenisation of its town centre in the Roman period.[56] Most of ancient Alexandria now lies either under modern building or under the sea, although recent excavations, both in one area of the modern city and underwater, are likely to add enormously to earlier knowledge derived from the underground necropoleis.[57]

Funerary contexts contribute much material evidence of Greek and Roman date (as for earlier periods), from the cemetery of Kom Abou Billou (ancient Terenouthis) in the Delta to Hawara and Er-Rubayyat in the Fayum, the source of many mummy portraits in Graeco-Roman style, to Tuna el-Gebel (the necropolis of Hermopolis) and sites like Akhmim (Panopolis) and Thebes which have produced mummies of the Ptolemaic and Roman periods.[58] Necropoleis were, of course, places of activity and employment for the living as well as repositories for the dead (sacred animals as well as humans), as we see most clearly at Saqqara.[59] But the interpretation of funerary evidence poses particular challenges; what exactly do the tombstones of Kom Abou Billou tell us of the beliefs of those who set them up? And what may be inferred from a mummy whose every surface (and that of the coffin too) is replete with symbolic decoration?

Material culture, no less than writing, needs to be 'read', and requires the interpreter to understand its symbolic language. The sheer bulk and range

---

[55] See e.g. Petrie (1889), cf. Drower (1985); *P. Fay.* plates (Grenfell and Hunt).
[56] Bailey (1991); note also the Italian excavations at Antinoe: *Antinoe (1965–1968): Missione Archaeologica in Egitto dell'Università di Roma* (Rome, 1974).
[57] See Breccia (1922); La Riche (1996).
[58] See especially Walker and Bierbrier (1997), Doxiadis (1995).
[59] D. J. Thompson (1988), 155–89.

of material evidence to survive from Greek and Roman Egypt, together with the intricacy and sophistication of the Egyptian iconographic tradition, modified in its latest stage to reflect the taste of a partially hellenised population, makes the interpretation of this culture a peculiarly daunting but fascinating occupation.

2 Royalty and religion

Introduction

In Greek and Roman Egypt, as in most of the ancient world, women were normally excluded from public positions or roles. This chapter presents the main exceptions – royalty, goddesses and priestesses – and also reviews more generally women's involvement in religious life.

Compared with the other Hellenistic kingdoms, the Ptolemies accorded an exceptionally prominent role to the women members of their dynasty (see **Section I**). Like queens elsewhere, they might hold royal property, and had some financial independence; more unusually, several of them ruled as regents or even in their own right. Their prominence met with diverse reactions. Some seem to have achieved considerable popularity among both Greek and native subjects. Following the deification and death of Arsinoe II, cult of individual queens was joined to cult of the living rulers and their ancestors to enhance such ruler cult as a long-term focus for loyalty to the dynasty. Some queens, in contrast, provided classic examples for later hostile writers of the ill effects of allowing women to wield political power. The texts also illustrate how the Ptolemies, while remaining fundamentally a Greek dynasty with a Mediterranean focus, both acted and were presented, especially in religious contexts, as traditionalist successors to the Pharaohs. The situation changed dramatically when Egypt was made a province of the Roman Empire in 30 BC (**Section II**). Now the ruling family was not only alien but lived outside Egypt. Under the Julio-Claudian emperors there was still some personal contact, including possession of imperial properties, between Egypt and female members of the imperial family. Thereafter contact was normally indirect and ritualised, reflecting both Egypt's physical distance from the court and Roman reluctance to allow the imperial women to appear to have any independent public role, although they still, of course, had a part to play in dynastic propaganda. This role was restricted by the end (through Christianity) of the imperial cult in the fourth century, but at the same time the potential for direct contact was reopened by the women again being allowed personal possession of imperial properties.

Both the Egyptian and the Greek pantheons had a wide range of female deities, in both cases including major deities (**Section III**). The texts illustrate the conception, role and worship of some of these female deities. They exemplify the introduction into Egypt of new deities brought by Greek and other immigrants under the Ptolemies (and even earlier), and the tendency towards syncretism (equating deities from different pantheons). Female deities, principally Isis and some of the deified royal women, provide important examples of the development of state-supported syncretistic cults; indeed the cult of Isis became one of the most popular cults, for men as well as women, across the whole Roman empire. Theophoric names (i.e. names that refer to specific deities) were popular for both sexes; but women more often than men were named after Egyptian goddesses. On the whole, as the following texts show, deities did not have gender-specific roles (i.e. there were few deities especially for women). Women tended to worship and petition both male and female deities (**Section V**). Their ability to make offerings as individuals depended on their social and economic situation. All-female cult associations were a feature of Egyptian religion and, though relatively rare, provided some exception to the general exclusion of women from forms of public organisation. And although the chief priests of most cults were male, Egyptian cult included some specifically female priesthoods, and priestly status, which was hereditary, could pass through the female line (**Section IV**). The prominence of the Ptolemaic royal women was reflected in the creation of special priests and priestesses of their cult; these disappeared under Roman rule, and the Roman imperial cult in Egypt gave no special role to women.

The spread of Christianity and of the organised church offered women new roles in religion, which increasingly became subject to formal definition, and also introduced new restrictive attitudes (**Section VI**). Women provided early converts, martyrs, saints, and nuns, but never, it seems, anchorites or priests. Christianity also brought the idea that virginity was a state of grace, and the maternal role-model of Mary, whose cult and representation as mother, drawing on pagan precedents, became extremely popular in Egypt as elsewhere. The broader social effects for women of the spread of Christianity are illustrated in subsequent chapters.

I   Ptolemaic Queens

For the general history of the Ptolemaic dynasty see Bianchi (1988), Bevan (1927) and Will (1979–82); more specific treatment of its female members can be found in MacCurdy (1932), Pomeroy (1990) ch.1 and Whitehorne (1994). This section aims to present the different faces of some of the better-known Ptolemaic queens, with particular emphasis on their place in the cult of the royal family.

1.   Women and diplomacy at the court of Ptolemy I

Plutarch, *Life of Pyrrhus* 4.4
Alexandria, *c.* 300 BC

This episode, recounted in a second-century AD biography, illustrates the influence
and marital uses of women at the Ptolemaic court. In 302 BC his enemies forced
Pyrrhos, the young king of Epirus, out of his kingdom; he became a companion
of the Antigonid king Demetrios, and came to Alexandria as a hostage for him in
301 BC. In 297 BC, with the aid of Ptolemy I, Pyrrhos regained his kingdom.

Pyrrhos provided Ptolemy with proof of his strength and endurance both
in hunting and athletics, and paid special court to Berenike since he saw that
she was the most powerful of Ptolemy's wives and the one with the most
virtues and intelligence. He was as clever at eliciting aid from his superiors
as he was disdainful of his inferiors, and because he lived an orderly and sensible life, he was chosen out of many young princes to take as his wife
Antigone, one of Berenike's daughters, whom she had had by Philippos
before marrying Ptolemy.

2.   The influence of Arsinoe II

(Excerpt from) *Syll.*³ 434–5
Athens, 268–265 BC

Arsinoe (*c.* 316–270 BC), the daughter of Ptolemy I and Berenike I, was married
first to Lysimachos, king of Thrace, then to Ptolemy Keraunos, and finally to her
brother Ptolemy II. This brother–sister marriage, perhaps Macedonian or Persian
in origin or else mistakenly thought to be in Pharaonic tradition, set a trend (cf.
3.69 note 3). This excerpt comes from an inscription of the vote at Athens (the
'Decree of Chremonides') to join the alliance of Greek city-states organised by
Ptolemy II against Antigonos Gonatas of Macedon. Arsinoe II was prominent in
projecting the Ptolemaic image of concern for and patronage of the old Greek *poleis*
– note her funding of the construction of a massive round building for the mystery-
cult on Samothrace (McCredie, 1992). Whether this posthumous reference indicates a real influence on Ptolemaic policy is debatable: see Pomeroy (1990), 17–20.
But undoubtedly her image was widely disseminated in a variety of visual media –
coins, busts, reliefs, vases – in both Greek and Egyptian styles (see **Plates 1** and **2**;
cf. **Plate 3**).

Since . . . there are those who are attempting to overthrow the laws and
ancestral constitutions of the individual cities, King Ptolemy (*II*), in accordance with the policy of his predecessors and of his sister, is giving open

1   Arsinoe II: a Greek image
Silver dekadrachm (Fitzwilliam Museum, Cambridge)
Alexandria, *c.* 270–242/1 BC

On coins, Ptolemaic kings and queens represented themselves as 'Greek' rulers. This silver
dekadrachm, issued by either Ptolemy II (after Arsinoe's death) or Ptolemy III, portrays on its
obverse (front) the head of Arsinoe, with the horns of Zeus–Ammon, and wearing a diadem
and veil in the style of a goddess, perhaps Hera or Demeter (cf. **Plate 6**). The reverse shows
a double cornucopia bound with a fillet, symbolising prosperity and fertility, and bears the
legend: 'Of Arsinoe Philadelphos (brother-loving)'.

encouragement to common freedom for the Greeks. And the Athenian
people have made an alliance with him, and the vote has been taken to urge
the Greeks to adopt the same policy.

3.   Berenike I, Arsinoe II and the Adoneia

Theokritos, *Idyll* 15, lines 106–11
Alexandria, 270s BC

Theokritos, from Syracuse, was one of the poets who received patronage from
Ptolemy II and whose poems contain flattering references to the dynasty. *Idyll* 15 is
a dramatic presentation of the Adoneia (the festival of Adonis, a young fertility god
who died annually and was revived by his lover, in the Greek version the goddess
Aphrodite) through the chatter of two Syracusan women settled in Alexandria (lines
1–99, translated as **6.262**), and culminating with a hymn to Adonis. By sponsoring
festivals of this type (see **7**; also **4**) Ptolemaic queens helped to create a Greek cultural milieu in Egypt, thereby also enhancing the public image of the dynasty
among Greek settlers.

SINGER (of the Adonis hymn): 'O Kypris (*Aphrodite*), daughter of Dione,
you have made Berenike immortal from being mortal, so men say, by

dripping ambrosia[1] into her woman's heart. To please you, you of many
names and many shrines, the daughter of Berenike, Arsinoe, beautiful as
Helen,[2] nurtures Adonis with all good things . . .'

[1] The staple food (nectar) of the immortal gods. Berenike I had not been deified, but court
   flatterers declared that she had become immortal.
[2] Helen of Troy.

4. Divine honours for Arsinoe II

P.Lond. VII 2046
Philadelphia, *c.* 254 BC

Arsinoe II seems to have achieved considerable popularity, and was the first
Ptolemaic queen to receive cult in both Greek and Egyptian temples (see **6**).[1] The
name Arsinoe (like that of Berenike) was used for women even in Egyptian priestly
circles, which did not in general adopt Greek nomenclature. A festival called the
Arsinoeia, modelled on other festivals (see **3** and **7**), was established. Towns and villages, such as Philadelphia and Arsinoe, were named after her (this honour was also
paid to some later queens); the newly expanded area of the Fayum (earlier known
as 'The Lake') was renamed the Arsinoite nome by 256/5 BC; Arsinoe became joint
patron deity of the nome along with Souchos, the crocodile god. The involvement
of Zenon (see **Ch.3 Arch. A**) suggests royal prompting behind this initiative (contrast **5**).

To Zenon, greetings from Peteërmotis, [known to(?)] you from the
Serapeum.[2] I petitioned you then about the temple of Arsinoe which is to
be built in order that I might come here. So, if you agree, let me serve under
you here – I am not alone, but have family – so that I may offer prayers both
for the king and for your own well-being. I have written to you so that no
one else pushes in, but it is I who serves you. Farewell.

[1] Initially in conjunction with the cult of her younger sister Philotera; see Thompson (1988),
   127, 131; Fraser (1972), I 669. For the cult of Philotera, see also **45**.
[2] Serapeum: a temple complex of Serapis, probably that nearby at Memphis (see **33** and **37**),
   where Peteërmotis, it seems, had already met and approached Zenon.

5. Berenike II as Aphrodite

P.Enteux. 13
Pelousion (Arsinoite nome), 28 January 222 BC

Greek settlers, such as the husband of the woman named Asia here, might take the
initiative in spreading the royal cult, as also other new cults. For the assimilation of
Ptolemaic queens to Aphrodite (or, for the Egyptians, Hathor or Isis), the goddess
of beauty and love, see also **3** (with **Plate 1**), **12** and **13**; more generally, see

2 Arsinoe II: an Egyptian image
(Detail from) north wall of room VII, temple of Isis
Philae, 270–246 BC

In Egyptian contexts, the Ptolemies were represented as Pharaonic rulers. The reconstruction of the temple of Isis at Philae began under Ptolemy II Philadelphos, who is shown in this and other relief scenes making offerings to Isis (wearing the lyriform cow's horns of Hathor embracing the solar disc) and to his deified sister–wife Arsinoe (standing behind Isis). Arsinoe wears the red crown of Lower Egypt, surmounted by the high plumes of Isis; a miniature version of Hathor's crown surmounts the red crown, and below are the ram's horns of Ammon with the uraeus, or royal cobra (**2.6** note); see Quaegebeur (1988). This differed from the traditional queen's crown, and was modelled on the crown of Hatshepsut (see **Plate 4** introduction).

Quaegebeur (1978b). An inscription of 186–181 BC (*I.Fay.* III 150) shows two descendants of Machatas still acting as priests of this shrine. Although petitions such as this were formally addressed to the king, they were actually dealt with by a local official; there survives a large dossier of petitions all acted upon by the strategos Diophanes; see Lewis (1986), ch. 4 (and for other examples, **29, 4.122, 130**).

To King Ptolemy, greetings from Asia. I am wronged by Poöris, the owner of our billet. My husband Machatas was billeted in the village of Pelousion. He made a division with Poöris (*of Poöris' house*) and built a shrine to the Syrian goddess[1] and Aphrodite Berenike in his part. There was a half-finished wall between Poöris' part and that of my husband. When I wanted to complete the wall to prevent access to our part of the house, Poöris stopped the building. It was not that the wall concerned him, but he

3   Greek cult of Berenike II: a faience queen vase

The 'Xanthos' vase (Antalya Museum 571)
Xanthos, Lycia, after 243 BC

Several Ptolemaic queens (Arsinoe II, Berenike II, and Arsinoe III) are depicted on faience *oinochoai* (wine-pourers), used for pouring libations in Greek cults of the queens. Although faience is a distinctively Egyptian form of glazed ware (blue or blue-green in colour), the depictions of the queens are Greek in style, and many have Greek inscriptions. This example, from a part of the Ptolemaic overseas empire, represents Berenike II, the wife of Ptolemy III, and is inscribed, 'For the good fortune of Queen Berenike'. She wears a Greek *chiton* and *himation*, holds a cornucopia in her left hand, and pours a libation from a plate in her right hand. An altar (not visible here) inscribed 'of the benefactor gods', dates the vase to after 243 BC, when Ptolemy III and Berenike II took this title. The vase (24 cm high; diameter 18.8 cm) is light-blue in colour, the hair a darker blue, the lettering green, and the base gilded. On these vessels and their use, see D. B. Thompson (1973).

despised me since my husband has died.[2] So I beg you, King, to order Diophanes the strategos to write to Menandros the *epistates* that, if the wall appears to be ours, he should prevent Poöris stopping us building it, so that, taking refuge with you, King, I may receive justice. Farewell.

(*2nd hand*) To Menandros: if possible, reconcile them; otherwise refer him to me for investigation. Year 25, Loios 26, Choiak 13.

[1] Atargatis, whose cult had become established in Egypt before Alexander's conquest. Machatas, who has a Macedonian name, may have set up the shrine to Atargatis for his wife, whose name suggests an Eastern origin.
[2] For use of this image of 'womanly weakness' see **3.73**.

6.   The development of ruler cult under Ptolemy III

(Excerpts from) *OGIS* I 56 (the 'Canopus Decree')
Kanopos, 4 March 238 BC

On the death of his sister-wife Arsinoe II, Ptolemy II instituted a Greek cult at Alexandria of her, served by a priestess called a 'basket-bearer' (*kanephoros*). Earlier, in 272/1, he had instituted a dynastic cult of himself and Arsinoe as the 'brother–sister gods' (*theoi adelphoi*), linked to the cult of Alexander the Great. To this Ptolemy III added cult of himself and Berenike II as the 'benefactor gods' (*theoi euergetai:* see **Plate 3**), so reinforcing the image of family unity and continuity. The priests of these cults were cited as part of official Greek dating formulae, as at the start of this document (also **34**; other examples in **4.118–20, 124, 126; 5.182–4**).

In Egyptian temples Arsinoe II was the first Ptolemaic queen to receive her own cult, served by priests and regularly joined to that of the local god or goddess. This inscription, in hieroglyphs, Demotic Egyptian and Greek (the version translated), of decisions taken at a meeting of the senior Egyptian priests shows the extension of the Ptolemaic ruler cult within the Egyptian temples. All priests were now to serve in the royal cult, and a fifth 'tribe' of priests was instituted in honour of the current rulers. Furthermore Berenike, the recently deceased daughter of Ptolemy III, was deified as a 'temple-sharing goddess' (*sunnaos thea*) on the precedent of Arsinoe II. The traditional Egyptian ritual described here followed her mummification.

On the ruler cult and these priestly decrees in general, see Thompson (1988), ch.4, Hauben (1989); on queen cult, see Quaegebeur (1978b) and (1988); on the deification of this Berenike, see Dunand (1980).

(*Lines 1–10*): In the ninth year of Ptolemy son of Ptolemy and Arsinoe, the brother–sister gods, when Apollonides son of Moschion was priest of Alexander, of the brother–sister gods and of the benefactor gods, when Menekrateia daughter of Philammon was *kanephoros* of Arsinoe Philadelphos, on the seventh of the month Apellaios, and the seventeenth of the Egyptian (month) Tybi, a decree (was made):

The chief priests and the prophets and those who enter the innermost shrine to clothe the gods, the *pterophoroi*,[1] the sacred scribes and the other priests have congregated from the temples throughout the land for the fifth day of (the month) Dios, when the king's birthday is celebrated, and for the 25th, when he received the kingdom from his father; they have sat in council on this date in the temple at Kanopos of the benefactor gods and they have decreed:

Since King Ptolemy son of Ptolemy and of Arsinoe, the brother–sister gods, and Queen Berenike, his sister–wife, the benefactor gods, continually bestow many great privileges on the temples in the country and have further increased the honours made to the gods, showing constant concern, combined with heavy outlay and expense, for Apis and Mnevis[2] and the other renowned sacred animals in the land . . .

(*Lines 20–27*): With good fortune, it has been decided by the priests throughout the land to increase the existing honours in the temples to King Ptolemy and Queen Berenike, the benefactor gods, and their forebears, the brother–sister gods, and their grandparents, the saviour gods. The priests in the temples of the land are to be further named priests of the benefactor gods and this title is to be recorded in all official deeds and the additional priesthood of the benefactor gods is to be engraved on the rings which they wear. To the existing four tribes of the community of priests in each temple there shall be added a further tribe, to be named the fifth tribe of the benefactor gods, since also with good fortune the birthday too of King Ptolemy, son of the brother–sister gods, chanced to take place on the fifth of Dios, and this was the beginning of many blessings for mankind . . .

(*Lines 46–76*): And since, while the priests from the whole country, who
annually foregathered in his presence, were still in attendance on the king,
the young daughter born of the benefactor gods King Ptolemy and Queen
Berenike, and named Berenike, who was also immediately recognised as
princess, while still a maiden chanced of a sudden to be translated into the
everlasting firmament, the priests immediately instituted major mourning
at the event. And deeming it appropriate, they persuaded the king and
queen to establish her as a goddess together with Osiris[3] in his temple at
Kanopos . . . And after this with great care and attention they explained the
customary ceremonies for her deification and the completion of the period
of mourning, as is the practice in the case also of Apis and Mnevis, and it
was decreed to establish in all the temples of the land everlasting honours
for the princess Berenike, offspring of the benefactor gods.

She joined the gods in the month of Tybi, which is when in the beginning the daughter of Helios[4] also died, she whom her father in his love
named sometimes his 'crown' and sometimes his 'sight'; and in most of the
first-class temples they celebrate a festival and sacred voyage during this
month when the deification of Tefnut first took place. For this reason they
would establish in all the temples of the land also for the princess Berenike,
offspring of the benefactor gods, a festival in the month of Tybi and a ceremonial voyage for four days from the 17th when her voyage and the
completion of mourning first took place. And there shall be a sacred statue
for her, of gold and set with precious stones, in each of the first- and the
second-class temples, and it shall be placed in the innermost shrine. The
chief priest or one of those priests chosen to clothe the (statues of the) gods
shall carry the statue in his arms whenever there are processions outside and
festivals for the other gods so that seen by all it may receive reverence and
obeisance. It shall be called that of Berenike, mistress of the maidens. And
the crown attached to her image shall differ from those of her mother
Queen Berenike; it shall consist of two ears of wheat in the centre of which
will be the cobra insignia[5] and behind it a commensurate papyriform sceptre
of the type regularly carried in the hands of goddesses; around this shall be
entwined the tail of the crown in such a way as to show clearly, from the
form of the crown, the name of Berenike written in hieroglyphs.

And whenever the festival of the Kikellia[6] is celebrated in the month of
Choiak before the voyage of Osiris, the daughters of the priests shall prepare
a further statue to Berenike, mistress of the maidens, and to this they shall
both perform sacrifices and the other rites performed at this festival. And,
in the same way, any other maidens who wish may perform the rites performed to the goddess; she is to be celebrated in hymns both by those
maiden-priestesses chosen for this and by those who look after the needs of
the gods; they shall place upon her the individual crowns of the gods whom
they serve as priestesses, and as soon as the harvest comes, the sacred maidens
shall bring the ears of wheat to be laid beside the goddess' statue, and both

male and female cantors shall sing to her, daily and during the festivals and celebrations of the other gods, whatever hymns the sacred scribes may write and give to their musical director; and copies of these shall be recorded in the sacred books.

And whenever food-allowances from the temples are granted the priests, whenever they have been supplied to the body of priests, then there shall be given to the daughters of the priests from the sacred revenues, from whatever day they are in service, the allowance that is to be agreed by the priestly councillors of each temple, according to the account of the sacred revenues; and the bread given the women shall have its own shape and shall be called the 'bread of Berenike'.

And the supervisor and chief priest appointed in each of the temples and the temple scribes shall inscribe this decree on a stone or bronze pillar in hieroglyphs, in (*Demotic*) Egyptian and in Greek, and they shall set it up in the most visible position in the first-, second- and third-class temples, so that the priests in the land may be seen to honour the benefactor gods and their offspring, as is right.

[1] *Pterophoroi* were sacred scribes whose Greek title (literally 'plume/feather-bearers') describes their ceremonial headdress.

[2] Apis and Mnevis were the sacred bulls of Memphis and Heliopolis, buried after a seventy-day period of mummification and mourning (see **33**, also **23**).

[3] The main deity of Kanopos. This Egyptian god, with whom a deceased pharaoh was identified, was recognised as Dionysos by the Greeks.

[4] Helios is the Greek sun-god, here, as elsewhere, identified with the Egyptian sun-god Re, who was the father of Tefnut (on whom see **Plate 9a**).

[5] The cobra was a symbol of royalty, and the cobra-head fitted to the royal crown was termed the uraeus (see **14**).

[6] The Greek name for an Isis festival (which was later attached to that celebrated on 25 December).

7.   Court women in a coup d'état

(Excerpts from) Polybius, xv.27.1–2; 29.8–30.1; 33.7–12
Alexandria, 203 BC

When Ptolemy IV died in 204 BC, his sister–wife Arsinoe III was assassinated as part of a plot by a court clique led by Agathokles, who seized power nominally as regent for the young Ptolemy V. Agathokles was the son of Oinanthe, an influential mistress of Ptolemy III; his sister Agathokleia, another member of the plot, is also known to have owned a Nile barge (see **10** and Hauben (1993) on other upper-class Alexandrian female shipowners). The episode shows how women of the Greek nobility in Alexandria, such as those who attended the women's festival of the Thesmophoria and the *syntrophoi* of the queen (those 'brought up with' her), could play a prominent role in political crises. The procedures of public humiliation and killing recounted here are echoed in 'martyrdoms' at Alexandria centuries later (see **53–5**).

One scheme in particular among those carried out by Agathokles' group had the effect of heightening the anger both of the masses and of Tlepolemos.[1] They took Danae, who was the latter's mother-in-law, out of the temple of Demeter, dragged her unveiled through the middle of the city, and imprisoned her, in order to make clear their hostility towards Tlepolemos . . . (*A popular revolt began to stir*) . . . In her dangerous situation, Oinanthe went to the Thesmophoreion since the shrine had been opened for some annual sacrifice. To begin with she fell on her knees and entreated the goddesses[2] with ritual incantations. Then she sat by the altar and kept quiet. The majority of the women, pleased to see her in despair and in danger, said nothing, but the relatives of Polykrates and some other women of noble family, not realising that the crisis-point was upon them, came forward and tried to console Oinanthe. 'Don't come near me, animals!' she shouted at the top of her voice, 'I know you well – that your thoughts are hostile to us and that you are praying to the goddesses for the greatest disaster to strike us. However I still trust, if the gods are willing, that I will make you taste of your own children.' With these words, she ordered her bodyguards to drive them back and to beat up any who refused. All the women seized on this excuse to withdraw, raising their hands to the gods and praying that she should come to experience what she was intending to do to the women near her.

Revolution had already been decided on by the men, and now, when in each house the anger of the women was added, the blaze of hatred was redoubled . . . (*Next day the palace was stormed, and Agathokles was taken to the stadium and killed.*) . . . Then Agathokleia (was brought), naked together with her sisters, and after them all their relatives. Last of all they hauled Oinanthe out of the Thesmophoreion, and came to the stadium, bringing her naked on a horse. All alike were handed over to the mob. Some bit them, some stabbed them, others cut out their eyes. Whenever one of them fell, they ripped their limbs apart, until they had in this way mutilated them all. For a terrible savagery accompanies the angry passions of the people who live in Egypt.

At the same time, some young girls who had been *syntrophoi* of Arsinoe (*III*), on learning that Philammon, who had been responsible for the queen's murder, had arrived back from Cyrene three days before, rushed to his house, forced their way in, killed Philammon with blows from stones and sticks, strangled his son who was a mere child in age, and, together with these, dragged out Philammon's wife naked into the square and slaughtered her.

[1] A rival of Agathokles.

[2] I.e. Demeter, a goddess of agricultural fertility (see **36**), and her daughter, originally called Kore, who was abducted by Hades, king of the Underworld, and became his wife and queen under the name of Persephone. The Thesmophoreion was the temple of the two goddesses whose festival, the Thesmophoria, celebrated a mystery cult concerned with death and regeneration.

8. The ruthlessness of Kleopatra III

Pausanias, *Guide to Greece* 1.8.6–9.3

Kleopatra III, niece and second wife of Ptolemy VIII, was one of the longest-reigning and most powerful Ptolemaic queens. Her power may be illustrated in the priestly appointments made for her (see **34**), and *P.Köln* II 81, a dating protocol from the 'regency' of Kleopatra III (105/4 BC), shows how later she usurped the position of priest in the royal cult that was normally held by the king (Koenen, 1970). The following brief account in Pausanias' guidebook description of Athens (second century AD) is an example of the later negative tradition concerning the Ptolemies, in which the scheming power of the royal women symbolises the decadence of the dynasty.

In front of the entrance of the theatre which they call the Odeion are statues of Egyptian kings. All of these are called Ptolemy, but each has his own epithet. They call one Philometor (*mother-loving*)[1] and the other Philadelphos (*sister-loving*)[2] . . . The Ptolemy (*IX*) named Philometor was the eighth in line from Ptolemy (*I*) son of Lagos, and he acquired this epithet through mockery. For we know of none of the kings who was so hated by his mother. He was the eldest of her children but his mother did not allow him to take the throne; she managed to get him sent away to Cyprus by his father. Various reasons are given for Kleopatra's ill-will towards her son, including the fact that she reckoned that her younger son would be more malleable. For this reason she persuaded the Egyptians to take (*Ptolemy X*) Alexander as their king. When the people opposed her, she then sent Alexander to Cyprus as governor in name, but in practice hoping rather to intimidate Ptolemy (*IX*) through him. And finally she covered with wounds the most supportive of her eunuchs and was brought before the people claiming that she was the victim of Ptolemy's plot, and that the eunuchs had suffered thus at his hands. The Alexandrians made to kill Ptolemy, and when he got away first on board ship, Alexander came back from Cyprus and they made him king. Kleopatra met retribution for the banishment of Ptolemy and she died at the hands of Alexander, whom she herself had made king of Egypt.

[1] Normally known as Ptolemy IX Soter II (Philometor).
[2] Normally known as Ptolemy X Alexander (Philadelphos).

9. Vineyard of Berenike

P.Tebt. III 720 (*BL* IX 358)
Hephaistias (Arsinoite nome), 247–245 BC

Normally in the Greek world there were severe limitations on women owning and managing property (Schaps, 1979; van Bremen, 1996, esp. ch. 7), but Ptolemaic queens and princesses, following the precedent of Macedonian queens, owned and controlled in their own right considerable landed and other property in Egypt, and could use their wealth independently (**Ch.5 Sect. I** introd.; *Pros. Ptol.* IV 8523–31). The 'garden'-land ringing villages was virtually the only type of land in the Arsinoite nome under the Ptolemies which could be privately owned (cf. **Ch.5 Sect. I** introd.). This Berenike, the daughter of Ptolemy III whose deification is ordained in **6**, also appears to have had a bank account in her own name. The name of the banker is restored from other texts, see Bogaert (1994), 302; the money was presumably drawn by the manager of Berenike's holdings in this area.

[X acknowledges that he has received from Pyth]on, banker at Krokodilopolis, for the provision of 20 mattocks for work in the vineyard of Berenike, the daughter of the king, which lies near Hephaistias in the nomarchy of Timotheos, at four drachmas each, eighty drachmas.

10.   Nile barge of Kleopatra II

P.Lille I 22
Arsinoite nome, 2 April 155 or 30 March 144 B C

Because little land could be privately owned, boats were an important form of private property in Ptolemaic Egypt; queens (Hauben, 1980) and upper-class Alexandrian women (see **7** introd.) owned such barges, which were often used for the transport of tax-grain (Thompson, 1983).

Year 26, Phamenoth 4. 300 artabas of wheat.
Year 26, Phamenoth 4. Paremphis, captain of the queen's barge which is without a name device,[1] for which the same Paremphis is lessee, acknowledges the loading at the harbour of Ptolemais, destined for the royal granary at Alexandria, from the produce of year 25, being recorded through Herakleodoros on behalf of the royal scribe, three hundred artabas of tax-wheat.

[1] Other boats carried ensigns (or some other forms of marking); for instance, a barge of Agathokleia (see **7**) was marked with the goddess Isis (*P.Heid.* VI 368, of 212 B C).

11.   Land of Kleopatra II

(Excerpts from) *BGU* XIV 2438 (for the date, see Scholl, 1990, 977)
Herakleopolite nome, second century B C

These lines from a document listing revised measurements of land, including kleroi (see Glossary), subject to a variable tax in wheat reveal that, in addition to land belonging to the *Idios Logos* ('privy purse') of the monarchy, Kleopatra II held further extensive holdings in her own name. Presumably these plots of land were leased out, with the rents going directly to the queen, while the lessees paid the taxes due on them to the state.

(*Lines 40–2*): (Village of) Phys:
(Difference of) measurement of the kleros of Amyntas: (an increase? of) 3¼ arouras, 17½ (artabas of wheat?).
Of the *Idios Logos*: instead of 294 (ar.) sown, 256 (ar.), a reduction of 38 (ar.), 123½ (art.).
Of the queen: instead of 210 (ar.), 194½ (ar.), a reduction of 15½ (ar.), 51 (art.).

(*Lines 46–54*): Around Phebichis; (Village of) Sithis:
Leased land: instead of 55¼⅛ (ar.), 54¼⅛ (ar.), a reduction of 1 (ar.), 2½¼ (art.).
Of the queen: instead of 94½ (ar.), 87 (ar.), a reduction of 7½ (ar.), 21 (art.).

(Village of) Tosachmis:
Leased land: instead of [. . .], [. . .], a reduction of 4+ (ar.), [. . . (art.)].
Difference of measurement (of the kleros) of Dionysios son of Pen(. . .), from the [. . . (an increase? of)] 8½⅛ arouras, 29⅛ (art.).
Of the queen: instead of 242 (ar.), 239½ (ar.), a reduction of 2½ (ar.), 7½$\frac{1}{32}$ (art.).

12. Kleopatra VII as pharaoh

I.Fay. III 205
Arsinoite nome, 2 July 51 BC

Kleopatra VII was the last, arguably the most powerful, and certainly the most famous, queen of the dynasty. Born in 69 BC, she succeeded her father in 51 BC. At first she reigned alone, but later jointly with her younger brothers – first Ptolemy XIII, and then Ptolemy XIV (47–45). Finally, from 45 BC, a joint reign is attested with Ptolemy Caesar, known as 'Caesarion' (little Caesar) because he was, allegedly, Kleopatra's son by Julius Caesar (see **Plate 5**). The following Greek text was inscribed on a votive relief (illustrated in **Plate 4**) dedicated in the first year of Kleopatra's reign by an Egyptian priest, in which she is depicted as a male pharaoh.

On behalf of Queen Kleopatra goddess Philopator, the (holy) place of the association of (Isis) Snonaitiake,[1] of whom the president is the chief priest (*lesonis*) Onnophris. Year 1, Epeiph 1.

[1] On Isis in this form (perhaps 'Isis the great, Nanaia'), see Wagner and Quaegebeur (1973), 59–60 n. 2.

4 Kleopatra VII as pharaoh
Votive relief; Musée du Louvre, Paris
(inv. E 27113)
Arsinoite nome, 2 July 51 BC

This limestone votive relief, dedicated in the
first year of Kleopatra's reign, portrays the queen
as a male pharaoh making an offering to Isis. In
pharaonic times women rulers had been rare,
and the only significant case, Queen Hatshepsut
(ruled *c.* 1504–1482 BC), was represented as a
man (Ray, 1994). Probably this relief was
originally prepared as a dedication to Kleopatra's
father. See Bianchi (1988), 188–9. For the text
of the dedication, see **2.12**.

5 Kleopatra and Caesarion
(Detail from) rear wall of temple of
Hathor
Dendera (Upper Egypt), before 30
BC

Kleopatra and her son and co-ruler
Ptolemy XV Caesarion are shown here
making offerings to the divinities of the
temple; her crown shares elements with
that of Hathor/Isis (cf. **Plates 2** and **12**),
although they are not identical. Kleopatra
stands in a subordinate position behind her
son, although in reality he was too young
to share power (he was aged seventeen at
the time of her death). The small figure
behind Caesarion is his *ka* (spirit). See
Hamer (1993), 14–16.

6   Kleopatra VII as Hellenistic queen
Silver tetradrachm (Fitzwilliam Museum, Cambridge)
Phoenicia, *c*. 34 BC

This coin portrays on one side a bust of Kleopatra wearing the *tainia* – the headband, often called a 'diadem', of a Hellenistic king (cf. **Plate 1**) – and a pearl necklace and dress embroidered with pearls; the Greek legend reads 'Queen Kleopatra the new goddess', a reference to her self-identification with Isis/Aphrodite (see **2.13**). The other side portrays a bust of Antony, with the Greek legend 'Antony imperator for the third time, triumvir'.

13.   Kleopatra VII meets Mark Antony

(Excerpts from) Plutarch, *Life of M. Antonius* 26–7
Asia Minor, 41 BC

Kleopatra hoped to use first Julius Caesar and then Mark Antony to make an alliance with Rome which would preserve and even increase her empire. Plutarch's account of Antony and Kleopatra, from which this and **14** are taken, was written in the early second century AD, and marks an important stage in the development of the romantic legend of Kleopatra which still prevails today. Shakespeare, for example, drew on Plutarch, known to him through the English translation (from Amyot's earlier French translation!) of Sir Thomas North, for his *Antony and Cleopatra*. The first paragraph here also inspired Tiepolo's painting *Antony and Cleopatra*. Although the scene has undoubtedly been embellished by Plutarch (and his sources), Kleopatra's representation of herself as Aphrodite (Isis) does reflect her propaganda, and follows that of previous queens (see **5**). For Roman views and images of Kleopatra VII, see Wyke (1992); for later views, Hamer (1993) chs. 2–5. The second paragraph of this passage is the only evidence of any Ptolemaic monarch learning the native Egyptian language. In one document (*BGU* XIV 2376) Philopatris (father-land-loving) is added to her more usual title of Philopator (father-loving), which may also suggest a special attempt to win the loyalty of her Egyptian subjects.

She received many letters of invitation from him and from his friends, but so despised and disdained the man that she sailed up the river Kydnos in a gold-prowed barge, with purple sails spread, and rowed along by silver oars to the sound of the flute mingled with pipes and lutes. She lay beneath a gold-spangled canopy, adorned like Aphrodite in a picture, and young boys, like Loves in pictures, stood on either side and fanned her. So too the most beautiful of her serving-maids, wearing the robes of Nereids and of Graces, stood some by the rudders and some by the bulwarks. Wonderful scents from many types of incense permeated the river banks. Some of the populace escorted her on either side from the river mouth, and others came down from the city for the spectacle. The crowd in the market-place poured out, until finally Antony himself, seated on his tribunal, was left alone. And the word went all around that Aphrodite was coming to revel with Dionysos for the good of Asia . . .

Her beauty, so they say, was not entirely hard to match, and would not turn heads at first sight. But the experience of spending time with her exerted an irresistible pull, and her appearance, combined with her conversational skills and the general atmosphere which surrounded being in her company, provided quite a spur. Her speaking voice was sweet, and she had the facility of attuning her tongue, like an instrument with many strings, to whatever language she wished. There were few foreigners she had to deal with through an interpreter, and to most she herself gave her replies without an intermediary — to the Ethiopians, Troglodytes, Hebrews, Arabs, Syrians, Medes and Parthians. It is said that she knew the languages of many other peoples too, although the preceding kings had not tried to master even the Egyptian tongue, and some had indeed ceased to speak Macedonian.[1]

---

[1] I.e. the Doric dialect of Greek traditionally used by Macedonian aristocrats, as distinct from the *koine* ('common' Greek) which developed in the Hellenistic world.

14. Kleopatra's suicide

Plutarch, *Life of M. Antonius* 85
Alexandria, 30 BC

Octavian (the future emperor Augustus) defeated Antony and Kleopatra at the battle of Actium in 31 BC, and then captured Alexandria in 30 BC. Following Antony's example, Kleopatra took her own life, probably to avoid the humiliation of appearing in Octavian's triumph in Rome. No one knew quite how she poisoned herself and her attendants. The claim that she used an asp, as described also by Galen (XIV.235–6 Kühn; cf. **15**), was probably a deliberate attempt to imply that she became immortal, for the asp/cobra was a traditional Egyptian symbol of divine kingship (see **6** note 5); hence Charmion's proud comment on the deed.

After making these laments, Kleopatra wreathed and kissed the urn (*containing Antony's ashes*), and ordered a bath to be prepared for her. After bathing, she reclined and ate a splendid lunch. And a man arrived from the country carrying a box. When the guards enquired what he was bringing, he opened it, pulled back the fig-leaves and showed that the container was full of figs. They were amazed at their beauty and size; he smiled and invited them to take some; they trusted him and told him to take the box in. After her lunch Kleopatra took a tablet she had written and sealed and sent it to Caesar (*Octavian*). Then she made the rest leave, except for her two special women, and locked the doors . . . (*Octavian sends men to stop her suicide*) . . . but when they opened the doors, they found her dead, lying on a gold couch and dressed as queen. Of her women, the one called Eiras[1] was dying at her feet, while Charmion, already stumbling and heavy-headed, was arranging the diadem which was on Kleopatra's head. 'Well done, Charmion,' said someone sarcastically. 'Indeed, very well done,' she replied, 'and appropriate for the descendant of so many kings.'

[1] Eiras' name suggests that she may have been Jewish (Heinen, 1989).

15. Kleopatra's cures for hair-loss

Galen, *De compositione medicamentorum secundum locos* (XII.403–4 Kühn) Second century AD

Galen was a Greek doctor of the second century AD, whose voluminous writings are an invaluable source for ancient medical traditions and practices. Kleopatra acquired such a reputation for her beauty, and for artful improvement of it, that compilations of remedies and recipes, especially for hair-care, were attributed to her, whether or not she had ever composed any, along with treatises on metrology – essential for getting these recipes right (or making drugs)! The recipes comprise a normal mixture of 'scientific' and 'folk' remedies.

In the 'Cosmetics' of Kleopatra medicines for hair-loss are recorded in her own words, more or less as follows. 'Against hair-loss: make a paste of realgar[1] and blend it into oak gum, apply it to a cloth and place it where you have already cleaned as thoroughly as possible with natron.'[2] Indeed I myself (*Galen*) have added foam of natron to the above recipe, and it worked nicely . . . 'Another: rub in a pounded mixture of heads of mice. Another: anoint with a paste of mouse-dung, after rendering the spot raw with a cloth.'

[1] A natural form of arsenic monosulphide.
[2] A natural form of sodium carbonate.

II   Roman Imperial women

Many of the women of the Julio-Claudian dynasty (31 BC–AD 68) were prominent and influential, and had links with Egypt through property or ancestry (**16** and **17**). There was a reaction against this public prominence under the Flavian emperors, but the part of the imperial women in the

propaganda of dynastic continuity and loyalty continued and developed
from then through the second century. When Hadrian visited Egypt in AD
130–1 he was accompanied by his wife Sabina, niece of his adoptive father
Trajan, who brought her own retinue, which included the grand-daughter
of a Neronian Prefect of Egypt (**6.244–5**); **18** illustrates the importance of
women to the line and legitimation of the Antonine emperors. The power
of the forceful women of the Severan dynasty (AD 193–235) was more
openly admitted (**19**). The end of the imperial cult with the Christianisation
of the empire ended this route for provincial contact with the women of
the Roman and Byzantine court, but under the Theodosian dynasty (AD
379–450) imperial properties in Egypt were again assigned to women (*P.Mil.*
II 63; *P.Oxy.* L 3582 and 3585; see more generally Holum, 1982), and the
patronage links which accompanied land-ownership re-emerge strikingly a
century later in the case of the empress Theodora (**20**).

16.   Dedication on behalf of Augustus and family

SB I 982
Pelousion (Delta), 8 January 4 BC

Women of the emperor's family were included in the fairly standardised public
Graeco-Roman cult of the imperial household which imperial officials throughout
the empire were expected to support, as seen here. However individual cult of them
was not usually encouraged (**18** is one of the exceptions), and they were never

represented in traditional Pharaonic-style reliefs on Egyptian temples. Livia was Augustus' last wife, whom he married in 38 BC; the epithet 'Augusta' was officially given her in AD 14 by Augustus' will, but this honour seems to have been long anticipated in the east. On Livia, see further **Plate 7** and Grether (1946), Purcell (1986), Fischler (1994). Julia was Augustus' only child (by Scribonia); in 17 BC he had adopted Gaius and Lucius, her sons by Agrippa (died 12 BC), intending them to succeed him, but they died in AD 4 and 2 respectively.

On behalf of Emperor Caesar Augustus son of a god, and Livia Augusta, and Gaius Caesar and Lucius Caesar the sons of the emperor, and Julia the daughter of the emperor, and Gaius Turranius Prefect of Egypt, Quintus Corvius Flaccus son of Quintus, formerly epistrategos of the Thebaid, (while acting) as *iuridicus* at Pelousion set up this throne and altar. Year 26 of Caesar, Tybi 13.

17.   Sheep of Antonia

P.Oxy. II 244
Oxyrhynchos, 2 February AD 23

When he conquered Egypt Augustus took over for himself the personal property of the Ptolemies (see **9–11**), which he and his Julio-Claudian successors then assigned to relatives and courtiers as revocable gift-estates, a practice which ceased under the Flavians (Crawford, 1976; Parássoglou, 1972). Women of the imperial family – especially his wife Livia – were among the recipients and, like Ptolemaic queens, exercised direct control of the property assigned to them. This Antonia was the younger daughter of M. Antonius (Mark Antony); she was married to Drusus, brother of Tiberius, and their children included the future emperor Claudius (Kokkinos, 1992). The manager of her Oxyrhynchite interests attested in this text wrote in Latin, so was probably a slave she had sent out from Italy. She is also known to have used a prominent Alexandrian Jew, Tiberius Julius Alexander, to supervise her affairs in Egypt (Josephus, *Jewish Antiquities* XIX.276); her patronage of this family, evident in Alexander's acquisition of Roman citizenship, was presumably inherited from her father, and was passed on to Claudius and Nero, under whom Alexander's elder son, of the same name, held various equestrian posts and became Prefect of Egypt.

To Chaireas strategos from Kerinthos slave of Antonia (wife) of Drusus. Since I wish to transfer from the Oxyrhynchite to the Kynopolite nome for the sake of pasturage the three hundred and twenty sheep and one hundred and sixty goats and the accompanying lambs and kids which I have on the register in the Oxyrhynchite nome in the present ninth year of Tiberius Caesar Augustus, I submit this memorandum so that you write to the strategos of the Kynopolite to put the declared sheep and [. . .] on the register [. . .].

(*2nd hand; in Latin*) Cerinthus, slave of Antonia (wife) of Drusus, I have presented this, year 9 of Tiberius Caesar Augustus, Mecheir on the eighth day. (*3rd hand*) Chaireas to Hermias strategos of the Kynopolite, many greetings. Kerinthos, slave of Antonia (wife) of Drusus, has presented a return, since he wishes [. . .

18.   Cult of Faustina

(Beginning of) *P.Oxy.* III 502
Oxyrhynchos, 1 March AD 164

Faustina was the deceased wife of the reigning emperor Marcus Aurelius, and the daughter of his predecessor and adoptive father Antoninus Pius. Beginning with the Flavian dynasty it had become customary to deify deceased female members of the imperial family, but the provision of a separate priest at Oxyrhynchos for Faustina is exceptional (and the reason for it unknown). Since the priest comes from the urban élite, the cult was probably attached to the civic cult of the imperial family (see **19**).

Dionysia daughter of Chairemon, with her guardian her son Apion alias Dionysios son of Diogenes, priest of Faustina Augusta, both from Oxyrhynchos city, has leased . . . (*a house in Oxyrhynchos to another woman*).

19.   Municipal honours to the Severans

(Excerpt from) *BGU* II 362
Ptolemais Euergetis, 11 and 14 April AD 215

This excerpt comes from an account of expenditure by the town council concerning the temple of Jupiter Capitolinus in the capital city of the Arsinoite nome. The dedication of the temple (imitating the Capitolium at Rome) and other entries – such as for the festival of the nome deity Souchos (early March), a visit by the Prefect (16 March), and the birthday of Rome (21 April) – show the official nature of cult in this temple which represented the public loyalty to Rome and its rulers of the local town council, recently created here, as throughout all Egypt, by Septimius Severus. Julia Domna was Septimius Severus' wife, and mother of the current emperor Severus Antoninus (Caracalla); for her role in the dynasty and title 'mother of the camps' (*mater castrorum*) see Birley (1988), ch.8; Turton (1974); cf. **44**.

(*Page xi, lines 8–19*): 16 (Pharmouthi): Birthday of the god Severus, father of our lord emperor Severus Antoninus: crowning of all (the statues) in the temple, 20 drachmas;

>   oil for lighting lamps in the [enclosure], 6 dr.;
>   pine-cones, incense and so on, 12 dr.;

labourers carrying the wooden statue (in procession) in [the theatre, 16 dr.];

crowns [for this statue, 4 dr.].

19: Holy day for the acclamation of our lady Julia Domna as 'mother of the invincible camps': crowning of all (the statues) in the temple as before, [x] dr.;

oil for lighting lamps, [x] dr.

20. The healing hand of Theodora

P.Cair.Masp. III 67283
Aphrodite, *c.* AD 546/7

Theodora was an intelligent, dynamic and beautiful woman of non-aristocratic origin, who exercised considerable influence and power in the reign of her husband the emperor Justinian (see Moorhead, 1994). This draft of a petition addressed to her through the local clergy, which must be dated shortly before her death in 548, implies that the imperial estates at Aphrodite had been assigned to her, and that she could exert influence on imperial administrators in Egypt in favour of her dependants, in this case villagers who were tenants of her land. Aphrodite was a former nome capital which had lost its civic status but retained the right to collect the taxes it owed independently of the regional authority, that is the pagarchy of Antaiopolis. This petition refers to one attempt by a pagarch to end this independence, on the alleged grounds that Aphrodite was in arrears with its payments. The petition is the earliest surviving document written by Dioskoros, a prominent inhabitant of Aphrodite, whose papers and writings give a fascinating insight into sixth-century Egypt (see **Ch.3 Arch. L**; MacCoull, 1988). Dioskoros wrote both in Coptic and Greek; this piece, in Greek, is highly rhetorical and vivid. The left half of the text of the petition is missing; where necessary the probable general sense is indicated in brackets.

[(From the men of the village of Aphrodite?), to . . . and Vic]tor(?), deacon, and the most admirable [. . .]ios and Victor, our [. . . greeting. (We report to our most august mistress that his brilliance Julianus(?) wishes), against] custom, to drag us into the pagarchy of the (city) of the Antaiopolites, of which he has gained control [. . . although we are] under the authority of the *dux*[1] and our mistress' agents. And we are at a loss to imagine the grounds [(of this attack on our independence?) . . . For] the competent local office knows that we have never been in arrears [. . . (But this Julianus has not shrunk?)] from plundering our property more than the places ravaged by barbarians, on the pretext [(of tax-arrears) . . . and,] as already said, they have plundered in an indescribably evil manner. Indeed even [. . . so that we are not able] to pay our [customary] contributions to the public dues, or to live a modest life in possession of our animals and [. . . for] in the [fields?] they have left us [nothing] and in the village absolutely none of the furnishings of a decent life for us. [. . .] the foul killings that have occurred as part of this plague, which has struck and brought shrieking, [. . . (and all the crimes)] which surrounded us then, for which a papyrus has no room unless it narrates with no break [. . .] carrying off booty [. . .] Therefore, in view of our complete and utter inability [. . .] to live in peace, as regards this matter which is so serious for us, [we have decided?] to approach our most august [mistress . . . through] the godfearing [bishop(?) of the (city)] of the Antaiopolites, to ask that she watch over our humility(?) and ward off from us [(our enemy?) . . . thus enabling us] to exist quietly and to discharge [peacefully] what concerns the august (*i.e. imperial*) taxes and the supplementary [grain-shipment (*i.e. for Constantinople*) . . . so that] we may be healed by the [hand] of our most august mistress and your eminence (*i.e. the dux*) [. . . who] make [safe] from undermining and uprooting the property of your dependants. (*There follows a page and a half of subscriptions by the individual petitioners.*)

¹ The chief imperial military and civil authority of the region, whom the petitioners hope that Theodora will get to restrain the pagarch.

III   Goddesses

The traditional Egyptian pantheon included important female deities such as Hathor, goddess of love; there were also female zoomorphic deities such as Thoeris and Bastet (see **Plates 8** and **9**; and, in general, Dunand, 1991). Cult of these traditional deities continued through to the Christian period, but Egyptian religion was flexible and open: the cult of Isis, for example, grew enormously in popularity from the late Pharaonic period onwards and spread through the Greek and Roman worlds (**24–6** and **Plates 10–12**). Greek settlers under the Ptolemies (and earlier) brought Greek deities such as Aphrodite (**5, 43**) and the Syrian goddess Atargatis (**5**), who were sometimes identified with local deities (**23**). A new Ptolemaic and then a Roman ruler cult also developed (**4–6, 18, 19, Plates 1–7**).

21.   Thoeris, goddess of childbirth

PSI Congr. XVII 14
Oxyrhynchos (?), second-first century BC

Thoeris (Taweret in Egyptian; equated with the Greek goddess Athena) was the patron deity of Oxyrhynchos but achieved wider recognition as the main Egyptian goddess of marriage, childbirth and infancy, and as a protector of women generally (see Quaegebeur, Clarysse and Van Maele, 1985). As such she is a rare case of a female deity with a gender-specific role (see **Plate 8**). In this question to an oracle (for the procedure, see **47**), it is not clear whether Tausorapis' malady related specifically to childbirth; Thoeris may be invoked because of her more general role as a protectress

8 The goddess Taweret (Thoeris)
Fitzwilliam Museum, Cambridge (inv. E.22.1955)
Second–first century BC

Taweret (Thoeris in Greek) was the goddess of childbirth (see **2.21**). She was depicted, as in this wooden statue (27.5 cm in height), as a pregnant hippopotamus, standing upright, with post-natal breasts, human arms, leonine legs and paws, and a crocodile's back and tail.

of women (or possibly simply as the patron deity of Oxyrhynchos, if that is the origin of the document; cf. **35**).

To our Lady Thoeris, and to Thonis and Harpebekis and Harpokrates: if Tausorapis will become healthy in her present malady, bring back this (slip) to me.

22.   A dancer of Boubastis

P.Mich.inv. 4394a (ed. W. Clarysse and P. J. Sijpesteijn, *Archiv* 41, 1995, 56–61)
Karanis, second–first century BC

The cat-headed goddess Bastet was called Boubastis by the Greeks; her nome (the Boubastite nome) was in the Delta. Closely linked to Sekhmet, the lioness-goddess of war (see **Plate 9**), she was often honoured by worshippers through the dedication of mummified cats, later buried in catacombs; cf. **28**. Boubastis was the goddess of love and also of music, dancing and rejoicing. Dancers of Boubastis are known from several texts, and dancing remained a popular form of entertainment

9   Bastet and Sekhmet, feline goddesses

The lioness and the cat are two aspects of the same female deity, called Sekhmet (or Tefnut) and Bastet respectively (see **2.22** and **28**). Their connection is best shown in the legend of Tefnut, the daughter of the sun-god Re (see the solar disc and uraeus on the goddess' head in **(a)**), who was sent out by her father Re to punish mankind. As a ferocious lioness, she started to kill all mankind, but was appeased by a trick, when instead of human blood she drank wine, and thus changed into the benevolent cat-goddess Bastet.

(a)   Statuette of Sekhmet (Brussels Museum inv. E.7618)
Late Pharaonic/Graeco-Roman period

A bronze statuette, with the necklace picked out in gold paint.

(b)   Statuette of Bastet (Brussels Museum inv. E.7671)
Late Pharaonic/Graeco-Roman period

A bronze statuette, of the type called 'a housewife Bastet'. She carries a one-handled basket, and an aegis with the head of Sekhmet and a uraeus on top. Her right hand probably once held a sistrum.

throughout this period (see **5.215–16** and **Plate 29**). Dancers came from a priestly milieu, at least under the Ptolemies. For the clichés at the start of this letter, perhaps addressed to an official, compare **4** and **23**.

To my lord, from your dancer. I pray to all the gods that they may give you health and good fortune, and ever greater success with the kings. May they give you favour and standing and success, and may the goddess Boubastis give you health.

23.   Burial of the Hesis cow

P.Zen.Pestman 50
Aphroditopolis (Atfih), 9 January 257 BC

The Hesis was the cow of Aphroditopolis with particular markings which was regarded as an incarnation of Hathor; when the current cow died, it was taken for mummification, for which the ruler might pay, as he did for the Apis bull (see **33**; Thompson, 1988, 114–25). Note that the Egyptian priests, petitioning Apollonios the *dioiketes* (**Ch.3 Arch. A** introd.) in Greek, refer to Hathor as both Aphrodite and Isis. For the conventional wish for royal favour, cf. **22**.

The priests of Aphrodite to Apollonios [the *dioiketes*], greeting. In accordance with what the king has written to you, to give a hundred talents of myrrh for the burial [of the Hesis]; please order that these [be given. For,] as you are aware, the Hesis cannot be brought up to the nome unless [we have] ready all that they may require for the burial, because [mummification starts?] on the same day. Know that Hesis is Isis: may she grant you favour [before the king]. Farewell. Year 28, Hathyr 15.

24.   Isis, sister-queen

Diodorus Siculus, 1.27.1–2
Mid-first century BC

In the developed Egyptian tradition Isis was the sister–wife of Osiris, who after his death had conferred immortality on his body and borne his son Horos, ruler of the world. The cult of Isis grew enormously in popularity from the late Pharaonic period; for general surveys see Witt (1971), Heyob (1975), Solmsen (1979). The Ptolemies encouraged the cult of Isis to unify their kingdom and increase their prestige. They funded the construction of temples, notably the one at Philae, and some Ptolemaic queens associated themselves with her (see **12** and **Plate 2**). Within Egypt this support was continued by the Roman emperors, as is illustrated by Augustus' early confirmation of the revenues to her temple at Philae (**Plate 10**), although their attitude to the cult in Italy was more ambivalent.

This text, written by a Sicilian Greek historian who had visited Egypt in the

10   Augustus and Isis
(Detail from) Kalabsha Gate, Ägyptisches Museum, Berlin
Kalabsha, shortly after 30 BC

The reconstructed 'Kalabsha Gate', discovered in fragments when the Kalabsha temple was
moved to a level above the Aswan dam, is displayed at the Ägyptisches Museum,
Charlottenburg, Berlin. Its relief scenes of the emperor Augustus and Isis must date from
shortly after the Roman conquest of Egypt, for in the cartouches, Augustus is named 'the
Roman', and 'Caesar the god, son of the god', instead of 'imperator Caesar', his standard title
throughout most of his reign. This scene shows Augustus as Pharaoh, presenting the symbol
for fields to the goddess, signifying her possession of the whole *dodekaschoinos* (the Nile valley
south of Aswan for 110 km), which paid a tithe to her great temple at Philae (cf. **Plate 2**).
See Winter (1977).

company of Roman envoys, reveals Isis' new emblematic importance in that he
attributes to her (and exaggerates) some social peculiarities of Egypt – some women
rulers, marriage on equal terms (cf. **Ch.4 Sect. I**), and brother–sister marriage (see
3.69).

They say that the Egyptians made a law contrary to the general practice of
mankind that men may marry their sisters, because of the success of Isis in
this respect. For Isis lived as wife with her brother Osiris, and when he died
she vowed she would never accept the partnership of another man. She
avenged her husband's murder and continued thereafter to rule entirely
according to the laws. In sum, she was responsible for the most and great-

11 Isis as a nursing mother
Wall painting (Kelsey Museum Archives 7.2256; now in Cairo)
Karanis, third century A D

This wall painting of Isis suckling Harpokrates (the infant Horos), from a niche in House B50 at Karanis, shares stylistic features with some Fayum mummy portraits. Worshippers in temples dedicated statuettes of Isis and Harpokrates in huge numbers; periodically the priests had to clear them out, and hence they are commonly found in ancient rubbish tips (Tran Tam Tinh, 1973; cf. **Plate 16**). Although the cult of Isis seems to have declined by the end of the third century A D, this motif may have influenced Christian iconography of Mary with the infant Jesus (cf. **Plate 14**).

est benefactions to all mankind. This, they say, is the reason that it was handed down that the queen should receive greater power and respect than the king and that, among private individuals, the woman should be master of the man, and in the dowry-contract husbands should agree to obey the wife in all matters.

25. Praises of Isis

(Excerpts from) *P.Oxy.* XI 1380
Oxyrhynchos, early second century A D

Hymns listing the particular attributes, at various places, of a deity and the deity's powers and achievements (this part being called the 'aretalogy'), were common both in Greek and Egyptian tradition. This papyrus text, although full of gaps, is one of the longest of the several surviving versions in Greek of the hymn to Isis, which have been found (mostly inscribed on stone) throughout the east Mediterranean and date from the third–second century B C until the second century A D. For a translated example, see Burstein (1985), no. 112; on Isis and these hymns in general, see Griffiths (1970), Bergman (1968). They claim to, and probably do, derive from an Egyptian exemplar (see the Demotic example in *P.Tebt.Tait* 14). The major legible sections of the text are translated here.

Her cult similarly gave rise to representations in both Greek, Egyptian and mixed styles (**Plates 10–12**). As her popularity grew, Isis displayed unusual megalomania for a polytheistic goddess, subsuming the identity and annexing the epithets and functions of other major goddesses, both Greek and Egyptian, such as Hathor, Aphrodite and Artemis, while being reluctant to share her cult or temples with other deities.

12   The cult of Isis in Hellenic form
Graeco-Roman Museum, Alexandria (inv. 25783)
Ras el-Soda, Alexandria, mid-second century AD

A marble statue of Isis. Over her *chiton* she wears her characteristic rectangular wrap tied over her chest in the 'Isis knot' (Goldman, 1996). Her left hand holds a situla for the sacred Nile water, while her left foot stands on a small crocodile. Her right hand (found separately) had a serpent coiled around it. Her crown consists of a solar disc between two horns, surmounted by two feathers (cf. Merkelbach, 1995, plate 86).

. . . (*Lines 7–13*): at Aphroditopolis of the Prosopite (nome), commander of the fleet(?), of many forms, Aphrodite; in the Delta, giver of favours; at Kalamisis, gentle; at Karene, affectionate; at Nikiou, immortal, giver; . . . (*lines 17–24*): at Hermopolis, of beautiful form, sacred; at Naukratis, father-less,[1] joy, saviour, almighty, greatest; at Nithine of the Gynaikopolite, Aphrodite; at Pephremis, Isis, queen, Hestia,[2] lady of the whole land; . . . (*lines 83–5*): at Rome, warlike;[3] in the islands of the Cyclades, of threefold form, Artemis;[4] . . . (*lines 102–8*): among the Amazons, warlike; among the Indians, Maia;[5] among the Thessalians, moon; among the Persians, Latina; among the Magi,[6] Kore, Thapseusis; at Susa, Nania; in Phoenician Syria, goddess; on Samothrace, bull-faced; at Pergamum, mistress; . . .

(*lines 119– 65*): you who are also the first of all interpreters of the fifteen commandments, ruler of the world; (they call you) guardian and guide, lady of the mouths of seas and rivers, skilled in writing and calculation, under-standing, the one who also brings back the Nile over the whole land, the beautiful animal of all the gods, the glad face in Lethe,[7] the leader of the Muses, the many-eyed, the fair goddess on Olympus; you are the adorn-ment of women, full of affection, providing sweetness in the assemblies, the lock of hair(?) in festivals,[8] plenty to those observing lucky days, Harpokratis[9] of the gods, all-ruling in the processions of the gods, enmity-hating, true jewel of the wind and diadem of life, by whose command images and animals of all the gods – having [. . .] of your name – are worshipped.

O lady Isis, greatest of the gods, first of names, Io Sothis,[10] who rules over the mid-air and the immeasurable, who devises the weaving of [. . .]. It is your will that women in health come to anchor with men, all the elders at E[. . .] sacrifice, all the maidens who [. . .] at Herakleopolis are borne towards you and have dedicated the country to you, you are seen by those who invoke you faithfully. From you [. . .] in virtue of the 365 combined days, gentle and placable is the favour of your two ordinances, you bring the sun from rising to setting and all the gods are glad, at the rising of the stars the people of the country worship you without cease, and the other sacred animals in the sanctuary of Osiris, they become joyful when they name you; the [. . .] spirits (*daimones*) become subject to you . . . (*lines 174–81*): and you may bring destruction to what you will, and to the destroyed you may bring increase, and you purify all things. You have appointed every day for joy, you [. . .] having discovered all of the . . . of wine provided it first in the festivals of the gods . . . You became the discoverer of all things wet and dry and cold <and hot> of which all things are composed. You alone brought back your brother (*Osiris*), piloting safely and burying him fittingly; . . . (*lines 209–31*): you established your son Horos Apollo everywhere as the youthful lord of the whole world and . . . for all time. You made the power of women equal to that of men. And in the sanctuary you . . . nations . . . queen . . . lady [you protect] every country with your wings. You, lady of the land, bring the flood of rivers . . . and in Egypt of the Nile, in Tripolis the Eleutheros, in India the Ganges; owing to whom the whole and the . . . exists through all rain, every spring, all dew and snow, and all . . . and land and sea. You are also the mistress of all things for ever . . . (*lines 237–51*): you have dominion over winds and thunders and lightnings and snows. You, the lady of war and rule, easily destroy <tyrants> by trusty counsels. You made great Osiris immortal, and have delivered to every country . . . religious observances; so too you made immortal Horos who became a benefactor and good. You are the lady of light and flames. You [. . .] sanctuary in Memphis. Horos, having judged before that you had made him successor of him (*Osiris*) . . . (*lines 265–8*): you established him as lord of the throne of all and oracular king over his father's house for all time . . .

[1] In Egyptian tradition Isis was the daughter of the god Geb. The reference here is uncertain and the reading may not be correct.
[2] Protecting goddess of the household (Greek *hestia* means 'hearth').
[3] An example of an epithet appropriate to the place, since the Romans were notoriously militaristic.
[4] Greek virgin goddess of hunting and childbirth.
[5] The mother-earth.

6 Median priests.
7 The river of Hades, sometimes used to denote the Underworld in general.
8 The Greeks cut off a lock of hair as a tribute to the dead; the association of this with Isis is a punning reference to her cult at the town of Koptos (Greek *koptein* means 'to cut').
9 The female form of Harpokrates ('Horos the child'), an object which gives pleasure.
10 Isis was identified both with the Greek Io, who was transformed by Zeus into a cow, and with the dog-star Sirius, in Greek called Sothis, whose summer rising marked the beginning of the Nile inundation.

26. Epitaph of a deified daughter

I.Métr. 87
Tuna el-Gebel, second century(?) A D

This is the second of two Greek verse epitaphs from the so-called 'tomb of Isidora' at Tuna el-Gebel, the cemetery of Hermopolis, written on the wall to the left of the door of the inner chamber. A father addresses his young daughter, Isidora, who has become a divinity on her death. In Egyptian tradition those who drowned in the Nile were believed to be deified and were offered cult,[1] and death by drowning is the most likely explanation for Isidora's deification. The Greek for 'snatched away' (*harpagime*) by the Nymphs (line 4) implies a divine agency for her premature death; and the first poem (*I.Métr.* 86) is full of imagery which specifically suggests drowning (the Nymphs, daughters of 'the waters' or of the Nile, have built her burial chamber in the form of a conch-shell; the reference to Hylas, a mythical youth drowned in a fountain, also described as 'snatched away'). The fact that only three seasons offer her libations presumably reflects the tripartite division of the Egyptian calendar (see Ch. 1 p. 4). The approximate date of the text is inferred from the letter-forms and from coins found in the tomb.

> No more shall I sacrifice to you, my daughter, with lamentation,
> Now I know that you have become a goddess.
> With libations and prayers celebrate Isidora,
> The maiden[2] who has been snatched away by the Nymphs.
> Greetings, my child; Nymph is your name, and see – the Seasons
> each year pour the libations appropriate to them;
> Winter pours white milk, the oily blossom of the olive,
> And garlands you with narcissus, the most delicate flower;
> Spring sends here without our asking the product of the bee
> And the opening bud of the rose, the flower dear to Eros;
> The hot season then sends the drink from the press of Bacchus' vat,
>   and for you a crown
> Of a bunch of grapes, binding the grapes onto their stems.
> These, then, are for you; each year all these will be performed
>   here
> As a rite for the immortals. And that is why I myself[3]
> No more shall sacrifice to you, my daughter, with lamentation.

[1] Herodotus, II.90, with Lloyd (1976), 366–7.
[2] A pun: the word translated 'maiden' is the same as that for 'Nymph' – *nymphe*.
[3] The masculine gender of this word shows that it is Isidora's father speaking and not her mother.

IV Priestesses

In classical Athens women as priestesses played a crucial role within the city-state. In Pharaonic Egypt they might hold ceremonial posts; the appointment of 'god's wife of Amun' at Thebes (Robins, 1993, 149–56) is picked up under the Ptolemies when, from the first century BC, the wife of the high priest of Ptah becomes 'wife of Ptah' (although not so recorded in **39**). In Ptolemaic and Roman Egypt, priestesses are found in both Greek and Egyptian temples. The Egyptian priestly caste was a closed one: wives and daughters served within the temple communities, particularly as chantresses and musicians performing in temple rituals (but for a wider range of priestly functions open to them, see **28**; for a full list see *Pros.Ptol.* III, and IX 7081a–7273). Within the priestly community most daily contacts, economic dealings, and marriages fell within this close-knit group. The posts of priestesses in the Greek ruler cult of the Ptolemies seem to have been reserved for women from prominent Macedonian and other immigrant families (**34**). For priestesses in Ptolemaic temples, see de Cenival (1977), 29–30. On priests and temples in Greek and Roman Egypt in general, see Bowman (1996), ch. 6; Glare (forthcoming), ch. I.

27. Women and succession to priestly status

(a) *BGU* V 1210.§84
Egypt, Roman period

On the *Gnomon of the Idios Logos*, from which this rule comes, see **4.131**. The section about priestly privileges and obligations probably preserves, with some amendments, Egyptian traditions maintained by the Ptolemies. The brief statement is difficult to translate without tacit interpretation, but probably means that priestly status and rights could pass through the female as well as the male line.

Sacred things are preserved for a daughter.

(b) Oliver (1989) no. 232 (= *P.Col.* VI 123.25–7 revised)
Alexandria, AD 200

This ruling of Septimius Severus, made in response to a petition from an Aurelius Sarapion when the emperor was at Alexandria in AD 200, reveals that he had abrogated the right recorded in the *Gnomon*, **(a)**.

To Aurelius Sarapion: Recently we forbade priesthoods from passing down
in succession from the mother's side.

28. A cult association

P.Lille dem. 31 (ed. de Cenival, 1977, 21–4)
Arsinoite nome, third century BC

This unusual list of members of a female cult association is ordered according to
their function with a record of dues. The organisation of the cult and priestly titles
here are modelled on those of the better-known male cult guilds, with titles always
in the feminine form. Besides the male gods, Amun, Thoth and Horos, the priestesses serve female goddesses, Isis, Boubastis (the cat-goddess, see **22** and **Plate 9**)
and the female falcon. The 'wet nurse of the (sacred) cat' is a specifically female
responsibility; sacred cats were fed with bread and milk. Another text from the same
find mentions a mixed cult guild, with men and women listed separately in two
fragmentary columns.

> The superiors:
> Tasais, the (female) superior[1] of Boubastis, 12 dr.
> Tapchoiris, the (female) superior of Harmachis[2] (?), 9 dr.
> Haynchis, daughter of Nechtnibis, the wet nurse of the cat, 8 dr.
> Hemedjelet, the prophetess of the gods (*sc. sacred animals?*), 6½ dr.
> Renpnophris, daughter of Onnophris, the (female) general, 6½ dr.
> Senobastis, the (female) second-in-command, 5 dr.
> Semset, the chantress of Isis, the (female) superior of the (female) falcon,
>   5 dr.
> Taneirou, the chantress, the directrice of . . . 4½ dr.
> Tetosiris, daughter of Oaphres, the (female) superior of Amun, 4 dr.
> Tetosiris, daughter of Bienchis(?), the (female) superior of Thoth, 4 dr.
> Tekysis, the prophetess of Horos, 1½ dr.

[1] The traditional translation of the Egyptian priestly term which means 'great', here in the
  feminine form.
[2] Horos in the form 'Horos in the horizon', signifying the rising sun.

29. A thiasos of women

P.Enteux. 21
Kerkethoeris (Arsinoite nome), 13 January 218 BC

Egyptian women formed groups to join in cult (cf. **3** and **7,** for the Greek-style
women's festivals of the Adoneia and Thesmophoria) and for mutual support to
cover the cost of mummification. As often, it is something going wrong which leads
to documentation. For petitions to kings, and the dossier of the strategos
Diophanes, see **5**.

Therous and Teos to King Ptolemy, greeting. We are wronged by Temsois, Senemenopis, Teteim[.], Herieus and the other members of the women's cult association (*thiasos*) from Kerkethoeris in the Polemon division (*of the Arsinoite nome*). For Soeris, my sister and wife of the aforementioned Teos, who was a member of the aforementioned group and held the post of priestess for the group for four years, chanced to die. Apart from us she had no close relatives, but when those named were asked for the cost of her burial they did not pay it. We beg you therefore, sovereign, to order Diophanes the strategos to write to Ptolemaios the *epistates* so if even now they may agree to pay us (all will be well), but if not, that he may send them to Diophanes so they may be compelled to pay us, in order, O king, that through your help we may receive justice. Farewell.

(*2nd hand*) To Ptolemaios. Do your best to clear it up. If not, send them to us so the case may be tried through the correct court on 10 Choiak. Year 4, Daisios 27, Hathyr 29.

30. Transfer of benefices between women necropolis attendants

P.BN+P.Louvre dem. 2412 (ed. M. Pezin, 'Un contrat memphitique de partage de revenus liturgiques', *BIFAO* 87, 1987, 269–73)
Memphis, 305/4 BC

The *choachytai*, libation-pourers in the cult of the dead, were a minor grade of Egyptian priests working in the necropoleis, that is the burial areas. Like other Egyptian priesthoods, their position was hereditary. Their income came from payments for the performance of their duties, and families of *choachytai* controlled particular areas of the necropolis, as is seen in the following text (cf. the sale of temple land, another possible source of income, between two priestly families in **5.163**; also **184**). This Demotic contract shows how women in such families might inherit, control and dispose of benefices. In the form of a fictitious sale, Taous alias Heriobastis transfers to her niece Hedjenpaouni three types of benefice – part of a prebend (income from funerary duties) of a group of tombs and of an enclosure, which derive from her mother, father and grandmother, and appear to have come in part down the female side of the family; her son guarantees the transfer. Fig. 1 shows the family tree of those involved.

Year 13, third month of [. . . of the king] Alexander,[1] son of Alexander. The woman Taous alias Heriobastis, daughter of the *choachytes* Imouthes, whose mother is Nehoeris, has made a declaration to the woman Hedjenpaouni, daughter of the *choachytes* Pkoilis, whose mother is Nephersachmis, the daughter of my elder brother.

'You have satisfied my heart with the money for my ⅙ part of the prebend of the *choachytes* Imouthes, son of Pkoilis, whose mother is Hedjenpaouni, [my father, the father of your father, the prebend] which lies in the necropolis of Memphis; likewise for the ⅙ part of the prebend of the *choachytes'* daughter Hedjenpaouni, daughter of Petemestous, whose mother is

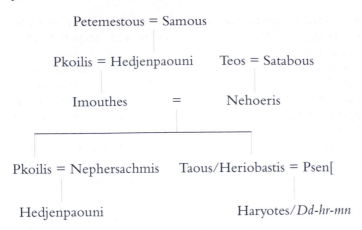

Figure 1   Family of Taous alias Heriobastis

Samous, the mother of my father, the mother of the father of your father, the (prebend) which lies in the necropolis of Memphis; likewise for the ⅙ part of the prebend of the *choachytes'* daughter Nehoeris, daughter of Teos, whose mother is Satabous, my mother, the mother of your father; likewise for the ⅙ part of every tomb, of every burial place, of every funerary monument, with every source of income [belonging to Imouthes, son of Pkoilis], my father, the father of your father (named) above, which lie in the necropolis of Memphis; likewise for the ⅙ part of the tombs, the burial places, the funerary monuments, the sources of income of the *choachytes'* daughter Hedjenpaouni, daughter of Petemestous, the mother of my father, the mother of the father of your father, which lie in the necropolis of Memphis; likewise for the ⅙ part of the tombs, the burial places, the funerary monuments, the sources of income, the prebends belonging to Nehoeris, daughter of Teos, whose mother is Satabous, my mother, the mother of your father, (named) above; [likewise for the ⅙ part of] the enclosure lying north of the house of the *choachytes* Imouthes, son of Pkoilis (named) above, which measures 70 divine cubits north–south, by 45 divine cubits east–west and lies in Thenis-Anchtawy outside the wall of Thenis and south of the temple-avenue of the great god Imouthes son of Ptah.

To you belong the prebends (listed) above, likewise the ⅙ part of their [?], likewise the ⅙ part of the tombs, the burial places, the funerary monuments, the income from the prebends (listed) above; likewise the ⅙ part of the enclosure (mentioned) [above]; [likewise] all which is in their name and all that may be added to them, from today and forever. I have no claim whatsoever to make against you concerning them. Anyone who will proceed against you on account of them, I shall cause him to stay away from you, and I shall be responsible for ensuring that you are freed from any written (claim) and absolutely anything else. To you belong all the deeds which have been drawn up concerning them, and all the deeds from which my title derives; they belong to you, with the rights (they impart). To you belongs what my rights derive from.

The oath (or) the testimony which you may be asked for, that I should make in their name, I shall make it, for the *choachytes* Haryotes alias *Dd-hr-mn*, son of Psen[ ], his eldest son, declares: To all that is outlined above, my heart is satisfied. I am far from you (*i.e. I make no claim on you*) in respect of all that concerns the ⅙ of the prebends (and) of all that Taous alias Heriobastis, daughter of Imouthes, my mother (named above), has written for you in respect of them. I have no claim whatsoever to make against you concerning them. Anyone who opposes you over them, I will make to leave you.'

Written by Harchebis son of [   ].

---

[1] I.e. Alexander IV, son of Alexander the Great and Roxane. Although he was murdered in 310 BC, Ptolemy (like the other Successors of Alexander) continued to use his name in regnal dating until he himself adopted the royal title (*basileus* in a Greek context, Pharaoh in an Egyptian one) in early 305/4, shortly after this document was written.

31. Tomb of a prophetess of Ammon

G. Wagner, 'Épitaphe d'une prophétesse d'Ammon', *ZPE* 106 (1995), 123–5
Kom Ombo, first century BC–first century AD

This small inscribed stela was discovered in 1989/90 near the eastern necropolis of Ombos (Kom Ombo). Prophetesses are only rarely attested (but cf. **32**), and no prophetess of Ammon was hitherto known. Ammon was not a major deity at Ombos; perhaps the prophetess was merely buried in Ombos, having served a temple of Ammon elsewhere.

Tomb of Temalis, prophetess of Ammon.

32. Prophetess of Jeme

(End of) *P.Lond.dem.* IV 6.9
Jeme, 175 BC

In Thebes, under the Ptolemies, the main priestess of the temple guaranteed contracts drawn up by temple scribes; the formula quoted here comes from the foot of a Demotic cession (transfer) of tombs between funerary workers. Jeme (Memnoneia in Greek; cf. **6.244**) was the Egyptian name for the area around the temple of Ramses III at Medinet Habu, on the west bank of Thebes. For a wife of the chief priest at Memphis, the 'rival' centre of Egyptian religion, see **39**.

Amenothes son of Totoes has written this; he writes in the name of the agents of the prophetess of Jeme.

33.   The 'Serapeum Twins'

UPZ I 18
Memphis, 163 B C

When the Apis bull died at Memphis in April 164 B C and, as usual, was mummified at the temple of Ptah in the valley, and later taken up to the vaults under the Serapeum (which can still be visited) for entombment, a pair of Egyptian twins were employed to play the parts of the sister-goddesses Isis and Nephthys in the ceremonies of mourning (cf. **Plate 43(c)**). This draft of a complaint to Ptolemy VI, written for them by their 'protector' Ptolemaios, summarises their story. A second version of the same petition is translated in **3.79**, along with other texts also relating to the twins (**Ch.3 Arch. B**). See further Thompson (1988), ch.7 on the twins, and, more generally, on the great temple complex of Serapis at Memphis (also **37**).

From Thaues and Taous, twins in the great Serapeum at Memphis. We are wronged by Nephoris, our mother. She left our father and set up house with Philippos son of Sogenes, a military man from Pyr[. . .]'s troop. But Philippos – for she was full of suspicion and ordered him to kill our father Hargynouti – grabbed a knife and chased after him. Our father's house is near the river; he plunged into the river and swam until he reached the island in the stream; and a boat picked him up and set him down in Herakleopolis, and he died there of a broken heart. His brothers went to fetch him, and brought him to the necropolis where they deposited him; and he is still without a grave. She took his possessions and is receiving a monthly rent of 1,400 bronze drachmas. She threw us out, and we, starving, went up to the Serapeum to Ptolemaios, one of those in detention. Ptolemaios was a friend of our father; he took us in and fed us. When the mourning[1] occurred, they took us down to mourn the god. The acquaintances of our mother persuaded us to take on her son Panchrates as our attendant. We sent him to collect what was owed us for year 17 from the royal treasury. And he stole what we had in the Serapeum and the measure of oil which he collected from the treasury on our behalf; and he went off back to his mother. Ptolemaios, who is in detention in the same temple, rescued us, on the god's orders . . .

(*On the back*) From Ptolemaios son of Glaukias, a Macedonian, in detention for the eleventh year.

[1] On the death of the Apis bull.

34.   Priestesses of the ruler cult

(Beginning of) *P.Cairo dem.* 30602 + *UPZ* I 130
Memphis, 6 April 115 B C

As the royal cult was expanded, new appointments occurred for both priests and priestesses from the major Macedonian families of the Greek cities of Alexandria and Ptolemais (see Clarysse and Van der Veken, 1983). In this dating formula to a Demotic contract multiple queenly priestesses are recorded, particularly for Kleopatra III (on whom see **8**). For the divine epithets of the Ptolemies, see **6** introd.

In year 2, 18 Phamenoth, of Queen Kleopatra (*III*) and Ptolemy (*IX*) mother-loving saviour god, when King Ptolemy mother-loving saviour god was priest of Alexander, of the saviour gods (*Ptolemy I and Berenike I*), and of the brother–sister gods (*Ptolemy II and Arsinoe II*), and of the benefactor gods (*Ptolemy III and Berenike II*), of the father-loving gods (*Ptolemy IV and Arsinoe III*), of the manifest gods (*Ptolemy V and Kleopatra I*), of the god whose father is holy (*Ptolemy Eupator*), of the mother-loving god (*Ptolemy VI*), of the young father-loving god (*Ptolemy VII*), of the benefactor gods (*Ptolemy VIII and Kleopatras II and III*), and of the mother-loving saviour gods (*Kleopatra III and Ptolemy IX*), when Krateros son of Krateros was *hieros polos*[1] of Isis the great, the wet nurse, the mother of the gods, when Aretine daughter of Theodoros was crown-bearer of Queen Kleopatra (*III*) saviour justice victory-bringing mother-loving goddess, when Kratera daughter of Theodoros was *athlophoros* of Berenike (*II*) Euergetis, when Theodoris daughter of Theodoros was fire-bearer of Queen Kleopatra (*III*) saviour justice victory-bringing mother-loving goddess, when Dionysia daughter of Dionysios was *kanephoros* of Arsinoe (*II*) Philadelphos, when Mnemosyne daughter of Nikanor was priestess of Queen Kleopatra (*III*) saviour justice victory-bringing mother-loving goddess, when Artemo daughter of Seleukos was priestess of Arsinoe (*III*) Philopator . . .

---

[1] This Greek priestly title ('sacred foal') derived from that of the cult of Demeter; in the Demotic here it is simply transliterated (*3yrw pwl3*), not translated as most other titles are, sometimes laboriously.

35.   A sacred virgin fails to perform

P.Mert. II 73, as re-ed. M. Vandoni, *Aegyptus* 47 (1967) 243–6 (*BL* VI 78–9)
Oxyrhynchos, AD 163/4

Women continued as priestesses in Roman Egypt (see in general Dunand, 1978). Their appointment and their revenues were now supervised by Roman officials, such as the *Idios Logos* and the High Priest (Stead, 1981; Glare, forthcoming).

From Taarthoonis, sacred virgin,[1] through [NN] priest of Athena Thoeris[2] and Isis and [Serapis and the gods sharing the shrine. Since I happened to be] elected by the body of the priests [of the above temple for . . . and the] *komasiai*[3] for the Fortune of our lords [Augusti, but am now unable] being gripped by illness, with regard(?) to all which it [concerns] our temple [to

supervise, according to the orders given] by Bienus Longus the former
[High Priest and in charge of the temples and by Timo(?)]krates the former
head of the *Idi[os Logos*, I declare all my sources of] revenue, both from
contributions and gifts [. . .], in year 4 of Antoninus and Verus our lords
[. . .], which fall to me . . . (*there follows a sadly lacunose list of revenues, mostly
contributions from associations of workers*).

[1] No patronymic is given for Taarthoonis, possibly because a 'sacred virgin' was deemed to
have left her natural family, or more simply because she is the daughter of the priest who
makes the declaration.
[2] cf. **21**.
[3] Processions in which the statues of the gods were carried.

36. A priestess of a mystery cult

P.Oxy. XXXVI 2782
Oxyrhynchite nome, third century A D

In an Egyptian village Demeter (see **7**) might be expected to stand for the Egyptian
Isis, but the title *hierophantes* is that of the main priest of the mystery cult of Demeter
at Eleusis near Athens, and the priestess' title means 'bearer of the ritual basket
(*kalathos*)' used in the cult of Demeter, suggesting that this cult was modelled on
that of Eleusis in mainland Greece. Earlier references to priestesses of Demeter in
Demotic texts (e.g. *P.Oxf. Griffith* 16, of 132 B C) also strongly suggest that the Greek
cult of this goddess was adopted in the chora of Egypt.

Marcus Aurelius Apollonios, *hierophantes*, to the *kalatephoros* of (the village
of) Nesmeimis, greetings. Please go to (the village of) Sinkepha, to the
temple of Demeter, to perform the customary sacrifices for our lords the
emperors and their victory, for the rise of the Nile and increase of crops,
and for favourable conditions of climate. I pray that you are well.

V   Religion and the individual

Women participated in all normal forms of religious activity. Private religious activity is difficult to illustrate because it usually did not involve written
records. Unsurprisingly the written evidence is biased towards Greek-speak-
ers (female literacy, even dictation, in Demotic is rarer), and to the Roman
period. It also privileges particular forms of activity, such as dedications by
wealthy and independent women. Oracles, dreams, magic spells and curses
are well attested because writing them down was often part of the procedure
of using them, and they seem to have formed an important part of everyday
religious experience in Egypt, as elsewhere in the ancient world. It may also
be noted that, as is shown in the early Ptolemaic census documents from the

Arsinoite nome (*P.Count.*), many more women's names than men's names, both Egyptian and Greek, were theophoric – that is based on the name of a deity (e.g. Taosiris, 'she of Osiris'; Isidora, 'gift of Isis').

37. Curse of Artemisia

UPZ II
Memphis, late fourth century BC

This is one of the earliest surviving Greek documents on papyrus from Egypt, and comes from the Ionian community established in Memphis (the 'Helleno-memphites'; see Thompson, 1988). Artemisia bears the name of the famous woman tyrant of Halicarnassus in the early fifth century (Herodotus, VII.99, VIII.68–9, 87–8, 93, 102–3, 107), but her father's name, which is that of the last native ruler of Egypt before the Persian conquest under Kambyses, may indicate a mixed Ionian-Egyptian family of high status (or aspirations).

O lord Oserapis[1] and the gods who sit with Oserapis, Artemisia the daughter of Amasis [appeals?] to you against the father of her daughter, who has deprived her of her funeral rites and burial. So if he has not treated me and his children rightly, indeed has treated me and his children wrongly, may Oserapis and the gods grant to him that he does not receive burial from his children, and that he does not bury his own parents. While the cry for help lies here, may he and what is his be destroyed evilly on land and on sea by Oserapis and the gods who sit in Poserapis,[2] and may he not receive the favour of Oserapis or of the gods who sit with Oserapis. Artemisia has deposited this appeal, appealing to Oserapis and the gods who sit with Oserapis to give judgement. While the appeal lies here, may the father of the young girl receive no favours at all from the gods. If anyone removes this document or wrongs Artemisia, the god will inflict punishment on him . . . (*the text becomes fragmentary*).

[1] The Apis bull of Memphis, mummified as Osiris (hence the composite name Oserapis: Osiris–Apis), who was in this period being redefined as Serapis for the new Greek (and other) immigrants.
[2] Egyptian for 'the House of Oserapis', that is the Serapeum (see **33**).

38. A sacred slave of Anoubis

P.Freib. IV 73, with W. Clarysse, *Enchoria* 16 (1988), 7–8
Philadelphia, 209/8 or 192/1 BC

This Demotic text is an example of a fictive contract by which a woman (or man) binds herself (or himself) to a deity as a 'servant' (Demotic *b3k*), and promises to make a regular token payment, symbolising servitude, to the deity, in return for the special protection of that deity. Anoubis, the Egyptian god of the Underworld, might be expected to be a particularly effective protector against malicious spirits of the dead.

Year 14 of King Ptolemy son of Ptolemy, may he live for ever. The servant of Anoubis the great god, Taosiris daughter of Petosiris, whose mother is Mesiesis, has said: 'I am your servant from this day forward and for ever more, and I give you every month 2.5 *kite* for my rent of service before Anoubis the great god. No spirit, no evil force, no demon, no angry monster, no man on the earth or of the Underworld, shall have power over me from this day forward and for ever more.' Written.

39.   Imouthes grants a son

BM Stele 147.6–12 (ed. Reymond, 1981, no. 20)
Memphis, 42 BC

Taimouthes (the name means 'she of Imouthes') was the wife of Psenptais, chief priest of Ptah at Memphis, and a contemporary of Kleopatra VII; she died aged thirty on 15 February 42 BC (see Thompson, 1988, ch. 4 for the family). This hieroglyphic inscription on one of her tombstones illustrates how the divine assistance of Imouthes was sought in the crucial business of producing a male child (cf. **6.230**). In Egyptian tradition Imouthes (Egyptian Imhotep) was the deified architect of the first pyramid, the step pyramid of Zoser near Memphis. The Greeks identified him with Asklepios, their god of healing, and hence he acquired a healing function. On the text, see J. Quaegebeur, *Ancient Society* 3 (1972), 93–6; for a translation of the complete inscription, Lichtheim (1980), 59–65.

Year 23, day 22[1] of Epeiph (= *25 July 58 BC*)of the king, lord of the two lands.[2] My father gave me as wife to the prophet of Ptah . . . *(further priestly titles)*, the chief priest of Ptah, Psenptais, son of Petobastis, deceased, and of Haynchis, deceased, the very great sistrum-player, dancer-musician of Ptah, the great, south-of-his-wall, lord of Anchtawy.[3] The heart of Psenptais, chief priest of Ptah, was full of joy. I became pregnant by him three times. I gave birth to no son, but only to three daughters. I prayed together with the chief priest to Ptah's divine son Imouthes, great god, great in his wonders, great in his works, he who grants sons to those who lack them. He heard our prayers, he listened to our entreaties. Imhotep, in all his majesty, came to the chief priest in a revelation and spoke to him: 'Let there be built within the sacred enclosure of the necropolis of Anchtawy, the place where my spirit dwells, a great monument. In return I shall grant you a son.' Psenptais awoke. He gave thanks to Imouthes. He straightway put in charge of the work the prophets, those who guard the sacred scriptures, the priests and the craftsmen of the golden house.[4] He instructed them to build a fine building within the sacred enclosure. They carried out all his instructions. He performed the ritual of the opening-of-the-mouth[5] for this great god.

He made a great sacrifice with all good things; he rewarded the craftsmen on behalf of the great god. He made their hearts glad with all good things. And in return for these deeds, the god made me conceive a male child. I gave birth to this son at the eighth hour of the day on 15 Epeiph, year 6 (= 15 July 46) of her majesty the Queen, Kleopatra, the lady of the two lands, life, prosperity and health.

[1] See Quaegebeur, *Ancient Society* 3 (1972), 94 note 89.
[2] I.e. Upper and Lower Egypt.
[3] The name for part of the headland of North Saqqara.
[4] Part of an Egyptian temple.
[5] A rite to activate a statue as a vessel for the deity, through the priest touching its mouth with special ritual tools (also performed upon mummies to bring the deceased 'to life').

40. Restrictions on entry to a sanctuary

SEG XLII 1131
Ptolemais (Upper Egypt), first century B C

Inscribed on a small conical basalt column are the number of days of purificatory intermission required after certain acts or events before entering a sanctuary. Since similar regulations survive from elsewhere in the Greek world, and Ptolemais was founded as a Greek city, these regulations probably come from a civic sanctuary for a Greek deity, possibly that of Asklepios. See further J. Bingen, *CdE* 68(1993), 219–28.

Men who enter into the [sanctuary] must wait to be pure in accordance with the following: For one's own [or another's] illness, 7 days. For death [. . . x (days). . . For] miscarriage [. . . x (days). The man?] of (a woman) who has given birth and is nursing, [x (days)]. And if she exposes (the child), 14. Men after (sex with) a woman, 2. Women, as in the case of men. After(?) miscarriage, 40. [After . . . x (days)]. A woman who gives birth and is nursing, 40. If she exposes the child, [x]. After menstruation,[1] 7. (After sex with) a man, 2, and [she shall bring?] myrtle.[2]

[1] See **Ch.6 Sect.V** introd.
[2] Myrtle was often used in Greek religion in a context of propitiation.

41. Endowment of a cult of Serapis

P.Oxy. II 242
Oxyrhynchos, 6 December A D 77

This report to the authorities for registration of a change in ownership reveals a woman, Thermouthion, selling to the priests of a cult of Serapis, perhaps for a notional price, a strip of land adjacent to the temple-enclosure which she had bought the previous year from another woman, Dionysia (whose father's name is not given); she wishes it to remain dedicated to the cult of Serapis. The narrative of these two sales, which seem to quote passages from the contracts of sale, is rather garbled in the middle, but the overall sense is clear.

[. . . We wish to notify for registration the sale made by us to (names) and (name)] daughter of Phatres, Apis son of Harpaesis, son of A[. . .], whose mother is Tausorapis daughter of Harthoonis, and the [(four or so)] priests of Thoeris, Isis and Serapis and of the great gods who share their shrine – and Harthonis and Paesis are in addition *stolistai*[1] of the same gods – of what the woman disposing of it acquired by purchase(?) from Dionysia alias Taamois daughter of Dionysia, daughter of Epimachos, in the month Kaisareios of the past ninth year. (The land lies) in the Serapeum of Oxyrhynchos city in the Hermaion[2] quarter. On the north [. . . which] Dionysia alias Taamois has relinquished(?), north of the enclosure-wall of the great god Serapis, extending half a cubit (from it), (are) some partially walled plots, with their existing fixtures. The condition of sale is that the plots sold are allowed to the lord Serapis for the use of the same god and that the remaining parts are walled. They are not to make a profit out of these plots so that they remain dedicated to the use of the same god and the temple, nor, indeed, are they allowed to sell to other people in any way what they have bought on these conditions from Thermouthion daughter of Dionysios, son of Thoonis, whose mother is Teseuris daughter of Petosorapis, together with her husband, Kephalon son of Harthoonis, son of Euboulos, whose mother is Thaesis, (acting) as guardian, all inhabitants of Oxyrhynchos city, for the price of 692 silver drachmas, (that is) 51 bronze talents 5,400 drachmas.[3] Farewell. Year 10 of Emperor Caesar Vespasian Augustus, Choiak 12. (*There follows a subscript by bankers attesting payment of the sales-tax on the purchase by one of the priests.*)

[1] Priests whose task was to clothe the statues of the deities.
[2] The temple of Hermes/Thoth.
[3] The old Egyptian unit of account, still occasionally used in traditional contexts.

42. Dedication of a statue to Aphrodite

I.Alex. no. 69
Alexandria, AD 80–1

This is the inscription from the base of a statue, erected as a posthumous thank-offering by a woman with Roman citizenship, whether a widow who had had a happy marriage or a freedwoman who had enjoyed a remunerative relationship with her former master. Note that statuettes of Aphrodite (or, for Romans, Venus) were often given to brides with their dowry (see **5.191** and **Plate 28**).

To the most great goddess Aphrodite, Claudia Athenarion according to her will, through Claudia Polla her daughter and heiress. Year 3 of Emperor Titus Caesar Vespasianus Augustus [. . .

43.   Dedication of Hathor chapel

OGIS II 675
Kom Ombo, 26 February A D 88

Few women, apart from queens, could afford to finance the construction of temples
or shrines. One of the exceptions was Petronia, apparently a widow, perhaps of a
Roman official or soldier. The facade of the chapel is decorated with scenes involving the Egyptian goddess Hathor, but the inscription, being in Greek, refers to the
goddess as Aphrodite.

On behalf of Emperor Caesar [[Domitian]][1] Augustus Germanicus and all
his family, to Aphrodite the greatest goddess, Petronia Magna and her children built the shrine when Gaius Septimius Vegetus was Prefect and
Artemidoros was strategos, seventh year of Emperor Caesar [[Domitian]]
Augustus [[Germanicus]] in the month of Phamenoth, on its first day.

[1] The later erasure of his name follows the official *damnatio memoriae* of Domitian.

44.   Temple offerings by women

P.Oxy. XII 1449. 7–16
Oxyrhynchite nome, A D 213–17

This list, submitted by the priests of several temples at Oxyrhynchos, illustrates the
sort of offerings found in smaller temples.

List of offerings for year 2[.] of [Marcus Aurelius Severus] Antoninus
Parthicus Maximus Britannicus Maximus Germanicus Maximus [Pius
Augustus], as follows:
  Objects in the temple of Neotera:[1] [A painted portrait of our lord]
emperor Marcus Aurelius Severus Antoninus Felix [Pius Augustus] and Julia
Domna the lady Augusta [and his deified father Severus] – some of the
offerings being inscribed with the names of the dedicators, . . . while in
other cases we are ignorant of the [dedicators because the offerings] have
been in the temple from antiquity – a traditional statue of Demeter, [most
great goddess, of which the head] is of Parian marble and the other parts of
the body of [wood – . . . was not] disclosed to us. And in regard to other
offerings which were dedicated in accordance with ancient custom for vows
or for pious reasons, . . . dedicated by Phragenes(?) son of Horion, a small
bronze statue of Neotera; 5 rings [dedicated by . . .] son of Didymos; a green
robe dedicated by the mother of An[. . .]; [. . .] dedicated by Kastor son of
Asklepiades; a small [. . .] on which is a statuette of Neotera [. . .]; a stone
[. . .] of well-cut stone; a rudder [representing Neotera; a statue of . . .] of
which the head is of Parian marble and the amulets are of plaster; a statue
of Typhon,[2] part of which [. . .] is glued together in the middle, and the

[. . .] in a casket; 2 small [gold lamps] full of brimstone(?) dedicated by
Sara[pion son of] Sarapion; another small gold l[amp] full of brimstone(?)
dedicated by Saraeus daughter of Achill [. . . another lamp full of brim-
stone(?)] dedicated by Ptolemais wife of [. . . of which the] weight is
described in the periodical lists; 10 children's armlets and 1 child's ring, (*the
papyrus continues but the text is full of gaps*).

[1] Another name of Isis, cf. **Plate 6**, applied to Kleopatra.
[2] The Greek name for the Egyptian god Seth, the brother of Osiris and enemy of Horos.

45.   Obeisance to lady Philotera

O.Max. inv. 279+467 ed. A. Bülow-Jacobsen, H. Cuvigny and J.-L.
Fournet, *BIFAO* 94(1994), 32–3
Maximianon, second century AD

Letters not uncommonly refer to the sender performing obeisance (*proskynema*) to
the local deity on behalf of the recipient; see **3.104–5, 108–9; 6.232** introd., **237**.
Serapias in this letter found at Maximianon in the eastern desert mentions her obeisance before the deified Philotera, sister of Arsinoe II and Ptolemy Philadelphos,
after whom a coastal city to the north of Myos Hormos was named (Strabo 16.4.5).
In a further letter, Serapias tells Ammonios that she has left Myos Hormos soon after
giving birth (O.Max. inv. 267; *BIFAO* 94, 1994, 33–4).

Serapias to Ammonios, her father and lord, many greetings. Above all I pray
that you are well, and I do obeisance on your behalf before lady Philotera.
I received from Nestereus 6 loaves. If I come to Myos Hormos, as I
announced to you, I shall send you a jar of fish-sauce with the first donkeys.
For I care as much about you as if you were my own father. And if I find
the linen for you, I shall buy it. If you have a drinking-cup, send it to me.
My brother greets you.
(*Upside-down in upper margin*) Send me the scalpel – don't forget.
(*Downwards in left margin*) Receive 1 jar . . . write to me about yourself. Greet
Proclus.

46.   Invitation to attend a festival

P.Oxy. I 112
Oxyrhynchos, third–fourth century AD

Probably Serenia lived in the city but was an important landowner in the area of
this cult.

Greetings, my lady Serenia, from Petosiris. Make every effort, lady, to come
out (*sc. of the city*) on the 20th for the birthday of the god, and let me know
whether you are coming out by boat or by donkey, so that it can be sent

for you. Take care not to forget, lady. I pray you are well, and long remain
so.

47.   Question to an oracle

P.Oxy. VIII 1149
Oxyrhynchos, second century AD

There were various ways in which deities could be consulted, and in which they
might give a response. Written oracle questions were often submitted on two slips
of papyrus, one with positive and one with negative phrasing; the deity answered by
returning the appropriate slip. For other examples of oracle questions, see **21, 6.249**.

To Zeus Helios,[1] great Serapis, and the (gods) of the same shrine, Nike asks:
<If> it is to my advantage to buy from Tasarapion the slave she has, Sarapion
alias Gaion, give me this (back).

[1] I.e. the Greek equivalent of the Egyptian god Amon-Re.

48.   A binding spell

SEG XXVI 1717
Antinoopolis, third–fourth century AD

The clay statuette of a woman pierced with needles shown in **Plate 13** was found
in a clay jar together with a rolled up lead tablet, roughly 11cm square, bearing the
following text, well written by a 'professional' hand. This type of spell to bind a
loved person is well attested in Egypt (see also **6.282–6**), but rarely found with the
accompanying statuette. The lover in this case, as is usual, calls on the spirit of a
dead person to do the binding (the jar was to be placed on his grave), and invokes
a syncretistic mix of Egyptian, Greek and Semitic deities and *nomina sacra* ('sacred
names'). Also usual is the use of mothers' names to identify the people involved.
Similar spells are collected in Gager (1992), ch. 2; on the implications for sexual
relations, see Winkler (1990); more generally on magical spells from Greek and
Roman Egypt, Faraone and Obbink (1991), and *P.Mich.* XVI 757 introd.

I entrust to you this binding (charm), gods of the Underworld, Plouton[1]
and Kore Persephone[2] Ereschigal[3] and Adondis[4] alias BARBARITHA and
Hermes Thoth of the Underworld PHOKENSEPSEU EREKTATHOU MIS-
ONKTAIK and to Anoubis the strong PSERIPHTHA who holds the keys of
the (gates) of Hades, and demon-gods of the Underworld, youths and
maidens (dead) before their time, year by year, month by month, day by day,
hour by hour, night by night. I adjure all the demons in this place to stand
by this demon Antinoos.[5] Rouse yourself for me and go off into every place,
into every quarter, into every house, and bind Ptolemais, whom Aias bore,
the daughter of Origenes, so that she is not fucked or buggered and does

13   Clay figurine of woman pierced with needles

Musée du Louvre, Paris (inv. 27145)
Antinoopolis, third–fourth century AD

This clay figurine, pierced with needles, of a woman kneeling with her hands bound behind her back, was found in a clay jar together with a rolled up lead tablet bearing the text translated in **2.48**. Instructions for using a figurine like this (with a different type of spell) are given in *PGM* IV 296–466, translated in Betz (1992), 44–7.

nothing for the pleasure of another man, except only for me Sarapammon, whom Area bore, and do not allow her to eat, to drink, to enjoy anything, to go out, to be able to sleep, away from me, Sarapammon, whom Area bore . . . (*more summoning of Antinoos*) . . . tear at her hair, her innards, until she does not reject me Sarapammon, whom Area bore, and I have her Ptolemais, whom Aias bore, the daughter of Origenes, subject for the whole time of my life, loving me, desiring me, telling me her thoughts. If you do this, I will release you.

[1] King of the Greek Underworld, also called Hades.
[2] Daughter of Demeter and wife of Plouton/Hades (see **7**).
[3] A female deity of Babylonian origin.
[4] Adonis (see **3**), or Adonai.
[5] The city of Antinoopolis was founded by Hadrian to commemorate his boyfriend Antinoos, who died here during Hadrian's tour of Egypt; possibly this is the Antinoos summoned.

VI   Christianity

Christianity, which by the fourth century was spreading rapidly in Egypt (Bagnall, 1993a, ch. 8), brought the cult of Mary, female saints and martyrs, and nuns. The following section concentrates on the roles and experiences

14 Mary with the infant Jesus
Berlin: Museum of Late Antique and Byzantine Art (acc. no. 4726)
Medinet el-Fayum, fourth–fifth century AD

A limestone stela (*c.* 55 × 34 cm), depicting a nursing mother sitting on a cushioned folding stool, framed by pillars. Although the crosses were added later, the scene seems to reflect the Christian reinterpretation of the earlier iconographic tradition of Isis suckling Harpokrates (**Plate 11**), to represent Mary with the infant Jesus (Effenberger, 1975; though cf. Forman and Quirke, 1996, 177–8). Traces of the original paint survive: a green curtain hangs between the black pillars, and there is yellow and brown on the dress and the cushion.

of women in Christian religion. For the effects of Christianity on the status and legal position of women, see **Ch.4 Sections IV–V**.

49. Amulet invoking Mary

P.Bon. 19
Provenance unknown, fourth century AD (?)

The cult of Mary gained in general popularity after the christological controversies of the fifth century AD and after she was credited with saving Constantinople in the sixth century (cf. Cameron, 1978), but her cult began earlier in Egypt and flourished to some extent independently of imperial developments. Her iconography drew on the earlier Egyptian traditional representation of Isis and Horos: **Plates 14** with **11**. Known hymns or prayers to Mary on papyrus from Egypt are listed in the commentary to *New Docs.* 2 (1982), no. 92, pp. 145–6; most of them repeat or elaborate the gospel passages about Mary. This invocation on a small scrap of papyrus was probably worn as an amulet.

. . . to the] most [ble]ssed [name?] of the holy god-bearing and ever-virgin[1] Mary, and saint Longinus[2] the centurion. One holy Father, one holy Son, one holy Spirit. Amen, amen, amen.

[1] God-bearing and ever-virgin (see also **50**): Greek *theotokos*, the chief epithet of imperial cult of Mary, and *aeiparthenos* (cf. **58**).

[2] The centurion in Matthew 27.54 and Luke 23.47, venerated by eastern Christians, particularly in Egypt.

50.   Date-clause invoking Mary

SB I 4665
Arsinoite nome, 10 February A D 656

The importance of Mary for Christians, and especially for official Christianity, is illustrated by the invocation of her at the start of dating formulae. (The main body of this document, a letter, does not survive.)

† In the name of our lord and master Jesus Christ, our god and saviour, and of our mistress the holy god-bearing and ever-virgin Mary, and of all the saints, year 373 of Diocletian,[1] Mecheir fifteen, sixth indiction. †

[1] After the Arab conquest Greek documents in Egypt were commonly dated from the year of accession of the emperor Diocletian.

51.   Women as well as men are fitted for martyrdom

Clement of Alexandria, *Miscellanies (Stromata)* IV.viii.58.2–60.1
Alexandria, *c.* A D 200

The writings of Clement, bishop of Alexandria and head of the Catechetical School there from A D 190 to 202, draw on Greek philosophical techniques and classical learning to present a model of the Christian life (see also **6.261**). He regards women as well as men as capable of Christian perfection, although this should not interfere with a wife's subordination to her husband.[1]

For the whole Church is full of those, both men and self-controlled women alike, who all their life have contemplated the life-engendering death for Christ. For the person whose life is conducted as ours is may philosophise without education, whether barbarian, or Greek, or slave, whether old man, or boy, or woman. For self-control is common to all human beings who have chosen it. And we admit that the same nature exists in every race, and is capable of the same virtue. As regards human nature, the woman does not exhibit one nature, and the man another, but both the same; so also with virtue. But if the virtue of a male, perhaps, were self-control and righteousness, and whatever qualities are thought consequent upon them, then it belongs to the male alone to be virtuous, and to the woman to be licentious and unjust. But it is offensive even to say this. Accordingly woman should practise self-control and righteousness, and every other virtue, in the same way as man, both free man and slave; since it happens that the same nature possesses one and the same virtue. That therefore the female nature is the same as the male, in so much as it is female, we do not say; for obviously it stands to reason that some difference should exist between them, in virtue of which the one is female and the other male. Thus pregnancy and parturition, we say, pertain to the woman, in so much as she happens to be female, not in so much as she is human. If there were no difference between man and woman, each of them would do and experience the same. In the respect, therefore, as there is sameness, as in regard to the soul, she will attain to the same virtue; but in the respect that there is difference, as in the distinct construction of the body, she is destined for pregnancy and house-keeping.

[1] Cf. IV.xix.123.2: 'The self-controlled woman, then, will first choose to persuade her husband to be her partner in what conduces to happiness, but if this is not possible, let her alone aim at virtue, obeying her husband in everything, so as never to do anything against his will, except as much as contributes to virtue and salvation.'

52.   A certificate of pagan sacrifice

P.Mich. III 158
Theadelphia (Arsinoite nome), 21 June A D 250

The growth of Christianity was accompanied by phases of conflict with pagans and with the Roman state (until the conversion of the emperor Constantine). The aim of the order by the emperor Decius that everyone should publicly offer cult to the imperial images was probably to foster general loyalty and unity in the empire, not to attack Christians in particular. However, local opponents of Christianity found it a handy tool (see **53**), and Christian writers refer to a 'persecution'.

To those in charge of sacrifices in the village of Theadelphia, from Aurelia Bellias, (daughter) of Peteres, and her daughter Kapinis. We have always sacrificed to the gods, and now in your presence according to the regulations I have made libations and sacrificed and tasted the sacred (offerings), and I request you to certify this for us.
(*2nd hand*) We, Aurelii Serenos and Hermas, saw you sacrificing.
(*3rd hand*) I, Hermas, have signed.
(*1st hand*) Year 1 of Emperor Caesar Gaius Messius Quintus Traianus Decius Pius Felix Augustus, Pauni 27.

53.   Women martyrs at Alexandria

Eusebius, *History of the Church* VI.41.1–7
Alexandria, A D 249/50

The church historian Eusebius here quotes from a letter of Dionysios who was bishop of Alexandria at the time of the Decian 'persecution'.

It was not with the imperial edict that the persecution began among us, but it preceded it by a whole year . . . First, they seized an old man named Metras, and ordered him to blaspheme. When he refused, they beat his body with sticks, stabbed his face and eyes with sharp reeds, led him to the suburb, and stoned him to death. Then they led a woman believer called Quinta to the temple of the idol,[1] and they tried to force her to do obeisance. When she turned away and showed disgust, they bound her by the feet and dragged her through the whole city over the paved stone surfaces, so that she was smashed against the granite stones, while they also whipped her. They brought her to the same place and stoned her to death. Then they all simultaneously made for the homes of the godfearing, and each falling on the neighbours they recognised, they harried, spoiled and plundered them . . . Furthermore, they then seized that marvellous aged virgin[2] Apollonia and knocked out all her teeth by hitting her jaw. They piled up a pyre in front of the city and threatened to burn her alive if she refused to say along with them the instructed impieties. She begged a brief respite and, granted this, she eagerly jumped into the fire and was burnt up.

[1] Probably the Serapeum (in Alexandria), possibly the Caesareum (see **54**).
[2] Cf. **58**.

54.   The killing of Hypatia

Socrates, *History of the Church* VII.15
Alexandria, March AD 415

The emperor Theodosius I (379–94) had made Christianity the official religion of the empire and had outlawed pagan worship. Hypatia was a pagan philosopher and teacher (see Dzielska, 1995), whose devoted pupils included men such as Synesius, later bishop of Cyrene (see Cameron and Long, 1993, 40–62).[1] Among the upper-class élite such 'tolerance' and intellectual interchange was still acceptable, but more militant Christians were deeply suspicious and hostile. The immediate background to the killing of Hypatia was complex. For a mixture of personal and public reasons, including a Christian pogrom against the Jews of Alexandria, the patriarch Cyril had annoyed the imperial governor Orestes, who himself had then been assaulted by a mob of monks brought to Alexandria to support Cyril. This account of Hypatia's death draws on the literary tradition of Christian martyrologies (such as **53**), and also recalls the public shaming and killing of prominent women in Ptolemaic times (see **7**).

There was a woman in Alexandria called Hypatia. She was the daughter of the philosopher Theon. She so excelled in her studies that she surpassed the philosophers of her time, and took over the Platonic school which derived from Plotinus,[2] and she explained all the branches of philosophy to those who wished. For this reason those wishing to study philosophy flocked from everywhere to her side. As she was honoured with the freedom to speak because of her studies, she addressed even officials face to face with decorum. Indeed there was nothing shameful about her presence in a company of men, for they all had the greatest respect and admiration for her because of her outstanding decorum. But hatred was then marshalled against her. Since she visited Orestes quite frequently, this stirred up a false accusation among the people of the church that it was she who was preventing Orestes from establishing friendly relations with the bishop. Some hot-headed men, led by a reader called Peter, plotted together and kept an eye out for the woman to return home from some outing. They threw her out of her carriage, dragged her to the church known as Kaisarion,[3] and after stripping off her clothes, killed her by (throwing) broken tiles. When they had torn her limb from limb, they brought the limbs together at a place called Kinaron, and destroyed them by burning. This affair brought considerable disgrace on Cyril and the Alexandrian church.

[1] An anecdote from the fifth-century AD philosopher Damascius' *Life of Isidoros* (frag. 102 Zintzen) tells how Hypatia repelled a young suitor among her pupils by showing him one of her 'woman's rags' (i.e. sanitary protection), asserting that it was her female physicality he loved and not a thing of true beauty.

[2] The third-century philosopher who developed a mystical form of Platonism which influenced several early Christian thinkers. He came from Lykopolis in Egypt and had studied at Alexandria, but had then lived and taught in Rome, so the misattribution of this school to him is presumably intended to increase Hypatia's standing.

[3] The Caesareum, formerly the temple of Augustus and focus of the imperial cult in Alexandria. In the 350s it had been converted into a church.

55.   The Egyptian Saint Thekla

(Excerpt from) The Martyrdom of Paese and Thekla (Reymond and Barns, 1973, pp. 34–5)
This version written in the Fayum, mid-ninth century

The active roles of early Christian women in Egypt are often described in martyrdoms, such as the Coptic martyrdom of Paese and Thekla. Although related to the much better-known story of Paul and Thekla (see **Ch.6 Sect. II** introd.), the Coptic story concentrates more on the daily life and perseverance of the early Christians in Egypt in the face of persecution. In this excerpt, Paese's sister Thekla, a wealthy young widow, tends the Christian victims of Diocletian's persecution. Ultimately however, both Paese and Thekla take a more active role, journeying to Alexandria to help the martyrs there, eventually being martyred themselves. The martyrdom of Paese and Thekla is part of the extensive cycle of martyrdoms attributed to Julius of Aqfahs, who appears as a contemporary of the martyrs, but the date of these compositions is probably sixth–seventh century. The feast day of Paese and Thekla was 8 Choiak. See further T. Orlandi, 'Paese and Tecla, Saints', in A. S. Atiya (ed.), *The Coptic Encyclopedia* (New York, 1991), VI:1865.

And he (Paese) had a sister, whose name was Thekla and who lived with her husband at Antinoou. She bore a son and she called him Apollonios; she

sent him to school before the Persecution happened. The husband of
Thekla passed on, being a very rich man; he passed on when he was still
young. Thus, Thekla became a widow, and she was very beautiful in appearance. She regularly went to church and she heard the words of the scriptures with her son. Thekla also frequently sent and bought much clothing
and mats. She loaded her servants with these things and sent them throughout the whole city, distributing them to the poor and needy. And this is how
she lived for three years. After the Persecution began, she waited on the
saints and she cared for them, and her love endured in the prisons, where
she cooked food and drew water for the saints, who ate from her hands. And
whenever she saw one who was naked, she brought him into her house,
clothing and feeding him. The angel of the Lord revealed himself to her on
many occasions. He spoke with her and she, herself, spoke with him many
times, saying: 'My Lord, help me.' And he would say to her: 'In the manner
in which you have clothed the naked, I will cause you, yourself, to be
clothed, both your body and your spirit, in clothing of light. And as for the
one(s) who will give a shroud for your body, I will cover their souls with
clothing of light, so that no dark force may have power over them.' Thekla
reflected in her heart about the words that the angel said to her – 'your body
will be clothed' – and she said: 'But what will happen to me? Is poverty
coming to me? Or will wild animals devour me and my body be buried with
love? But the will of God will be done.' Now, many rich men of the city
beseeched her, saying: 'We want to take you as wife.' But she herself was not
persuaded, and instead continued to devote herself to the saints, bandaging
their wounds. On their tortured bodies, she put oil and wine. Now the
saints blessed her, saying: 'May the lord protect all of you: you, your little
son and your brother. May you come into the number of the saints and may
you receive an inheritance in the heavenly Jerusalem.'

56.   My lady the teacher

SB XIV 11532
Alexandria, fourth century AD

Although women deacons are attested in other areas of the early Christian world,
and even a few women priests, in Egypt no woman holding office in the church
(outside nunneries) is yet attested; cf. *New Docs.* 1 (1981), no. 79. This fragmentary
letter (missing the beginning and the right-hand side) between Christians, perhaps
of a particular sect, provides the only possible, but partial, exception.

. . .] to you new in Alexandria [. . .] my lord brother Julianus [. . .] and if
you wish [. . .] what good we can. The [. . .] my lady the teacher. The [. . .]
who wrote to me and a letter [. . .] my lady Xenike, my lady Arsinoe, and
[. . .] of truth(?) the august free [. . .] Philoxenos and those with you. The

lord [. . .] the fine Phoibammon and all his [household greet] you. The grace of our lord Jesus Christ [be with you all].[1]

(*In left margin*) My lady the teacher.

(*On the back*) [Deliver to] Philoxenos, best of all men, teacher.

[1] An echo of 2 Corinthians 13.13.

57. Women become male to enter the Kingdom of Heaven

The Gospel of Thomas: Nag Hammadi Codex II 99.18–26 (Layton 1989, p. 92)

Nag Hammadi, composed late third century(?)A D

Tensions between the active involvement of women in the Christian religious life and attitudes towards women expressed in the New Testament fostered the notion that women could 'become male' in order better to serve God, an idea already hinted at in biblical texts and made explicit in the lives of early Christian women such as Perpetua. The transformation of women into men is reflected in the following passage from the conclusion of the Gnostic Gospel of Thomas, known from a complete Coptic version and Greek fragments from Egypt: Simon Peter asks that Mary be sent away from the group because she is not a man, but Jesus offers to make her a man so that she can remain with the disciples, and extends the offer to all women.

Simon Peter said to them: 'Let Mary go away from us, for women are not worthy of the Life.' Jesus said: 'Behold, I shall impel her, in order to make her male, so that she herself may become a living spirit, being like you males. For any woman who makes herself male shall enter the Kingdom of Heaven.'

58. A virgin bookworm

P.Lips. 43

Hermopolis Magna(?), fourth century A D

Use of the 'title' of ever-virgin (*aeiparthenos*), a cult epithet of Mary (see **49** and **50**), often, as in this case, in place of the normal patronymic, has a partial precedent in the 'sacred virgins' of pagan cult (see **35**), but is essentially a novelty which reflects the great importance that the early church put on virginity, and denotes women who had in some sense devoted themselves to a religious life, even if they were not all what we would call nuns (see **53**; in general Elm, 1994, esp. ch. 7). This text also illustrates the growing role of church authorities as arbitrators.

Pharmouthi 18, in the entrance of the catholic church, under Plousianos the most respected bishop. At the arbitration held between Thaesis the

ever-virgin (*aeiparthenos*) and the heirs of Besarion, the arbitration judgement delivered by the same bishop Plousianos as arbitrator in the presence
of Dioskorides son of Hymnion, town-councillor, and E[. . .] alias
Herakleios son of Eith[. . .], and [. . .] deacon, was that: either the heirs of
Besarion are to produce witnesses who will identify Thaesis, as regards the
theft of Christian books, as the one who did it, and she is to bring them
back, or she is to swear an oath that she has committed no theft, and then
everything which is left in the house <is to be divided> into two halves,
and Thaesis is to receive one half and the heirs the other half, and this is to
happen by the thirtieth of the same Pharmouthi.

59.   An exchange of Christian books

P.Oxy. LXIII 4365
Oxyrhynchos, fourth century A D

A petition, signed by Aurelia Soteira alias Hesychion, was cut down so that the back
could be used for this short letter, which may also be in Soteira's hand.

To my dearest lady sister in the Lord, greeting. Lend the Ezra, since I lent
you the little Genesis.[1] Farewell from us in God.

[1] D. Hagedorn, *ZPE* 116 (1997), 147–8, suggests that 'little Genesis' refers to Jubilees; cf.
    Epiphanios of Salamis, *Panarion* 39.6.1.

60.   Twenty thousand virgins

(Excerpts from) *Historia Monachorum in Aegypto* V. 1–6
Oxyrhynchos, mid-fourth century A D

This somewhat hyperbolic account of the popularity of monasticism, and of ortho-
dox Christianity in general, was written in Greek by an anonymous Christian
traveller (it is more often cited in the slightly later Latin version by Rufinus). The
'virgins' here are clearly nuns; the fourth century was indeed the period when their
numbers boomed (see **61**).

We also visited Oxyrhynchos, a city of the Thebaid, whose wonders cannot
be described adequately . . . There are said to be five thousand monks within
the city and as many others living outside it . . . Furthermore, there is not
a single heretical or pagan inhabitant in the city . . . On the basis of our
information from the holy bishop there, we declare that he has ten thousand monks under him and twenty thousand virgins. The nature of their
hospitality and their love I am unable to describe. The cloaks of each of us
were ripped apart by people dragging us in to stay with them.

61.   Two 'apotactic' nuns

P.Oxy. XLIV 3203
Oxyrhynchos, July A D 400

'Nuns', called *monachai* (*monachos* = monk), appear in the papyri in the fourth century (see Judge, 1981). The meaning of *apotaktikos* is not clear, but it may, as apparently here, denote city-dwelling monks and nuns who did not live in a self-contained community (cf. **60**). Clearly these sisters had not relinquished their personal property (cf. Elm, 1994, 235–8).

The year after the consul[ship of Flavius Theodoros] the most illust[rious, Epeiph . . .]. To the Aureliae Theodora and Tayris whose father is Silvanus, of the illustrious and most illustrious city of the Oxyrhynchites, apotactic nuns, from Aurelius Jose son of Judas, Jew, of the same city. I voluntarily undertake to lease from the first day of the next month Mesore of the present year 76/45,[1] at the start of the fourteenth indiction, from your property in the same city of the Oxyrhynchites in the Cavalry Camp quarter, one ground-floor room – a hall – and one cellar which is in the basement with all appurtenances, and I will pay for the rent of them annually one thousand two hundred myriads of denarii, total 12,000,000 denarii, and I will be obliged to pay the rent in six-monthly halves without delay, and whenever you wish I will hand back the same rooms clean and as I received them. † The lease-contract, in two written copies, is valid; and when asked, I assented.

(*2nd hand*) I, the aforementioned Aurelius Jose son of Judas, have leased the dining-room and will pay the aforementioned rent. I, Aurelius Elias son of Opebaios(?), have written for him since he cannot write.

[1] At Oxyrhynchos in this period documents were sometimes dated from the years of accession (as Caesars) of the emperors Constantius II (A D 324) and Julian (A D 355); see Bagnall and Worp (1978), 36–42.

62.   A nun's dispute with her mother

P.Lond. V 1731.1–20
Syene, 20 September A D 585

The popularity of monasticism is difficult to explain. This account of a family dispute, vividly if ungrammatically recounted in a string of subordinate clauses, suggests how personal reasons could contribute to the decision of an individual like Aurelia Tsone to become a nun.

(*Chi-rho monogram*) In the fourth year of the reign of our most divine master Flavius Tiberius Mauricius the eternal Augustus emperor and greatest benefactor, and the second year of the consulship of our same master, Thoth 23 of the fourth indiction, in Syene. Aurelia Tsone, daughter of Menas, whose mother is Tapia, nun (*monache*) originating from Syene . . . to Aurelia Tapia, daughter of Tsios by Mariam her mother, acting herself without a husband as guardian, my own mother, originating from the same Syene, greeting. Since formerly my blessed father Menas held you in the partnership of a legal marriage, and after my birth, when I was still young, through the workings of the devil and Satan you were divorced from him; and my afore-said father Menas gave you four coins of gold; and after my reaching the legal age I proceeded against you, accusing you over the same four coins, and saying that these had been given to you specifically for the necessary maintenance of me from childhood; for this reason, because I was main-tained by my father, after I had been thrown out by you and you joined with another man, I proceeded against you seeking to take these (coins); you dis-puted this, saying that the same four coins were (returned) for <your> release and dowry; and after many claims, counter-claims and opinions, it was later decided that I should receive the same four coins . . . (*acknowledges receipt of them*).

63.   A cloak for a widow

P.Wisc. II 64
Oxyrhynchos, 27 January A D 480

As the church became more organised and wealthy, it became an institutionalised source of charity, offering relief to those, like poor widows, whose social position left them without normal family support.

(*Chi-rho monogram*) The holy church to Peter, steward (of the church) of (Saint) Kosmas. Provide the widow Sophia, from the cloaks which you have which are fit for use, with one cloak, total 1 cloak only.

(2nd hand) † Farewell.

(*1st hand*): Year 156/125,[1] Mecheir 1 of the 3rd indiction.

[1] See **61** note 1.

64.   Wine for widows

P.Oxy. XVI 1954
Oxyrhynchos, late fifth century A D

Wine was one of the basic foodstuffs which might be provided by church charity, as in this order to a lay official of a church which seems to have assumed regular responsibility for a group (or set number) of widows.

To Victor wineseller. Give to the widows of (Saint) Michael 1 only double-jar of wine. Mesore 16, indiction 5, beginning of 6.

65.   Release from a spell

Palladius, *Lausiac History* XVII.6–9
Nitrian desert (west of Alexandria), written around AD 420

The spread of Christianity did not bring an end to the use of magic, for many of the extant love-charms from Egypt date from the fourth century or later (see **48**), and some involve people with apparently Christian names (e.g. *SB* XIV 11534). Indeed, as this text illustrates, the continuing belief in magic gave holy men an arena for demonstrating the power of their sanctity.

An Egyptian man, who was struck with desire for a married woman of free birth but was unable to entice her, consulted a magician and said, 'Seize her with love for me, or somehow arrange it so that her husband throws her out.' On receipt of the necessary, the magician used his magical spells and furnished her with the appearance of a brood mare. So when the husband returned home, he blanched when he saw a mare lying on his bed. The man wept and wailed. He tried to talk to the animal, but got no reply. He summoned the elders of the village. He took them in and showed them. He found no solution. For three days she did not take hay like a mare or bread like a man, but was deprived of both kinds of food. In the end, so that god would be glorified and the virtue of Saint Makarios would be shown, it entered her husband's head to lead her into the desert. He bridled her like a horse, and so led her into the desert. At their approach the brothers stood by the cell of Makarios, and fought off her husband and said, 'Why have you led this mare here?' He said to them, 'For her to receive mercy.' They said to him, 'What is wrong with her?' The husband replied to them, 'She was my wife, but has been transformed into a horse, and today is the third day that she has not touched any food.' They reported this to the saint who was praying inside. For God had revealed it to him, and he was praying for her. So Saint Makarios replied to the brothers and said to them, 'You are the horses, for you have the eyes of horses. For she is a woman, not changed in form, except only in the eyes of those taken in.' Then he blessed water and poured it over her naked body from the head down, and he prayed. And immediately he made her appear a woman to all. He gave her food and made her eat, and let her go, giving thanks to the lord, with her own husband. And he instructed her and said, 'Never stay away from the church[1] or miss the communion. These things happened to you because for five weeks you had not attended the mysteries.'

---

[1] For a woman's regular attendance at church cf. **4.153**.

66.   A Christian amulet

P.Oxy. VIII 1151
Oxyrhynchos, fifth century AD(?)

Another Christian response to pagan magic was to develop 'Christian' magic. This
papyrus was tightly folded and tied with a string, presumably to be worn as an
amulet (see **49**). In the style of pagan charms, this text includes garbled biblical and
liturgical passages or allusions, presumably thought to have power in themselves,
and identifies individuals by their mother's name, not their father's name, as is usual.

† Flee, hateful spirit! Christ pursues you; the Son of God and the Holy Spirit
have overtaken you. O God of the pool at the Sheep Gate,[1] deliver from all
evil your servant Joannia, whom Anastasia alias Euphemia bore. † In the
beginning was the word, and the word was with God and God was the word.
All things were made by him, and without him was not one thing made that
was made. O lord † Christ, son and word of the living God, who healed
every sickness and every infirmity, heal and watch over also your servant
Joannia, whom Anastasia alias Euphemia bore, and chase from her and put
to flight all fevers and every kind of chill, quotidian, tertian, and quartan,[2]
and every evil. Pray through the intercession of our lady the mother of God,
and the glorious archangels, and Saint John the glorious apostle and evangel-
ist and theologian, and Saint Serenus and Saint Philoxenos and Saint Victor
and Saint Justus and all the saints. On your name, O lord God, have I called,
which is wonderful and exceedingly glorious and frightens your enemies.
Amen. †

[1] See John 5.2, the healing of a cripple at the pool near this gate in Jerusalem (known in
   Hebrew as Bethesda).
[2] Fevers returning every day, every other day and every third day (counting inclusively).

67.   Appeal to a holy man

P.Lond. VI 1926
Upper Egypt(?), mid-fourth century AD

A more doctrinally correct way of seeking relief from worldly troubles, including
illness, was belief in the efficacy of prayer, but here too, patronage could be of assistance. This is one of an archive of seven letters (*P.Lond.* VI 1923–9) to an anchorite,
who clearly had a high reputation for spirituality and healing.

To the most honoured and Christ-carrying and adorned with every virtue
Apa Paphnouthis,[1] Valeria, greetings in Christ. I request and entreat you,
most honoured father, to ask for me [help] from Christ and that I may obtain
healing. I believe that in this way, through your prayers, I shall obtain

healing, for by ascetics and devotees revelations are manifested. For I am afflicted by a great disease of breathlessness. I have believed and believe that in this way, if you pray on my behalf, I shall obtain healing. I entreat God, I entreat you too; remember me in your holy intercessions. Even though in body I have not come to your feet, in spirit I have come to your feet. I mention also my daughters; remember them too in your holy intercessions, Bassiana and Theoklia. My husband also greets you many times; pray on his behalf too. My whole household also greets you. I pray you are well, most honoured father.

(*On the back*) To the most honoured father Apa Paphnoutios from his daughter Valeria.

[1] Apa was the Aramaic for abba, Father, often used as a title of respect for monks and other holy men. For the variant spellings of the name Papnouthis/Paphnoutios, cf. e.g. **Ch.3 Archs. B, D** and **G**.

68.   A Christian tombstone

IGA v 48
Alexandria, 19 March A D 409

One of the novelties of Christianity was to bring belief in an eventual bodily resurrection. The tortuous problems of the details of physical resurrection are elegantly avoided in this Greek inscription by use of the liturgical periphrasis ('judge her fit . . .'), which derives from the story of Dives and Lazarus (Luke 16.19–31).

††† God the almighty, the one who is, who was and who is to come, Jesus Christ, the son of the living god, remember the sleep and repose of your slave Zoneene, the most pious and law-loving.[1] And judge her fit to dwell, through your holy and light-bringing archangel Michael, in the bosom of the holy fathers Abraham, Isaac and Jacob. Because yours is the glory and power to the ages of ages, amen. She lived blessedly for 77 years. This is her memorial. Phamenoth 23, after the consulship of Bassus and Philippus.

[1] An epithet adapted from Judaism.

3 Family matters

Introduction

To us, 'family' has two senses: firstly a group of individuals, often but not necessarily related by blood or marriage, co-habiting as a household, and secondly the wider group of relatives with whom one has regular contact although they are not part of the same household. No word used in the papyri from Egypt has quite the same range of meanings, and ambiguities, as 'family'; but the texts do provide ample illustration of both household composition and the wider ramifications of family relationships.

Our main evidence for household composition, and for demography more generally, comes from census declarations submitted to the Roman authorities in Egypt between AD 11 and 257.[1] The data conforms to a model of low life expectancy at birth, on average perhaps twenty-five years for males and twenty-two years for females. Nearly half the infants and young children died before reaching five years of age. The regulations operative in Roman Egypt even excused provincials for not registering infants under three years old in the census.[2] But those children who did survive five years had better prospects; life expectancy for girls was then an additional thirty-eight years, and the approximately 45 per cent of female infants born who reached their fifteenth birthday could expect on average an additional thirty-two and a half years, thus bringing them to about forty-eight, and, in all likelihood, to or through the menopause. But only about 1 per cent of female infants born lived to see their eightieth birthday, and the population was thus a very young one. Infection and disease not only orphaned infants and children, but also thrust young adults into positions of considerable responsibility, including the burden of childbearing.

Social customs, however, such as the relatively early age of marriage for girls and the fact that nearly everyone married, spread the burden of childbearing among fertile women. Although very young brides of twelve and thirteen years are known, the majority of women in the villages married in their mid- and late teens, while those who lived in the metropoleis often delayed marriage until their later teens and early twenties. Their husbands were normally older than they (a pattern spread throughout the ancient Mediterranean); usually the gap was between two and thirteen years, but almost a quarter of young brides married men close to their father's age, some twenty to thirty years their senior. A woman who reached the menopause was likely to be a widow, and she would need to have given birth to about six live children in order to leave behind two surviving offspring. But many women never reached middle age, dying in childbirth, together with their infants.

In the Roman period close-kin marriages were popular, with perhaps nearly a quarter of the population participating in endogamous marriage between siblings and half-siblings. A number of distinct motives may have fostered such unions, even though, as anthropologists have noted, many societies prohibit them as incestuous, including the Romans.[3] For the socially ambitious and wealthy Greeks, the practice would preserve their bloodlines unmixed; maintaining family goods undivided and within family control may have motivated the thrifty; the poverty-stricken may have seen the practice as a means to avoid the expense of dowering a daughter; and the sensible, as a relatively easy way to find a bride for a young son, otherwise unable to obtain one in a competitive marriage market that favoured the older and financially established groom. The extension of Roman citizenship to the provincials of Egypt in AD 212 had considerable effect in curbing brother–sister marriage as a public phenomenon, although there is some evidence of the practice continuing, and the emperor Diocletian was still issuing prohibitions at the end of the third century (AD 291–5).

Partly because of the high mortality level, household composition varied considerably. Sometimes a single family member was left living alone, or grandparents died, leaving the younger generation and their children in the house. But multi-generational households were not uncommon, or households composed of adult siblings, spouses, and their children; domestic slaves or lodgers might also share the space. Grand houses in the Greek style, with separate quarters reserved for the men and their banquets, and large numbers of slaves, served the needs of wealthy families in Alexandria and the metropoleis, or on their country estates. In the Egyptian milieu of the villages, poverty dictated that very cramped quarters, often only a small portion of a house, served the needs of the less fortunate.[4] Families tended to congregate together, living within the same building or in adjacent dwellings.

The terms 'father' and 'mother', 'brother' and 'sister', not only designated members of one's biological family, but were also employed with increasing frequency in letters of the Roman period to express affective feelings.[5] Egyptian Christians from the fourth century AD onward greeted many as their 'brother or sister (in God)'. Metaphors drawn from family relationships, with their overarching implications of hierarchy – male over female, parents over children, and greater equality among siblings – were powerful concepts that shaped people's lives and defined men's and women's positions within a household. Sharing common living-space created quasi-familial relationships even among those with no kinship ties, and shared experiences fostered the use of kinship terms for one's friends and associates.

Throughout the period covered by this book, marriage and divorce remained private acts, not requiring official registration, although families who chose to have written contracts drawn up could register them in governmental archives, to be produced if a family dispute resulted in a court case. The Roman concern for preserving status distinctions did imply some official 'interference' in family matters, exemplified by declarations of birth and of death, as well as regulations about who could marry whom. Soldiers were particularly subject to restrictions on family life (Alston, 1995, 53–68), being forbidden by Roman law to marry until their military service was over; soldiers stationed in Egypt nonetheless established lasting relationships with women and produced children by them. These children were labelled 'fatherless' in official records, until the soldier was discharged from service, and obtained Roman citizenship for himself and his children and was entitled to make a legitimate Roman marriage with the children's mother. Retired soldiers often returned to their native villages, distinguishable from Graeco-Egyptians by the Roman names (*tria nomina*) they and their offspring bore, the emblem of their ability to use Roman legal forms and their exemption from capitation taxes.[6]

Occasionally single texts, like snapshots, vividly capture a family's activities at a particular moment; **Section I** contains some of these, together with examples of household and family registrations. But we often get a fuller picture of families, and women's roles within them, when we possess a number of papers belonging to the same family, known as archives.[7] In the last hundred years some archives were excavated and published as a group, but more were scattered by the antiquities dealers who bought them from peasant diggers and then sold off individual papyri to the highest bidder, fragmenting what was probably discovered as a unity, a family's records stored somewhere in their house, or discarded in a bundle on a rubbish heap. Many archives have had to be reassembled by scholars who have identified references to the same individuals in texts published separately. **Section II** of the chapter presents, in chronological sequence, selections from eleven archives, labelled alphabetically for convenient reference. Their chronological spread (mid-third century BC to mid-sixth century AD), and geographical provenance, are representative of our surviving evidence generally. Just over half of the archives derive from Fayum villages, with Upper Egypt, Hermopolis, Oxyrhynchos, and the temple complex at Memphis also represented, but not the almost undocumented Delta region, or Egypt's most important city, Alexandria. These archives also span several social levels, from those of wealth and property to temple priests, modest farmers, tradespeople, and low-level bureaucrats. The very poor also go unrepresented, since they had less property to protect with written proofs, and less access to the means of writing.[8]

Not all surviving archives give women a prominent role: some consist primarily of administrative papers relating to a man's public office, alongside which we may find rare glimpses of his family relationships (**A, E,** cf. **6.259**). But most of those chosen depict women in sufficient detail to show something of their character, or to trace common patterns, such as the attention a widowed mother frequently receives from her adult children (**E, G, J**). None of the individuals drew up their papers or composed their personal messages with the thought that outsiders, centuries later, might read them, and although we become unanticipated spectators of their private lives, allusions in letters well known to the recipients are seldom spelled out with a clarity sufficient for us to understand all nuances of their words. Sometimes we are puzzled by what is said. Disagreements and lawsuits, hatreds and jealousies, as well as the violence such emotions breed, seem to have the better chance of receiving commemoration in writing than do more gentle thoughts and affective emotions. Family matters were ever of great concern, causing joy and anguish within the household, as members quarrelled and reconciled, parted for journeys away from home and returned. Although family life was often strained by the intense relationships that close living engendered, caring for one's nearest and dearest had high priority. Family matters.

[1] See Bagnall and Frier (1994), 75–121; cf. Saller (1994) on the demography of the Roman empire as a whole.

[2] *Gnomon of the Idios Logos* §63; cf. **4.131**. But the census declaration **69** includes a girl of two years.

[3] Roman prohibition: **4.131** (§23). For bibliography on, and references to, endogamous marriages, see **69** note 3.

[4] For the parts of the Graeco-Egyptian house, see Husson (1983); on village housing, Hobson (1985).

[5] Often it is unclear whether or not kinship terms are being employed in non-biological relationships. For cases where the parties are certainly not related in the way a kinship term suggests, see e.g. **95**, and **2.45**; cf. also **5.172** and **173**.

[6] For soldiers, see Alston (1995), especially chs. 4 and 7; on Roman nomenclature, **Ch.4 Sect. III** introd.

[7] The term 'archive' is often applied loosely to any collection of texts relating to the same individual, although strictly speaking, it applies only to texts deliberately collected and kept together in antiquity. A collection compiled by modern historians from references to a single individual preserved separately is strictly a dossier; cf. Bagnall (1995), 40.

[8] Illiterates: **79** introd.; **86** introd.; **Arch. D** introd. and **90**; **Arch. F** introd. and **101, 103**; **Arch. K** introd.; see Hanson (1991b). See also **Ch.6 Sect. II**.

I   Perspectives on the family

This section assembles seven texts which view the family from different perspectives. The first four are declarations for official purposes of complete families (**69**), or of individual children (**70–2**). Then we have three graphic illustrations: of how a slave girl can take the role of a natural daughter (**73**); the affection of a soldier for his family, particularly his mother (**74**); and finally, the tensions arising from a family dispute over property (**75**).

69.   An endogamous family changes over time: extracts from census declarations

SB xx 14303 ii.21–iii.58
Arsinoe, 18 March A D 119 (1) and 22 July A D 133 (2)

The descendants of Dioskoros and his wife Zois were registered in the Roman census announced in Egypt for the year A D 117/18, and again fourteen years later, in the census of A D 131/2.[1] Declarations were commonly made in the year following the prefect's announcement. Our texts are not, however, the original declarations which the house owner submitted, but copies made by a scribe for an unknown purpose.[2] Both declarations show that this is a family of tenants, occupying a portion of a house they rented in the *metropolis*, Arsinoe.

In the earlier census (1) the mother of the family, Zois, is fifty-three years old, while her husband Dioskoros is presumably deceased, since he is not mentioned and because his seventy-year-old sister Isarous lives with his wife. Also in the household are Zois' grown children: a son Sokrates, his elder sister Aphrodous, and his younger sister, also named Aphrodous, whom Sokrates has married. Zois was aged about twenty when she gave birth to her eldest daughter, and her two subsequent children, Sokrates and his sister–wife, were both born by the time she was about twenty-five. It is surprising, then, that in the first declaration (1) Sokrates and the younger Aphrodous report no children. A groom who marries his sister tends to be somewhat younger than those marrying outside the family, and Sokrates is already thirty-two years old and his sister–wife, twenty-eight.[3] If children had already been born to the couple, they had not survived. By the next census fourteen years later (2), both Zois and her sister-in-law have disappeared and are presumably dead; Aphrodous, the elder sister, is also no longer present. Five children, three boys and two younger girls, have been born in rapid succession to Sokrates and the younger Aphrodous. The spacing of the children at two year intervals (except before the younger girl) suggests that Aphrodous nursed the children herself and that breast-feeding for a time after each birth temporarily reduced her fertility.[4] Whether subsequent children were born into the family is unknown.

(1) To Eudemos, strategos of the Arsinoite nome, Herakleides division, and to Hermaios alias Dryton, royal scribe of the same division, and to Herakleides and Euboulos, scribes of the *metropolis*, and to Herakleides, *exegetes*, and to the company of collectors of money taxes for the *metropolis*, and to Herodes, chief official of the Sacred Gate quarter, and to Maron, scribe for the census in the same quarter, from Philippiaina, daughter of Zoilos, son of Apollonios, daughter of a 'settler',[5] registered through another memorandum in the Moeris quarter, with her guardian who is her husband, Ploution, son of Komon, 'settler of the 6475'.

There belongs to me in the same Moeris quarter the 5th part of ¼ of a house and other plots in which (dwell) those inhabitants whose names are written below whom I am declaring for the house-by-house census of the past 2nd year of Hadrian Caesar, our lord, in the Sacred Gate quarter in which they were also registered in the house-by-house census of the 7th year of the deified Trajan. And they are, after other items:

Zois, daughter of Herakleides, son of Sokrates, 53 years old.

And her son Sokrates, son of Dioskoros, whose status has been scrutinised, 32 years old, without distinguishing marks.

And her daughter Aphrodous, 33 years old.

And another daughter Aphrodous, being married to her brother Sokrates, mentioned above, 28 years old.

And the elder paternal aunt of those mentioned above including Sokrates, Isarous, 70 years old.

Therefore I make my declaration.

Registered with the strategos and all the others. Year 3 of Hadrian Caesar, our lord, 22 Phamenoth.

(2) To Protarchos, strategos of the Arsinoite nome, Herakleides division, and to Hermaios, royal scribe of the same division, and to Maron, scribe of the *metropolis*, and to Didas, the tax collector of Moeris, and to Ptolemaios, chief official of the quarter, and to Deios, scribe for the census, and to Antoninus alias Hermaios, appointed (to the office), from Ploution, son of Komon, grandson of Heron, his mother being Ptollarous alias Ptolema, daughter of Apollonios, 'settler of the 6475', registered in the Moeris quarter and registered for the census through another memorandum.

There belongs to me in the quarter of Apollonios' Camp the . . . part of a house in which (dwell) those inhabitants whose names are written below whom I am declaring for the house-by-house census of the past 16th year of Hadrian, our lord, in the . . . quarter and they are, after other items:

Sokrates, son of Dioskoros, whose status has been scrutinised, 46 years old, without distinguishing marks.

And his wife, being his sister of the same father . . . and of the same mother, Aphrodous, 42 years old. Both registered for the census in the 2nd year in the Sacred Gate (quarter).

And the children from both of them: Dioskoros, registered among those who have been born after (the census), 12 years old;

and Onesimos, registered among those who have been born after (the census), 10 years old;

and Asklas, registered among those who have been born after (the census), 8 years old;

and a daughter Zoidous, 6 years old; and Herais, 2 years old.

Therefore I make my declaration.

Registered with the strategos and all the others. Year 17 of Hadrian Caesar, our lord, 28 Epeiph.

---

[1] For the mechanics and history of the fourteen-year census cycle, initiated soon after Egypt was made a Roman province, see Bagnall and Frier (1994), 1–30.

70. Registration in Latin of the birth of a girl

C. Pap. Lat. 156
Alexandria, 3 November A D 148

Registering the births of infants, including females, was required of Roman citizens, even those living in the provinces.[1] Here a father registers before the prefect
on 13 September 148 the daughter born to him and his wife, also a Roman citizen,
on the preceding 19 August. In November the father acquired a summary copy of
the Latin registration as it had been posted publicly. He had his copy written out
on a diptych, two wooden tablets fastened together. On the outer surface ink was
used for writing; on the protected inner surface the text was incised in the wax, and
this latter is translated below.

In the consulship of Gaius Bellicius Calpurnius Torquatus and Publius
Salvius Julianus, three days before the Nones of November, in the 12th year
of Emperor Caesar Titus Aelius Hadrianus Antoninus Augustus Pius, in the
month Hathyr, 7th day, at Alexandria in Egypt.
    The following copy was written out and compared with the declarations
of babies born, written on the whitened board and set up in the Great
Atrium, on which was written that which follows below:
    In the consulship of Gaius Bellicius Calpurnius Torquatus and Publius
Salvius Julianus, consuls, in the 12th year of Emperor Caesar Titus Aelius
Hadrianus Antoninus Augustus Pius when Marcus Petronius Honoratus was
prefect of Egypt: declarations of babies received outside of official scrutiny,
tablet 5 and, after other items,[2] on page 3, 18 days before the Kalends of
October:
    Tiberius Julius Dioskorides, with a census rating of 5000 sesterces, (says)
that his daughter Julia Ammonous was born from Julia Ammonarion 13 days
before the Kalends of September last . . .
    (*Witnesses*) Gaius Julius Priscus, Gaius Julius Serenus, Titus Fenius Macedon,
Marcus Servilius Clemens, Gaius Julius Lecinnianus, Titus Julius Eutychos,
Lucius Petronius Celer.

[1] Another example is *Sel.Pap.* II 303 (= *PSI* IX 1067; with *BL* VII 239) AD 236/7.
[2] See **69** note 2.

71. Sempronia Gemella registers the birth of twins 'from an uncertain father'

P.Mich. III 169
Karanis, (29 April) AD 145

This declaration, found in Karanis[1] was also (like **70**) written on a wooden diptych with wax interior. The Greek summary of the text, translated below, was written on the outer surface, perhaps because those in the village who needed to read it would have found the Latin copy less easy to understand. Sempronia Gemella submitted the notice about the twins, born to her and an 'uncertain father', 12 days before the Kalends of April (= 20 March); the birth was registered on 4 Pachon (= 29 April) in year 8 of Antoninus Pius (144/5).[2] Like Sempronia Gemella, the seven witnesses who signed the Latin copy of the registration were Roman citizens, as also was her guardian Gaius Julius Satorninus, a man from Karanis.[3]

The diptych was found in House B7 (**Plate 19**); Taesion/Taesis of House B1 (**Arch. G**) was Sempronia Gemella's neighbour, and another neighbour in House B17 was Sokrates, son of Sarapion and Thatres. Sokrates, one of the most important collectors of capitation taxes at Karanis, had two sons named Sarapion and Sokrates, who may have been Sempronia Gemella's twins, named Marcus Sempronius Sarapion and Marcus Sempronius Sokration in this official registration of their birth. Despite the official registration of the twins as born from an 'uncertain father', it is likely that she, and the rest of the village, knew their father's identity. Sempronia Gemella may have had personal and socio-legal reasons for not concluding a formal marriage agreement with Sokrates; as a Roman citizen, she could not marry a man of Graeco-Egyptian status without endangering her sons' Roman citizenship (see **4.131**, esp. §39 and §52). Further, she seems never to have lived in the same house with Sokrates; the diptych comes from House B7, and no papers of hers were found in Sokrates' House B17.[4]

I, Sempronia Gemella with my guardian Gaius Julius Satorninus, have summoned witnesses to the fact that two twin sons were born to me from an uncertain father and that the babies were called Marcus Sempronius, son of Spurius, Sarapion and Marcus Sempronius, son of Spurius, Sokration. I, Gaius Julius Satorninus, was registered as her guardian and I wrote about[5] her because she does not know letters.

[1] Cf. **Archs. G–J**, with **Plates 17–24**.
[2] The Latin version (translated in Lewis and Reinhold, 1990, 482) gives dates in full. See also Youtie (1975a) and Gilliam (1978).
[3] For Roman nomenclature, see **Ch.4 Sect. III** introduction.
[4] Van Minnen (1994a). Sokrates forwarded private letters for villagers: see **104** and **108**.
[5] The expression 'about', instead of the usual 'on behalf of', indicates that the scribe was primarily a Latin speaker and not totally familiar with the usage in Greek documents.

72. Apynchis and Tapasis, his sister–wife, register their eight-year old daughter

P.Petaus 2
Ptolemais Hormou, 14 February AD 185

This text illustrates the procedures by which the Graeco-Egyptian population reg-istered their offspring. It also exists in two copies, both written on papyrus, one addressed to the village scribe, the local official who kept population records for tax purposes (*P.Petaus* 1); the other (translated here) addressed to the royal scribe, the official with similar duties at the nome level. On brother–sister marriage, see refer-ences in **69** note 3.

To Hermophilos, royal scribe of the Arsinoite nome, Herakleides division, from Apynchis, son of an unknown father and his mother Tapholemis, and from his sister Tapasis, born from the same mother, who is also his wife, from the village of Ptolemais Hormou, with Apynchis as the guardian of Tapasis. We register our daughter Taesis, who was born to us both and is now eight years old in the present 25th year. Therefore, we submit this memorandum of her birth.
(*2nd hand*) To the village scribe of Ptolemais Hormou. Complete this as in similar instances, with the reckoning and the risk being yours if some aspect is not as it should be.
    Year 25 of Marcus Aurelius Commodus Antoninus Augustus Pius, 20 Mecheir.

73. Petition: Thermouthion's slave girl was injured on her way to a singing lesson

P.Oxy. L 3555
Oxyrhynchos, first/second century AD

This petition shows how in the absence of natural offspring, a slave could take on a daughter's role, both in the affections of her mistress, and in providing the prac-tical care an elderly parent could expect. Peina's name is unusual and, if derived from Greek, would mean 'Pearl', although if derived from Egyptian, it would mean 'Mouse'. The petition is expressed in unusually complex language for a docu-mentary text, and loss of clarity is sometimes the result, perhaps reflecting Thermouthion's consternation over the accident.

To Asklepi( )[1] strategos, from Thermouthion, daughter of Ploutarchos, from the city of Oxyrhynchos. I loved and took care of my serving girl, Peina, a homebred slave, as though my own little daughter, in the hope that when she came of age I would have her to nourish me in my old age, since I am a woman who is helpless and alone. The incident involved crossing the city on the 19th of last month, when a certain Eucharion, freedwoman of Longinus, was escorting[2] her to her lesson in singing and other skills, who at the moment of the departure from my house led Peina in with her right hand in bandages, and when I asked her the cause, (Eucharion) told me that the girl had been dashed down by a certain slave Polydeukes, as he was driving his donkey, so that, as a result, her whole hand (*or arm?*) was crushed, and most parts mutilated, while the rest was a gaping wound.[3] And because I did not then have someone in charge of the office of strategos,[4] I did (not ?) submit a petition about this matter, supposing her wound to be a superficial one, but it is incurable, and I am unable to endure the pain concerning my serving girl, because she is in danger of her life and because I am sorely pressed by my despair for her life; you too will feel distressed when you actually see it. Of necessity, then, I have fled to you as my defender and I ask that I be helped and receive from you (the benefit ?) . . .

[1] 'Claudius' was written before the strategos' name, but was then excised.
[2] The verb *paidagogein* is used for a slave when he escorts his master's sons to the school master (cf. **6.238**).
[3] We do not accept the translation suggested by Hagedorn in *ZPE* 65 (1986), 88.
[4] Apparently no strategos was in office on the 19th of the preceding month to whom Thermouthion could direct a petition.

74. A soldier schemes to visit his mother

P.Mich. III 203 (*BL* III 111 and 184; VII 109)
Pselkis, reign of Trajan

Aphrodous, mother of the soldier Satornilos, lives in the Fayum village of Karanis. Her son, stationed with a Roman frontier garrison far to the south at Pselkis in Nubia, hopes to find a way to visit Karanis within the next two months, or otherwise he will not see her until completion of another eighteen months tour of guard duty. His scheme is to get himself included in a military detail to deliver official correspondence to the prefect in Alexandria and to take advantage of the opportunity to pass by Karanis on his way.[1] Being detailed on such a mission would put the facilities of the offical postal couriers (*cursus publicus*) at Satornilos' disposal, but securing the assignment was difficult, and he feared he might incur a 'useless expense' by bribing the wrong person at the wrong time. While bribing an officer charged with selecting men in order to receive special treatment contravened Roman army rules, bribery was not unknown, and another soldier from Karanis observed about life in the camp that 'nothing happens here without money, and letters of recommendation do not help, unless one helps oneself' (*P.Mich.* VIII 468.38–41).

Satornilos to Aphrodous, his mother, very many greetings. Before all else I pray that you are in good health and enjoying good fortune. I want you to know that I sent three letters to you this month. I received all the monthly allowances that you dispatched to me with Julius and the basket of olives with Julius' slave boy. I want you to know that another baby boy has been born to me who was named Agathos Daimon.

If the gods wish it, whenever I find an opportune time to do it, I am coming to you with letters. I want you to know that it is already three months from the time I moved to Pselkis and I have not yet found an opportune moment for coming to you. I was afraid to come just now because people were saying that the prefect is in transit, lest he take the letters away from me and send me back to my unit, and I incur a useless expense. I want you to know that if another two-month period passes by and I do not come to you until the month of Hathyr, I have another eighteen months of sitting in the garrison until I return to Pselkis and come to you. Everybody who comes will testify to you how I am trying to come every day. If you want to see me a little, I want it a lot, and I pray to the gods every day that they soon give me an easy passage for coming. Everything in the army happens when an opportune moment arrives. If I find an opportune time I am coming to you. Feed my children's pigs so that if my children are there, they will find them. The next chance you get, please send to Ioulas, the son of Julius, the monthly allowance in whatever amount you can and treat him as if he were my son, just as you love me and I love my children. If his brother has free time, send him to me, in order that I dispatch in his care my children and their mother. Send me an extra jar of olives for my friend, and do not do otherwise. You know that whatever you give to Julius he brings to me just as he has promised me. Write me whatever he does. Salute Sokmenios, and his children, and . . . and Sabinus and Thaisas, and her children, and my brothers and Tabenka, my sister, and her husband. If she has had her baby, write to me. Salute Tasokmenis, my lady sister, and Sambas and Soueris, and her children, and Sambous and all our relatives and friends by name. All of us salute you – Gemella and Didymarion, and the newborn (?) Agathos Daimon, and Epiktetos. You all give greetings to Gemellos and . . . the wife of . . .lianos. And it was not a large concern . . . I pray that you all are well. Year [.] of Trajan, best Caesar,[2] our lord. 25 Phaophi.

(*Address on the back*) To Karanis, to my mother Aphrodous, daughter of . . . from Satornilos, soldier.

[1] We follow the interpretation of the letter by H. C. Youtie, *ZPE* 20 (1976), 288–92 (= *Script.Post.* I 282–6), and Speidel (1985).
[2] The Greek imitates Trajan's Latin title, *optimus princeps*.

75.   Petition: my uncles stole my property

P.Oxy. XXXIV 2713 (*BL* VI 111, VIII 261)
Oxyrhynchos, *c.* AD 297

This petition illustrates the downside of family relationships; an orphan claims that her two uncles had conspired to defraud her of her maternal inheritance (cf. **5.176**).

In the Roman period guardians of orphaned minors were required to submit to authorities yearly accounts of their management of the child's property (cf. *P.Oxy.* LVIII 3921); but here the matter was no doubt complicated by the fact that the two brothers and their niece lived as a single household. The allusion to woman's 'weakness' is a common motif of petitions submitted by women, designed (like the careful wording of the rest of the petition) to elicit the sympathetic attention of the official being addressed (cf. **2.5, 5.177**, and **Ch. 6 Sect. V** introduction).

To Aristius Optatus, most distinguished prefect of Egypt, from Aurelia Didyme, daughter of Didymos, from the . . . most glorious city of the Oxyrhynchites. It is a difficult matter to be wronged by strangers, but to be wronged by kin is worst of all. My mother's father Dioskoros had three children in all – Theon, Dioskoros, and Ploutarche, my mother – who inherited from him when he died. After some time, my mother also died, while I was under-age and already an orphan. My lord prefect, you know well that the race of women is easy to despise, because of the weakness of our nature. For all the things from the inheritance devolving upon us (for it was a single household and one family) were in the house there in which they were living – that is, the slaves, the immovables, the furnishings, and movable goods were all there undivided. In the meantime, my mother's brothers from the same mother plotted together with useless and foolish stupidity, intending to cheat me. Each one grabbed whatever he wanted of the slaves and all the rest, paying no attention to me whatsoever, but, so to speak, even pushing me off from the third part of the inheritance that falls to me. Now, at any rate, I have recovered, due to your ever-alert spirit, and I am beginning to realise that I should approach no one but you, the benefactor and guardian of me and everyone else. Thus I hurry to ask you, since you have seen me bereft, to command, whenever it seems good to you, that my uncles, brothers of my mother, be compelled to return to me what belongs to me, as heiress of my mother, together with the increments from that time until now from the slaves and rents and everything else. I shall eternally confess my gratitude to your spirit, once I take back my inheritance from my mother through your trustiness and your nobility. Farewell.
(*2nd hand*) I, Aurelia Didyme, submitted this petition. I, Aurelius Thonis, wrote for her because she does not know letters.

II   Archives

A.   The archive of Zenon, Philadelphia, *c.* 261–227 BC

Zenon, son of Agreophon, was born at Kaunos in Karia, on the south-western coast of modern Turkey.[1] Before the middle of the third century

BC he entered the service of Apollonios, finance minister (*dioiketes*) to Ptolemy II Philadelphos, and was representing Apollonios' interests on business missions abroad and within Egypt (261–256 BC; cf. **4.124**). Zenon eventually settled at Philadelphia in the Herakleides division of the Arsinoite nome (256–248 BC), overseeing large estates given to Apollonios by King Ptolemy in both the Memphite and Arsinoite nomes in return for his services to the crown. In the optimistic mood of building and expansion which characterised the activities of the Greek immigrants in this period, the village of Philadelphia was being laid out, largely under Zenon's direction. The nearly two thousand papyri that comprise his archive show Zenon and his associates at work; there are letters, appeals for help, reports, and accounts, by far the majority in Greek with a few bilingual receipts in Greek and Demotic, and a few items only in Demotic, including a letter. Zenon was well educated, writing his many letters and directives in concise, but correct, Greek. He had some interest in the great literature of the past, owning, for example, a copy of Euripides' *Hippolytos* (*P.Zen.Pestman* 15) and some poems probably by the archaic poet Archilochos; he commissioned two epigrams to commemorate his hunting dog Tauron, who died from wounds received while saving Zenon from an attack by a wild boar (*Sel.Pap.* III 109–10). Zenon was the most important man in the village and the neighbouring area, settling disputes among the local population and organising commercial enterprises that centred upon projects in the village. Zenon's responsibilities were many, and correspondents, especially Apollonios, chided him for being tardy in bringing a business matter to completion.

Most of Zenon's correspondence dealt with business matters. So overwhelmingly male was the milieu in which Zenon lived and worked that of approximately three thousand individuals whose names appear in the archive, only about sixty are women; and of the women named, by far the majority are mentioned only once. We know almost nothing of Zenon's private life: his father Agreophon visited him from Kaunos; one of his brothers, Epharmostos, lived with him for a time at Philadelphia; he also maintained contact with a family of cousins in Karia. After retirement in 249 BC, he neither returned to Karia, nor went to Alexandria, but stayed on in the countryside around Philadelphia for another twenty years. He never mentioned a wife or children, but was closely involved in the education and training of a number of young boys, apparently orphans of Greek soldiers who had died in the king's service. The lads received instruction not only in reading and writing, but also in music and gymnastics, sometimes at a gymnasium in Alexandria run by a certain Hierokles (*P.Lond.* VII 1941) and later in Zenon's career at a local gymnasium in Philadelphia where a certain Demeas was teaching (*P.Lond.* VII 2017). One boy, named Kleon, may have felt a particular fondness for Zenon, since he alone addressed him as 'father', in a memorandum (**76**) asking Zenon to send the allowance for himself and his widowed mother, including some wine that he Kleon must contribute to a festival of Hermes and the Muses, perhaps a celebration at the gymnasium.

Other documents from the Zenon archive are translated elsewhere in this book (**2.4, 23; 4.124; 5.162, 200–2, 207, 209**). The two texts included below are intended, not to provide an unproblematic illustration of Zenon's family life, but to raise the question how far Zenon's largely male-orientated pattern of sociability, more characteristic of earlier Greek society, left any place for close relationships with women.

[1] For more texts from the Zenon archive with English translation, see *P.Mich.* I, *P.Lond.* VII, *P.Col.* III–IV, and *Sel.Pap.* I, nos. 31, 66, 72, 88–93, 170–1, 179–83, 265–7, 346, 409–11. For an accessible survey of the Zenon material, see Clarysse and Vandorpe (1995); the orphan boys are discussed at 61–2. See also *P.Mich.* I, pp. 1–57, and *Pap.Lugd.Bat.* XXI A and B.

76. Kleon to Zenon, his 'father'

PSI V 528
Philadelphia (?), undated

Memorandum to Zenon, his father, from Kleon. Please send to us the provisions that are for both me and my mother, totalling with the oil, 17 drachmas. A wine jar is also ours, containing 6 large measures plus 3 small measures, also the contribution for the festival of Hermes and of the Muses, for everyone else has already contributed. Also give thought concerning the water, for we have been buying it for many days past. I have forwarded on to you in addition the letter Demetrios and Hippokrates sent to me concerning the fruit from the trees. At any rate, I replied to them, telling them, 'Go directly to Zenon, my father'. May you prosper.

77. Satyra to Zenon

P.Cair.Zen. I 59028 (*BL* III 37)
Alexandria(?), *c.* 258–257? BC

Satyra[1] was a zither player, based in Alexandria and Athribis in the Delta; an account of clothing showed that Zenon arranged for dispatch of at least one linen tunic to her in Alexandria on 23 May 257, and another to Athribis on 21 October of the same year, and perhaps this chiding letter played a role in the deliveries. Some ten years later Satyra's name also appeared among those receiving grain in Philadelphia from Zenon.

Satyra to Zenon, greetings. Apollonios made an order to give us clothing, both me and my mother, and you will find the memorandum Apollonios wrote about these matters. We have, in fact, received nothing since, although it is now the second year. Please look into the matter and make it clear to

Apollonios . . . to remember us so that we are not naked. And let him grant this, to have it privately from you.[2] Also inquire concerning our provisions, as we have only received them once, and these you sent so as to reach us during the festival of Demeter. Please also look into these matters, at any rate, if it seems good to you too – as quickly as possible. Farewell.

(*Zenon's note on the back*) From Satyra, the little girl,[3] to Zenon.

[1] Satyra is also mentioned in *P.Cair.Zen.* I 59087.17, 23; IV 59699 and 59700.
[2] Or, perhaps, 'And I seem to have this from you privately'.
[3] Zenon employed the diminutive *korasion*, 'little girl', only for Satyra; but she was apparently not a young child.

B.   The Serapeum archive, Memphis, mid–second century BC

The cult of Serapis was introduced by Ptolemy I, and in Alexandria, or when the cult subsequently spread outside Egypt, Serapis, together with Isis, appeared in anthropomorphic, hellenised, guise. In a more traditional Egyptian milieu, however, the god had much in common with the other Egyptian deities, and the Serapeum (the temple complex of Serapis near Memphis), was largely peopled by Egyptians. This archive of more than a hundred papyri, written in both Greek and Demotic over some twenty years, consists mainly of the papers of Ptolemaios, eldest son of the Greek soldier Glaukias, his brothers, and his friends.[1]

Although this archive, like the last, could scarcely be said to depict a 'normal' set of family relationships, the family of Glaukias began traditionally enough. He lived with his wife, perhaps an Egyptian woman, and four sons – Ptolemaios, Sarapion, Hippalos, and Apollonios – in a village not far south of the Serapeum. After Glaukias' death, his sons were left to fend for themselves. It was a disturbed period, of civil war between Ptolemy VI and his younger brother, invasion from Syria, and of repeated rebellions (see pp. 8–9 above). Some nine years before the archive begins, the eldest son Ptolemaios came to the Serapeum for an indefinite stay of divine service, choosing to be 'detained', as the Greek puts it, at the Astartieion (the shrine of the Phoenician goddess Astarte). Ptolemaios chose the life of a religious recluse, yet because he was a Greek living in a milieu dominated by Egyptians, he sometimes felt himself an outsider, and brief outbursts of enmity between him and some Egyptians serving in the Serapeum appear in his papers. He does seem to have enjoyed a cordial relationship with the Egyptian Harmais, his closest associate in the Astartieion. Service in the temple prevented Ptolemaios from leaving the area, and so his contacts with the outside world consisted largely of exchanges by letter, or occasional visits from his brothers. His father Glaukias had had an Egyptian friend, Hargynoutis, the father of twin daughters, Tages (her name is sometimes written 'Thaues') and Taous. The family of the twins Tages/Thaues and Taous also broke up, and they moved to the Serapeum as well, entrusting themselves to Ptolemaios and Harmais. Ptolemaios clearly cared for the twins, taking up their causes and petitioning the royal bureaucracy for the support the government promised, but did not always provide. Sometimes Ptolemaios was mistaken for their father, although how much older he actually was is unclear. He did hope they would care for him in his old age, but scholars have noted how Ptolemaios' reports about dreams often involved the twins, suggesting that possibly his interest in them was more than paternal (**80**).

Ptolemaios' youngest brother Apollonios eventually joined him at the Serapeum; after a few months Ptolemaios arranged for him to enrol in the army. Apollonios was also interested in the twins, and they appeared in his dreams as well (**82**). The brothers had enjoyed a Greek education, for both read and wrote Greek with ease, and the archive contains several literary works.[2] But they presumably spoke Egyptian with many at the Serapeum, including the twins, and some of the dream reports are in Egyptian Demotic (**81, 82**). Of Ptolemaios' brothers, only Sarapion seems to have married and settled down (**83**).

[1] The texts are published mostly in *UPZ* I; translations and discussion by Thompson (1988), 212–65, and Lewis (1986), 69–87; contemporary Demotic documents in Ray (1976).
[2] Underneath Ptolemaios' copy of the opening verses of Euripides' *Telephos*, spoken by a Greek who ruled over barbarians, Apollonios wrote: 'I am a Macedonian, I am a Macedonian.'

78. A petition from Ptolemaios' fellow recluse Harmais about a sister of the twins

UPZ I 2 (*BL* VIII 499)
Memphis, March 163 BC

The hostile behaviour of Nephoris toward her Egyptian husband and her twin daughters Tages/Thaues and Taous is evident in the petition Ptolemaios submitted on the twins' behalf (**2.33; 79**). In this text, dated to the same year as that petition, their younger sister Tathemis has also been deposited in the Serapeum under the protection of Ptolemaios' Egyptian colleague, Harmais. Whether or not Nephoris was responsible for abandoning the girl, she took a not inconsiderable sum of the money her daughter had collected at the temple, but did not carry out the business for which she claimed to take it – circumcision,[1] then clothing and a dowry for Tathemis, as the girl looked forward to marriage. Female circumcision probably involved excision of part or all of the clitoris. This is the only mention of female circumcision in the Greek papyri, and, in this instance, the operation is to be performed as the young Egyptian girl was reaching puberty (see Montserrat, 1996, 41–3). We are better informed about male circumcision: in the Pharaonic period it was performed on both infants and older boys of royal and priestly families. In the Greek and Roman periods, priestly families continued to circumcise their sons (see

BGU XIII 2216). Strabo, the geographer who visited Egypt shortly after the Roman takeover, seems to emphasise the difference in the extent of the operation on males, as opposed to females, by using different forms of the verb 'to cut': males they 'cut around' (*peritemnein*), but females they 'cut out' (*ektemnein*, XVII 2.5). The present text, however, uses 'cut around'. Although the fifth-century BC ethnographer, Xanthos of Lydia, told his Greek-speaking audience that clitoridectomy was a Lydian practice, designed to preserve a woman in her youthful beauty and analogous to castration in boys, most Greek and Roman references to clitoridectomy label it an Egyptian custom. Graeco-Roman medical writers advised clitoridectomy for women suffering from satyriasis, a continually enlarged clitoris.[2]

To Dionysios, one of the friends (of the king) and strategos, from Harmais, a recluse in the Great Serapeum for over four years now, living also off what I collect by begging in the temple.

I am being wronged by Nephoris, inhabitant of Memphis. Her little daughter Tathemis stays with me in the temple and she is also provided for from the distributions she collects.[3] When she had got together 1,300 bronze drachmas, she gave them to me for safekeeping. After a while Nephoris cheated me and claimed that it was about time for Tathemis to get circumcised, as the custom is among the Egyptians. She asked me to give her the 1,300 drachmas. She would take care (of the circumcision) in return and clothe the girl and give her a dowry when she would marry her off to a husband. If she did not do any of this and if she did not circumcise Tathemis by Mecheir of year 18, she would pay me 2,400 bronze drachmas instantly. On those terms I agreed and gave her the 1,300 drachmas in Thoth. Now she has done none of the things we agreed upon, and for this reason I am bothered by Tathemis who wants her 1,300 drachmas back. It so happens that I cannot go down to Memphis for business matters. I therefore ask you not to overlook me now that I am hard pressed, but be appalled at this affair. Take into account how she cheated me and give instructions, if you think it best, for her to be summoned to appear before you. If things are as I say, then force her to do justice by me, so that I can pay the money back to Tathemis and will no longer be bothered. If this happens, I shall receive considerable assistance. Farewell.

[1] Legislation has repeatedly banned all forms of female circumcision in present-day Egypt, but it is still practised clandestinely on female infants, little girls, and those approaching puberty, particularly along the Nile valley; the practice is found to some extent among all religious groups (Lightfoot-Klein, 1989, 27–45).

[2] Xanthos Lydiakos = *FGH* III C 765, F 4a. Clitoridectomy as an Egyptian custom: Ps.-Galen, *Introductio sive medicus* 10, XIV 706.12–15 Kühn; Philo Judaeus, *Quaestiones et Solutiones in Genesin* III 47 (*Philo* Supplement I, Loeb Classical Library); for the operation: Caelius Aurelianus, *Genecia* II 112; Muscio II 76; Paulos Aiginetes VI 70; Aitios, quoting Philoumenos, XVI 115; the chapter 'On the enlarged clitoris and clitoridectomy' is now lost from the text of Soranos' *Gynaecology*, but the chapter heading has been preserved in the table of contents.

[3] Or perhaps, 'from the gifts she gathers'.

79. A second copy of the twins' petition

UPZ i 19
Memphis, 163 BC

Ptolemaios' brother Apollonios wrote out the first version of the petition for the twins (**2.33**). This second version[1] was drafted by someone else (*1st hand*), likewise writing on the girls' behalf, but subsequently another party (*2nd hand*) also went through the document, correcting the main text (deletions indicated below by double square brackets) and adding words between the lines (raised text). The fact that this second hand added the name of Pachrates on the back of the present text underscores the fact that one of this later writer's intentions was to magnify the role of the twins' step-brother in the affair. The considerable differences between the first version and this second drafting raise questions, not only as to which version lies closer to what the girls themselves said, but also more generally about the extent to which scribes intervened in narrations from those illiterate in Greek and imposed their own wording on a text (cf. **Arch. K**, introd.). A final copy of the petition was handed to King Ptolemy and Queen Kleopatra on 8 October 163, although this did not end the matter, and the twins continued to petition, expanding their requests for assistance with other grievances.

(*1st hand*) To King Ptolemy and Queen Kleopatra his sister, mother-loving gods, greetings from Thaues and Taous, twins who perform services in the great Serapeum at Memphis, pouring libations to Osorapis[2] on behalf of you and your children. After we were wronged in quite a few matters by Nephoris and Pachrates, (*2nd hand*) her son we have fled to you in order to receive justice. The aforementioned Nephoris [[after she left our father, she lived with a certain Philippos and despite what she did, she did not have the face of a wrong doer, but also]] (*2nd hand*) living with a certain Philippos, a man from Memphis she [[contrived]] (*2nd hand*) kept contriving that the aforementioned Philippos would destroy him in the [[then]] prevailing time of unrest. He sat by the door of his house that was near the river in the Egyptian Market. When our father came out, he noticed and jumped into the river and was barely saved on an island; and he was picked up into a certain boat sailing along and he didn't dare disembark here anymore and he went off to the Herakleopolite nome. Because of our not being with him, he died from hopelessness. Although his brothers sailed up [[and brought]] and conveyed him to the burying grounds at Memphis, Nephoris has, until now, not had the courage to bury him. His possessions that were confiscated by the crown Nephoris has redeemed, after she sold half the house belonging jointly to us and to her for 7 bronze talents, and she carried off property worth 60 bronze talents and she rents to tenants for 1400 bronze drachmas a month. (*2nd hand*) and she doesn't share any of this with us. Not satisfied with all this, she cast us out so that we are in danger of perishing from starvation. When we noticed Ptolemaios, one of the recluses at the great Serapeum who was a friend of our father, we went up to him and we were from then on fed by him.

When the lamentation for the Apis bull took place, they brought us to mourn for the god. Then friends of our mother persuaded us to take her son as our attendant, and once this happened, he watched us for some time for an opportunity and he took our written (*1st hand*) token (*2nd hand*) from those in charge of these matters to the man in charge of oil distribution for one measure of oil (*2nd hand*) the customary amount to be given us by you [[so that we might get our yearly amount]] and once he secretly made off with this and plundered from us the bronze money we used to have (*2nd hand*) and other things, he went off to his mother, with the result that we do not even have the necessities. We therefore beg you to send our petition to Dionysios, of the friends (of the King) and strategos, so that he may write to [[Mennides]] (*2nd hand*) Apollonios the *epimeletes* and to Dorion the *antigrapheus*,[3] so that they not pay to her either the oil and kiki (*castor oil*) that belongs to us, or anything else of ours, and that he should compel her to return whatever of our father's she holds illegally, so that we are helped through you. May you prosper.

(*On the back; 1st hand*) Nephoris
(*On the back; 2nd hand*) Nephoris and Pachrates

---

[1] The translation of this text as Lefkowitz and Fant (1992), no. 407 was based on an early version of the Greek, not that by Wilcken in *UPZ* I. See also Thompson (1988), 239–42 for a translation of Apollonios' report about the twins' allowance of oil and kiki (castor oil) on 14 December 162 BC (= *UPZ* I 23).

[2] Cf. **2.37**.

[3] The *epimeletes* and the *antigrapheus* were officials who monitored distributions of supplies.

80.   Seven dream reports recorded by Ptolemaios

UPZ I 77 (*BL* II 2.172; IX 363)
Memphis, June 161 and June 158 BC

A note on the back of the papyrus indicates that Ptolemaios reported seven dreams, although not all were his own. Most reports of ancient dreams derive from literary sources, such as Artemidoros' *Dream Book*, and these reports from individuals about whom something else is known are more interesting. When a Freudian psychiatrist and a papyrologist examined Ptolemaios' dream reports more than sixty years ago, they concluded that Ptolemaios had a repressed sexual interest in the twins, especially Tages/Thaues.[1] Ptolemaios failed to write down the last dream because he ran out of papyrus; his note on the back summarised the dream's contents as 'What I saw regarding the queen (?)'.

The dream that Tages the twin saw on Pachon 17. She seemed in the dream to be walking down the street, counting nine houses. I wanted to turn away and I said, 'All these are no more than nine (houses).' They say: 'You are free to go.' I said, 'It is too late for me.'

The dream that Ptolemaios saw at the festival of the Moon on Pachon 25. I seem to see Tages rather sweetly singing (?), and well disposed, and I see Taous laughing, and her foot is big and pure.

(Pachon) 29. Two men are working in the vestibule, and Taous is sitting on the steps and joking with them. And as soon as she hears Chentosneus' voice she immediately turns black. They said they would teach her a lesson . . .

Dream of Ptolemaios on Pachon 15. Two men came to me and said to me, 'Ptolemaios, take the money for the blood.' They count out to me 100 bronze drachmas and for Tages the twin, a purse full of bronze four-drachma coins. They tell her, 'Here's your bronze money for the blood.' I told them, 'She has more bronze money than I.'

The dream that I (Ptolemaios) saw on Pachon 20. I seem to be counting (the days of the month) Thoth of year 20 up to the 20th day.

Year 23, Pachon 4. I (Ptolemaios) seemed in the dream to be calling upon the very great god Ammon, calling upon him to come to me from the north with two other (gods). I seemed (to see) a cow in the compound and she is in labour. He (*Ammon*) takes hold of the cow and lays her down on her side. He puts his hand into her privy parts and draws out a bull.

May that which I (Ptolemaios) saw in the dream turn out well for me. Pachon 23, on my birthday.[2]

---

[1] For the Freudian analysis, Storch and Heichelheim (1931). Sauneron (1959) discusses other Egyptian material on dreams; Lewis (1986), 82–4, translates additional dreams from the archive.

[2] On birthdays, see **6.232** introd.

81. Two Demotic dream reports from the twins

O. Petersburg 1129[1]
Memphis, August ? 160 BC

The first dream. The dreamer (*Tages/Thaues?*) sees herself in Memphis. She is told that her mother Nephoris is threatened by the rising inundation. She swims to her and brings her safely to the temple of Anoubis.

Another dream. I find myself in the house. They say: 'Horos the scribe marries (?) the girl, the sister (Taous?).' I must talk to her so that I can know whether he made love to her. I say to him: 'Love her, the sister.' If he loves her, she will love him. I write down . . . all the words. Written in year 21, Mesore . . .

---

[1] Based on the paraphrase by Sethe (1913), 61.

82. Four dream reports from Apollonios, brother of Ptolemaios

P.Bologna 3171 and 3173[1]
Memphis, undated

Like the preceding dreams, these too were written in Demotic script. Some of the reports refer to the twins.

I dreamt: I see a woman. She was going forward. They made her stop, saying to her, 'Rest'. She is in her house with her husband and her children, and she is content. I find a loaf of bread and some cabbages (?) and I eat them.

Second (dream). I dreamt: I see a tomb, being in ruins, while its front (?) is open. It was desecrated. One lives in it. I see a woman who is having sex. I give some coins and candy to her son Haryotes. I speak to a(nother?) woman, saying, 'The possessions of Phatres are hers since he killed himself.'

First (dream). I am going along the avenue of the Serapeum with a woman called Tages, a virgin. I am talking to her, saying, 'Tages, is your heart weary because of the sex I had with you?' She said: 'She will be hard against me, my sister Thotortais,[2] when they say that I am going upon her (?).'[3]

Second (dream). A man says, 'Apollonios is a Greek word,[4] Peteharenpois is an Egyptian word.'[5] The one who speaks, he is a priest.

[1] As republished by Bresciani et al. (1978), 95–104; the translation in Lewis (1986), 83, relies on an older edition of the Demotic. See also Ray (1987).
[2] A slip of the pen for Taous?
[3] Perhaps 'when they say that I am going upon her (?)' is a comment by the dreamer.
[4] Or, perhaps, 'Apollonios speaks Greek'.
[5] Or, perhaps, 'Peteharenphois speaks Egyptian'.

83. Invitation to the wedding of Sarapion, Ptolemaios' brother

UPZ I 66
Herakleopolis, 16 August 153 BC

Sarapion's bride was the daughter of a neighbour back home in Herakleopolis, and although Ptolemaios had quarrelled with her father Hesperos several years earlier, this did not stop Sarapion from wooing and winning the girl. The actual wedding was to take place later, between 26 August and 24 September. For other wedding invitations, see **6.250**.

Sarapion to Ptolemaios and Apollonios his brothers, greetings. If you are well, then I too am well. I am married by contract to the daughter of Hesperos and I intend to take her in Mesore. Please send me half a container of olive oil. I have written so that you may know. Farewell, year 28, Epeiph 21.

PS. Be here for that day, Apollonios!

(*Address on the back*) To Ptolemaios and Apollonios.

C. The archive of Dryton and Apollonia alias Senmonthis, Pathyris, *c.* 174–95 BC

The thirty to forty texts in this bilingual archive from Upper Egypt were purchased from dealers by European collectors, beginning at the end of the nineteenth century. Many of the documents are fragmentary, and scholars continue to debate details about the persons of the archive and which documents belong to the archive (e.g. **84**). The cavalry officer Dryton, son of Pamphilos, married his second wife Apollonia alias Senmonthis,[1] daughter of Ptolemaios, and they settled in Pathyris; their marriage contract was registered before the *agoranomos* in Latopolis on 4 March 150. At this time, Apollonia alias Senmonthis was probably in her late teens, and over the next twenty-four years she bore him at least five daughters (by 29 June 126; see **86**). Dryton was a full generation older than Apollonia alias Senmonthis, in his forties at the time of this marriage. He had an under-age son Esthladas from his previous marriage to Sarapias, a woman who was, like Dryton, a citizen of Ptolemais, the Greek polis in Upper Egypt, and of Cretan descent. Apollonia alias Senmonthis and Dryton lived the rest of their lives in Pathyris some miles south of Thebes, where Egyptian nationalism was strong (Dryton's transfer to Pathyris may have occurred when Ptolemy VI augmented his garrisons in Pathyris and other towns of the Thebaid, in order to contain native restlessness in the region during his planned invasion of Syria).

Apollonia alias Senmonthis was a local girl (**85**), and she and her three sisters inherited a house in Pathyris from their father Ptolemaios, an infantryman also in the king's service. The family employed double names, one Greek, the other Egyptian, and she continued the practice with her five daughters. The women's documents were sometimes drawn up in Greek, sometimes in Demotic, and at times they retained copies in both languages. There is no evidence, however, that any of the women were able to read or write either language. The use of the Egyptian legal forms enabled them to conduct business without a guardian. Dryton and his son Esthladas appear less bi-cultural, bearing only Greek names in their written documents. Both men read and wrote Greek, conducting their business and correspondence in that language, although after his father's death Esthladas was involved in contracts in both Greek and Demotic (*P. Grenf.* II 26). During their army service father and son perhaps learned to speak Egyptian in order to communicate with the troops under their command.

Ptolemaios, the father of Apollonia alias Senmonthis, died intestate; perhaps he was following Egyptian practice whereby it was not customary to make a separate will, but to make inheritance provisions in a marriage contract. As a result, his daughters experienced difficulties in claiming their inheritance (**85**). By contrast, Dryton wrote at least three wills, the earliest in early summer of 164 BC and his second on the same day he registered his marriage contract with Apollonia alias Senmonthis.[2] The third will (**86**), known in multiple copies, was made twenty-four years later in order to provide for the couple's five daughters. The marriage of Dryton and Apollonia alias Senmonthis lasted for at least twenty-five years, but their documents – contracts, wills, and receipts – furnish no information about the couple's affective feelings for one another, and assessments about the quality of their marriage have varied considerably: for a negative view, Pomeroy (1990), 103–24; for a more positive one, Lewis (1986), 88–103; both include translations of further texts. The marriages of two of Dryton's daughters ended in divorce (**87** introd.), as did those of two granddaughters (*P.Bad. dem.* 6, 100 BC; *P.BM dem.* 10514 ined., 95 BC).

[1] Sometimes written 'Semmonthis' (**85, 86**).
[2] For Dryton's first will, see Messeri Savorelli (1990); his second will is *P.Grenf.* I 12 + *SB* I 4637 + P.Cairo 10349 (perhaps another copy in *P.Bad.* II 5 = Scholl, 1990, 56); for the notice of marriage to Apollonia Senmonthis, *SB* XVIII 13330 and Clarysse (1986). The practice of making a will on the occasion of a man's marriage may have been a fairly common phenomenon, cf. *BGU* IV 1050 (reign of Augustus).

This family tree, and those that appear for the more complex archives below, includes those family members mentioned in the introduction to the archive, or in the texts themselves. A reference to a more extensive family tree, if one has been

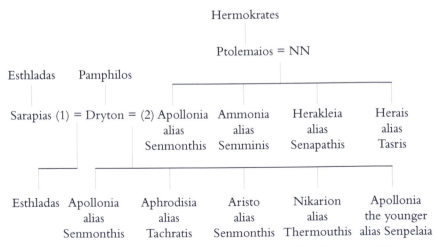

Figure 2   Family of Dryton and Apollonia alias Senmonthis

constructed, is given in the notes to the introduction to each archive. For an explanation of 'NN', please see Notes for the Reader, p. xiv.

84. Copy of a popular song, 'A Young Woman's Complaint before the Closed Door'

P. Grenf. 1 1
Thebaid (?), after 174 BC?

A young woman has been betrayed by her lover and she gives voice to her sorrows, standing alone before his closed door. The song explores a woman's emotions in an erotic encounter (cf. **6.285–6, 289**). It may derive from a longer, dramatic mime, or may have been an independent poem (cf. Theokritos, *Idyll* 2, trans. Bing and Cohen, 1991, 149–57). A poem in which a rejected lover lamented in front of his beloved's closed door was called a *paraklausithyron*, and versions of the motif became increasingly popular among Hellenistic and Roman poets.[1] This is the only poem we possess in which the poet pictured a woman in the role of rejected lover, although some argue that *CIL* IV 5296 is also a *paraklausithyron* in a woman's voice. This text is Pack[2] 1743; see also I. U. Powell, *Collectanea Alexandrina* (Oxford, 1970) 177–80.

This text is in Dryton's own hand. In the fragmentary contract on the front side of the papyrus (*P. Grenf.* 1 10; a loan of wheat, dated 174 BC) the description differs from that given in Dryton's second will – Dryton in the loan of wheat had a fancy, brushed-up hair-style, and was 'sallow-complexioned' (literally, 'honey-coloured'), while he was bald and probably 'fair-complexioned' in 150 BC.[2] But the passage of time and the different perceptions of scribes can account for these discrepancies; much greater divergencies in physical descriptions of undoubtedly a single person are not uncommon; cf. the case of Nahomsesis, an Egyptian woman who was a contemporary of Dryton at Pathyris (**5.184**).

> The choice was from us both,
> we were yoked together – the lady of Cyprus, Aphrodite,
> is surety for love. Pain grips me,
> whenever I remember –
> how he used to kiss me, all the while treacherously
> intending to desert me,
> both the inventor of my unsettledness and the creator of my love.
> Eros took hold of me,
> I don't deny that I have him in my mind.[3]
> Beloved Stars and Mistress Night, my partner in passion,
> now escort me once again to him toward whom Aphrodite
> drives me, I who am betrayed – and also strong Eros, in his turn.
> I have a mighty fire as guide along my path –
> it burns also in my soul.
> In this he wrongs me, in this he pains me,
> that deceiver of hearts:
> before this so haughty and denying that Aphrodite

was the cause of our passion,
he has done me an extraordinary injustice.
I am about to go mad, for jealousy grips me.
I burn to a crisp at being deserted.
Indeed, (I ask) only this: Throw your garlands my way,
for they will cheer me when I am alone.
My lord, do not push me away, locked out,
but take me. I am content – even eager – to be your slave.
Maddening passion (?) involves much hard labour,
for one's got to be always striving, bearing, and patient.
If you cling to one man, you will only get crazy,
because a single-object passion drives you mad.
Be warned – I have an unconquerable will when I quarrel. I am
    enraged
when I remember I shall sleep alone.
But you, you are running away elsewhere to cheer yourself up.
If we are angry now, right away
we ought also to be reconciled.
Is this not why we have friends,
who will decide who is the one doing wrong?

(This is the end of the first column in the papyrus. The poem continues for at least one more column, only small bits of which are preserved.)

¹ Copley (1956) remains the fullest discussion of the *paraklausithyron* in English. Other examples: Theokritos *Idyll* 3 (trans. Bing and Cohen, 1991, 157–60); *Anthologia Palatina* V 23, 103, 145, 164, 189, 191, 213, 281 (*The Greek Anthology* I, Loeb Classical Library); for Latin examples, Barsby (1973), 70–81.

² The editor's restoration [*leuk*]*ochros;* but also possibly ([*melan*]*ochros*), a misspelling of 'dark-complexioned', *melanchros*, as in *PSI* XIV 1402.12. Lewis (1986), 88–9, argues that the poem did not belong to Dryton, son of Pamphilos.

³ Or, perhaps, 'I don't deny it', with 'that I have him in my mind' as a later addition to the poem.

85.   Petition of Apollonia alias Senmonthis and her sisters to Santobithys

SB I 4638 (*BL* III 171; VIII 311; IX 240)
Pathyris, between April and August–September 135 BC

To Boethos, kinsman (of the King) and epistrategos . . . from Apollonia alias Semmonthis and Ammonia alias Semminis and Herakleia alias Senapathis and Herais alias Tasris, daughters of Ptolemaios, belonging to the Cyrenaeans settled in Pathyris. We are wronged by Kallimedes, son of Apollonios who is (also called) Patous, son of Psemmonthes, infantryman, and by his wife Kalibis and their sons Orseus and Panobchynis. When our aforementioned father Ptolemaios, son of Hermokrates, who was an infantryman (in the troop) of Diodotos, died and left his property to us without a will, the accused, being overbearing and despising us because we had been left as under-age young girls,[1] as if in accordance with kinship, came against us with his accomplices and others. Although they were neither registered as next-of-kin, nor named as our guardians in accordance with a will, they secretly seized the house that belongs to us in Pathyris and forcibly occupied it, and, after opening the house and appropriating the furnishings left to us by our father and the titles to the land, they carried them off. From then on, always falsely claiming our things for themselves and harming us in every way, they sorely oppressed us. Once we came of age, we necessarily entered into our rightful inheritance, having paid the taxes due to divine Berenike. Yet, when they did not give back our property, we submitted a petition in the 30th year (*152/1 BC*) to Herakleides, who was chief of police of the Pathyrite nome, before whom, having reached an agreement, they barely gave back any contracts. But rather, having plundered these, plus both contractual agreements and other papers, they destroyed the profits realisable through them, and, having assessed the furnishings, they made no move to pay back (their value?), thinking to deprive us by excluding them with their oath,[2] obviously being liable for theft of booty, since they claimed property of other people, even of orphans. Although we have many times petitioned for these things, he (*Kallimedes*) prevailed in making us unsuccessful. In the 32nd year (*150/49 BC*), having surrounded us together with Ones, the former deputy-inspector, they forcefully carried off 13 artabas of wheat, and Ones carried off 3 artabas of barley from our house, and then even appropriated the aforementioned house. As a result also before Santobithys . . .

(*Note on the back*) (Petition) of Herakleia and Apollonia and Ammonia. (Forward) to Santobithys.

---

[1] For this and similar motifs in petitions, see also **75, 87**; **5.177**; cf. **Ch.6 Sect. V** introd.
[2] Or, perhaps, 'by washing them off with their oath'.

86. Copy of Dryton's third will

P.Grenf. I 21 (*BL* III 70; VIII 140; IX 95)
Pathyris, 29 June 126 BC

This will (*diatheke*) is of the standard Greek form, but the witnesses listed in a fragmentary copy of the same will (*Pap. Lugd. Bat.* XIX 4) underscore the extent to which King Ptolemy's supposedly Greek troops in Pathyris lived in an Egyptian cultural milieu. Five men witnessed the official registration of Dryton's will of 126 BC before the *agoranomos*, yet only one witness was able to sign his name in Greek – Ammonios, son of Areios, a cavalryman like Dryton. Nonetheless, Ammonios,

nearly forty years Dryton's junior, is known from other documents to have been literate in Demotic, as well as Greek. The other four men were Egyptians and they witnessed the will by signing in Demotic. The official copy with the Demotic signatures is apparently no longer extant, but the surviving copy, with the five signatures translated into Greek, contained a note appended to the signatures: 'these four used native letters because in these places there are not a sufficient number of Greeks' (*Pap.Lugd.Bat.* XIX 4 ii.1–25).

Dryton's property is divided in roughly equal shares between Esthladas on the one hand and the five daughters by his second marriage on the other. This may be thought to favour the single son over the five daughters; but represents an attempt to achieve a balance between the offspring of Dryton's two marriages.

Year 44, Pauni 9, in Pathyris, before Asklepiades the *agoranomos*. The following testamentary arrangements were made by Dryton, son of Pamphilos, Cretan, of the *diadochoi* and of the *epitagma*-unit, cavalry officer over men, while he was of sound body and mind, with his wits about him.

May I be master of my property, while I enjoy good health, but if I should suffer some mortal fate, I leave and give my property, both in land and movables and livestock, and whatever I may subsequently acquire as follows: the horse on which I ride in military service and all my armour to Esthladas, son from me and Sarapias, daughter of Esthladas son of Theon, a citizen (*of Ptolemais*), with whom I used to live as my wife in accordance with the laws and with the will that I had registered through the record office in Little Diospolis before Dionysios, the *agoranomos*, in the 6th year of the reign of Philometor (*164 BC*). This previous will both specified other matters and appointed as guardian Hermokrates(?), being my kinsman. Also of the household slaves, being 4, those whose names are Myrsine and her . . . (I give to Esthladas), while the remaining 2 female slaves, whose names are Eirene and Ampelion, I give to (my daughters) Apollonia and her sisters, being five girls in all. Also (I give to Esthladas) the vineyard belonging to me in Kochlax of Arabia[1] of the Pathyrite nome and the wells constructed from baked brick in the vineyard, and the other appurtenances; also the wagon with its harness; and the dovecote and another one, half-constructed; and a courtyard, whose neighbours are: on the south, vacant plots belonging to the same Esthladas; on the north, a vaulted apartment belonging to Apollonia the younger; on the east, a vacant plot belonging to Petras . . . son of Esthladas; on the south, a vacant lot belonging to Esthladas as far as the doorway which opens to the west.

The remaining quarters and furnishings and . . . and the vacant plot, earmarked for a dovecote, beyond Esthladas' door and to the west of the vaulted apartment, I give to Apollonia and Aristo and Aphrodisia and Nikarion and Apollonia the younger,[2] being five girls in all, my daughters from my wife Apollonia alias Semmonthis, the wife with whom I am living in accordance with the laws. Also the two female slaves (mentioned above) and the cow they are to possess for their households in equal shares in accordance with the division I have made. Esthladas must give to them 4 square cubits from the vacant lot assigned to him, opposite his doorway which opens to the west, as space for a bake-oven.

The remaining buildings and vacant lots in Great Diospolis (= *Thebes*) in the Ammonieion Quarter and the Potters' Quarter – Esthladas is to have one half-share, while Apollonia and her sisters are to have one half-share. Also all my other possessions, contractual agreements for both produce and money, and all movable property, in half-shares (one half to Esthladas and the other half to Apollonia and her sisters). Esthladas and Apollonia with her sisters are to pay expenses in common for the building of the specified dovecote, until they bring it to completion.

Also to Apollonia alias Semmonthis, my wife, for a period of four years, if she remains in my house and is without blame, for her provisions and for her two daughters, each month 2½ artabas of wheat, ¹⁄₁₂ of kroton (*castor oil*), 200 bronze drachmas. After the four years they are also to give in common the same amounts to the two younger girls for eleven years. They are also to give to Tachratis for dowry 12 bronze talents out of their joint funds. Whatever property Semmonthis clearly acquired for herself while she was Dryton's wife, let her continue to have possession of this, while those who proceed against her concerning these properties . . . Year 44 Pauni 9.

¹ A region on the eastern bank of the Nile opposite Pathyris.
² In **87**, Dryton's daughters are identified by both Greek and Egyptian names.

87. Petition from the daughters of Dryton and Apollonia alias Senmonthis to Phommous

P.Lond. 11 401, p. 13
Pathyris, 115–110 BC

In his will of 126 BC (**86**) Dryton required that Esthladas and his daughters provide a dowry for their sister Aphrodisia alias Tachratis. Her marriage to Psenesis ended in divorce on 25 March 123 BC (*P.Bad.dem.* 7) and another sister, whose name is lost, also divorced her husband Herienupis (*P.Bad.dem.* 8). The sisters continued to co-operate with one another, however, and in 100 BC, three of them – Thermouthis, Senmonthis, and Senpelaia – paid their taxes together (*WO* 1618 and cf. 1617).

To Phommous, kinsman (of the King) and epistrategos and strategos of the Thebaid, from Apollonia alias Senmonthis and Aphrodisia alias Tachratis, both daughters of Dryton, living in Pathyris. We own, together with our sisters Aristo alias Senmonthis and Nikarion alias Thermouthis, and Apollonia the younger alias Senpelaia, a half-share of our father's plots of land, being 4 in number in both the Peritheban and Pathyrite nomes, and similarly with regard to the domestic slaves. The plots of land include: in

Kochlax of Arabia[1] in the aforementioned Pathyrite nome, a half share of 2½ arouras, more or less, of a vineyard plot; to the east of this, a garden plot with wells and farm buildings and a wine press; a plot of unwatered land; another plot of non-revenue producing land, and all the appurtenances that our father owned as long as he lived, but after his death we were owners of the rest (except for . . .). Ariston, son of Athenodotos, from Great Diospolis (= *Thebes*), quite violently occupied the vineyard plot and its appurtenances, in times of unrest,[2] and he unjustly claims for himself the half share that belongs to us. And he has planted a certain part with vines, despising us because we are women and because we are not able to go to the aforementioned property, since we live in another place. As a result, we, having fled to you, ask, if it seems (good to you), that you call him up and investigate, and, if things are as we have written, that you compel him to relinquish the half-share of the vineyard we have described and the plants growing in it and the adjoining areas, and also to pay for the crops he carried from them, and, because of the violence he has committed, that you condemn him in a manner befitting those who hate wickedness, so that we may receive help. May you prosper.

[1] See **86** note 1.
[2] Probably a reference to dynastic struggles that followed after the death of Ptolemy VIII in 116 BC.

D.   The archive of Tryphon, Oxyrhynchos, AD 8/9–66

Tryphon, son of Dionysios and Thamounis/Thamounion, was born at Oxyrhynchos in AD 8/9.[1] In AD 11/12, Tryphon's 64-year-old grandfather, Tryphon son of Didymos, headed an extended household which included three adult sons: Didymos, aged 38; Dionysios (Tryphon's father), aged 33; and Thoonis, aged 22. About a year after 11/12, Dionysios and his wife produced a second son named Thoonis; their youngest son Onnophris was born considerably later. Perhaps there were other children who did not survive infancy. The adult men of grandfather Tryphon's household were weavers, as also were, in the following generations, Tryphon, the central figure of the archive, his brother Onnophris, and Tryphon's two sons by his second wife Saraeus.

Some forty documents, all written in Greek, refer to Tryphon and his family, yet Tryphon acknowledged that 'he did not know letters', and others signed for him; his second wife Saraeus was also illiterate in Greek. Throughout his life he both loaned and borrowed money, which he seemed able to pay back on time; he bought half a house from a nephew of his mother in AD 55. Originally the family lived in the 'Hippodrome quarter'

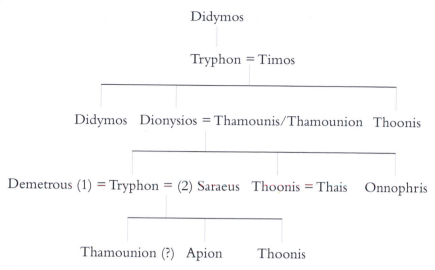

Figure 3   Family of Tryphon and Thamounis/Thamounion

of Oxyrhynchos, but by AD 44 they had moved to 'Temenouthis quarter'; Tryphon's mother was still alive at the time of the move, but his father, Dionysios, had died, as had the grandparents. In the same year Tryphon's brother Thoonis deserted Oxyrhynchos, leaving unpaid tax debts; a decade later he had returned to Oxyrhynchos, where we find him acting as guardian for his wife Thais, daughter of Amenneus, who was buying ½₂ of a two-storey house from her eighteen-year-old nephew.[2]

Neither Tryphon's mother nor his brother Onnophris appear in the family's papers after AD 44, and what had been a multi-generational family now becomes a nuclear household consisting of Tryphon, his second wife Saraeus, and eventually their three children.[3] The eldest was a girl, perhaps named Thamounion after Tryphon's mother, followed by two sons, Apion, named after Saraeus' father, and Thoonis, born *c.* AD 53, and named after Tryphon's brother and uncle. In AD 37, Tryphon reported to the authorities that Saraeus had suffered a miscarriage as a result of physical attacks on her (**89**). In AD 50, she was again attacked while pregnant, and perhaps miscarried again (*P.Oxy.* II 324 and 316 = *SB* X 10244 and 10245). In AD 54 Tryphon bought a loom; two years later, he was teaching weaving to his elder son Apion, while Thoonis was apprenticed to another weaver in AD 66 (*P.Oxy.* II 275).[4] Already in AD 52, Tryphon claimed to the authorities that his eyesight was failing, and was released from tax obligations on the orders of the prefect – but whether he was trying to hoodwink the authorities with his claim, or whether impaired vision interfered with his weaving remains unclear (*P.Oxy.* I 39).

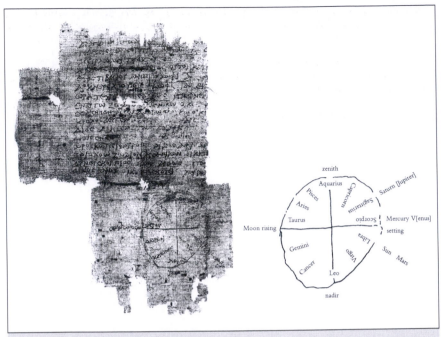

15   Earlier horoscope from the archive of Tryphon the weaver
P.Oxy. II 235 (Cambridge University Library ms. Add.4051)
10 pm on either 28 or 29 September A D 15–18 or 19–22

Beneath the text of the horoscope (see **Ch.3 archive E** introd.), giving the positions of the
sun, moon and planets 'at the fourth hour of the night' (about 10 pm), is a diagram with the
signs of the zodiac: anticlockwise from the top – Ὑδροχόος, Aquarius; Ἰχθύες, Pisces; Κριός,
Aries; Ταῦρος, Taurus; Δίδυμοι, Gemini; Καρκίνος, Cancer; Λέων, Leo; Παρθένος, Virgo;
Ζυγός, Libra; Σκορπ(ίος), Scorpio; Τοξότης, Sagittarius; Αἰγό(κερως), Capricorn.

Two horoscopes survive among Tryphon's papers, the later one for a
birthday of 3 January 46 (*P.Oxy.* II 307), possibly that of his first son Apion,
born about this time.[5] The year of the earlier horoscope is lost because of
damage, but the day and time of the birth are preserved: 10 pm on either
28 or 29 September (*P.Oxy.* II 235, illustrated in **Plate 15**). Astronomical
and other data point to a year between A D 15–18 or 19–22. Someone
attached a note at the beginning of the horoscope, addressing 'dearest
Tryphon', and promising to try hard with the 'times that had been given'.
It must have been commissioned by either grandfather Tryphon, son of
Didymos, or by his grandson Tryphon, son of Dionysios, depending on
how much time elapsed between the actual birth and the request that the
horoscope be cast.

[1] The archive was partly published in *P.Oxy.* I and II; full publication and a summary in
Biscottini (1966); texts not fully reported in *P.Oxy.* II were republished as *SB* X 10220–49.

Discussions of Tryphon and his family: Morris (1978), esp. 271–3; Whitehorne (1984); Gagos et al. (1992), esp. 189 and note 36. The name of Tryphon's mother is preserved in five texts as 'Thamounis', in four texts as 'Thamounion'; and once in both forms (*P.Oxy.* II 251.3, 28, 38).

2 On the family's social milieu, see Crossan (1992), 19–30, cf. 43–6.
3 For Tryphon's marriage contract with Saraeus, see **4.132**. Concerning the children of Tryphon, we follow the original editor (Biscottini, 1966).
4 Translation and discussion in Lewis and Reinhold (1990), 133–4, §36. Compare the actions of a contemporary weaver, also from Oxyrhynchos, Pausiris son of Ammonios (*P.Mich.* III 170–2; *P.Wisc.* I 4 and further texts, discussed in Gagos et al., 1992).
5 For Greek and Roman astrological practices and horoscopes, see Barton (1994).

88. Tryphon's first wife Demetrous deserts him

P.Oxy. II 282 (*BL* III 130; VIII 234)
Oxyrhynchos, between 26 January 29 and 22 May AD 37

Demetrous and Tryphon had probably been married only a few years at most when she deserted him; by the time he made the marriage contract with his second wife Saraeus on 22 May 37 (**4.132**), Tryphon was about twenty-eight, and it is unlikely that he was unusually young when he married for the first time.

To Alexander, strategos, from Tryphon, son of Dionysios, of Oxyrhynchos city. I married Demetrous, daughter of Herakleides, and I, for my part, furnished her with the expected things, even beyond my means. She, however, began to despise our common union, and has finally left my house. She (and an accomplice)[1] carried off property belonging to me which is listed below. So I beg you to have her led before you in order that she receives what she deserves and returns my property. I retain and will continue to retain my rights with regard to the matters I have with her. Farewell.

    The stolen articles are: a . . . phaion worth 40 drachmas.[2]

1 The verb 'carried off' is plural, perhaps indicating that Demetrous had a helper; in **89** Demetrous' mother Thenamounis operated in concert with her daughter.
2 The papyrus breaks off at this point, and presumably other items taken by Demetrous were listed.

89. Tryphon's former wife Demetrous attacks his new wife Saraeus

SB X 10239 (*BL* VII 217; VIII 357)
Oxyrhynchos, after 25 June–21 July AD 37

Not long after the 'unwritten' marriage agreement with Saraeus (**4.132**) Tryphon's first wife Demetrous, acting together with her mother, attacked Saraeus, who was by this time pregnant, causing her to miscarry.[1] Demetrous and her mother seem to have disappeared from the lives of Saraeus and Tryphon after this point, although a subsequent attack was made on Saraeus about A D 50 by a woman whose name is lost from the papyrus, serving as ring-leader to other women (*P.Oxy.* II 324 = *SB* X 10244).

To Sotas strategos, from Tryphon, son of Dionysios, of Oxyrhynchos city. At a late hour on the Augustal day[2] of the present month Epeiph in the 1st year of Gaius Caesar Augustus, the women Thenamounis . . . and her daughter Demetrous, although they had absolutely no cause against me nor against my wife Saraeus, made a senseless attack on her and provoked her, although she was pregnant and . . . with blows . . . a miscarriage. So I come to you and ask that the women charged be led before you in order that they receive . . .

[1] Harm done to pregnant women during attacks is frequently mentioned in petitions; see also **6.229**.

[2] I.e. a day on which events important to the imperial house (e.g. a birthday) were commemorated, cf. **6.232** introd.; in the reign of Gaius (Caligula) there were six imperial holidays in the month of Epeiph.

90. Thamounis/Thamounion borrows money from her son Tryphon

SB X 10238 (*BL* VII 217)
Oxyrhynchos, 20 December A D 37

Tryphon's mother Thamounis/Thamounion, no longer young, was still playing an active role in family affairs; she was certainly a widow by the time of this transaction.

Thamounis, daughter of Onnophris, Persian,[1] with her guardian Leon (?), son of Aperos (?), to my son Tryphon, greetings. I acknowledge that I have from you at the Serapeum at Oxyrhynchos city through the bank of Ploutarchos, son of Sarapion, sixteen drachmas of silver in imperial and Ptolemaic coinage, equals 16 drachmas principal, to which nothing at all has been added, and I shall repay these to you on the thirtieth of (the month) . . . in the coming third year of Gaius Caesar Augustus Germanicus, without any delay . . .[2] for payment of taxes . . . on behalf of Thoonis, son of Dionysios. If I do not repay in accordance with what has been written, I shall pay you as penalty the aforementioned principal sum plus a half and the interest customary for the overtime, with it being your right to proceed against me and all my property, just as if from a legal decision. This receipt is authoritative wherever produced and for anyone who produces it. Year 2 of Gaius Caesar Augustus Germanicus, Choiak 24.

(*2nd hand*) I, Thamounis, have as principal the sixteen drachmas of silver which I shall also repay. I, Leon (?), son of Aperos (?), am registered as her guardian and I have written on her behalf because she does not know letters. Year 2 of Gaius Caesar Augustus Germanicus, Choiak 24. (*3rd hand?*) Year 2 of Gaius Caesar Augustus Germanicus, Choiak 24, the payment was made through the bank of Ploutarchos, son of Sarapion.

[1] See Glossary.

[2] It has been suggested that the beginning of this sentence should read: '[The money is, in fact, useful to me] for payment of taxes [on behalf of my son] . . .' This wording is without parallel and unlikely to be right.

91. Saraeus appears in court accused of baby-snatching

P.Oxy. I 37 (*BL* VIII 230)
Oxyrhynchos, 29 March A D 49

Saraeus gave birth to her first son Apion on 3 January 46, if one of the horoscopes in the archive does mark Apion's birth, and she nursed her baby for some time thereafter. After weaning Apion, Saraeus undertook the nursing of another child, implying that Saraeus and her family found themselves currently short of cash, because nursing contracts of the sort Saraeus presumably signed placed heavy restrictions on a married woman (see **5.213–14**). The child Saraeus agreed to nurse was 'raised up from the dung-heap', a foundling abandoned by its parents and taken in by Pesouris to raise as his slave (cf. **6.230** introd.). According to Saraeus the slave child died during the second year she was nursing it, but Pesouris claimed that the surviving baby was his slave. The case came before the strategos, who decided in Saraeus' favour, thus vindicating Apion's freeborn status and keeping him with his parents.[1] Pesouris did not accept this judgement, but continued to harass the family with his attempts to 'carry off into slavery' the little Apion. Tryphon finally appealed to the prefect (*P.Oxy.* I 38 = *M.Chr.* 58).

From the minutes of Tiberius Claudius Pasion, strategos. Ninth year of Tiberius Claudius Caesar Augustus Germanicus Emperor, Pharmouthi 3, before the tribunal. Pesouris against Saraeus. Aristokles was advocate for Pesouris: 'Pesouris, for whom I am speaking, raised up from the dung-heap a male slave child named Heraklas in year 7 of Tiberius Claudius Caesar (*AD 46/7*). He turned the baby over to the defendant, and a nursing contract was handed over here (*in Oxyrhynchos*) to Pesouris' son. In the first year she took her wages for nursing. When the stipulated day came round in the second year she also took them again. The proof that I speak the truth is the written receipt through which she agreed that she had received her wages. When the slave child became emaciated, Pesouris snatched him away. After this, when Saraeus found an opportune moment, she penetrated the house of my client and grabbed the child away, and she wants to carry the slave child off on the pretext of (its being) freeborn. I have, first of all, the written contract of nursing; and second, I have the receipt (of wages) for nursing. I ask that these contractual agreements be safeguarded.' Saraeus: 'I weaned my

own baby, and their slave child was turned over to me. I received from
them eight staters in all.[2] After this the slave child died, although .[3] staters
remained for me. Now they want to snatch away my own child.' Theon:
'We have documents concerning the slave child.'[4]

The strategos ruled: 'Since from its appearance the baby seems to belong
to Saraeus, if she and her husband will sign a sworn affidavit that the slave
child turned over to her by Pesouris has died, my opinion, in accordance
with the rulings from our lord prefect, is that she should have her own child,
provided she pays back the money she received.'

[1] The strategos' decision, made on the grounds of the child's resemblance to Saraeus, may
reflect ethnic bias, if the child looked to him 'Egyptian' rather than 'Greek'. Infant exposure was apparently practised more widely among the hellenised metropolitan population
than among the Egyptian lower classes; Bagnall and Frier (1994), 151–3; cf. **6.230**.

[2] I.e. 32 dr., a low salary in comparison with contemporary nursing contracts (cf. **5.213–14**);
perhaps the scribe made a mistake.

[3] The numeral lost here specified the amount of money Saraeus had yet to earn on the
nursing contract when the slave child died.

[4] Theon, who also spoke on the side of Pesouris, was probably the son to whom the nursing
contract was originally handed over: van Minnen, *ZPE* 96 (1993), 119.

E.   The archive of Apollonios the strategos and Aline, AD 113–20

This archive of over two hundred Greek papyri was unearthed by clandestine diggers in Hermopolis, either in the family's city residence, or in their
suburban villa, since the family seems to have owned more than a single residence. The papyri were subsequently sold by dealers to different institutions, mainly in Europe.[1] The earliest documents in the archive belonged to
the strategos' grandfather, also named Apollonios, and to his father Herakles,
showing them as landholders in the Hermopolite nome, certainly by the end
of the first century AD and perhaps already fifty years earlier under the Julio-
Claudian emperors. By the time of Apollonios the strategos this wealthy
family not only owned estates in the Hermopolite and perhaps the
Lykopolite nomes, but also had business interests in weaving and textiles.
The women of the family supervised much of the weaving, together with
servants and slaves (**94–5**, **97**). Apollonios himself rose to the highest office
in the bureaucracy available to Graeco-Egyptians during the Roman
Principate, becoming strategos of the Apollonopolite (Heptakomias) nome
by 12 June 114; he was still serving some five or more years later. The many
documents he brought back north with him on returning home after his
term of duty provide much information about the management of nome
affairs. The large number of letters between family members suggests that,
because Apollonios was a high government official, he and his family were
able to make use of official postal couriers and, because of their social promi-

nence, were also informed about those travelling between the Hermopolite and Apollonopolite nomes.

Apollonios had the misfortune to be in office when the Jewish revolt spread to Egypt from Cyrene with the appearance there of a 'Messianic' figure, on its way eastward to Mesopotamia and northward to Cyprus; within Egypt the uprising began in Alexandria and advanced southward towards Hermopolis in Middle Egypt. Although the strategos was a civilian official, Apollonios was nonetheless involved in the fighting in various areas, even campaigning as far north as Memphis. By late autumn of 117 Apollonios had twice written to the prefect, requesting a leave of sixty days so that he could attend to his private affairs and restore to order his estates in and around Hermopolis – these had suffered, he claimed, because of his absence 'and also because of the attack of the impious Jews' (*Sel.Pap.* II 298 = *C.Pap.Jud.* II 443).[2] The uprising brought separation to Apollonios' family, although some of the womenfolk may have preferred to remain near the more sophisticated and hellenised attractions of Hermopolis, as opposed to the more Egyptian atmosphere in the *metropolis* of Heptakomia. Apollonios' mother Eudaimonis resided more or less permanently at Hermopolis, watching over her granddaughter Heraidous, perhaps the first child of Apollonios and his wife Aline to survive infancy. Aline, however, was not infrequently with her husband and, although she was separated from Heraidous, other unnamed children were with her and Apollonios (e.g. *P.Alex.Giss.* 59 = *SB* x 10652c).

Many of the letters cannot be precisely dated, leaving uncertainty about the chronology, not only of the Jewish revolt, especially in its later stages, but also of Apollonios' family affairs. The seriousness of Apollonios' official duties preyed upon the minds of family members and was underscored by a friend at the close of a fragmentary letter: 'for you know, better than I do, the magnanimity the situation requires, and, if it is not present, look out for fellows of this kind!' (*P.Alex.Giss.* 38 = *SB* x 10646.17–19). Apollonios' wife Aline and his mother Eudaimonis, perhaps a widow since no husband is mentioned, worried about his safety during the hostilities.

The family unquestionably belonged to the upper levels of Graeco-Egyptian society, and the majority of Apollonios' correspondents seemingly wrote closing greetings to their letters in their own hands; this includes at least some of the letters from both Eudaimonis and Aline. Even if scribes wrote the body of letters for these women, the fact that they were able to write a closing greeting shows that both Eudaimonis and Aline were literate.[3]

Friends and family employed kinship terms lavishly, greeting one another frequently as 'brother', 'sister', 'mother', 'father', in their letters, although in some instances the letter itself suggests that the 'mother' or 'sister' addressed was not in fact related by blood (**95**). Earlier scholars thought that Apollonios and Aline were brother and sister, as well as husband and wife,

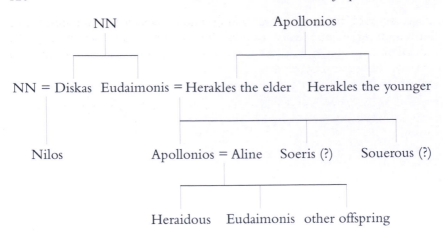

Figure 4   Family of Apollonios and Aline

because Apollonios and Aline did on occasion refer to each other as 'brother' and 'sister', while Eudaimonis sometimes called Aline 'my daughter' in letters addressed to Aline and Apollonios. But the fact that in two letters to Apollonios alone (*P.Alex.Giss.* 57.2–3, 59.4 = *SB* x 10652A and c) she referred to Aline as 'your wife', excludes this possibility. Aline and Apollonios had several children, although names are known only for two girls, Heraidous and the baby Eudaimonis (named after her grandmother). Like others in the household, grandmother Eudaimonis hoped that one of Aline's pregnancies would produce a boy (**94**).

---

[1] Other texts with English translation: *C.Pap.Jud.* II 436–44 and *Sel.Pap.* I 115, II 298, 354, 423. Also part of the archive are *P.Brem.* 1–82 and *SB* x 10277–8; *P.Giss.* 3–27, 41–7, and 58–93; *P.Flor.* III 326–34; *P.Alex.Giss.* 14–61 = *SB* x 10639–53. Discussion of the archive in *C.Pap.Jud.* II, pp. 225–7.

[2] The Jewish community nearly disappears from the Egyptian evidence for more than a century after the revolt.

[3] As was Heraidous, **94–5**; cf. **6.236–7**. Pomeroy (1988), 719–20, overemphasises the fact that Eudaimonis and Aline employ scribes, for her intention was to caution against a facile generalisation from Heraidous' education to the assumption of literacy for her female relatives.

92.   Eudaimonis to Apollonios

C.Pap.Jud. II 437 (*BL* VII 59)
Hermopolis, 30 June AD 115 (?)[1]

Eudaimonis alludes to rumours that reached Hermopolis about the outbreak of hostilities in the Jewish revolt, taking place further to the north.

. . . at any rate, if the gods are willing, and especially the unconquerable
Hermes, may they not defeat you. For the rest, may you be well for my sake
with all your people. Heraidous salutes you, your daughter whom the evil
eye may not touch. Epeiph 6.
(*Address on the back*) To Apollonios.

¹ The chronology of the letters, vis-à-vis that of the revolt, is much debated; we follow
Schwartz (1962), 354.

93.   Aline to Apollonios

C.Pap.Jud. II 436
Hermopolis, beginning of September A D 115 (?)

Instead of spending the Egyptian New Year's day with his wife Aline in
Hermopolis, Apollonios rushed back to his post. Fragmentary letters from
Eudaimonis to Apollonios, probably dating from the same time as this anxious letter
from Aline, tell of his mother's worry for her son's safety. She began one letter with
'Because of (?) the hostilities near us, I persevere night and day with my prayers to
all the gods and goddesses that they take part together in protecting you'
(*P.Alex.Giss.* 58 = *SB* x 10652B).

Aline to Apollonios her brother, many greetings. I am very worried about
you, because of events that are said to be taking place and because you left
me suddenly. Neither drink nor food do I approach with pleasure, but
staying awake continually night and day, I have a single anxiety, about your
safety. Only my father's care arouses me, and on the first day of the new year
– I swear by your safety – I would have stayed in bed without eating a bite,
if my father had not come and forced me. Please, then, keep yourself safe
and do not put yourself in danger alone without a guard; but, like the strategos here who puts the burden on the magistrates, you too do the same . . .
my father . . . because the name of my brother was proposed . . . but god
will . . . him. If, at any rate, brother, . . . from your affairs . . . write to me
. . . to you . . . is coming up . . . of your safety . . .
(*Address on the back*) To Apollonios my brother.

94.   Eudaimonis to Aline

C.Pap.Jud. II 442 (*BL* V 19; VI 24; VIII 68)
Hermopolis, 16 July A D 116 (?)

By this time Aline has joined her husband in the Apollonopolite (Heptakomias)
nome.

Eudaimonis to Aline her daughter, greetings. I pray first of all that you may
be delivered of your child in due course and that I get news that it's a boy.

You sailed up river on the 29th and on the next day I finished drawing down
(? the wool).[1] With difficulty I got the material from the dyer on 10 Epeiph.
I am working together with your slave women to the best of my ability. I
cannot find women able to work with us, for they are all working for their
own mistresses. Our people have been walking around the whole *metropolis*, offering (?) higher wages. Your sister Souerous was delivered of her child.
Teeus wrote to me, praising you, so that, my lady, I know my orders remain
in force. For she left all her own people and set out to join you. The little
girl (*Heraidous?*) salutes you and is assiduous with her lessons for school.[2]
Know that I am not going to pay attention to god (*Hermes?*) until I am
reunited with my son safe and sound. For what purpose did you send me
the 20 drachmas, when I am having a difficult time? Already I have before
my eyes the notion that I shall be naked throughout the winter.
(*2nd hand*) Farewell. 22 Epeiph.
(*1st hand, written in the left margin*) The wife of Eudemos does not leave my
side and I am grateful to her.
(*Address on the back, 3rd hand*) To Aline my daughter.

[1] Apparently the verb 'draw down' is a technical term in weaving, as well as in the building
  trade ('pulling down a building'), in agriculture ('harvesting fruit crops'), and in navigation
  ('hauling boats down to water'). Eudaimonis may be referring to 'carding and combing the
  wool' or to 'spinning it', preparatory to turning it over to the dyer. Aline uses the same
  term in the following letter (**95**).
[2] See **6.236–7**.

95. Aline to Tetes

P. Giss. 78
Heptakomia (?), late in the reign of Trajan

Tetes, addressed affectionately as 'mother' by Aline, was an older woman, perhaps
a slave belonging to the family. The first editor of the text remarked that the signature in the 2nd hand at the bottom was 'delicate'.

Aline to Tetes her mother, greetings. You told me about the sale of the garments. Now please expedite also the remaining items. I have made certain
that I finished drawing down[1] your . . . necessarily, in fact, as you know, also
because of the . . . until (the matter?) is finally (?) brought to a successful
conclusion.[2] When my little Heraidous wrote to her father, she did not send
a greeting to me, and I do not know why.
(*2nd hand*) I pray that you are well.
(*Address on the back*) To Tetes my mother.

[1] See **94** note 1.
[2] The suggestion in *BL* I 462, 'brought to completion for the good of the *metropolis*' seems
  less likely.

96.   Eudaimonis to Apollonios

P.Flor. III 332 (*BL* VII 54)
Hermopolis, *c.* 30 September of an unknown year, late in the reign of
Trajan

Eudaimonis to Apollonios her son, greetings. It does not escape you that
two months ago today I went to the intractable Diskas, since he would not
wait for your arrival. Well, he is now seeking, along with other friends of
his from the gymnasium, to attack me in your absence, supposing that he
can gain his ends unjustly. I have already done my part, and have neither
bathed nor worshipped the gods through fear about your unfinished business, if indeed it is still unfinished. Do not let it be unfinished any longer,
lest I be dragged off to the law courts. Before all, I pray that you are healthy,
together with all my little children and their mother. Keep writing to me
about the health of you all, so that I might have a consolation for my
journey. Farewell, my lord. Phaophi 3.

   At your wedding the wife of Diskas my brother brought me 100 drachmas. Since now Nilos her son is about to marry, it is only fair that we too
give a return gift, even if there are unresolved claims against them.
(*Address on the back*) To Apollonios her son.

97.   Eudaimonis to Apollonios

P.Giss. 21 (*BL* V 34)
Hermopolis, *c.* 20 December of an unknown year, late in the reign of
Trajan

The note 'And you made a mistake!' was added between the lines in a much smaller
hand, according to the editor of the text.

Eudaimonis to Apollonios her son, very many greetings. I was quite overjoyed to hear that you are well, as was your sister Soeris. From the day on
which you sent to me, I have been hunting for the Spartan-style garment,
but only found a worn-out Pergamene one instead. You are well aware that
you gave us raw wool (?) for producing the white garment. (*2nd hand*) And you
made a mistake! (*1st hand*) As a result, you are expending one pound and a stater
in weight. At any rate, you are to buy it and send it, so that it may be speed-
ily dispatched. Please, stay at home so that you do not distress me . . . Salute
your sister Aline. Soeris thanks you very much and wrote me a letter about
this. Little Heraidous salutes you and her mother.
(*2nd hand*) Farewell, my child. Choiak 24.
(*Address on the back*) To Apollonios strategos of the Apollonopolite nome.

98.   Eudaimonis to Aline

P.Giss. 23
Hermopolis, late in the reign of Trajan

The first editor suggested that the 'Souerous' of this letter was the same person as 'Soeris', whom Eudaimonis called Apollonios' sister in the previous letter (**97**). Eudaimonis also called Aline's sister 'Souerous', when announcing to the pregnant Aline that Souerous had already given birth to her child (**94**). Other scholars have argued that 'Soeris' and 'Souerous' are two different women, because of the divergent spellings of their names (but see **Arch. K**, introd. note 2).

Eudaimonis to Aline her daughter, many greetings. I have as the most compelling of all my prayers the one for your health and that of your brother Apollonios and of your (children) whom the evil eye may not touch. Next, thanks be to god that you . . . Souerous salutes you and also Heraidous. Farewell . . .
(*Written in the bottom margin*) But she (?) made . . .
(*Written in the left margin*) After you have sent them to me . . . a suit (?) for Heraidous. Pauni . . .
(*Address on the back*) To Aline from Eudaimonis.

99.   Teeus to Aline

P.Giss. 77 (*BL* III 68; IX 94)
Hermopolis, *c.* 19 November of an unknown year, late in the reign of Trajan

Teeus[1] to Aline her mistress, greetings. Before all, Heraidous salutes you and I salute all your people. When they were here with us, . . . of mine, when I am leaving . . . Then I knew that you sent the tunic to me. I praised you very much before all the gods, because you have clothed me. I hope it turns out, then, that I shall pray on your behalf under the happy circumstance that you have given birth to a baby boy and . . . the women have been summoned by (?) . . . to Amounis. . . . It seems as if I am close to you (?) and if you are going to give me something, . . . a little . . .[2] instead of me and send me what you have. Farewell mistress, Hathyr 23.
(*Address on the back*) Deliver to Aline.

[1]   Like Tetes (**95**), Teeus was probably a servant in the household in Hermopolis.
[2]   It is not clear whether Teeus is asking for a present of food (a misspelling of *paropsidion*), or a garment with a border (a phonetic spelling of *paruphidion*).

F. The archive of Kronion, farmer of Tebtynis, and his family, AD 107–53

The nearly seventy documents that make up the archive of Kronion were found by Italian excavators on the cellar floor of a building, apparently thrown there with other discarded papyri and flammable materials, such as palm fibres, perhaps for use as kindling.[1] Kronion's family may thus never have lived in the building. All Kronion's papers were written in Greek, yet (like Tryphon's family, **Arch. D**), no family member is known to have been literate in Greek, and the notation 'I wrote on their behalf because they do not know letters' appears frequently. Several times Hippalos, son of Chrates, an old man of the village, and no doubt a respected and trustworthy figure, signed contracts for them, including Kronion's will of AD 138 (**101**).[2] Both Kronion and his son Harphaesis held the minor priestly office of *pastophoros* in the main temple at Tebtynis, dedicated to the crocodile god Soknebtynis (equated with Greek Kronos; hence the name 'Kronion'). The family probably spoke Egyptian among themselves, and other family members bore Egyptian names.

Kronion's family were long-standing residents of Tebtynis. In AD 35, Kronion's father Cheos sold three arouras of sacred land inherited from his own father; the sale contract recorded the consent of Cheos' mother Thaesis to this sale of family property (*P.Mich.* V 260–1). Her age in AD 35, 'about forty years', suggests that she was about fifteen years old when she gave birth to her son Cheos, who was 'about twenty-five years' at the time of the sale. Cheos married Taorsenouphis, and their child Kronion, the central figure of the archive, was born in AD 63, when his father was fifty-three years old. Kronion's own wife Thenapynchis (born *c.* AD 69) was also about fifteen years old when she bore her first child, Kronion, in 84/5. Four other children followed: a daughter Taorsenouphis (born 88/9); another son Harphaesis, and then another daughter Tephorsais (born 105). The fifth child, a son Harmiysis, mentioned only once in family papers (**101**), seems to have left his natal household early, neither sharing the family's farming activities nor its closely entwined social structure – for the family practised endogamous marriage in the extreme. The eldest son Kronion married his sister Taorsenouphis, and Harphaesis married his sister Tephorsais. Perhaps the fact that there was no sister for Harmiysis to marry hastened his departure from the family home. The marriage of Kronion the younger and Taorsenouphis ended in divorce after about twenty-seven years, in AD 138 (**102**). Their eldest child, a son named Sasopis, was born in 111. Other children may have died in infancy before the birth, more than ten years later, of their other two surviving children: a son Pakebkis and a daughter Tephorsais, both still minors at the time of their parents' divorce. Given the family's modest wealth, Taorsenouphis brought a surprisingly large dowry

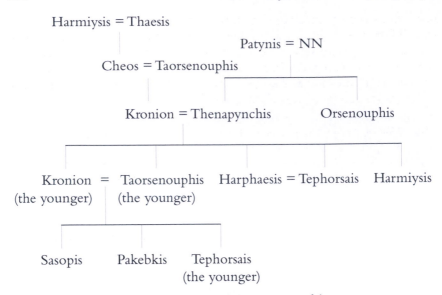

Figure 5   Family of Kronion and Taorsenouphis

at her marriage to her brother, consisting of gold jewellery, uncoined silver, and probably also garments, not mentioned in their divorce agreement, to a total value of about one thousand drachmas. After all, Taorsenouphis' dowry goods would remain a family asset because of the endogamous marriage. As it turned out, the younger Kronion converted his wife's gold and silver to cash for his personal use. Tephorsais also brought her brother a dowry of similar value. In view of these sizeable dowries, the sisters inherited only a small sum through their father's will (**101**);[3] Kronion divided the bulk of his inheritance equally between his two younger sons, Harphaesis and Harmiysis, and his under-age granddaughter, Tephorsais, perhaps intended for her future dowry. Kronion the younger, who had offended his father, was virtually excluded from the inheritance.

In contrast to the dowry provisions, other information about the family's economic affairs suggests that continual shortages of cash forced them into borrowing money and seed wheat for planting. Kronion's two daughters Taorsenouphis and Tephorsais owned some land, occasionally using portions of it as security on loans (e.g. **103**). The elder Kronion supplemented the family's holdings by leasing land from others, often at some distance from Tebtynis, such as the twenty-five arouras around the village of Kerkesis; he managed the cultivation, taking out leases until he was approaching seventy years of age, but from about AD 135 onward his sons, especially Harphaesis, took over direction of family affairs and the undertaking of leases. Chronic debt ever threatened, and the family found it increasingly difficult to repay loans. At its largest extent the household consisted of six adults and at least four children – ten mouths to feed. Poverty may also have motivated Kronion's son Harmiysis to abandon the family enclave, yet divorce and death proved more threatening to family cohesion. The elder Kronion's wife Thenapynchis died before AD 138; Kronion disappears after September 140, when he was about seventy-eight years old.

[1] The archive is published as *P.Kronion*; discussion in Kehoe (1992), 149–58, and Lewis (1983), 69–73. The archive's discovery is described from excavation records by Gallazzi (1990).

[2] Hippalos' name should not be restored in *P.Kron.* 15.12–13; for illiterates' need to identify a 'trustworthy' person to read and write for them, see Hanson (1991b).

[3] This was normal practice; Hobson (1983).

100. Kronion petitions to have the lady Akousarion return his donkey

P.Kron. 2
Tebtynis, 7 April 127 (or 128?)

Given the economic difficulties that plagued Kronion's family, the loss of a donkey, a versatile beast of burden, was a misfortune. Nothing further is heard about the affair, and perhaps the donkey's whereabouts were discovered.

To Andromachos, strategos of the Arsinoite nome, Polemon division, through Sabinus, former gymnasiarch, who is carrying out the functions of strategos, from Kronion, son of Cheos from the village of Tebtynis. I turned over to Akousarion a black, female donkey of mine in the *metropolis*. When I wanted to get my donkey back from Akousarion, I learned from her that my donkey had suddenly run away from her courtyard toward Tebtynis. Since after my return to Tebtynis, I did not find my donkey, I therefore ask that Akousarion be led before you with a view toward me recovering my donkey, in order that I may be benefited by you. [Eleven]th (*or twelfth?*) year of Emperor Caesar Trajan Hadrian Augustus, Pharmouthi 12.

101. Kronion's will

P.Kron. 50 (*BL* VII 74)
Tebtynis, 13 June 138

Kronion wrote this will aged about seventy-five; the document was witnessed and sealed by the requisite six witnesses and registered at the record office in Tebtynis.[1] He left the bulk of his estate to his two younger sons and his only granddaughter. His eldest son Kronion was cut off with a token amount of money, because of the wrongs he had done his father; these surely included the younger Kronion's divorce

from his sister Taorsenouphis, finalised some 2½ months after this will was written
(**102**).

In the twenty-second year of Emperor Caesar Trajan Hadrian Augustus,
Pauni 19, in Tebtynis of the Polemon division of the Arsinoite nome.
Kronion, son of Cheos, son of Harmiysis, his mother being
Taorsenouphis, from the village Tebtynis, about seventy-five years old,
with a scar on his right hand, acknowledges that after his death he has
ceded to three heirs, both those born to him from his deceased wife
Thenapynchis, daughter of Patynis – his sons Harmiysis and Harphaesis –
and also to the daughter of other children of Kronion himself, namely of
Kronion (the younger) and Taorsenouphis (the younger) – Tephorsais (the
younger), under-age – all the things of any kind that he, Kronion the
father, might leave behind him, the property, furniture, implements,
household goods, and other properties, as well as all the debts owed to him
and anything else in any way, to each of them equally a third part. To the
other three children of Kronion himself – Kronion (the younger) and
Taorsenouphis (the younger) and Tephorsais: (he acknowledges) to have
designated for Kronion (the younger) only forty drachmas of silver
because of the fact that he has been wronged by him in many matters over
the course of his lifetime, as Kronion the father affirms; to the two daughters Taorsenouphis (the younger) and Tephorsais, apart from the gold and
silver jewellery and clothing which he affirms to have prepared for them
as gifts, he gives as a present to each . . . drachmas of silver. The funeral
of Kronion the declarant and the preparation of his mummy are the
responsibility of the three heirs, Harmiysis and Harphaesis and his granddaughter Tephorsais (the younger), being under-age, and also the paying
out of the aforementioned legacies and of other debts, public or private,
that he seems to owe. For the time that Kronion the declarant lives on, he
is to hold total authority over all his possessions to manage as he chooses.
He who wrote the subscriptions was Onnophris, son of Th . . . xosis,
about sixty-two years old, with a scar on his forehead.

   Witnesses: Hippalos, son of Chrates, about sixty-eight years old, with a
scar on his right forearm; Soterichos, son of Eutychos, about forty years old,
with a scar on each eyebrow; Kronion, son of Tyrannos, about thirty-two
years old, with a scar on his left calf; Zoilos alias Tyrannos, son of Kronion,
about thirty years old, with a scar on his right knee; Aretion, son of Ision,
about forty years old, with a scar on his right foot; Diogenes, son of Horion,
about twenty-six years old, with a scar on his forehead. These are the six
witnesses to this cession.

   (*2nd hand*) I, Kronion, son of Cheos, acknowledge to have ceded after
my death to my children Harmiysis and Harphaesis and to my granddaughter Tephorsais, my three heirs in common, equally, all things of any
kind whatsoever I may leave behind – property, all household goods, et

16 Amulet of Isis and Harpokrates
Kelsey Museum 26024 (Bonner 1950, no. 29)

Amulets were commonly worn as pendants or set in rings or beads, both to protect the wearer from harm and to serve as a seal for documents (see **3.101**). This example, made of lapis lazuli, shows Isis seated on a high-backed chair holding the infant Harpokrates on her knees (cf. **Plate 11**).

cetera – but to my son Kronion to have designated only forty drachmas, because he wronged me, and to my two daughters Taorsenouphis and Tephorsais, to each . . . drachmas, and in regard to the other specifications as aforementioned. And I seal with a carving of Isis and Harpokrates.[2] I, Onnophris, son of Th . . . xosis, wrote for him, because he does not know letters.

(*3rd hand*) I, Hippalos, son of Chrates, am a witness and I seal with a carving of Harpokrates.

(*4th hand*) I, Soterichos, son of Eutychos, am a witness and I seal with a carving of Serapis.

(*5th hand*) I, Kronion, son of Tyrannos, am a witness and I seal with a carving of Athene.

(*6th hand*) I, Zoilos alias Tyrannos, son of Kronion, am a witness and I seal with a carving of Hermes.

(*7th hand*) I, Aretion, son of Ision, am a witness and I seal with a carving of Serapammon.

(*8th hand*) I, Diogenes, son of Horion, am a witness and I seal with a carving of Isis and Serapis.

(*9th hand*) Twenty-second year of Emperor Caesar Trajan Hadrian Augustus, Pauni 19. This was registered through the registry office in Tebtynis.

[1] A great many documents produced through this record office have survived, particularly from the first century AD (published in *P. Mich.* vols. II and V; see also **5.168, 185; 6.229, 252**). Hobson (1984) discusses the roles of women attested in this evidence.

[2] For a seal depicting Isis holding Harpokrates, see **Plate 16**; cf. **2.24** and **Plate 11**.

102. Divorce agreement between Taorsenouphis (the younger) and Kronion (the younger)

P.Kron. 52
Tebtynis, 30 August 138

More than two months after Kronion wrote his will (**101**), his married children Taorsenouphis and Kronion signed this formal agreement of divorce. Two months after that, on 24 October 138, the younger Kronion entered into a complicated financial arrangement with a woman of considerable property, Diogenis, daughter of Lysimachos alias Louppos, for whom Kronion had been working for several years as manager on one of her farms. Kronion's family also leased land from Diogenis' brother Heron, an important man in the *metropolis*. The arrangement with Diogenis required Kronion to repay 1800 drachmas, plus interest, outstanding from his farm accounts for the year A D 137, or else to remain with Diogenis, carrying out all tasks assigned to him on the farm or in the village, in lieu of principal and interest, receiving food and clothing from Diogenis and with her paying his public taxes. Nothing more is known about this arrangement, but a receipt for grain taxes, dated some two years later, suggests that the upheaval caused by the divorce was temporary and that after a short hiatus the younger Kronion was again farming together with his brother Harphaesis and his own elder son Sasopis.[1]

Copy of agreement. Year 2 of Antoninus Caesar our lord, in the month Sebastos 2, in Tebtynis of the Polemon division of the Arsinoite nome. They acknowledge to each other – Kronion, son of Kronion, about 54 years of age, with a scar on his left forearm, and she who was his wife, being also his sister from the same father and the same mother, Taorsenouphis, about 50 years of age, lacking distinguishing mark, with her guardian, the father of them both, Kronion, son of Cheos, about 76 years old, with a scar on his right hand – that they have cancelled their living together, which they had established with each other without a written contract and that it is possible for both of them to manage their own affairs as each chooses, and for Taorsenouphis to live with another man without recrimination of any sort. The jewellery that all the aforementioned affirm Kronion received from his sister Taorsenouphis – gold, weighing one mina and ten quarters, and uncoined silver, weighing twenty-eight staters – and which he converted into cash for his own use, the declarant Kronion must repay to his sister Taorsenouphis in equivalent jewellery within sixty days from the present day, with the right of execution belonging to Taorsenouphis herself against her brother Kronion and against all the property belonging to him. Insofar as other matters that relate to their living together, they will not proceed against one another concerning any pretext in any fashion whatsoever, not Kronion against Taorsenouphis with regard to any property she has bought, in consideration of the fact that she paid out its price from her own funds, nor concerning any other matter at all, whether in written or unwritten (arrangement) until the present day. There were born to them from each other the sons Sasopis and Pakebkis and a daughter Tephorsais.

¹ Contract with Diogenis: *P.Kron.* 16 (*BL* VII 73); land leased from Heron: *P.Kron.* 35 (AD 135/6) and *P. Kron.* 39 (26 May 139); receipt for grain taxes: *P.Kron.* 40 (23 July 140). The suggestion (Lewis, 1983, 73) of a romantic involvement between the younger Kronion, aged 54, and the 45-year-old Diogenis seems unlikely, considering the difference in their social and economic standing.

103. The daughters of Kronion borrow money from Didyme

P.Kron. 17
Tebtynis, 25 September 140

Because Taorsenouphis and Kronion the younger were now divorced, the elder Kronion here acts as guardian for his daughter; her sister Tephorsais' guardian is her husband-brother Harphaesis. The lender, Didyme daughter of Heron, belonged to a prominent local family (see *P.Kron.* p. xxxi). Tephorsais and Taorsenouphis subsequently defaulted on this loan, and in AD 144 Tephorsais formally notified the keepers of the property register (the *bibliophylakes enkteseon*) that two of their arouras were mortgaged to Didyme as security for the debt (*P.Kron.* 18 with *BL* VIII 158; cf. also *P.Kron.* 20).

Fourth year of Emperor Caesar Titus Aelius Hadrianus Antoninus Augustus Pius, Thoth 28 in Tebtynis of the Polemon division of the Arsinoite nome. Taorsenouphis, about forty-five years old with a scar on her left calf, and Tephorsais, about thirty-five years old with a scar on her left hand, both daughters of Kronion, son of Cheos, each acting with a guardian – for Taorsenouphis, her father, Kronion, son of Cheos, about seventy-eight years old with a scar on the little finger of his left hand; for Tephorsais, her husband, who is also her brother, Harphaesis, about forty-eight years old with a scar on his left thumb – both women being Persians of the *epigone*¹ and mutually guaranteeing the repayment, acknowledge to Didyme, daughter of Heron, son of Amais, about forty-six years old with a scar on her left calf, with her guardian, her first cousin on her mother's side Harpaesis, son of Herakles, about .. years old, with a scar on his left hand, that they have from her, Didyme, immediately from hand to hand, a loan at interest with a capital sum of three hundred seventy-two drachmas, the return of which they will necessarily make in Thoth of the coming fifth year without postponement. If they do not pay back on the above-mentioned appointed day in accordance with what has been written, (they acknowledge) that it is possible for Didyme, or for someone acting on her behalf if she should choose, to enjoy the use to her own benefit of two arouras of land, beginning from the same fifth year, out of the four arouras of the katoikic allotment belonging to her, Tephorsais, in the vicinity of the village Tebtynis in the so-called 'Development of

17   Letters found in the house of Taesion
Kelsey Museum Archives, 5.2036
Room C, House B1, Karanis

The two folded letters from Apollinarios (see **Ch.3 Archive G**) lie just as the excavators found them (centre of photograph).

Stasikrates',[2] from whichever extremity or section of it Didyme chooses, with all public taxes on the two arouras payable by Tephorsais. But if Didyme does not wish to enjoy use of the land, (they acknowledge that) the right of execution is hers against the borrowers, or against one of them, and against all the property belonging to them, as if in accordance with a judgement. He who wrote the subscriptions below was Hippalos, son of Chrates, about seventy- . . . years old, with a scar on his right forearm.

(*2nd hand*) We, Taorsenouphis and Tephorsais, both daughters of Kronion, each with her guardian – Taorsenouphis with her father, Tephorsais with her husband Harphaesis – acknowledge to have from Didyme with mutual guarantee the three hundred and eighty-two[3] drachmas as a loan that we shall repay in the month Thoth of the fifth year, and if not, that she will enjoy the two arouras around Tebtynis as indicated above. Hippalos, son of Chrates, wrote for them because they do not know letters.

(*3rd hand*) Didyme, daughter of Heron, with her guardian her first cousin on her mother's side Harpaesis, son of Herakles: the agreement has been

18   Karanis: plan of areas excavated in the 1924–5 and 1925–6 seasons
Boak and Peterson (1931), Plan 1

House 5006 (see **Ch.3 Archive H**) was probably situated in Area F in the vicinity of the 'newly discovered temple', or 'north temple', as it was later called. Area G is not plotted on this map.

made with me as indicated above. Maron, son of Maron, wrote for them because they do not know letters.

[1] See Glossary.
[2] 'Development' seems a proper translation for *diaita*, known elsewhere with the meaning 'building', a translation that is inappropriate here.
[3] Apparently an error for 372 drachmas, the figure mentioned not only in the body of the contract, but also in the subsequent arrangements with Didyme (*P.Kron.* 18.18).

G.   The archive of Taesion/Taesis and House B1 in Karanis, later second century AD

Excavations at Karanis, a village at the north-east edge of the Fayum, were carried out by the University of Michigan between 1924 and 1935, and the co-operation between archaeologists and papyrologists offered a unique opportunity to maintain the connections between papyri, material objects,

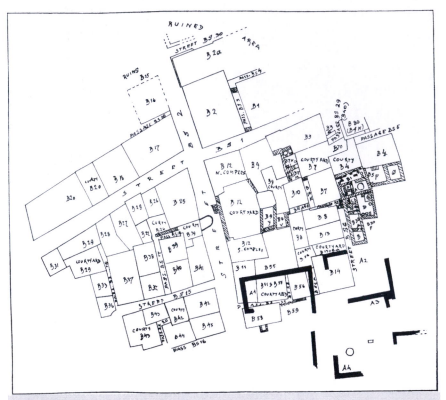

19   Karanis: plan of Area G
Boak and Peterson (1931), Plan II, Area G

House B1 (of Taesion, **Ch.3 Archive G**) lies to the right of the plan on Street BS1, only
partially excavated. To reach House B7 (of Sempronia Gemella; **3.71**), continue right along
Street BS1 to Passage BS29. House B17 (of Sokrates; **3.71**) is at the intersection of Streets
BS1 and BS2.

and the ancient context of a village.[1] Two letters were found in House B1,
both from Apollinarios, a young man who joined the Roman fleet in the
latter decades of the second century A D. **Plate 17** shows Apollinarios' letters
as excavators found them. Apollinarios sent one letter (**104**) to his mother
Taesion/Taesis shortly after he arrived at Portus, the harbour at Ostia built
by the emperor Trajan for imperial Rome; he sent the second letter not long
afterwards (**105**).[2] Apollinarios was assigned to Misenum, the large naval base
at the north end of the Bay of Naples. Whether the letter Apollinarios mentioned dispatching from Cyrene (see **104**) ever reached Karanis is unknown,
since only two letters were found in Taesion/Taesis' house. Nor do we know
whether Apollinarios ever returned to Karanis.

Taesion/Taesis was apparently a widow, and she may have shared House

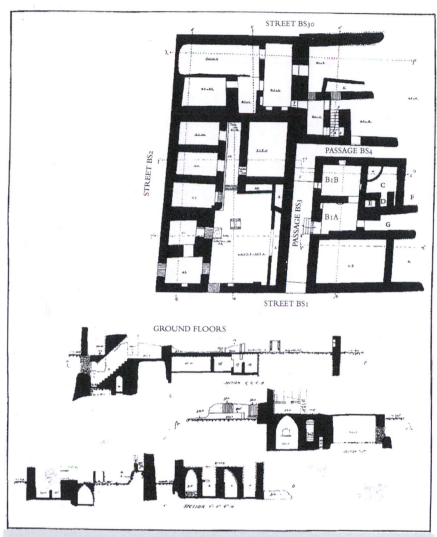

20   Karanis: detailed plan of the block including House B1
Boak and Peterson (1931), Plan IIIB

House B1 (Taesion's house: **Ch.3 Archive G**) was entered from Passage BS3 by three steps
(**Plate 21**), bringing one into Room A, and from there into Rooms B and G. Room C, in
which Taesion kept her letters from Apollinarios (**Plate 17**), was in the more secluded part of
the house. The elevation diagram shows the presence of staircases and vaulted cellars (cf.
2.61, 5.196).

21 Karanis: steps leading into the House of Taesion
Kelsey Museum Archives 5.2405

A view north along Passage BS3, showing the three steps leading to the right into House B1, Room A (see **Plate 20**). Beyond the steps, at the corner with Passage BS4, stands a large stone storage jar.

B1 with her two sons, another Apollinarios and Kalalas/Karalas, and their children, for these were the people greeted by Apollinarios in his letters. Taesion/Taesis' house B1 was situated in Area G (**Plates 19–20**).[3] The narrow Passageway BS3 opened onto the larger Street BS1 and into Passageway BS4 (**Plate 20**), and three steps led from Passageway BS3 directly into Room A (**Plate 21**). Taesion/Taesis kept the letters in the interior Room C. The living quarters are to the north, or upper part of the plan of the house, while cubicles for the storage of grain occupied the southern portion and were on the same level as room C. Because House B1 was never completely excavated, the total extent of the living quarters remains unknown. No courtyard was unearthed, and excavators speculated that Taesion/Taesis used the adjacent passageway as her courtyard. Other, better preserved, courtyards belonging to houses in Area C on the north-east side of Karanis show that the open courtyards housed ovens for baking the family's bread, and mills for grinding the family's grain (**Plate 22**).

[1] For the method, van Minnen (1994a).
[2] For more soldiers' letters, see **74** (also to a mother), and White (1986), 157–66 (nos. 101–5).
[3] For some of Taesion/Taesis' neighbours, also living in Area G, see **71**.

22   Karanis: Area C
(a) Courtyard with an oven
Kelsey Museum Archives, 5.3994

A close view of the oven in House C119, marked 'K' on plan (c).

(b) Courtyard with milling equipment
Kelsey Museum Archives, 5.3767

The courtyard with mills for House C113 (marked C113N on plan (c)). In the foreground are a mill-base and millstone; behind lie storage bins and an oven (to left).

(c) Overall plan of area C
From Husselman (1979), Map 11

104.   Taesion/Taesis' son Apollinarios joins the Roman fleet

P.Mich. VIII 490
Karanis (sent from Portus), later second century AD

Apollinarios to Taesion his mother, many greetings. First of all, be in good health for me, as I am making obeisance on your behalf before all the gods. From Cyrene I encountered a man travelling in your direction and I felt it necessary to tell you about my well-being. You, too, tell me soon about your well-being and that of my brothers. Even now from Portus I am writing to inform you, for I have not yet gone up to Rome and been assigned. When I do get my assignment and know into which section I am going, I will inform you immediately. You, too, do not hesitate to write to me concerning your safety and that of my brothers. If you do not find a man travelling toward me, write to Sokrates[1] and he sends it on to me himself. I greet my brothers many times and Apollinarios and his children, and Kalalas and his children, and all those who love you. Asklepiades greets you. Farewell in good health. I arrived at Portus on Pachon 25.
(*2nd hand*) Know that I was assigned to Misenum, for I learned it later.
(*Address on the back*) Deliver to Karanis, to Taesion, from Apollinarios her son.

[1]   For Sokrates, see **71** introd.

105.   Apollinarios to Taesion/Taesis

P.Mich. VIII 491
Karanis (sent from Misenum), later second century AD

Apollinarios to Taesis, his mother and lady, many greetings. First of all, I pray that you are well. I, too, am well and I make obeisance on your behalf before the gods here in this place. I want you to know, mother, that I arrived safe and sound at Rome in the month Pachon on the 25th and I was assigned to Misenum. I do not yet know my century,[1] for I had not gone to Misenum when I was writing this letter to you. I beg you, mother, do look after yourself – do not worry about me, for I have come to a fine place. Please write a letter to me about your well-being and that of my brothers and all your people. If I find someone, I write to you; I shall not hesitate to write to you. I greet my brothers many times, both Apollinarios and his children and Karalas and his children. I greet Ptolemaios, and Ptolemais and her children, and Heraklous and her children. I greet all those who love you individually by name. I pray you are well.
(*Address on the back*) Deliver to Karanis to Taesis, from Apollinarios her son, from Misenum.

[1]   A recruit was assigned to a ship, identical with a 'century' in the organisational terminology of the Roman fleet, when he arrived at the naval base. In the Roman infantry 'century' designated a unit under the command of a centurion.

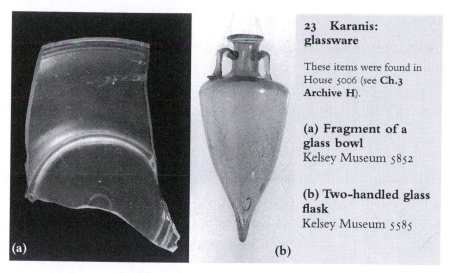

23 Karanis: glassware

These items were found in House 5006 (see **Ch.3 Archive H**).

(a) Fragment of a glass bowl
Kelsey Museum 5852

(b) Two-handled glass flask
Kelsey Museum 5585

H. The archive of Gaius Julius Niger and House 5006 in Karanis, AD 154–214

House 5006 was excavated in 1924, and although its position was never plotted on published maps, it was probably situated in the northern portion of Karanis, not far from the North temple (**Plate 18**).[1] Some fifty papyri and ostraka found within the house, belonging to two different families, reveal something of the house's history over the course of more than a century. Various objects left behind in the house no doubt belonged to its inhabitants: an attractive oil lamp; three substantial fragments of a deep bowl; a two handled flask used as a storage for unguents and perfumes (**Plate 23**). Toys found in the streets of Karanis (**Plate 24**) illustrate what playthings would have been available to the children of the house.

The documents reveal that three siblings, Gaius Minucius and his sisters Minucia Gemella and Minucia Thermoutharion, inherited House 5006 from their parents about AD 90, when the sisters were in their twenties (*P.Mich.* IX 554). They had Roman names because their father served in the Roman military. Minucia Thermoutharion later married Gaius Valerius Heraclitanus, also a Roman citizen, and about AD 94 she produced a daughter, Valeria Diodora. In AD 138, when Valeria Diodora was forty-five years old and married to Limnaios, son of Petheus, she was wealthy enough to loan out 408 drachmas; the contract gives her distinguishing marks as a mole near her left eyebrow and a scar on her right calf (*BGU* II 472). In AD 154 she sold House 5006 to the cavalry veteran Gaius Julius Niger for 800 drachmas (cf. **106**). This time her mole was described as on the nose (*P.Mich.* VI 428); her husband Limnaios was again her guardian, and wrote for her because she was a 'slow writer'.[2]

24   Karanis: children's toys
After Gazda (1983), fig. 53

Back row: wheeled horse, doll, miniature chair with a rag doll.
Middle row: toy weaver's comb, miniature scribal writing stand, top, clay dog, another
reading and writing stand with a toy clay lamp set on it.
Front: baby's rattle.

Gaius Julius Niger and his wife Ptollois had two sons, one born some
months after he purchased House 5006; their son Gaius Apolinarius Niger
married, and, after his death his widow Tasoucharion, a citizen of the Greek
city Antinoopolis, declared the house along with considerable other properties in a census declaration of AD 189 (**106**). Tasoucharion stated that her
father was unknown, but, given the relative wealth and social prominence
associated with Antinoopolite citizenship, it is likely that her father was a
veteran of the Roman forces who died before formalising his relationship
with her mother Sarapias. Until the reign of Septimius Severus, soldiers
were forbidden to marry during their period of military service, although
many soldiers did take 'unofficial' wives, living with them and fathering
their children while still on active duty (cf. **4.139**); and already in 119 the
emperor Hadrian gave such unions limited recognition, permitting children
acknowledged by their father during service to inherit his property. The
names of Tasoucharion's own children, Gaia Apolinaria and Gaius Gemellus
Horigenes (more commonly known as Gemellus alias Horion) reflect their
inheritance of Roman citizenship from their father. Nothing more is heard
about the daughter, but Gemellus alias Horion, born in AD 171, lived as an
adult in House 5006; most of the papyri found there belong to him. His

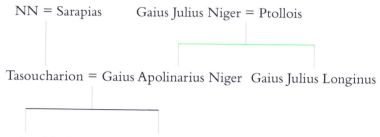

Figure 6   Family of Gaius Julius Niger and Ptollois, later owners
of House 5006

petitions to officials suggest that he felt himself increasingly in difficult circumstances and unable to protect either himself or his mother (**107**).

¹ 'House 5006' belonged to a numbering system the excavators followed for their first two
seasons, 1924–5 and 1925–6, but abandoned thereafter – see Johnson (1981), 107. For the
families of Minucia Thermoutharion and C. Julius Niger, see Alston (1995), 132–3,
129–32.
² For 'slow writers', see **Ch.6 Sect. II** introd. and **Plate 36**.

106.   Tasoucharion declares her property for the census

P.Mich. VI 370
Karanis, 9 August AD 189

This census declaration is atypical in the absence of personal descriptions for
Tasoucharion and her children, and in lacking any reference to occupants of the
buildings belonging to the family. Apparently Tasoucharion and her children were
absentee landlords, employing Sarapion, son of Esouris, to manage their property
in Karanis, including House 5006 (described in the census document as 'formerly
the property of Valeria Diodora'). The family members presumably made their personal declarations in the quarter of Antinoopolis where they resided. Any tenants
of their Karanis properties would have appeared in the personal declarations submitted by the head of each tenant household (cf. **69**).

To Ammonios, strategos of the Herakleides division of the Arsinoite nome,
and Harpokration alias Hierax, royal scribe of the same division, and the
village scribe of Karanis, and the census officials of the same village, from
Sarapion, son of Esouris, of the village Karanis. Those represented by me,
Tasoucharion, whose father is unknown, her mother being Sarapias, an
Antinoite,¹ the mother of those mentioned below, possess a house and
courtyard and a third share of another house in the village; and Gaia
Apolinaria and Gemellus Horion, her children, Antinoites, possess in

common and equally, a house and two courtyards, formerly the property of
Valeria Diodora, and a third part of two houses and two courtyards, and in
another place one half of a house and courtyard, and of another courtyard,
and in another place a house and courtyard and two courtyards, formerly
belonging to Gaius Longinus Apolinarius, a veteran, and a house and courtyard formerly belonging to Ptolemais, and in another place a third part of a
house and courtyard, which I declare for the house-by-house registration of
the past 28th year. Therefore I submit my declaration.

(*2nd hand*) I, Ptolemaios, have received copies of this for examination.

(*3rd hand*) I, Isidoros, also have one.

(*4th hand*) I, Souchammon, also have one.

(*5th hand*) I, Ptolemaios, also have one.

(*6th hand*) Twenty-ninth year of Aurelius Commodus Antoninus Caesar our
lord, Mesore 16.

---

[1] Roman citizenship enabled the family to make use of Roman law and exempted its male
members from capitation taxes; Antinoite citizenship exempted them from performing
liturgies in other cities where they owned property; cf. the family of Marcus Lucretius
Diogenes (**4.148**; **6.270**), who also possessed Roman and Antinoite citizenship.

107.   Gemellus alias Horion complains to the strategos

P. Mich. VI 423–4
Karanis, 22 May AD 197

In his petition Gemellus alias Horion complains that attackers had been harassing
him and his property for some time, invading his fields when the harvest was at
hand. On at least two occasions, they tried to cast a spell on his fields and on those
working in them, using a *brephos*. *Brephos* has the general meaning 'infant', but this
brephos was more probably a still-born child or aborted foetus.[1] The repeated phrase
'to encircle . . . with their envy' seems to refer to casting a spell on the unwitting
party. Gemellus alias Horion did not write the body of his document, but he signed
his name at the bottom.

To Hierax alias Nemesion, strategos of the Herakleides division of the
Arsinoite nome, from Gemellus alias Horion, son of Gaius Apolinarius,
Antinoite. I sent a petition, my lord, to the most glorious prefect, Aemilius
Saturninus, informing him of an attack made against me by a certain Sotas,
who despised me because of my poor eyesight and who with violence and
audacity wanted to seize my property, and I received in return his sacred
subscription[2] directing me to petition his excellency the epistrategos. Then
Sotas died and his brother Julius, who also proceeded with their characteristic violence, invaded my cultivated fields and carted off not only a not
insignificant amount of hay, but also cut off dried olive shoots and heath
plants from my olive orchard near Kerkesoucha. When I was there at the
time of harvest, I learned what he had done. Not satisfied with this, he again

invaded with his wife and a certain Zenas, bringing with them a *brephos*. They wanted to encircle my cultivator with their envy so that he would abandon his own cultivating after a partial harvesting of my crops from another plot of mine, and they themselves gathered it up. After these events, I went to Julius together with public officials so that there would be witnesses to these things. Again, in identical fashion, they threw the same *brephos* at me, wanting to encircle me too with their envy in the presence of Petesouchos and Ptollas, elders of the village of Karanis who also currently function as secretaries of the village, and Sokras their assistant. In the presence of these officials, Julius took the *brephos* off to his own house, after having gathered up from the fields what crops remained. Through the agency of these same officials and the collectors of grain taxes in the same village I made a report on the facts of the case. As a result, I, compelled by necessity, submit this petition and I ask that it be put in the record so that the right to proceed against them before his excellency the epistrategos may remain for me in regard to the bold actions perpetrated by them and as concerns the public rents for the fields owed to the imperial treasury, because they wantonly gathered up my crops.

(*2nd hand*) Gemellus alias Horion, about 26 years old, infirm in his eyes.

(*3rd hand*) Year 5 of Lucius Septimius Severus Pius Pertinax Augustus, Pachon 27.

[1] As argued by Aubert (1989), 437.

[2] The prefect's response to Gemellus alias Horion written on the petition he had submitted.

J. The archive of Satornila and her sons, late second century AD

This dossier of letters was purchased by a group of institutions in Europe and America buying papyri on the Egyptian antiquities market in the 1920s, and the papyri were divided among the contributing institutions.[1] Satornila, the mother and grandmother of this family of Roman citizens, boasted five grown sons: Sempronius, Maximus, Valerius, Satornilus, and Longinus. Satornila herself may be a widow (no husband is mentioned), but whether she and her extended family inhabited a single house, or adjacent ones, is unknown. She had nurtured the boys in their infancy and childhood, and now her sons, especially Sempronius, were repaying the debt that children owed their parents[2] through concern for her health and happiness, expressed by letter when they were away from the family home in a Fayum village, perhaps Karanis. Sempronius was frequently in Alexandria, for he mentions making obeisance on his mother's behalf every day before lord Serapis, no doubt in the Serapeum there, commonly mentioned by correspondents from Alexandria (**108–9**, cf. *Sel.Pap.* I 121). Longinus also wrote a letter to Maximus, informing him that their brother Sempronius was currently 'conveying bread to the soldiers' in the vicinity of Taposiris in the Delta, a day's journey by boat from Alexandria (*P.Mich.* III 206). Sempronius often addressed letters to his brother Maximus (see the backs of **108–9**; cf. *Sel.Pap.* I 121), including notes for Satornila, but one letter (**110**), also with a note to Satornila, was addressed to his brothers Valerius and Satornilus.

These letters underscore not only the difficulties of maintaining communication with one's family, but also the importance of finding someone reliable to carry a letter. Sempronius' letters were written by different hands, one of which might be his own; but the letters translated below do not exhibit a change of hand between body and closing greeting; if he made use of a scribe, it was not his habit to pen a closing greeting. Various motives have been suggested for Sempronius' practice of sending several letters on a single sheet of papyrus (not unparalleled; cf. *Sel.Pap.* I 162, *P. Brem.* 61). Was he a penny-pincher? Or was he seizing the opportunity to send several letters with a traveller heading toward home? Or was Sempronius, knowing that his mother Satornila would demand that a letter from him be read to her immediately upon its arrival, trying to control what would reach her ears by carefully placing his communications to her before (**109**), or after (**110**), his letters to his brothers? The inclusion of letters to Satornila in communications addressed to her sons suggests that Satornila herself was illiterate.

The letters are undated, but a relative chronology can perhaps be reconstucted by following what is said to and about Maximus' wife, a woman never named in the correspondence as preserved.

---

[1] The archive was first identified by Bell (1950); additional texts in Sijpesteijn (1976), republished as *P.Mich.* XV 751–2, *P.Mich.* III 206 (Longinus Celer to Maximus) and 209 (Satornilus to Sempronius), and *P.Heid.* VII 400 (Sempronius to Satornila). We follow Sijpesteijn in excluding *PSI* VIII 943 from the archive. Bell's argument that the archive came from Karanis was based on a false connection between Sempronia Gemella (**71**) and this family. A connection with Karanis might possibly be re-established, however, through the Sokrates who forwarded a letter to Sempronius (**108**; cf. the contemporary Sokrates in **71** and **104**).

[2] Sempronius wrote to Maximus in *Sel.Pap.* I 121.27–30: 'for we ought to honour as divine the lady who gave us birth, especially since she is so very good. I wrote this to you, brother, knowing the sweetness of one's revered parents.' The Greek concept of *gerotrophia*, the child's nourishing of an aged parent in return for care received during helpless infancy, is explicitly enunciated in *P.Oxy.* VIII 1121.11–12 (AD 295); for the virtue, see also **73**, **5.209**, **6.273**.

108.   Sempronius to his mother

P.Mich. XV 751
Alexandria, late second century AD

Sempronius to Satornila his mother and lady, very many greetings. Before everything, I pray that you are well, and at the same time I make obeisance on your behalf every day before lord Serapis. I am surprised that you did not write to me, either through Celer or through Sempronius, for when I returned from my journey I encountered them and kept asking them what was the reason they did not bring a letter for me. They said it was because of my being away. After I did learn about your well-being, I was less troubled. So now I beg you, my lady, do not hesitate to write to me about your well-being. I received a letter through Sokrates and another short one through Antonianus . . .[1] Now I write to you so that you remember. Up to now his letter to you fell on deaf ears, and you wrote your second letter to us about these matters. I write about these things, because I too kept wanting to do all I could and to come to you – first of all to give thanks for your good and child-loving nature and second also concerning these matters. Even now I have not found an opportunity, but while I was away I did write to you concerning these same matters. Greet Maximus and his wife and Sempronius Kyrillos and Satornilus and Gemellus and Julius and his family and Helene and her family and Skythikos and Kopres, Chairemon, Thermouthis and her children. Farewell my lady, always. (*Address on the back*) Give to Maximus from Sempronius his brother.

[1] The next twelve lines are very fragmentary. We sometimes translate supplements suggested in the notes.

109.   Two letters from Sempronius

P.Mich. xv 752
Alexandria, late second century A D

Although Sempronius seemed at first to postpone telling Satornila about his clothing ('going to write another time' was supplied by the editor), he apparently changed his mind, adding the note in the margin.

Sempronius to Satornila my mother and lady, very many greetings. Before everything I pray that you are well and next that my sweetest brothers are also well, and at the same time I make obeisance on behalf of you all every day before lord Serapis. When I discovered a man sailing upcountry toward you all, I felt compelled to greet you by letter. I beg you, my lady, do not hesitate to write to me about the well-being of you all so that I may live with less worry. I am going to write to you another time (?) about my clothing . . .[1]
(*In the margin*) The garment you are making for me with the purple border on which you added . . . having . . . of purple at the hem and on both the collar and the sleeves . . . there should also be . . . on the . . .
  Sempronius to Maximus his brother, very many greetings. Before everything else I pray that you are well. I received your letter in which you write that you have dispatched two letters to me. Know, brother, that I received

only one. You write to me about Lobotes, how he is . . . It is not easy to
please every man . . . don't blame me as though I were being careless . . .
but I have carried out all the things you have told me to do . . . I greet your
wife and your children. Farewell to you, brother.
(*Address on the back*) Deliver to Maximus his brother from Sempronius.

---

[1] There follow fifteen fragmentary lines, in which Sempronius again greeted individuals
named in previous letters.

110.   Three letters from Sempronius

P.Wisc. II 84
Place of writing unknown, late second century A D

Preceding the two letters preserved on this papyrus sheet are the very ends of the
lines of a first letter, presumably to Sempronius' brother Valerius (see the address on
the back). Satornilus, recipient of the second letter, once wrote to Sempronius, 'I
regard you not only as my brother, but as my father, my lord and god' (*P.Mich.* III
209).

Sempronius to Satornilus his brother, greetings. I received two letters from
you, one concerning the matters I informed Maximus about and the other
about our lady mother – how she was in danger and was still constrained by
her illness. In any case, please realise, brother, that I am quite upset and, at
the same time, do not sleep during these nights until you let me know how
she is getting along in this weather. Do not say foolish things when you find
a man sailing down toward me. Comfort our brother Maximus however you
can. I also wrote to Valerius our brother about him. I hope that he too is by
no means unaware how difficult life is now for us with regard to . . .[1] But
after this, what can we do to help? For he is not the only one who is bereft
of her, but also all the rest of us. As a result, then, like women (?) unable to
do anything – but you do not have an obligation to dwell upon human frail-
ties especially at such a time.[2] Farewell.
    Sempronius to Satornila his mother, greetings. As soon as you receive my
letter, tell me how you are getting along, for I am very upset until I learn
about your situation. With regard to my brother Maximus, I am now about
to write to you how to comfort him . . . not . . . excessively . . . for, he says,
. . . But my inopportune situation does not leave me (?) . . . in order that
he himself not swerve from his grief into something else. I know that you
also grieve over him, but, my lady, come to your senses because of my brothers; this, too, you ought to do because perhaps he did love his daughters and
his (?) sister Siborra, but what can we do in a situation in which god is
powerless? Farewell.
(*Address on the back*) Deliver to Valerius his brother and Satornilus his brother
from Sempronius.

[1] Presumably the name (a very short one) of Maximus' recently deceased wife has been lost here.

[2] Or, assuming with the editor that the feminine ending on 'unable' was a mistake for a masculine ending, 'Therefore, regard us as not being able to do anything, but do not be humble especially at such a moment.'

K. The archive of Paniskos and Ploutogenia, Philadelphia, *c.* 297/8 AD

This archive of seven letters was found at Philadelphia in the Fayum.[1] Most were written by Paniskos to his wife Ploutogenia during his absence at Koptos in the Thebaid over the course of about six months. In one letter Paniskos referred to the short-lived revolt under Lucius Domitius Domitianus, who, with the assistance of a deputy named Achilleus, controlled Egypt for almost a year.[2] The emperor Diocletian came in person to quell the revolt and presided over the fall of Alexandria after a siege of eight months. Not only are the exact year, or years, of the revolt debated, but so is the reason for Paniskos' presence in Koptos, the centre of the revolt, yet also an important trading station in times of peace. He may have been a soldier, fighting imperial troops under the commander Achilleus, or a merchant, caught in the midst of hostilities and in need of weapons to assure safety for himself and his associates. Paniskos urged Ploutogenia to join him, bringing with her various items, including his shield, helmet, and lances, but it seems she never did so. The couple had a daughter Heliodora, named after her maternal grandmother; she was young enough to be living at home. The correspondence also refers to other kin: Ploutogenia's brother and sister, and possibly a brother of Paniskos. The mothers of both Paniskos and Ploutogenia were evidently still living.

Ploutogenia and Paniskos both had pagan names; but they lived during a period when the Christian religion was spreading in Egypt, although it did so covertly until the cessation of active persecution of Christians by the Roman state (AD 311) and the so-called edict of Milan in 313 restoring property to the Christian Church. Until these acts of reconciliation, there was plentiful cause for Christian converts to maintain reticence about their faith; persecutions of Christians occurred some fifty years earlier under the emperor Decius (**2.52–3**), and the great persecution under Diocletian began in 303. Sporadic attacks against the clergy and church property were not uncommon until the Roman government publicly reversed its earlier hostility.[3] Paniskos' archive has appeared in modern collections of Christian letters, because both Paniskos and Ploutogenia begin some letters with the phrase 'I pray for your health each day before the lord god', and both use the phrase 'if god wills it'.[4] But such phrases guarantee neither participation in, nor even sympathy toward, the new faith, because people who were obviously pagans also refer at times to 'god', rather than 'gods'.[5]

Ploutogenia and Paniskos were probably illiterate: their letters are written in the fast and flowing cursive of several different, practised scribes, and neither Ploutogenia nor Paniskos add concluding greetings in their own hands, as literates often do. Paniskos employed one scribe for his first letter, which uses the conventional pagan greeting 'I pray for your health each day before all the gods' (**111**). A different scribe wrote the three letters that contain the references to 'god', and these same three letters exhibit other similarities, such as not referring to Ploutogenia by name, but merely as 'wife' (**112, 114**; *P.Mich.* III 219). The scribes were certainly responsible for the erratic spelling of the letters, but we can be less confident about the extent to which scribes and other writers felt free to alter the actual words and phrases dictated to them by illiterates.[6]

[1] *P.Mich.* III 214–21 (for 215 as the bottom portion of 219, see *BL* VI 81). For the dating of the revolt of Domitianus to A D 297/8, see Thomas (1976), 266–7.
[2] *P.Mich.* III 220, addressed to 'Protogenia'; Youtie (1976) argued that the various spellings of Ploutogenia's name (also **113**) provide a good example of the fluid orthography that prevailed in the writing of personal names throughout antiquity.
[3] Van Minnen (1994b), and Bagnall (1993a), 261–93, discuss the Christianisation of Egypt. For claims about the couple's religious loyalties: *New Docs.* 2 (1982), no. 22; Naldini (1968), 110–23; Farid (1977).
[4] **112, 114, 115,** and *P.Mich.* III 219.
[5] See **93, 94, 98, 110** introd.
[6] The comparison of **79** with **2.33** raises similiar questions about scribal interference.

III.   Paniskos to Ploutogenia

P.Mich. III 214 (*BL* IX 159)
Koptos, *c.* A D 297/8

Paniskos to my wife Ploutogenia, mother of my daughter, very many greetings. First of all, I pray for your health each day before all the gods. Furthermore, I want you to know, sister, that we have been staying in Koptos near your sister and her children so that you won't be grieved when you come to Koptos, because your kinsmen are here. And just as you want above all to greet her many times, so she prays to the gods daily, since she wants to greet you together with your mother. Once you have received this letter of mine, do whatever is necessary so that, whenever I send for you, you may come immediately. And when you come, bring ten fleeces of wool, six jars of olives, four jars of honeyed wine, and my shield – only the new one – and my helmet. Also bring my lances. Also bring the paraphernalia for the tent. If you discover a good opportunity, come here with gentlemen; have Nonnos come with you. Bring all our clothes with you when you come. Bring your gold jewellery with you on the trip – but don't wear it on the boat.[1]

(*Written on the back*) Salute my lady daughter Heliodora. Hermias[2] salutes you both.

(*Address on the back*) Deliver to my wife and my daughter from Paniskos, father.

---

[1] The comment 'but don't wear it on the boat' was added in the left margin, for the letter had already filled the front side of the papyrus.

[2] Apparently Ploutogenia's brother.

112. Paniskos to Ploutogenia

P.Mich. III 216 (*BL* III 111, VI 81, VII 109)
Koptos, 16 June A D 297 (?)

Paniskos to his wife and his daughter, many greetings. First of all I pray before the lord god that I receive you back in good health together with my daughter. It is already the second letter I am writing to you in order that you come to me, but you have not come. If, in fact, you do not want to come, write back to me. Bring my shield, the new one, and my helmet, and my five lances, and the accessories for the tent. You wrote to me, saying 'I sent to Heraiskos . . . and I gave a talent to Antoninus so that he would give it to you.' At any rate, do not neglect . . . of the soldiers and . . . If, anyway, you have (weaving) materials, bring them with you and cut them (from the loom) here. I greet my daughter many times and your mother and by name those who love us. I pray you are well. Pauni 22.
(*Written in the bottom margin*) You also wrote to me that you picked up twenty-three (?) shields, but Tammon none. Temnas remained down there. I greet you both.
(*Address on the back*) Deliver to his wife from Paniskos in the house (?) of Par[. . .

113. Paniskos to Ploutogenia

P.Mich. III 217[1]
Koptos (?), *c.* A D 297/8

Paniskos to Ploutogenes his wife, greetings. I told you when I left not to go away to your house, but you have departed nevertheless. If you want to, you do it, not taking account of me, but I know that my mother does these things. Look – I have sent three letters to you and you have not written me even one. If you do not want to come up to me, no one is forcing you. I wrote these letters to you because your sister here compels me to write. Since it is not possible for you to write about this matter, then write other things about yourself; I have heard other things that are not connected with you. Send to me my helmet and my shield and my five lances and my breastplate and my sword belt. I greet your mother Heliodora. When the one who carries letters came to me, he said, 'When I was about to set out, I said to your wife and her mother to give me a letter to carry to Paniskos, but they didn't give me one.' From Psinestes I sent one talent to you through Antoninus. I pray you are well.

(*Address on the back*) To Ploutogenes, his wife.

[1] We do not accept the textual emendations suggested in *BL* III 111.

114. Paniskos to Ploutogenia

P.Mich. III 218 (*BL* III 111)
Koptos, *c.* A D 297/8

Paniskos to his wife, many greetings. I greet my daughter Heliodora many times, and you, pay attention to her. I want you to know that if you have need of something, I have written to Aion.[1] Even if you have gone to Heliopolis, send word with regard to these things. I dispatched the fleeces for you, so that, if you want, you can use them for yourself. Also pay attention to your flocks, and make the three gold *solidi* into anklets for my daughter. Also prepare the material for your tunic and your overcloak. And if the god wills and I come, I am sending Achaos there. Also get my leather cloak ready and if they want something, pay attention to them. Know, then, that I am writing you as a brother, not as your . . .[2] I pray you are well.

(*Written in the left margin*) I greet your mother many times and Nonnos with his children and Sarapion.

(*Address on the back*) Give to his wife from Paniskos in the house of Mopsarion.

[1] Apparently Paniskos' brother, see *P.Mich.* III 219.
[2] Although the suggestion for this line in *BL* III 111, 'not as one who is a stranger to you', gives acceptable sense, and seems to echo Ploutogenia's words to her mother (**115**), it does not match the traces of ink on the papyrus.

115. Ploutogenia to her mother

P.Mich. III 221
Alexandria, *c.* A D 296–8

Ploutogenia to my mother, many greetings.

First of all I pray before the lord god that you are well. Already it is eight months since I have come to Alexandria, but you have not written even one letter to me. Once again you do not hold me as your daughter, but as your enemy. Give the bronze vessels which you have with you to Atas, and receive them all back from Atas. Also write to me how much money you received from Koupineris and do not be careless. Pay attention to the (irrigation) machine and to your flocks; do not hesitate and do not wish to annoy . . .

If your daughter is about to marry, write to me, and I will come. I greet you
together with your children. I greet by name those who love us. I pray you
are all well for a long time to come.

(*Address on the back*) Give to my mother from Ploutogenia, her daughter.

L. The archive of Flavius Dioskoros, Aphrodite, AD 506–85

Flavius Dioskoros' family resided for some generations in the village of
Aphrodite, across the Nile from Antaiopolis, the *metropolis* of the Antaiopolite
nome. The bulk of the family's papers were discovered by chance in 1905–7,
and further texts came to light through clandestine diggings.[1] A significant
portion of the archive has been edited only recently,[2] and other rolls, both
Greek and Coptic, have yet to be opened for transcription and study. This
bilingual archive, with documents and literature in Greek and Coptic, reflects
the sophisticated and Christianised milieu in which the family lived.

Psimanobet, whose Egyptian name means 'son of the gooseherd', is
the first member of the family known to us; his son, the elder Dioskoros,
had at least three children by his wife Thaumasia: Besarion, Apollos, and
a girl whose name is lost. The bulk of the archive published so far concerns the later generations of the family, beginning with Besarion and
Apollos. Apollos was energetic and ambitious. He and Phoibammon son
of Triadelphos, the husband of his niece Anastasia alias Tekrompia,
significantly increased the family's fortunes, moving it into the élite class
of villagers, through leasing land from absentee landowners and sub-
leasing it to local farmers.[3] During his long life Apollos not only served
in minor public offices, but also journeyed to the imperial capital
Constantinople in AD 541; he became a monk in his later years and
established a monastery. Apollos died about 546/7, and by the end of his
life he had gained the honorific *nomen* 'Flavius' which distinguished
important citizens of the late Roman empire from the more humble ones
who bore the *nomen* 'Aurelius'.

Apollos' son Flavius Dioskoros (after whom the archive is named), born
about 520, was well schooled in Christian and pagan literatures in both
Coptic and Greek, and he wrote both languages fluently. His library
included a collection of the comedies of Menander, and, like his father, he
once journeyed to Constantinople (AD 551). Dioskoros not only drafted
documents of various types for family members, fellow villagers, and citizens of Antinoopolis, where he resided for some years (see **4.155–6**), but
also wrote poems in classical Greek metres, dedicating them to various not-
ables in the area (**117**).

What is striking about this archive from an upwardly mobile family of the
sixth century AD is how few names of its women were recorded in family
papers. Admittedly, many texts have yet to be read and published; but in the

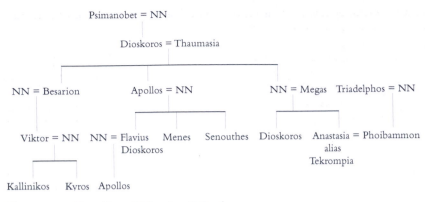

Figure 7   Family of Flavius Dioskoros

third and fourth generations of Dioskoros' family, at least five wives and
mothers are not mentioned by name: the wives of Apollos and his son
Flavius Dioskoros, of Besarion and his son Victor; and for Apollos' daughter, the mother of Anastasia alias Tekrompia. These women's existence must
be deduced from the legitimate children they bore their husbands. Aurelia
Anastasia alias Tekrompia is the only woman known by name in these
generations, and she appears in only one transaction (**116**).

---

[1] For the archive, Gagos and van Minnen (1994) with a family tree as Fig. 1, p. 131, and
MacCoull (1988). 'Aphrodite' is the Greek form of the village's name; in Coptic it is
'Aphrodito'.
[2] E.g. **116**, and Kuehn (1993).
[3] See Keenan (1980) and (1984).

116.   Settlement of a dispute

P.Vat.Aphrod. 10.1–24 (as corrected by Gagos and van Minnen, 1994,
50–2)[1]
Antinoopolis, *c.* A D 537

Anastasia alias Tekrompia together with her husband Phoibammon, purchased a
piece of land (perhaps a vineyard) from Eudoxia, Antonia, and Kollouthos, children
of a brother or a sister of Nikantinoos. They were unaware that the property had a
lien on it; it had been mortgaged some years before by the parents of Nikantinoos
to the parents of Iosephios in the name of their son. Instead of resorting to the
courts and legal means of redress, Nikantinoos, who had now paid off his parents'
mortgage, and Apollos, representing his niece Anastasia and her husband, reached
a compromise settlement through the assistance of mediators: Anastasia and
Phoibammon were to reimburse Nikantinoos for his expenses in cancelling the
earlier mortgage. The top portion of this text was published in 1980 among other
papyri from Aphrodite in the Vatican Museum; in 1991 a more substantial bottom

portion came to light at the University of Michigan, further clarifying the arbitration process in which Anastasia was involved.

Aurelius Nikantinoos, contributorial tax payer of the village of Aphrodite, living here in the fair city of the Antinoites, to the Aurelii Phoibammon, son of Triadelphos, who is also a contributorial tax payer, and to his wife Anastasia alias Tekrompia, daughter of Megas, both of whom originate from the same village of Aphrodite, through you Apollos, son of Dioskoros, chief citizen of the village already named, uncle on her mother's side to the aforementioned Anastasia, greetings. I acknowledge to you the following:

I, the aforementioned Nikantinoos, contributorial tax payer, made a settlement with you, the aforementioned Phoibammon and Anastasia his wife, through you, the aforementioned Apollos, chief citizen, in the civil courthouse of the area, concerning the debt, now, in fact, paid by me, on behalf of the redemption of a deed of security, which was made for the parents of Iosephios in the name of their son, regarding a piece of land that was mortgaged as security to him by my parents and that was sold to you, the aforementioned Phoibammon and Anastasia his wife, by my nephew and nieces some little time ago – I mean, in fact, Eudoxia and Antonia and Kollouthos – according to the force of the sale of the same piece of land that took place to you from them and which have their own validity.

After many things were said and set in motion toward this matter here between me, Nikantinoos, and Apollos, chief citizen and the one who is taking the place of you, the aforementioned, before a court case and before preliminary hearings, in the end good friends, having become mediators for us and having taken up the matter, decided that I, the same Nikantinoos, was to receive from you on behalf of the total discharge of the debt paid by me in order to redeem the mortgage of the aforementioned piece of land, seven gold solidi less two carats each. . .

[1] For the complete document, *P.Vat.Aphrod.* 10 + P.Mich. inv. 6922, about 120 lines in length, see Gagos and van Minnen (1994).

117. Flavius Dioskoros writes a wedding song for Patrikia

P.Lond.Lit. 100c
c. AD 566

This poem in dactylic hexameters, or 'epic' metre, was Dioskoros' first attempt at writing a wedding song (*epithalamion*), although he eventually wrote several more. Throughout the poem Dioskoros was keen to display his knowledge of old myths from pagan antiquity, as well as to sing fulsome praises of the bride and groom from important local families. Because of the poem's learning and pretentiousness, as well as its apparent mistakes in metre, it is at times difficult to follow, especially when the text becomes fragmentary after line 20. While the papyrus breaks off before the poem's conclusion, the initial letter of each line has already spelled out the message 'To Patrikia, bride of Paulos . . .' and so the amount of text missing may not be not extensive. Line 12 exists in two versions, underscoring the fact that this was the poet's working copy.

> Hermes, splendidly striving in magnificence,
> had it in mind to sing a memorial of you, Tritogeneia.[1]
> He shouted out your song and he swore a mighty oath,
> having followed you everywhere, because from your countless virtues
> 5   the mother that bore you clearly was in love with the shining sun.
> I call upon your name, foam-born[2] one who is hymned by all;
> surely you were filled by the beauty of the much beloved Lady of
>   Paphos,
> as she stood with Eros, yet Desire forged your loveliness.
> Well-born because of your ancestor Kallinos with his halls, you
> 10 hoped for Paulos as your desirable husband, much-beloved,
> godlike, charming, equal to Bellerophon,
> {charming bridegroom . . . .}
> charming bridegroom, from his feet to the hair of his head.
> Bridegroom, I am composing the hymn for your quite noble
>   marriage;
> you were given a bride more skilful than the Graces, composers of
>   song.
> 15 Do not be afraid to treat with reverence the delicate railing of your
>   marriage bed.
> Oh guardian of life, saviour of homes, bearer of the sceptre . . .
> May all of you give Paulos a sweet, harmonious marriage with
>   Patrikia . . .
> [May you all keep] diseases continually apart from the life . . .
> of beloved Patrikia together with Paulos . . .
> 20 Give to them the . . . of a harmony that cannot be shattered . . .
> to them, as they lift children and grandchildren on their knees,
> a shining life, praiseworthy for its peace . . .

[1] 'Tritogeneia' was a traditional epithet for the goddess Athene; its etymology was disputed throughout antiquity. Here it refers to Patrikia, although the sense in which Dioskoros intended the comparison between Patrikia and Athene is unclear; perhaps he was appealing to Athene's status as a virgin goddess, or as a patroness of skilful weavers, or alternatively, he may have been appealing to one of the more obscure etymologies of Tritogeneia, such as 'born on the third day'.

[2] 'Aphrogeneia' (literally 'foam-born') is a punning allusion to the goddess Aphrodite (also 'Lady of Paphos'), yet seemingly also a reference to the fact that Patrikia was born in the village of Aphrodite. For a different interpretation of these and other lines, see MacCoull (1988), 81–4.

4 Status and law

Introduction

Law provides the basic framework within which many of the central elements of women's lives developed. That is not to claim that it either fully accounts for the patterns of behaviour we see (or, still more, those we cannot discern from the documents) or even puts firm limits to those patterns. Legal requirements were evaded, broken, reinterpreted, and built upon. But women's legal status and competence had much to do with their marriages, their livelihoods, and their property.

The range of legal influences on women in Egypt over the thousand years that concern us in this book was very large. The fact that the language of most of the documents is Greek might lead one to imagine that Greek law was a dominant influence. But there was no unified system of Greek law; laws varied from one city to another (most, apart from Athens, poorly documented), so that Alexandria, Naukratis and Ptolemais each had its own laws, while the Greek law of the Egyptian chora was different again. The large majority of the population at all times was basically Egyptian in language and culture, even though much of its documentation was produced in Greek and many people were bilingual. Egypt's own legal system, already well developed long before the arrival of the Greeks, continued to operate under Ptolemaic rule; its impact can be seen, not only in documents written in Egyptian (**Section I**), but increasingly through traces in Greek papyri. The Romans again brought a complex legal system with them when they conquered Egypt. Although this applied formally only to Roman citizens, a tiny minority at first, it slowly influenced the Hellenistic practices inherited from the Ptolemaic period, and when Roman citizenship was extended to the entire population in AD 212, Roman law officially became applicable to all. In practice, however, Roman forms operated in part as an overlay on existing habits and only gradually and incompletely supplanted these.

After Constantine gained control over Egypt in AD 324, it had an avowedly Christian emperor and a government operating on the Christian week. The next several centuries saw many imperial laws invoking Christianity in support of one or another enactment, and Christian influence has often been seen in the documents of this period. Defining this influence, however, generally has proved difficult, and disentangling it from other strands even in imperial legislation a frustrating exercise. Every document presented here falls somewhere along this complicated line of development. A few provide virtually pure examples of one legal system or another; most do not. Even the purest need careful scrutiny to see how far the social realities at work are those presupposed by the legal framework.

I   The Egyptian background

The treatment of women in Egyptian law had evolved over several millennia by the time Alexander arrived in Egypt, and the Greeks who settled there in the aftermath of his conquest found a well-established set of patterns very different from what they were used to. Egyptian women were free of the legal disabilities found in much of the Greek world. At least as early as the sixth century BC, the woman's consent to a marriage, even one arranged by her family, was required. Marriage itself needed no specific ceremony, no particular documentation, and not even consummation for its validity, but continued cohabitation was the normal indicator that a marriage existed (Tyldesley, 1994, ch. 2).

Married women retained full rights to their own property and could engage in business transactions like money-lending without the need of the husband's approval. This freedom extended to the ability of either party to terminate a marriage unilaterally, without being required to specify any grounds. Mutual agreement to end a marriage is more commonly mentioned in documents and was equally effective.

The surviving documents generally reflect this very free legal regime without telling us much of the underlying social and attitudinal realities. For example, the abstract freedom of divorce for both parties is restricted in marriage settlement **119** by a contractual penalty for the man if he initiates the divorce. In **120**, the brevity and simplicity of the legal language of divorce obscure any payments that one spouse had to make to the other and leave the reader in the dark about the motives for the separation. There is considerable evidence in Egyptian literature to suggest that the Egyptians took a much more relaxed attitude toward the sexual activity of unmarried women than the Greeks, but very much disapproved of adultery with married women (cf. **121**). These attitudes reflect a high value placed on harmonious marriage but no strong sense of male property rights in women. The financial terms of documents connected with marriage often try to reinforce the solidity of marital ties with financial incentives, thus restricting in practice the complete liberty (especially for men) granted by the underlying legal framework.

Documents **118–21** date from the Ptolemaic period, but were written in Egyptian (in the Demotic script) and reflect practices already prevalent before the late fourth century BC. Demotic marriage settlements were interested only in the property rights resulting from a marriage: what gift a husband had to pay to his wife, what goods a wife brought into a marriage, and what proprietary rights she might enforce in case of divorce. At the time of the wedding the parties might enter into a contract over property rights, but there was no legal duty to do so. Most marriage settlements were in fact drawn up many years after the actual marriage, at a time when children had already been born. In these respects they differ sharply from Greek marriage and divorce contracts, which are interested both in property and in personal rights, including a prohibition of bigamy and the right of a woman to remarry.

Demotic marriage settlements may be divided into two types (Pestman, 1961). In the first type (**118**), a bridal gift is made by the husband to the wife, usually a rather small amount of money. In the Ptolemaic period this 'gift' was often fictitious, the wife receiving the money only in case of divorce (cf. above). In the second type (**119**), the wife gives to her husband a sum of money called a feeding allowance, here translated as 'endowment,' and receives from him in return an annual allowance of food and clothing. The entire property of the husband serves as a security that he will return the money when the wife asks for it, that is, in case of divorce.

118. An Egyptian marriage settlement

P.BM dem. 10394 (*Rec.dém.biling.* no. 7)
Thebes, 226 BC

This marriage settlement of the first type (Pestman, 1961; see introd. above) belongs to a small archive concerned with a man named Melas and his wife. The other texts of the archive (published in *P.Lond.dem.* IV 35–9, dated between 226 and 210 BC) deal with sales of land and houses in Hermonthis. Although both Melas and his father-in-law bear Greek names, all of the texts are in Demotic and follow Egyptian legal practices.

Year 21, Epeiph, of the reign of King Ptolemy, son of Ptolemy and Arsinoe, the brother–sister gods, when Galestes son of Philistion was priest of Alexander and the brother–sister gods and Berenike daughter of Sosipolis was *kanephoros* before Arsinoe Philadelphos.[1]
The Greek Melas son of Apollonios and Rwrw has said to his wife Senobastis daughter of Ptolemaios and Senminis:

'I have taken you as a wife. I have given you 1 deben (= *20 drachmas*) of money, i.e. 5 staters, i.e. 1 deben of money again, as your bridal gift. If I repudiate you as a wife, be it that I hate you, be it that I love another woman instead of you, I shall give you 2 deben of money, i.e. 10 staters, i.e. 2 deben of money again, not including the 1 deben of money mentioned above, which I have given you as your bridal gift, to make in full 3 deben of money, i.e. 15 staters, i.e. 3 deben of money again. Your eldest son is my eldest son and master of all and everything that I possess and that I shall acquire. I will give you the third part of all and everything I possess and which I shall acquire.

This is the list of the goods-of-a-woman which you have brought into my house:

a shawl (*bridal veil?*)	1 deben and 6 kite
a coat	2.5 kite
1 cloak	1 deben
1 . . . (of bronze)	1.5 kite
one ladle (of bronze)	1 kite
1 . . . (of silver)	1 deben
one necklace	4 kite
one bed	2 kite
another bed	1 kite
a pair of . . .	1 kite
one woman's . . . (of silver)	1 kite

to make in all 5 deben of money, i.e. 25 staters, i.e. 5 deben of money again, as the value of your goods-of-a-woman, which you have brought with you into my house.

I have received them from you, in full and without any remainder. My heart is satisfied with them. If you are inside (my house), you will be inside with them, if you are outside (my house), you will be outside with them. To you belong their proprietary rights, to me the right of administering their disposition.

If I repudiate you as a wife or if you want to go yourself, I will give you your goods-of-a-woman mentioned above or their price in money as written above. I will not be able to impose upon you an oath in order that you take it concerning your goods-of-a-woman mentioned above, saying, "You have not (really) brought them with you into my house." You are the one who has the rights over them against me, without me speaking about any deed or anything at all.'

Herieus, son of Harsiesis, has written it.

---

[1] For ruler cult titles in dating formulae, see **2.6**.

119.   An Egyptian marriage settlement in two parts

P.Mich.inv. 4526, ed. E. Lüddeckens, *Ägyptische Eheverträge* (Äg.Abh. 1, 1960), 148–53, no. 4D
Philadelphia, 199 BC

This text belongs to a family archive found at Philadelphia and dating to the third and second centuries BC. Most of the texts are still unpublished.

Marriage documents of the second type usually consist of two parts (Pestman, 1961). One is an I.O.U. from the husband, in which he states that he has received a certain sum of money from the wife, the second a deed of payment, in which the husband states to his wife that he has sold her his entire property (as collateral) and has received the purchase-money for it (that is, the sum given to him in the first part of the deed). But this 'sale' is not complete as long as it is not accompanied by a 'deed of cession' or 'statement of no title', by which the husband waives his claims to the property in question. Such a deed of cession is not part of the marriage settlement, and therefore the 'sale' is not a transfer of property from husband to wife, but only a kind of mortgage on the husband's property. Only in the event of divorce and the husband's failure to meet his obligation to return the money to his wife can he be obliged to draw up a 'deed of cession'.

(Texts 1 and 2 both begin with the following dating formula and introduction):
Year 6, Choiak, of King Ptolemy son of Ptolemy and Arsinoe, the father-loving gods, when Andromachos son of Lysimachos was priest of Alexander and the saviour gods, the brother–sister gods, the benefactor gods, and the father-loving gods, when Themisto daughter of Hegisistratos was *athlophoros* of Berenike Euergetis, when Soteris (?) daughter of Ptolemaios was *kanephoros* of Arsinoe Philadelphos.[1]
The farmer and servant of Hathor, mistress of Aphroditopolis, the great goddess, Pais[2] the younger, son of Pais and Eseremphis, has said to Nebuotis, daughter of Psammetichos and Taarmotnis:

(Text 1)
'You have contented my heart with 21 deben of pure silver of the treasury of Ptah, i.e. 20 deben 9 $\frac{2}{3}$ $\frac{1}{6}$ $\frac{1}{10}$ $\frac{1}{30}$ $\frac{1}{60}$ $\frac{1}{60}$ kite, 21 deben of pure silver of the treasury of Ptah again, as your endowment. To the children which you have borne to me and the children which you will bear to me belongs everything that I possess and all that I shall acquire. Your eldest son is my eldest son among the children which you have borne to me and the children you will bear to me. I give you 72 (measures) of emmer with the hin-measure,[3] i.e. 48 measures of barley with the hin-measure, i.e. 72 measures of emmer again, and 2 deben 4 kite of pure silver of the treasure of Ptah, i.e. 2 deben 3 $\frac{2}{3}$ $\frac{1}{6}$ $\frac{1}{10}$ $\frac{1}{30}$ $\frac{1}{60}$ $\frac{1}{60}$ kite, i.e. 2 deben 4 kite of pure silver of the treasury of Ptah again, as your maintenance, every year in the house you want.
You are entitled to the arrears (in payment) of your food-and-clothing allowance, which will come to my charge. I shall give them to you.
Everything that I possess and that I shall acquire is security for your above-mentioned endowment and for the arrears (in payment) of your above-mentioned food-and-clothing allowance.
I shall not be able to say to you: "Receive back your above-mentioned endowment from my hand." (But) on the day that you want it back from me, I will give it to you.
I will not be able to impose an oath upon you except in the house of judgement.'

Written by Onnophris son of Peteesis.

(Text 2)

'You have contented my heart with the money of the value of all I possess and all that I shall acquire (house, arable land, courtyard, building plots, wall, vineyard, orchard, male and female slave, cow, she-ass, all my livestock, every allowance, every title-deed, every possession on earth of a free man), which I have and which I shall acquire. It all belongs to you from this day onward. I have given it to you for money. I have received its price.

My heart is satisfied with it, because it is full without remainder. No person on earth will have power over it except you. Every person who will come up against you on its behalf, I will keep him off from you. I will keep it free for you, on any day, from every document, every title-deed, everything on earth. To you belongs every document that has been made concerning it and every document that has been made to me concerning it, and to my father, and to my mother, and every document by which I am entitled to it. They all belong to you with their legal rights. To you belongs that by which I am entitled to these things.

The oath or the proof which will be imposed upon you in order to make me take it concerning them, I will take it.

I will make for you the above-mentioned deed of payment of all I possess and all I shall acquire.

You have a claim on me on the basis of the legal rights of the deed of endowment of 21 deben which I have made for you to make two documents complete. You have a claim on me concerning them and their legal rights, so that I must do for you according to them.'

Written by Onnophris son of Peteesis.

[1] For these ruler cult titles, see **2.6** and **34**.
[2] Corrected from Patous; cf. E. Lüddeckens et al., *Demotische Namenbuch* (Wiesbaden, 1986), p. 398.
[3] The hin contained about 0.5 litre.

120.   An Egyptian priest divorces his wife

P. Tor. Botti 16[1]
Jeme, 29 December 114 BC

This example of no-fault divorce from the Ptolemaic period is, like all surviving Demotic divorce agreements, addressed by the man (Harpaesis) to the woman (Tateosiris). He releases her from all obligations connected with the marriage, explicitly stating that her having produced children frees her from any claim. He renounces all ability to lay claim to her marital services in the future or to interfere with a subsequent marriage; the formula includes, in fact, his directive to her to find a new husband. Whereas Egyptian marriage agreements deal almost exclusively with property rights, the divorce contracts do not mention property. There is no indication of an equivalent document written from the woman to the man. Such documents show clearly the ability of the Egyptians to end marriages without continuing entanglements, but they give no clue to the actual circumstances of the separation, or even to which party initiated the divorce. For later texts from the same family archive, see **5.165**. For the opening dating formula, cf. **2.34**.

Year 4, Choiak 10, of Queen Kleopatra and King Ptolemy Philometor Soter, and when the priest of Alexander and of the saviour gods, of the brother–sister gods, of the benefactor gods, of the father-loving gods, and of the manifest gods, and of the god whose father is holy, and of the mother-loving god, and of the father-loving god, and of the benefactor gods and of the saviour mother-loving (god), and the *athlophoros* of Berenike Euergetis, and the *kanephoros* of Arsinoe Philadelphos, and the priestess of Arsinoe Philopator, were as they are written in Rhakotis (=*Alexandria*), (and in) Psoi in the Thebaid (=*Ptolemais*):
The *pastophoros* of Amon of Jeme, Harpaesis son of Esnechates and Thatres, has said to the woman Tetosiris daughter of Pachombekis and Senimouthis:

'I have repudiated you as wife; I am far from you[2] regarding (the) right to (you as a) wife. I have no claim on earth against you in the name of (your being my) wife. I am the one who says to you: "Take yourself a husband." I shall not be able to stand in your way in any place where you will go in order to take yourself a husband, from today onwards. If I shall find you with any other man on earth, I shall not be able to say to you, "You are my wife." You are contented with your contract for a wife, on account of your children whom you have borne to me, without any legal document, without anything on earth with you.'

Harsiesis son of Chestephnachthis has written this, who writes in the name of Espmetis son of Osoroeris, the prophet of Jeme.
(*signatures of four witnesses*)

[1] With important corrections by K.-Th. Zauzich in *Enchoria* 2 (1972), 88. Our translation is based on that of Pestman (1961), 72–7.
[2] The normal formula of Demotic contracts for renunciation of claim.

121. Oaths of fidelity on the occasion of a divorce

U. Kaplony-Heckel, *Die demotischen Tempeleide* (Äg.Abh. VI, 1963), nos. 6 and 1
Jeme, **(a)** 15 September 117 BC and **(b)** (23 January 79 or 16 January 50 BC)

On the occasion of a divorce, a woman might have to swear an oath to her ex-husband that she had been faithful to him during the time of the marriage and/or that she had not taken away any of his possessions.[1] Pestman (1961), 56, remarks, 'The wife is put to the oath by her husband. If she takes the oath, she is deemed innocent of the adultery she is charged with; if she refuses to take the oath, she is found guilty.' There are no cases where a husband takes a similar oath for his ex-wife, probably an indication of inequality of expectations in marriage. These two examples are representative of a stereotyped genre.

(a) Copy of the oath which Tikos will take at the gate of Jeme in the temple of Montou lord of Meten[2] in year 53, Mesore 30, to Psenesis: 'By the bull of Meten, who resides here, and every god who resides with him, I did not go to anybody when I was married with you. I do not have anything which is concealed from you for a value of more than 20 deben.' If she takes the oath, I give (*he will give*) her 2 talents and 50 deben. If she refuses to take it, she will deduct the things which she makes known from the 2 talents and 50 deben.

(b) Copy of the oath which Taminis daughter of Plilis will take at the gate of Jeme in the temple of Montou lord of Meten in year 2, Tybi 14, to Phagonis (*or* Pachel) son of Permamis: 'By the bull of Meten, who resides here, and every god who resides with him, I did not sleep, I did not have intercourse with anybody since I was married with you in year 22 until today. There is no falsehood in the oath.' If she takes the oath, he should keep off from her and he must give her 4 talents and 200 deben.

---

[1] There is also one instance in which such an oath is taken by a man to the husband of a woman.
[2] That is, in the temple at what is now Medinet Habu.

II   Greek and Egyptian in a colonial society

The Greeks who settled in non-Hellenic parts of the empire conquered by Alexander and divided by his successors, from Anatolia to Afghanistan, tried very hard to maintain their Hellenic culture. Their determination in this regard may well have been strengthened by the fact that so many of the settlers came not from the famous city-states of classical Greece but from what people like the Athenians and Spartans regarded as areas of marginally Hellenic character, like Macedonia and Thrace. Remains of Greek education and institutions can be found wherever these people settled.

In no sphere was it harder to maintain ancestral ways than in the role of women, and particularly of marriage customs. Greek cities in general had a very restrictive set of rules governing women.[1] In Athens, the best known, women had little legal independence and were expected to be under the control and protection of their fathers or husbands. Their world was that of the household, not of public life. The nearest male relative, normally the father, gave the woman in marriage at his own discretion. Certainly social and economic realities limited the ability of many people to realise these ideals in daily life, and there are signs that some families subverted women's theoretical inability to own real property. But the underlying ideology of women's roles and limits remained widely accepted.

In Egypt, the foreign settlers lived for the most part not in separate communities but in smaller groups scattered among the local people, particularly in rural villages. Most of the Greek settlers were men, as is to be expected from the fact that most of them were veterans of Alexander's armies. Intermarriage with the Egyptians was thus virtually unavoidable. Indeed, we know that Alexander's men had to a large extent acquired non-Greek concubines in the course of the army's progress across Asia; settling down more permanently with an Egyptian woman would not have seemed strange. Even where Greek women were available, it would be unlikely that one could find a spouse from one's own native city, and the extreme particularism of Greek cities and their institutions could hardly survive under such circumstances. For that matter, it is not clear that these men had much interest in preserving some of the more restrictive aspects of the societies they had left.

The legal environment of Ptolemaic Egypt was thus very complex. The three Greek cities of Egypt (Alexandria, Naukratis, and Ptolemais) each had its own laws, but other Greeks in Egypt were governed both by royal legislation and by legal norms from their home cities, which were themselves enormously varied. The Egyptians continued to use their own laws and practices, developed over millennia. A given individual might operate under one legal system in one transaction, a different one in another, depending on the nationality of the parties, the language used, and the place where litigation took place.

The papyri of the Ptolemaic and early Roman periods show the survival of many Greek forms, but numerous cases in which those forms come to surround substantively Egyptian practice. The most obvious element of continuity is the use of the Greek language. Another is the requirement that Greek women have legal guardians, *kyrioi* in Greek (see **122** for a request to have one appointed). A third is the Greeks' habit of acquiring slaves, particularly for domestic service (**124**). The earliest Greek marriage contract (indeed, the first dated Greek document) surviving from Ptolemaic Egypt (**123**) is full of legal language redolent of fourth-century Athenian usage and embodies the normal family-controlled, male-operated marriage system known for the classical period.

But such continuity of practice did not last very long. The other documents, though all in Greek, show a woman acting as guardian of a child, allowable in Egyptian but not Greek legal practice (**125**); a woman giving herself in marriage (**126**); a no-fault divorce by mutual consent (**127**); and two women settling between themselves the aftermath of a marriage ended by the husband's death, including the fate of an unborn child (**129**). These come from such diverse sources as Alexandria and country villages, and the women involved show in general very different levels of Hellenism. But in all cases the colonial setting has witnessed the opening up of a range of possibilities for legal activity for women impossible to imagine in the classical Greek city. (For women's conduct of property transactions, see **Ch.5**, especially **164, 182–3**; cf. Rowlandson, 1995.)

¹ The bibliography on women in Greek law is vast: see esp. Schaps (1979), Just (1989), Sealey (1990).

122.   A widow requests a guardian

P.Enteux. 22 (*BL* VII 46)
Arsinoite nome (Themistos division), 13 January 218 BC

This is a typical example of a petition addressed to the king (here, Ptolemy IV Philopator) but read and acted on by the strategos of the local area (see **2.5**). The petitioner is a widow, Nikaia, whose husband had died seven years earlier, leaving his son as executor of his estate and 'guardian' or legal representative of his widow. After the son's death, Nikaia needed a male *kyrios* to figure in legal acts and, at the same time, to provide practical assistance given her advanced age; she requests her late husband's brother-in-law be registered in this role. The request is, despite the language of supplication, a formality, and the strategos disposes of it as a routine matter.

Nikaia's own origins are unclear; the term 'Persian' used to describe her indicates Hellenic status but obscures family origins (see Glossary). Her husband's origins are not stated, but the brother-in-law is a Thracian, from the fringe of the Greek world. The Greek practice of requiring a legal representative was, we see here, adhered to strongly by these borderline Greeks in a country with no tradition of such representation of females.

To King Ptolemy, greetings from Nikaia daughter of Nikias, Persian. My husband Pausanias died in the 23rd year, leaving behind a will of the same year, in the month of Panemos, by which he left behind [. . .]naios, his own son, as my guardian. But it has happened that he too died in year 4, in the month of Daisios (in Egyptian reckoning, Hathyr), and that I have no kinsman to be registered as my [guardian. Therefore] lest for this reason the property left to me by my husband be ruined, [since I am without] a guardian with whom I will be able to make arrangements about this property, I beg you, King, to order Diophanes the strategos that there be granted to me as guardian Demetrios the Thracian, one of the men (under the command) of Ptolemaios son of Eteoneus [of the x] hipparchy, a one-hundred-aroura holder, to whom also Pausanias gave his sister in marriage; and to order the strategos to commit these matters to writing so that they may be on record for me. And because, as I am rather old and have become weak, I am not able to go to Krokodilopolis, I have sent the above-mentioned Demetrios to present my petition, I ask for Diophanes to write to

Dioskourides the *epistates*, (*sc. ordering Dioskourides*) to record a physical description of me and the guardian whom I am requesting and to send a copy to Diophanes. For if these things come to pass, I shall have obtained, King, the benefit that comes from you. Farewell.

(*2nd hand*) To Dioskourides. Take some of the village elders and go to Nikaia and if . . . send a clear record of their descriptions to us. Year 4, Daisios 27, Hathyr 29.

(*On the back*) Year 4, Daisios 27, Hathyr 29. Nikaia daughter of Nikias, Persian, concerning what she requests.

123. Two Greeks marry in Egypt

P.Eleph. 1 (*BL* II 2.52, V 27, VI 35)
Elephantine, 311 BC

This marriage contract is the earliest dated Greek papyrus from Egypt, just twelve years after the death of Alexander the Great, and it follows closely marriage practices of the contemporary Greek world. The contract relates to the marriage of a man from Temnos (a city on the coast of Asia Minor) and a woman from the island of Kos. Though classical inhibitions against marrying someone from another city have disappeared in this colonial world, the dominant role of the bride's father in the arrangements reflects Greek practice. The need for a woman to have male assistance is also reflected in the mention of 'those helping Demetria' in case of any problems. Uncertainty about the availability of suitable legal process may be reflected in the careful provisions for arbitration. The dowry is the equivalent of several years' ordinary income and shows that we are dealing with well-off Greeks, among whom marriage customs tended to remain more conservative. Characteristic also is the double standard in the behaviour expected of the spouses: Demetria is hemmed in by the broad restriction against anything tending to bring shame on her husband, while Herakleides agrees not to add a second wife to the household, have children by another woman, or to 'do evil against Demetria'. There is no sign of Egyptian influence in any of the provisions.

In the reign of Alexander son of Alexander,[1] in the seventh year, in the satrapship of Ptolemy,[2] in the fourteenth year, in the month Dios. Marriage contract of Herakleides and Demetria. Herakleides (the Temnitan) takes as his lawful wife Demetria the Koan, a free man a free woman, from her father Leptines, Koan, and her mother Philotis, (Demetria) bringing clothing and ornaments to the value of 1000 drachmas, and Herakleides is to supply to Demetria all that is proper for a freeborn wife, and we shall live together wherever it seems best to Leptines and Herakleides consulting in common. If Demetria is discovered doing any evil to the shame of her husband Herakleides, she is to be deprived of all that she brought, but Herakleides shall prove whatever he alleges against Demetria before three men whom they both approve. It shall not be permitted for Herakleides to bring home

another wife in insult of Demetria or to have children by another woman
or to do evil against Demetria on any pretext. If Herakleides is discovered
doing any of these things and Demetria proves it before three men whom
they both approve, Herakleides shall give back to Demetria the dowry of
1000 drachmas which she brought and shall moreover forfeit 1000 drachmas
of the silver coinage of Alexander. Demetria and those aiding Demetria to
exact payment shall have the right to exact payment, as derived from a
legally decided action, upon Herakleides himself and upon all Herakleides'
property both on land and on water. This contract shall be normative in
every respect, wherever Herakleides may produce it against Demetria, or
Demetria and those aiding Demetria to exact payment may produce it
against Herakleides, as if the agreement had been made in that place.
Herakleides and Demetria shall have the right to keep the contracts severally
in their own custody and to produce them against each other. Witnesses:[3]
Kleon, Gelan; Antikrates, Temnitan; Lysis, Temnitan; Dionysios, Temnitan;
Aristomachos, Cyrenaean; Aristodikos, Koan.

[1] Alexander IV, posthumous son of Alexander the Great.
[2] Ptolemy son of Lagos, king in all but name by this time.
[3] This is a typical Greek contract, with six witnesses.

124. Sale of a young slave girl

P.Cair.Zen. I 59003
Birta (Transjordan), 259 BC

The Ptolemies tried to keep their Greek subjects from enslaving the native population of Egypt (for unpaid debts, for example), preferring to see them import from
outside Ptolemaic territory to meet their perennial demand for slaves. Here we have
a Greek in the service of the finance minister of Ptolemy II buying a slave-girl while
in Transjordan; her ethnic identity is only partly preserved, but Sidonian appears to
be the best restoration. Many, if not most, slaves were used for household service,
and women predominated in this slave population. For the purchaser, Zenon son
of Agreophon, see **Ch.3 Arch. A**, and **5.207**.

[In the reign of] Ptolemy son of Ptolemy and of his son Ptolemy, year 27,
[the priest] of Alexander and of the brother–sister gods and the *kanephoros*
of Arsinoe Philadelphos being those in office in Alexandria,[1] in the month
Xandikos, at Birta of the Ammanitis:[2] Nikanor son of Xenokles, Knidian,
in the service of Toubias, sold to Zenon son of Agreophon, Kaunian, in the
service of Apollonios the *dioiketes*,[3] a Sidonian (?) [slave-girl] named
Sphragis, about seven years of age, for fifty drachmas. [Guarantor . . .] son
of Ananias, Persian, of the troop of Toubias, kleruch.[4] Witnesses: . . . judge;
Polemon son of Straton, Macedonian, of the cavalrymen of Toubias,
kleruch; Timopolis son of Botes, Milesian, Herakleitos son of Philippos,

Athenian, Zenon son of Timarchos, Kolophonian, Demostratos son of Dionysios, Aspendian, all four in the service of Apollonios the *dioiketes*. (*Docket*) Deed of sale of a slave-girl.

[1] The holders of these priesthoods of the Ptolemaic dynastic cult (cf. **2.6**) for the current year were not known in Palestine when this contract was drawn up.
[2] Modern Amman, in Transjordan.
[3] Finance minister of Ptolemy II, and Zenon's employer.
[4] For the terms 'Persian' and 'kleruch', see Glossary.

125. A mother acts as 'guardian' for her orphaned son

SB XVI 12720.1–20
Arsinoite nome, 142 BC

This petition to Pankrates, an official of the military administration, requests official action to register the boundaries of a landed estate forming part of a swap of allotments between two cavalrymen. One of the two is now dead, and in his place his orphaned son (who would succeed to his father's military position and landholding) joins the other cavalryman in the joint request for official clarification. In the part of the original text not printed here this detailed description of the land is provided, including an elaborate computation of its area.

The papyrus is noteworthy for the mother's guardianship of her orphaned, under-age son, which is explicitly said to derive from her marriage contract with the late Ariston. The term used, *prostatis*, is unique in the documents and apparently has a non-technical sense of 'protector' or 'patron' like its masculine cognate form. Thais' responsibility for her son appears to take the place of the guardianship (by a male) normally found in the case of minor surviving children. Egyptian marriage contracts sometimes provide for the mother's guardianship, and the use of a non-technical term here may have been intended to get around the impossibility of such an appointment in Greek legal practice. We see thus the incursion into a Greek-speaking milieu of less restrictive Egyptian practices allowing women a larger share in the management of their own and their children's affairs: see Montevecchi (1981).

To Pankrates, chief bodyguard[1] and official in charge of the *syntaxis*,[2] from Antimachos son of Aristomedes, Macedonian, one of Apollonios' men of the 3rd hipparchy,[3] a 100–aroura holder, and from Herakleides son of Ariston, Thracian, of the same hipparchy, an orphan, with his *prostatis*, appointed on the basis of a contract of marriage, being his mother Thais, daughter of Apollonios.
Since the party of the aforesaid orphan and his mother are raising additional doubts concerning the boundaries of the allotment of 40 arouras in the vicinity of Kerkesoucha and the village of Ares of the Polemon district, which the aforesaid Antimachos happens to have assigned (to them), in return for that (allotment) which Ariston, the father of Herakleides, gave to

him in exchange, in the vicinity of Boubastos of the Herakleides district, we ask you to order that a letter be written to Nikolaos, *epistates* of the 5th hipparchy, of Ar. . .'s men, ordering him to make assignment of the named allotment of 40 arouras in accordance with the list of measurements and outlines submitted to Antimachos, a copy of which has been appended below. When this has been achieved we shall have experienced benefaction from you. Farewell.

(*A copy of the detailed description of the land follows.*)

¹ Sc. of the king; a term belonging to a hierarchy of honorific court titulature.
² An official responsible for administering the allotments of land given to military settlers. See Geraci (1981).
³ A subdivision in the landed military establishment.

126. A Macedonian woman gives herself in marriage

P.Giss. 2 (*BL* I 168, II.2 61, VII 59)
Krokodilopolis (Arsinoite nome), 16 September 173 B C

The parties in this contract are members of the propertied Hellenic stratum of society, a cavalryman and the daughter of another cavalryman, both men holding very large allotments (about ten times what was required to support a family). A slave is included in the dowry. The language and provisions of the agreement are entirely Greek in character (including the unequal behavioural requirements for the two parties), and the woman has her father as guardian. What is curious is that in the face of this visibly conservative Greek set of practices the woman gives herself in marriage rather than being given away by her father (*ekdosis*; see Modrzejewski, 1981). Probably this action is a reflection of Egyptian custom, in which women could act as principals in marriage agreements.

In the reign of Ptolemy son of Ptolemy and Kleopatra, manifest gods, the eighth year, in the priesthood of Herakleodoros son of Apollophanes for Alexander and the saviour gods and the brother–sister gods and the bene-factor gods and the father-loving gods and the manifest gods and the mother-loving gods; the *athlophoros* of Berenike Euergetis being Sarapias daughter of Apollonios; the *kanephoros* of Arsinoe Philadelphos being Aristokleia daughter of Demetrios; the priestess of Arsinoe Philopator being Eirene daughter of Ptolemaios;¹ on the seventeenth day of the month Peritios, Mesore seventeenth, at Krokodilopolis of the Arsinoite nome. With good fortune.

Olympias daughter of Dionysios son of Maketas, with her own father Dionysios, a Macedonian of the second hipparchy, a hundred-aroura holder, as her guardian, has given herself to Antaios, an Athenian of the men under Kineas of the second hipparchy, a one-hundred-aroura holder, so as to be his wedded wife, bringing as dowry reckoned in bronze ninety-five talents and her slave-girl by name of Stolis and her (*Stolis'*) nursling child named

NN, worth five bronze talents, making a total of [one hundred] bronze talents. And let Olympias be beside Antaios, in obedience to him as [is fitting for a wife] to her husband, managing jointly with him their property; and let Antaios furnish Olympias with [life's necessities and] furniture and clothing and all else that befits a [married] woman, both when he is at home and when he is abroad, [according to his means]; and let it not be allowed for him [to introduce] another woman into Olympias' presence or have a concubine or a boy lover,[2] [nor let it be allowed for him to beget children] from another woman in Olympias' lifetime, or to inhabit another [house of which] Olympias shall not be mistress, or cast her out, or insult her [or injure her], or alienate any property to Olympias' [detriment]. If he should be proved to do any of these things or not to supply her with [furniture or clothing] or the rest as [written above, let Antaios immediately pay back to Olympias] the dowry [and a fifty percent fine. By the same token, let it not be allowed to Olympias] to be absent by night or [by day] from [Antaios' house without Antaios'] permission . . .

Apollonios, Macedonian of the men under Kineas in the second hipparchy, hundred-aroura holder. Witnesses: Philios, Macedonian; Demokratides, Thessalian, both being men under Kineas in the second hipparchy; Diogenes, Cyrenaean, of the men under Diodoros in the 1st hipparchy, all three being one-hundred-aroura holders; Menophilos, Macedonian, *taktomisthos*,[3] one of the men formerly under Aristonikos; Alexandros son of Horion, Cretan; Sarapion son of Zopyros, Persian, both of the *epigone*.[4]

[1] For the ruler cult in dating formulae, see **2.6** and **34**.

[2] Greek *paidikon*, the term for a boy who was the passive partner in a man-boy relationship. It is interesting that the contract forbids Antaios not only to bring a concubine or boy into the common household but to have either at all.

[3] A military rank.

[4] See Glossary.

127. A no-fault divorce for a short-lived marriage

BGU IV 1103 (*BL* I 97)
Alexandria, 27 March 13 BC

This divorce agreement belongs to the only sizeable group of papyri from Alexandria, preserved because the paper was sold for wrapping mummies and deposited in a cemetery in the Herakleopolite nome (see also **129, 6.257**). It comes from the earliest decades of Roman rule in Egypt, when the process of transforming the Ptolemaic structures of government and society was still young, and gives insight into a population otherwise poorly documented. The marriage dissolved by this agreement lasted only five months or a little less, producing no offspring, and the parties separate by mutual agreement. The only issues at stake are the return of the relatively modest dowry and the freedom of both parties to remarry without being vulnerable to legal challenge. This agreement, as a record of actions already taken, served mainly to protect against future litigation.

To Protarchos[1] from Zois daughter of Herakleides, with as guardian her brother Eirenaios son of Herakleides, and from Antipatros son of Zenon. Zois and Antipatros agree that they have separated from one another, severing the union which they had formed according to an agreement made through the same tribunal in Hathyr of the current 17th year of Caesar, and Zois acknowledges that she has received from Antipatros by hand from his house clothes to the value of one hundred and twenty drachmas and a pair of gold earrings, which he received as dowry. The marriage agreement shall henceforth be null, and neither Zois nor any other person acting for her shall take proceedings against Antipatros for collection of the dowry, nor shall either party take proceedings against the other about cohabitation or any other matter whatsoever up to the present day; from which day it shall be lawful both for Zois to marry another man and for Antipatros to marry another woman without either of them being liable. In addition to this agreement being normative, the one who transgresses it shall moreover be liable both to damages and to the established fine. Year 17 of Caesar, Pharmouthi 2.

[1] Head of an Alexandrian tribunal at this time and addressee of the numerous Alexandrian documents submitted for official registration.

128. Husband deserts wife and baby for another woman

BGU VIII 1848
Herakleopolite nome, 48–46 BC

Dionysia daughter of Herakleios submits a petition to the strategos. Nearly two years earlier, she says, her husband Apollonios deserted her and their baby. Going to Alexandria, he reportedly took up with another woman by whom he fathered another child. It is unclear whether Apollonios' arrangement in Alexandria is to be construed as extra-marital concubinage or as a second marriage. In any case, Dionysia seeks the return of a 2000–drachma dowry, a clear signal of her own view that her marriage to Apollonios is over; but the dowry apparently no longer exists in liquid form. According to Dionysia, Apollonios had instructed his father Isidoros to sell some real estate (a house and some land) to obtain the cash that she seeks, but Isidoros has not acted upon those instructions. It is, accordingly, against her father-in-law Isidoros that Dionysia principally lodges her complaint. It is certain that Dionysia has given up on her marriage to Apollonios and likely that Apollonios wants to terminate the marriage so as to be free to formalise his union with the woman in Alexandria.

To Eurylochos, kinsman[1] and strategos and official in charge of the revenues, from Dionysia, the daughter of Herakleios, of those from Tilothis.[2]

Apollonios, son of Isidoros, grandson of Pau . . . by contract of marriage and other legal arrangements, together with his parents Isidoros and Philista, made off with my dowry of 2000 silver drachmas, for repayment of which they also gave surety for one another – it is now nearly two years ago (*that this was done*) – and he left me with the female child, which we conceived together for ourselves, in rags, and he has journeyed by boat down to Alexandria, and, as I am informed, being ill-disposed toward me and the child, he has joined himself there to another woman, from whom he has also produced a child, and he has told his father by letter to sell his house and allotment for cash and to return to me the dowry; and I with the child am being sufficiently tended to in every way by my brother, since I lack even basic nourishment, and since Isidoros is not making any change in his behaviour whatsoever, I ask you, if it seems appropriate, to order him to be summoned before you and to help compel him to return to me for life's necessities the dowry, so that I may receive it back. Farewell.

¹ Sc. of the king; part of the hierarchy of court titulature.
² A village in the Herakleopolite nome.

129.   Pregnant widow allowed to expose her infant

BGU IV 1104
Alexandria, 8 BC

Dionysarion daughter of Protarchos married Hermias son of Hermias in the early autumn of 10 BC. Eighteen months later Hermias[1] was dead, leaving Dionysarion pregnant. In this document Dionysarion acknowledges that she has recovered her dowry from Hermias' mother Hermione. Dionysarion renounces litigation about the dowry and about the expenses for the delivery of her baby, obtaining in turn freedom to expose the infant if she chooses and a guarantee that a subsequent remarriage will not provoke any litigation from Hermias' family. The coupling of these provisions might suggest that Dionysarion's remarriageability would be impaired by having a young infant by her deceased husband. This document belongs to the same group of Alexandrian legal texts as **127**.

To Protarchos from Dionysarion, daughter of Protarchos, with her brother Protarchos as guardian, and from Hermione, daughter of Hermias, female citizen (*of Alexandria*), with her brother's son, Hermias the son of Hermias, as guardian. Dionysarion agrees that the agreement which the deceased son of the said Hermione, Hermias son of Hermias, submitted with the said Hermione as surety through the same tribunal in the year 21 of Caesar, Phaophi, is invalid;[2] (and) Dionysarion has received from Hermione, on behalf of her said deceased husband, by hand out of the house that dowry which she had brought to Hermias with Hermione as surety: clothing worth two hundred and forty drachmas and earrings and a finger-ring . . .

and one hundred silver drachmas. And she agrees that the . . . agreement is invalid together with everything mentioned in it; neither Dionysarion nor anyone on her behalf shall take action against Hermione or against the estate left behind by the deceased Hermias, whether with respect to the dowry or the marriage or any other matter whatsoever, written or unwritten, from past times down to the present day. Since Dionysarion is also pregnant, she shall not bring action about the expenses of the child's birth because of being compliant about these matters; and she is allowed to expose her infant and to be joined to another man in marriage; and in addition to the agreement's being normative, if she transgresses (it) [she is liable] to both damages and the set penalty. We ask (to have this registered).

Year 22 of Caesar, Pachon . . .

---

[1] No fewer than five men named Hermias are mentioned in a few lines. Hermias 1 had a son Hermias (2) and a daughter Hermione, who married another Hermias (3). Each of these children had sons named Hermias (4 and 5). It is Hermias 5, son of Hermione and Hermias 3, who was Dionysarion's husband under the contract here terminated. The description of the parties makes it very unlikely that Hermione married her brother, i.e. that Hermias 2 and Hermias 3 were the same.

[2] That is, cancelled and with no future effect.

130.   Woman scalded by bath-attendant

P.Enteux. 82
Trikomia (Arsinoite nome), 220 BC

This complaint suggests something of the social and ethnic complexity in which Greeks living in the Egyptian villages found themselves. Philista, who describes herself as a 'working woman', i.e. working with her hands, complains about an Egyptian bath-attendant. The petition, though addressed like most petitions to the king, goes in fact to Diophanes, the strategos of the district (see **2.5**; cf. **122**); the culprit is in the custody of an Egyptian police chief. The village's *epistates* (superintendent) is probably Jewish. It is striking that the women's bath employed a male attendant, which one might think incongruent with Greek concern for the protection of women's modesty. The ancients assumed that servants and slaves did not count as people for purposes of modesty, however much this might trouble the servants. Several examples of Greek *tholos*-baths (note 2) have been discovered in the Fayum: see **Plate 25**.

To King Ptolemy, greeting from Philista daughter of Lysias, one of the settlers in Trikomia.[1] I am wronged by Petechon. For while I was bathing in the bath of the aforesaid village on Tybi 7 of year 1 (he being bathman in the women's rotunda),[2] and had stepped out to soap myself, when he brought in the jugs of hot water, he emptied one (?) over me and scalded my belly and my left thigh down to the knee, so as to endanger my life. On finding him, I handed him over to the custody of Nechthosiris the chief

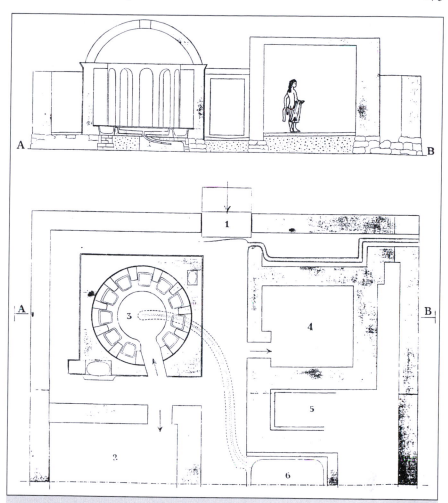

25 Plan of a bath-house
After Schwartz and Wild (1950), plate XIV
Dionysias (Arsinoite nome), before *c.* AD 200 (?)

The characteristic element of Greek baths in Egypt, as elsewhere in the Hellenistic world, was the *tholos*, a vaulted rotunda. Around the periphery of the paved floor was a ring of shallow semicircular basins covered with waterproof plaster, in which the bathers sat. Numerous examples have been found in Egypt, from cities and *metropoleis* and villages; for that excavated at Dionysias, see Schwartz and Wild (1950), 51–62 (cf. **4.130, 6.254, 286**).

Key: 1: entrance   2: changing room?   3: *tholos*
     4: sweating room   5: hot anteroom   6: cold plunge bath.

policeman of the village, in the presence of Simon the *epistates*. I beg you, therefore, O king, if it please you, as a suppliant who has sought refuge with you, not to allow me, a woman who earns a living with her hands, to be so lawlessly treated, but to order Diophanes to write to Simon the *epistates* and Nechthosiris the chief policeman that they are to bring Petechon before him in order that Diophanes may inquire into the case, hoping that having sought refuge with you, O King, the common benefactor of all, I may obtain justice. Farewell.

(*Response*) To Simon, send the accused. Year 1, Gorpiaios 28, Tybi 12.

(*Docket*) Year 1, Gorpiaios 28, Tybi 12. Philista vs. Petechon, bathman, about having been scalded.

[1] A Fayum village with a large Jewish colony in the third century BC; the Greek suggests that Lysias was a military settler (*katoikos*) there.

[2] '*Tholos*' (partly restored) in Greek; the word indicates that the room's floor plan was round, the roof (perhaps) vaulted. On the separation of male and female bathing, and for references to baths excavated in Egypt, see Meyer (1992); on Greek baths generally, the standard work is Ginouvès (1962).

III   Roman transformations

The Roman conquest introduced into Egypt a modest foreign military presence, Roman legionaries of diverse ethnic backgrounds, some of whom would settle in Egypt as veterans (Alston, 1995, ch. 3), and a handful of Roman citizens of equestrian status in the higher reaches of the provincial government. Roman law was also introduced, but, since ancient law tended to operate on principles of legal personality rather than those of legal territoriality, it generally speaking applied only to the Roman citizens in the province; the rest of the population continued to be subject to the Graeco-Egyptian legal norms inherited from the Ptolemaic period (e.g. **132**; but see **138**).

Roman citizens at first were few in number but increased over time, partly as a result of grants of Roman citizenship to the local upper classes, especially citizens of Alexandria (the emperor Claudius was notably generous in granting citizenship). But Roman citizens remained a small minority in Egypt until AD 212, when Caracalla bestowed Roman citizenship on inhabitants of both sexes throughout the empire, including Egypt. All Roman citizens needed (at least) three names, the *tria nomina*: the *praenomen* (personal name), *nomen* (*gens*, 'clan', name) and *cognomen* (family name); newly-created Roman citizens would adopt the *praenomen* and *nomen* of the Roman who had obtained the grant for them, keeping their own name as *cognomen*. For example, a Graeco-Egyptian called Didymos enfranchised by the emperor Claudius (Tiberius Claudius Caesar) would become 'Tiberius

Claudius Didymos'. All the provincials who acquired citizenship from Caracalla adopted his *nomen* Aurelius (fem. Aurelia) in their official nomenclature (in practice his *praenomen* Marcus was dropped), preceding the name by which they were normally known (see **140** and following texts).

Both before and after 212, the clearest imprint of the Roman 'law of persons' (i.e. that part of law that governed creation and changes of status) in the documentary papyri is to be found in references (explicit or implicit) to the emperor Augustus' laws on rules concerning marriage and status (cf. **131**). Female Roman citizens in Egypt were subject to the same laws as Roman women in (say) Italy or anywhere else in the empire. They married in accordance with the Julian law on marriage, and had the arrangement formalised by conferral of a dowry on their husbands, usually by their fathers (**136**, cf. **141**). Like all Roman women they were subject to perpetual guardianship (*tutela*) by male kinsmen (**140**), unless privileged with full legal independence by the Augustan *ius trium liberorum* ('right of three children') (**141, 142**). But, since non-Roman marriages were also dowered (cf. **132** introd.) and women required a male guardian (*kyrios*), whether in general or for some specific legal act (see especially **133** introd.), it is difficult to decide whether Roman or non-Roman women possessed the greater legal and proprietary freedom. Consequently the real effects on women, either of Augustus' efforts at social control in the rules collected in the *Gnomon of the Idios Logos* (**131**), or of Caracalla's grant of citizenship in 212, remain unclear.

Slavery was another area of legal concern to the Roman administration, because of its inherent ambiguity. Slaves were income-producing property (**144**), yet also persons who could have children, or form relationships with their freeborn owners (**139**); and, if manumitted, their descendants would be fully absorbed within the freeborn community. Therefore manumission, whether by Roman (**139**) or Graeco-Egyptian law (**134**), was closely regulated, and had to conform to the correct procedures.

131. Roman rules on women's status and property

BGU v 1210 (*Gnomon of the Idios Logos*) (excerpts)
Second century AD

The *Gnomon of the Idios Logos*[1] is a set of rules, mainly from the emperor Augustus, but revised down to the second century. The main extant copy was written after AD 149 and probably emanates from Theadelphia (Arsinoite nome).[2] Many of the surviving 115 clauses regulate status, marriage, and inheritance: only a representative sample is included here (see also **2.27(a)**, clause 84). Clauses 24–32 clearly reflect the Augustan inheritance legislation (see Brunt, 1987, 558–66 and 725). The terms *astos* (pl. *astoi*) and *aste* (pl. *astai*) are used throughout for male and female citizens of the Greek cities of Egypt (Alexandria, Naukratis, Ptolemais and, after 130,

Antinoopolis), but sometimes Alexandrians' rights are distinguished from those of the other cities.

Of the rulebook which the Deified Augustus handed over to the administration of the Private Account, and of those occasional additions to it either by emperors or senate or the prefects at the time or administrators of the Private Account, I have appended for you a summary of its main regulations, so that by applying your memory to a shortened version of the document, you may more easily master its topics.

6. An Alexandrian cannot bequeath to his wife from whom he has had no progeny more than a fourth part of his wealth; but if he has children by her, he can give his wife a share no greater than that which he assigns to each one of his sons.

15. Freedwomen of *astoi* are not allowed to make wills, just as *astai* are not.

23. Romans cannot marry their sisters or their aunts, but it is granted them to marry their brothers' daughters. Pardalas (*a former administrator of the Private Account*), indeed, confiscated the property of siblings who had married.

24. The dowry brought by a Roman woman over fifty years of age to a husband less than sixty years of age the treasury confiscates after her death.

25. Likewise also that which is brought by a woman less than 50 years old to a husband over sixty years of age is confiscated by the treasury.

28. If a woman is 50 years old, she does not inherit.[3] If she is less and has 3 children, she inherits; a freedwoman (inherits), if she has four children.

30. Those inheritances left to Roman women who have 50,000 sestertii and are unmarried and childless, are confiscated.

31. A Roman woman can leave to her husband the tenth part of what she owns; anything more than that is confiscated.

38. Children born to an *aste* and an Egyptian man remain Egyptians and inherit from both parents.

39. The children of a Roman man or woman who marries by ignorance an Egyptian[4] follow the lower status.

41. If an Egyptian takes from the dung-heap a child and adopts it, he is after death fined one quarter (of his property).

46. It has been granted to Roman men or *astoi* who by ignorance marry Egyptian women to be exempt from liability and for the children to follow the paternal status.

49. Freedmen of Alexandrians may not marry Egyptian women.

50. Norbanus confiscated the property of a freedwoman of an *astos* who had children by an Egyptian; but Rufus gave (the property) to the children.

52. Marriage between Romans and Egyptians is [not] allowed.

53. If Egyptian women married to discharged soldiers style themselves as Romans, the matter is subject to the rule on usurpation of status.

54. Ursus (*Egyptian prefect c.* A D *84–85*) did not permit a discharged soldier's daughter, who had become a Roman citizen, to inherit from her mother, who was Egyptian.

69. An Egyptian woman who had sent slaves out (of Egypt) with her sons through Pelousion . . . was condemned to pay 1 talent, 3000 drachmas.

[1] Cf. S. Riccobono, *Il gnomon dell'Idios Logos*; also *BL* II 2.25–6, III 18, IV 7, VI 15, VII 19, VIII 43.

[2] A first-century copy of a few sections is found in *P.Oxy.* XLII 3014. The Berlin papyrus contains a more complete copy of a later revision.

[3] This clause reflects the Augustan legislation on inheritance, intended to promote fertility, which possibly applied only to inheritances outside the immediate family.

[4] *BGU* V 1210 has 'or with *astoi* Egyptians', which is clearly garbled. The copy in *P.Oxy.* XLII 3014 probably had only 'with Egyptians', which makes sense; probably 'or with *astoi*' was a later marginal alteration.

132.   Financial formalisation of an unwritten marriage

P.Oxy. II 267 (*BL* VI 96, VII 129, VIII 234)
Oxyrhynchos, A D 37

This contract is cast as a receipt for a sum of 72 drachmas: 40 drachmas as a loan in cash and 32 drachmas in valuables. But this sum, though having all the appearance of a dowry, is to be repaid after five months (the earrings at once, in case of separation). It was in fact repaid five years later, but the couple remained together for at least twenty-three years. At the time of the contract, the couple were living together without a contract. Contracts of the kind found here are not uncommon. Apart from providing the husband with some working capital for the household, they gave the wife a certain amount of leverage over the husband and gave him an incentive not to divorce her. The legal antecedents of this transaction lie in Egyptian marriage law, but it uses Greek banking institutions to carry out its objectives (Gagos et al., 1992, esp. 189–92).

The framing of the contract suggests considerable tentativeness in the relationship, and in fact Tryphon was fairly recently separated from his first wife,
Demetrous, who just six weeks after this agreement attacked Saraeus and her
mother. Saraeus was at that time pregnant, and may indeed have been pregnant
already when the loan agreement was drawn up (see further **Ch.3 Arch.D**, and
Whitehorne, 1984).

Tryphon, son of Dionysios, Persian of the *epigone*, to Saraeus, daughter of
Apion, with as guardian Onnophris son of Antipatros, greeting. I acknowledge that I have received from you at the Serapeum in Oxyrhynchos city,
through the bank of Sarapion son of Kleandros, forty silver drachmas of
imperial and Ptolemaic coinage, and for the value of one pair of gold earrings, twenty silver drachmas, and for a milk-white *chiton*, twelve silver
drachmas, making in total a principal of seventy-two drachmas of silver, to
which nothing at all has been added, concerning which I am satisfied. And
I will repay to you the seventy-two drachmas of silver on the 30th of
Phaophi in the coming second year of Gaius Caesar Germanicus New
Augustus Emperor without any delay. If I do not repay in accordance with
the above terms I will pay to you the said principal with the addition of half
its amount, for which you are to have the right of execution upon me and
upon all my property, as in accordance with a legal decision. If we separate
from each other, you shall be empowered to have the pair of earrings at their
present value. And since we are living together without a marriage contract,
I further agree if likewise owing to a quarrel we separate from each other
while you are in a state of pregnancy, to . . . so long as you . . . This receipt
is authoritative wherever and by whomsoever it is produced.
(*Date, signatures.*)

133.   Alexandrian woman appoints legal representative

P.Oxy. II 261 (*BL* VIII 234)
Oxyrhynchos, AD 55

The parties here are Alexandrian citizens living in Oxyrhynchos. Demetria appoints
her grandson as her legal representative for some litigation she has undertaken
against a third party, because 'womanly frailty' prevents her from taking part herself.[1]
Demetria was evidently elderly, since adult grandchildren are her closest surviving
relatives, but her reason for using a representative is not simply old age; compare
the reason ascribed to the older jurists by Gaius (*Inst.* 1.144) for the institution in
Roman law of guardianship *propter animi levitatem* ('on account of their instability
of judgement'). It is interesting that the representative was different from her *kyrios*,
who was her granddaughter's husband.

Second year of Nero Claudius Caesar Augustus Germanicus Emperor, on
the . . . th of the month Neos Sebastos, at Oxyrhynchos city in the Thebaid.
Demetria daughter of Chairemon, female citizen,[2] with, as her guardian,

the husband of her granddaughter Demetria, female citizen, namely Theon
son of Antiochos, of the Auximetorean tribe and the Lenean deme,[3]
acknowledges to her own grandson, the brother of her granddaughter
Demetria, Chairemon son of Chairemon, of the Maronean deme, in the
street,[4] that touching the claims which the acknowledging party Demetria
brings against Epimachos son of Polydeukes or which Epimachos himself
advances against her, being unable to attend the court by reason of womanly
frailty, she has appointed her aforesaid grandson Chairemon as her legal
representative before every authority and every court, with the same powers
as she, Demetria, who has appointed him, would have had if present; for
she consents to this appointment. The contract is authoritative.

[1] See generally Clark (1993), 56–62. This case, which by 'womanly frailty' refers to some
specific impediment, should be distinguished from the petitions where women themselves
manipulate the general stereotype of female weakness to gain sympathy for their cases; see
5.177.
[2] I.e. of Alexandria: cf. **131** introd.
[3] These are subdivisions of the Alexandrian citizen body, used here to identify Theon's legal
status.
[4] I.e. in public before a notary.

134.   **Woman slave owner frees woman slave**

P.Oxy. XXXVIII 2843 (*BL* VII 153, VIII 262)
Oxyrhynchos, 24–8 August, AD 86

In this draft manumission, both the manumitter, Aline, and her slave, Euphrosyne,
are women. Euphrosyne (herself the offspring of a slave woman) is said to be about
thirty-five years old, by which point she is likely to have served her function of producing slave children. Slave women were typically manumitted after their reproductive peak, in their mid-thirties to mid-forties, and virtually no slave women over
forty-five appear in the census declarations. Males were freed earlier, probably on
the basis of accumulated earnings; hardly any past the early thirties are attested in
the census.

   Aline is, like all women in Roman Egypt who could not take advantage of the
ius liberorum (she was not a Roman citizen), represented by a male guardian, her son.
Euphrosyne's situation is less clearly known. Her 'ransom' is paid for her by one
Theon, presumably from her own funds. His relationship to her is unknown; the-
ories that he was a banker or an intended husband have been shown to be
unfounded. The contract is careful to specify that Theon will not be able to attempt
to collect the tax and ransom from Euphrosyne. Possibly he was an acquaintance of
the manumitting family discharging a function that required a third party. The draft
is incomplete: blank spaces were left to fill in later the exact date, the location of
Aline's and Euphrosyne's scars (a means of identification), and the name of the
certifier.

Fifth year of Emperor Caesar Domitianus Augustus Germanicus, month of
Hyperberetaios, intercalary day (*blank space*), month Kaisareios, intercalary

day (*blank space*), in Oxyrhynchos city in the Thebaid, before the *agoranomoi* Theon, Dios, and Dionysios. Aline, daughter of Komon, son of Dionysios, and of Kleopatra daughter of Dionysios, from Oxyrhynchos city, age about . . years, height medium, complexion honey-coloured, face long, scar (*blank space*), accompanied by her guardian who is her own son Komon the son of Mnesitheos son of Petesouchos, of the aforesaid city, age about . . years, height medium, complexion honey-coloured, face long, scar on the left eyebrow, acting in the public street, has set free, under sanction of Zeus, Earth and Sun, the female slave Euphrosyne who is her property, age about 35 years, height medium, complexion honey-coloured, face long, scar (*blank space*), home-born from the female slave Demetrous, on payment of ten drachmas of coined silver and the ransom money which Theon son of Dionysios, son of Leon and Isione, of the aforesaid city, age about 43 years, height medium, complexion honey-coloured, face long, scar on the right calf, has agreed to hand over for her to the aforesaid owner Aline, i.e., 800 drachmas of imperial silver coin, in bronze ten talents, 3000 drachmas; neither Theon nor anyone else connected with him has a right to claim the ransom money [or the tax in any way] from Euphrosyne who is being man-umitted, or from those acting on her side, nor . . . in any way. The certifier of the manumission is (*blank space*).

135. Husband and in-laws wrangle over deceased wife's property

P.Fam.Tebt. 20
Alexandria, AD 120/1

The situation described in this agreement is the counterpart of that seen in **141**. Herakleides married (without any written agreement) Apia alias Herakleia, who died not long after giving birth to a child. Her property passed after death to the child and was thus retained by Herakleides as the child's surviving parent and guardian. Apia's relatives, however, sued to recover the property, alleging that the child had since died (in which case the property should revert to Apia's family rather than to Herakleides), and that Herakleides had substituted another child in order to avoid returning the property. This agreement is the settlement of the case reached after the child (or substitute child, depending on one's point of view) died. Herakleides apparently had returned the property and agreed not to make future claims against it.

Copy. To Boukolos, former *agoranomos*, former priest of Alexander founder of the city (*sc. Alexandria*) and of the age classes, priest, chief judge and supervisor of the *chrematistai* and the other courts, through his son Sarapion, also former priest of Alexander founder of the city and of the age classes, temporarily performing the duties of chief judge, from Herakleia also called Isidora, daughter of Mysthes, who is absent and on whose behalf her brother Ptolemaios son of Mysthes is acting by virtue of an agreement executed through the registrar's office at Ptolemais Euergetis in the Arsinoite nome, in the month of Epeiph of the past year (*July 120*), and from Ptolemaios himself and Lysimachos son of Didymos, son of Lysimachos, whose mother is Apia, and from Herakleides son of Sarapion, son of Herakleides, all of them from the *metropolis* of the Arsinoite nome.

Whereas Herakleides was married without written contract with Apia also called Herakleia, daughter of Herakleia also called Isidora and the latter's deceased husband Kronion brother of Lysimachos, and as during the marriage she became pregnant through him and was delivered, the child . . . (whereas), moreover, Apia also called Herakleia having died, Herakleia also called Isidora and her said brother Ptolemaios and Lysimachos and (on the other side) Herakleides have attended before Eudemos, strategos of the Herakleides division of the Arsinoite nome, the party of Herakleia also called Isidora argued that the child borne by Apia also called Herakleia had died and that Herakleides had adopted another one; Herakleides himself, however, argued that the child which he had taken up was really the child borne by Apia also called Herakleia, as appears according to their own information from the record drawn up in the presence of the strategos in the month of Epeiph of the 4th year of Hadrian the lord (*July 120*), which proves also that the case has been held over to the higher court. Since it has happened, as both parties concede, that the infant itself, either of Apia also called Herakleia or an outsider, has died, they have now settled the whole controversy and Herakleia also called Isidora and Ptolemaios and Lysimachos agree with each other that they will not proceed against Herakleides either on account of the charge taken down in the minutes of the strategos or of any other matter with or without written document from past times until today; and their opponent, Herakleides, that he will proceed neither against Herakleia also called Isidora and Ptolemaios and Lysimachos nor against any of the possessions left by Apia also called Herakleia, neither on the strength of the minutes nor of any other . . . Herakleia also called Isidora and Ptolemaios and Lysimachos not suffering any harm with respect to any other debt contracted with or without a written document. So we request. (*Date*).

136. Roman bride brings big dowry

P.Mich. VII 434
Early second century AD

A Roman father, C. Antistius Nomissianus, marries his daughter Zenarion to a Roman citizen groom, M. Petronius Servillius. The document is of interest for its allusion to the *Lex Iulia de maritandis ordinibus* of 18 BC and for its formulaic reference to procreation as the purpose of marriage. These features are Roman, but the detailed written list of dowry items, even though written in Latin, has been viewed as a Greek inspiration. For Roman practice, the father's unilateral oral promise of a dowry, expressed in formal words, the so-called *dotis dictio*, would have been legally binding in itself. Such a promise is referred to toward the beginning of the present document. The list that follows is of items actually delivered to the groom. This inventory would serve as evidence and no doubt as a 'check list' in case the marriage ran into difficulties. The (evidently) seven Roman citizen witnesses hint at some connection between this transaction and the ancient Roman ceremonial mode of conveyancing known as *mancipatio*.[1]

The document has appeared in many editions and been the subject of much scholarly discussion; its provenance is unknown. The meanings of some of the dowry items are generally identifiable, but at times obscure in their specifics.

Gaius Antistius Nomissianus has given in matrimony his virgin daughter, Zenarion, in accordance with the Julian law concerning marriage which was passed for the purpose of procreating children, to a groom whose name is Marcus Petronius Servillius; and he has made a verbal promise[2] of a dowry to him and he has given all these things which are written below: two and three-quarters arouras of ancestral katoikic land near the village of Philadelphia in the place (called) Kor . . . and near the same village ancestral sandy land (?) . . . vineyard; and in gold a large earring (weighing) two and a half quarters, *cottatia* (weighing) one and a half quarters, makes 4 quarters; and silver *claria* each one equal in weight to 7 staters; and in assessed clothing: a tunic and little cloak and a Skyrine cloak,[3] worth 430 Augustan drachmas and a *heratanion* and a striped garment; and bronzes, a Venus[4] and a small jar (worth) 48 Augustan drachmas; and a mirror and boxes . . . and two ointment flasks and another jar, 7 and a quarter minas in weight; and a wooden arcla (*casket?*), a chair, a small box, a hamper, and an ancestral slave woman, Herais, and items above and beyond the dowry: a tunic and a little cloak, somewhat worn. Likewise also Marcus Petronius Servillius has stated that he has brought in his own ancestral property near the village of Philadelphia: . . . two arouras of grainland in the place . . .
Remains of six signatures of 'sealers' (sphrageis) to the contract survive (a seventh is apparently lost), five in Greek, one in Latin; all apparently have the Roman tria nomina.

[1] This ceremony involved witnesses, a scale-holder, and a prescribed ritual. See Berger (1953), 573 for a description.
[2] Technically the *dotis dictio* of Roman law.
[3] The meaning is unclear: either 'of Skyrine manufacture' (i.e. from the island of Skyros) or perhaps a colour reference.
[4] See Burkhalter (1990b); cf. **5.191**.

137.   Wife deserts husband and child

P.Heid. III 237 (*BL* V 43, IX 103)
Theadelphia (Arsinoite nome), third century A D

Although Roman centurions had no legal standing as civil juridical officials, they tended, like the Capernaum centurion whose son Jesus heals in Matthew 8.5–13 =

Luke 7.1–10 (cf. John 4.43–54), to be accorded great informal authority (Alston, 1995, 86–96), through their control of the most immediate means of official coercion. Local people therefore often appealed to them for assistance. Here, a husband complains of desertion by his wife, who has remarried, apparently without having formally divorced him. The petitioner's reference to the seizure of his farming tools may be designed particularly to attract the centurion's attention; if prevented from farming his land, he will be unable to pay his taxes. Some of the other items seem to have been dowry items (compare those in **136**) that the absconding wife was not entitled to remove.

To Claudius Alexandros (?), centurion, from NN son of Panetbeous, public farmer[1] from the village of Theadelphia. The wife with whom I was living [NN, from whom] I have begotten a child, becoming dissatisfied about her marriage with me, [seized] an opportune absence of mine, and left my house . . . months ago, without a so-called [divorce?], taking away her own goods and many of mine, among which were a large white unfulled cloak and an Oxyrhynchite pillow, and a striped dilassion (*a garment*), materials for two *chitons*, and other farmers' working implements. And although I have many times sent to her seeking to recover my things, she has not responded or returned them, and yet I am supplying to her the cost of support for our child. Besides, having now learned that one Neilos son of Syros from the same village has lawlessly taken her and married her, I submit (this petition) and request that she and Neilos may be summoned before you in order for me to be able to obtain legal redress and get back my things and be helped. Farewell.

[1] I.e. tenant cultivator of government-owned land.

138.   A father attempts to end his daughter's marriage against her will

P.Oxy. II 237 coll.VI.4–VIII.7
Oxyrhynchos, AD 186

Dionysia in this remarkable and long petition to the prefect of Egypt sets out her case against her father Chairemon. The first five columns deal with a financial dispute between the two; much of this section is damaged, in part because of trimming the papyrus roll suffered when the back was used for copying *Iliad* Book V. The next two plus columns describe the dispute over Chairemon's attempts to take his daughter away from her husband against her will. This is the part printed here. The petition then reverts to the financial disagreement. The two are, however, closely connected, because Chairemon's attempt to end the marriage was a product of the property dispute, in which Dionysia and her husband Horion stood together against her father in a matter concerning her property and dowry. Dionysia's victory in the property litigation produced her father's attempt to remove her from Horion in accordance with what he claimed was ancestral Egyptian law. The central portion of this papyrus deals with Dionysia's case, submitted to the prefect, against Chairemon's attempt.

The citations from the minutes and opinions of various Roman officials appear unanimously to recognise in 'Egyptian' law a provision giving a father continued rights over his married daughter and her property, even to the point of being able to remove her from her husband. The Roman testimonies consistently reject this as too harsh and defer to the woman's wishes. Roman *patria potestas* is clearly not applicable here, because the women are not Roman citizens, who alone were subject to that distinctive legal custom. The use of the term 'Egyptian' here, however, refers only to the legal status of the Greek-speaking persons involved, on the 'Egyptian' side of the line dividing Egyptians and Romans in the Romans' binary conception of legal status in the Egyptian countryside (i.e. outside the few Greek cities). It is in fact Greek law, not Egyptian, that provided the harsh rule criticised and set aside here by the Roman magistrates.[1]

(Chairemon), however, once more renewed his attacks upon me without cessation, but recognising the impossibility of accusing me any longer concerning my rights to possession after such elaborate inquiries and so much correspondence had taken place, turned his schemes against me in another direction; and though your highness had like the other prefects proclaimed that applications concerning private suits were not to be sent to you, he not only wrote but came in person and mutilated the case, as if he were able to deceive even you the lord prefect. Ignoring entirely both the circumstances under which the letter of Rufus[2] was written, my petition to Rufus, his answer, the inquiry held by the strategos, the report of the keepers of the archives, the letter written to you on the subject by the strategos, the reply to it which your lordship sent to me on my petition, and the orders consequently issued to the keepers of the archives, he merely wrote to you a letter as follows:

'From Chairemon, son of Phanias, ex-gymnasiarch of the city of the Oxyrhynchites. My daughter Dionysia, my lord prefect, having committed many impious and illegal acts against me at the instigation of her husband Horion, son of Apion, I sent to his excellency Longaeus Rufus a letter in which I asked to recover in accordance with the laws the sums which I had made over to her, expecting that this would induce her to stop her insults to me. The prefect wrote to the strategos of the nome in the 25th year, Pachon 27 (*22 May 185*), enclosing copies of the documents which I had submitted, with instructions to examine my petition and to act accordingly. Since therefore, my lord, she continues her outrageous behaviour and insulting conduct toward me, I claim to exercise the right given me by the law, part of which I quote below for your information, of taking her away against her will from her husband's house without exposing myself to violence on the part of any agent of Horion or of Horion himself, who is continually threatening to use it. I have appended for your information a selection from a large number of cases bearing upon this question. Year 26, Pachon (*April/May 186*).'

Such was his letter. He could not indeed cite a single insult or any other act of injustice against himself with which he charged me, but malice was the root of his abuse and assertion that he had been shamefully treated by me, saying that forsooth I turned a deaf ear to him, and a desire to deprive me of the right which I retain over the property. Stranger accusation still, he professes that he is exposed to violence on the part of my husband, who, even after my marriage contract with him which stated that I brought him this right unimpaired, gave his consent to me and afterwards to my mother . . . when we wished to agree to Chairemon's mortgaging the property in question for a total sum of 8 talents. Since that time (he has continued) attempting to deprive me of my husband, being unable to deprive me of my property, in order that I may be unable to get provision even from my lawful husband, while from my father I have had neither the dowry which he promised nor any other present, nay more, I have never received at the proper times the allowance provided.

He also appended the judgements of Similis[3] as before, and other similar cases quoted by the *archidikastes* in his letter to Longaeus Rufus, unabashed by the fact that even Rufus had paid no attention to them as a precedent on account of their dissimilarity (to the present case) . . . But your lordship exercising your divine memory and unerring judgement took into consideration the letter written you by the strategos, and the fact that a searching inquiry into the affair had already been held, and that . . . was a pretext for plotting against me; and you answered the strategos as follows:

'Pomponius Faustianus[4] to Isidoros, strategos of the Oxyrhynchite nome, greeting. The complaint which I have received from Chairemon, ex-gymnasiarch of the city of the Oxyrhynchites, accusing Horion, the husband of his daughter, of using violence against him, has by my orders been appended to this letter. See that the matter is decided in accordance with the previous instructions of his excellency Longaeus Rufus, in order that (Chairemon) may not send any more petitions on the same subject. Farewell. Year 26, Pachon 30 (*25 May 186*).'

On receipt of this letter, Chairemon brought it on Epeiph 3 (*27 June 186*) before Harpokration, royal scribe and deputy-strategos; and I appeared in court through my husband, and not only welcomed your orders and desired to abide by them, but showed that a decision in accordance with the previous instructions of Rufus had already been reached. For while Chairemon had written to protest against my possession as being illegal, Rufus, as was proved both by his answer to Chairemon and his reply to my petition, desired that an inquiry should be held to investigate the justness of my possession, and gave orders to the strategos on the subject. The strategos did not fail to execute them. He held a searching inquiry on the evidence of the keepers of the archives, and wrote to the prefect a report on the whole case . . . (*The decision of the deputy-strategos was*) '. . . that the strategos carried out Rufus' instructions by the commands given to the keepers of the archives, and by writing the aforesaid letter on the subject. But since Chairemon in the petition which he has now sent to his excellency the prefect asked to take away his daughter against her will from her husband, and since neither the letter of his late excellency Rufus nor that of his excellency the prefect Pomponius Faustianus appears to contain any definite order on this question, his excellency the prefect can receive a petition concerning it giving a full account of the facts of the case, in order that judgement may be given in accordance with his instructions.'

On all points then, my lord prefect, the affair being now clear, and the malice of my father towards me being evident, I now once more make my petition to you, giving a full account of the case in accordance with the decision of the royal scribe and deputy-strategos, and beseech you to give orders that written instructions be sent to the strategos to enforce the payment to me of the provisions at the proper times, and to restrain at length his attacks upon me, which previously were based upon the charge of an illegal possession, but now have the pretext of a law which does not apply to him. For no law permits wives against their will to be separated from their husbands; and if there is any such law, it does not apply to daughters of a marriage by written contract and themselves married by written contract. In proof of my contention, and in order to deprive Chairemon of even this pretext, I have appended a small selection from a large number of decisions on this question given by prefects, procurators, and *archidikastai*, together with opinions of lawyers, all proving that women who have attained maturity are mistresses of their own persons, and can remain with their husbands or not as they choose; and not only that they are not subject to their fathers, but that the law does not permit persons to escape a suit for the recovery of money by the subterfuge of counter-accusations; and (thirdly) that it is lawful to deposit contracts in the public archives, and the claims arising from these contracts have been recognised by all prefects and emperors to be valid and secure, and no one is permitted to contradict his own written engagements. In this way too he will at length cease from continually troubling the prefecture with the same demands, as you yourself wished in your letter.

'From the minutes of Flavius Titianus, sometime prefect.[5] Year 12 of the deified Hadrian, Pauni 8 (*2 June 128*), at the court in the marketplace. Antonius son of Apollonios appeared and stated through his advocate, Isidoros the younger, that his father-in-law Sempronius at the instigation of his mother had made a quarrel with him and taken away his daughter against her will, and that when the latter fell ill through grief the epistrategos Bassus, being moved by sympathy, declared that if they wished to live together Antonius ought not to be prevented, but all to no effect. For Sempronius ignoring this declaration presented to the prefect a complaint of violence and had brought back an order that the rival parties were to be sent up for trial. Antonius therefore claimed, if it pleased the prefect, that he should not be separated from a wife affectionately disposed towards him. The advocate Didymos replied that Sempronius had had good reason for having been provoked. For it was because Antonius had threatened to charge him with incest that he, refusing to bear the insult, had used the power granted by the laws and had also brought . . . accusations against the other. Probatianus on behalf of Antonius added that if the marriage had not been annulled the father had no power either over the dowry or over the daughter whom he had given away. Titianus said: "The decisive question is with whom the married woman wishes to live." Read over and signed by me (the prefect).'

'Extract from the minutes of Paconius Felix, epistrategos.[6] Year 18 of the deified Hadrian, Phaophi 17 (*14 Oct. 133*), at the court in the upper division of the Sebennyte nome, in the case of Phlauesis, son of Ammounis, in the presence of his daughter Taeichekis, against Heron son of Petaesis. Isidoros, advocate for Phlauesis, said that the plaintiff therefore, wishing to take away his daughter who was living with the defendant, had recently brought an action against him before the epistrategos and the case had been deferred in order that the law of the Egyptians might be read. Severus and Heliodorus, advocates (for Heron), replied that the late prefect Titianus heard a similar plea advanced by Egyptian parties, and that his judgement was in accordance not with the inhumanity of the law but with the choice of the daughter, whether she wished to remain with her husband. Paconius Felix said, "Let the law be read." When it had been read Paconius Felix said, "Read also the minute of Titianus." Severus the advocate having read: "Year 12 of Hadrian Caesar the Lord, Pauni 8, etc.," Paconius Felix said, "In accordance with the decision of his highness Titianus, they shall find out from the woman," and he ordered that she should be asked through an interpreter what was her choice. On her replying, "To remain with my husband," Paconius Felix ordered that the judgement should be entered on the minutes.'

'Extract from the minutes of Umbrius, *iuridicus*. Year 6 of Domitian, Phamenoth (*Feb./March 87*) . . Didyme, defended by her husband Apollonios, against Sabinus also called Kasios: extract from the proceedings. Sarapion: "Inquire of the parties who are Egyptians, amongst whom the severity of the law is untempered. For I declare to you that the Egyptians have power to deprive their daughters not only of what they have given them, but of whatever these daughters may acquire for themselves besides." Umbrius said to Sabinus, "If you have already once given a dowry to your daughter, you must restore it." Sabinus: "I request . . ." Umbrius: "To your daughter of course." Sabinus: "She ought not to live with this man." Umbrius: "It is worse to take away (a wife) from her husband . . ."'

'Copy of a lawyer's opinion. Ulpius Dionysodoros, ex-*agoranomos*, lawyer, to his most esteemed Salvistius Africanus, prefect of a fleet and judicial officer, greeting. Since Dionysia has been given away by her father in marriage, she is no longer in her father's power. For even though her mother lived with her father without a marriage contract, and on that account she appears to be child of a marriage without contract, by the fact of her having been given away in marriage by her father, she is no longer the child of a marriage without contract. It is about this point probably that you write to me, my good friend. Moreover, there are minutes of trials which secure the rights of the daughter against her father in respect of the dowry, and this too can help her.'

[1] See Modrzejewski (1988), 392–4.
[2] The prefect of Egypt, Longaeus Rufus, mentioned in the next paragraph.
[3] Flavius Sulpicius Similis, Longaeus Rufus' predecessor as prefect.
[4] Rufus' successor as prefect.
[5] Under Hadrian; he is well-attested because he was responsible for the census of 131/2.
[6] Epistrategos (regional governor) of Lower Egypt.

139.   The natural family of a Roman veteran

BGU I 326 (*BL* I 435, II.2 15, III II, VIII 23–4)
Karanis, AD 189–94

This document, the will of Gaius Longinus Kastor, a resident of Karanis and veteran of the praetorian fleet of Misenum (near Naples), has been called 'one of the very few examples of pure Roman law found in Egypt'. It presents in writing all the formalities of the traditional 'will by copper and scales', a fictive sale, and mentions all the 'actors' in that little ceremonial drama: the 'estate purchaser' (*familiae emptor*), the scale-holder (*libripens*), and five Roman citizen witnesses. The original was drawn up in Latin in autumn 189. On 7 February of a subsequent year, perhaps only days or weeks before his death, Kastor added codicils in his own hand. The will was officially opened and read on 21 February 194. The waxed tablets of the original will and codicils have not survived; what we have is a Greek translation on papyrus, probably made at the behest of one of Longinus Kastor's heirs.

The primary heirs are two slave women, Marcella and Kleopatra, whom Kastor also manumits by the terms of his will. Both are stated to be over thirty years of age and therefore not subject to one of the restrictions on testamentary manumission enacted in the Augustan *Lex Aelia Sentia* of AD 4. If Marcella dies, her share of the estate is to go to Sarapion, Sokrates, and Longus; if Kleopatra dies, Neilos is to receive her share. The will also includes a legacy, whose property terms are set forth in detail, in favour of Kleopatra's daughter, Sarapias, also emancipated in the will.

Because, until about the time of this will, Roman soldiers were prohibited from marrying, and because wills were (and are) by and large meant to devolve the testator's property in specific ways upon next of kin, it is reasonable to speculate that Marcella or Kleopatra, or both, were Kastor's common-law wives; that Sarapias was not only Kleopatra's daughter, but his as well; and that Sarapion, Sokrates, Longus, and Neilos were his sons; see Watson (1966). Kastor as a veteran could have married upon honourable discharge, but Roman law insisted upon monogamy, and Longinus' own 'discharge papers' (*diploma*), while granting him the chance to legitimise a 'common-law' union, would also have included a proviso against bigamy. Kastor's children were therefore all illegitimate, 'spurious' (*spurii*) in Latin, or in Greek 'fatherless' (*apatores*), not because their father's identity was unknown, but because they were not products of an acknowledged Roman-law marriage. The result is an irony: Kastor's will turns out to be subject to the 5 per cent tax on inheritances because his heirs (primary and secondary) were not his legal kin. For a more extended discussion, see Keenan (1994).

Translation of a will. Gaius Longinus Kastor, honourably discharged veteran of the praetorian fleet of Misenum, has made a will. I order that Marcella my slave woman, over thirty years of age, and Kleopatra my slave woman, over thirty years of age, become free . . . Let them in equal shares be my heirs. Let all others be disinherited. Let them enter upon the inheritance, each for her own share, whenever it seems proper to each to bear witness that she is my heir; it shall not be possible to sell or mortgage it. But if the above-written Marcella suffers the lot of human kind, then I wish her share of the inheritance to devolve upon Sarapion and Sokrates and Longus. Likewise for Kleopatra, I wish her share to devolve upon Neilos. Let whoever becomes my heir be liable to give, to do, to provide all these things that have been written in this my will, and I commit them to her trust.
Let my slave woman Sarapias, daughter of Kleopatra my freedwoman, be free, to whom I also give and bequeath: five arouras of grainland which I hold in the vicinity of the village of Karanis in the place called 'Ostrich'; likewise, one and a quarter arouras of wadi-land; likewise, a third share of my house and a third share of the same house which I earlier bought from Prapetheus son of Thaseus;[1] likewise, a third share of a palm-grove which I hold very close to the canal called 'Old Canal'. I wish my body to be carried out[2] and wrapped by the care and piety of my heirs. If I leave behind anything in writing after this, written in my own hand, in any way whatsoever, I wish this to be valid. Let evil malice[3] be absent from this will.
The household and property of the will just made were bought by Julius Petronianus for one sestertius coin, the scale holder being Gaius Lucretius Saturnilus. (He acknowledged.) He (*the testator*) has called as witness Marcus Sempronius Heraklianus. (He acknowledged.) The will was made in the village of Karanis in the Arsinoite nome on the 15th day before the Kalends of November[4] in the consulship of the two Silani, in the 30th year of Emperor Caesar Marcus Aurelius Commodus Antoninus Pius Felix Augustus Armeniacus Medicus Parthicus Sarmaticus Germanicus, Hathyr 21 (*17 Nov. 189*). If any further writings I leave behind written in my own hand, I wish these to be valid.
Opened and read in the Arsinoite *metropolis* in the Augustan Forum in the office of the five percent tax on inheritances and manumissions on the 9th day before the Kalends of March in the consulship of the present consuls, in the 2nd year of Emperor Caesar Lucius Septimius Severus Pertinax Augustus, Mecheir 27 (*21 Feb. 194*). The remaining sealers: Gaius Longinus Akylas (he acknowledged); Julius Volusius, Marcus Antistius Petronianus, Julius Gemellus, veteran.
Translation of codicil tablets. I, Gaius Longinus Kastor, honourably dis-

charged veteran of the praetorian fleet of Misenum, have made codicils. Marcus Sempronianus Heraklianus, a friend and a man of worthy repute, I have made trustee on his own good faith. To my kinsman, Julius Serenus, I give and bequeath 4000 sestertius coins. I have written this in my own hand on the 7th day before the Ides of February (7 Feb.). Longinus Akylas and Valerius Priscus have sealed them. Sealers: Gaius Longinus Akylas (he acknowledged); Julius Philoxenos, Gaius Lucretius Saturnilus (he acknowledged); Gaius Longinus Kastor; Julius Gemellus, veteran.

Opened and read on the same day on which the will was unsealed.

(*2nd hand*) I, Gaius Lucius Geminianus, expert in Roman law, translated the above copy and it is in conformity with the original will.

[1] Prapetheus is identified only by his mother's name; he thus had no legitimate father.
[2] For burial.
[3] A calque of the Latin *dolus malus*.
[4] A mistake for 'December', if the Egyptian date is correct.

140. Women ask the governor for male guardians

The two following documents both reflect the growing use of fully Roman legal forms in third-century Egypt. The *lex Iulia et Titia*, of Augustan date (apparently confirmed by a decree of the Roman senate; see **(a)** and **(b)** below), provided for a provincial governor to name a tutor for a woman if none was provided by a will or by statute. Under Roman law, women needed a male tutor when they conducted important business (e.g. making a will, or selling or manumitting a slave), unless they were exempted by virtue of having three children. The tutors had a formal rather than substantive role (see further, Modrzejewski, 1974; Arjava, 1996, 112–23; 1997). Text **(a)** is an original petition in Latin, with signatures in Greek and the prefect's response in Latin. Text **(b)** is a request similar to the first, but with the answer in Greek, not Latin; it seems to be a copy rather than the autograph original.

(a) *P.Oxy.* IV 720 (*BL* I 327, III 132, VI 98, VII 130, VIII 237)[1]
Oxyrhynchos, 5 January A D 247

(*Latin*) To Gaius Valerius Firmus, prefect of Egypt, from Aurelia Ammonarion. I ask you, my lord, to give me as guardian Aurelius Ploutammon in accordance with the *lex Iulia et Titia* and the decree of the senate. Dated in the consulship of our lords Philippus Augustus for the 2nd time and Philippus Caesar.

(*Greek*)   I, Aurelia Ammonarion, have presented the petition.

I, Aurelia (*sic, for Aurelius*) Ploutammon, assent to the request.

Year 4, Tybi 10.

(*Latin*) In order that . . . may not be absent, I appoint Ploutammon as guardian in accordance with the *lex Iulia et Titia*. I have read this.

[1] See also Sanders (1933).

(b) *P.Oxy.* XII 1466 (*BL* VII 139)
Oxyrhynchos, 21 May AD 245

(*Latin*) To Valerius Firmus, prefect of Egypt, from Aurelia Arsinoe. I ask you, my lord, [to give me as guardian according to the *lex Iulia et Titia* and the decree of the senate Aurelius] Herminos. Year 2, Pachon 26. Sheet 94, vol. 1.[1]

(*Greek*) Translation of the Latin:[2]
To Valerius Firmus, prefect of Egypt, from [Aurelia Arsinoe. I ask you, my lord, to give me] as guardian according to the *lex Iulia et [Titia]* [Aurelius Herminos. Presented] on the 12th day before the Kalends of June in the consulship of the Emperor Philippus Augustus and Titianus. I, Aurelia Arsinoe daughter of Sarapion, [have presented the petition, requesting that Aurelius Hermi]nos should be appointed my guardian. I, Aurelius Tima[genes (?), son of . . . wrote for her as she is illiterate.[3] I, Aurelius Herminos son of Dionysios, consent to the petition. Year 2, Pachon 26.] Unless you have the right to another guardian, [I grant you the guardian] for whom [you ask].

[1] This note indicates the location of this petition in the official archives.
[2] In Roman law, only Latin was permitted for some types of document; translations were for convenience only.
[3] Relatively few women, except of the wealthiest class, were literate; cf. **142**, and **Ch.6 Sect. II**.

141. Mother recovers widowed daughter's dowry

P.Coll.Youtie II 67
Oxyrhynchos, AD 260/1

This document records the repayment of a young widow's dowry to her parents by the guardian of the child of the marriage, into whose hands the estate of the child's late father has come. Although the text does not explicitly say so, the first items listed (down to 'five thousand drachmas on account') clearly constituted the *pherne*, the dowry proper, as opposed to the supplementary paraphernalia (see p. 313 for this distinction). Thus, contrary to the editor's interpretation, no part of the dowry was kept back to form the child's inheritance (Wolff, 1979; cf. Rowlandson, 1996, 157–8). The parties to the agreement are all members of the wealthiest stratum of Egyptian society (Rowlandson, 1996, 111–12), and the goods enumerated in the receipt amount to about ten talents in value, a sizeable fortune even in the third century.

The widow's father, who would normally have issued this receipt, is not in Oxyrhynchos, having gone to serve as governor of the Hermopolite nome, to the south (the third member of this prominent family to hold that position). His wife Dioskouriaina therefore issues it on his behalf. As the mother of three children she acts without a guardian (see **142**), and she undertakes to have her husband confirm her actions upon his return, or else to stand responsible for them herself, which, as a member of a wealthy Alexandrian family, she no doubt felt able to do with confidence.

Aurelia Dioskouriaina, daughter of Dioskourides, former eutheniarch and councillor of the most illustrious city of the Alexandrians, acting without a guardian by right of children according to Roman law, to Aurelius Menon (?), son of Theon, his mother being Claudia, from the city of the Oxyrhynchites, one of the victors in the sacred games from among the ephebes,[1] guardian of my minor grandson, Aurelius Epimachos, gymnasiarch[2] of the same city, son of Epimachos and however he was styled, with the agreement of the minor's uncle on his father's side, Aurelius Severus, gymnasiarch and councillor of the same city, greeting. I acknowledge that I have received and recovered from you the things conferred by my husband, Aurelius Spartiates, also called Chairemon, former gymnasiarch and councillor of the same city, upon our mutual daughter, Aurelia Apollonarion, when she was married to the since-deceased father of the minor, in accordance with their marriage contract, all the goods, in full by weight and valuation, which are: of gold, in goods, altogether, by the Oxyrhynchite standard, seventeen minas' weight less one quarter, and a necklace and an earring at valuation of fifteen hundred drachmas; and . . . twenty-seven pounds; and all the clothing at valuation of five thousand drachmas; and also, out of the four talents and two thousand drachmas in silver coin contributed towards the purchase of other dower goods, five thousand drachmas on account; and all the contributed paraphernalia with gold jewellery and clothing and linens and brasses and stoneware in kind, in full; and out of the one talent contributed towards the purchase of slaves, three thousand drachmas on account; and the two slaves contributed by me, Dioskouriaina; all of which shall be bestowed upon the same daughter of mine when she is married to another husband.

And I shall provide that same husband of mine, when he returns from the office of strategos of the Hermopolite nome, which he has taken in hand, either to approve this receipt or to issue another while I recover this one. If he should do neither of these things, you are to have the right of prosecution against me concerning these things, while (the right of prosecution?) remains to both of them, that is, to my husband and to the child, concerning the remainder and all the rights he has according to the contract. Let the text be authoritative, written in triplicate, which you shall publish through the public records office whenever you choose, if my husband either should not approve this receipt or should not issue another receipt, without asking my permission, because I have now approved the future publication by you. Formally questioned by you, I have assented.
Year 1 of Emperors Caesars Titus Fulvius Iunius Macrianus and Titus Fulvius Iunius Quietus, Pii Felices Augusti.

[1] A local title of athletic distinction.
[2] The magistrate in charge of the gymnasium, where the city's youth were trained in athletics.

142.   Mother of three seeks legal independence

P.Oxy. XII 1467 (*BL* VIII 246)
Oxyrhynchos, 15 July AD 263

Aurelia Thaisous alias Lolliane applies to the prefect of Egypt for permission to conduct her affairs without a guardian, on the basis of being the mother of three children (the *ius trium liberorum*), as specified in the Augustan *lex Iulia* and the *lex Papia Poppaea*.[1] For good measure she mentions that she is literate, a legal irrelevancy. The prefect does not explicitly grant the privilege, but he does assure Thaisous that her application will be kept on file. The lively formulation of the petition suggests the value that Thaisous set upon this mark of legal independence.

. . . [Laws long ago have been made], most eminent prefect, which empower women who are adorned with the right of three children to be mistresses of themselves and act without a guardian in whatever business they transact, especially those who know how to write. Accordingly, as I too enjoy the happy honour of being blessed with children and as I am a literate woman able to write with a high degree of ease, it is with abundant security that I appeal to your highness by this my application with the object of being enabled to accomplish without hindrance whatever business I henceforth transact, and I beg you to keep it without prejudice to my rights in your eminence's office, in order that I may obtain your support and acknowledge my unfailing gratitude. Farewell. I, Aurelia Thaisous also called Lolliane, have sent this for presentation. Year 10, Epeiph 21. (*Annotation*) Your application shall be kept in the [office].

[1] See Arjava (1996), especially 77–8, 119–22. The three did not all have to be still alive for the right to be claimed.

143.   Jewish synagogue buys freedom of mother and children

P.Oxy. IX 1205 (*BL* V 78, VI 101, VIII 242)
Oxyrhynchos, AD 291

This remarkable manumission concerns (like **134**) a female house-born slave near the end of her reproductive years. But here two children of hers are also set free, suggesting that this is no ordinary case. Other indications support that view: the ransom has been paid by the 'synagogue of the Jews' through two men, one from Palestine. One of the woman's children is named Jacob; the name of the other is lost. However, the description of the guardian of one manumitter as 'astounding' (*paradoxos*), connecting him with the athletic aristocracy of Oxyrhynchos, suggests that the manumitters were gentiles. It is unclear what occasion brought the Jewish community to discharge its moral obligation to liberate their coreligionists from slavery only when Paramone was forty years old.

Translation of manumission. We, Aurelius . . . of the illustrious and most illustrious city of the Oxyrhynchites, and his sister by the same mother Aurelia . . . daughter of . . . the former *exegetes* and councillor of the same city, with her guardian . . . the astounding . . ., have manumitted and discharged among friends[1] our house-born slave Paramone, age 40 years, and her children . . . with a scar on the neck, age 10 years, and Jacob, age 4 years, . . . from all the rights and powers of the owner: fourteen talents of silver having been paid to us for the manumission and discharge by the synagogue of the Jews through Aurelius Dioskoros . . . and Aurelius Justus, councillor of Ono in Syrian Palestine,[2] father of the synagogue . . . And, the question being put, we have acknowledged that we have manumitted and discharged them, and that for the above manumission and discharge of them we have been paid the above-mentioned money, and that we have no rights at all and no powers over them from the present day, because we have been paid and have received for them the above-mentioned money, once and for all, through Aurelius Dioskoros and Aurelius Justus. Transacted in the illustrious and most illustrious city of Oxyrhynchos . . . in the second consulship of Tiberianus and the first of Dion, year 7 of Emperor Caesar Gaius Aurelius Valerius Diocletianus and year 6 of Emperor Caesar Marcus Aurelius Valerius Maximianus, Germanici Maximi Pii Felices Augusti, Pharmouthi . . . nineteenth day.
. . . Paramone and her children . . . and Jacob . . . (I witness) the agreement as stated above. I, Aurelius . . . (wrote for him) as he is illiterate.
Aurelius Theon also called . . . of the money . . . rights . . . of Dioskoros . . . Justus . . . the (talents) of silver . . . manumit . . . illiterate.

[1] Latin *inter amicos*, an informal mode of manumission.
[2] A city in the region of Lydda, inland from the Levantine coastal city of Joppa.

144.   Woman claims her due from parents' slave

P.Oxy.Hels. 26 (*BL* VIII 274)
Oxyrhynchos, 13 June A D 296

This petition records a woman's complaint about the failure of a man, who she says is her slave, to pay her an *apophora* (contribution). The slave was part of her inheritance, jointly with her sister, from their parents. Despite Tapammon's terminology, however, it is likely that the 'slave' had been manumitted by the will. Freedmen did typically have duties toward their patrons, and the dispute here probably concerned just what was due to Tapammon.
   It is interesting that, although Tapammon claims the right to act without a

guardian by virtue of the *ius liberorum* (cf. **142**), she uses a male intermediary in filing this complaint (see also **145**). The right to act independently was no doubt worth recording, even if Tapammon found it practically desirable to have Sarapiades act on her behalf.[1]

In the consulship of our lords the Emperor Diocletian Augustus for the 6th time and Constantius the most noble Caesar for the 2nd.
To Aurelii Dionysios also called Apollonios and Demetrianos son of Ploution, both former gymnasiarchs and councillors of the illustrious and most illustrious city of the Oxyrhynchites, the most distinguished *nyktostrategoi*,[2] from Aurelia Tapammon daughter of Thonios and Allous from the same city, acting without a guardian in virtue of her children, through her foster father Aurelius Sarapiades son of Didymos also called Hierax, from the same city. I own by inheritance from my parents along with my sister Dioskouriaina a slave whose name is Sarmates, house-born from the slave woman Thaesis. And from the time of the death of my parents he supplies us with his contribution. But now he absents himself, will not stay in our service, and will not provide us with any contribution, with what object I do not know. Therefore, since I cannot endure the insolence of a household slave, I present this written petition requesting that through your care the slave may be compelled to pay the contribution he owes and that it may be arranged (?) that he should stay in our service.
Year 12 and 11 of our lords the Emperors Diocletian and Maximian Augusti and year 4 of Constantius and Maximian the most noble Caesars, Pauni 19. Aurelia Tapammon has presented through me, Aurelius Sarapiades. I, Aurelius Ischyrion, wrote it for her.

[1] For the practice of male relatives representing women who enjoyed the *ius liberorum*, see generally Beaucamp (1992), 193–267.
[2] City officials in charge of law and order.

IV   Freedom and responsibility in developed Roman society

Despite restrictions on women's private-law independence in both Greek customary and Roman civil law, the papyri create a sense of growing extension of women's freedom in both the private and the public spheres as the Roman passes into the late Roman period (Bagnall, 1993a, ch. 5). This freedom was furthered by the 'right of three children' that became available to some Roman-citizen wives from the time of Augustus onward (see preceding section), but went beyond it. The third to the sixth centuries provide examples of some extraordinarily 'high-class' and wealthy female landlords (**151; 5.174–5, 179, 192–3**). Women possessed wide proprietary powers in disposing of their property after death (**145–8**), and neither Christian doctrine nor imperial legislation appear in practice to have curtailed their grounds for divorce (**154, 156**; Clark, 1993, 17–27; Evans Grubbs, 1995).

The government's growing financial and liturgical pressures on wealthy families drew women closer to public spheres of activity (cf. van Bremen, 1996). Women did not serve the government in person, but came to do so in name (**150**), while the liability of their property to government claims upon that of their male kinsmen became for them a matter of no small concern (**149**).

With added legal freedom and public responsibility came greater personal protection. Marriage contracts, earlier almost exclusively concerned with property arrangements, now included more elaborate specification of marital duties, enshrining the woman's right to proper treatment in marriage, perhaps because this could no longer be taken for granted (**155**; cf. **157**, and by implication, **152–4**). Men continued to assist at the business dealings of their daughters, sisters, and wives; and fathers, then as now, were concerned that their daughters be well treated by their husbands (especially **152**). Similarly paternalistic concerns were formulated by the emperor Justinian himself.[1] If the financial entanglements and disentanglements of marriages and divorces remained a focus of the law, the ethical notions of respect and love between marriage partners and of marriage as intended for the procreation of children also found their expression.

[1] Clark (1993), 58, citing a law of AD 531, and passim. On the theme of women's frailty see Beaucamp (1994).

145. Woman names daughter heir, blasts daughter-in-law

P.Lips. 29
Hermopolis, AD 295

This 'Greek testament' illustrates the persistence of Greek testamentary practices for generations after Caracalla's grant of universal Roman citizenship of 212.[1] Aurelia Eustorgis addresses her will to her adult daughter, making her sole heir to Eustorgis' estate. Eustorgis is at pains to make clear that the widow of her late son Sarmates has no claim against the estate and is to receive nothing from it. Sarmates' death appears to have been recent, to judge from the reference to 'the care of his corpse', and there is at least one large sum receivable by his estate. Eustorgis appears to have been Sarmates' heir, perhaps by intestacy. Clearly Tameis, the daughter-in-law, had pursued her claims with vigour and (in her mother-in-law's view) rapacity.

[Aurelia Eustorgis . . . with a scar on her] left [. . .], styling herself as without guardian by the *ius liberorum* [according to Roman custom], [registered in] the most brilliant city of Hermopolis in the West Fort District, with the assistance[2] of [Aurelius] Triadelphos, [son of Hermophilos, registered in the] West City District, to my own daughter, Aurelia Hyperechion also called Ammonarion, [greetings].

May I have good health and [benefit from] our property; but if (may it not happen!) some mortal event should come upon me, which I wish may not happen, I appoint you as sole heir according to all the laws so that you may be fully empowered to go wherever you wish, inasmuch as you have become of legal age. On account of this reason, I have devolved upon you all my property through this Greek testament, being of sound intention and mind. For suspecting that a mortal illness has come upon me, but being of sound intention and mind, I have drawn up this my will so that it may not be possible for anyone to go against my dispositions, and so that Aurelia Tameis, the former wife of my deceased son, Sarmates, may <not> enter our house, which is in the West Fort District, nor meddle with any property that belongs to me or to him, my deceased son, on the grounds of the care of his corpse, you my above-described daughter and heir being self-sufficient with our and Sarmates' friends. For I, too, though independent, have suffered at her hands, as a result of which I do not wish her to inherit any of our [property], especially since she has no claim against me or against my deceased son, pursuant to her declaration to me in a third written quit-claim that she had been paid in full for the property of hers which she alleged our son had. I wish you to know, that of what was owed to my same son [by] NN, gymnasiarch of Alexandria, for the price of linen, twelve talents of new silver, he had delivered to me only one (talent) . . . and of Theban (wine) one hundred *knidia*,[3] with respect to your pursuing him at law concerning the balance owed me by him. The Greek testament, which I have issued to you in double copy, is valid as if deposited in a public archive, and having been asked the formal question, of sound intention and mind, I have agreed. Year 11 and 10 of our lords Diocletian and Maximian, Augusti, and year 3 of our lords Constantius and Maximian, the most glorious Caesars, in the consulship of Nummius Tuscus and Annius Anullinus, the most excellent. (*2nd hand*) I, Aurelia Eustorgis, have made this testament as stated above. I, Aurelius Triadelphos, son of Hermophilos, am present with her and have written on her behalf as she is illiterate.

[1] The requirement for Roman wills to be in Latin, and to follow a strict formula (see **139**) posed such problems for the new Roman citizens of the eastern empire that Severus Alexander relaxed the regulations, acknowledging the validity of wills written in Greek and employing customary Greek wording; see Rowlandson (1996), 140.

[2] See **144** for men assisting women who possess the *ius liberorum*.

[3] A measure.

146. Woman names mother heir, leaves legacy to husband

P.Princ. II 38 (*BL* III 149)
Hermopolis, *c.* AD 264

Though fragmentary, the will preserves several key elements of the standard Roman will. The testator names an heir (her mother, Aurelia Asklatarion); she disinherits all others; she grants the heir the standard hundred-day period for pronouncing formal acceptance of the inheritance (*cretio*, see Gaius, *Institutes* 2.170). The 'days of distinction' that are mentioned are the days of special mourning following the death of the testator. Finally, Serenilla leaves a legacy to her husband of several parcels of land.

The disinheriting was probably not motivated by hostility (Champlin, 1991, 107ff., esp. 110–11). Since no secondary heirs are named, Serenilla was evidently willing to let her estate pass to her other heirs by the rules of intestate succession if her mother predeceased her. Note that Serenilla has two guardians: her husband as *kyrios* (by Greek tradition) and a *curator (minoris)*, required by Roman law from the early third century onward for girls aged aged between 12 and 25 (see Arjava, 1996, 114–15, 120).

Aurelia Serenilla also called Demetria, daughter of Philippianos also called Kopreus, former councillor of Hermopolis the Great, ancient and most brilliant (city), with her guardian (*kyrios*) Aurelius Hermeinos also called Achilleus, son of Eudaimon, *eutheniarch*[1] of the said Hermopolis, and her *curator* Aurelius Valerius Longus, [veter]an from the same Hermopolis, has made a will and has pronounced it for commitment to writing:

'Let Aurelia Asklatarion alias Koprilla,[2] my mother, be my heir. Let my other (family members)[3] be disinherited. Let her enter upon my inheritance within my 100 days of distinction, when she learns of it and can bear witness that she is my heir. To Aurelius Achilleus also called Hermeinos, *kosmetes*,[4] my husband, I leave in the vicinity of Ibion Peteaphthi *machimos*-assignment land[5] from the allotment of Naubes, of those arouras which I hold in one parcel . . . five arouras, and near the same village from the . . . which I have in partnership with Aline, three arouras . . .'

(The land provisions become increasingly damaged. Serenilla's curator and a house are mentioned in later lines, but no connected sense is possible.)

[1] A civic official responsible for the food supply.
[2] The alias Koprilla is, like the father's alias Kopreus, derived from the Greek word for dung. For these names see Pomeroy (1986), Hobson (1989), 163–4.
[3] The first edition read 'sons' here, corrected by Wilcken (see *BL* III 149); Champlin (1991), 110 n. 28 cites it without knowledge of Wilcken's correction.
[4] An official of the gymnasium (of Hermopolis).
[5] A land category term deriving from the Ptolemaic period.

147. Woman gives house to daughter, provides for funeral

SB VIII 9642(1) (*BL* VII 213–4, VIII 353)
Tebtynis, *c.* AD 112

An alternative to disposition of property by will was the document type called *donatio mortis causa*, a gift effective upon the death of the giver (cf. **5.217**, and **148** for a *donatio* in a very different form). One-third of the surviving agreements of this type were made by women, a much higher share than of formal wills (see *P.Mert.* III 105A). The use of this legal form for the transmission of property allows the giver to separate this transaction from the disposition of the rest of the estate (avoiding any threat that might be caused by the failure of the will) and to attach conditions to the gift (here, care after death). In this document, Tamystha, a fifty-year-old woman, gives her half-share of a house in the village of Talei, together with its contents, to her daughter. Tamystha retains the use of the house for the remainder of her life, and Taorsenouphis' receipt of the house is conditional upon her payment of twenty drachmas to her brother Heron and to her provision of a proper burial for her mother. It is not said if the twenty drachmas for Heron are his sole share of the estate. It is entirely possible that Tamystha has landed property disposed of by another *donatio mortis causa* or through a will, and that Heron has received or will receive a portion (even a majority) of this. The usual six witnesses attest to the deed of gift.

[Tamystha, daughter of Apollonios (son of Herakleides) and Thenpetenouphis, from the village of Talei, with as guardian] her brother on both her father's and her mother's side, Satabous, about fifty years old, with a scar on his left hand, [acknowledges] that she, the acknowledging party Tamystha, has agreed that after her death there shall belong to her daughter Taorsenouphis, born to her from her deceased husband, Sabion, son of Heron, the share that belongs to her of an old house and courtyard, amounting in all to one-half, purchased from Ptolemais and Didis and Ta . . . and held in common and undivided, with all the appurtenances, in the aforesaid village of Talei, of which the neighbours and the other rights are set forth in the contracts relating to it; and also the furniture which shall be left by the same Tamystha and the utensils and the household gear and clothing and sums due her of any kind whatsoever, on condition that Taorsenouphis shall provide a fitting funeral and laying out for her mother Tamystha, and shall give to her brother, Heron, the twenty drachmas of silver which their mother Tamystha agrees has been given to him. For as long as she lives the acknowledging party, Tamystha, shall have complete power with respect to the possessions that are the subject of this agreement, to administer them as she wishes.

The subscriber is Ischyrion, son of Ischyrion, about 26(?) years old, with a scar on his left knee. The witnesses are Eutychos, son of Areios, about 62 years old, with a scar in mid-forehead; Sagathes, son of Areios, about 39(?) years old, with a scar on his right shin; Ptollarion, son of Eutychos, about . . years old, with a scar on his left eyebrow; Pakebkis, son of Psoiphis, about 42 years old, with a scar on his right eyebrow; Onnophris, son of Panesis, about 21(?) years old, with a scar on his right calf; Psenkebkis, son of Pakebkis, about 4[.]? years old, with a scar on his right eyebrow.

I, Tamystha, daughter of Apollonios son of Herakleides, my mother being Thenpetenouphis, acknowledge that I have agreed that after my death there shall belong to my daughter Taorsenouphis the half share of the house and court and the property that shall be left by me, and I agree to the other stipulations as aforesaid. Ischyrion, son of Ischyrion, wrote for them because they are illiterate.

I, Eutychos, son of Areios, bear witness as aforesaid.

I, Sagathes, son of Areios, bear witness as aforesaid.

I, Ptollarion, son of Eutychos, bear witness as aforesaid.

I, Pakebkis, son of Psoiphos, bear witness as aforesaid.

I, Onnophris, son of Panesis, bear witness as aforesaid.

I, Psenkebkis, son of Pakebkis, bear witness as aforesaid.

Registered through Lourios, who has charge of the registry office at Tebtynis.

148. A woman divides her property between her husband and son

P.Diog. 11–12
Ptolemais Euergetis, AD 213

This document, in which a woman arranges for the distribution of her property after her death, is curious in form and remarkable in contents. Technically it must be considered a *donatio mortis causa*, like **147**, a document not meeting the specifications to be considered a will but taking effect at death with retroactive force. It is, however, not written in the formulary typical of such texts, but in an idiosyncratic formula, and lacks registration at the public record office. The document is drawn up shortly after Caracalla's grant of universal Roman citizenship, but Isidora does not yet bear the name Aurelia nor does the document show any signs of Roman legal practice.

These irregularities may be the result of the situation in which it was written. Isidora was the second wife of Marcus Lucretius Diogenes, and the pair had been married less than four years, how much less we do not know. With an infant son whose nurse is specifically provided for, she may well (as the editor speculates) have died shortly after childbirth, certainly very young. This may therefore represent an informal testament drawn up with Isidora on her deathbed, drawing on the family members and friends within easy reach as witnesses rather than the usual group of outsiders to the family circle.

Year twenty-two of Emperor Caesar Marcus Aurelius Severus Antoninus Parthicus Maximus Bretannicus Maximus Germanicus Maximus Pius Augustus, in the month of Hadrianos, in Ptolemais Euergetis of the Arsinoite nome. I, Isidora daughter of Ptolemaios, from the *metropolis* of the Arsinoite nome, from the quarter of the Sacred Gate, with as guardian my husband Marcus Lucretius Diogenes, Antinoite,[1] and however else he is named, having established a division of my property, have allotted to my son Isidoros, on the day before my death, any fields and buildings and gold objects and clothing belonging to me . . . which I have according to the agreement (of my marriage) made with my husband Lucretius Diogenes, with the exception of my two slaves and 500 drachmas of silver. These I confer upon my husband, Lucretius Diogenes. I do not wish him to reclaim my two slaves, nor the 500 drachmas, since I have allotted them to him in advance. I have a pair of gold bracelets weighing 2 minas, and a pair of arm-bands weighing 3 minas, and likewise other objects of gold weighing 5 quarters, and clothing and bronze objects. I have bequeathed all these to my son. I have bequeathed the pair of gold bracelets to be sold and the proceeds to pay for my funeral. Let my mother Harpokratiaina and my husband Lucretius Diogenes, father of my son, take charge of my son and provide to his nurse support on his behalf from all my possessions. I have bequeathed all these things in the presence of Sarapammon son of Valerius, lessee of the six-witness (document?)[2] for the village of Philadelphia, and of my mother Harpokratiaina and of my sister NN and of Aurelius Egnatius son of Apollinarios and my aforesaid guardian and husband Lucretius Diogenes and Marcus Aurelius Serenus. The division is authoritative.

I, Isidora daughter of Ptolemaios, have bequeathed to my son the aforesaid (possessions) through the aforesaid witnesses as aforesaid. I, Marcus Lucretius Diogenes her husband and guardian, wrote for my wife Isidora because she is illiterate, and I was present at the division.

I, Sarapammon, lessee of the village of Philadelphia, wrote the division as aforesaid.

[1] See **3.106**.

[2] A term not found elsewhere; Sarapammon evidently leased a government contract allowing him a monopoly on the drawing up of these formal documents in his village.

149. Woman burdened by responsibility for unproductive public land

P. Oxy. VI 899 (*BL* I 328, III 133, IV 60, VI 99, VII 132, VIII 238)
Oxyrhynchos, A D 200

This long and complex document is part of a petition from Apollonarion to the strategos of the Oxyrhynchite nome, seeking relief from the responsibility for a quantity of public land imposed upon her. (The Roman government sought to protect its tax revenues by assigning unwanted public land to solvent individuals, who had at least to pay the taxes on it, whether they cultivated it or not: see Rowlandson, 1996, 88–92.)

The case appears to have proceeded from an original petition (surviving in sections 1–3) of Apollonarion to the *dioiketes* (a financial official of the province), which quoted decisions of earlier governors of Egypt supporting the principle that women should not be burdened with compulsory cultivation of land (sections 2–3). The *dioiketes'* favourable decision (now lost) was communicated by the then acting strategos to the local officials (embedded in section 4), but evidently this did not have sufficient effect, and Apollonarion petitioned the *dioiketes* again. This petition is partly surviving in sections 4 and 5, partly lost; the *dioiketes'* favourable response is also lost. Apollonarion then wrote the present document (incorporating all these earlier ones) to the new strategos to ask him to order the local officials to co-operate (section 6).

The basis for the rulings exempting women is nowhere clearly stated. Apollonarion describes herself as 'a woman without a husband or helper', and both the perceived vulnerability of women to mistreatment in business affairs and their assumed inability to carry out the physical labour of cultivation are likely to have led to the official decision. But the large size of Apollonarion's compulsory assignment (undoubtedly in excess of two hundred arouras) suggests that she possessed enormous landed wealth; compulsory assignments were usually proportionate to, but only a small fraction of, a person's total landholding. Her protestations of bankruptcy are therefore probably rather overstated.

(1) [To his highness the *dioiketes* Flavius Studiosus, from Ap]ollonarion also called [Aristandra, daughter of Aristandros, her mother being Di]dyme daughter of [. . . of Oxyrhynchos] city. [(*Two very fragmentary lines*) . . . I cultivate . . .] 20 arouras near the *metropolis*, . . . arouras near Chysis in the pastures of Dionysias, and . . . arouras near . . . and 110 arouras near Ision Panga, and 38½ arouras near Seryphis, and . . . arouras near Senekeleu and Ke. . . As long as I had the power I cultivated these and [paid . . .] the taxes, but since it has befallen me as the result both of the extra levies ordained . . . by his excellency the prefect Aemilius Saturninus and of other causes and . . . to have perforce spent nearly the entire year on them, not only being hard pressed . . . but also in consequence [having sacrificed?] both my household stock, my personal ornaments, and . . . and a large quantity of other property worth a considerable amount for quite a small sum . . . I am hence reduced to extreme poverty. For which reason, in order that I may not become a wanderer . . . as I have only . . . to live on, I present this petition, and beg you [to take pity on] what has befallen me, and to release me from the cultivation of the aforesaid [lands, and to write to] the strategos of the Oxyrhynchite nome instructions that the official in each village shall provide for the cultivation being performed [by others]; for men are the persons suitable for undertaking the cultivation, as you yourself, my lord, know . . . owing to your innate kindness, I have appended . . . in order that I may be completely benefited through you. Farewell.

(2) Year 18 of the deified Aelius Antoninus (*Pius=AD 154*), Th[oth . . ., in the case of . . .]etis daughter of Ptollion: Saturninos, advocate, said, 'Ptollion the father of my client was [during his lifetime?] appointed [to cultivate] crown and public land near the villages of Bousiris, Thinteris, and . . . in the Herakleopolite nome. He died leaving her as his heir, and since the village scribes of these villages are, contrary to the regulations forbidding

this, imposing her father's assignment upon her, and it has been decided by prefects and epistrategoi from time to time that women are not to be forced to undertake this duty, she too requests, citing these judgements, that she may be released from the assignment, which pertains only to men.'

(3) Parmenion said, 'Let the judgements upon such cases be read.' There was read . . . a decree of Tiberius Alexander in the 2nd year of Galba (*AD 68/9*), forbidding women to be made cultivators, . . . and (a decision of) Valerius Eudaimon the prefect to the same effect in the 5th year of Antoninus (*141/2*), . . . and another of Minicius Corellianus, epistrategos in the 10th year of Antoninus Caesar the lord (*146/7*); whereupon Parmenion said, 'In accordance with the judgements read out, Tathun[. . . should be] released from the cultivation . . ., and . . . other cultivators be appointed in her stead for the land.' I, Apollonarion also called Aristandra, have presented the petition. Signed, the 7th year, Phamenoth 6 (*2 March 199*).

(4) So far the copy of the letter and the petition; acting in conformity with which the royal scribe of the nome and deputy strategos Ammonianos wrote instructions to the officials of the villages where the lands are situated as follows: 'Ammonianos, royal scribe and deputy strategos, to the village scribe of Chysis and those of the other villages. I send you a copy of the petition presented to me by Apollonarion also called Aristandra, to which is joined a letter of his highness the *dioiketes*, and also a petition concerning the cultivation for which she declared herself not to be liable, in order that you may, in accordance with the judgements on the subject, hold an inquiry and report to me. Signed, the 7th year, Pachon 27 (*22 May 199*).'

(5) The transfer of obligation to other cultivators ought accordingly to take place in conformity with your letter, and the rents should be exacted from those who have been cultivators; I therefore entreat you, if it please your Fortune, to order that stricter instructions be written to the present strategos of the nome to compel the officials to make the transfer in accordance with the orders they received, and the collectors to exact the dues from the replacement cultivators of the land, and not to harass me, a woman without a husband or helper, following your previous instructions in this matter, that I may obtain relief. Farewell. Presented by me, Apollonarion also called Aristandra. Year 8, Tybi 1[.] (*6–15 January 200*). Signed. Signed by me Aufidius Ammonios.

(6) Thus far the petition, the list, and the letter; in accordance with which I entreat you to instruct the local officials to make the transfer of obligation as I requested, and the collectors to exact the dues from the proper persons. Year 9, Thoth 1. I, Apollonarion also called Aristandra, daughter of Aristandros,

have presented (this). I, Cornelius son of Pekysis, have been appointed her guardian. I, . . . assistant, have brought the petition. Year 9, Thoth 1 (*29 August 200*).

150.   A wealthy woman serves the public

P.Oxy. XXXVI 2780 (*BL* VII 153, VIII 262)
Oxyrhynchos, 16 July AD 553

The late Roman state only increased the pressure on well-to-do landowners to discharge public duties. Most civic offices were discharged by wealthy men at their own expense. It may seem paradoxical that the richest and most powerful residents of the empire accepted a system that placed on them great burdens and risks, but they gained thereby low basic rates of taxation and the political and social power that went with their visible control of public functions.

These burdens rested essentially on the family property, but they were normally discharged by the family's adult male members, regardless of in whose name the property was registered, a significant part of it often in women's names in fact. Occasionally, however, a woman held the public offices, perhaps because her house had no eligible male at the time (cf. Lewis, 1990). Such is Flavia Gabrielia, a very high-ranking woman holding at once all the principal civic offices: *logistes, prohedros*, and father of the city. It is unlikely that she actually carried out public business, but her property in effect bore the responsibility for any shortfalls in the revenues and expenses for which those offices were liable. In this document Gabrielia receives the acknowledgement of a water-supplier for the public bath of the city for receipt of his salary for the first portion of the year about to begin.

Year 27 of the reign of our most god-like and pious master Flavius Iustinianus, the eternal Augustus and Emperor, and in the 12th year after the consulship of Flavius Basilius the most illustrious, Epeiph 22 of the 1st indiction in the city of the Oxyrhynchites. To Flavia Gabrielia, the most honourable and magnificent patrician, who obtained the offices of *logistes* and *prohedros* and father of the city of this illustrious city of the Oxyrhynchites, on behalf of the House of Timagenes of noble memory for the fortunate *logisteia*[1] of the second indiction through you, the worshipful Christophoros, her deputy, Aurelius Timotheos, water-supplier of the public bath of the same city, son of Paulos. I agree that I have received from your honour now already on account of my salary for the first instalment of the fortunate *logisteia* of the 2nd indiction 2 gold solidi on private standard otherwise . . . through the most admirable John, your honour's weigher, total 2 gold solidi on private standard, and for the security of your honour I have made this declaration to you, which is valid written as a single copy and in reply to the formal question I gave my assent. I, Aurelius Timotheos, son of Paulos, the aforesaid, have made this declaration having received the said 2 solidi on private standard on account of my salary for the first instalment of the *logisteia* of the 2nd indiction and all is satisfactory to me as written above. I, . . . son of . . . wrote for him on request as he is illiterate. Completed by me, Justus, deacon.

[1] The term of office of the *logistes*, lasting one year.

151. Wealthy woman caught in cash squeeze

PSI 1 76
Alexandria, A D 572 or 573

This affidavit, drawn up in duplicate by Flavia Christodote for signature by the *defensor civitatis*[1] of Alexandria, sets out her claims against Flavius Eustathios, an Alexandrian banker. Christodote, though wealthy in land, had considerable debts and was hard-pressed by creditors. She was, in turn, owed a considerable sum by her brother, Kometos. Kometos arranged for Eustathios to pay Christodote on his behalf, in effect refinancing his obligations through the banker. But Eustathios failed to pay on the agreed-upon date. The surviving copies were not in fact submitted to the *defensor*, and we do not know if other copies were. The affidavit, though clear enough in itself, omits key information about the case (where was Kometos, and what was he doing? Who were Christodote's creditors?), and the outcome of events is entirely unknown. On this text, see further Keenan (1978).

The sum at stake here, sixty-one pounds of gold, is enormous by the standards even of the wealthiest families of the Egyptian countryside (Christodote lived in Oxyrhynchos), something like 1500 times the annual income required to support a family in modest comfort. Even if it amounted to the entire value of her property (which is doubtful), Christodote was a multimillionaire. The rhetorical force of the document certainly shows that she both operated with confidence in the higher levels of finance and employed top-quality lawyers to present her case.

In the reign of our most divine and most august ruler, Flavius Justinus, the eternal Augustus and Emperor . . .
I, Flavia Christodote, with God, illustrious daughter of John of glorious memory, deceased patrician, give affidavit to you, Flavius Eustathios, the most brilliant count and banker, concerning the matters set forth below.
The good faith of contracts, when preserved, places those who execute them in praise and preserves in purity the disposition of those who have made the contracts; in precisely the same manner, when trampled, it assur-edly produces the opposite results. So then, Your Magnificence recalls that It[2] reached settlement with me in writing concerning my most renowned brother, the lord Kometos, for sixty-one pounds of gold, with the total interest on them [for repayment] within an agreed-upon term day, and (behold!) the term day passed by and It did not satisfy the terms of Its agree-ment, so that I therefore am prepared in the future to go to the queen of cities and to obtain my rights through the blessed and justifacient Crown. For I have a case (?) against no one but your Brilliancy which on behalf of

my aforementioned most renowned brother entered into the settlement with me for the same sixty-one pounds of gold. The fact that I am wrestling with debts and am hourly harassed by my creditors is known to all; but in addition, the real property left behind for me in the (province) of Arcadians, from which I derive my essential nourishment, is under the circumstances about to be handed over to my creditors, so that the consequent damage focuses on Your Brilliancy which till now has not furnished me with what is owed to me by It, so that I might be able to free myself from my creditors.

Therefore, whether as a result of this culpability some damage may grate against me and I shall be in jeopardy with respect to the real property left behind for me in the (city) of (the) Oxyrhynchites, or whether I shall incur expenses by reason of my living away from home, these I intend to demand back from Your Brilliancy which is unwilling without litigation to make satisfaction to me for Its agreement. Therefore, in order to remove every plea and so that Your Brilliancy may know that as a result of Its procrastination It is liable to me both for the expenses that naturally occur to me because of your delaying and for those that are about to be taken from my estate by my creditors because of my inability to pay my debts, amounts equivalent to what I have not received from Your Brilliancy, those agreed upon by It for me in behalf of my most renowned brother, therefore I have utilised the present affidavit, sent to It through the most eloquent *defensor* of the (city) of (the) Alexandrians, with my subscription and His Eloquence's, a copy of which I have retained in my possession for my own protection with the aforementioned most eloquent defensor's signature. And I beg It by the Holy and Consubstantial Trinity and the victory and safety of our gloriously triumphant rulers, Flavius Justinus, the eternal Augustus, greatest benefactor and emperor, and Aelia Sophia, our most august empress, not to depart from the (city) of (the) Alexandrians until It makes satisfaction to me for the gold that was agreed upon for me by It, as mentioned above.

[1] A municipal offical, concerned with justice.
[2] Use of the third person form of address (It = Your Magnificence = you) is characteristic of the floridly polite late antique style.

152.   Father ends daughter's marriage to 'lawless' husband

P.Oxy. I 129
Oxyrhynchos, sixth century A D

This document, in which a father removes his daughter from her husband (cf. **138**) because of his behaviour, illustrates both how the woman's interest is protected by her father, and the expectation that a woman be properly treated in a marriage (see also **154**). The habitual formalism of Byzantine use of honorific titles produces the irony that the doer of 'lawless deeds' is addressed as 'my most honourable son-in-law'. Another copy of the document, which does not survive, was kept by the father.

. . . eleventh indiction. I, John, father of Euphemia, my daughter subject to my power[1], do send this present deed of separation and dissolution to you, Phoibammon, my most honourable son-in-law, by the hand of the most illustrious *defensor*[2] Anastasios of this city of the Oxyrhynchites. It is in substance as follows: 'For since it has come to my ears that you are giving yourself over to lawless deeds, which are pleasing neither to God nor to man, and are not fit to be put into writing, I thought it well that the marriage between you and her, my daughter Euphemia, should be dissolved, seeing that, as is aforesaid, I have heard that you are giving yourself over to lawless deeds and that I wish my daughter to lead a peaceful and quiet life. I therefore send you the present deed of dissolution of the marriage between you and my daughter Euphemia, by the hand of the most illustrious *defensor* aforesaid with my own signature, and I have taken a copy of this document, subscribed in the hand of the said most illustrious *defensor*. Wherefore for the security of the said Euphemia my daughter I send you this deed of separation and dissolution written on the 11th day of the month Epeiph in the eleventh indiction.'
I, John, the aforesaid, father of Euphemia, my daughter, send the present deed of separation and dissolution to you, Phoibammon, my most honourable son-in-law, as is above written.

[1] I.e. still under *patria potestas*.
[2] See **151**, note 1.

153. **Woman complains of violent and abusive husband**

P.Oxy. VI 903 *(BL* III 133)
Oxyrhynchos, fourth–fifth century A D

This remarkable affidavit lacking all indication of date, use, or addressee shows the seamy side of a marriage that began, in traditional Egyptian fashion, without written documentation and was provided with contractual support only after some time. The parties, owners of a number of slaves, were both clearly well-to-do land-owners. Their slaves found themselves caught in the middle of bitter domestic strife. Among notable elements in the woman's description of events are: the role of the bishops as mediators, her reliance on her husband to regulate her tax payments to the state, and the constant violence of the husband's treatment of slaves.

Concerning all the insults uttered by him against me. He shut up his own slaves and mine together with my foster-daughters and his overseer and his son for seven whole days in his cellars, having insulted his slaves and my slave

Zoe and almost killed them with blows, and he applied fire to my foster-daughters, having stripped them completely naked, which is contrary to the laws; and, saying to the same foster-daughters, 'Give up all that is hers', they said, 'She has nothing with us'; and, saying to the slaves as they were being beaten, 'What did she take from my house?' they said under torture, 'She has taken nothing of yours, but all your property is safe.' Zoilos went to see him because he had shut up his foster-son, and he said to him, 'Have you come on account of your foster-son or of such a woman, to talk about her?' And he swore in the presence of the bishops and of his own brothers, 'In future I will not hide all my keys from her' (he trusted his own slaves but he did not trust me);[1] 'I will stop and not insult her.' And a marriage contract was made, and after these agreements and the oaths he again hid his keys from me; and when I had gone out to the church on the sabbath,[2] he had the outside doors shut on me, saying, 'Why did you go to the church?' and speaking many terms of abuse into my face and through his nose; and concerning the 100 artabas of wheat due to the state on my account, he paid nothing, not a single artaba. Having got control of the books, he shut them up saying, 'Pay the price of the hundred artabas', having himself paid nothing, as I said previously; and he said to his slaves, 'Provide helpers, to shut her up also.' Choous his assistant was taken off to prison, and Euthalamos gave security for him which was not enough. So I took a bit more and gave it for the said Choous. When I met him at Antinoopolis[3] having my bathing-bag(?) with my ornaments, he said to me, 'Anything you have with you, I shall take because of the security which you gave to my assistant Choous for his dues to the state.' His mother will bear witness to all this. He also persistently vexed my soul about his slave Anilla, both at Antinoopolis and here, saying 'Send away this slave, for she knows how much she has got possession of', probably wanting to get me involved, and on this pretext to take away anything I have myself. But I refused to send her away. And he kept saying, 'After a month I will take a courtesan for myself.' God knows this is true.

[1] This sentence is inserted between the lines.
[2] I.e. Saturday.
[3] The couple perhaps had property at Antinoopolis, or some other reason for spending time there as well at Oxyrhynchos.

154. A turbulent marriage to violent husband ends in divorce

P.Oxy. L 3581
Oxyrhynchos, fourth–fifth century A D

Like the preceding affidavit, this petition recounts a troubled relationship that began without legal formalities, hit difficulties, was patched back up with mediation by clergy, was provided with contractual sanctions for misbehaviour, and in the end collapsed again. Here, the husband's violence is against the wife; indeed, she claims that their original union was unwilling on her part. The most outrageous part of the husband's deeds, however, is his endangerment of the wife by his behaviour toward soldiers billeted in their house and his persistent involvement with another woman, which the complainant here describes virtually as bigamy. The wife has already sent him a divorce notice, without much effect. Although it is difficult to disentangle the course of events from the sensationalist and ex parte narrative presented in this petition, it is clear that the petitioner (who signed the subscription herself) seeks financial redress.

The mention of unilateral repudiation of the husband by the wife is of great interest, because most evidence for divorce in this period concerns separation by mutual agreement. The lack of a date, however, makes it difficult to correlate this repudiation with the history of imperial legislation on divorce.

[To Flavius] Marcellus, tribune and officer in charge of the peace, from Aurelia Attiaina from the city of the Oxyrhynchites. A certain Paul, coming from the same city, behaving recklessly, carried me off by force and compulsion and cohabited with me in marriage . . . a female child by him . . . taking [him] into our house . . . his objectionable course of action and all my property . . . leaving me, with my infant daughter too, in . . . he cohabited with another woman and left me bereft. And after a time he again beguiled me through priests (*presbyteroi*) until I again took him into our house, stating in writing for me that the marriage was abiding and that if he wished to indulge in the same objectionable behaviour he would pay a fine of two ounces of gold, and his father stood surety in writing for him. And when I took him into our house, he tried to behave in a way that was worse than his first misdeeds, scorning my orphan state, not only in that he wrought devastation in my house but also, when soldiers were billeted in my house, he robbed them and ran away, and I endured insults and punishments to within an inch of my life. So, concerned not to run such risks again on his account, I sent him through the *tabularius*[1] a deed of divorce through the *tabularius* of the city, in accordance with imperial law. Again behaving recklessly, and having his woman in his house, he brought with him a crowd of lawless men and carried me off and shut me up in his house for <not?> a few days, and when I became pregnant, he again left me and cohabited with his same so-called wife; and now he tells me he will stir up malice against me. Wherefore I appeal to my lord's Staunchness to order him to appear in court and to have exacted from him, in accordance with his written agreement, the two ounces of gold and whatever damages I suffered on his account, and for him to be punished for his outrages against me. I, Aurelia Attiaina, presented this.

[1] A tax official, who also acted (as here) as a private notary.

155.   Proper behaviour in marriage

P.Cair.Masp. III 67310 + *P.Lond.* V 1711
Antinoopolis, AD 566–73

This marriage contract is unusual in form, drawn up after consummation of the
marriage it legitimises. It is an acknowledgement of indebtedness on the husband's
part, possibly cloaking a gift to his new wife whose virginity has by experience been
found intact (cf. **158**).[1] Corrections and above-the-line additions, and the absence
of names and signatures, indicate that this text is a draft or model. The actual marriage contract composed on its basis has survived in *P.Lond.* V 1711, which, however,
is very much damaged at its beginning, the very section where the Cairo draft text
is reasonably well-preserved. Both texts come from the archive of Dioskoros of
Aphrodite (**see Ch.3 Arch. L**) and date from 566–73, when Dioskoros was a lawyer
and notary in Antinoopolis, the provincial capital of the Lower Thebaid. The translation below starts with the front side of the Cairo papyrus.

Lately, in accordance with friendly and peaceful disposition, I joined myself
to Your Propriety by a giving[2] in legal marriage, based on sound expectations, if God should think best, also for the procreation of legitimate children; and, having found your sacred and secure virginity, I have proclaimed
it. Wherefore I have come to this guarantee in writing by which I agree that
I owe and am indebted for your wedding gifts or gifts before marriage,
agreed upon and pleasing between me and you, for 6 good-quality imperial solidi, less 36 carats, by the scale and standard of Antinoopolis. And I am
ready to furnish these to Your Nobility whenever you want, without any
neglect or delay, at the risk and wealth and expense of my property, general
and particular. And I agree no less in addition to support you legitimately
and to clothe you in likeness to all my family members of like status and in
proportion to the wealth available to me, as far as my modest means will
allow; and not to show contempt for you in any way or to cast you out from
marriage with me except by reason of unchastity or shameful behaviour or
physical misbehaviour established through three or more trustworthy free
men, be they country residents or city residents; and never to leave your
marriage bed or to run to other disorder or wickedness, provided however
that Your Propriety is obedient to me and preserves all benevolence towards
me and sincere affection in all fine and useful deeds and words, and is subject
to me in all ways that it befits all women of nobility to display toward their
own well-endowed and most beloved husbands, without insult or fickleness
or any other type of disdain whatever; rather you are to be full-time house-
keeper and husband-loving on my account, in keeping with the good and
proper disposition that will be displayed to you by me.

*The back of the Cairo text, which continues by detailing what will happen if the
husband fails to keep his part of the agreement, is somewhat damaged. The corresponding part of the London document is well-preserved, and is translated below:*

But if it should happen that I at some point in time disdain you in the above proclaimed manner, or cast you out without reasonable cause as above written, I, your aforementioned husband Horouonchis, am ready to furnish to Your Propriety, by reason of penalty for the said disdain, 18 solidi, deposited by me on demand without any prevarication or delay of trial or judgement or any pretext or blame or any kind of indisputably legal exception; you, too, however, my aforementioned bride and wife Scholastikia, being liable to the very same penalty if you should disdain me with respect to the above set forth agreements . . . [and] I your husband additionally agree not to invite any inconsequential man home to your presence or to hold a drinking-party in your presence with friends or relatives or anyone else if you are opposed to their presence. And for the security of either party and for our mutual-loving marriage, I have drawn up this agreement of union, or marriage contract, it being authoritative and secure wherever it is produced. And, having been asked the formal question, I have willingly and voluntarily agreed, not overcome by duress or fraud or violence or deceit or compulsion; and I have issued to you for security that which is written below (*sic*), and for each and every one of the clauses contained in it and for the payment of the penalty (if this should happen), putting under mortgage to you all my property, present and future, by way of pledge and by right of mortgage. And I the aforementioned husband Horouonchis agree in addition that I cannot at any occasion or time introduce other wives above my lawful wife, and if I do so I shall pay the same penalty.

[1] On this and other late antique marriage contracts, and payments for virginity, see Kuehn (1993), 103–9.
[2] Greek *ekdosis*; cf. **126** introd.

156. 'No-fault' divorce blames evil demon

P.Lond. V 1712
Antinoopolis, 15 July A D 569

This contract of divorce also comes from the archive of Dioskoros of Aphrodite (see **155** introd.). The husband is apparently an oarsman on a galley of the official fleet. The divorce is typical in blaming 'an evil demon' for the couple's marital discord and avoiding placing any blame on either party.[1] The document in its drafting seems to wander between subjective and objective formulations. The woman, Kyra, agrees in an additional clause added after the conclusion of the agreement to give up to the man, Mathias, the child with whom she is currently pregnant if he pays the expenses of childbirth without her having to sue him for the money.

In the reign and consulship of our most divine ruler, Flavius Justinus, the eternal Augustus and Emperor, fourth year, the twenty-first day of Epeiph in the third indiction, at Antinoopolis the most illustrious, we have established and made with one another this written separation or divorce in two identical copies, on the one side, Aurelius Mathias son of Phoibammon and Helene, oarsman, and on the other side, Aurelia Kyra, daughter of John and Tanoe, both originating from the city of the Antinoites. We agree with one another as to the matters set forth below. Since some time ago we were joined with each other for a legitimate <marriage> and community of life, with good hopes and for the procreation of children; but now, a dispute having grown up between us because of an evil demon, we have separated from one another; we have at this point come together for this written separation; we agree and each party agrees that it has received back its personal property in full, that we have and will have no cause against each other, whether for furnishings or for goods, whether for wedding-gifts, whether concerning the marriage or any other matter whatsoever, small or large, written or unwritten, thought or unthought, intentional or unintentional, ordered or not ordered; and we are not charging one another and we shall never make any charge in any court whatsoever, or outside court, because we have been completely released and paid in full and have been reconciled with one another; and it shall be possible for each one of us to enter into marriage with someone else if he (or she) should wish, without hindrance or impediment or reproach; and in addition to all these things, they have on each side sworn the most terrifying oath to abide by all the terms written herein and in no way to transgress them; but if one of us transgresses the written terms, the transgressing party agrees to pay to the abiding party, by way of penalty, two gold solidi, by fact and force exacted and deposited, in addition to which this dissolution, which we have agreed upon with one another, remains in every way authoritative and secure; and having been asked the formal question we have agreed to all the terms. And it has been additionally decided between us that, if the foetus of the above-written Kyra should survive and be born, on condition that Mathias, oarsman, give for the expense of the said childbirth six gold [carats] without judgement or trial, his father should receive the little child.

[1] On the evil demon, see Dickie (1993), 9–26.

V   Continuity and change in the Coptic texts

Coptic law has recently been defined as 'the particularities of legal practice evidenced in documents written in the Coptic language from roughly the sixth to the ninth centuries' (*The Coptic Encyclopedia* v, s.v. Law, Coptic). The earlier Coptic documentation is not in fact neatly separable from the Greek, some of which has been presented in the preceding section. The notary Dioskoros of Aphrodite, for example, was skilled in writing both

Greek and Coptic, and drafted marriage and divorce contracts in both languages.[1] It comes as no surprise, then (especially given the high percentage of Greek loanwords in Coptic), that there is some coincidence of terminology in Greek and Coptic contracts of marriage and divorce, or that Coptic divorces, like the Greek, include 'no-fault' divorces that accord both parties the right to remarry or, should they so choose, to enter monastic life. As in earlier periods of Egyptian history, marriage contracts of the late antique period are relatively uncommon, and those Coptic contracts that do survive tend to be concerned with property rights and settlements (Till, 1948). This probably reflects the relatively informal attitude that Egyptians (as opposed to Romans, and less so Greeks) had towards the act of marriage. The few known marriage documents in Coptic range over a broad period of time, from the sixth to the thirteenth century. Presented below is a series of documents that is not reflective of existing Greek documentation.

[1] See **155–6** and **Ch.3 Arch. L**; also MacCoull (1988), ch.2.

157.   Father marries off daughter

CPR IV 23
Akhmim, 29 August A D 610

This short text from Akhmim (Shmin in Coptic; Greek Panopolis) is one of the earliest known Coptic marriage documents. It is not a marriage contract proper, but a contract in which a father agrees to allow a man to marry his daughter, specifying a fine to be paid if the father breaks the agreement. Marriages arranged by parents, often through an intermediary, are frequently alluded to in Coptic documents; in other cases, however, the woman appears to exercise some initiative in the matter. The present contract gives little information about the circumstances surrounding the marriage, such terseness being common in Coptic documents of the period. Its use of Greek and Coptic and its list of witnesses are very typical for any Coptic legal document.

(*Greek*) In the name of the lord and ruler Jesus Christ, our God and saviour, (in) the reign of our most serene ruler Flavius Phocas, eternal Augustus and Emperor, sixth year, day 1 of Thoth, 14th indiction.
(*Coptic*) I, Pachom, son of Psate, the dye-seller and citizen of Shmin, although now I live in Tin in the district of Psoi, make this contract and write to Dioskoros, son of Arsenios, from this same town. I rejoice and agree that, if God grant that we live, from now on I give my daughter to you as wife. But if I deceive you and take her from you and give her to another, then it is necessary for me to pay three gold solidi as a fine. This contract is firm and valid everywhere.
(*2nd hand*) †I, Moses, son of Papnoute, the priest, am witness to this contract, as I was instructed.†

(*3rd hand*) †I, Johannes, son of Abraham, the priest from Tin, am witness to this contract, as I was instructed.†

(*1st hand*) I, Paulos, son of Megas, from Tin, was instructed and I made this contract with my hands and I act as witness to it.†

(*Back*) †The contract of Pahom the dye-seller and man of Shmin.

158.   A daughter-in-law is found not to be a virgin

KRU 67.13–46
Jeme, eighth century A D

The monk Paham, in his long and detailed will,[1] sets out clearly the problems connected with his son's marriage: Paham had opposed the match in the first place, the bride turned out not to be a virgin, and the couple (so the father says) lived together in discord for quite some time, but they eventually parted and lived separately until the death of Paham's son, which was followed by that of all of the children of the marriage. In the following excerpt, Paham sets out his views on the marriage.

I, Paham, have written this will with my own hand, while dwelling on the mountain of Jeme as a monk . . . I know that a person does not know his own way (in life), and I said, lest an illness come upon me and I die suddenly, with no one near me to whom I might send my words concerning the few meagre possessions that I have from my father and my mother and their home, since [. . . I had] three small children. I went and became a monk. I left them alive, and the three of them dwelled in the world. As for the eldest son, Papnute, he took a wife against my wishes. I was very grieved about this, for his life did not run smoothly from the time that he married her, quarrels and disturbances happening in his affairs. They came south to me and told me the reason: her virginity had not been intact (*at marriage*). I said that I wanted to have nothing to do with him, because he had not listened to me. I left it to God, the true judge, and the prayers of my holy father (*the superior*). After he (*my son*) left, his mind was deceived with flattering words, and she remained with him. He begat children with her, but his heart was distressed. He used to come and tell me his troubles on many occasions. He made me even more sad, but I didn't want to send him away on account of (my service to) God; for he was my flesh and blood. I set aside a small place for him, so he could live in my house, together with his possessions: silver, gold, bronze and clothing. But when I had acted for him, things happened to him that were ordained in another place. God called after him, in the manner of any person, and he died with his children at once. He left no living heirs behind him. Now, as God had made him and his children strangers to this world, I, myself, made him stranger to (*i.e. disinherited from*) my entire dwelling-place, which came to me from my father and his wife.

As for the inherited property in my possession, no one acting as his representative shall get it, because of the house that I gave him, in which he lived until his death with his wife . . . And his wife, herself, swears an oath concerning what she brought to it (*the marriage*), and takes it back, in a (fair) share. You, Jacob (*Paham's second son*), should treat her like the childless widows that live near you in your village, and kindly allow her to go home, back to the village she came from.

---

[1] For a German version of the entire long will see Till (1954), 169–77. Our translation is based on MacCoull (1986), 49–50.

159. Divorce agreement

E. Balogh and P. E. Kahle, Jr., 'Two Coptic Documents Relating to Marriage', *Aegyptus* 33 (1953), 331–40
Hermopolis, sixth–eighth century A D

Documents for divorce from late antique Egypt are even rarer than marriage contracts, but this does not mean that divorce itself was infrequent. As with marriage, divorce was relatively informal in the Coptic textual evidence and a document of divorce was only drawn up when there was a question concerning property settlement. The clause permitting the remarriage of the divorced man and the provision for a fine should the wife prosecute the husband are standard. The present text suggests that the divorce was initiated by the wife, who provides a brief account of the circumstances surrounding the separation that was formalised by this document. But the separation may in fact have been by common consent, with a corresponding document, containing similar terms, drawn up by the husband for the wife.

I, Dophile, daughter of the late Antone, man of Shmoun,[1] write to my husband [. . .], the son of George of Shmoun, saying: [Since] I was given to him as wife, I did not remain with him and I [decided] to leave him. We agreed with each other and were separated from each other. If you want to take (another) wife, I shall not be able to prosecute you. And if you want to take her as wife, namely Doketsh, I shall not ever be able to prosecute you. If I want to prosecute you myself, I shall pay six solidi without (recourse to) judgement or law. By almighty God and the health of those who [rule] over us, I swear that I shall not ever take action against you.
(*2nd hand*) †I, Dophile, daughter of the [late] Antone man of Shmoun, I agree to this (?) as it is written.†
(*3rd hand?*) †I, Kosma, son of the late [Apa] Kyre man of Shmoun, I am witness.†
(*3rd hand?*) †I, Shenoute, son of the late Johannes man of [Shmoun], I am witness.†

---

[1] The Coptic name for Hermopolis.

160.   Complaints over unpaid alimony

W. C. Till, 'Eine koptische Alimentenforderung,' *Bulletin de la Société
d'Archéologie Copte* 4 (1938), 71–8
Seventh century A D (?)

Even with a settlement, divorce in the Coptic documentation was not free from
problems. The most frequent violation of divorce settlements appears to have been
the non-payment of alimony. In this text, an invalid woman begs an unspecified
official to help restore the alimony payments that her former husband has ceased to
pay. In doing so, she gives a brief narrative of the break up of her marriage and the
subsequent events that led to her current predicament. The implicit interaction
between the woman and her ex-husband's new wife is not uncommon in such cases.
The person to whom the text is directed is not named, but the form of address suggests that it was probably a religious official, a local priest or bishop. Pleas to local
religious leaders from abandoned or widowed women are common among Coptic
documentary texts; such officials were often an important part of women's support
networks.

Be so good, by the glory which God granted you, and hear of my maltreatment, so that God bless you. May your lordship hear of my maltreatment
by Paul, my husband: I bore him three sons before I became sick and, God
knows, since I became sick I bore another son. When he saw that God
brought the sickness onto me, he cast me aside. He went off with another
(woman) and he left the children abandoned. After plenty of quarrels
between me, him and the other woman whom he took, [it was agreed] that
he should give me yearly alimony, consisting of 4 artaba-measures of barley,
4 *xestes*-measures of oil and 4 [measures] of wine, and a dress each year, and
a cloak each year. But he also deprived me of the alimony and has not paid
to me since last year, except for a mere artaba-measure of barley. I ask for
nothing except the alimony which he established for me, for I am sick and
I live on it. God bless you.

161.   Repudiation of a wife

Ep 270
Sixth–seventh century A D

The actual mechanics of divorce were fairly simple if there was no property settlement to consider. A spouse could leave or, depending on the ownership of the
house, simply force the other spouse to leave. The most common reason for divorce,
whatever its mechanics, was remarriage. In this brief text, a man divorces his first
wife, marries his second and also marries his daughter to his new son-in-law, presumably to secure the familial relationship. An earlier fragmentary text on the same

document (not translated here) seems to allude to an earlier separation between the couple in which Tecoshe went to the nearby town of Jeme.

Shenetom, the fisherman, son of Pcale, living in Pashme,[1] has thrown out his wife Tecoshe. He has married Teret, daughter of Komes, son of Pare, and he has given his daughter to her son. 10th indiction.

[1] A village in the district of Koptos.

5 Economic activities

Introduction

The documentary evidence of the papyri tells us far more about the economic lives of women than we can deduce from any literary evidence. Although it would be difficult to maintain that many women had 'careers' in the modern sense of the term, except in a very few specialised areas, the evidence from Egypt suggests that women's economic activities were not confined to circumstances in which they were either working as slaves or working because they needed to do so in order to survive. They must also have supplied much routine labour in contexts which do not find description in the written evidence. What we have in the papyri certainly suggests that the somewhat restrictive legal institutions and provisions did not inhibit independence and initiative as much as we might expect.

This chapter is divided into two sections. **Section I** traces in chronological sequence the developments in women's capacity to possess agricultural land, and to participate in agricultural work or management. **Section II** looks at the range of women's other economic activities: property ownership, the use of money, and types of employment, particularly in weaving and prostitution. In **Section II**, the texts are grouped by subject matter as much as by date.

I Women and agricultural land

The early Ptolemies were responsible for important agricultural improvements in Egypt, introducing better strains of wheat and new varieties of vine, and extending and improving the quality of the agricultural land. Development may have been particularly intensive in the Fayum, but was clearly widespread throughout Lower and Middle Egypt. However, women's participation in these developments, and access to the possession of arable land in their own right, was significantly restricted by the conditional system of land tenure (Rowlandson, 1995). Much land was allocated in temporary grants to groups who performed certain important functions within the state: thus soldiers received allotments (kleroi) of kleruchic land; high officials received gift-estates or *doreai*; and newly acquired royal land

26 A woman and child at the harvest
(Detail from) Tomb of Petosiris
Tuna el-Gebel, late fourth–early third century BC

The lavish family tomb of Petosiris, high priest of Thoth at Hermopolis between the last years of Persian rule in Egypt and the reign of Ptolemy I, is notable for the relief scenes in its colonnaded entrance hall (*pronaos*); although Egyptian in conception and style, they exhibit some Greek influence, such as in the depiction of the figures. But the presence of a woman (with a male child) in this harvesting scene, albeit apparently in the subordinate role of gathering crops reaped by the man, is closer to Egyptian gender roles than to those of the Greek world. For reference to detailed studies of the tomb, and for translations of some of its inscriptions, see Lichtheim (1980), 44–54.

was held by royal farmers, also almost exclusively male. The groups of immigrant entrepreneurs developing the Fayum in the mid–third century attested in the Zenon correspondence and other contemporary groups of papyri were resolutely male, although women were included among their native workforce (as perhaps in **162**). Even by the late second century BC, no woman seems to have held land in the Arsinoite village of Kerkeosiris.

However, on the temple and royal lands of Upper Egypt, where older traditions prevailed, Egyptian women are found throughout the Ptolemaic period possessing arable land in their own right. Egyptian custom also seems to have allowed women to perform agricultural work in the fields, as we see from the reliefs on the Tomb of Petosiris (**Plate 26**).[1] Upper Egypt remained a predominantly Egyptian milieu despite some Greek influence from military units and from Ptolemais, the Greek city founded by Ptolemy I (cf. **Ch.3 Arch.C**); and women are regularly documented in Egyptian, and later also Greek, contracts, buying or selling, inheriting, and leasing arable land (**163, 165–6**). Even in Lower Egypt, not only queens (cf. **2.9**) but also non-royal women might possess vineyards: the most striking example is Eirene daughter of Orpheus who possessed a vineyard and garden on royal and gift-estate land in the Arsinoite 'model-town' of Philadelphia (**164**).

By the first century BC, a major change had begun to take place in the tenure of kleruchic land, which before the end of the Ptolemaic period had become heritable, not only by sons who could be expected to take over the obligations of military service associated with it, but also by daughters (**167**). It was, however, left to the Roman administration when Egypt became a Roman province in 30 BC to take the final step and make kleruchic land fully private property (now called katoikic land), along with certain other categories of land, for instance 'bought land' (*eonemene*). This facilitated the wide-scale acquisition of agricultural land by women, both through inheritance and by purchase. It appears from land registers and other evidence throughout the Roman period that about one-third of landowners were women, perhaps owning between 16 and 25 per cent of the land.[2] Women from the imperial family of the Julio-Claudian dynasty are also documented as possessing Egyptian estates, for instance Antonia the Younger (see **2.17**).

Women at all levels of society can be found during the Roman period buying and selling agricultural land. The sale transactions, however, sometimes involved buying from or selling to close relatives (as indeed had been true of sales from the Ptolemaic period: **163**, cf. **2.30**); and one suspects that rather than being 'market transactions', these were employed to adjust the effects of the inheritance system (**168**). Although the Roman administration treated land as the property of single individuals, owners, both male and female, were in fact locked into a nexus of family and local connections which must have restricted the extent to which any individual really exercised a wholly free disposition over his or her property (cf. Rowlandson, 1996, chs. 5 and 6).

Although agricultural land was not included in the core of a bride's dowry, the *pherne*, in the Roman period it was occasionally given as a supplementary element (see **Ch.6 Sect.III** introduction; cf. **4.136**). The desire to provide for a daughter's future marriage may also have motivated purchases of land by parents on behalf of their daughters (**171**). According to the rules of intestate inheritance, women inherited private land on the same terms as other property; and this was no doubt a major factor in explaining the extensive ownership of land by women. However, it is interesting to see that even a woman who herself owned agricultural land might discriminate, when drawing up her will, between male and female heirs, reserving the agricultural land for the males (**170**).

As well as being the titular owners of land, women in the Roman period certainly could play an active role in agriculture. Women are documented undertaking various types of agricultural work for wages (**169**). Private letters from the Roman period commonly reveal women's involvement in agricultural management and decision-making (**172–3**, **180**). Women are also documented borrowing wheat in quantities which suggest that it was intended not merely to provide food for a household, but to finance a year's agricultural activities on credit (**178**). In contrast, it apparently remained extremely rare for women to undertake a tenancy of agricultural land: scarcely a handful of examples survive among nearly one thousand land leases of Roman or Byzantine date (**165(b)**), although leasing of land by women to male tenants was not uncommon (**179, 181**, cf. **172**).

Thus the Roman administration faced a dilemma in its policy towards female landowners. Male landowners were required to cultivate, or at least to pay the taxes on, unproductive public land. Women were officially exempted from this burden on the grounds of their weakness and unsuitability to agricultural tasks (**4.149**); yet some women evidently did not find agricultural management beyond their capabilities, and particularly by the third and fourth centuries A D, there were women who clearly derived enormous wealth from agriculture and associated activities (**174**, cf. **175**). The increasing prominence of female landowners may indeed be partly the result of their exemption from some of the burdens imposed on men, a privilege the Roman administration was increasingly reluctant to concede (cf. **176**). More generally, the pleas of weakness by women claiming assistance from public officials should not necessarily be understood literally, but represent a conscious strategy by articulate women to further their own ends by invoking an officially sanctioned image of female weakness (**177**).

[1] Cf. Herodotus' remark that Egyptian women engage in commerce and trade, while the men stay at home and do the weaving; quoted above, p. 3.

[2] Hobson (1983), Bagnall (1993a), 130.

162. Petition by a widow named Senchons to Zenon

P.Mich. I 29
Philadelphia, July 256 B C

An Egyptian widow complains to Zenon (see **Ch.3 Arch.A**), in a letter full of misspellings due to 'Egyptianisms'[1] that Nikias (an overseer of transport: see *P.Mich.* I 34) has summarily taken her ass, which she needs to carry beehives to the honeybearing pastures. Greek immigrant entrepreneurs of this period, such as Zenon and his associates, often owned hives which they leased to Egyptians, in return for a rent; tax was also paid to the king. This case illustrates Egyptian women's involvement in outdoor agricultural tasks (cf. **Plate 26**). The terse style, and reminder that Zenon himself and the king will suffer if the ass is not returned, are typical of petitions of this early period, even from a humble Egyptian woman to a man of great influence as Zenon was.

To Zenon, greeting, from Senchons. I petitioned you about my she-ass which Nikias took from me. If you had written to me about her, I would have sent her to you. If it seems good to you, tell him to return her, so that we may carry our beehives to the pastures, lest they be ruined both for you and the King. If you look into the matter, you will be persuaded that we are useful to you. I beg you and supplicate you not to keep me waiting, for I am a widow. Farewell.

(*Docket on the verso*) Year 30, Pachon 2[.]. Senchons, about an ass.

---

[1] Clarysse (1993): the writer was not Senchons herself, but a professional Egyptian scribe, using a rush pen.

163.   Sale of temple land between two women

P.Berl.dem. 3142 and 3144 (ed. Grunert, 1981)
West Thebes (Memnoneia), 9 July–7 August 199 BC

Formal Demotic contracts of sale normally consist of two parts, sometimes, though not always, made up at the same time and then written on the same papyrus. The first part is the 'writing for silver' or money-document (sẖ n ḏb3 ḥḏ, *syngraphe praseos*) in which the seller states that his (or her) heart has been satisfied with the money given by the buyer. The second part is the cession-document (sẖ n wy, *syngraphe apostaseos*), by which the seller withdraws any further claim on the sold property. Either part without the other may serve a function other than that of sale: a money-document without a cession-document may for instance be a mortgage or a will, a cession-document without a money-document may be drawn up when a party has lost a battle in court. A comparison of the phraseology of the typical example below with that of a Greek sale such as **165** shows that the Demotic sale is generally more elaborate and sophisticated in the formulae by which the purchaser's title to the property is guaranteed.

P.Berl.dem. 3142 and 3144 constitute the money-document and the cession-document for a sale of three plots of land, of about 2.5 arouras of agricultural land in the Memnoneia between two women, Senminis and Tanouphis. One year later the buyer Senminis sold half of the land to a certain Psenchonsis, son of Amenothes and Tanouphis, *pastophoros* of Amenhotep (P.Berl.dem. 3146). He may be a son of Tanouphis, who is the vendor in the present documents. In that case the sale is perhaps not a commercial transaction, but one of the many ways in which priestly families exchanged property (and family ties) among each other (cf. **2.30**).

The texts are dated to year 6 of the reign of the rebel king Haronnophris (Pestman, 1995b; see p. 8 above); P.Berl.dem. 3146 belongs to year 7 of his successor Chaonnophris, who continued the numbering of the regnal years of his predecessor.

(a) P.Berl.dem. 3142

Year 6, Pauni, of Pharaoh Haronnophris, may he live forever, beloved of Isis, beloved of Amon-Re, king of the gods, the great god.

The woman Tanouphis daughter of Psenthotes, her mother being Ata, has said to the woman Senminis daughter of Pachnoumis, her mother being Tamenos:

'You have satisfied my heart with the money of half of my ⅙ portion of the three plots of land which are in the temple estate of Amon on the island of the artisans on the west side of Thebes. Their list: 2 plots of land, taken together measuring 11 arouras with their surplus of measurement;

(neighbours)   South: the land of Pamonthes, son of Pachnoumis

North and West: the land of Taoueris daughter of Timolaos

East: the canal of Libys

The other plot of land, measuring 5 arouras with their surplus of measurement;

(neighbours)   South: the lands of Herieus son of Phatres

North: the land of Psenamounis son of Pachnoumis

East: the canal of Libys

West: the land of Pachnoumis son of *Pa-ws.t*

Total of the neighbours of all three plots of land mentioned above, of which I gave you half of their ⅙ portion.

I have given it to you. It belongs to you. Your half of the ⅙ portion of the three above-mentioned plots of land is it. I have received their price in money from you, complete without any remainder. My heart is satisfied with it. I have no claim whatever against you in his (*sic*) name. No person at all, myself included, shall be able to exercise authority over it except you from this day onwards. As for anyone who will proceed against you on account of them in my name or in the name of anyone at all, I shall cause him to stay away from you. I shall clear it (*sic*) for you from any document, any title-deed, from anything at all at any time. To you belong their documents and their title-deeds, wherever they are. Every document which has been drawn up for me about it (*sic*) and every document by virtue of which I am entitled in respect of them, it belongs to you, with the right conferred by them. To you belongs that by virtue of which I am entitled in respect of them. The oath or the proof which will be imposed upon you in the courthouse concerning the rights (conferred by) the above-mentioned document, which I have drawn up for you, to cause me to swear it, I will swear it, without alleging any title-deed or anything on earth against you.'

Written by Panechates son of Herieus.

(b) P.Berl.dem. 3144

Year 6, Pauni, of Pharaoh Haronnophris, may he live forever, beloved of Isis, beloved of Amon-Re, king of the gods, the great god.

The woman Tanouphis daughter of Psenthotes, her mother being Ata, has

said to the woman Senminis daughter of Pachnoumis, her mother being
Tamenos:

'I am far from you concerning your half of my ⅙ portion of the three plots
of land which are in the temple estate of Amon on the island of the artisans
on the west side of Thebes. Their list: 2 plots of land, taken together measuring 11 arouras with their surplus of measurement;

(neighbours) South: the land of Pamonthes, son of Pachnoumis
                     North and West: the land of Taoueris daughter of Timolaos
                     East: the canal of Libys

The other plot of land, measuring 5 arouras with their surplus of measurement;

(neighbours) South: the lands of Herieus son of Phatres
                     North: the land of Psenamounis son of Pachnoumis
                     East: the canal of Libys
                     West: the land of Pachnoumis son of *Pa-ws.t*

Total of the neighbours of all three plots of land mentioned above, of which
half of their ⅙ portion belongs to you, as I have made for you a document
of money concerning them in year 6, Pauni, of the pharaoh, may he live for
ever.

It belongs to you. Your half of the ⅙ portion of the three above-mentioned
plots of land is it. I have no claim at all against you in their name from today
onward. As for anyone who will proceed against you on account of them
in my name or in the name of anyone at all, I shall cause him to stay away
from you, whereas you are able to constrain me by the right conferred by
the document of money, which I have drawn up for you about them in year
6, Pauni, of the pharaoh, may he live forever, to carry out for you its obligations at any time, besides the document of cession above, to fulfil the two
documents. And I shall carry out for you their obligations at any time,
without a blow.'

Written by Panechates son of Herieus.

164. Arrangement for the management of garden land belonging to Eirene daughter of Orpheus

P.Mich. III 182
Philadelphia, 4 March 182 BC

Eirene daughter of Orpheus is one of few female landholders from the Ptolemaic
period whose activities are known from more than one text (*Pros.Ptol.* IV 8147;
discussed by Pomeroy, 1990, 158–60). By 185/4 BC, she was in possession of the
crown land and gift-estate mentioned below, consisting of vineyard, orchard and
garden land; in 183/2, she leased the crops of the orchard to Leontiskos and his
partners in return for their paying the state dues on this land. She also took on

the substantial loan from Nikandros of 44 talents 4800 drachmas at interest mentioned below. In the text translated here, Leontiskos and his partners (who had in
fact not paid the state dues of the previous year) contract with Nikandros to repay
Eirene's loan, in lieu of rent on the orchard, which they had again leased from
Eirene for the following year. Despite apparently gaining no economic benefit
herself from the arrangements described here, Eirene seems to have been a well-
to-do woman, who was probably literate (see *P.Mich.* III 183), and appears to have
supervised her own business actively, hiring labourers to work on the vintage, and
keeping detailed accounts.

Year 23, Panemos 28, Tybi 28, in Krokodilopolis of the Arsinoite nome.
Leontiskos son of Leontiskos, Persian of the *epigone*, and Thymos son of
Megakles, Macedonian of the *epigone*, and Tesenouphis son of Petous,
Arsinoite, agree with Nikandros, Syracusan of the troop of Theodoros of
the second hipparchy, holder of an eighty-aroura allotment, that they will
pay to him on behalf of Eirene daughter of Orpheus, Macedonian
woman,[1] to be credited against the loan, with interest, of 44 talents and
4800 drachmas granted in accordance with the mortgage of a vineyard and
garden belonging to her located in Philadelphia of the Herakleides division, contracted in year 23, month of Daisios: 48 talents of bronze money[2]
(which is) the rent of the olive, fig and pomegranate crops located in the
aforesaid garden on royal and gift-land[3] within a single boundary which
Leontiskos, Thymos and Tesenouphis have leased from Eirene for year 24,
according to contracts of lease; and (they agree) that they will make payments to Nikandros or to whomsoever he orders, in Philadelphia, according to the clauses in the contracts, from Pauni of year 23 to Thoth of year
24, 2 bronze talents per month; and in Phaophi, 8 bronze talents; in Hathyr
of the same year 15 talents; and in Choiak of the same year the remaining
17, Nikandros or his agents providing them with receipts for each
payment.

And if they do not make payments according to the stated terms, let
Leontiskos, Thymos and Tesenouphis immediately pay as penalty to
Nikandros what they owe plus half as much again. But if they in no way
infringe the contract, let Nikandros receive on Eirene's behalf the aforesaid
48 bronze talents towards the loan on mortgage and the interest in accordance with what was stated above, and whatever remainder they owe to him
in connection with the mortgage. If there is any shortfall in respect of the
48 bronze talents whether through ruin, risk or failure of the crops concerned in the aforesaid leases which Eirene made with the aforesaid men,
having received this from Eirene let him make a cancellation of the mortgage in the time specified therein.

If Nikandros, having received from the aforesaid men the 48 bronze
talents stated above, either does not credit them to Eirene or furthermore
having received the shortfall, does not make a cancellation of the mortgage,

let Nikandros immediately pay to Eirene a fine of one thousand silver drachmas of old Ptolemaic coin, and nonetheless let it be obligatory for Nikandros to make a cancellation of the mortgage. Let this agreement be binding everywhere.

[1] I.e. a woman of Macedonian ancestry.

[2] From *c.* 211 BC, monetary calculations in the Ptolemaic papyri were made in the progressively depreciating bronze currency rather than in silver, as was common earlier. Note that the penalty if Nikandros fails to cancel the mortgage after repayment is stated in the valuable old silver drachmas.

[3] We cannot tell whether Eirene's land lay on part of the former gift-estate which Apollonios the *dioiketes* held at Philadelphia (see **Ch.3 Arch. A** introd.). Note that Eirene's possession of this land was sufficiently secure to enable her to use it as security for a loan. However the reading here of the word meaning 'purchased', i.e. from the state (*BL* III 110), is very doubtful.

165.   Tatehathyris and the land 'The Point'

Pap.Lugd.Bat. XIX 2 and 3
West Thebes (Memnoneia), 109 BC

The documents relating to Tatehathyris were preserved with the family archive of her husband Totoes, discovered in two pots at Deir el Medina in 1905.[1] Tatehathyris (born *c.*129) married Totoes early in 109 BC. Her father Psenminis had died the previous autumn, and on 8 May, she and her brother Pikos (born *c.*136–134) drew up a division of their father's land ((**a**)). Pikos received two-thirds of the paternal inheritance, the double portion accorded to an eldest son by Egyptian custom, assuming responsibility for organising their father's funeral arrangements and for two-thirds of the cost.[2] Tatehathyris' share of the inheritance was the 7½ arouras known as 'the Point', the history of which can be reconstructed in detail (Pestman, 1978). It had descended with other property to Tatehathyris' father from her paternal grandmother Lobais. On 12 January 109 (before the inheritance was divided, and almost certainly before her marriage) Tatehathyris leased it out for two years. However, on 20 October 109, another lease ((**b**)) was made for the same land by Totoes to a different tenant, a woman, without any indication that the land belonged to his wife, not to himself! The next year Tatehathyris leased the land, along with other property, to her brother. In 104 Totoes acted as lessor, leasing it to a cavalryman, yet the next spring Tatehathyris received rent for it from her brother. And again in 101, it was leased out by Totoes.

In Greek contracts, Tatehathyris appears with a male guardian as the law required. In Egyptian legal transactions, women needed no guardian; yet Pestman has shown that in reality a male was sometimes present. It appears that before her marriage, or in transactions with other family members, Tatehathyris herself was formally a contracting party, even if she was actually accompanied or represented by a man, as in (**a**), while after her marriage, Totoes often simply acted in her stead in dealings with outsiders, as in (**b**) (Pestman, 1995a; *New Primer* p. 52)

(a)   Division of inheritance between Pikos and Tatehathyris

Pap. Lugd. Bat. XIX 2
8 May 109 BC

Although Tatehathyris acts without a guardian in this Demotic agreement, the use of masculine gender forms suggests that in fact a man may have been speaking on her behalf: Pestman (1995a), 84–5 (referring also to *Pap. Lugd. Bat.* XIX 1 = *P. Tor. Botti* 43).

Year 8, Pharmouthi 22.
Pikos son of Psenminis says to Tatehathyris daughter of Psenminis, his younger sister:
'I agree with you concerning the division, you agree with me concerning the division of 21 arouras of land, which our father gave us. I have given you the parcel of lands, which are on 'the Point', which cover 7½ arouras and their extension of measurement,[3] of which the neighbours are: South: Pasemis son of Thoteus; North: the field of Onnophris son of Psenminis; West: Onnophris son of Psenminis; East: the water of pharaoh,[4] as inheritance. You have given me 456⅓ deben and 6 artabas of wheat; on your head (there are still) 48 deben.[5] Whichever of us withdraws from doing everything in accordance with every word above, he shall give 5 talents before Montou,[6] 5 before Jeme and 5 to pharaoh, whereas he will (nevertheless) be forced to act in accordance with every word above.'

(b)   Totoes leases his wife's land to Tachrates

Pap. Lugd. Bat. XIX 3
20 October 109 BC

Quite apart from the fact that the land belongs not to the lessor, Totoes, but to his wife, this lease presents anomalies. The produce which the tenant pays Totoes cannot be rent, since she receives payment in return. The arrangement seems in effect to be a labour contract to grow a fodder crop (*arakos* was a legume, possibly wild chickling) with the intention, not of producing much yield, but of enriching the land by ploughing most of the crop back into the soil. Moreover, the final docket on the back (in Greek) suggests that Tachrates did not actually undertake any work herself; the land was apparently sub-leased, to Phibis, by a man who was presumably acting on her behalf as Totoes acted for Tatehathyris.

(*Greek*) Year 9, Phaophi 2, in the presence of Apollonios, the person in charge of the office of the *agoranomos* of the Memnoneia and of the lower toparchy of the Pathyrite (nome). Totoes, son of Smanres, has leased to Tachrates, daughter of Pesouris, Persian woman,[7] with her own son,

Pamonthes son of Psenamounis, as guardian, the land belonging to him in Pestenemenophis,[8] (measuring) 7½ arouras, whose neighbouring properties are: on the south: the land of Pasemis son of Thoteus; on the north: the land of Onnophris son of Psemminis, a hollow path running between them; on the east: (the canal) of Patinis; on the west: the land of Onnophris son of Psemminis, or whoever are the neighbours on all sides; for the sowing of the 9th year, to grow *arakos* on the above-written land, (Totoes?) being responsible for measuring out to the royal treasury the appropriate dues for the land that shall be inundated; on condition that Tachrates shall give to Totoes a half aroura's produce of *arakos* and that Totoes shall give to Tachrates two artabas of wheat on the threshing floors in return for the half aroura's produce of *arakos*. And the landlord may not lease out (the land) to others within this time period, nor may the tenant abandon the land (within) this time period; but (after the time has lapsed) let her (*Tachrates*) hand over his land and let him lease it out to whomever he wishes.
I, Apollonios, have handled (this business).
(*On the back*) *Demotic:* The lease of the land which Tachrates has made.
Demotic: The lease of land which Tachrates has made for (the land called) 'The Point'.
Greek: Petechonsis the elder has (?sub)leased to Phibis.

[1] The archive comprises 53 papyri, spanning the period from 189 to 100 BC: 42 Demotic, 7 Greek, 4 bilingual, published in *PSI* IX 1014–25 (Greek) and *P.Tor.Botti* (Demotic, with corrections by Zauzich in *Enchoria*, I–III). Pestman (1978, 1985a and b, 1995a) has greatly elucidated many aspects of the archive, and has re-published several texts. See also **4.120**.
[2] Psenminis was not buried until four years later; in a receipt dated 16 August 105, Pikos acknowledged receipt of Tatehathyris' share of the expenses and undertook 'to prepare him for burial and place him to rest in a tomb without having requested more money, grain, or anything else at all' (Pestman, 1985b, text 2 = *P.Tor.Botti* 29).
[3] I.e. any excess land not recorded in the cadastre.
[4] The canal of Patinis (see **(b)**), which ran along the western side of the valley near the desert edge: Pestman (1978).
[5] Presumably Tatehathyris' compensation to her brother for her receiving slightly over one third of the 21 arouras.
[6] The local god; cf. **4.121**.
[7] See Glossary.
[8] An area west of the Nile.

166. Sale of arable land by three women

Sel.Pap. I 27
Pathyris, 15 November 107 BC

Three sisters, Taous, Sennesis alias Tatous and Siephmous, sell 3½ arouras of arable land in the northern plain of Pathyris in the Thebaid to Peteharsemtheus son of Panebchounis and his brothers. Although the document is written in Greek, the milieu of Pathyris remained very Egyptian throughout the Ptolemaic period, and this is reflected in the wording of the document, the character of the property transactions' and the fact that women own land there. See Lewis (1986), 139–52, particularly on the family of Peteharsemtheus, the purchaser here.

(*Summary*). Year 11=8,[1] Phaophi 28. Taous and Sennesis and Siephmous have sold to Peteharsemtheus and his brothers 3½ arouras for 9 bronze talents.

(*Text*). In the reign of Kleopatra and her son Ptolemy surnamed Alexander, mother-loving gods, year 11 which is also the eighth, the priests and priestesses and *kanephoros* being those currently in office, on the twenty-eighth of the month of Phaophi, in Krokodilopolis; before Paniskos, *agoranomos* of the upper toparchy of the Pathyrite (nome). Taous daughter of Harpos, about 48 years old, of medium height, fair-skinned, round-faced, straight-nosed, with a scar on her forehead, and her sisters Sennesis alias Tatous daughter of Harpos about 42 years old, of medium height, fair-skinned, round-faced, straight-nosed, with a scar on her forehead, and Siephmous daughter of Pachnoumis, about 20 years old, fair-skinned, round-faced, straight-nosed, without mark, all three being Persian women, with their guardian the husband of the said Taous, Psennesis alias Krouris son of Horos, Persian of the *epigone*, from the village of Gotnit of the lower toparchy of the Latopolite (nome), about 45 years old, of medium height or less, dark-skinned, somewhat curly-haired, long-faced, straight-nosed, with a scar on the lower lip, have sold the high land, grain-bearing, undivided, in two parcels,[2] which belongs to them in the northern part of the plain of Pathyris, three and a half arouras with the attached surplus[3] out of 7 arouras in the 40 arouras, of which the neighbours are: of the first parcel, south: land of Patous son of Horos and his brothers; north: land of Chesthotes son of Melipais; east: land of Aes and his brothers; west: an embankment; and of the other parcel, south: land of the aforesaid Chesthotes; north: land of Chesthotes son of Panemgeus; east: land of Thrason and his brothers; west: the embankment; or whatever the boundaries are on all sides.

Peteharsemtheus son of Panobchounis, about 36 years old, of medium height, fair-skinned, rather curly-haired, long-faced, straight-nosed, and his brothers Petesouchos and Phagonis and Psennesis, all four Persians of the *epigone*, from Pathyris, have bought the land for nine bronze talents, each paying an equal share.

Negotiators and guarantors of everything regarding this sale are: Taous and Sennesis alias Tatous and Siephmous the vendors, who have been accepted by Peteharsemtheus and Petesouchos and Phagonis and Psennesis the purchasers. I, Paniskos, have registered it.

[1] That is, year 11 of Kleopatra III and year 8 of her co-ruler Ptolemy X Alexander.
[2] 'High land' signifies the ordinary, permanent land, which was not liable to be washed away in the Nile flood. 'Undivided' refers to the ownership of the land, not to its physical condi-

tion (which was in two separate parcels): the three women each held an equal joint share of the common property.

³ See **165** note 3.

167. Petition to the strategos by the daughter of a cavalry kleruch

SB VIII 9790
Herakleopolite nome, mid-first century B C

This opening to a petition, in which Rhodokleia, the daughter of a cavalry kleruch, refers to her succession to her father's property, including his kleros, demonstrates that before the end of Ptolemaic rule in Egypt a daughter's succession to her father's kleros in the absence of male heirs was officially permitted.

To Alexander, strategos of the Koites (toparchy),[1] from Rhodokleia daughter of Menippos, orphan, one of the inhabitants of Phebichis. After the death of my aforesaid father, in accordance with the ordinances of our greatest kings I was authorised through the record office relating to cavalry[2] to succeed to the twenty arouras left by my father from the allotment near Molothis because he had no male progeny; and the ownership of his other property fell under my [. . .

[1] Of the Herakleopolite nome, where the villages Phebichis and Molothis were located.
[2] The bureau which kept the records relating to the allocation and possession of kleroi.

168. Conveyance of a vineyard by Lysimachos to his sister Hero

P.Mich. V 266
Tebtynis, 31 January A D 38

This text, preserved in a large archive of papers from the Tebtynis record office from the mid-first century A D, records one of a complex series of property transactions between members of a single family (see **185**). Such transactions within a family may often have been intended to adjust the distribution of property resulting from inheritance; here we may also see the consequences of a recent financial embarrassment suffered by the family. Hero daughter of Lysimachos had five brothers, and was married to one of them, Didymos the Younger (on sibling marriage see **3.69** note 3); in A D 35/6 Didymos transferred to Hero some arable land in return for a price which included part of the dowry which the couple had received from their father (*P.Mich.* V 262). In the present text, their brother Lysimachos agrees to transfer to Hero, without remuneration, ownership of a vineyard which he had earlier bought from Didymos. Another text (*P.Mich.* V 232) shows that Lysimachos, Didymos, an elder brother, and the three sons of a deceased brother, had in A D 36 defaulted on a massive debt, and had given up to the creditors the large area of land inherited from their father (82 arouras) on which it had been secured. Hero herself was not directly involved in the debt, but it is possible that the two transfers of land to her were either in return for financial assistance she had earlier given her brothers, or a means of preventing the creditors seizing yet more of the brothers' property. See further Rowlandson (1981), esp. 377f.; and more generally *P.Mich.* v, pp. 14–22. Herakleides son of Maron (a member of another prominent Tebtynis family) and his daughter Arsinoe give their consent to the transaction because, as we know from another text (*P.Mich.* v 350), Arsinoe seems to have been Lysimachos' wife; she and her father would have a legal interest in Lysimachos' property if it formed the security for Arsinoe's dowry.

Lysimachos son of Lysimachos to Hero, my sister by the same father and mother, with her guardian her own kinsman Herodes son of Ptolemaios,[1] greeting. I acknowledge that, whenever you command me, I must convey to you through the record office of Tebtynis the vineyard with the vines trained on trees belonging to me near Ibion Eikosipentarouron, of one and a half arouras, which I have bought from Didymos, the brother of both of us, who is also your husband. I am to receive absolutely no remuneration, and no guarantee is forthcoming except for my descendants and those who may bring suit in my name. Let this note of hand be binding. The second year of Gaius Caesar Augustus Germanicus, Mecheir 5.
(*2nd hand*) I, Herakleides son of Maron, agree to render my daughter Arsinoe agreeable to the sale whenever it is completed as stated above without her receiving anything. Year 2 of Gaius Caesar Augustus Germanicus, Mecheir 5.

[1] Normally Hero's husband would act as her guardian, but he was excluded here because of his involvement in the transaction, and a more remote kinsman was chosen.

169.   A woman contracts to work at an oil-press for a daily wage

P.Fay. 91
Euhemeria (Arsinoite nome), 16 October A D 99

Here a woman named Thenetkoueis contracts to work at the olive-press of Lucius Bellenus Gemellus for one season of oil manufacture for the standard daily wage for such work in the village of Euhemeria; she receives an advance payment of sixteen drachmas. Lucius Bellenus Gemellus, her employer, was a discharged army veteran and substantial landowner at Euhemeria and neighbouring villages; a collection of documents relating to him found together in a house in Euhemeria is published in *P.Fay.* (see pp. 44, 261–3). From another of these (*P.Fay.* 92) we learn that Gemellus also employed girls in the task of winnowing, as well as men and boys in various capacities.

Phaophi 18; Agreement of Thenetkoueis with Lucius. Third year of Emperor Caesar Nerva Trajan Augustus Germanicus, Phaophi eighteenth, in Euhemeria of the Themistos division of the Arsinoite nome.

Thenetkoueis daughter of Heron, olive-carrier,[1] Persian woman,[2] about twenty-six years old with a scar on her right shin, with as guardian her kinsman Leontas son of Hippalos, about fifty-four years old with a scar on his forehead to the right, agrees with Lucius Bellenus Gemellus discharged from military service from the legion, about sixty-seven years old with a scar on the left wrist, that she has received from him directly in cash from the house sixteen drachmas of silver as non-returnable caution money. Therefore Thenetkoueis must carry at the olive-press belonging to Lucius Bellenus Gemellus in Euhemeria, from whatever day he orders her, the olives which constitute the produce of the present third year, performing all that befits an olive-carrier until the completion of the oil-making, and receiving from Lucius Bellenus the same daily wage as the other olive-carriers in the village; and Lucius shall deduct the sixteen drachmas of silver by instalments from her wages. If Thenetkoueis does not act in accordance with the aforewritten conditions, she shall pay back to Lucius double the earnest money, and Lucius Bellenus shall have right of execution against her and against all her property as if in accordance with a legal decision. The signatory on behalf of Thenetkoueis is Leontas the aforementioned.

(*2nd hand*) I, Thenetkoueis daughter of Heron, Persian woman, with as guardian my kinsman Leontas son of Hippalos, agree that I have received from Lucius the sixteen drachmas of silver as earnest money, and I shall carry in the oil-press from the day you bid me, receiving from you, Lucius, wages at the same rate as the other carriers, and I shall do everything as agreed. I, Leontas, have also written for Thenetkoueis since she does not know letters.

(*1st hand*) Registered in year [3], Phaophi 18, through Heron in charge of the record office of Euhemeria.

(*3rd hand*) I, Lucius Bellenus Gemellus, through Epagathos,[3] have received the aforementioned (drachmas?), and I make no further claim.

(*In the left-hand margin, at right-angles*) Sixteen silver drachmas. Fifth year of Emperor Caesar Nerva Trajan Augustus Germanicus, Tybi 12.

---

[1] The precise significance of this term is not known, but it presumably referred to the task of feeding the olives into the press.

[2] See Glossary; here Thenetkoueis is so described because she has received an advance payment.

[3] Bellenus' estate manager.

170. Taarpaesis bequeaths land and other property to her descendants

P.Köln II 100 (*BL* VIII 156)
Oxyrhynchos, 24 August AD 133

Taarpaesis alias Isidora, described as 'about 59 years old', here bequeaths to her son Ptolemaios and her two daughters Berenike and Isidora alias Apollonarion property consisting of both houses and arable land in Oxyrhynchos and in three villages of the Oxyrhynchite nome: Phoboou, Ophis and Posompous Aristomachou. Without knowing the value of the different items of property, we cannot tell the relative value of the shares which the son and the two daughters received, although Ptolemaios' share seems likely to have been considerably larger. Also, Taarpaesis clearly seems to have decided to leave no agricultural land to her daughters: the bulk went to her son Ptolemaios, while one aroura was left to Ision, her grandson by Berenike. Some of the property had been acquired by inheritance from Taarpaesis' mother or father; some had presumably been bought. Another beneficiary of the testament is Psenesis alias Ision, who receives the usufruct of some of the property for the duration of his life. Very probably, he was in fact the father of Taarpaesis' children, who were illegitimate; he was perhaps prevented from marrying Taarpaesis by the restrictions on marriage between persons of different status groups (cf. **3.71, 4.131**).

Copy. Seventeenth year of Emperor Caesar Trajan Hadrian Augustus, first extra day of the month of Kaisareios, in the village of Pim[. . .]¹ Taarpaesis alias Isidora daughter of Apollonios son of Apollonios whose mother was Tsenamounis, of Oxyrhynchos city [with her guardian her half-brother Apollon son of Apollonios son of Apollonios] whose mother was Diogenes, from the same city, being sane and in her right mind, has made the following will before the notary in the street:
'As long as I survive I am to have complete power over my own possessions, to make whatever disposition I choose [about them and to alter and revoke] the present will, and whatever disposition I make shall be valid. But if I die leaving the present will having made no other disposition, I leave as my heirs [my children Ptolemaios and Berenike and Isidora alias Apollonarion] all three styled children of myself, each of them if they live, and if not, their children:
To Ptolemaios, from the buildings I possess in Oxyrhynchos city [in the south Dromos quarter, of a house and light well and courtyard and fitments] and entrances and exits; and in the village of Phoboou of the same Oxyrhynchite nome, in the north-west portion of the village, of walled vacant lots and of my quarter share of an orchard [and of the date-palms and other trees therein and of a cistern of well-baked brick and] fitments and all appurtenances and entrances and exits; and in the middle part of the same village, of a walled vacant lot inherited from my father, in which is a house and courtyard and entrances and [exits, and near the same Phoboou, from the former landholding of Etearchos in one plot] 3⁷⁄₁₆ arouras of arable land; and from the former holding of Apollonios son of Lykios 1²⁹⁄₃₂ arouras; and near Ophis in the same Oxyrhynchite [nome (?) ⁵⁵⁄₆₄ arouras]; and near Posompous Aristomachou in the same Oxyrhynchite nome in one plot 4 arouras; and near the same Posompous Aristomachou in another parcel, inherited from my mother [1 aroura.
And to Berenike and to Isidora also called Apollonarion,] each of them

through the agreement made with their husbands on the conditions all contained therein and through this same testament, jointly in equal shares: of what I possess formerly the property of Herais daughter of Teos and others in [Oxyrhynchos city in the same South Dromos quarter, a half share of a house and] light well and fitments and entrances and exits; and in the aforesaid village of Phoboou in the eastern part, inherited from my father, a half share of a house and courtyard and fitments and [entrances and exits.

And I also leave to the son of one of my daughters, Berenike, Ision son of] Herakleides, the remaining [1] aroura which I have near the aforesaid Ophis from the (kleros) of Pyrrhias son of Allous with that of Tryphon.

All the furniture and equipment and household goods and loans, written and [unwritten, and everything else, is to belong to Psenesis alias Ision son of Ptolemaios . . .] since he was always good to me and made me much provision, if he lives, and if not, to my aforesaid son Ptolemaios. And [until his] death, the same Psenesis alias Ision [shall also enjoy the usufruct and right of habitation and rents] of all my property after the taxes on the land have been paid. And from the time that Psenesis alias Ision dies, my daughter Berenike [alone] for the duration of her life shall have the usufruct after the taxes and [of the 1 aroura bequeathed to her son Ision. If it happens that either Ptolemaios or Isidora] alias Apollonarion die childless, let whatever is bequeathed from my property to Ptolemaios be shared jointly and equally between both my daughters, Berenike and Isidora alias Apollonarion; [or what is bequeathed to Isidora alias Apollonarion is to go to Berenike, but Psenesis] alias Ision shall enjoy the usufruct, right of habitation and rents from it for as long as he lives.

No one shall infringe these testamentary provisions of mine in any way; [and whoever does so shall forfeit to whoever abides by them the damages and a penalty] of 1000 silver drachmas, and a like sum to the Treasury, and no less. To no one else do I leave a single one of my possessions. This testament is authoritative.'

(*Lines 18–27 contain the subscription of Taarpaesis, with a detailed repetition of the provisions.*)

(*Line 28*) I consent to all the other provisions set out. I am about 59 years old with a scar on the sole of my right foot, and my seal is Aphrodite. I, Apollon son of Apollonios whose mother was Diogenes, half-brother of the aforesaid [woman, have subscribed for her as her guardian . . . I, Theon] son of Onnophris son of Thonios, have written on their behalf as they do not know letters, and I am about 53 years old with a scar on my left foot. I, Papontos son of Abau son of Apollonios, cousin of the aforementioned Taarpaesis [alias Isidora, witness her will . . .] and my seal is Apis.[2] (*There follow the signatures of another five male witnesses; and certifications by four of them that they recognised their seals*).

---

[1] Probably Pimpasi; see *P.Oxy.* LVII 3911.10 note.

[2] I.e. the seal has a representation of the Apis bull. The other seals described in the omitted section have representations of Aphrodite, Ammon, Hephaistos and the ibis. See also **3.101**.

171.   A woman bids to purchase confiscated property on behalf of her daughter

P. Turner 24
Oxyrhynchos, A D 148–54

Ptolemais daughter of Agenor applies to the strategos to purchase sixteen arouras of confiscated katoikic land (see Glossary) on behalf of her daughter, Claudia Areia. A motive for this purchase appears to be consolidation of their property: either mother or daughter already own the neighbouring land on all sides. But the purchase may be made in the name of her daughter as a means of increasing the girl's provision for a future marriage; there are several other examples of purchases of land on behalf of unmarried daughters (see Rowlandson, 1996, 193f.).

To Aelius Aphrodisios, strategos, from Ptolemais daughter of Agenor son of Philiskos from Oxyrhynchos city, mother of Claudia Areia, through the scribe Hermes. I wish to purchase for my daughter, Claudia Areia and however she styles herself, from the properties put up for sale near the epoikion of Artapatou in the middle toparchy, from the allotment of Simias, 16 arouras of katoikic land, of which the neighbours on all sides are myself and my daughter Claudia Areia, at a price of 3600 drachmas. When my bid is confirmed on these terms, I shall pay the whole amount on her behalf to the public bank . . . but for the rest, we shall be completely without obligation, and ownership shall remain with Claudia Areia and her descendants and those acting for her.

172.   Letter of Arsinoe to Sarapias about rent-collecting and other matters

P. Oxy. XXXIII 2680
Oxyrhynchos, second–third century A D

This letter from one woman to a close relative or friend (the terms 'sister' and 'brother' are not necessarily to be understood literally, cf. **173(b)**, and **3.95**) sandwiches arrangements about rent-collecting between comments about a gift of pickle that is to accompany the letter. It is significant in suggesting that a woman might go in person to collect rent from a tenant, as well as in its implication of the very extensive use of letter-writing, for communication not only between the two women, but also between them and the tenant.

Arsinoe to her sister Sarapias, greeting. Since Achillas was going downstream, I decided I must greet you in writing. About the matter which you wrote to me that it was completed, you will do well to give it to Achillas my brother for him to bring it to me. Receive from the same Achillas a jar of pickles . . . If the roads are firm I shall go off at once to your farmer and ask him for your rents; if indeed he will give them to me, for you should

have sent me a letter addressed to him. Nevertheless, if you have again
instructed him in advance to give them to me, I shall go off and collect them.
Greet Polykrates and all your people. Poletas greets you, as does Demetrous.
If you want anything sent to you, write to me, and I shall send it to you
immediately. I topped up the jar of pickle because it had sunk in; the bottom
layers are better than the top ones. Farewell; Choiak 27.
(*Back*) From Arsinoe to Sarapias wife of Polykrates.

173.   Women's letters concerning agricultural management

Letters from the Roman period show that women sometimes took decisions about
agricultural management, even where they did not necessarily carry out the work
(see also **180**). Women had good reason for concern that tax payments were up to
date, since they might risk imprisonment for debts owed by their menfolk, presumably because officials regarded the men, if left free, as more capable of clearing the
debt (see **(b)**; cf. *P.Oxy.* XLVIII 3409.17–20: 'send their wives to the city and lock
them up so that the males can be released').

(a) *P.Oxy.* VI 932
Oxyrhynchos, late second century AD

Thais writes to a male friend or relative, or more probably her estate manager,
giving instructions on various agricultural matters. The letter is written in rather
clumsy Greek, leaving the sense at times unclear.

Thais greetings to her own Tigrios. I wrote to Apolinarios to come to do
the measuring in Petne.[1] Apolinarios will tell you how the deposits and
public dues[2] stand; what name[3] they are in, he will tell you himself. If you
come, take out six artabas of vegetable-seed[4] and seal them in sacks so that
they are ready, and if you can, go up to search out the ass. Sarapodora and
Sabinos greet you. Do not sell the young pigs without me. Farewell.

(b) *P.Oxy.* XXXVI 2789
Oxyrhynchos, third century AD

Kleopatra's two letters, to her 'father' and 'brother' (perhaps just terms of politeness,
cf. **172**), were written on a single sheet of paper (cf. **Ch.3 Arch. J**).

Kleopatra to her father Epaphroditos, very many greetings. Do all you can
to measure out to Moros the builder five artabas of barley, since I am being
pressed by the *dekaprotos*;[5] for I am about to be imprisoned. Do see that you
don't neglect it. I pray for your health.
Kleopatra to Moros her brother, greeting. I wrote to my father
Epaphroditos that he should measure out to you five artabas of barley, so
that you can sort out the matter of the *dekaprotos*, and from now on you

will be competent in this matter. Do see that you don't neglect it. I pray for
your health.

[1] A village in the middle toparchy of the Oxyrhynchite nome.
[2] Both the deposits and public dues would be in grain. Farmers kept surplus wheat on
account in the local granary, from which they could draw in order to pay their land tax
(the 'public dues' mentioned here: normally one artaba of wheat per aroura).
[3] The 'name' refers to the name under which the deposit is listed in the granary records. It
is clear that, whether through administrative inefficiency or through efforts to evade regulations, 'names' were often either out-of-date or actually fictitious.
[4] An oil-producing crop.
[5] A tax-collecting official.

174.   A wealthy lady declares her grain stocks

P.Oxy. XLII 3048
Oxyrhynchos, 17–18 March AD 246

Several documents of the mid-240s suggest that Oxyrhynchos was experiencing a
grain shortage, which prompted the *iuridicus*, one of the provincial officials, to order
all holders of private stocks of grain to register them by the following day. This text
contains copies of both the order itself and of the declaration by Calpurnia
Herakleia alias Eudamia. Calpurnia Herakleia belonged to an élite Alexandrian
family (hence her father's Fellowship of the Alexandrian Museum), and owned very
substantial landed estates in the Oxyrhynchite nome,[1] as we know not only from
this text but also from a document of the previous year (*P.Oxy.* XLII 3047), in which
she declared that lands at five different villages, amounting to a total of over 1700
arouras, had failed to receive irrigation from the year's flood. Of the six villages listed
in the text printed here, only one (Thmoinepsobthis) occurs also in *P.Oxy.* XLII
3047; presumably Calpurnia was a landowner at all the villages where she held
stocks of grain. Also noteworthy are the various categories of worker employed on
her estates.

On the authority of Aurelius Tiberius the most excellent *iuridicus*:
All those who are holding grain in the city and in the nome are to declare
it – so that the city can have its nourishment and the public necessities can
be fulfilled – tomorrow, that is Phamenoth 22, without any loss to themselves, for each will receive the price which our most illustrious prefect has
fixed, 6 denarii;[2] in the knowledge that if anyone is discovered not to have
registered it, not only their grain but also the house in which it is found will
be confiscated to the most sacred treasury. Year 3, Phamenoth 21.

Copy of declaration:
To Aurelius Tiberius the most excellent *iuridicus*, from Calpurnia Herakleia
alias Eudamia, daughter of Calpurnius Theon, former Fellow of the
Museum and however he was styled, acting through Aurelius Pekyllos alias
Theon, former gymnasiarch and *prytanis*, councillor of the city of

Oxyrhynchos, and Chairemon alias Demet(rios?) and however he is styled, her guardians:[3] I declare in accordance with your orders the grain which I have in the hands of my managers:

In my estate near Souis, 3020 artabas; in Dositheou 245(+) artabas; and in Ision Tryphonis 220 artabas; and in Thmoinepsobthis 460 artabas; and in Lile 280 artabas; and in Satyrou 820 artabas.[4] From the above-mentioned, monthly allowances are given to the managers and bailiffs and farmers and servants and monthly workers;[5] and in Satyrou . . . already pledged from the past month of Mecheir to Kopres and [. . .]pos, cooks in the city, because the oil has gone bad from long keeping, 287 artabas.

Year 3, Phamenoth 22.

[1] See further Rowlandson (1996), esp. 110.
[2] I.e. 24 drachmas, well above the normal market price at this period.
[3] The Greek word *epitropoi* might here mean 'managers' rather than 'guardians'.
[4] The first three villages were all in the Oxyrhynchite lower toparchy, the other three all in the eastern toparchy.
[5] Rathbone (1991), 89–91 discusses the meanings of terms used for the employees of large estates.

175.   A female owner of flocks of sheep and goats

SB VIII 9912 (*BL* VI 161)
Neiloupolis (Arsinoite nome), 23 May A D 270

Valeria Elpinike, a woman of high status (probably the wife or widow of a high-ranking imperial procurator), here acknowledges the transfer of one of her flocks of sheep and goats from the Arsinoite to the Memphite nome. From other texts relating to the shepherd Kalamos and his associate Neilammon we see that she was one of several wealthy estate owners, both male and female, in the district near Theadelphia in the Arsinoite nome who derived part of their substantial wealth from flocks. It is also noteworthy that Elpinike abruptly and unilaterally terminated the five-year lease when it had at least two and a half years to run; see further Rathbone (1991), 202–11.

Valeria Elpinike alias Philoxene the most excellent, through Aurelius Pekysis son of Polion, chief shepherd, to Aurelius Kalamos son of Hatres from the village of Neiloupolis, greeting. Since you leased right from the first year of the rule of Claudius, the month of Choiak, the flocks formerly belonging to Flavia Isidora alias Kyrilla, to the number of fifty, both male and female, equal numbers in fleece and sheared, and five goats; and my manager Aurelius Dionysios, former *kosmetes* and councillor of Alexandria, has ordered them to be transferred into the Memphite nome . . . I agree that I have received them and taken them over from you and taken them away into the Memphite and handed over according to his instructions the animals equal numbers in fleece and sheared and five goats to Aurelius Sabinos, chief shepherd, without distinguishing mark, all in full, and when asked the

formal question I gave my consent. Aurelius Pekysis, about 57 years old, scar
on his face.

1st year of Lucius Domitius Aurelianus Pius Felix Augustus and 4th year of
Julius Aurelius Septimius Vaballathus Athenodorus the most illustrious king,
consul, Emperor, general of the Romans, Pachon 28.

176. Petition by two sisters to the strategos about a misappropriated inheritance

P.Cair.Isid. 64
Karanis, *c.* A D 298

The two daughters of Kopres, Taësis and Kyrillous, complain to the strategos of the
Arsinoite nome about their uncle's misappropriation of their paternal inheritance.
They evince particular indignation that he had left them responsible for the arable
public land (which in the village of Karanis at this time was clearly largely unproductive, but still subject to relatively high taxation), even though as women they
should be exempt from such obligations (cf. **4.149**), and could in any case be
expected to meet the obligations on it only if they had actually received their father's
inheritance.

To Aurelius Heron, strategos of the Arsinoite nome, from Aurelia Taësis and
Aurelia Kyrillous, both daughters of Kopres from the village of Karanis. Our
father, noblest of strategoi, left some movable property when he died. But
his brother Chairemon appropriated all that he left, and handed over to us,
the women, arable arouras of public land, although we are not able to meet
the rents on these arouras. And at that time we approached the headman of
the village who was then in office, Serenos alias Harpokras; and he ordered
him to hand over to us all the property left by our father. But he (*Chairemon*)
takes no thought for us, and therefore we include an inventory of the estate,
and beg and beseech your clemency to order him, namely Chairemon, to
hand these things over to us so that we may be able to have the benefit of
our own property. Farewell. This is the property: 61 full-grown sheep; 40
full-grown goats; 1 grinding-mill; and 3 talents of silver; and 2 artabas of
wheat; and two slaves, of which he has sold one, a female.

177. A widow petitions the prefect for redress against two unscrupulous business managers

P.Oxy. 1 71 col.2 lines 1–16 (*BL* 1 314)
Found at Oxyrhynchos, A D 303

Here a female landowner invokes her defencelessness (see **3.75**) and inability to
manage her estates without male help in order to claim the assistance of the prefect
of Egypt against two dishonest managers.

To Clodius Culcianus, the most excellent prefect of Egypt, from Aurelia Gle[. . .] the most illustrious, living in Arsinoe. You give help to all, my lord prefect, and render to all their due, but particularly to women because of their natural weakness. Therefore I myself petition your highness in the full confidence of obtaining assistance from you. Having large [estates] around the same Arsinoite nome, and paying a considerable sum in taxes – I mean the payments for public purposes and supplies for soldiers – and being a weak and widowed woman, for my sons are in the army and absent upon foreign service, I engaged as my assistant and manager of my affairs in the first place a certain Secundus and subsequently Tyrannos besides, thinking that they would preserve my good name. But these men conducted themselves dishonestly and robbed me, and, depriving me of the property I placed in their hands, they never submitted to me proper accounts; and similarly, by giving way in the business they conducted, they stole from me two oxen from those which I have for [ploughing? or irrigation?] of my same estates, despising my lack of business sense. (*The rest of the text, in which she seeks redress from the prefect, becomes increasingly fragmentary.*)

178.   Loan of wheat to Aurelia Tamaleis

P.Col. VII 176
Karanis, 8 September AD 325

This is one of several similar texts from fourth-century Karanis documenting loans in kind made to both male and female villagers by well-to-do creditors. In each case, the loan is made at the beginning of the Egyptian year, to be repaid after the harvest. Aurelia Tamaleis, the borrower here, is the elder sister of Aurelia Tetoueis, who is documented as borrowing wheat and money in six further texts; and probably (on the assumption that she was twice-married) the mother of Valerius son of Antiourios and Aion son of Sarapion, also well-known individuals from the Karanis archives: for further details see *P.Col.* VII, pp. 4–9 and 201ff. Loans of this sort seem to be the product, not of a sudden financial crisis on the part of the borrower, but of habitual reliance on credit to finance the costs of the year's agriculture until the harvest was gathered in (see Bagnall, 1980).

Aurelia Tamaleis daughter of Hatres, whose mother was Tapaeis, from the village of Karanis, about thirty years old with a scar on the wrist of her right hand, acknowledges that she has received and had measured out to her from Eutropios son of Archias of Arsinoe, through his agent Poeris, 38½ artabas of wheat including the additional one half;[1] which she, the acknowledging party, must of necessity repay on the appointed day in the month of Pauni of the present year, from the crop of the 14th indiction, by the four-choinix measure, in quality fresh, clean, unadulterated, and in good condition, without delay; and that upon a request for payment, Eutropios shall have right of execution upon the acknowledging party, and upon all her possessions as if in accordance with a legal decision; and, when asked the formal question, she gave her consent. In the consulship of Paulinus and Julianus the most illustrious, Thoth 11.

I, Aurelia Tamaleis, have received the thirty-eight and a half artabas of wheat, and I shall repay them on the appointed day as stated. I, Chaireas, wrote for her because she is illiterate.

(*Back*) Note of hand of Tamaleis [daughter of Hatres for] 38½ artabas [of wheat].

[1] I.e. the 50 per cent normally charged on loans in kind, whatever their duration, had already been incorporated into the figure of 38½ artabas; Tamaleis had therefore actually received 25⅔ artabas.

179. The landholdings of Aurelia Charite

P.Charite 7 and 8
Hermopolis, A D 347 and 348

Charite daughter of Amazonios was among the wealthiest landowners in fourth-century Hermopolis, with estates of around 500 arouras. The many surviving documents, particularly leases and rent receipts, relating to her ownership and management of her landed estates have been collected as *P.Charite*, with a useful introduction (in German). Below are two typical examples from her papers (see also **193**). Several of her tenants were by no means peasants themselves, but were either councillors of Hermopolis, or, as in the two cases here, soldiers from a local military unit. Charite was literate and also possessed the right to dispense with a guardian (cf. **4.142**). However, in (**b**), as in many of her papers, only the subscription is actually in her own hand; a business manager or secretary would be responsible for writing the body of the contract (see **Plate 27**; cf. Bagnall, 1993a, 247).

(a)   Offer to lease land from Aurelia Charite

P.Charite 7
Hermopolis, 22 October A D 347

To Aurelia Charite, daughter of Amazonios, ex-magistrate and councillor of Hermopolis the most glorious, from Flavius Cassius, *promotus* of the detachment of *Mauri scutarii* stationed under the command of the *praepositus* Almesianus in the same Hermopolis. I voluntarily and of my own free will wish to lease from you for the present year only, of the crops of the felicitous 7th new or 22nd indiction, the fifteen arouras belonging to you within the embankment of Magdola Mire[1] from the allotment (worked by the villagers?),[2] to sow and plant with whatever I choose, at a total rent of thirty artabas of wheat, which rent I shall measure out in the month of Epeiph of the same 7th indiction without delay; wheat that is new, clean, unadulterated, free of earth, free of barley, sieved, by the Athenaion-measure.[3] It is

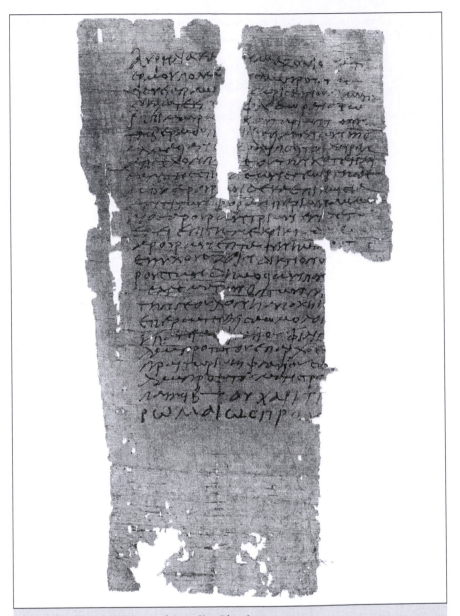

27   The handwriting of Aurelia Charite
P.Charite 8 (Österreichische Nationalbibliothek, Vienna G 2.097 verso)
Hermopolis, AD 348

A wealthy landowner like Aurelia Charite, even though literate herself, would employ a
professional scribe or business manager to write the body of her legal and business
documents, appending her signature at the bottom. In this rent receipt (translated in
5.179(b)), Charite's signature, on the last two lines, follows the fluent cursive of the
professional writer (see **Ch.6 Sect.II** introduction).

your responsibility to see to the cleansing and measuring on the threshing floors of the *metropolis* of all the public dues, impositions, *annonai*, and extra charges which fall on you, the landowner. This lease is authoritative, and in answer to the formal question I have given my consent. The consulship of Vulcacius Rufinus, the most illustrious prefect of the sacred praetorium, Phaophi 24.

I, Flavius Cassius, have taken on the lease as stated.

(b)　Receipt for rent

P.Charite 8 (see **Plate 27**)
Hermopolis, 27 May A D 348

Aurelia Charite daughter of Amazonios from Hermopolis the glorious, literate, acting without a guardian by right of children, to Flavius Doratianus, cavalryman of the *Mauri scutarii* stationed in the same Hermopolis under the command of the *praepositus* Almesianus, greeting. I have received from you the half that belongs to me of the crop which you farmed on my ten arouras on a sharecropping arrangement instead of rent: that is, three arouras near Ammon and seven arouras in the marsh near the Nekrike canal[4] – from the crop of the lucky seventh indiction in full, all public dues of all kinds being the responsibility of myself, the landowner. This receipt is authoritative, and when asked the formal question, I gave my consent. The consulship of Flavius Philippus the most illustrious prefect of the sacred praetorium, and Flavius Salias the most illustrious Master of Horse, Pauni 2. I, Aurelia Charite, have been paid in full, as agreed.

[1] A village in the Hermopolite nome.
[2] We expect a person's name here, but the Greek appears to say 'through them'.
[3] One of the many different grain measures used in Egypt; see Rathbone (1983), with earlier bibliography.
[4] This canal may have linked the city of Hermopolis to its necropolis at Tuna el-Gebel: Rea (1985), 70.

180.　Women in the archive of Papnouthis and Dorotheos

P.Oxy. XLVIII 3403 and 3406
Oxyrhynchos, fourth century A D

The brothers Papnouthis and Dorotheos, tax collectors and estate managers, are known from a group of papyri published in *P.Oxy.* XLVIII 3384–429 (with LVI 3875). They were fluent writers; it is possible that their mother, Maria, was also literate, if the letter **(a)** below was written in her own hand. In that letter, and even more in **(b)**, a letter from Klematia, the female landowner for whom Papnouthis worked, we see women involved in the details of economic affairs and agricultural management. Neither letter can be dated precisely, but the archive spans the middle of the fourth century A D.

(a)   Letter of Maria to her son Papnouthis

P.Oxy. XLVIII 3403

To my lord son Papnouthis from his mother, Maria, very many greetings. You have again been persisting in your neglect and have sent me no word concerning those things I instructed you about. So you will do well to send me the money. Your wife, too, says herself that you should send her money for the wages of the wool-workers. Don't neglect it, and send them quickly. Make haste to write to us about the work. I pray for your health for a long time.

(b)   Letter of Klematia to Papnouthis

P.Oxy. XLVIII 3406

From Klematia, landowner, to Papnouthis, manager at Sadalou, greeting. Measure out six artabas of wheat and lentil mixture into Pagas' boat so that we may have it here, and help Pagas so that we may have the extra payments of the vintage there; and try also to bring wool up with the boat, and do not delay because of the baked brick. And collect from Paymis the two jars of honey for the festival, as well as the honey-cakes, and from Pagas the wool.

181.   Lease of land by a daughter to her father

P.Lond. III 1007 b and c, pp. 264–5 (*BL* I 297, III 95, VII 88)
Tarrouthis (Antaiopolite nome), 8 May A D 558

This sixth-century lease of land from the Antaiopolite nome is unusual in that the lessor is the daughter of the tenant, and the land is a gift to her from her uncle, the tenant's brother. Such family relationships would not be unusual between the parties to a sale contract (cf. **168, 185**), but are very rare in leases, where landlord and tenant are normally unrelated, and indeed are often of different social classes and places of origin (cf. Rowlandson, 1996, ch. 7). Our text breaks off suddenly after a rather confused statement of the boundaries to the two parcels of land; perhaps the scribe rejected this version in favour of a fairer copy, but we cannot of course be sure that a full contract was ever completed.

(c) In the reign of our most divine master Flavius Justinianus the eternal Augustus and Emperor, thirty-second year, in the seventeenth year after the consulship of Flavius Vasileius the reputable and most reputable, Pachon 13, start of the seventh indiction. To Aurelia Eudoxia daughter of Apollos alias Phellos from the village of Tarrouthis in the Antaiopolite nome, from Aurelius Apollos alias Phellos, your aforesaid father, son of Phoibammon, whose mother is Maria, a slow writer, farmer, from the same village. I, the aforesaid Apollos alias Phellos, acknowledge that I have voluntarily and of my own free will leased from you for a five-year period calculated from the crops of the present seventh indiction inclusive, the land given to you my aforesaid daughter Eudoxia by my most discreet full brother [. . .] (b) the priest of the monastery of the Antaiopolite, from the said village of Tarrouthis according to a written deed of gift made previously to you by him, half the arouras as stated there, however many they are, in arable land and vineyard with all their movable and immovable and self-moving accoutrements [as set out in?] the same written deed of gift according to the appended detailed statement, [the boundaries of the?] arouras, whatever their extent, being on the west the road there and on the east the vineyard belonging to me the aforesaid Apollos alias Phellos and the aforesaid Eudoxia my daughter; the northerly portion of these arouras whatever their extent, that is, from their northern limit southwards to the share of the other half of them, and from their eastern limit westwards to their western limit; and a half share of the dry vineyard, whatever its extent, which is on the east of the same road, that is the [. . .] share of it whatever its extent (*here the text abruptly ends*).

II   Women in the non-agricultural economy

There is plentiful evidence for the activities of women in a range of economic areas other than agriculture. The evidence for the Roman imperial period (30 BC − AD 284) is generally fuller and better than that for the Ptolemaic and Byzantine eras, but since that reflects the survival of papyrological evidence as a whole, it implies no striking conclusion about changes in the role of women. But it is worth keeping in mind the historical differences and developments over the whole period which could have caused changes in the economic behaviour of women: for example, the comparatively stronger position of Egyptian law in the Ptolemaic period, or the increasingly predominant role of the Christian Church from AD 300 onwards.

One important area of evidence concerns the ways in which women controlled and disposed of non-agricultural property, particularly houses or parts of houses. We can draw some conclusions about the amount of property owned or controlled by women and their degree of economic independence. Here the native Egyptian inheritance laws were clearly influential, and although the influence of Greek law might have eroded their power from the Ptolemaic period onwards, it should not be thought that the necessity for women to act with a guardian (*kyrios*), unless they enjoyed dispensation, involved any real curtailment of their ability to conduct legally valid transactions. Studies of the situation in Fayum villages during the Roman period (where, it must be admitted, the Greek influence may well have been stronger than in some communities in Upper Egypt, for example) shows that women may have accounted for up to one-third of the owners and controllers of real estate. This was a result of a partible inheritance system which tended to keep property within the family as far as possible, and to guarantee the prosperity of all members of a family, male and female, without simply making equal divisions (Hobson, 1983, 1984).

Women could thus buy and sell houses and parts of houses or other assets in real and movable property. Leases are also common, as are the various means by which real property could be used to secure loans or to provide necessary cash. Women appear as money-lenders as well as borrowers (**183–4, 188–90, 193**). It is important to note that whatever degree of independent economic activity existed it was not obviously affected by marital status – perhaps an important survival of the influence of Egyptian law. However, in times of financial difficulty, a family was perhaps most likely to draw first on the resources brought by the wife into the marriage, hoping to preserve the paternal property intact.

The range of assets held by women is varied but not particularly large. Apart from the expected personal possessions and money, often brought to a marriage as part of a dowry (see below), we find houses, parts or annexes (*exedrae*)[1] of houses, plots of ground in towns and villages. There is little basis for any distinction between the towns and the villages in this respect. We also find ships (see **2.7** introd.), camels, slaves and revenue-producing enterprises of other kinds: milling equipment, a pottery, a fullery, a religious precinct (**186–7, 194, 197, 217, 2.30**). Such a range shows that the economic activity of women was certainly not confined to their domestic role, even if the weight of the evidence does emphasise the latter (Hobson, 1984). It is difficult to assess the degree to which that means that the real economic independence of women was curtailed. The answer may, indeed, not be susceptible to precise measurement derived from written documentation and was perhaps in any case less important to the large proportion of the female (and male) population who could not directly control the documentation which regulated their lives.

The texts which illustrate economic transactions tell us something about the ways in which women could raise and use money, many of which were not specific to women. Two areas in which they did have a specific and gender-related role were the use of the dowry and the provision of wet-nursing which amounted to the fiduciary sale of a child (**213–14**, cf. **3.91**). Loans and speculations in various forms make it clear that from the Hellenistic period on, and certainly to a very great degree in the Roman period, this was a highly monetised province, a feature which applies to villages as well as towns, to women's lives as well as men's (Howgego, 1992).

As well as using assets, women could also engage in non-agricultural activities to make money. The two most prominent and traditional areas (apart fom wet-nursing) are weaving and prostitution, both of which are illustrated in the selections which follow (**200–6, 207–8**). Weaving was a cottage industry centred on peasant families, in which women played an important part, especially in spinning the yarn. Garments were made mainly of wool or linen. There is no evidence in ancient Egypt for the widespread use of cotton. Owners of large establishments, who might be quite well-to-do, also clearly involved female members of the family in the business (cf. particularly **3.94**). Apprenticeship contracts, especially involving female slaves, are common.[2] Textile production was an important part of the activity on the estate of Zenon at Philadelphia in the third century BC, as the letters from the Zenon archive show (**200–1**). **201(a)** is of particular interest since it illustrates the range of garments produced by a group consisting of two men (father and son?), a mother and a wife; it is noteworthy that in **201(b)** there is a suggestion that the women workers would be paid at a lower rate than the men. The pattern of production seems to have involved spinning taking place at home and weaving in workshops.[3]

There are a number of references in the papyri to women engaging in prostitution, both willingly and unwillingly. They are attested in a Ptolemaic census list, and in the Roman period the Koptos Tariff attests a tax on prostitutes.[4] No doubt prostitution played a larger role than is reflected on paper and the same may be true of other personal and domestic functions which are so heavily represented in the servile inscriptions from the city of Rome, for which there is no counterpart in the towns and villages of Egypt; it is notable, for example, that there are no females at all mentioned in the will emanating from the wealthy Alexandrian household of the Tiberii Julii Theones (*P.Oxy.* XLIV 3197) yet there must have been many such female slaves, given the prevalence of home-breeding. The general service-contract was another means of exploiting female labour (**198–9**). Other documents show that women could sell beer or wine (**209–10**), entertain as flute-players or dancers (**215–16**) and perform a variety of other waged jobs which are formal enough to be recorded in documents where occupations are listed.[5] No doubt much of this was supplementary to, or a substitute for, male earning-power and, no doubt, as in other similar societies the actual share of work of all kinds performed by women was very much greater than formal documentation will ever tell us.

[1] For the range of meanings of this word see Husson (1983), 73–7.
[2] **204**; in general see Préaux (1939), 96–114, Wipszycka (1965).
[3] For this, and further evidence, see Thompson (1988), 46–59.
[4] *P.Count.* 3.91 (229 BC), *I.Port.* 67.16–17. See Bagnall (1991a).
[5] *P.Count.* 3 (229 BC) also lists temple-dancers (*sompheis*), a policewoman and a female tailor.

182.   The daughter of a Greek settler buys a plot of ground

SB XIV 11376
Hibeh, 239 BC

In this contract of the early Ptolemaic period the daughter of a privileged Greek military settler originally from the colony of Cyrene in Africa, acting with her father as legal guardian, buys from another military settler a plot of ground for the substantial sum of 500 silver drachmas. The credit arrangement made in the sale is unusual; it is couched in the form of a fictional loan without interest, allowing a period of ten days during which the vendor has to provide a certificate of sale; this presumably covers the interval during which the transfer and registration formalities can be completed.

In the reign of Ptolemy, son of Ptolemy and Arsinoe, brother–sister gods, the 8th year, when Onomastos son of Pyrrhon was priest of Alexander and the brother–sister gods and the benefactor gods, and Archestrate daughter of Ktesikles was *kanephoros* of Arsinoe Philadelphos, in the month Peritios, in Tholthis in the Oxyrhynchite nome. Theodote daughter of Leon, Cyrenaean, acting with her father Leon, Cyrenaean, private of Zoilos' troop, as her guardian, has lent to Zenion from Aenos, private of Antiochos' troop, 500 drachmas of silver produced to view[1] in the presence of the designated witnesses, without interest. In lieu of the 500 drachmas which he has received from Theodote let Zenion give to Theodote a certificate of purchase of the plot of ground (?) . . . belonging to him, either at the registry in Herakleopolis or at the registry in Oxyrhynchos within 10 days from the day on which Theodote gives Zenion notice to do so. If he does not give to Theodote the certificate after the aforementioned days, Zenion shall repay to Theodote twice the amount of the loan of 500 drachmas, and Theodote shall have the right of execution upon Zenion in accordance with the edict. This contract shall be binding wherever it is produced.[2] The witnesses are Eurymedon . . .

[1] The phrase 'produced to view' means that the money sum has been personally inspected by the witnesses to the contract. The sum of 500 silver drachmas is considerable. Towards the end of the third century a depreciated bronze coinage became the standard currency; see **164** note 2.

[2] These are the normal legal formulae in such contracts. The names of witnesses, normally six, would have followed in the lost portion of the papyrus.

183.   A woman makes a loan with the right to occupy property in lieu of interest

BGU VI 1273.1–40 (*BL* IX 26)
Oxyrhynchite nome, 30 August 221 BC

Another contract between members of Greek immigrant families from Cyrene. This is the inner text of a contract written in duplicate on both sides of a papyrus. Demetria lends Apollonios a capital sum of 400 drachmas, of which he has the use, and receives the use of a tower belonging to Apollonios instead of interest. If he fails to repay the capital by the agreed date, he pays interest on three-quarters of the capital sum while Demetria continues to occupy his property in lieu of interest on the remaining quarter. Apollonios may be using this as a way of exploiting a piece of inherited residential property for which he has no direct personal need.

In the first year of the reign of Ptolemy, son of Ptolemy and Berenike, benefactor gods, when Nikanor son of Bakchias was the priest of Alexander and the brother–sister and the benefactor gods, and Aristomache daughter of Ptolemaios was *kanephoros* of Arsinoe Philadelphos, the eighteenth of the month Gorpiaios, in the village of Takona in the Oxyrhynchite nome. Demetria daughter of Apollodotos, Cyrenaean, acting with her guardian Apollophanes son of Apollodotos, Cyrenaean of the *epigone*, has lent to Apollonios son of Patron, Cyrenaean of the *epigone*, four hundred drachmas in bronze money produced to view, bearing interest at the rate of two drachmas per mina per month, but in lieu of the interest on this loan Apollonios has leased to Demetria his tower[1] inherited from his father in the village of Takona in the Oxyrhynchite nome, doors and all, for 1 year from the month Hyperberetaios of the first year, on condition that Demetria and her associates (?) shall inhabit this tower for the agreed term of the contract, using it in whatever manner they wish and having a right of way through the existing passage from the tower to the street. The neighbouring properties of the tower are, on the south the house of Sosibios, on the east the portion of the property of Apollonios' brothers, on the north a public street, and on the west a public street. This loan Apollonios shall repay to Demetria in the month Gorpiaios of the second year with the interest.[2] If he fails to repay it according to the written agreement, Apollonios shall continue to pay to Demetria interest on three hundred drachmas for the subsequent time at the rate of 2 drachmas per mina per month, but in place of the interest on the remaining one hundred drachmas Demetria and her associates (?) shall inhabit this tower, occupying and using it in whatever manner they wish and having a right of way as stated in writing, until Apollonios repays to Demetria the four hundred drachmas constituting this loan and the interest on the three hundred drachmas for the extra time in excess of the year, and Apollonios shall guarantee to Demetria and her associates the use of this tower and passage and doors during the aforementioned year and for the ensuing time until Apollonios repays to her this loan of four hundred drachmas and the interest on the three hundred drachmas as stated above. If he fails to guarantee as stated in writing, Apollonios shall forfeit to Demetria this loan of four hundred drachmas increased by half and the net interest on the three hundred drachmas, and Demetria shall have the right of execution in accordance with the ordinance[3] and the lease shall be no less binding for the term of the contract, and it shall be lawful for Demetria and her associates to countereject anyone who tries to eject them from this tower and passage without being liable to any penalty or legal action. This contract shall be binding wherever it is produced. Witnesses: Timolaos, Thessalian, decurion, Parmenion, Persian, private, both of the troop of Philon;

Perdikkas son of Polyarchos, Persian, Philonades son of Lysanias, Cyrenaean, Demetrios son of Themison, Cyrenaean, Noumenios son of Kallixenos, Chalkidian, all four of the *epigone*.[4]

[1] The word *pyrgos* ('tower') denotes a structure of a traditional Egyptian type, either circular or rectangular, which could have either residential or agricultural/commercial uses; see Husson (1983), 248–51, Nowicka (1970).

[2] The reading 'with the interest' is rejected by M. Kuschnik, *ZPE* 74 (1988), 166; the use of the tower was substituted for the payment of interest in money.

[3] The royal ordinance defining legal procedures.

[4] The names of the witnesses show that this comes from the context of the privileged military settlers. The term '*epigone*' literally means 'descent' but its significance when used in conjunction with the ethnics is as a status designation, apparently for persons without claim to a specific military rank (see e.g. Oates, 1963; Goudriaan, 1988).

184.   A shrewd businesswoman forecloses on a loan

Pap.Lugd.Bat. xix 6 (*BL* viii 202)
Pathyris, 18 February 109 BC

This text comes from the small archive of Nahomsesis, a woman of a priestly family from Pathyris.[1] Although Nahomsesis' business transactions were conducted through Greek contracts (which were duly registered with the Ptolemaic bureaucracy), she did not make use of the customary male guardian (*kyrios*). Yet she does not appear to have been able to read or write Greek (whether she was literate in Demotic is unknown), and was indifferent to discrepancies and even mistakes in personal details about herself. Her name was rendered into Greek with five different spellings, although we can be confident that the documents all refer to the same individual because of the rarity of the name, Nahomsesis, daughter of Spemminis. Her descriptions also reveal considerable discrepancies: about 112 BC she was described as 'about 30 years,[2] middle height, dark-complexioned, straight-nosed'; only three years later she was said to be 'about 45 years, middle height, sallow-complexioned, flat-faced, straight-nosed, scar on her forehead'.

Despite this apparent indifference to legal formalities, Nahomsesis seems to have conducted her business affairs successfully. On 10 November 110 BC Harkonnesis, a cavalryman, had borrowed 9 artabas of wheat from Nahomsesis, promising to repay about one hundred days later 13½ artabas (i.e. 9 artabas at 50 per cent interest; the contract was designed to hide the high rate of interest not uncommon for loans of produce). As security for the loan, Harkonnesis put up a quarter of two parcels of royal land he had bought a few years earlier, filing a document of sale, in which the 13½ artabas represented the sale price for his mortgaged land, and the base figure on which Nahomsesis' payment for the tax on sales was calculated (C). By 18 February 109 Harkonnesis had not yet repaid his debt, which became subject to a penalty for non-repayment of 50 per cent of the principal (making a total of 18 artabas); and what had been a fictitious sale now became a real one with the 18 artabas representing the sale price, already paid by Nahomsesis the buyer (A–B). Two other documents filed on the same day show that Harkonnesis ceded the quarter of his grain land to her and that Nahomsesis acknowledged Harkonnesis' repayment of the loan of wheat (*Pap.Lugd.Bat.* XIX 7A/B).

(*A; 3rd hand*) Year 8 Mecheir 2. Harkonnesis, son of Phigeris, sold a quarter of 2 parcels of high land[3] in the Latopolite nome. Nahomsesis, daughter of Spemminis, was the buyer. 18 (artabas) of wheat (was the price).

(*B; 1st hand*) Year 8 in the reign of Queen (Kleopatra) and King Ptolemy, the mother-loving saviour gods, while King Ptolemy, the mother-loving saviour god, was priest of Alexander, of the saviour gods, of the brother–sister gods, of the benefactor gods, of the father-loving gods, of the gods manifest, of the god Eupator, of the god Philometor, of the god the new Philopator, the god Euergetes, the mother-loving saviour gods; at the time of the *hieros polos* of Isis, Great mother of the gods, of the *athlophoros* of Berenike Euergetis, of the *kanephoros* of Arsinoe Philadelphos, of the priestess of Arsinoe Philopator, who are (in office) at Alexandria; and in the time of the priests and priestesses and the *kanephoros* who are (in office) at Ptolemais of the Thebaid.[4] In the month Phaophi 22, in Pathyris before Sosos, public notary.

Harkonnesis, son of Phigeris, Persian of the wage-receiving cavalrymen, about 50 years old, good-sized, dark complexioned, long-faced, straight-nosed, sold a quarter of two parcels of the grain-bearing high land which belongs to him in the lower toparchy of the Latopolite nome: the first, of 8 arouras, whose neighbours are on the south, land of Pasemis; on the north, the hollow[5] called Tpachis; on the east, land of the ibis-guards; on the west, land of Pasemis with a hollow in the middle. The other, of two arouras, (whose neighbours are) on the south, a dike; on the north, land of Patsantis; on the east, the base of a dike; on the west, a hollow; or whatever the neighbours are on all sides. Nahomsesis, daughter of Spemminis, Persian, bought for 13½ artabas of wheat. Harkonnesis the seller was the guarantor whom Nahomsesis the buyer accepted.

I, Ammonios, agent of Sosos, have transacted the business.

(*C; 2nd hand*) Year 8 Phaophi 22. Nahomsesis, daughter of Spemminis paid into the bank at Pathyris which Patseous directs a provisional payment for the 10 per cent sales tax on the sale of a quarter of 2 parcels of grain land in the lower toparchy of the Latopolite nome, one of 8 arouras and the other of 2 arouras, that she bought from Harkonnesis, son of Phigeris, for 13½ artabas of wheat (equals) 2 talents and 4200 bronze drachmas, on which the tax is 1620 bronze drachmas, which, with the surcharge, makes 1950 bronze drachmas in all.

---

[1] See Pestman (1981b). Nahomsesis' uncle by marriage, Patous, was a witness to Dryton's third will; see **3.86** introd.

[2] A mistake for 'about 40 years'? *BGU* III 996 iii.8 with *BL* VIII 38. See *Pap.Lugd.Bat.* XIX 6 introd. for further details of Nahomsesis' name and descriptions.

[3] See **165** note 2.
[4] For this lengthy dating formula, cf. **2.34**.
[5] Probably a canal bed that was dry for part of the year.

185.   A mother sells two rooms to one of her sons

P.Mich. v 253
Tebtynis, 28 August AD 30

A Demotic contract, with Greek subscriptions, for the sale of two rooms by a
mother to her son. Transactions of this sort between family members were frequently used to adjust the effects of the traditional Egyptian system of partible
inheritance (see **168**, **2.30**). For the use of contracts written in Demotic in the early
Roman period see Zauzich (1983). This is one of a small group of papyri recording transactions of members of this family. Thermouthis and her husband Eutychos
had five sons, three of whom were called Eutychos. The elder appears as a property owner also in *P.Mich.* v 269 and 308; he also acts as a scribe. The reference at
the end of the Demotic version to the handing over of documents with the property illustrates the importance of the written word in this society.

(*Demotic*) Year 16 of Tiberius Caesar Augustus, fifth intercalary day. The
woman Thermouthis, daughter of Marepsemis, her mother being Demario(n),
has said to Sisois the elder, son of Sisois, who is called Takn-lin, her son
being present and acting for her as guardian . . . who is called Eut(ycho)s,
his mother being Thermouthis: You have satisfied my heart (with the)
money of the price of my half share of this room which is built which is
equipped with beams and doors downstairs . . . together with my half share
of the way of entrance and exit, together with my half share of this bedroom
(in) the third storey, he having authority against her in the gate of the courtyard, (in the) Souchos town of Tebtynis (in) the division of Polemon, on
the south side of the canal Moeris, (in the) Ar(si)noite nome. The boundaries of the entire, undivided house: south, the house of Petenefer. . .(?),
together with its courtyard; north (the) house of Kames and his brothers;
west, the royal road; east, the courtyard of this room. No man in the world,
myself included, shall be able to exercise authority over them, except you,
from this date. He that shall come to you on account of them, I will cause
him to be far from you in respect of them, of necessity, without delay, and
I will cause it to be clear for you from every writing, every document,
everything in the world. Yours is every writing [which has been made] concerning them and every writing which has been made (for) my father (or)
my mother concerning them and every writing which has been made for
me concerning them. Yours . . . together with their law. The oath (and the)
confirmation which shall be required of you (to) cause that I make it, I will
make it.

(*Greek*) I, Thermouthis, daughter of Marepsemis whose mother is Demarion, acting with my son, Eutychos the third, son of Eutychos, as guardian acknowledge that I have sold to my elder son, Eutychos, son of Eutychos, the half share, belonging to me by inheritance from my mother, of the ground floor of a house, and on the roof another half share of a so-called bedroom, unplastered, and of all the appurtenances, in Tebtynis, and of the entrances and exits. The neighbours of the whole house are: on the south the house and court of Petenephies, son of Orseus Achis (?); on the north the house and courtyard of Kames and others; on the west the royal road; and on the east the plots of the sons of Nephies. In return for this we have received from Eutychos the elder, son of Eutychos, the agreed and established price, in full, from hand to hand, out of the house, and we shall guarantee the sale with every guarantee as free from both public and private encumbrances and from every impost as aforementioned. I, Eutychos son of Eutychos, wrote for my mother because she does not know letters, and I have been appointed her guardian. (*2nd hand*) Eutychos the elder, son of Eutychos. The sale was made to me as aforementioned.

186.   A female villager registers her ownership of six camels

P. Grenf. II 45a (*BL* III 75, IX 96)
Soknopaiou Nesos, 29 January A D 137

Soknopaiou Nesos was a remote village on the north shore of Lake Moeris which almost entirely lacked agricultural land; instead its economy was based on the activities of its temple, and on the long-distance haulage of goods, both to and from the oases and from the west of the lake to Memphis (cf. **211**). Thus wealth in this village often consisted in the ownership of camels. From the elaborate system of annual registration of camels (along with other livestock) we can see that women also shared in this form of wealth. As with other forms of property, they are also found buying and selling these valuable commodities (see **187**). Note also the restricted and distinctive nomenclature in this remote village (cf. **204**).

Soknopaiou Nesos: 6 camels.
To Vegetus alias Sarapion strategos, and Hermeinos royal scribe of the Arsinoite nome Herakleides division, from Taouetis daughter of Stotoetis from the village of Soknopaiou Nesos with her relative Stotoetis son of Stotoetis as her guardian. The six camels in the vicinity of the village which I registered in the previous 20th year I also now register for the present 21st year of the lord Hadrian Caesar, at Soknopaiou Nesos. (*2nd hand*): 6 camels placed on the records of the strategos; 21st year of the lord Hadrian, 4th Mecheir. (*3rd hand*): 6 camels placed on the records of the royal scribe; 21st year of the lord Hadrian, Mecheir 4. (*4th hand*): I, Ptolemaios, have counted 6.

187.   A priestess sells two camels

M.Chr. 260
Soknopaiou Nesos, 13 January AD 144

Here another Taouetis, a priestess of Soknopaiou Nesos, sells two female camels to
a fellow priest for 500 drachmas. It is interesting to note that another surviving
papyrus, *P.Lond.* II 304 (pp. 71–3) contains the declaration to the royal scribe she
made shortly afterwards that she no longer possessed any camels, having sold the
two mentioned in this text and another three to a different purchaser (also male).

The seventh year of Emperor Caesar Titus Aelius Hadrianus Antoninus
Augustus Pius, Tybi 18, in Soknopaiou Nesos in the division of Herakleides
of the Arsinoite Nome. Taouetis daughter of Harpagathos son of Satabous,
priestess, of the same village (*i.e. Soknopaiou Nesos*) about 21 years old
without distinguishing mark, with as guardian her relative Stotoetis son of
Stotoetis son of Stotoetis, about 35 years old with a scar on his left thumb,
agrees with Satabous son of Satabous son of Satabous, priest of the fifth tribe
about ( )[1] years old without distinguishing mark, that she, the acknowledging party, has sold to him the two female camels belonging to her branded
'N' and 'H' on the right flank, unblemished, and that she, the acknowledging party, has received all the agreed price in full from Satabous of five
hundred drachmas of Augustan silver, and that she, the acknowledging
party, guarantees all matters relating to this sale in every respect with every
guarantee, and that Satabous will register them in the present year's declaration, and all public taxes on them are his[2] responsibility. (*2nd hand*)
Subscriber, Sykos, also known as Papees, son of Neilos, about 40 years of
age with a scar . . . (*3rd hand*) I, Tatouetis, daughter of Harpagathos, acting
with my relative Stotoetis son of Stotoetis as guardian, acknowledge that I
have sold to Satabous the two female camels which belong to me, branded
'N' and 'H' on the right flank and I have received the price of 500 drachmas of silver and I will guarantee this with every guarantee, as aforementioned. I, . . . have written on her behalf. Drawn up in the registry of
Soknopaiou Nesos. (*Back*) *Red stamp.*

[1] No age is filled in.
[2] Or 'her' if the suggestion in *BL* I 17 is accepted.

188.   A loan between two women

P.Tebt. II 389
Tebtynis, 22 April AD 141

A straightforward contract of loan between two women, both acting with relatives
as legal guardians, transacted through a private bank in the Treasuries' quarter of the

Arsinoite *metropolis*. The statement that the loan is in accordance with a contract of mortgage (*hypallage*) seems to mean that this agreement is subject to, or a condition of, a previous agreement of loan made on a mortgage. This again emphasises the extent to which the availability and use of money depended on ownership of property.

Fourth year of Emperor Caesar Titus Aelius Hadrianus Antoninus Augustus Pius, Pharmouthi 27, by a draft of the bank of Sabinus[1] in the Treasuries' quarter. Isidora daughter of Herakleides son of Meledemos, with her relative Apion son of Apion as her guardian, (acknowledges) to Tamystha daughter of Origenes son of Origenes with her son Ptolemaios son of Ptolemaios as guardian the loan of the capital sum of three thousand five hundred drachmas of silver, total 3500 dr., for one year from the present month Pachon, at the interest of a drachma per mina per month, which sum she will repay in the month Pharmouthi of the coming 5th year of Antoninus Caesar the lord with the interest accruing upon it, four hundred and twenty drachmas, in accordance with a contract of mortgage which Tamystha has made upon her legal rights over a capital sum, and which was drawn up through the registry.

[1] This is a private bank. Such institutions received money on deposit from private individuals and paid out on instruction. The extent of their role in tax collection is not precisely clear, but the handling of taxes and other state funds was the main function of the public banks. See Johnson (1936), 445–8, Bogaert (1994).

189. Repayment of a loan by the children of the deceased wife of a veteran soldier

P.Oxy. LV 3798 (*BL* IX 204)
Oxyrhynchos, 24–8 August A D 144

This document records the return of a loan which had been made at the standard rate of interest (12 per cent) by the wife of a veteran soldier named Gaius Veturius Gemellus. By the date of this document the wife, Artemis daughter of Eudaimon, who was not a Roman citizen, had died, and the return of the loan was acknowledged by her son and daughter, who probably were Roman citizens. However, it is likely that they inherited as her heirs under Egyptian law, since prior to the *senatus consultum Orfitianum* of A D 178 children could not inherit in Roman law from an intestate mother.

C. Veturius Gemellus and Lucia Veturia alias Thermouthion, both children of C. Veturius Gemellus, veteran, whose name is engraved,[1] in association with their deceased mother Artemis, daughter of Eudaimon son of Eudaimon, whose mother is Thermouthion, whose name survives on the bronze stela at Rome, Lucia Veturia alias Thermouthion acting with C. Veturius Gemellus the father both of herself and of Veturius Gemellus as her guardian, to Epimachos son of Epimachos grandson of Epimachos, whose mother is Tateos (?), from Oxyrhynchos city, greetings. I acknowledge[2] that we have received back from you through the bank of Agathos Daimon and his partners at the Serapeum[3] in Oxyrhynchos city a capital sum of three hundred drachmas of money, and the interest on these of a drachma (per mina per month) from Hathyr of the past year up to the present day, the capital having been lent to you by our mother Artemis – since she died intestate, we declare that we are her only children and heirs – in accordance with a note of hand through a bank, dated in the month of Phaophi of the same past year, which we have delivered to you for cancellation, and that we have no claim against you or your agents about anything whatsoever up to the present day. The receipt is binding. Year 7 of Emperor Caesar Titus Aelius Hadrianus Antoninus Augustus Pius, Mesore . . . intercalary day.

(*2nd hand*) I, C. Veturius Gemellus, have received back, along with my sister, the three hundred drachmas and the interest and I have no claim, as aforesaid.

(*3rd hand*) I, Lucia Veturia alias Thermouthion, daughter of C. Veturius Gemellus, veteran, have jointly received it back, as aforesaid. I, C. Veturius Gemellus, veteran, have been registered as guardian of my daughter and I wrote on her behalf because she does not know letters.

(*4th hand*) I, Epimachos the younger son of Epimachos grandson of Epimachos, gave my assent. I, Eudaimon the elder son of Pesyris (?), wrote on his behalf because he does not know letters.

(*5th hand*) Seventh year of Emperor Caesar Titus Aelius Hadrianus Antoninus Augustus Pius, . . . intercalary day. The draft (is) through Agathos Daimon . . . the banker (?)

(*Back*) . . . Epimachos.

[1] C. Veturius Gemellus is known to have been enrolled in an Ituraean cohort in AD 103 at the age of 21. This reference to the bronze stela at Rome, where the names of discharged veterans were publicly displayed, is unusual in a document of this type; it is a regular element in the formulae of military diplomas (discharge certificates).

[2] The singular rather than plural verb is probably just a scribal slip.

[3] The Serapeum at Oxyrhynchos was not only a temple but also the nucleus of a commercial centre (cf. **214, 3.90, 4.132**).

190.   Credit transactions from the archive of Koloje

Jeme, seventh–eighth centuries AD

The archive of Koloje, consisting of thirty ostraka written in Coptic, dates to the seventh or eighth century AD and comes from the town of Jeme, by the temple of Medinet Habu on the west bank of the Nile opposite Thebes (for detailed discussion, see Wilfong, forthcoming(a), ch. 5). All the texts are connected with money-lending or loans of agricultural products (mainly wheat) in which her husband and her son were also involved. But Koloje, a businesswoman living in the centre of a thriving town, was able to act quite independently of her male relatives. The first of the documents reproduced records the transfer of a chain as security for a cash loan to another woman; the second is an acknowledgement of a loan of wheat and a promise to repay; the third, which may well be in the hand of Koloje herself, is a declaration that no deceit has been practised with regard to a necklace deposited as security.

(a) *OMH* 72

I, Mariam, daughter of Pebo, the woman of Petemout, write to Koloje, daughter of Phello, the woman of Jeme, saying: 'Seeing that I deposited the chain with you for two solidi, now, behold, I declare on this day, which is the fourteenth day of the month of Epeiph, that I have no [means] of proceeding against you on its account, ever, neither I nor any heir of mine, nor any man acting as my representative. Whosoever shall desire, from today until any time to come, to proceed against you concerning the chain, shall give four solidi as fine and shall come in and comply with this release.'

(b) *OMH* 50

Pses, son of Lase, writes: he owes to Koloje, daughter of Hllo, son of Katharon, one *shokas*[1] of wheat, 'and I shall give it to you in Paone (=*Pauni*) together with its interest, which is two *maje* to the artaba, without any objection'. I, Pses, son of Lase, assent to this sherd. I, Isaac, son of Paul, was requested and wrote with my hand, and I am witness. I wrote on the twenty-fifth of Paone, under Abraham, son of Atheris. Matthew, son of Shai, witness. Mark, son of Samuel, witness.

(c) *OMH* 93

By the place that is here, as to this gold necklace for two gold solidi, I have not removed anything from it, for these two solidi and their interest.

[1] The *shokas* and *maje* are measures: the *maje* one-twelfth of an artaba, and the *shokas* an uncertain multiple of the artaba – probably two artabas.

191.   Instruction to recover pawned property

P.Oxy. I 114 (*BL* I 316, II.2 93, IX 176)
Oxyrhynchos, second–third century AD

This text illustrates the provision of commercial services in a society which lacked the modern range of banking facilities. The author of the letter has raised cash by pawning her personal effects (cf. **6.253**; on pawnshops see Husselman, 1961) The rate of interest seems exorbitant, 48 per cent compared to the normal 12 per cent

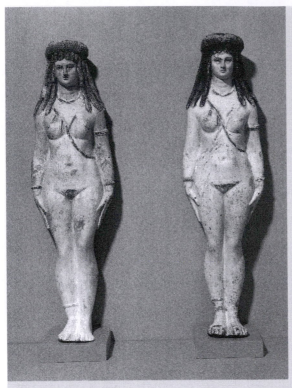

28   Statuettes of Aphrodite–Isis
British Museum, London
EA 26265–6
Tuna el-Gebel?,
Ptolemaic–Roman period

This pair of terracotta figurines is said to have been found, each in a wooden box, in a tomb probably at Tuna el-Gebel. The goddess' naked body, painted white by a thin application of clay, is protected by the amuletic qualities of her torque, armlet, bracelets, anklet, and chain with magical knot passing over her right shoulder and left hip. The diagonal marks from her left shoulder to right hip represent a fringed sash, painted in two colours. The pubic hair is also prominently picked out with paint. Similar statuettes from the Roman period show the goddess clothed, but raising her dress to display the pubic hair, a gesture known as *anasyrmene* ('exposure') which emphasises women's sexual and reproductive role; Goldman (1996), 251; Montserrat (1996), 167–9. Statuettes of Aphrodite were sometimes included in dowries, presumably to symbolise the bride's sexual and reproductive maturity (cf. **2.43, 4.136, 5.191**).

(cf. Cicero, *Att.* 5.21.11, for loans made at this high rate by Brutus to the people of Salamis in Cyprus). The list of pawned items reads like a list of dowry goods; see **6.252**. For statuettes of Aphrodite, see Burkhalter (1990b); cf **Plate 28** and **2.43**.

Now make it your concern to redeem my property from Sarapion. It is pawned for two minas and I have paid the interest up to Epeiph, at the rate of one stater per mina. There is a dalmatic cape the colour of frankincense, a dalmatic cape the colour of onyx, a tunic and a white cape with a real purple border, a striped face-cloth of the Lakonian type, a purple linen garment, 2 armlets, a necklace, a blanket, a statue of Aphrodite, a cup, a large tin flask and a wine-jar. Recover the 2 bracelets from Onetor. They have been pawned since Tybi of last year for eight hands (?)[1] at the rate of a stater per mina. If our cash is insufficient owing to the carelessness of Theagenis, if, I repeat, the cash is insufficient, sell the bracelets to make up the money. Many greetings to Aia and Eutychia and Alexandra. I pray for your health. Xanthilla greets Aia and all her friends. (*Back*) [To . . .] from Eunoia.

[1] The meaning of this phrase is not clear.

192.   A woman attempts to buy cheap wheat

SB XVI 12607
Provenance unknown, second–third century A D

This document shows an attempt to take advantage of low prices of wheat by indulging in commodity speculation. The person on whose instructions the estate managers are acting, referred to as 'little Theodora', may be the owner of the estate or the owner's daughter.

Dionysios to the most esteemed Hermes and Dioskoras, greeting. I learned from . . .on, the inspector,[1] that the majority of those from whom taxes are being demanded are not responding because of the cheapness of the crops. For he was saying that wheat is selling in your locality for 12 drachmas. And when she heard this the little Theodora wanted you to procure as much as you can for her. If this is the situation then, buy as many artabas of wheat as you can for two talents,[2] but only good clean seed, and let me know with what measure you receive it. However much you buy, therefore, let me know so that I may enter the price in the daily account[3] against your names . . . (*Back*) To Hermes and Dioskoras, estate managers.

[1] The *episkeptes*, a government official responsible for determining the area of taxable cultivated land.
[2] Two talents will buy about 1000 artabas, a very large quantity; these must be wealthy people.
[3] For accounting in estate management see Rathbone (1991), 331–87.

193.   Aurelia Charite takes a loan with mortgage of a courtyard

P.Charite 34
Hermopolis, 3 January A D 318 or 348

For the archive of Aurelia Charite, a wealthy landowner from Hermopolis Magna in Middle Egypt, see **179** introduction. Not surprisingly, her family also owned urban property in Hermopolis, and Charite here takes a loan of 640 talents for one month without interest, mortgaging a courtyard which she has inherited from her father, a councillor of Hermopolis.

Aurelia Charite, daughter of Amazonios formerly councillor of Hermopolis, to Aurelios Dios son of Helladios, formerly councillor of the same
city. I acknowledge that I have received and had measured out to me by you
from your house as a loan at interest a capital sum, with interest included,
of six hundred and forty talents of the coinage of the Augusti, total 640
talents, which I shall repay to you in the following month of Tybi without
delay. And when the day for repayment arrives, if I have not repaid I will
pay you interest for the intervening time until repayment has been made.
And as surety for the loan of this money I mortgage to you the courtyard
which I have received by inheritance from my deceased father in the South
Garrison quarter in which there is a verandah and a cellar and a fodder store
and cisterns of well-baked brick, of which the neighbours are on the south
the sons of Anoubion, son of Ammon, flax-worker, on the north a public
street, on the east property of myself Charite and on the west another public
street. This courtyard I shall keep unencumbered by any other loan . . .
Bond. Charite daughter of Amazonios. Capital with interest included, 640
talents. Tybi, 7th indiction.

194. A woman renounces any claim against her sister on an inherited millstone

BGU II 405 (*BL* I 44, II.2 17)
Philadelphia, 6 March A D 348

This text illustrates yet another type of property which might come into the possession of women: here two sisters had jointly inherited from their father a millstone
and grain-grinding machine. Aurelia Valeria, having sold it (whether to her sister
Nemesilla or to a third party is unclear) as her portion of the inheritance, renounces
any further claims on it against Nemesilla, from herself or her descendants.

In the consulship of Flavius Philippus the most illustrious prefect of the
sacred praetorium,[1] and Flavius Salias, the most illustrious master of horse,
Phamenoth 10. Aurelia Valeria daughter of Alypios to Aurelia Nemesilla,
my full[2] sister, of the village of Philadelphia of the Arsinoite nome, greeting. Since we were allotted a stone for crushing grain and a device for grinding grain by inheritance from our father, and I singly have taken the stone
and sold it for the portion falling to me, I hereby acknowledge that I have
no share in the aforesaid device for grinding grain, but am estranged and
alienated from it, and no one shall take proceedings against you about it, nor
shall I, Valeria, nor my children, nor heirs, nor anyone else; and I have issued
to you this written bond of assurance. This agreement is authoritative and
in answer to the formal question I have given my assent. I, Aurelia Valeria
the aforesaid have issued this assurance that I have no share in the device and

I agree to the written terms as stated. I, Aurelius Sarapion son of Julianus, from Alexandria, living in the same village, have written on her behalf, as she does not know letters.

¹ At this period, a high civil official.
² The editor reads *homogastrio* ('maternal') here, but since the women were sharing an inheritance from their father, *homognesio* ('full') is a more probable reading.

195.   A contract of deposit

P.Ryl. IV 662
Antinoopolis, AD 364

A contract of deposit for a sum of 11,600 talents drawn up at Antinoopolis between two women acting jointly and a third woman. The difference between a contract of deposit and a contract of loan is that the latter normally specified a rate of interest and repayment of the capital at a fixed time, whereas the former stated, as here, that the sum deposited was repayable on demand. Early in the empire when serving soldiers were not permitted to contract legally valid marriages the deposit formula was used by soldiers and their 'wives' to conceal dowries in unofficial 'marriages'.

Dated in the year after the consulship of Julianus, for the fourth time, and of Flavius Sallustius, the most illustrious prefect of the sacred praetorium.¹ Aurelia Thaisa, daughter of Papnouthis whose mother is Tanophris, from the Arsinoite nome and resident in the most illustrious city of Antinoopolis, and Aurelia Thaesis, daughter of Archias whose mother is Tanois from the same city of Antinoopolis, being mutual sureties for repayment, to Aurelia Tabinis of the same city of Antinoopolis, greeting. We acknowledge that we have received from you on deposit free of all risk and not subject to any deduction eleven thousand six hundred talents of silver, total 11,600 talents,² which sum we will repay to you at whatever time you choose without delay or prevarication. If we fail to do so, we will make restitution to you in accordance with the law governing deposits, you having the right of execution on us being mutual sureties, jointly and severally as you may choose, for payment or on all our possessions as though in accordance with a legal decision. This deed of deposit which we have herewith issued to you for your security is binding and confirmed and in response to the formal question we have given our consent. Mecheir 18. We, Aurelia Thaisa daughter of Papnouthis and Thaesis daughter of Archias the aforementioned, hold on deposit the eleven thousand six hundred talents, and will restore them as aforesaid. I, Aurelius Dorotheos, son of Antinoos, have written for them since they do not know letters.

¹ See **194** note 1.
² For comparison, in AD 360 a pound of meat cost 96 talents (*P.Oxy.* VII 1056).

196.   A woman takes out a lease on three rooms

P.Oxy. XVI 1957
Oxyrhynchos, 28 March AD 430

In late antiquity, leases of houses or rooms in houses occur not infrequently, and women appear both as lessors (cf. **2.61**) or, as in the text translated here, as tenants. It would be interesting to know why Didyme should require the use of two dining rooms and a further room; it is unfortunately characteristic of legal documents such as this contract of lease that we are not told such details. Note that Didyme acts without a guardian (**Ch.4 Sect. III** introd.), but has a man present and signing on her behalf, since she was illiterate.

After the consulship of Flavii Florentinus and Dionysios the most illustrious, Pharmouthi 2. To Flavius Flavianus son of Agathinos [. . .] from the glorious and most glorious city of the Oxyrhynchites, from Aurelia Didyme daughter of Horos, from the same city, acting without a guardian. I voluntarily undertake to lease from the present [month of Pharmouthi] of the present year 106/75,[1] the current thirteenth indiction, the three rooms belonging to you in the same city in the Cavalry Camp quarter, complete, a dining room and another dining room situated above the vault and in the light well a single[2] room with all its fitments; and I shall pay you for their rent annually half a gold solidus, which I shall of necessity give you each year in two six-monthly instalments, and whenever you wish, I shall hand back to you the same rooms in the condition I received them. The lease written in a single copy is authoritative, and when asked the formal question, I gave my consent. I, Aurelia Didyme the aforesaid, daughter of Horos, acting without a guardian as she affirmed herself, have taken on lease the aforesaid rooms and shall give the rent as stated. I, Aurelius Theodoros son of Theodoros [have written on her behalf] in her presence since she does not know letters.

[1] A date by the eras of Oxyrhynchos; see **2.61** note 1.
[2] The word *monochoron* used here presumably means a room separate from the rest of the building.

197.   Lease of a potter's workshop in a monastery from the heirs of Helen and from Mariam her sister

P.Cair.Masp. I 67110 (*BL* VII 34)
Aphrodite, 25 July AD 565

Two sisters, Helen and Mariam, had jointly inherited from their father a one-third share of a potter's workshop within ancestral property, now a monastery. In this contract Psais, a potter, undertakes to lease, for the duration of his life, the pottery with its accompanying fittings, cistern and furnaces, in return for an annual rent of 2400 jars. Helen too had died, probably not long before the contract was made, so it is addressed to her heirs, whoever they are, and the co-owner, her sister Mariam.

After the consulship of Flavius Basileius the most reputable, 24th year, Mesore 1 of the fourteenth indiction. Aurelius Psais whose father was Jeremiah, and mother was Maria, potter from the village of Pte[. . .] of the Antaiopolite nome now living in the village of Aphrodite, to all the heirs, whether sons or daughters, of Helen daughter of Romanus son of Victor [. . .] and to Mariam her full sister, landowners in the same village of Aphrodite, greeting. I have leased from you voluntarily and with conviction (?) for the entire period of my life,[1] calculated from today the aforestated day, which is Mesore 1 of the current fourteenth indiction, for the sub-sequent entire duration of my life, your patrimonial third share complete of a complete potter's workshop situated in the south of the same village of Aphrodite, near the holy place of Abba Michael, being in your paternal farmstead, near the pottery of the holy monastery of Abba Sourous your ancestor, adjoining it on the north part, which forms the two-thirds share to complete the whole pottery, facing west, with your third share of the cistern there and of all things proper to it and fittings, namely the two long rooms being within the (monastery of) holy Michael, and the long room in front of the guest-room facing north, with one third of the furnace and pitch-furnace, on condition that I shall have this under my control for my work, and give to you annually for fixed rent acceptable (?) jars without pitch two thousand four hundred − total 2400 jars − in due time without dispute. Let the lease be authoritative and guaranteed, and when asked the formal question, I gave my consent. I, Aurelius Psais son of Jeremiah, afore-said, potter, have taken on the lease as stated. I, Aurelius Horoonchis son of Menas, at his request, wrote for him since he does not know letters. I, Aurelius Kallinikos son of Hermaos witness it as stated. I, Aurelius Iohannes son of Kyriakos witness the lease as stated.
Drawn up by me, Kyros, notary.
(*Back*) Lease made by Psais son of Jeremiah with the heirs of Helen daugh-ter of Romanus and Mariam her sister.

[1] This provision is very unusual in leases from Egypt.

198. Agreement to provide services in lieu of interest on a loan

SB IV 7358; re-ed. H. C. Youtie, *ZPE* 13 (1974), 235–7
Karanis, A D 277–82

A woman from Memphis receives from a resident of Karanis the sum of three talents which she has used to pay off a debt incurred by her father. The recipient, instead

of paying interest on the loan, binds herself to remain in service with the lender, performing weaving and general domestic duties. This form of service, called *paramone*,
was relatively common: see Westermann (1948), Adams (1964), Samuel (1965), esp.
301–6, Hengstl (1972); cf. Hopkins (1978), ch.3. If the father is still alive it may be
imagined that he is in effect selling his daughter into service to pay off a debt.

Aurelia Taesis, daughter of Asklepiades, whose mother is Sarapous, from the
city of Memphis, has acknowledged that she has received from Aurelia
Thaisarion, daughter of Komon, from the village of Karanis, the capital sum
of eighteen thousand drachmas, that is three talents, and Aurelia Taesis has
acknowledged in addition that she has expended this for a debt of her aforementioned father Asklepiades, and that she, the acknowledging party, must
of necessity remain in service with Aurelia Thaisarion, performing weaving
work of which she is capable and domestic duties in place of the interest on
the capital. And if she wishes to leave, she must of necessity make repayment of the aforementioned three talents of silver without any delay and
until the repayment (?) Aurelia Thaisarion shall have the right of execution
upon the acknowledging party Aurelia Taesis and all her possessions as if by
legal judgement. Let this document, which is made in a single copy, be
binding wherever produced. And in answer to the formal question, I have
given my consent. I, Aurelia Taesis, have the aforementioned three talents
of silver and I shall remain to do service in the weaving trade and other
domestic duties. And if I leave, I shall repay the aforementioned sum, as
aforementioned. And in answer to the formal question I have given my
consent. I, Aurelius Horion son of Soterichos, from the Phremei quarter,
have written on her behalf since she is illiterate.

199.   A contract to provide service (*paramone*)

P.Köln II 102
Oxyrhynchos, 30 March A D 418

In this contract of *paramone* (see **198**) a village woman binds herself to provide
general services for a resident of the *metropolis* for a sum of two solidi.

After the consulship of our masters Honorius the eternal Augustus for the
11th time and Flavius Constantius the most illustrious, Pharmouthi 4.
Aurelia Asenneth daughter of Paulos whose mother is Thekla from the
village of Alkonis in the Oxyrhynchite nome to Aurelius Chairemon son of
Serenos from the illustrious and most illustrious city of the Oxyrhynchites,
greetings. I acknowledge that I have personally received from you out of
your house on account of advance payment for the service which I undertake for you gold solidi, single, bearing the image of our masters, of full
weight and genuine, number 2 as a capital sum in return for which I will

remain with you and blamelessly and of my own free will perform the tasks
enjoined upon me by you and whenever I wish to leave you or when you
yourself wish it, I shall necessarily hand over to you in full the aforementioned two gold solidi without delay, you having the right of execution on
me and all my possessions. The document, written in duplicate, is authoritative, and in answer to the formal question I have given my consent. I,
Aurelia Asenneth daughter of Paulos have received the two solidi on
account of payment for service and am in agreement with everything as
aforementioned. I, Aurelios Hermeias . . . have written on her behalf [since
she is illiterate]. Note of hand of Asenneth, daughter of Paulos.

200.   Request from a female weaver for fleeces

P.Mich. I 16
Philadelphia (or Memphis?), 3 June 257 BC

Bia, the female weaver referred to in this letter to Zenon (see **Ch.3 Arch. A**) may
well be a slave (see Thompson, 1988, 53–5).

Nikon to Zenon, greeting. Bia is asking for the two rams' fleeces which you
left behind for spinning yarn. Write to us therefore whether they should be
given to her. For she said that she is in need of woollen yarn and because of
this is behind schedule. I have written to you previously about these matters.
Farewell. Year 29, Pharmouthi 25. (*Back*) To Zenon. About fleeces. Nikon,
about 2 fleeces, if they should be given to Bia. Year 29, Daisios 11.

201.   Two letters to Zenon offering the services of weavers

(a) *PSI* IV 341
Philadelphia, 22 November 256 BC

Here two brothers offer to Zenon the services of themselves and their female relatives as weavers. For weaving on the estate of Apollonios (see **Ch.3 Arch. A** introd.)
see Rostovtzeff (1922), 116–17; Préaux (1939), 105; Clarysse and Vandorpe (1995),
63–8; cf. Thompson (1988), 53–5.

Apollophanes and Demetrios, brothers, craftsmen in all the skills of weaving
women's clothing, to Zenon, greetings. If you please and you happen to
have the need, we are ready to provide what you need. For hearing of the
reputation of the city and that you, its leading man, are a good and just
person, we have decided to come to Philadelphia to you, we ourselves and
our mother and wife. And in order that we might be employed, bring us
in, if you please. If you wish, we can manufacture cloaks, tunics, girdles,

clothing, sword-belts, sheets; and for women: split tunics, tegidia,[1] full-length robes, purple-bordered robes. And we can teach people, if you wish. Instruct Nikias to provide us with lodging. And, to save you wondering, we will provide you with guarantors, men of substance, some from here and some in Moithymis. Farewell. Year 30, Gorpieion 28, Thoth 28. Apollophanes and Demetrios, brothers.

(b) *PSI* VI 599 (with p. xviii, *BL* VIII 399)
Philadelphia, undated

In this memorandum a family of weavers offers to work for Zenon, proposing alternative methods of compensation for their work, which, according to their estimate for preparing the yarn and weaving a piece of cloth, would take three men and one woman six days. Zenon could pay them as a group for each piece (1 drachma for cleaning and combing the flax and 3 drachmas for weaving it), or he could pay a daily wage of 1½ obols for each man per day, ½ obol for the woman, making an assistant available to them.[2] The daily wage proposed for the woman was thus only one third of that asked for each male weaver, perhaps because she was sometimes occupied with domestic chores and did not spend all her time weaving. The fact that the weavers asked for any salary for her contrasts with the more strictly domestic economy that prevailed in classical Athens (on which see Pomeroy, 1994, 41–5, 57–67).

To Zenon, greetings from the weavers. We have come here to work. So that we may receive our due, you need to give us 1 drachma for each talent-weight of washing and carding and 3 bronze drachmas for weaving each piece of linen cloth. Even this is not sufficient for us, (because) each piece requires 3 men and one woman six days to finish and cut off from the loom. If you do not accept these conditions, give us each 1½ obols a day and the woman ½ obol, and furnish us with an assistant able to help with the weaving equipment for 5 drachmas and 2 obols, to be deducted from our wages. Farewell.

[1] An item of female clothing, but it is unclear precisely what it means.
[2] Following the calculations in Clarysse and Vandorpe (1995), 64–5, the weavers' total earnings by piecework would be 20 drachmas each month; if paid by the day, with the monthly (?) salary of the assistant charged to them, their total earnings would be 19 drachmas 4 obols each month.

202. List of female textile-workers

P.Cair.Zen. II 59295
Philadelphia, 250 BC

This short list giving the number of women engaged in wool-working in three Fayum villages emphasises the high numbers involved in this domestic mode of production; cf. **180(a)**, **3.94**.

List of women working wool according to the registration of the 30th year:

Mouchis	320
Oxyrhyncha	314
Tebtynis	150
Total	784

203.   List of female textile-workers

BGU x 1942
Provenance unknown, second–first century B C

A list of female textile workers, probably slaves, and all with Greek names, alpha-betically[1] arranged (α to θ). If the remaining two-thirds of the alphabet produced a similar proportion of names, a large establishment of over forty workers is implied. The high proportion of women unable to work because of illness is noteworthy. On this text see Bingen, *CdE* 42 (1967), 228, Lewis, *BASP* 11 (1974), 149.

Apollonia	. . .
Arkadia	unwell
Aristonike	wool-working[2]
Gaza	shaking the weft
Dionysia	wool-working
Dianoia	wool-working
Demarion	unwell
Helenis	unwell
Euthene	shaking the weft
Hermione	spinning
Eirene	. . .
Ebenion	unwell
Herakleia	unwell
Theophila	wool-working

[1] Unusual at this early period.
[2] The verb here seems to refer to the process of carding the wool, see Lewis, *BASP* 11 (1974), 149.

204.   Apprenticeship contract for a female slave

Stud.Pal. XXII 40 (*BL* II.2 167, III 238, V 145, VI 196, VIII 481)
Soknopaiou Nesos, 20 October A D 140

Contracts of apprenticeship show slave-girls, apparently about twelve or thirteen years old, being apprenticed to master weavers on the same terms as young boys, both free and slave.[1] Once trained, slave-girls could work within the master's household, or be hired out for a wage (**3.94**; also *P.Wisc.* 1 5). No freeborn girls are documented as apprentice weavers, despite the plentiful evidence of free adult women working as weavers, including Aurelia Libouke of Karanis, who (acting without a guardian 'because of her right of children') accepted a young slave-girl as apprentice in A D 271 (*SB* XVIII 13305). Nor is it certain that any freeborn women were among the few females who paid the weavers' tax, paid in the Roman period by professional weavers aged fourteen or over.[2]

The terms of this apprenticeship contract, from the archive of Segathis,[3] a woman from the Fayum village of Soknopaiou Nesos, are not unusual; they reflect the general practice in other skills too, such as shorthand-writing.

The fourteenth year of Emperor Caesar Titus Aelius Hadrianus Antoninus Augustus Pius, Phaophi 23, in the village of Soknopaiou Nesos in the division of Herakleides in the Arsinoite Nome. Segathis daughter of Satabous son of Tesies from the village of Soknopaiou Nesos, about 60 years old, with a scar above her mouth, with her guardian Stotoetis, son of Stotoetis, grandson of Stotoetis, about 40 years old with a scar on his right hand, has handed over to Pausiris son of Panemmeus, weaver, about . . . years old, with a scar on his right hand, her slave girl whose name is Taorsenouphis to learn the skill of weaving for a period of one year and two months, commencing on the first day of the present month of Hathyr of the 14th year of Antoninus Caesar the lord. The child shall be fed and clothed by Pausiris. All public taxes pertaining to the trade shall be paid by Pausiris and the girl shall not be absent from the house of Pausiris by day or by night without his authority. And for whatever number of days she is idle through the fault of her mistress or is sick or neglects her duties, she shall remain for an equal number of days in compensation after the set time. And after the set time Pausiris shall return the girl having been taught the craft to the best of his ability. And if he does not return her he shall pay compensation of one hundred drachmas of silver and an equal amount to the public account. And if her mistress takes the girl away within the period she shall pay an equal amount of compensation. Satabous son of Abous, about 30 years old with scars on his forehead and his mouth and between his eyebrows is the subscriber . . . I, Pausiris son of Panephremis, acknowledge that I have received the girl to learn the craft for the aforementioned period of time and I shall do each of the specified things as aforementioned. I, Satabous, have written on his behalf since he is illiterate. I, Segathis daughter of Satabous with my guardian Stotoetis son of Stotoetis, have handed over the girl to learn the craft of weaving for the aforementioned period of time and I shall do each of the specified things as aforementioned. I, Pakysis, have written on their behalf since they do not know how to write.

[1] Apprenticeship contracts, *didaskalikai*, are listed by Herrmann (1957), 119, updated in the introductions to *P.Wisc.* I 4, *P.Oxy.* XLI 2977, *P.Oxy.Hels.* 29, and *BASP* 22 (1985), 255–6. Of 28 apprentice contracts for teaching various aspects of weaving (including two from the archive of Tryphon: **Ch.3 Arch.D**), 19 relate to freeborn boys, 3 to slave boys, and 6 to slave girls (**204** and *P.Mich.* 346a, *P.Oxy.* XIV 1647, *PSI* III 241, *SB* XVIII 13305, and probably *P.Ross.Georg.* II 18.450–8).

[2] The woman in *BGU* III 617 was certainly servile; other receipts for weaver's tax do not specify the woman's status, but the absence of patronymic makes servile status probable (*O.Mich.* 111; *P.Coll.Youtie* I 36; cf. *PSI* IX 1055).

[3] For the name see *BGU* XI 2043.4 and note.

205.   Letter from Apollonia to Philetos giving an account of expenses incurred in weaving

P.Oxy. XXXI 2593

Oxyrhynchos, second century A D

This letter from Apollonia to Philetos is interesting for its technical language and for the systematic account Apollonia gives of what she has spent on ready-spun warp and on wool for the woof and spinning expenses, some of which she has done herself and some of which she has contracted out.

Apollonia to Philetos, greetings. I send my very best wishes to you and Herakleides, and I have sent to you by Onnophris the younger the yarn for weaving Herakleides' outfit: 7 minas of woof, weighing . . . staters, that is 110 reels; and warp from Lykopolis weighing 90 staters, that is 75 balls. Of which the cost is: for the warp, at twenty-one drachmas per 30 staters weight, total, 63 drachmas; and the price of the wool for the woof, 36 drachmas. 30 staters' weight has already been spun for the cost of one stater (?),[1] and I gave one stater's weight of wool of my own towards the cost of the manufacture, 4 drachmas. I sent out three minas to be spun, at an obol per stater weight, in all 17 drachmas 5 obols, and I myself spun the other four minas and put into them a coloured black thread – put three minas of these into the cloak of the outfit. We send you very best wishes. Goodbye. The warp has been soaked here with me. (*2nd hand*) Year . . . Thoth. (*Back*) Deliver to Philetos for Herakleides.

[1] The stater is a weight of approximately 14 g. It can also refer to a denomination of money (4 dr.), but elsewhere in this document the writer uses only drachmas and obols.

206.   Letters from Tayris about weaving equipment

P.Oxy. XXXI 2599

Oxyrhynchos, third–fourth century A D

Some of the names in these letters from the woman Tayris are strongly suggestive of either a Jewish or a Christian context, but it is impossible to be sure which.

Tayris to my lord father Apitheon, greetings. Send us two weaver's combs and two ounces of storax and also two large hair combs. Just as you said to me 'I shall send things like that to the place for you', send them. Buy the purple of which you were saying, 'I shall buy it'. So then, tell the sister of

Dioskoros' wife to say to Didyme, 'If, as you said, you are making double thick material (?),[1] go on making it, if you are not, work on my father's purple and tow.' I send good wishes to Esther (?) and your sister Susanna. So then, Kyra, just as you said, 'I shall send you some towels', send them, and I shall send you some Egyptian ones. I send good wishes to you, Kyra, along with your sister and your mother's sister.

Tayris to my lord brother Theodore, very many greetings. Buy me, my lord brother, three towels and the . . . pair of boots which you mentioned and three pairs of slippers for the baths. Take the half-pound of fine tow (?) which I gave you to use (and) [either] make it into a face-cloth or bring the price of it. Send me two large combs. Just as you said to me 'I shall buy . . .' remember your oath when you depart. As to the little book (?) in the bag, do not give it to anyone. Bring it when you come. As to the half-pound of fine tow (?) . . . Tell the son of Herakleianos . . . the two talents, if you think proper . . . buy purple. I send good wishes to you, Herakl. . . and your husband. I send good wishes to Theod. . . Come quickly so that we may see you.

[1] The meaning of the word *dikarutida* is uncertain.

207. Letter about trade in prostitutes

PSI iv 406
Philadelphia, third century b c

A memorandum to Zenon (see **Ch.3 Arch. A**) in which he is asked to investigate the activities of two men who are allegedly engaged in trading female slaves as prostitutes to Palestine; see Scholl (1990), 42; (1983), no. 6; Orrieux (1983), 44–5; Harper (1928); and cf. **4.124**. The quality of the Greek leaves much to be desired and some of the details are obscure.

Memorandum to Zenon from Herakleides the driver. Concerning the things which Drimylos and Dionysios have done to the slave girl. (One of them?) misused her and gave her to the desert guard. They decked her out with whatever she had. And she is in Pegai with the desert guard. They bought another girl from the Ammonites and they sold her in Ptolemais. This is the fourth time he has brought a sacred priestess down to Joppa.[1] And he went away to the Hauran taking a female slave with him and got 150 drachmas. And when he returned from there he collected a band of Nabataeans. And when a disturbance arose he was taken off to prison in fetters for seven days. And Drimylos bought a slave-girl for 300 drachmas. For each day they went out on to the streets and made a splendid profit. And because they were doing this they did not keep their mind upon the livestock but Drimylos each day warmed two bronze cauldrons of water for his sweetheart. And he sold the female ass and the onager. And there are witnesses of these events. Concerning more of these affairs, if you ask me, you will find the whole truth.

[1] Despite the description of the girl as a 'priestess', it seems unlikely that this is to be connected with the practice of temple-prostitution. The passage is too obscure to offer any firm interpretation.

208. A leading councillor of Alexandria murders a prostitute

BGU IV 1024 col. VI (*BL* I 88–9, VII 17, IX 25)
Hermopolis, end of fourth century A D

This extract comes from a long dossier of texts from Hermopolis recording legal proceedings before a high official. The cases all seem to concern murder or prostitution, and may be a collection of precedents for use by lawyers. This particular case concerns the accusation of a councillor of Alexandria by the mother of a prostitute who claims to have been deprived of her means of livelihood because the man had murdered her daughter. See Keenan (1989), 15–23, Bagnall (1993a), 196–7.

Against a certain leading councillor of Alexandria called Diodemos who was the lover of a public prostitute. Diodemos was completely besotted with love for the prostitute. Diodemos regularly employed the company of the prostitute in the evening hours. Diodemos murdered the prostitute and when Zephyrios found out, he ordered Diodemos to be imprisoned. On the following day, at the morning greeting ceremony, the councillors of Alexandria asked Zephyrios that Diodemos should be freed and that the case against him be discussed. The councillors' request seemed to Zephyrios unreasonable. He nevertheless promised that he would free Diodemos, but he was lying. When Zephyrios came out of his house after the greeting the local people asked him not to free Diodemos. So, finding an excuse, Zephyrios said to the councillors: 'I am no longer able to free Diodemos in accordance with my announcement to you since the rest of the non-residents and the people of the province have found out about the statement made against Diodemos, being in the pay of the ranting mob (?).' So they persuaded me, saying 'It is to your advantage and ours that Diodemos should be kept under guard in prison . . .' So they (*the Alexandrian councillors?*) asked that Diodemos should be brought out of the prison and given a hearing. Diodemos thought carefully and considering . . . agreed that he had murdered the prostitute. And the mother of the prostitute, a certain Theodora, a poor old woman, asked that Diodemos should be compelled to provide for her a subsistence allowance as a small recompense (*for the loss of her daughter's life?*). For she said: 'It was for this reason that I gave my daughter to the brothel-keeper, so that I should be able to have sustenance. Since I have been deprived of my means of livelihood by the death of my daughter, I therefore ask that I be given the modest needs of a woman for my subsistence.' The prefect said: 'You have slaughtered a woman who makes a shameful reproach of her fortune among men, in that she led an immoral life but in the end plied her trade . . . Indeed, I have taken pity upon the wretch because when she was alive she was available to anyone who wanted her, just like a corpse. For the poverty of the mother's fortune so overwhelmingly oppressed her that she sold her daughter for a shameful price so that she incurred the notoriety of a prostitute . . . . full of toil . . . but so that you may not wish to . . . the . . . sanctity of the council-chamber, it is my instruction, as if purging the dignity of the city and the council-chamber, that you should be executed by the sword as a murderer. As for Theodora, the impoverished old woman and mother of the deceased who, because of the poverty which constricted her, dragged her own daughter away from the path of virtue, on account of which she has lost her, she shall inherit one tenth of the property of Diodemos. This is what the laws suggest to me and the considerations of clemency are in harmony with what is permitted under the law.'

209. The owner of a beer-shop complains to Zenon about the abduction of her daughter

P.Lond. VII 1976
Philadelphia, 253 BC

A female owner of a beer-shop complains to Zenon (see **Ch.3 Arch. A**) about the deception of her daughter by a vine-dresser who has 'carried her off' despite the fact that he already has a wife and child.

Haynchis to Zenon, greetings. I take beer from the large beer-shop and dispose of 4 drachmas worth daily,[1] and pay regularly. But Demetrios the vine-dresser, having deceived my daughter, has carried her off and conceals her saying he will set up house with her without my consent. And she helped me to manage the shop and supported me in my old age. Now therefore since she has gone away I am making a loss and I do not have the necessities of life. And he has another wife and children here, so that he cannot consort with the woman he has deceived. I therefore ask you to help me on account of my old age, and return her to me.

[1] This appears to mean that the woman buys beer from a larger brewery and resells it at a profit. The manufacture and distribution of beer was a royal 'monopoly' in the Ptolemaic period, see Préaux (1939), 152–8.

210. A widow is accused of deceiving her husband's partner

P.Oxy. XXII 2342 (*BL* IV 65–6, VII 148)
Oxyrhynchos, 16 March AD 102

This petition to the prefect of Egypt, written in somewhat laconic and obscure Greek, illustrates a widow's capacity for independent action in financial and business matters when the surviving sons have been disinherited. A wine-seller from Oxyrhynchos attempts, probably for a second time, to claim redress against the widow of his deceased partner whom he accuses of having realised the capital worth of the business and retained the proceeds for herself. On Pasion and Berenike, see Cockle (1987), 196; Pasion's will survives (*P. Oxy.* III 493).

To my lord the prefect C. Minicius Italus, from Apion son of Apion, from Oxyrhynchos city, wine-merchant. In the second year of Trajan Caesar the lord, Pasion son of Sarapion, my partner and debtor, died in Alexandria, having disinherited his children because of their dereliction of duty, and left his wife Berenike as his heir. She kept the whole stock of wine to herself under lock and key and appropriated the whole amount which she realised by its sale when she learned of her husband's death away from home. She is under pressure from her evil-scheming sons not to tell the truth about her conduct nor to come to an agreement. And she has neither paid out the money which she held as capital nor given up the documents but is keeping the entire deposit and is daily deceiving me. We went before Dios the strategos and she said: 'There are written documents worth three thousand drachmas and others secured on the wine to the value of five thousand.' Seeing that she was lying, Dios asked her for the daily account-book of her husband Pasion which he himself would often produce, showing a total of five thousand two hundred and forty-nine drachmas and four obols in respect of all transactions, written and unwritten. Having been instructed not to produce the account-book because of the prosecution she concealed it and hoodwinked the strategos. He, on the pretext of urgent business (?) dismissed us . . .[1] For these reasons, having been wronged, I have recourse to you, the benefactor of all mankind, and I ask you, if it seems good to you, to instruct the strategos of the nome in writing to settle the case as far as possible. Farewell. Handed to the prefect in Kos,[2] Phamenoth 20.

[1] The translation here follows the sense suggested by Van Groningen, *CdE* 32 (1957), 348–51. Lines 29–35, which are fragmentary and obscure, are omitted.
[2] Kos was the chief town, either of the Herakleopolite nome, or of the Koite toparchy.

211.   Receipt from a female camel-keeper

P.Aberd. 30 (*BL* III 211)
Soknopaiou Nesos, *c.* AD 139

A receipt from a female camel-keeper (cf. **186–7**), of payments due to her for transporting grain from the village of Dionysias in the Fayum to the Nile harbours. The payment was in arrears and the complexities of the bureaucratic procedures were due to the fact that it had to be made by authorities of a region other than the one in which she resided.

To the controllers of disbursements of the division of Themistos, from Taouetis, daughter of Totes, camel-keeper, of the village of Soknopaiou

Nesos in the division of Herakleides, acting with Tesenouphis, son of Tesenouphis, as my guardian. I acknowledge that I have had measured out to me and have received from the grain-collectors of the granary of the village of Dionysias, from the granary of the village, the [artabas of wheat] which Dion strategos of my own division informed me that his predecessor as strategos had written were due to me for wages for the transport of the public grain which I conveyed from the [granaries] of the division of Themistos . . .

212. Sale of a slave girl rescued from exposure

P.Kellis 8
Kellis (Mothite nome, Dakleh Oasis), A D 362

It is often thought that, because of the cultural preference for boys, girls were more likely to be exposed 'on the dung-heap' to die, unless picked up and reared for their economic value by a stranger (see **213**, **6.230**). Here we chance on the story of one such girl who was brought up as a slave in a small hamlet, nursed by the woman of the couple who rescued her, and then sold by them while still very young to a resident of the local urban centre.

Aurelii Psais, son of Pekysis, grandson of Palitous, and Tatoup his wife, both from the village of Kellis in the Mothite nome, residing in the hamlet of E . . ., to Aurelius Tithoes, son of Petesis, carpenter, from the same village in the same nome, greetings. We acknowledge that we have sold and conveyed to you from now for all time the slave-girl belonging to us, raised from the ground and reared by me, the aforementioned woman, with my own milk, at a price agreed between us of two solidi of imperial, unalloyed and newly minted gold, total 2 solidi, which we have received from you from your hand in full on all the terms written herein to which we give assent, in order that you the purchaser from henceforth possess, own and have proprietary rights over the slave-girl sold to you and have the right to control and manage her in whatever way you choose, the guarantee resting on us the sellers throughout against every litigant or claimant. Let the sale, having been written in two copies with the signature of the man subscribing on our behalf, be authoritative, guaranteed and legal everywhere it may be produced, and having been formally questioned we have assented. In the consulship of Mamertinus and Nevitta the most illustrious, Thoth according to the Greek calendar.
(*2nd hand*) We, the aforementioned Aurelii Psais son of Pekysis and Tatoup his wife, have sold the aforementioned slave girl . . . and we have received the price in two solidi of gold and we shall guarantee the sale for you with every guarantee as aforesaid and having been formally questioned we have assented. I, Aurelius Timotheos, son of Harpokration, former magistrate, have written for them at their request because they do not know letters.

(*3rd hand*) I, Aurelius Demosthenes, son of Polykrates, from the village of Kellis, am a witness.

(*4th hand*) I, Aurelius Horion, son of Timotheos, from the village of Kellis, am a witness.

213. Contract for a wet nurse

BGU IV 1058 (*BL* VIII 39–40)
Alexandria, 29 March 13 BC

About forty nursing contracts survive from Roman Egypt, mostly from Alexandria and the hellenised *metropoleis*.[1] In most cases, the wet nurse was employed to nurse, not a freeborn infant, but a slave, either born in the house of its master or 'picked up from the dung-heap'. The number of female infants said in the contracts to have been 'picked up' is double that of male infants (cf. **212** introd.). For the sexual restrictions placed on wet nurses, see Bradley (1980).

Several aspects of this nursing contract concluded between two members of a wealthy Alexandrian family are unusual: first, the fact that the mother Philotera agrees to furnish her own slave as wet nurse for the infant slave girl Agalmation her son Sillis had 'raised up'. Second, the fact that the 288 drachmas salary for the nursing her slave is to carry out over time is to be paid to Philotera immediately, and not in instalments; perhaps the arrangement conceals a loan by Sillis to his mother. And third, the fact that should the infant Agalmation die, Philotera must find another slave child, likewise picked up from the dung-heap, to nurse in its place. Otherwise the provisions are typical for nursing contracts.

To Protarchos.[2] From Sillis son of Ptolemaios, of the deme Philometoreios, and from his mother Philotera daughter of Theodoros, Persian woman,[3] with her guardian, her husband Ptolemaios son of Sillis, of the deme Philometoreios. Regarding the matters at issue, Philotera agrees that she will furnish her slave Zosime for the duration of two years from Pharmouthi of the present (year) 17 of Caesar, to raise and nurse at Philotera's house the raised-up slave child that Sillis entrusted to her, a suckling female named Agalmation. The stipulated salary for milk and nourishment each month with oil and bread is 12 drachmas, while the total sum for the two years of nursing is 288 silver drachmas which Philotera has right away received from Sillis in cash. And if the above mentioned child should happen to suffer something mortal within the two years, Philotera must pick up another child and furnish her slave as nurse, disposing her completely (to the task) for the two years to which she has agreed, receiving nothing more, because she received an 'immortal' child[4] to nourish. Further, from the present moment she (agrees) to furnish her slave who is to take suitable care of herself and of the child, not spoiling her milk, neither engaging in sexual intercourse, nor becoming pregnant, and not nursing another child in addition; (she agrees that) whatever things she takes for the baby, or has entrusted to her, she will preserve intact and give back, whenever she is asked, or she will pay the value of each, except that she be released of any clear wear and tear that is also obvious, nor will she abandon the nursing within the time. If she transgresses any of these conditions, she is to pay the amount she took for the nursing with a penalty of half and damages and expenses and another 500 drachmas as fine, with the right of legal action belonging to Sillis against both Philotera herself and all her property, as if from a legal decision. While all guarantees of protection that exist, and whatever ones might be introduced, are invalid, the agreement which Philotera made to Sillis remains valid and confirmed with regard to the slave child . . . .[5] We ask (that this contract be registered). (Year) 17 of Caesar, Pharmouthi 4.

[1] Masciadri and Montevecchi (1984); a chart (pp. 32–5) summarises the information contained in the contracts.
[2] For other legal documents submitted to Protarchos, head of an Alexandrian tribunal, see **4.127, 129**.
[3] See Glossary.
[4] The child is 'immortal' in the legal sense that if the baby dies, another must be found and nourished in its place.
[5] The last word in this sentence might be 'also to be nourished', perhaps pointing to an additional slave child.

214. Acknowledgement of wet-nursing services

P.Oxy. I 91
Oxyrhynchos, 13 October AD 187

A man from Oxyrhynchos acknowledges to a woman the receipt of wages which she has paid to him for the wet-nursing service provided for her baby daughter by the man's female slave. The element of exploitation of the slave is obvious, but many women were no doubt able to provide such services if they had given birth to children who did not survive. In this case the baby is freeborn but there are many examples of wet-nursing contracts for slave children and foundlings (e.g. **213**; cf. **3.91**).

Chosion son of Sarapion, son of Harpokration, whose mother is Sarapias, of Oxyrhynchos city, to Tanenteris daughter of Thonis, whose mother is Zoilos, of the same city, acting with her guardian Demetrios son of Horion whose mother is Arsinoe, of the same city, greeting. I acknowledge that I have received from you through Heliodoros and his associates overseers of the bank at the Serapeum in Oxyrhynchos city for which the promise of payment was given by Epimachos, four hundred drachmas in imperial coin for wages, oil, clothes and all other expenses during the two years in which my slave Sarapias nursed your daughter Helena, registered as your daughter who, when you took her back, had been weaned and had received every care; and I acknowledge that I neither have nor shall have any complaint or charge to make against you either in connection with this transaction or with any other matter whatsoever up to the present time. The receipt is authoritative. Year 28 of Emperor Caesar Marcus Aurelius Commodus Antoninus Pius Felix Augustus Armeniacus Medicus Parthicus Sarmaticus Germanicus Maximus Britannicus, Phaophi 15. (*2nd hand*) I, Chosion son of Sarapion, have received the four hundred drachmas for the nursing and I have no complaint against you, as aforementioned. I, Tanenteris daughter of Thonis, acting with Demetrios son of Horion as my guardian, agree and I have taken my daughter, as aforementioned. I, Ploution son of Hermes, have written on their behalf since they do not know letters.

215. Engagement of a flute-player by a female dancer

CPR XVIII 1
Theogenis, January–February 231 BC

This and the following document are examples from a number of contracts (in this case an abstract) of this kind engaging performers (cf. *P.Lond.* VI 1917 where four flageolet players are hired) who were sometimes organised in companies. Olympias appears to be a single performer but it is not clear whether Artemisia and her colleagues formed a company. See Westermann (1932), 16; Grassi (1973), 117–35.

Sosos son of Sosos, Syracusan of the *epigone*, has hired himself to Olympias . . . from Attika (*?Athenian*), dancer, acting with Zopyros, son of Marikkos (?), Galatian of the *epigone*, as her guardian, to work with her as a flute-player for twelve months from the month of Hyperberetaios of the 16th year for a wage of forty-five bronze drachmas per month. And Sosos has received in advance from Olympias 50 bronze drachmas. He shall not fail to appear at any festival or any other engagement at which Olympias is present and he shall not provide service for anyone else without the authority of Olympias. The keeper of the contract is Olympichos, son of Herodotos, Kleopatreus . . .[1] Sosos is about 30 years of age, large, with honey-coloured skin. Olympias is about 20 years of age, short, with white skin and a round face. Zopyros is about . . . with honey-coloured skin and a large face. Olympichos is about 40 years of age, of medium height, with honey-coloured skin, a large face and a bald forehead. The contract was written in year 16, Hyperberetaios.

[1] The significance of this term is unclear; it may designate Olympichos' deme.

216. Engagement of castanet-dancers

P.Corn. 9
Philadelphia, AD 206

A village woman engages three castanet-dancers to perform in a private house on generous terms. Dancing of this kind appears to have been traditional in Egypt; see

29   A 'Coptic' textile depicting female dancers
Flemish private collection; De Moor (1993) cat. 60
Circa fifth–sixth century AD

This scene (35 x 25.5 cm), worked in purple wool on the neck area of a tunic of undyed
linen, shows four arched niches containing dancers, alternately male and female; the women
wear long tunics and the men animal skins.

Herodotus, II.60 and **2.22**. For a bronze figurine of a castanet-dancer clothed in a
transparent linen dress, see Perdrizet (1911), 63–4 and plate 29; for a 'Coptic' textile
depicting castanet dancers, **Plate 29**.

To Isidora, castanet-dancer, from Artemisia, from the village of Philadelphia. I wish to engage you with 2 other castanet-dancers to perform at my
house for six days from the 24th of the month Pauni according to the old
reckoning,[1] receiving for all of you wages of 36 drachmas per day and for
the whole six days 4 artabas of barley and 20 pairs of loaves, and we will
safely guard whatever garments or gold ornaments you bring down, and we
will provide two donkeys for you when you come down and the same when
you return. (*2nd hand*) Year 14 of Lucius Septimius Severus Pius Pertinax
and Marcus Aurelius Antoninus Pius, Augusti and Publius Septimius Geta
Caesar Augustus, Pauni 16.

[1] This is a late use of the old Egyptian *annus vagus*, as opposed to the fixed year introduced
by Augustus, which intercalated an extra day in each fourth year.

217. A widow bequeaths a fullery to her sons

P.Coll.Youtie II 83
Oxyrhynchos, 12 December AD 353

A woman from Oxyrhynchos uses the form of the *donatio mortis causa* (see **4.147**) to leave equal shares in her fullery to her two sons. On fulling, see Wipszycka (1965), 129–45.

In the consulship of our masters Constantius Augustus for the 6th time and Constantius the most illustrious Caesar for the 2nd time, Choiak 16. Aurelia Ammonia also known as Zois, daughter of Hermon, from the glorious and most glorious city of the Oxyrhynchites, acting in virtue of the 'right of children',[1] to my children Aurelius Paulos and Dionysios, both sons of my deceased husband Aurelius Her[. . .] greetings. Since you, Dionysios, have for a long time since the death of your father remained with me, your mother, and have worked at the fulling trade and have not abandoned me but have treated your mother kindly, I acknowledge that I have ceded to both of you, my children, in common and in equal shares all the fulling works and offices (?)[2] that I have built up and fostered through my labours and everything else pertaining to that trade on condition that it should remain with me for as long as I survive and after my death you two, Paulos and Dionysios, shall have possession of it with your children and descendants and shall have the power to use, control and administer it without hindrance. The guarantee is authoritative . . . and in response to the formal question I have given my consent.

[1] See **4.142**.
[2] The meaning of the term *psepheia* is obscure.

6 Being female

Introduction

The events of birth, marriage, and death punctuated the lives of women in Greek and Roman Egypt, for biology determined their destiny, even as social customs sanctioned and reinforced women's intimate relations with these most important moments in a family's life from one generation to the next. In this chapter we present women's activities arranged according to the life cycle, from birth (**I**) through education (**II**), marriage and married life (**III**), to sickness and death (**IV**). Wives and daughters were responsible for running the household, overseeing daily preparation of food, baking of bread, bringing water from the well, weaving clothes, even in wealthy homes where slaves and hired help were available to perform menial tasks. When there were no slaves, as seems to have been the case in many village households, women did the work themselves, congregating in an inner courtyard with friends and women from the neighbourhood (cf. **Plates 21–2**). Grown children, both men and women, looked homeward in good times and in bad, no matter how great the distances that separated them, and the letters they sent home underscore how family members were a source of physical support and emotional strength throughout one's lifetime. Correspondents laced their letters with complaints of having received no replies to earlier letters, or reported the safe arrival of baskets of items which the letter-carrier had also brought. Affective relationships between parents and children, between siblings, between husbands and wives, exemplify how much home and family meant to these people of two millennia ago. Their world, often so different from our own, appears more familiar when we confront family members speaking their private messages to one another.

The chapter concludes (**V**) by exploring some of the potentially conflicting and contradictory images that characterise the women of Greek and Roman Egypt. Juxtaposed against the petitions which manipulate the stereotype of women's weakness and helplessness in order to gain redress for grievances we find, not only the misogynist maxims that were often part of the school curriculum (**242**) and literary portrayals of women as sexually potent or aggressive (**288–9**, cf. **3.84**), but also magical texts in which a woman was the active party (**285–6**).

Throughout this chapter, even more than previous ones, it is important to be aware of the perspectives from which our views of women are derived. Many of the texts in this chapter were explicitly written by men, either addressing women directly, or voicing concerns about women to others. Even those in which women employ the first person and purport to speak in their own voice may have been either wholly composed, or at least written down, by men. In both literary texts and funerary inscriptions, whether in Greek or Egyptian, male writers assumed women's voices (**262, 272–4, 289**). The Roman aristocrat Julia Balbilla does, however, speak in her own voice, when flattering the emperor Hadrian and his wife Sabina during their tour of Egypt, and when boasting of her own illustrious ancestry in her elaborate poetic programme (**244–5**), although even her words had to conform to the conventions of the genre.

The scribe waiting with his portable writing-stand on the street corner to be hired by villagers or townspeople to write an important letter or to compose a necessary document was not simply a passive transcriber of words dictated to him, but shaped what his clients wished to say into the appropriate format and phraseology.[1] Women who could read and write, and sign the documents that concerned them, might be able to verify the scribe's official version of their narratives (cf. **Plates 27, 36, 40**). In private letters, women's voices may emerge, despite the scribal interventions (especially in the case of illiterates) and repetition of standard formulae.[2] Literate women composed and wrote letters themselves, and, even when using a scribe, often affixed a final greeting, or appended notes in the margins and between the lines, strengthening our belief that they inspected what a scribe had written down to their dictation. Although we cannot be completely certain which letters were written by the hand of a woman, those written entirely in the awkward capitals of someone not in the habit of writing frequently may well have been penned by the woman herself.[3]

The binding spells and magical charms of attraction are also couched in formulaic expressions. Handbooks offered collections of spells, which refer vaguely to the one who desires and the one who is desired as 'this man' and 'this woman'; the common implication is that the person who took action was male and the object of his aggression was female.[4] Nonetheless, those spells that were personalised through the addition of the names of the pursuer and the pursued show that women also played the role of aggressor. For the spell to be effective, women must have intoned the magic words in their own voices, or risked attaching their beloved to whoever recited the charm (**285–6**). The aggressive woman from Egyptian and Greek milieux was not simply a figure of literary imaginations.

A further recurrent theme of the chapter concerns the ways by which women, and men, attempted to gain control over the uncertainties of the future. Religion (in the form of oracle questions and prayers), magical charms and medical prescriptions all represent ways of trying to ensure greater control over the precariousness of human existence. These alternatives, far from being sharply differentiated, interlocked and overlapped with one another through shared assumptions and techniques. The area of women's health, in particular, shows a complex interrelationship between medical and popular perspectives.

Throughout this chapter, arrangement by topic takes precedence over chronological sequence. On several occasions we have taken the liberty of presenting fuller versions of texts from the manuscript tradition, rather than the more fragmentary versions preserved on papyrus (**218, 238, 247,** cf. **241** introd.).

[1] For the extent of scribal interference in petitions, compare **2.33** with **3.79**.
[2] See especially **Ch.3 Arch. K.**
[3] **Plates 30, 41**; cf. **225** and **Ch.3 Arch. E.**
[4] See **282–6**; Winkler (1990) discusses the intellectual and emotional complexities exhibited in the erotic spells.

I   Birth, infancy and childhood

218.   *Predictions of Astrampsychos*: **The unknown future**

In addition to visiting an oracular shrine and submitting questions to the god (see **249**), a simple way to secure divine advice about a human problem was to go to the local oracle seller who helped you 'consult' his copy of the *Predictions of Astrampsychos*. Our most complete copies of the *Predictions* consist of a list of about ninety questions, numbered in sequence, some thousand possible answers arranged in groups of ten ('decades'), with each decade numbered, and a concordance that shows how to move from question to answer. The arrangement of each numbered decade, although appearing to be random, has in fact been carried out with care. According to the introductory letter of instructions about how to use the *Predictions*, the oracle seller told the customer to pick a question from the list, and noted its number. He then asked the customer to choose any number between one and ten. The customer's choice, it was thought, would reflect divine guidance; 'Assure the customer that God will put the number in one's mouth', says the Christian version of the introductory letter. The oracle seller then added the two numbers together and in the customer's presence used the concordance to determine which decade contained the response to the question posed. For example, if a man wanted assurances that his prospective bride was going to present him with a dowry, his question was 'Am I going to get the dowry?', number 49. Suppose he picked 4 as the number 'the gods put into his mouth'. The concordance would indicate which decade contained the answer to question 49 + 4, or '53'. Since answers to question 49 actually appeared in each of ten decades, it did not matter if the customer had said '8' instead of '4' as the number that 'the gods put into his mouth'; the concordance would then indicate a different decade which also included an answer to question 49. In five decades the answer was positive: 'You are getting the dowry', and in the other five its prediction was negative: 'You are not getting a dowry'. Most of the ninety questions were orientated to be appropriate for a male questioner, but the men's concerns often involved the future of their womenfolk, whether indirectly, with questions involving good luck in business ventures, or in attaining public office, or directly, as in the following examples that concern birth of children.

Fragmentary copies on papyrus show that the *Predictions* were revised over time. The number of answers was sometimes expanded from the simple five positive and the five negative answers, to yield a greater variety in the repertory of responses, presumably to meet the demand of customers for more nuanced predictions. Gods' names were added to the numbers in the concordance during pagan centuries and to the numbered decades, so that the oracle seller could instruct the customer to ask a particular god, under whose name he found his answer. In Christian centuries names of Old and New Testament figures replaced the pagan gods, demonstrating the continuing popularity of the *Predictions*.

The translation below, taken from the fullest copy of this oracle book, preserved in a thirteenth-century manuscript, illustrates the development of additional responses beyond the simple positive and negative answers to questions regarding the birth of children. Note that this translation does not preserve the original arrangement of answers in decades, but instead extracts from the decades in which they appear all the possible answers to each question.[1]

Question 24: Is my wife going to give birth?
> *Repertory of different answers:* She is going to give birth and be in danger.[2]
> > She is going to give birth with much pain.
> > She is going to give birth, but does not raise the child.
> > She is going to give birth to the creature engendered, and you, be quiet.
> > The creature engendered is not going to be raised.

Question 30: Am I to raise the child that has been conceived?
> *Repertory of different answers:* The child conceived is to survive.[3]
> > The child conceived is going to live and be raised.
> > You will raise the child conceived.
> > The child conceived is not going to survive.
> > The child conceived is not going to live.
> > The child conceived is not going to be raised.

Question 47: Will I beget children?
> *Repertory of different answers:*
> > You are going to beget children and raise them.
> > You will not beget children now.[4]
> > You are going to beget children right away.
> > You need to be childless now, in my opinion.
> > You will beget a son and a daughter.
> > You are going to beget children – don't worry.
> > You are not going to beget children now – don't expect to.
> > You have the lot of a childless person.
> > You are going to beget children and take no pleasure in it.

Question 59: Will my wife abort?
  Repertory of different answers: She will abort and be in danger.[5]
    She will not abort, don't worry.
    She is going to prevail with regard to her growing (?) womb.

[1] Cf. **247**: *Predictions* regarding marriage. Our description of the procedure follows Browne (1970). Browne (1983) published the Greek text of the Christian version. Fragments of the earlier pagan versions on papyri: *P.Oxy.* XII 1477, XXXVIII 2832–3 (re-edited by Browne, 1974); *P.Oxy.* XLVII 3330; *P.Leid.Inst.* 8.
[2] The first answer appears in more or less the same form in six decades; the remaining four once each.
[3] The first answer appears in five decades; the next answer twice; the remaining four once.
[4] This second answer appears in more or less the same form in three decades; the rest once each.
[5] The first answer appears in the same form in five decades; the second answer in four decades; the third answer once.

219.   A family letter about a pregnancy

P.Oxy. XLVI 3312 (*BL* VIII 269)
Oxyrhynchos, second century A D

This letter and the two that follow (**220–1**), all directed to family members or close friends, look to impending births (cf. Adam, 1983; Montevecchi, 1979). The damaged beginning of this letter leaves it unclear whether the writer is a man or woman.

. . . [Salute] . . . and his children – may the evil eye not touch them – and Isidora, your sister, and Athenais. Be sure to write to me about Dionysarion, how many months (pregnant) she is. Gaia greets you, as well as both her children and husband. Know, then, that Herminos has gone to Rome and become a freedman of Caesar so that he may take on official duties. Salute all your people by name, and all those with me greet you. I pray you are well. (*Address on the back*) . . . of . . . at (?) Oxyrhynchos (?).

220.   A daughter reports about her pregnancy and other matters

SB V 7572 (*BL* III 189; IX 247)
Philadelphia, early second century A D

Thermouthas probably wrote this letter herself (see **Plate 30**).

Thermouthas to Valerias her mother, very many greetings and always good health. I received from Valerius the basket in which there were twenty pairs of wheat cakes and ten pairs of other cakes. Send me the blankets at the price (we agreed upon) and fine quality wool, four fleeces. Give these items

(a) Front: Thermouthas' letter

(b) Back: Address (written transversely)

30   Letter of Thermouthas to Valerias

SB v 7572 (= P.Mich.inv. 188)

Philadelphia, early second century AD

This letter (see **6.220**) is probably written by Thermouthas herself. Despite the awkward penmanship and somewhat uncertain orthography and grammar, it seems wrong to label this a 'letter of an illiterate woman', as in Pestman, *New Primer*, 40. Cf. **Plates 27, 36, 40, 41**.

to Valerius. Also, I am at the moment seven months pregnant. And I greet Artemis and little Nikarous and Valerius, my lord (I long for him in my mind), and both Dionysia and Demetrous, many times, and little Taesis, many times, and all those in your house. And how is my father doing? Please send me news, because he was ill when he left me. I greet grandma.[1] Rodine sends you greetings. I have set her to the handiwork; again I have need of her, but I am cheerful. Phaophi 8.

(*Address on the back*) Deliver to Philadelphia, to Valerias, my mother.

[1] Or the word *maman* may designate Thermouthas' wet nurse.

221.   A man's concern for Theonilla who is pregnant

PSI VIII 895 (re-ed. Manfredi, 1993)
Oxyrhynchos, late third–early fourth century A D

The writer's name is lost, though the masculine participles indicate that he was male. He may have been Theonilla's husband, as well as her brother.

. . . you, coming to . . . I (?) have come here. Now I repeatedly received your (?) letters that make clear to me . . . that you (?) are coming. But, even if your absence especially grieves me . . . But this I entrust to you, beseeching and pleading your daughter (?) to offer . . . to my sister Theonilla during each hour and to advise her about things that are suitable, so that she is in no way aggrieved. For I myself know and have been persuaded that our common parents look down on her, and I repeatedly pleaded with them by letters to furnish the same concern for her and to make all the customary preparations for her delivery.[1] For the god knows that I wanted to send unguents and all the other things to be used for the delivery. But in order that . . . occur again, I am being detained by no one of those you know. In fact, I have sent a copy of the whole account to my lord father without having added one silver coin, but I have asked him through letters . . . the accounts of my colleagues . . . with regard to our affairs. If you want, read my letter . . . to (?) my father. This I now ask of you . . .

(*In the left margin*) . . . to Antiochos, concerning the money which I mentioned . . . and . . . the same Theonilla to you [. . .

(*Address on the back*) to . . . son of . . .]onios . . . mphionis.

[1] See Hanson (1994b), section I.

222.   Obstetrics in Egypt

Soranos, *Gynaecology* II 6

The king's divine birth (as an embodiment of the sun-god) played a central role in Egyptian religion. From the fourth century B C throughout the Ptolemaic and early

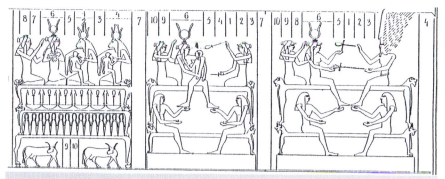

31 The divine birth of Horos
(Detail from) interior of Birth House (after Chassinat, 1939, plate xv)
Edfu, late second–early first century BC

The scenes from the north wall of the *naos* (inner chamber) of the mammisi at Edfu show
(right to left): Hathor and Amun making love, Hathor giving birth to Horos, the new king,
and Horos being suckled by two goddesses.

Roman periods, large temple-building projects, such as those at Dendera, Edfu and
Philae, included a separate 'birth-house' (*mammisi*) devoted to the celebration of the
divine birth, which was depicted in relief on the walls (**Plate 31**).

The hieroglyph which determines words relating to birth pictures a woman
sitting, with the head and arms of a child extending beneath her (**Plate 32**), very
close to the posture depicted in a scene of childbirth on a mummy label of the third
century AD (**Plate 42**). What appears to be a birth stool was excavated in a tomb
of the XVIII dynasty (*c.* 1500 BC); a similar stool is represented in a terracotta birth
scene of the Roman period (**Plate 33**).[1] By the time of the New Kingdom, childbirth sometimes seems to have taken place in a specially built, secluded structure,
perhaps in the garden or on the roof of a house; these are known to us only from
illustrations (Robins, 1993, 82–4).

There are parallels between the 'fertility tests' in an Egyptian medical papyrus
from the XIX or XX dynasty (*c.* 1314–1085 BC) and those in the *Hippocratic Corpus*,
Greek medical texts compiled largely in the late fifth–early fourth centuries BC;
these have, in turn, close ties with earlier, oral traditions of Greek medicine (cf.
Sect.V introd.; Iversen, 1939). Although separated by a millennium, both Egyptian
and early Greek medical men claim to rely on the ability of smells to traverse
passageways in the body of a woman who was able to conceive a child. The Greek
version instructs: 'Clean a clove of garlic, cut off the head, and insert into the vagina,
and next day see if she smells it through her mouth. If she smells it, she will conceive; if not, she won't.' Scholars disagree whether or not such prognostic tests
developed independently in Egypt and the Greek world, or whether Greek medicine borrowed them from Egyptian traditions (von Staden, 1989, 1–31).

In the third century BC under Ptolemy II Philadelphos, the Greek doctor
Herophilos not only undertook systematic dissection of corpses at the Museum in
Alexandria, but also practised vivisection, cutting up the condemned criminals
given him by the king. Although Herophilos' interests spanned most of medicine,

(a)

33   Egyptian birth stools
(a) Wooden stool (Egyptian Museum, Cairo no. 56.353)
Gournah, XVIII dynasty (*c.* 1500 BC)

This birth stool, constructed in wood and certainly portable, seems similar to the stool called for by the Hippocratic doctor of *Superfetation* 8, as an alternative to the large and cumbersome delivery chair. No wooden examples have survived from the Greek world (Hanson, 1994b).

(b) Terracotta figurine (British Museum, GR 1992.8.11.1)
First–second century AD

A pregnant woman, draped and veiled, is seated on a birth stool; see *JEA* 80 (1994), p. 181.

(b)

he was the first Greek doctor, so far as we know, to write a book entitled *Midwifery*. It is difficult to gauge how much influence Herophilos' many anatomical discoveries had beyond the city of Alexandria, but one of his contemporaries at the Museum, the poet Kallimachos, alluded to the anatomist's work both in isolating the fourth tunic of the eye and in advocating a sitting position for delivery that offered support for the parturient's back.[2] Herophilos' *Midwifery* and his anatomical writings are lost, but passages from them are preserved in the later medical writers of the Roman period, Soranos and Galen, both of whom went to Alexandria for training. Soranos' own work, *Gynaecology*, circulated in Greek-speaking Egypt, as a papyrus fragment demonstrates.[3] Soranos gave the following description of birth:

. . . The midwife is to insert her fingers (into the parturient's) vagina gently at the moment of dilatation. She is to pull the foetus forward, relaxing her grip when the uterus compresses itself together, but grasping gently and pulling when it dilates. If, in fact, she were to pull when the uterus is compressing, she would cause inflammation, or haemorrhage, or even an external prolapse. The servants who stand at the sides of the parturient are to press with their hands on the mass, gently moving it downward in the direction of her lower parts. At last the midwife herself is to receive the infant, covering her hands first with pieces of cloth, or, as those in Egypt do, with scraps of thin papyrus, so that the baby won't slip off and won't be squeezed, but may rest in quiet.

[1] For birth stools in Greek medical writers, see Hanson (1994b).
[2] Most (1981), 188–96; von Staden (1989), 394–5.
[3] *PSI* II 117, part of Book III (= Mertens-Pack[3] 1483; Mertens-Pack[3] 2347 may also derive from Soranos, see Hanson and Green, 1994). Temkin (1991) gives an English translation of Soranos' treatise. Throughout antiquity many doctors continued to go to Alexandria for their medical training; for Galen's studies in Alexandria, see Nutton (1993).

223.   Christian birth amulet

PGM CXXIIIa 48–50
Provenance unknown, fifth century AD

For a woman giving birth. 'Stride out from your tomb, Christ summons you.'
(Set) a potsherd on the right thigh.

224.   Petronilla and the birth of her dead husband's child

P.Gen. II 103 (*BL* VIII 136)
Arsinoite nome, August–September AD 147

The death of a baby's father prior to its birth occasioned serious problems for a pregnant widow; cf. **4.129**. Petronilla, a Roman citizen widowed while pregnant, wanted to vindicate her baby's right as heir to her dead husband, Herennius Valens.[1]

The relevant clause of the Roman praetor's edict, 'Concerning a belly that has to be inspected and a birth that must be watched over' (*de inspiciendo ventre custodiendoque partu*), ruled: 'In cases where a widow says she is pregnant, she must take care that the fact (of her pregnancy) is announced to those to whom these matters will be of concern, or to their agent, twice in a month, so that they may send, if they want, women who will inspect her belly. The women to be sent, moreover, are to be free, up to five in number, and these are to do their inspecting all at the same time, lest one of them, while she is inspecting, touch the belly when the woman herself is unwilling. She must give birth in the house of a totally honest woman whom I shall appoint', etc. (*Digest* XXV 4.10). The procedure was designed to protect not only the interests of a legitimate child posthumously born, but also the interests of the deceased father's family, lest an unscrupulous widow try to foist off on them a suppositious baby, brought in by a midwife in a basket.[2] Petronilla claims to have followed the inspection procedure as best she could before giving birth to a boy, Lucius Herennius.[3]

Kinsmen of Petronilla's deceased husband continued to dispute the child's legitimacy even after the inspection procedure (*P.Gen.* II 104), and Petronilla's decision to petition the *iuridicus* Calvisius Patrophilos, asking him to choose a guardian for her child, resulted from a subscription appended at the bottom of her earlier petition. Petronilla gave the *iuridicus* the names of two possible candidates, and he passed the names on to Maximus alias Nearchos, strategos of the Herakleides division of the Arsinoite nome, where Petronilla lived. Neither candidate, however, was from the Arsinoite nome, so Maximus wrote to Ptolemaios, strategos of the Aphroditopolite nome, where the two candidates lived. A copy of Ptolemaios' response to Maximus became part of the dossier, which concludes with a letter from the strategos Maximus, returning the matter to *iuridicus* and restating the testimony of the scribe of the *metropolis* in the Aphroditopolite nome that one candidate was better suited than the other to serve as the infant's guardian.

The first column in the dossier, directed to the *iuridicus* from Petronilla, mostly now lost, contained the opening portions of the description of the inspection procedure she followed. The translation starts at the top of the second column, towards the end of Petronilla's petition to the *iuridicus*. The body of this was no doubt penned by a professional scribe, but Petronilla appears to have added the closing greeting herself (*2nd hand*).

. . . (the woman) to whom you ordered me to go. She reported to you that she had examined me in the company of the midwife; she acknowledged that I was pregnant, but that it was not possible for me to give birth at her house; instead she promised that she would watch over me, if I continued until all my time was fulfilled and nothing happened that was my fault. May I be benefited.

(*2nd hand*) Farewell. (*1st hand*) Year 11, Thoth 27.

(*3rd hand*) Summon her.[4] (*4th hand*) A copy of a letter which Ptolemaios wrote to Maximus.

Ptolemaios, strategos of the Aphroditopolite nome, to the most honourable Maximus alias Nearchos, strategos of the Arsinoite nome, Herakleides division, greetings. You wrote to me that Calvisius Patrophilos, the distinguished *iuridicus*, sent a copy of the letter he wrote you concerning the appointment of guardians for the minor, Lucius Herennius . . . in order that (?) I might indicate which of the two, submitted by his mother, Petronilla, to the post of guardian, was the more trustworthy for the post in accordance with what the distinguished *iuridicus* wrote: Aelius Apollonios, former gymnasiarch of Antinoopolis, but currently auditor (*eklogistes*) of the Memphite nome, and a landowner in this nome, or Longinius Menenius former gymnasiarch of Aphroditopolis and a landholder in the same nome. I indicate, therefore, that the scribe of the *metropolis* has testified under oath that the more trustworthy of the two is Aelius Apollonios. Therefore, I write to you, sir, so that you may know. Farewell, sir.

(*5th hand*): Year 11 of Emperor Caesar Titus Aelius Hadrianus Antoninus Augustus Pius, 29 Thoth.

Copy of a letter.

Maximus alias Nearchos, strategos of the Arsinoite nome, Herakleides division, to Calvisius Patrophilos, the distinguished *iuridicus*, greetings. You have indicated to me concerning the appointment of a guardian for Lucius Herennius, minor, that I ought to determine the more trustworthy of those submitted by his mother and write to you, upon receiving the letter (?) concerning (?) Longinius Menenius . . . Aelius Apollonios, former gymnasiarch of Antinoopolis, but currently auditor of the Memphite nome, or Longinius Menenius former gymnasiarch of Aphroditopolis and a landholder in the same nome. By the strategos of the Aphroditopolite nome [it was . . .] and it was declared . . . by the scribe of the *metropolis* under oath that the more trustworthy for the post of his guardian was Aelius Apollonios. As a result I write to you, sir, so that you may know. Farewell, sir. Year 11 of Emperor Caesar .. . . .

[1] Wilcken (1906) first recognised the importance of this text; see also Gardner (1984) and (1986), 53.

[2] The fear of a suppositious child was vivid in the Greek and Roman world: Hanson (1994b).

[3] Following the Roman pattern of nomenclature, Petronilla's son by (Lucius?) Herennius Valens was named Lucius Herennius (Valens?); a girl would have been Herennia. Roman naming patterns are so conservative that the names of a man's children (and his freedmen and women) can usually be deduced from his own name. Petronilla's name is a diminutive feminine form (presumably her father's name was Petronius); such diminutives are common among Roman women's names.

[4] For the text at this point (*contra BL* IX 91), see Evans Grubbs and Hanson (forthcoming).

225.   A grandmother suggests a name for her daughter's baby girl

P.Münch. III 57

Provenance unknown, second century BC

The official form of names for Graeco-Egyptians followed the general Greek pattern: 'x son (or daughter) of y'; the mother's name and those of both paternal and maternal grandfathers could be added for more precise identification. Graeco-Egyptian naming choices display greater flexibility than the Roman (see **224** note

3), although the same names tend to repeat in families, the first son often being named after his paternal grandfather ('papponym').[1] In this letter a grandmother suggests that a newborn girl child be named 'Kleopatra', possibly after the contemporary queen (**2.8, 11**); but 'Kleopatra' was a common Macedonian name, like those of the addressees of this letter, and probably had some special family connotation. It is likely that the mother wrote this letter herself (see plate in *P.Münch.* III, Abb. 10).

Your mother to (?) . . . rek.a . . . ,[2] Ptollis, Nikander, Lysimachos, and Tryphaina, greetings. If you all are well, it would be as (I wish). I pray to the gods to know that you all are healthy. We received the letter from you in which you (Tryphaina) announce that you have given birth to your child. I kept praying to the gods every day on your behalf. Now that you have escaped, I am spending my days in the greatest joy. I sent you a flask full of olive oil and . . . pounds[3] of dried figs. Please empty out the flask and send it back to me safely, because I need it here. Don't hesitate to name the little one 'Kleopatra', so that your little daughter . . .

[1] Hobson (1989).
[2] The opening of this letter is unusual, and the mother should have mentioned her own name. Perhaps the broken letters after 'your mother' conceal both her name and the name of her first child (e.g. 'Your mother Geore, to K.a . . . , Ptollis', etc.).
[3] The numeral is missing.

226. A father decides on his daughter's name

P.Mil. II 84 (*BL* VI 77)
Provenance unknown, fourth century AD

There survives only a small portion of this letter written by the father of a newborn girl, addressed probably to his mother.

. . . Andrias and Nikias salute you, and also little Lampadis. If it had happened that I engendered a male, I was intending to give it my brother's name. As it was a little girl child, she was called by your name. I also salute the wife of the adjutant (*a military officer*).

227. Birth of a seven-month child

SB XVI 12606
Oxyrhynchos, third century AD

This letter[1] and the next (**228**) seem to reflect the superstition that a seven-month child is born lucky and survives, but the eight-month child dies, and in each instance a concerned younger relative of the parturient – brother or sister – is writing to a grandparent of the infant.

The notion that the eight-month child did not survive its birth, but the seven-month child did, permeated the writings of Greek medical authors. The notion is intertwined with the Greek superstition that 7 is a lucky number possessing mystical properties. Hypertensive disorders, such as the eclampsia that develops during the final trimester in about one quarter of all modern pregnancies, may have endowed the 'unlucky eight-month child' of the Graeco-Roman world with a degree of medical reality, so that fact and fiction interweave and reinforce one another, contributing to the longevity of the notion into modern times (see further Hanson, 1987 and 1994a). What helped to make the notion appealing in the Greek world was the fact that in a period of high infant and maternal mortality, there was no appeal from the judgement that a baby born dead, or already dying, was an eight-month child; and the conviction that eight-month babies always died exonerated birth attendants, both doctors and midwives alike, from accusations of negligence and offered some consolation to the bereaved family that the baby's death was inevitable. For the seven-month child, although weak and puny, there was hope, and so the baby born alive, yet smaller than expected, was cautiously labelled a seven-month child, not an eight-month child, in order to give the little one greater potential for survival.

For the possible identity of Techosous as a landowner, see Nielsen (1994), esp. 135–6.

Zoilos to Theodora his mother, greetings. When I was in Thallou today at my brother's, I found everyone in good health, but Techosous, my sister, was dreadfully ill. I expect that today she will bear a seven-month child. If, then, she comes through the delivery successfully, I will let you know the outcome. Inaaroous, the little one's father, who brings this letter to you, together with Akes, son of Pachoimis, the weaver, and also with the others, have come to Oxyrhynchos to complete an obligation that was placed upon them in the affairs of the most estimable Hieronikes. Please give to them the key to the room of the . . . in the gateway, for Eudaimonis says that they have come first to your side so that they might remain there until they receive hospitality from your lord. Salute all those at our house. Eudaimonis and Techosous and all those here salute you. She (?) even paid the same men for expenses . . .

[1] See H. C. Youtie, *ZPE* 36 (1979), 70–3 (= *Script.Post.* II 562–5).

228.   Thaubas announces the death of her sister and her baby, an eight-month child

P.Fouad I 75 (*BL* IV 32; VII 57)
Oxyrhyncha (Arsinoite nome), 15 October A D 64

Herennia and her father Pompeios are known from five letters to Pompeios from family and friends – his sister Charitous, his wife (?) Heraklous, two letters from Herennia, and this letter from Herennia's sister Thaubas, announcing Herennia's death.[1] Herennia employed others to write the two letters she sent to her father

Pompeios, but she was literate enough to append a greeting in her own hand to one of them (*SB* VI 9122). In this letter Thaubas also makes use of a scribe, without adding a greeting in her own hand. In addition to Thaubas, Herennia had another sister Thaisous and three brothers: Pompeios, Syrion, and Onomastos. Herennia and her husband also had at least one older child, born before 18 January 57, a little Pompeios named after his grandfather and uncle (cf. **225** introd.).

Thaubas to Pompeios, her father, many greetings. Please come home as soon as you receive my letter, because your poor daughter Herennia has died. And she already came safely through a premature delivery on the ninth of Phaophi. You see, she gave birth to an eight-month child, dead; she lived on for four days, but then died herself. She received a funeral from us and her husband, as was right, and has been transported to Alabanthis. So, if you come and want to, you can see her. Alexander greets you and so do his children. Farewell. (Year) 11 of Nero Claudius Caesar Augustus Germanicus Emperor, Phaophi 18.

(*Address on the back*) To Oxyrhyncha to the place called . . . to Pompeios.

¹ Other letters with English translation from this family's papers are *P.Mert.* II 63, Eitrem and Amundsen (1951); also White (1986), nos. 90–2.

229.   Petition: my pregnant wife was attacked and suffered a miscarriage

P.Mich. V 228
Areos Kome (Arsinoite nome), 23 November AD 47

A villager accuses an associate (or perhaps his employer) of having attacked his pregnant wife as a result of a quarrel over wages, making her miscarry and suffer risk to her own life (cf. **3.89**). The petition starts with a summary of the parties involved in the dispute.

About 26 years old, with a scar on the left side of his neck and his left forearm. His wife Tanouris, daughter of Heronas. Against Bentetis, son of Bentetis. From Thouonis, son of Akousilaos, of Areos Kome, 26th of the present month Neos Sebastos of the 8th year of Tiberius Claudius Caesar Augustus Germanicus Emperor.

(*2nd hand*) To Apollonios, strategos of the Arsinoite nome, from Thouonis, son of Akousilaos, of Areos Kome of the Polemon division, on the 26th day of the present month Neos Sebastos of year 8 of Tiberius Claudius Caesar Augustus Germanicus Emperor. When I was calculating accounts with Bentetis, son of Bentetis, a shepherd of Oxyrhyncha in the same division, with regard to how much he owes me for salary and provisions, and when he wanted not to pay me, but to cheat me, he behaved in an insulting manner to me and to my wife Tanouris, daughter of Heronas, in the aforesaid Areos Kome. In addition, he also pelted my wife unsparingly with hard blows on every part of her body he could, although she was pregnant, so that she gave birth to a dead foetus, and she herself lies in her bed and is in danger for her life. As a result, I ask you to write to the elders of Oxyrhyncha to send the accused to you for the judicial proceedings to take place. Farewell. Year eight of Tiberius Claudius Caesar Augustus Germanicus Emperor, Neos Sebastos 27. Thouonis about 26 years old, with a scar on the left side of his neck and his left forearm.

230. Hilarion writes to his wife Alis about children

P.Oxy. IV 744 (*BL* I 328, II.2 97, III 132, VII 130, VIII 237, IX 181)
Oxyrhynchos, 17 June 2 BC

The Greek practice of exposing unwanted children was dressed up in myth and literature with hopes that the exposed child would be picked up by others. The notion appeared in the myth of Oedipus, and Euripides' *Ion* demonstrated how tokens accompanying an exposed baby might later reveal its true lineage from freeborn parents, a theme also frequent in New Comedy. Exposure was the usual fate of malformed neonates, with the intention that they should die, but for healthy infants fiction at least held out a chance of survival.

The late first-century BC historian Diodorus claimed that Egyptians raised all children in their desire for an ever-expanding population, adding that no child, even one born from a slave woman, was considered a bastard, for children could be raised to puberty in Egypt easily and with little expense ('no more than twenty drachmas'), since they went naked and wore no shoes.[1] However, the papyri provide ample evidence of infant exposure in Greek and Roman Egypt (see **4.129**), and particularly of infants 'picked up from the dung-heap' for rearing as slaves.[2]

The following letter is often cited for the father's decision to raise only a boy; compare the preference for male offspring shown in **2.39**; **3.94, 99**.

Hilarion to his sister Alis, very many greetings. Also to my lady Berous and Apollonarion. Know that we are even now in Alexandria. Do not worry. If they actually set out, I am going to remain in Alexandria. I ask you and beg you, take care of our little one, and as soon as we get our pay, I intend to send it up country to you. If, among the many things that are possible, you do bear a child and if it is a male, let it be, but if it is a female, cast it out.[3] You have told Aphrodisias, 'Do not forget me'; but how can I forget you? I ask you, then, not to worry. Year 29, Pauni 23.
(*Address on the back*) Hilarion to Alis, deliver.

---

[1] Diodorus, 1.80, reflecting the Greek tradition of the 'otherness' of the Egyptians (cf. Herodotus, *Histories* II.35, quoted above, p. 3, and **2.24**). He further states that Egyptians considered fruit-bearing trees to be masculine, and the non-fruit-bearing feminine, 'opposite to the Greek way'.

[2] **3.91, 5.212–3**; cf. **4.131§41**. For bibliography on exposure, see Bagnall and Frier (1994), 151–3, esp. note 57.

[3] The translation in Fantham et al. (1994), 164, inexplicably stopped with 'cast it out'.

231. Valeria and Thermouthas urge Thermouthion to nurse a freeborn baby

P.Mich. III 202
Provenance unknown, 5 May A D 105

Although Valeria includes Thermouthas in her opening greeting to Thermouthion, she refers only to herself in the body of the letter ('. . . I asked . . .'). Valeria apparently wrote the letter in her own hand (see *P.Mich.* III, plate VII).

Valeria and Thermouthas, the two of them, to Thermouthion, their sister, greetings. As I asked you after I sailed downstream, with regard to the child of Thermouthas, you should take it and raise it. If you do this, you will be glad. As far as the two houses are concerned, you are going to enjoy yourself and amuse yourself. You will get five staters. If you do decide to nurse the child, you will find a wage that is greater than the usual one, because it is freeborn.[1] You will find amusement for yourself and for your parents,[2] if you do it. Sail downstream in the boat so that you can return with us together with the baby. Bring five staters from my mother, if you come downstream, so that we may go back up – or take whatever you want. I am asking you to sail downstream so that you may be fortunate, because a free baby is one thing, but a little slave, another. Farewell.
Year 8 of Trajan our lord, 10 Pachon.
(*Address on the back*) Give to Thermoutheion in Esoeso[3] at the house of . . . a Theudous, from Valeria.

[1] Cf. the wet-nursing contracts, **5.213–14,** and **3.91.**
[2] This seems to be the meaning of the phrase, although the Greek merely says, '. . . you will find your own pleasure and parents if you do it'.
[3] We follow Pestman (*New Primer* p. 134) in not accepting the correction in *BL* III 111 for line 32.

232. Birthday celebrations

P.Oxy. XXXVI 2791
Oxyrhynchos, second century A D

Royal birthdays were celebrated with festivities: accounts in the Zenon archive noted expenditures of 12 drachmas for the birthday of Ptolemy II (*P.Ryl.* IV 557, *P.Cair.Zen.* III 59358). Birthdays of Roman emperors and of members of the imperial family were celebrated each month and were called 'Augustal days' (see **3.89**). Gods also had birthdays: a correspondent of Apollonios the strategos (**Ch.3 Arch. E**) closed his letter with the note that he made obeisance on Apollonios' behalf at the festival of Isis on the night of the goddess' birthday (*P.Brem.* 15).
　　More ordinary folk seemed particularly eager to celebrate a child's first birthday, and two nursing contracts from the Arsinoite nome, both from a roll of contracts

fastened together for official registration, specify a present to be given to the wet nurse on the child's first birthday, in one instance a pair of gold earrings (*C.Pap.Gr.* I 30–I). A man reminded his friend in a letter that the next day was his birthday and he requested that the friend send him a tasty fish as his present (*P.Princ.* III 165, second century AD). The will of Akousilaos (Oxyrhynchos, AD 156) stipulated that after his death his wife, and, after her death, his son were to give one hundred drachmas to his slaves and freedmen for a feast the latter were to celebrate at his tomb every year on the anniversary of his birthday (*P.Oxy.* III 494 = *Sel.Pap.* I 84). For birthdays see also **279(b)**, and **3.80**.

Diogenes invites you to dine at the first birthday of his daughter in the Sarapeum tomorrow which is Pachon 26 (or 16?) from the 8th hour.

233.   Teeus gives her grandson in adoption to his uncle, a monk

P.Lips. 28
Areos Kome (Hermopolite nome), 31 December AD 381

Roman law did not permit a woman to give up a child for adoption, but the sixty-year-old grandmother Aurelia Teeus, most probably a widow, is an equal partner in this contract she makes with her younger son, Aurelius Silvanus, for him to adopt his elder brother's orphaned son. The boy's uncle agrees, not only to safeguard the child's considerable inheritance from his deceased parents until he comes of age, but also to make him his heir, as if he were his own son.

(*1st hand*) In the consulship of Flavius Eucherios, most illustrious, and Syagrios, most illustrious, commander (*of the imperial praetorian guards*), 5 Tybi.

Aurelia Teeus, daughter of Paesis and her mother Thaesis, about 60 years old, with a scar on her left knee, from Areos Kome in the Hermopolite nome, with the assistant I have willingly brought in for myself who also writes for me, since I do not know letters, Aurelius Proous, son of Koulos, headman of the same Areos Kome, and Aurelius Silvanus, son of Petesis and the aforementioned Teeus, appending his subscription below, a monk, from the same Areos Kome, greet one another. Since the elder son of me, the aforementioned Teeus, died – Papnouthios was his name – and left his son who is called Paesis, about 10 years old, more or less, it has seemed best that I, his brother Silvanus, adopt the child out of respect with a view toward being able to raise him in decent and appropriate fashion. In accordance with this, I, Teeus, turn over to you, Silvanus, the aforementioned child for adoption together with his inheritance from his father and mother consisting of lands and buildings and movable goods belonging to the house inventories, with the intention that he is to be your legitimate and first-born son, as if he were engendered by you from your own blood. On my part, I, Silvanus, receive from you, my mother, for adoption the aforementioned son of Papnouthios, whom I shall feed and clothe in decent and appropriate fashion as my own legitimate and physical son, as though he were born from me. I also receive his inheritance from his father and mother consisting of lands and buildings and movable goods belonging to the house inventories, on the condition that I watch over these things for him and restore them to him when he comes of age, all in good faith. Further, he who has been adopted by me is to be the heir of my property, as stipulated above. This contract of adoption is authoritative and has been written in identical duplicate copies so that a personal copy is with each of us for safe-keeping. And when asked, we assented.

(*2nd hand*) I, the aforementioned Aurelia Teeus, daughter of Paesis, made this contract of adoption and I agree to all its written provisions, as stipulated. I, the aforementioned Aurelius Proous, son of Koulos, headman of the village, assisted her and wrote for her, because she does not know letters.

(*3rd hand*) I, the aforementioned Aurelius Silvanus, son of Petesis, monk, made this contract of adoption and I have received his inheritance from his father and his mother, and I agree to all its written provisions, as stipulated.

(*1st hand*) It was written by me, Philosarapis.

234.   An impoverished widow surrenders her daughter for adoption

P.Oxy. XVI 1895
Oxyrhynchos, AD 554

A widowed mother, too poor to bring up her daughter, gives her up for adoption. For widowhood see **269**; and generally Beaucamp (1985), and Krause (1994).

In the 28th year of the reign of our most godlike and pious master, Flavius Justinianus the eternal Augustus and Emperor, the 13th year after the consulship of Flavius Basilius the most illustrious, . . . Aurelia Herais daughter of John and Susanna, from . . . to . . . -seller, son of Menas, and to Maxima your wife, daughter of . . . greeting. . . . years ago, more or less, my husband died, and I was left, toiling and suffering hardship for my daughter by him in order that I might provide her with necessary sustenance; and now, not having the means to maintain her . . . she being now nine years old, more or less, I have asked you . . . to receive her from me as your daughter, and I acknowledge that I have handed her over to you from now for ever as your legal daughter, so that you shall supply her needs and fulfil the position of parents to daughter, and I have no power henceforth to take her away from you. If I do so, I agree to pay you for all the expenses of her maintenance . . . pledging for the rights of this agreement all my property present and future, in particular and in general, as security and by right of mortgage. This agreement, written in a single copy, is authoritative, and in reply to the formal question I have given my consent. (*2nd hand*) I, Aurelia Herais daughter of John . . .

235. A mother donates her son to a monastery in return for his recovery from serious illness

KRU 86.17–32
Jeme, eighth century AD

The monastery of Apa Phoibammon was one of the religious institutions located on the mountain that overshadowed the Egyptian town of Jeme near Thebes (see further Wilfong, forthcoming (a), ch. 1). A number of similar donations, all written in Coptic, were kept on record at the monastery as testimony, not only to the piety of parents and other relatives, but also to the greater glory of God and the holy monk Phoibammon, because in many instances the little boys being donated were said to have been seriously ill prior to the donation, and their subsequent recovery was attributed to their having been given over to the service of God. Tachel's narrative claims that, although she promised her son Athanasios to the monastery, she later reneged on her promise and kept him with her. Tachel mentions no husband, and so perhaps he has died. She interprets the boy's subsequent serious illness as God's way of punishing her and she intends her fulfilment of the earlier promise to save her child's life.

Since, in the time in which we were, a male child was born to me – Tachel, woman and freewoman – in his seventh month, I promised him as a servant to the holy monastery of Apa Phoibammon in the mountain of Jeme, so that, if God would save him from death, I should give him to the holy monastery. Afterwards, when God caused that this little boy, whom I named Athanasios at his holy baptism, grow and get bigger, my lost reason cast me into a great sin, as I made schemes for this little boy, so that I should not (have to) give him to the holy place. When God saw the lawless thing I did, he cast the boy into a great sickness, which lasted such a long time that it was reckoned by everyone who saw him that he was dead. When I remembered the sin and the reckless thing I did, I returned again and begged the holy one in his monastery, saying: 'If you will beseech God and He will grace this boy with a cure, I will put him into the monastery forever, according to my first agreement.'

II   Education

Young girls from the families documented in the papyri acquired a variety of skills which prepared them for their adult lives as wives and mothers, such as spinning, weaving, clothes-making, the preparation of food, and the direction of domestic workers and slaves. However, the acquisition of domestic

34 Mummy portrait of Hermione, 'grammatike'
Girton College, Cambridge
Hawara, Arsinoite nome, *c.* AD
14–37.

This portrait on linen, still intact within the intricate mummy wrappings, is one of a group discovered by Petrie in 1911. It is usually dated by the hairstyle to the reign of Tiberius, although Walker and Bierbrier (1997), 37–9 argue for a later date, *c.* AD 40–50. It is most famous for the inscription, 'Hermione, *grammatike*'; see **Ch. 6 Section II** introduction and note 2. Hermione presents a serious expression, and her only jewellery is a pair of globular earrings. X-rays have confirmed that the mummy is that of a woman aged between sixteen and twenty-five, with a slender bone structure.

skills, learned in the traditional manner from mothers and female relatives in the home, suffers the same fate as most domestic labour performed by women, in remaining almost completely invisible to the written documentation. Paradoxically, slave-girls' training in skills such as weaving is better documented than that of freeborn girls; the education of a slave was an investment which could be expected to yield future income from her work, either in the master's household or hired for wages (see **5.204**; cf. **3.73**).

It will already be apparent that the papyri offer a wealth of evidence for women's literacy and illiteracy. Women more often than men were forced, 'because they do not know letters', to turn to others to subscribe their names to Greek documents. But we know that the twin girls of the Serapeum archive (**Ch.3 Arch. B**) attended the Egyptian school of Thothes, and were literate in Egyptian; and a number of women had enjoyed sufficient instruction in writing Greek to draft their own letters or to sign documents (e.g. **2.59, 4.142**, and see further below).

While tuition in the Egyptian scripts was largely conducted within the ambience of the temples, opportunities for a Greek education, particularly during the Roman period, were more plentiful in the *metropoleis* than in the villages, and more available to the élite classes who could afford private tutoring for their children. Mothers who could themselves read and write may have begun their children's education, as has been suggested in the case

35 Limestone statue of a woman holding a book
Rijksmuseum van Oudheden, Leiden inv. F 1980/1.7
Oxyrhynchos, mid-third century A D

Numerous funerary statues or reliefs from Oxyrhynchos have reached
the museums of Europe and America, and Leiden has a good
collection (Schneider, 1982). This finely-dressed woman carries a
book roll in her left hand, presumably to advertise her literacy. She
wears an elaborate necklace, and bracelets on each wrist.

of Aurelia Charite whose clumsy letter forms resemble those written by her
mother.[1] Mothers seem to have taken particular interest in their children's
progress; one mother in the village of Karanis reported to her husband,
probably a soldier in Roman service, that he should not worry about the
children: 'they are well and are kept busy with their teacher' (*P.Mich.* VIII
464.8–10). The 'teacher' in this case was a woman (*deskale*), and other female
teachers are attested at the elementary level. Fewer women are known
among the teachers of more advanced students, and the title '*grammatike*',
added to Hermione's name in her mummy portrait (**Plate 34**), has been
taken as a complimentary epithet indicating she was 'skilled in letters', or
'skilled in literature', rather than a formal indication of her professional
competence.[2]

The ability to write fluently was a matter of considerable pride for a
woman, even of the élite class: a funerary statue from Oxyrhynchos shows
a well-dressed woman holding a book roll in her left hand, indicating to posterity her skill with letters (**Plate 35**; cf. **4.142**). Most adult women had less
occasion than men to write and sign documents in their own hand and less
opportunity to practise with pen and ink. In between the literate and those
'who did not know letters' were 'slow writers', such as Sentia Asklatarion,
a landowner who rented plots near the village of Theadelphia to the illiterate farmer Soterichos between the years 127 and 133. One rent receipt, in

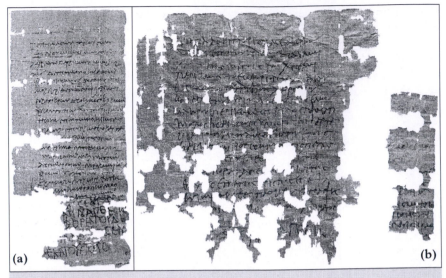

(a)   (b)

36   Sentia Asklatarion, a 'slow writer'
(a) *P.Soter.* 18, AD 127/8 (b) *P.Soter.* 19, AD 128/9
Theadelphia

Practised scribes wrote the body of these rent receipts issued by the landowner Sentia
Asklatarion. (a) shows Sentia Asklatarion's own signature at the bottom: 'I, Sentia
Asklatarion, have received the rent for the past eleventh year.' The fragmentary lines at the
bottom of (b) show that of her guardian Lucius Ignatius Crispus; cf. *P.Soter.* 20–1.

which Sentia Asklatarion acted without a guardian (not obligatory for such
documents), is signed in her own large and cumbersome letters; but in other
receipts, her guardian Lucius Ignatius Crispus signed for her, noting that she
was a 'slow writer', although he was no more dextrous at writing than she
(**Plate 36**).[3]

The ability to write at all, however, suggests that the writer could also
read to some extent. A fragmentary third-century AD papyrus preserves a
scene involving Odysseus' attempt to enter Troy in disguise, either part of
an original play for stage performance, or an advanced composition of a
school student.[4] In the scene, Odysseus is pictured as carrying letters for
Helen to read, an element not found in the original Homeric account
(*Odyssey* IV 241–51); this late Roman writer imagines Helen as belonging
to the class of wealthy women whom one expected to be literate.

In the Ptolemaic period some of the more hellenised villages, as well as
the Greek cities of Alexandria, Naukratis, and Ptolemais, possessed gymnasia, cultural centres for social, athletic, and religious activities for the Greek-
speaking population. The Roman government fostered gymnasia and other

civic institutions in the nome *metropoleis* as a means to institutionalise privileges of birth and wealth into a system of civic rights and responsibilities; and the gymnasium, in particular, provided a social base for the urban upper classes (see **3.96**). Girls as well as boys were sometimes registered with the gymnasium officials as a way of situating proper young women in the hellenised social and intellectual milieu.[5] Undoubtedly the family of Apollonios the strategos took pride in the intellectual accomplishments of young Heraidous: her perseverance with lessons and her ability to write a letter to her father (**236–7**; cf. **3.94–5**).

Portions of a Ptolemaic school book from the Arsinoite nome, copied on a papyrus roll nearly 2½ metres in length, reveal something of the curriculum employed for pupils at elementary and middle levels.[6] Students' early tasks were to master the alphabet, numbers, and syllables (cf. **239**), and to copy word lists, often grouped around a particular topic (cf. **240**), and short passages (cf. **241–2**). The first piece of literature more advanced students encountered was likely to be Homer's *Iliad* or *Odyssey* (**243**; cf. **267**). Teaching methods based on copying and memorising such materials remained more or less the same throughout antiquity. Christians inserted some of their own literature into the curriculum, and Psalms were a particularly popular source for short passages. Lives of martyrs and saints also circulated widely, in Greek and later in Coptic. The Greek *Acts of Paul and Thekla*, recounting the story of young Thekla, who forsook a comfortable life as daughter and bride-to-be of noble and wealthy families in Iconium in southern Asia Minor, in order to follow the apostle Paul, circulated in Christian Egypt. Three copies have been discovered in Egypt, all three distinctive for their small format and two particularly handsome in appearance; perhaps they were 'name-day' presents for young girls named Thekla, a name that became increasingly popular in Egypt during Christian centuries.[7] Two of the codices were found in cities (Antinoopolis and Oxyrhynchos), their luxurious production implying that their owners were from a milieu similar to that of Heraidous, daughter of a wealthy urban family. Egypt also produced its own holy martyr Thekla, whose story exists only in Coptic versions (see **2.55**), in which she is pictured, not only as sending her boy to school, but also writing him a letter from prison.

Alexandria was throughout the Ptolemaic and Roman periods the cultural and scientific centre of the eastern Mediterranean; her academic pretensions eclipsed those of Athens, and she vied with Rome, and later Constantinople, as the intellectual capital of the ancient world. The international community of scholars and poets working in the Alexandrian Museum included some women; and, although their writings are now lost (as are those of many of their male contemporaries), later works have preserved references to them: from Agallis of Corcyra, pupil of the grammarian Aristophanes of Byzantium, to Hypatia, her father's pupil and teacher of pagan philosophy, who was murdered by a Christian mob early in the fifth century AD (**2.54**).[8]

1 *P.Charite*, p. 2; see **Plate 27**.
2 Cribiore (1996), Appendix I, lists instructors at the elementary level mentioned in the papyri; of thirty-four examples, ten seem to have been women. On Hermione '*grammatike*', see Kaster (1988), 354, and Turner (1980), 77, who translates as 'Hermione, literary lady'.
3 *P.Soter.* 18–21; cf. Valeria Diodora (**Ch.3 Arch.H** introd.), and Phoibammon (**5.181**). See further Youtie (1971).
4 *P.Köln* VI 245.18–19, discussed in Parca (1991), 55–7, 78–9.
5 Two registrations of girls are known from Oxyrhynchos: *P.Corn.* I 18 (AD 291) and *P.Oxy.* XLIII 3136 (AD 292); cf. *P.Ups.Frid* 6 introduction, pp. 63–6.
6 Guéraud and Jouguet (1938) = Pack[2] 2642.
7 *P.Fackelmann* 3, ed. M. Gronewald, *ZPE* 28 (1978), 274–5 (third century AD, papyrus, 4 x 4.6 cm); *P.Ant.* I 13 (fourth century AD, papyrus, 7.2 x 8.7 cm); *P.Oxy.* I 6 (fifth century AD, vellum, 7.3 x 6.7 cm). For an English translation of the *Acts of Paul and Thekla*, see Schneemelcher (1991), II 239–46.
8 See Pomeroy (1977) for the Ptolemaic period, and ead. (1988), 716–17 for the Roman period.

236.   A gift for the teacher of Heraidous

P.Giss. 80
Hermopolis (?), *c.* 13 December of an unknown year, late in the reign of Trajan

Only the bottom portion remains of this letter from the archive of Apollonios the strategos (**Ch.3 Arch.E**). The identity of the writer is unknown; as the next letter (**237**) indicates, many were concerned with Heraidous' schooling.

. . . Heraidous salutes you and so does Hemou . . . (?) and Helen and Tinoutis and her papa and all in the house, and the mother of our very sweet Heraidous. The doves and the chickens which I am not in the habit of eating, send to . . . the teacher of Heraidous. Helene, mother of Apollonios, has asked you to keep her son Hermaios under your hand. All the things I did not eat when I was visiting with you . . . send to the daughter's teacher so that he may put in much effort for her. I pray that you are well. Choiak 17.

237.   A book for Heraidous to read

P.Giss. 85 (*BL* III 68)
Hermopolis (?), *c.* 30 August of an unknown year, late in the reign of Trajan

This letter from Hermaios to Apollonios the strategos is severely mutilated except at its close.

. . . I (Hermaios) thank you alone (Apollonios) so very much in front of lord Hermes and I do not omit making my obeisance on your behalf each day. Little Heraidous salutes you and (so does) your mother Helene. I, Hermaios, likewise salute you. I beg you to . . . to the administrator, so that he may furnish me with things suitable for school, such as a book for Heraidous to read. Farewell, my lord. Thoth 2.

238. The school curriculum

Dionisotti (1982), 98–100 (excerpts)

This description of events at school is taken from a bilingual Latin–Greek school book of the ninth–tenth century; but school texts on papyrus from Egypt exhibit many of the same teaching materials.[1] For example, important components of the later bilingual school books were the alphabetical glossary and word lists arranged by topics, such as the alphabetical list of occupations from early Roman Tebtynis (**240**), and practice passages for copying and reading aloud, such as those from Roman and Byzantine Egypt (**241–3**). Bilingual conversations about everyday activities were likewise employed in Egyptian schools of Byzantine times.[2]

Girls shared the same elementary curriculum as boys, although the content seems largely directed towards male interests and prejudices (cf. **241–2** especially), and only boys appear in this everyday conversation.

I went into school and I said, 'Greetings, teacher; greetings, instructor'[3] and he greeted me in return. He gives me a manual and orders me to read five pages in his presence. I read accurately and well. Then I gave the manual to another. Next I went to the assistant teacher. I greet him and my fellow pupils, and they greeted me in return. Then I sat in my place on a bench or chair or step or stool or large chair. While I am sitting down, the slave who carries my school box hands me my little tablets and my writing case, my straight-edge, my tablet, and my lupines.[4] I subtract, I do maths, I compute, I count and I shall count, I add and I subtract, I multiply, I divide . . . I cross out and I write an addition above the line, and I write and show it to my teacher. He praised me because I wrote well. I reread what I wrote word by word. I recite. I recited before you. Lies, I do not lie. 'If you speak truly', my pedagogue said to me, 'let us go home so that we can go to the Greek and the Latin teacher'. Then we are dismissed for sports, for Latin and Greek studies. We entered the school of the Greek teacher and the lecture room of the Latin teacher. I learn my texts thoroughly. If I am ready, I hand them in immediately. If not, I read them again . . . I took the text, verses, notes. The unknown book is explained to me, or the unknown passage. Explication is offered. I take my place, and others together with me read extemporaneously; the rest repeat it accurately. The younger boys practise interpretation and syllables, declensions, a lot of grammar, speech, all in front of the assistant teacher . . . The older boys go to the teacher, they read a text about the *Iliad*, another about the *Odyssey*. They take up a theme, a hortatory speech, a debate, history, comedy, narratives, every kind of oration, causes of the Trojan war . . .

[1] Dionisotti (1982). Recent catalogues of school texts from Egypt: Debut (1986), Cribiore (1996). Cribiore includes photographs of Greek and Coptic texts; see also *P.Rain.Unterricht (MPER* NS xv) (Greek); *MPER* NS xviii (Coptic).

[2] A good example from Egypt is the trilingual (Latin-Greek-Coptic) phrasebook, *MPER* xviii 270, fifth–sixth century A D, in which the Latin was written in Greek characters, with phrases such as 'If everyone has drunk, wipe off the table'; 'Set the lamps in the midst and light them' (270 col. 1 recto 4–12).

[3] Part of the passage's pedagogic technique is to present synonyms, as 'teacher', 'instructor', and frequently below. Not all are replicated in the translation.

[4] The 'straight-edge' was to keep the child's writing on line, and the lupines were perhaps seeds from the plant to be used as counters.

239. Practices of the Greek alphabet and a Greek syllabary

P.Rain.Unterricht (MPER NS xv) 7
Hermopolis (?), first century A D

This pupil's hand seems that of a beginner, for the letter forms are still unsure. Many examples of alphabets and syllables, written on papyrus and ostraka by students, are known.

1	αβγδεζηθι]κλμνξοπρστυφχψω	*(Greek alphabet)*
2	ωψχφυτσ]ρποξνμλκιθηζεδγβα	*(Greek alphabet backward)*[1]
3	]θυπτησφλεγμοδρωψ	*(letter-practice, nonsense words)*
4	]ψχθωινπληκτρονσφι[ξ	*(letter-practice, nonsense words)*
5	αωβψγχ]δφευζτησθριπκολξμν	*(first letter, last letter, etc.)*[2]
6	ᾱ β̄ γ̄ δ̄ ε̄ ϛ̄]ζ̄ η̄ θ̄ ῑ κ̄ λ̄ μ̄ ν̄ ξ̄ ō π̄ [Ϙ̄ρ̄σ̄	*(numerals 1–10, 20–200)*
7	τ̄ ῡ φ̄ χ̄ ψ̄]ω̄ Ἀ Ἀ Β Γ Δ Ἐ Ϛ drachmas	*(numerals 300–6,000)*

12	δα	ζα	θα	*(syllables)*
13	δε	ζε	θε	
14	δη	ζη	θη	
15	δι	ζι	θι	
16	δο	ζο	θο	
17	δυ	ζυ	θυ	
18	δω	ζω	θω	

[1] The letter 'θ' was inadvertently omitted from the published transcript, but can be seen on plate iii in the edition.

[2] Line 5, as presented here, was read from plate iii in the edition and is not what appears in the published transcript.

240.   Alphabetical list of occupations

P.Tebt. II 278 col. I 1–12
Tebtynis, early first century AD

The list was written in a practised hand, probably marking it as an exercise written
by the teacher for pupils to copy. All the occupations listed are masculine ones.

ἀρτοκόπος	baker
βαφεύς	dyer
γναφεύς	fuller
δοροξύς	spear maker
ἐλεουργός	oilworker
ζωγράφος	painter
ἡπητής	tailor
θωρωκοποίς	breastplate maker
ἰατρός	doctor
κλειτοποίς	locksmith
λάξος	mason
μυλοκόπος	millstone maker

241.   A short exercise in writing and reading aloud: a fable

P.Leid.Inst. 5
Provenance unknown, second century AD

This animal fable was written by a pupil, still struggling with the techniques of
writing (**Plate 37**). In preparation for reading the passage aloud to the teacher, the
student set oblique strokes marking the ends of most words, to serve as a guide for
phrasing; cf. **238**. The fable is known in other versions in both Greek and Latin
(see *P.Leid.Inst.*, pp. 8–9), although these are in verse, while this copy on papyrus
is prose. The poetic version closest to the fragmentary papyrus reads: 'A wild ass
and a lion were partners, / although the lion excelled in strength and the ass in his
swiftness. / When they had a plentiful catch of animals, / the lion divided it and
made three parts, / saying, "I shall take my first part, / because I am king; I shall
take also that part, / because I am an equal partner; this third share / will bring
some trouble to you, if you don't want to run away." Take stock of yourself!
Neither get involved / with a more powerful man, nor be his partner' (Perry,
Aesopica 339).

With good luck! A lion and a donkey became friends with one another . . .
from the hunt. When they went out . . . after they hunted down many
[animals] . . . [the lion divided it into three] parts and said, 'I shall take the
first one, because . . . ruler, [give me] the second one, [because I am your]

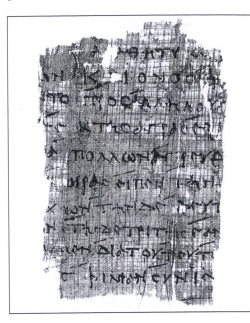

37   A school text
P.Leid.Inst.5
Provenance unknown, second
century AD

The student has marked the ends of
most words with oblique strokes as a
guide for reading the passage aloud.
The exercise seems to illustrate what
the student in **6.238** is describing,
since the strokes would aid in
'reading according to syllable'. The
text (an animal fable) is translated in
6.241.

partner, [but if you touch] the third one . . . On account of this [story] . . .
into friendship with someone stronger' . . .

242.   A short exercise in writing and reading: Opinions of Menander

MPER NS XVIII 269 I, folios IIa–IIIa, lines 55–83
Provenance unknown, sixth–seventh century AD

The so-called *Opinions of Menander*, single lines of pithy sayings in iambic trimeter
(the metre most often used for dialogue in both comedy and tragedy), were also
popular in the schools. Students copied a few *Opinions* on ostraka or scraps of
papyrus for practice in writing and reading. This copy, derived from a bilingual
(Greek–Coptic) school book of eight pages, was written by a skilful hand, probably that of the teacher. In this school book the *Opinions* are arranged alphabetically
according to the first Greek word in each line; we have translated all those with the
initial letter *gamma*, including the Greek words for 'old man' (*geron*), 'letters' (*gram-
mata*), 'woman' (*gyne*), and 'marry' (*gamein*).

> An old man in love is a dreadful fate in the end.
> Learn letters and you will have fair hopes.
> One must learn one's letters, and he who has learned them has
>   intelligence.
> 4   Silence confers attractiveness upon all women.

The man who is in a rush to marry is heading for regret.
Never trust your life to a woman.
Don't touch a woman and you'll not be opening a tomb.[1]
8   A woman knows nothing she doesn't want to know.
If you're an old man, don't marry a younger woman.
If you marry a woman, you'll be opening a tomb.

[1] The Coptic version adds the adverb 'soon'.

243.   'A book to read'

P.Oxy. XLIV 3160 ii.12–25
Oxyrhynchos, third century AD

More copies of Homer's *Iliad* and *Odyssey* have appeared on papyrus than any other works of ancient literature, and the two epics were used extensively in the schools for more advanced pupils (**238**). This example is part of a book-by-book treatment of the *Odyssey*, presenting first a summary of a book's contents, followed by a word list with synonyms for Homeric words, many obsolete in the contemporary Greek. This passage summarises *Odyssey* Book II, in which Odysseus' son Telemachos decides he must learn whether or not Odysseus died at Troy by visiting his father's old comrades who have returned from the Trojan war: the aged Nestor in Pylos, and King Menelaos and his wife Helen, now reunited in Lakedaimon. After the summary appear more than fifty Homeric words from *Odyssey* II with synonyms as vocabulary aids for the student.

. . . to sail away to Pylos and Lakedaimon, and once he got there, to make inquiry about his father. If he learned he was still alive, he intended to hold out another year; but if dead, to prepare a memorial tomb for him and send his mother back to the household of her father Ikarios, so that he could give her in marriage to whomsoever he wanted. Even though he was laughed at by the suitors with regard to his plans, with the help of Athena he put together a boat and a crew and sailed away.

244.   Julia Balbilla commemorates the visit of the emperor Hadrian

I.Memnon 28
Memnoneia, 20 November AD 130

Egypt attracted many tourists from elsewhere in the Greek and Roman world. An important attraction was the massive pair of colossal statues of Amenhotep III (1390–1352 BC) on the west bank of the Nile opposite Thebes. The northern statue, thought to depict the Homeric Memnon, son of Tithonos and the Dawn (hence the Greek name 'Memnoneia' for the district), was famed for emitting a twanging sound at sunrise, allegedly caused when the Persian king Kambyses mutilated the statue, though perhaps actually originating in an earthquake of 27 BC. By the fourth century AD, the statue was silent, as it remains today (Bowersock, 1984); but during its heyday, hearing 'Memnon's voice' and writing a signature or message on the statue's legs were an important part of one's tour. More than one hundred Greek and Latin inscriptions cover the legs of the statue.

Julia Balbilla was travelling in the entourage of the emperor Hadrian and his wife, the empress Sabina, as the imperial couple journeyed up the Nile in late autumn of AD 130. On the first day of their visit, Memnon did not emit his customary sound, but on the second day, he performed three times for the visiting dignitaries, and Julia Balbilla was moved to commemorate the experience by composing four poems, which were inscribed by a stonecutter on the statue's leg. The poems are in epic dialect, using many words from Homer; the metre, however, is not the Homeric dactylic hexameter, but elegiac couplets, more associated with personal expressions of emotion. Balbilla's poems advertise not only her association with the imperial household, but also her own excellent education.[1]

> (Poem of) Julia Balbilla, when Augustus Hadrian heard Memnon.
> I was told that the Egyptian Memnon, warmed by the rays
> of the sun, spoke from Theban rock.
> When he saw Hadrian, ruler of all, before the rays of the sun,
> 4   he greeted him as much as he could.
> But when Titan, driving forth with his white horses through the air,
> was casting a shadow on the second measure of the hours,
> as if a brazen vessel had been struck, Memnon cast forth his noise
>   again,
> 8   deep-toned, and in greeting, he even emitted a sound for the third
>   time.
> Lord Hadrian then greeted Memnon in return and
> he left behind for posterity some lines cut in stone to reveal
> what things he had seen and what he had heard.
> 12 It was clear to all that the gods love him.

[1] Balbilla's other inscriptions are *I.Memnon* 30–1; cf. those of Caecilia Trebulla, *I.Memnon* 92–4.

245. Julia Balbilla commemorates the visit of the empress Sabina

I.Memnon 29
Memnoneia, 20 November AD 130

Balbilla closes this poem with an overview of her own ancestry: a maternal grandfather Balbillus the wise, who served as prefect of Egypt, and a paternal grandfather who was king of Commagene. If Balbilla's brother reached a consulship at Rome in AD 109, it is likely that by the time of her trip to Egypt in 130 Balbilla was no longer young.

When I was present at Memnon with Empress Sabina.
Memnon, child of Dawn and old man Tithonos,
who sits opposite the Theban city of Zeus,
or Amenoth, Egyptian king, as the priests skilled in
4 the myths of old say – receive my greetings, and may
you sound out and salute also her,
the noble wife of the emperor Hadrian.
A barbarous man, the godless Kambyses,
8 smote off your tongue and your ears.
Surely through his pitiful death, he has
paid the penalty, struck by the same point
of the sword by which he ruthlessly killed the divine Apis bull.
12 I do not expect your statue to perish, but, for the rest,
I have preserved through my intelligence your immortal soul.
Pious were my parents and my ancestors, both Balbillus the wise
and King Antiochos – Balbillus was the father of my royal mother,
16 while King Antiochos was the father of my father.
This is the lineage from which I draw my noble blood,
and these are the verses I wrote, I, Balbilla the pious.

246. A Greek letter to women of the family who know no Greek

SB XVIII 13867
Provenance unknown, mid-second century AD

This letter illustrates the obstacles to written communication for those women who were not only illiterate, but did not even understand spoken Greek. By the second century AD, Egyptian Demotic script was rarely used except for certain specialised purposes, and thus Greek was effectively the only language available for letter-writing. The writer begins by addressing the unknown man who will translate his letter into Egyptian so that his mother and sister (despite their Greek names) can understand it. Nevertheless, it seems that the family was accustomed to communication by letter, and Ptolemaios writes more fully and intimately than many letter-writers from Egypt. He begins by explaining his previous silences. Another sister, who is unnamed, is staying with or near the writer, and much of his letter narrates events that involve him, a man named Karas, and this unnamed sister. He conveys his disappointment to his sister Rhodous that she did not join him for a festival on the twenty-fifth, presumably a festival of Serapis and Isis, and he urges her to come up country for a later festival. The final episode involves yet another woman, the sister of Ammonios.

By Serapis! You, the man who reads this letter, whoever you are, expend a little effort and translate for the women the matters written down in this letter and communicate it to them.
    Ptolemaios to Zosime his mother and Rhodous his sister, greetings. You

all blame me through letters and through messengers as though I have done wrong, so I swear by all the gods that I have done nothing of the matters mentioned, except only with regard to the donkey of Karas. You all seem to set up an ambush against me, and if you have some anger because, although I heard, I still sent no word – well, I was kicked by a horse and was in danger of losing my foot, or even my life. But I blame you all because you did not make inquiry after me, neither through messages nor through letters. If the gods are willing, it would be well . . .[1] but I also detained him and he enjoyed himself night and day for four days. On the next day, when there was no longer anything to drink, he stood by me, asking, 'Do you want a pound of meat to be purchased for you?' I said, 'Yes', and immediately gave him two four-obol coins for the pound of meat. After he took my two four-obols, he neither brought back the meat nor my money, nor have I seen him up to now. Well, I am writing to you not because of the money, but for the sake of his opinion of my sister. But I restrained her from mentioning to him about the money he owed her, because of my respect for you all. By the gods, I was very disturbed to hear how far the matter of a small bit of copper has been carried. But Rhodous . . . I was disturbed that you did not come up for the twenty-fifth[2] of the god. Anyway, I do urge you to come up for the seventieth of the god – to come to me, just as if to your own, for the same warm feelings remain. Advise the old lady to come up too. With regard to the letter you sent me, I did not receive it and I said the following: 'By Serapis, I do not have it, for I am no fool.'. . . She . . .ing and watching sometimes, where I straightway was going to recommend my own opinion, for she is absolutely without any sense. Because you stayed away from me, for four days I was in agony, lest she were ill, or she suffered something else, at which point I sent my sister with Karas as my pretext. Once I learned about her safety, I revealed everything. Ammonios her brother said to my sister that she went away. When I heard that she was gone, I became overjoyed because she was neither sick, nor was anything troubling her. But I am annoyed that she didn't say good-bye to me, but went off without me. But, there is nothing odd about their lack of sense. For my part, I kept wanting to send the entire matter to you. I pray you are well. Greet Tapsois and her mother Isarous.

[1] The bottom of the first column has broken off here; serious damage also occurs in col. ii, after 'I am no fool'.
[2] 'Twenty-fifth' and 'seventieth' presumably refer to festival days of a religious calendar.

III   Marriage and married life

For both men and women, embarking on marriage was a major step, for which supernatural advice might be sought (**247–9**), even though many marriages were terminated relatively soon, either by divorce or by the death of one partner. Although the state required no official registration of marriages, and Egyptian tradition required no formal contract or ceremony (**Ch.4**, esp. **Sect. I**), marriage was often an occasion for families to celebrate with feasting and rejoicing (**250–1**). It also occasioned the transfer of wealth to the newly married couple, in the form of the bride's dowry. Dowries consisted primarily of money, jewellery, and clothing, and sometimes metal or wooden utensils (**252**; cf. **4.123, 126–9, 141**). While these items had some practical use, they were luxuries rather than necessities for equipping a marital home; and the emphasis in marriage documents is on their monetary value as much as their immediate usefulness. The dowry formed a financial reserve, to be drawn on if necessary by pawning the goods;[1] one bride's jewellery was apparently hidden so securely in a wall cupboard that it came to light only forty years later during some building work (*Sel.Pap.* II 278). In the Roman period, dowries tended to become more elaborate than in the Greek marriage documents of the Ptolemaic period; and supplements to the dowry proper (*pherne*) were often given. The *parapherna* consisted of similar items to the *pherne*, jewellery, clothing or utensils; but differed in not normally being given a total monetary value (**252**; cf. **4.141**). Only exceptionally did dowries include the kinds of property which a girl might inherit from her parents, such as land, slaves, or houses (**4.126, 136**; cf. Rowlandson, 1996).

The jewellery and clothing brides brought in their dowries were surely too valuable for everyday wear (though see **254**; cf. **3.111**), but they offer close parallels to the way women are shown in the funerary 'mummy portraits' (see **Plate 38**; cf. **Plate 47**). Despite the often striking realism of these paintings, they offer more than a literal depiction, conveying the subject's social position through their repertory of visual symbols.[2] The parallel between the accoutrements of women in the portraits and the typical content of dowries may, therefore, be not coincidental, but a conscious portrayal of the deceased as married women. So care is needed in using the portraits as evidence of women's actual appearance. Nevertheless, in combination, papyrus documents, mummy portraits, and other funerary representations tell us much about women's dress and physical appearance, at least when they were 'in their best'.

The Ptolemaic and Roman periods apparently mark a change in both jewellery and clothing from the styles traditional in Egypt towards those common throughout the Greek and later the Roman world.[3] The basic items of clothing for both men and women consisted of a mantle or cloak (*himation*), covering a tunic (*chiton*) or sometimes two tunics.[4] Lists and inventories may distinguish garments for the two sexes simply by gendered adjectives: 'men's tunics' and 'women's tunics', or 'men's cloaks' and 'women's cloaks'. Gender distinctions in the garments themselves were shown through size, the fineness of weave, the elaborateness of decoration and embroideries, and, perhaps most obviously, by colour. Men are usually

38 Mummy portrait of young woman
Kelsey Museum 26801
Provenance unknown, early second century AD

This young woman, whose hairstyle is typical of the reign of Trajan, is wearing fine jewellery. Two necklaces are picked out in gold leaf: the upper one of thick gold loops, with three pendant dark red stones, mounted in gold, suspended from rectangular plates at the front; the lower one of long pendants, tipped with pearls, suspended from a gold chain. Her earrings, of the common bar and pendant type (cf. **Plate 39(c)**), are of unusually complex construction. See Root (1979), 52; Parlasca (1969), 66.

shown wearing white or unbleached garments (typically decorated with purple vertical stripes), whereas women favoured more diversity of colour, often bright shades of pink, mauve, blue and red. Despite minor differences of proportion (women's mantles were somewhat longer and narrower than men's), the clothes of both sexes shared the same simple construction. The mantle was simply an oblong length of cloth 'cut from the loom' (**265; 3.94**), and shaped about the body with belt and brooches. Ribbons and shawls often cinched the fabric under a woman's breasts or at her waist, providing both decoration and a means to shorten a long garment when her physical activity demanded more strenuous movement and a shorter skirt. The *chiton* consisted of two rectangular pieces of fabric sewn together along the selvage to fit across the shoulders, or might even be woven in a single piece, leaving a vertical slit for the neck opening. From around the mid-third century AD, both men and women began to adopt the 'Dalmatic' tunic with wide, loose sleeves. Respectable women in Egypt are sometimes shown with tunics reaching above the ankle, shorter than was customary elsewhere in the Greek world. But, although short-tunicked slave women appear frequently in tomb paintings of the Pharaonic period, we are less well informed about women's everyday working garments in the Ptolemaic, Roman and

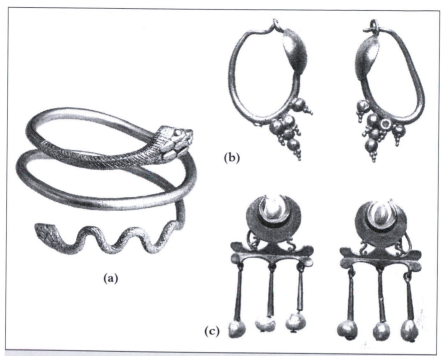

(b)

(a)

(c)

39 Items of jewellery

The jewellery surviving from Graeco-Roman Egypt follows the patterns common throughout the Mediterranean world at this period, rather than continuing Pharaonic traditions. Surviving examples of jewellery confirm the accuracy of the representations on mummies and mummy portraits (Walker and Bierbrier, 1997, 162–76).

(a) Snake bracelet
Benaki Museum, Athens, inv. 1717

A type commonly depicted on mummies. The woman painted on the plaque in **Plate 42** can just be seen to wear a snake bracelet on each arm.

(b) Granular earrings
Benaki Museum, Athens, inv. 1665

(c) Bar earrings
Benaki Museum, Athens, 1671

A type very popular from the first to third centuries A D.

Byzantine periods. Another garment, worn particularly by women, was the *maphor(t)ion*, a cape or shawl covering the neck and shoulders (**258**; cf. **5.191**). The sandals surviving in some quantity from Graeco-Roman Egypt (forty-one examples from Karanis alone) are made from plaited and sewn palm fibre rather than leather, but their strap arrangements are similar to those found elsewhere in the Roman empire; unsurprisingly, they lack the sophistication of fashionable Alexandrian footwear (**261(b)**).

In the Roman period, hairstyles seem to have followed closely the fashions of Rome, and the styles adopted by women of the imperial family; information about these styles would be disseminated not only through personal contacts with Romans from the court (**244–5**, cf. **2.17**), but also by coin images, and by the public display of busts of imperial women, such as Livia wife of Augustus (**Plate 7**). Egypt was noted in the ancient world for cosmetics, as for other branches of arcane knowledge; Kleopatra herself was supposedly an authority on the subject (**2.15**). The portraits depicting women's eyes cosmetically highlighted with liner, and the unguent jars and cosmetic implements found in burials, suggest that women in Egypt did attempt to make the most of their beauty by applying make-up, but probably no more than women elsewhere in the empire. Moralising condemnations of the excesses of female adornment are a literary genre, not to be read literally (**260–1**).

On the other hand, a married woman was expected to undertake serious responsibilities, bearing legitimate children for her husband in order to perpetuate the household into a next generation. Marriages were normally virilocal, the bride moving in to live with her husband's family (in brother–sister marriages, of course, it was already her own home); and she would be expected to share in the household management, assuming full control as the older members died. Archaeological excavations of ancient villages in the Fayum suggest that the typical house contained about fifty square metres of living space for its inhabitants (Hobson, 1985). These cramped quarters were often expanded, however, by an interior courtyard largely open to the air and usable for most of the year in the mild Egyptian climate. Here food was prepared and baked, small children cared for, and animals fed (**Plate 22**; cf. **3.106**). Many houses also had basement cellars for storage (**4.153**). Wealthier families enjoyed not only more space and a second courtyard, but also possessed slaves for routine household chores; nevertheless, élite women were personally involved in preparing clothing for family members.[5] Both food and clothing received frequent notice in letters, because those entrusted with delivering them at a distance were not always reliable carriers. Women's letters frequently mention exchanging baskets of food and delicacies, and raw wool for spinning, underscoring their responsibilities for the family's food and clothing (e.g. **220**, **225**; **3.94**, **95**, **97**; **5.172**). The mistress of a wealthy household might undertake considerable responsibility, supervising slaves and helping to deal with her husband's business interests, a role which goes beyond that prescribed for the ideal wife by Xenophon in his idealised overview of household management in fourth-century BC Greece (Pomeroy, 1994).

[1] **253, 5.191.** Divorce agreements sometimes refer to the husband's having dissipated his wife's dowry on his own use: **257; 3.102; 4.128.**

[2] Montserrat (1993). More generally on the portraits, see Parlasca (1966) and (1969), Corcoran (1995), Doxiadis (1995), Borg (1996), Bierbrier (1997).

[3] See especially Walker and Bierbrier (1997). On jewellery, see also Andrews (1990), 199–200; cf. **Plate 39.** Further illustrations of textiles and women's clothing, jewellery, and hairstyles may be found in: Vogelsang-Eastwood (1994), van't Hooft et al. (1994) – Egyptian; Sebesta and Bonfante (1994) – Roman; Bruhn (1993) – Byzantine.

[4] On clothing in Graeco-Roman Egypt, see King (1996), Walker and Bierbrier (1997), esp. 16, 177–80. Relatively few examples of clothing survive from the Ptolemaic and Roman periods, because most surviving textiles come from funerary contexts which prohibited wool, a popular clothing fabric for the living. Textile evidence becomes more plentiful from *c.* AD 300; cf. Kendrick (1920).

[5] One burial at Antinoe, of a woman named Euphemia who was clearly wealthy, included a set of equipment for spinning, weaving and embroidery; Guimet (1912), 10.

247. *Predictions of Astrampsychos* about marriage

See **218** (*Predictions of Astrampsychos* on childbearing) for the sources for the *Predictions*, and methods of consultation. Questions 52 and 90 each have only two answers (one positive and one negative, each repeated five times).

Question 21: Am I going to marry and is it profitable for me?
  Repertory of answers: You will marry the wife you want.[1]
        You will not marry just yet and don't expect to.
        You will marry and you will blame yourself.
        You will marry the wife with whom you are having daily intimacy.
        You cannot marry just yet and in the meantime keep quiet.
        You will marry, but your wife does not stay.
        You will marry, but you will change your mind.
        You will not marry now, but wait.
        You will marry and you will have to dissolve your marriage.
Question 52: Am I to inherit from my wife?
  Repertory of answers: You are going to inherit from your wife.
        You are not going to inherit from your wife.
Question 90: Am I to divorce my wife?
  Repertory of answers: You will not separate from your wife.
        You will divorce your wife.

[1] Several answers are mutilated, but the first answer appears in more or less the same form four times; the others once each. Some of these responses are considered to be very late additions.

248. Isis asked to choose a wife

(End of) P.Berl. 13538 (ed. Zauzich, 1978)
Elephantine, Ptolemaic period

The writer of this Demotic letter was in dispute with the people of Syene (Aswan), and threatened with removal from office; one bone of contention was his lack of a wife. He therefore asks the addressee, Hartephnachtes, director of the holy cloths, to inquire of the oracle of Isis which of two women he should marry (cf. **249**).

(*Line 20, recto*) One says to me from all the people who live in Elephantine and Syene: 'There is no woman in your house.' Please, take a man with (?) you, (*verso*) and ask in the presence of Isis concerning the woman whom I will take into my house: Sentayris, the daughter of Pachnoumis, or Sentares, the daughter of Espmetis. And send me the answer in order to assure me. This is a very important matter: I shall not write anything like it to you. If there are things here which you need, send a letter to me about them. Written in year 3, Hathyr day 7.

249. Three questions to oracles about marriage

Inquirers at oracular shrines consulted the god by submitting two slips of papyrus, with their question phrased positively on one, and negatively on the other. The deity responded by returning the appropriate slip. The same basic format persisted throughout antiquity, despite changes of language and religion; Christian examples survive in both Greek and Coptic, their questions now directed to martyrs and saints, such as St Kollouthos, protector of Antinoopolis. Of those translated here, **(a)** is in Demotic; **(b)** and **(c)** are in Greek.[1]

(a) Botti (1955); (corr. Pestman, in Veenhof, 1983, p.194)
Tebtynis, second century BC

My great lord Soknebtynis[2], the great god. Your servant Stotoetis son of Imouthes is the one who says: 'If it is a good thing for me to sit down[3] with Tanous, who was borne by Taapis,[4] so that she may become my wife, may this letter be taken out for me.' Written.

(b) *W.Chr.* 122
Soknopaiou Nesos, 26 April AD 6

To the very great and mighty god Soknopaios,[5] from Asklepiades son of Areios. If it is not[6] granted to me to marry[7] Tapetheus the daughter of Marres — may she not become the wife of somebody else — show it and confirm to me this writing. In the past Tapetheus was the wife of Horion.[8] Year 35 of Caesar, 1 Pachon.

(c) *P.Oxy.* IX 1213
Oxyrhynchos, second century A D

To Zeus Helios, great Serapis, and fellow gods. Menander asks: if it is permitted for me to marry, return (this slip) to me.

¹ Other oracle questions are **256, 2.21, 47**; also *Sel.Pap.* 1 193–5. For Christian examples,
   Youtie (1975b) and *PSI Congr.XVII* 20–1.
² Soknebtynis, 'Souchos, lord of Tynis', was the local crocodile god of the village Tebtynis.
   This oracle slip was found, with several others, by the Italian excavators not far from the
   main temple of the village.
³ I.e. 'marry'; ancient Egyptian marriage was brought about by two persons living together.
⁴ As in magical texts, identification by the mother's name is preferred as more certain than
   the patronymic.
⁵ Soknopaios, 'Souchos, lord of Pai', was the local crocodile god of the temple village
   Soknopaiou Nesos.
⁶ An example of the negatively phrased question.
⁷ The Greek means literally 'to live together with'.
⁸ This short postscript by the questioner informing the god about the precise circumstances
   of his situation is exceptional, and of religious interest in its assumption that the god is not
   omniscient.

250.   Five wedding invitations

These invitations, mostly from the *metropolis* Oxyrhynchos, are stylised in form
and lack the addressee's name: presumably the invitation was delivered by a
servant known to the recipient, making an address superfluous. The wedding banquets began in the early afternoon ('the 8th hour' is about 2 p.m.), and although
invitations were often delivered only a day before the banquet, preparations began
long in advance (cf. **251**). For a wedding invitation from the Ptolemaic period, see
3.83.

(a) *P.Fuad I Univ.* 7 (*BL* III 61)
Oxyrhynchos (?), second century A D

Agathos invites you to dine for the marriage of his daughter tomorrow,
which is the 16th, from the 8th hour, at the house of the president of the
athletic club (*xystarches*), which is where also . . . the masters (live ?) . . .

(b) *P.Oxy.* III 524
Oxyrhynchos, second century A D

Dionysios invites you to dine for the marriage of his children¹ at the house
of Ischyrion tomorrow, which is the 30th, from the (?)th hour.

(c) *P.Fay.* 132
Euhemeria (Arsinoite nome), third century A D

Isidoros invites you to dine with him for the marriage of his daughter at the
house of Titus the centurion from the 9th hour.

(d) *P.Oxy.* XII 1579
Oxyrhynchos, third century A D

Thermouthis invites you to dine at the marriage of her daughter in her house tomorrow, which is the 18th, from the . . . hour.

(e) *P.Oxy.* XII 1487
Oxyrhynchos, fourth century A D

Theon son of Origenes invites you to the marriage of his sister tomorrow, which is Tybi 9, from the 8th hour.

[1] Probably a brother–sister marriage: see **3.69** note 3.

251. A letter about wedding preparations

P.Oxy. XLVI 3313
Oxyrhynchos, second century A D

The lavishness of the wedding plans suggests that the senders of this letter and its recipient Dionysia are people of wealth and status. The letter may also give hints about family relationships: Dionysia could be the second wife of Alexander and stepmother of the groom Sarapion, while Alexander's daughter Aristokleia may have returned to her father's house with her children after being widowed or divorced.

Apollonios and Sarapias to Dionysia, greetings. Your wonderful announcement about the wedding of the most excellent Sarapion has filled us with joy, and we would have come right away to serve him on a day long-awaited by us and to share in the celebration; but, because of the court sessions[1] and because we are just recovering from illness, we were not able to come. There are not many roses here yet; on the contrary, they are scarce, and from all the estates and from all the garland makers we were barely able to collect the thousand that we sent to you with Sarapas, even by picking those that should have been picked only tomorrow. We had as much of the narcissus as you wanted, so we sent four thousand instead of the two thousand you wrote for. We wish that you did not despise us as such misers that you scorn us by writing that you had sent their cost, when we too consider the young ones as our own children; and honour and love them more than our own; and so we rejoice equally with you and their father. About the other things you want, just write to us. Salute the most excellent Alexander and his Sarapion, Theon, and Aristokleia (may the evil eye not touch them!), and Aristokleia's children. Sarapas will testify to you about the roses, that I have done everything possible to send you as many as you wanted, but we could not find them.
(*2nd hand*) We pray you are well, lady.
(*1st hand, address on the back*) To Dionysia, wife of Alexander.

[1] I.e. the prefect's *conventus*.

252. A village girl brings jewellery, clothing, and utensils to her marriage

P.Mich. II 121 recto IV i (*BL* VI 80)
Tebtynis, A D 42

This abstract of a marriage contract, drawn up through the record office of Tebtynis (cf. **3.101**), illustrates the range of items found in the dowry of a bride from an apparently quite humble village family.[1] Tamarres' was among the more valuable of the dowries recorded at Tebtynis from A D 42–6; the sixty-seven examples range in value from 18 to 1600 drachmas, with a median of 80 drachmas (Hopkins, 1980, 342).

Herakleides, son of Harmiysis, about 22 years old, with a scar on his left eyebrow, and his parents, Harmiysis, son of Orseus, about 45 years old, with a scar on his left shin, both of them Persians of the *epigone*, acting as sureties for one another, and his wife, the mother of Herakleides, Heraklea, daughter of Androniskos, Persian, about 40 years old, with a scar in the middle of her forehead, acting with her guardian Harmiysis, from the village of Phenameni that is in the Herakleopolite nome above Memphis, acknowledge to Klesis, son of Psosneus, about 65 years old, with a scar above the right side of his upper lip, that they have from him for the sake of his daughter Tamarres, a dowry, consisting of: 200 silver drachmas, including a robe with a value of 60 silver drachmas, and in *parapherna* without valuation, a pair of gold earrings of three quarters,[2] and a gold choker of one and a half quarters, and silver bracelets of a weight of 12 drachmas of uncoined silver, and a bronze pitcher, and a bronze mirror, and 2 bronze water jars, and a tin water jar of a weight of 5 minas, and a *chiton* with golden flowers, and 2 cloaks, and a white shawl. Those who are marrying are to live together. The dowry consists of 200 silver drachmas.

The signers are: Eutychos, son of Eutychos, about 32 years old, with a scar on his right knee, and for the other party, Soterichos, son of Herodes, about 32 years old, with a scar on the ankle bone of his right foot. The rest, as usual.

[1] Other marriage contracts are: **4.118–19, 123, 126, 136, 155**; for dowries see also **127–9**, and especially **141**; cf. **132**, and **Ch.3 Arch.F** introd.

[2] In the *parapherna*, quarters, drachmas and minas are all units of weight; but the total of 200 silver drachmas for the *pherne* expresses a monetary value.

253. Gold earrings in the pawnshop

P.Coll.Youtie II 96
Provenance unknown, 14 December A D 192

Isidora would be given this receipt when she pawned her gold earrings for cash (cf. **5.191**).

Year 33, Choiak 18.
Isidora, a seller of knick-knacks, for a pledge, a pair of gold earrings, 24 dr(achmas).

254. A woman and her mother lose their jewels in a fight at the baths

P.Ryl. II 124
Euhemeria (Arsinoite nome), first century AD

This rough and ungrammatical draft is one of a group of petitions surviving from mid-first century AD Euhemeria. It was no doubt intended, like the others in the series, for either the strategos or the *epistates phylakitikon* (chief of police). For village bath-houses, see also **4.130** and **Plate 25**. The floor of a circular bath at the site of Euhemeria was seen in 1989 by several of the contributors to this volume.

From Hippalos son of Archis, public farmer from the village of Euhemeria of the Themistos division. On the 6th Tybi, while my wife Aplounous and her mother Thermis (were bathing?), Eudaimonis daughter of Protarchos, and Etthytais daughter of Pees, and Deios son of Ammonios, and Heraklous attacked them, and gave my wife Aplounous and her mother in the village bath-house many blows all over her body so that she is laid up in bed, and in the fray she lost a gold earring weighing three quarters, a bracelet of unstamped metal weighing sixteen drachmas, a bronze bowl worth 12 drachmas; and Thermis her mother lost a gold earring weighing two and a half quarters, and . . . (*the text becomes fragmentary*).

255. Thais' marriage agreement: she will not put drugs in her husband's food and drink

PSI I 64 (*BL* I 390, IV 87, IX 311)
Oxyrhynchos, first century BC

In this unique marriage agreement (in the form of an oath), Thais swears, not only to offer fidelity and affection to her husband, but also to abstain from adding love potions as she prepares his food and drink. The document does not spell out his responsibilities to Thais, although he presumably supported her for as long as she lived with him. Thais' position in the relationship seems exceptionally weak. The text is mutilated at the point where the financial arrangements between the couple are spelled out, but the husband must have given Thais all the items which she agrees to refund should she desert him without due cause. On the other hand, Thais herself seems to have provided her husband with a marriage loan of five bronze talents.[1] Thais' signature at the bottom is in her own unpractised hand **(Plate 40)**.

40 Thais' marriage agreement
PSI I 64
Oxyrhynchos, first century BC

Thais signed this marriage agreement (see **6.255**) at the bottom in her own hand; unlike the scribe who drew up the document, she was not a practised writer.

Thais, daughter of Tarouthinos, swears to . . . son of Hermogenes, by Osiris, and Isis, and Horos (?), and Zeus, and all the other gods and goddesses to remain with you for as long as you live, dwelling with you as your legitimate wife, neither sleeping away from your bed, nor being absent from your house even for a day, and to be affectionate to you and to . . . neglecting nothing of yours. (*mutilated lines containing the financial arrangements*) If I, being wronged in no way, . . . (decide?) to separate from you and leave you . . . I shall pay back everything, taking nothing for myself. But with regard to the five talents of bronze through the loan, I shall annul the loan and shall surrender it with no excuse whatsoever. If you give me other items of gold jewellery in addition to the aforementioned . . . I shall not take these away with me, but shall give them back to you, taking nothing for myself. I will not be together with any other man, in the way of women, except with you, nor shall I prepare love charms against you, whether in your beverages or in your food, nor shall I connive with any man who will do you (harm) on any pretence. (Year) 2, Choiak.

(*2nd hand*) I, Thais, have sworn the oath written above and I shall do as prescribed.

[1] Thus *BL* IV 87. For the nature of such loans, see Gagos, Koenen and McNellen (1992); cf. **4.132**.

256. A husband questions an oracle about his wife's return

SB XVIII 14043
Soknopaiou Nesos, second century A D

See **249** for questions to oracles about entering into marriage, and for the procedure of consultation.

To our Lord Soknopaios, great god, and fellow gods. Etrenion asks you: if it is not to be permitted that my wife Ammonous come back up to me of her own free will, but that I must make the first move in order for her to come, return (this slip) to me.

257. An unwilling bride seeks to divorce her abusive and spendthrift husband

BGU IV 1105 (*BL* II.2 23)
Alexandria, 10 B C

A wife who suffered physical abuse in her marriage, or whose husband squandered the dowry she had brought, could have recourse to both blood relatives and officialdom for assistance in obtaining a divorce (see also **4.152–4**; cf. **128**). Much of Tryphaine's complaint against her husband Asklepiades is expressed in allusive phrases and ungrammatical language, and presumably a subsequent lawsuit would sort out the matters not directly connected with the return of her dowry. Her statements about the abuse she suffered at Asklepiades' hands are, by contrast, clearly expressed, as is her intention to recover her dowry of sixty drachmas. The restorations and interpretation of the text followed here are essentially those of Naber (1930), and Häge (1968), 49–50.

To Protarchos.[1] From Tryphaine, daughter of Dioskourides. Asklepiades, to whom I am married, persuaded my parents, although I, Tryphaine, was unwilling, to give me to him as my caretaker, and, while they (?)[2] were lodging in accordance with (?) an agreement formalised for him through your tribunal, (Asklepiades) entered into the marriage, (receiving ?) also on my behalf a down payment on my dowry consisting of clothing worth forty drachmas and twenty drachmas of coined silver. But my accuser, Asklepiades, since he kept going off (?) throughout the marriage for no reason, squandered the aforementioned goods, abused me and insulted me, and, laying his hands on me, he used me as if I were his bought slave. As a result, since I have dispatched my father Dioskourides to deliver my notice and to formalise matters in accordance with my divorce, I ask that you send someone with him from your tribunal who will get my divorce finalised, as is proper, and who will deliver a copy of this notification to Asklepiades, so that without delay he will either contest the matter further in court, or pay back to me my 60 (drachmas). And I further ask that you award (?) to Dioskourides the expenses of the other (items?), which are, in fact, 66 (drachmas), but that you thoroughly proceed against him (*Asklepiades*), in a manner that despises malefactors, for injuries and expenses, so that I have received assistance.

[1] See **4.127** for a no-fault divorce submitted to the same official.

[2] The translation assumes the logical interpretation of 'they' as Tryphaine's parents, although the grammatical construction implies that 'they' should refer to other, unnamed persons. Naber argues that Tryphaine's father ran an inn, connecting the 'lodgers' with the 'others' whose expenses were to be awarded to her father Dioskourides; but it seems more likely that only Tryphaine's own family is involved.

258. Clean laundry despite a wife's death

P.Oxy. LIX 4004
Oxyrhynchos, fifth century A D

This letter begins with condolences about the death of Makaria, wife of Kanopos, but it quickly veers off to other topics. This is typical of ancient letters, which often eschew elaborate laments over a death, once feelings of sadness and helplessness have been expressed (cf. **268** and **3.110**). Theodoros asks Kanopos to sail down to him because the Nile flood has begun (that is around mid-July), bringing garments which either need fulling or have already been fulled (cf. **5.217**).

To my lord, my truly most honoured brother, Kanopos, (from) Theodoros. We were very sad when we heard the fate of Makaria, your wife, and not without reason did your son Gratianos long for her so much, and also her other sons. Still, what can we do in the face of the human condition? So, please comfort yourself and shoulder the burden and come to me at the (village) of the Islands[1] with my lord Valentinos, for I have need of your nobility, and again I shall have you conveyed by boat. So do not delay, because it is the rising (of the Nile). When you come, please deign to bring whatever laundry[2] you have on hand. The items are: Nathanael's tunic; a white blanket, Synkletike's tunic, Kyra's cape, Kyra's tunic. I greet Didymos and Philoxenos and all your people.

(*2nd hand*): I pray that you are well for many years, lord, my most honoured brother. About the wheat, don't be concerned. I have not dispatched it myself so that it could be measured out for you when you come.

(*Address on the back, 1st hand ?*): To my lord, my truly most honoured brother Kanopos, (from) Theodoros.

[1] Probably situated on the east bank of the Nile opposite the border between the Oxyrhynchite and Kynopolite nomes.

[2] *Gnapsima*, a hitherto unknown word; its form suggests (garments) 'that should be fulled', or possibly 'that have been fulled'.

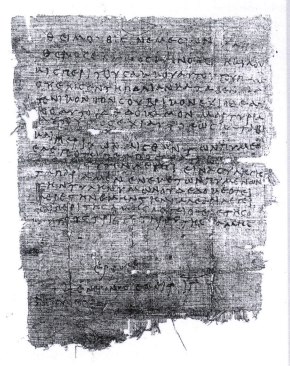

259.   Thermouthis manages her husband's affairs in his absence

SB XIV 11585
Philadelphia, 7 July AD 59

Nemesion, tax collector of Philadelphia, is well known from an archive of some 130 documents and letters, revealing his business activities as collector of capitation taxes for the village, an owner of flocks and farmlands, and a lender of money to impoverished fellow villagers.[1] Uniquely in the archive, this letter is addressed to Nemesion by a woman, Thermouthis. That she was a close relative is evident from its content; but proof that she was his wife, looking after Nemesion's business interests in the village during his absence in the *metropolis*, comes only from a tax receipt of AD 69/70, in which two young men stated that their parents were Nemesion and Thermouthis.[2] The whole letter may be in Thermouthis' own handwriting (**Plate 41**).

Thermouthis to Nemesion, greetings. I want you to know that Lucius[3] has come. With regard to his thick tunic that you have in the *metropolis*, if you come down, bring it back with you. He has the hood to it here. I already gave it to him on his word alone, so he might have it until your arrival. And with regard to the wages of the shepherds, he said, 'I am sending a soldier . . . right away, so that he may seize whatever remains of the shepherds' belongings'. Our mattress he has not given me: 'Bring my old one', he says. And with regard to the shovel, he says that you asked them three staters for the shovel. Farewell. Year 5 of Nero, Epeiph 13.

(*Address on the back*) Deliver to Nemesion.

[1] Nemesion's career as a minor bureaucrat within the Roman system of tax collection is discussed by Hanson (1989a); for examples of his handwriting, see Hanson (1984).
[2] *P.Graux* II 9–11 introduction (pp. 11–12); the tax receipt is *BGU* VII 1614A.7–8.
[3] A business associate of Nemesion: Hanson (1992).

260.   A wife's virtues, according to a Neopythagorean letter

P.Haun. II 13
Provenance unknown, third century AD

The Pythagorean school of philosophy produced a large body of writings over many centuries, including a series of letters, purportedly written by women to other women, defining a woman's proper conduct: her behaviour within a marriage, her response when her husband or lover proved unfaithful, how she should care for infants, how to behave toward maids.[1] The genre of literary letters developed in Hellenistic times and remained popular in the Roman and later periods, and scholars' conjectures about the original date of composition of these particular Neopythagorean letters have ranged from the fourth century BC to the second century AD.

This text of one letter was copied onto the back of a papyrus document. It is written, not in the Doric dialect of the original letters, but in the everyday Greek of the Hellenistic and Roman periods, the 'Common' (*Koine*) dialect; apparently the letters were re-edited and their dialect converted to make them more accessible to contemporary readers. Melissa's advice to Klearete in this letter on woman's quietness, self-restraint, and avoidance of luxury is commonplace in the Graeco-Roman world.

Melissa to Klearete, greetings. Spontaneously you seem to me to possess most of the virtuous accomplishments. The fact that you eagerly want to hear about a woman's adornment promises fair hope that you are going to perfect yourself in virtue. So the prudent[2] and free woman should dwell with her lawful husband, embellished by her quietness, pure white and clean with her clothing, simple but not expensive, unaffected but not elaborately worked and overdone. For she must shun the [. . .] and garments woven with purple or gold threads. For these are useful to prostitutes for hunting more men, but the adornment of a woman who is attractive to one man, her own, is her way of behaving, not her clothes. The free and prudent woman should look shapely to her own husband, but not to her neighbour, having on her face the blush of modesty more than of rouge and white lead, and also having nobleness and decorousness and prudence in place of gold and emerald. For the prudent woman ought not to direct her love of beauty toward lavish expenditure on her dress or her body, but on good management of her household and preservation of her family. She should please her own husband, a prudent man,[3] by carrying out his wishes, for to the decorous woman a husband's wish must be writ as the law by which she lives out her life. Further, she ought to consider that the fairest and greatest dowry she has brought with her is her orderliness. Also she ought to have faith in the beauty and wealth of her soul rather than in that which attaches to money and good looks, because time, jealousy, sickness, and fate all take away money and bodily appearance. The adornment of the soul, however, is present until death for those women who possess it.

[1] Pomeroy (1990), 61–7 argues for the authenticity of their female authorship.
[2] Xenophon was the first Greek writer whose works survive to connect 'prudence' (*sophrosyne*) in both men and women with good administration of the household; Pomeroy (1994), 275.
[3] The characterisation of her husband as 'a prudent man' is an addition to the *Koine* version.

261. Clement of Alexandria on female adornment

Alexandria, *c.* A D 200

A similar association between female virtue and avoidance of excessive luxury and bodily adornment is found in the Christian writer Clement of Alexandria (see also 2.51). His *Paidagogos* ('*Instructor*') provides a systematic exposition of the behaviour and appearance proper to virtuous men and women, from the baths to the bedroom, and from hairstyles to footwear (on which see (b) below). But the most graphic passages are those condemning the various forms of excess in adornment, particularly by women. This is summed up in an extended comparison between women who adorn their bodies excessively and Egyptian temples, whose external splendour contrasts with the unworthy animal deities within ((a)); note, too, how the animal imagery is pursued in the allusion to the biblical serpent's temptation of Eve.

(a) *Paidagogos* III ii.4.2–5.4: Against embellishing the body

But those women who beautify their exterior and let their inner depths go to waste, are unaware that they adorn themselves in the manner of Egyptian temples; in which the gateways and vestibules are carefully constructed, and the groves and sacred enclosures, and the courts surrounded with innumerable pillars; the walls gleam with imported stones, and there is no lack of skilled engraving; and the temples shine with gold, silver and electrum and glitter with multi-coloured gems from India and Ethiopia; and the sanctuaries are veiled with gold-embroidered hangings. But if you penetrate to the deepest enclosure, eager to view something greater, and seek the resident image of the temple, and if a *pastophoros* or another of the priests, having solemnly surveyed the sacred place, singing a hymn in the Egyptian tongue, draw back the hanging a little, to reveal the god, he will provoke you to hearty laughter at the object of veneration. For it is not a god to be found inside, which you have sought with such eagerness, but a cat, or a crocodile, or indigenous serpent, or some such beast unworthy of the temple, but worthy of a den, or hole, or the mire. The god of the Egyptians appears as a wild beast rolling on a purple couch.

Similar to this seem to me those women who wear gold, who occupy themselves in curling their tresses, and engage in anointing their cheeks, and painting their eyes, and dyeing their hair, and practising the other pernicious arts of luxury, bedecking the outer covering of the flesh – in true Egyptian fashion – to attract their idolatrous lovers. But if one draws aside the hanging of the temple – I mean the headdress, the dye, the clothes, the gold, the paint, the cosmetics – that is, the web consisting of them, with a view to finding the true beauty within, he will be disgusted, I know well. For he will not find the image of God dwelling within, as is worthy, but instead of it a fornicator and adulteress who has occupied the sanctuary of the soul, and the true beast will be detected, 'an ape smeared with white lead', and that deceitful serpent, devouring the understanding part of woman through her vanity, has her soul as its hole; filling all with deadly poisons, belching up the venom of his own error, this serpent seducer transformed wives into harlots – for love of finery is not for a wife, but a courtesan; such women think little of keeping house beside their husbands; but, loosing their husbands' purse-strings, they expend its resources on their pleasures, that they may have many witnesses to their seeming beauty, and the whole day they spend with their bought slaves, devoting their attention to beauty treatment.[1]

(b) *Paidagogos* II xi.116–17.1: On shoes

With regard to shoes, too, pretentious women act in the same manner, displaying in that respect also much looseness. Shameful, in truth, are 'those sandals on which golden flowers are fastened',[2] but they think it worth fastening nails in spiral pattern onto the soles, and many women, too, carve erotic embraces upon them as if, in beating the rhythm of their footsteps on the ground, by their gait they would impress on it their wantonness of spirit. So one must bid farewell to the gold-plated and bejewelled frivolities of sandals, and Attic and Sikyonian half-boots, and the Persian and Etruscan high boots; and, setting out the correct aim as is the custom with our truth, one must choose what accords with nature. For the use of shoes is on the one hand for covering the feet, and on the other for protection, saving the sole of the foot from stumbles and from the roughness of mountain tracks.

Women should be allowed a white shoe, except when they travel, and then they should use an oiled one. When travelling, women need nailed leather soles. Furthermore, they should generally wear shoes; for it is not appropriate to show the foot bare, and besides, a woman easily slips and comes to harm. But for a man it is quite appropriate to go unshod, except when on military service.

¹ Note also later in the chapter: 'For thrice, not once, (women) deserve to perish, who use crocodiles' excrement, and smear themselves with the froth of putrid humours, and stain their eyebrows with soot, and rub their cheeks with white lead'; for crocodile dung as a cosmetic, see Hanson (1998).
² A quotation from comedy.

262. Two married women at a festival

Theokritos, *Idyll* 15, lines 1–99
Alexandria, 270s B C

The poet Theokritos, son of Praxagoras and Philinna, came to Alexandria about 275 BC, to join the circle of court poets who enjoyed the patronage of King Ptolemy II Philadelphos and his sister–wife Arsinoe II. Many of Theokritos' poems (*Idylls*) were bucolic tales of shepherds, although he also composed a panegyric for King Ptolemy II, which begins with praises for his parents, Ptolemy I Soter and Queen Berenike – she was pictured as being overjoyed that baby Ptolemy was born in the likeness of his father (*Idyll* 17.63–4) – and culminates with a catalogue of Ptolemy II's wealth and good deeds. *Idyll* 15 also compliments the dynasty through its Alexandrian setting, depicting the conversation of two women, Gorgo and Praxinoa, as they visit the royal palace for the Adonis festival. Like Theokritos himself, these women and their husbands have left their native Syracuse in favour of Alexandria's economic opportunities and cultural splendours. Theokritos' poetry continued to find readers in Egypt throughout the Roman and Byzantine periods, and four fragmentary papyrus copies of *Idyll* 15 have been identified.¹

The poem opens with Gorgo's arrival at Praxinoa's home, and their preparations to set out for the festival. By line 40 the women are bidding Praxinoa's baby good-bye, for he is to stay at home with his nurse, Phrygia; and they set out along with their servants, Eunoa and Eutychis. Once inside the palace, a female singer sang a hymn in praise of Adonis, beloved of Aphrodite (lines 100–45), not translated here (see **2.3** for lines 106–11).

GORGO: Is Praxinoa at home?
PRAXINOA: Gorgo, dear, how long it's been (since you have been here)! I'm inside. I'm surprised you've come now. Eunoa, get a chair for her, and put a cushion on it.
GORGO: That's nice.
PRAXINOA: Please sit down.
GORGO: Oh, my flighty soul! I scarcely reached you alive, Praxinoa, with all that crowd and the many horses! Everywhere boots, and men in uniform.

The street was unending, and you always move further away!

PRAXINOA: That's my crazy one, for he came and took me to the
ends of the earth, not to a house, so that we shouldn't be
neighbours to one another – spitefully, the jealous brute is always
like that.

GORGO: Don't talk about your husband Dinon like that, dear, when
the little one is present. See, lady, how he looks at you. Cheer up,
little Zopyrion, sweet baby, she is not talking about your daddy.

PRAXINOA: The baby understands, by the goddess.

GORGO: Daddy is nice.

PRAXINOA: But that daddy of his the other day – in fact, the other
day, we said, 'Papa, buy soap and rouge from the stall' – but he
came home with salt for us, the thirteen foot booby.

GORGO: Mine acts the same way, a real spendthrift, my Diokleidas.
Seven drachmas he spent yesterday on mere dogs' hair, pluckings
of old bags, five skeins of the stuff, all filthy, adding work to
work. But come on, get your wrap and cloak. Let us go to
splendid King Ptolemy's palace so that we can see the Adonis.
I hear that the Queen is getting ready a magnificent
occasion.

PRAXINOA: All wealth in a wealthy house.

GORGO: But if you've seen it, you can give an eyewitness account to
someone who didn't see it. It's time to move.

PRAXINOA: It's always festival time for those who do not have to
work. Eunoa, good-for-nothing, take up the spinning and put it
down again out there – the cats use it for a soft sleep. Get a move
on, bring water, quick. We need water first, but she brings soap.
Give it anyway, but not so much, you wastrel! Pour on the water.
You wretch, why do you drench my tunic? Stop it! I've had
enough of a wash, thank god. Now, where's the key to the big
chest? Bring it here.

GORGO: Praxinoa, that full-gathered robe fastened with a brooch
really suits you. Tell me, how much did it cost you off the loom?

PRAXINOA: Don't make me think of it, Gorgo – more than two
minas pure silver. And I put my heart into making it up.

GORGO: Well anyway, it has turned out most successfully.

PRAXINOA: It's good of you to say so. (*To Eunoa*) Come, bring my
cloak and hat for me and put them on properly. I'm not going to
take you, baby. The Bogey-horse bites! You can cry as much as you
want, I won't risk your being lamed. Come on. (*To the child's nurse*)
Phrygia, take the little baby and play with him; call the dog inside,
and lock the courtyard door.

O ye gods, what a big crowd! However are we to get through this
crush, and how long will it take? Ants, numberless and

immeasurable! You've conferred a great many benefits on us,
Ptolemy, since your father (*sc. Ptolemy I*) went off to join the gods.
Nowadays no criminal harms the passerby, sneaking along in
Egyptian fashion; wicked games such as men welded into a mass of
deceit used to play, all as bad as one another, those idle good-for-
nothings.

50

Sweetest Gorgo, what are we to do? The royal war-horses! My dear
sir, do not trample me! That bay horse has reared up straight. See
how wild it is! Reckless Eunoa, won't you stand back? It'll kill the
man who is leading it. How relieved I am that I left my baby back
home.

GORGO: Cheer up, Praxinoa; now, see, we've got behind them and
they have gone off to their proper place.

60   PRAXINOA: I am beginning to recover myself already. Ever since I
was a child, I've been particularly afraid of two things: a horse and
the clammy snake. Let's hurry. There's a big crowd flowing toward
us.

GORGO: Say, mother, are you coming from the palace?

OLD LADY: I am indeed, my children.

GORGO: Then it is easy to get inside?

OLD LADY: The Greeks got into Troy through trying, my pretty
child. Just try and everything gets done.

GORGO: That old lady went off after some oracular utterances.

PRAXINOA: Women know everything, even how Zeus married Hera.

GORGO: Look, Praxinoa, what a large crowd there is around the gates
of the palace!

PRAXINOA: Marvellous. Gorgo, give me your hand, and you, Eunoa,
take hold of Eutychis' hand. Hold on to her tight, or you'll get
separated. Let's all go in together. Hold on tight to us, Eunoa. Oh
dear, dear me, Gorgo: my summer cloak has been torn right in

70   two! In the name of Zeus, if you care for your life, sir, look out for
my cloak.

1ST MAN: I can't help it, but still, I'll try to watch out.

PRAXINOA: The crowd is all bunched together. They're pushing
together like hogs.

1ST MAN: Cheer up, madam, we're in a good place.

PRAXINOA: May you be in a good place for years on end, kind sir,
for protecting us. What a nice and kind man! Eunoa's being
squeezed. Come on, you coward, force your way. Super! 'All
women aboard', as the groom said when he locked the door of the
bridal chamber.

GORGO: Praxinoa, come here a minute, and look first at the
embroideries – fine and ever so pretty. You'd say they were the
embroidered robes of the gods.

80   PRAXINOA: Mistress Athena! What excellent women wove these,
     what excellent (*male*) artists drew the accurate pictures! How true
     to life they stand, how truly they move! They're alive, not woven!
     Mankind really is a clever creature. The thrice-beloved Adonis
     himself, how wonderfully he reclines on his silver couch, sprouting
     the first down of manhood from his temples. Oh, Adonis, who is
     beloved even in the Underworld!

   2ND MAN: Oh you nuisances, stop your endless cooing like doves.
     They'll wear me out with all their oohing and ahhing.

   PRAXINOA: Indeed! Where is that man from? What business is it of
     yours if we are cooing? Buy your slaves before you order them
90   about. Are you giving orders to ladies of Syracuse? And, for your
     information, we're from an old Corinthian family, just like
     Bellerophon himself. We are speaking the dialect of the
     Peloponnese – I suppose it's proper for Dorians to speak their
     Doric dialect! May there not, Persephone, be any master over us,
     except the one we have. I don't care. Don't waste your breath on
     me.

   GORGO: Hush, Praxinoa. She's about to sing the Adonis song, the
     daughter of the Argive woman, the famous singer, I mean, who last
     year won the contest to sing the song of mourning. She'll sing
     something impressive, I know it for sure. She's already beginning
     her act.

[1] *P.Hamb.* III 201, Arsinoite nome?, first century AD; *P.Oxy.* XIII 1619, Oxyrhynchos, fifth
century AD; Pack^2 1487, Antinoopolis, *c.* AD 500; Pack^2 1488, Arsinoite nome, *c.* AD 500.

263.   Ahwere, the magician's wife

(Excerpt from) P.Cairo 30646 (Spiegelberg 1906–8)[1]
First century BC

Several of the best preserved fictional narratives in Demotic surviving from the
Ptolemaic and Roman periods belong to 'cycles' around characters loosely based
on historical figures: Setna Khaemwese, a son of Ramesses II of the XIX Dynasty,
and the seventh-century King Petubastis. The first Setna story, from which this
excerpt and **288** are taken, exemplifies the characteristic 'story within a story' structure of Demotic narrative fiction. Lichtheim (1980) includes more of the Setna
cycle, as well as the regrettably fragmentary story of Prince Pedikhons and Queen
Serpot, which recalls the Greek story of Achilles and the Amazon Queen
Penthesilea. On Demotic literature, see further Tait (1994) and (1996).

While exploring the ancient tombs of the Memphite necropolis, Setna is
somehow led to enter the tomb of Naneferkaptah, a prince and magician of long
ago. Naneferkaptah's ambitions as a magician had led to the destruction of his family
at the hands of the god Thoth; his sister–wife Ahwere and his son Merib are not

even buried with him. Nevertheless, his magical powers enable them to be present in spirit and, at the beginning of what is preserved of the story, Ahwere is narrating to Setna how her attempt to have a go-between persuade Pharaoh that she should marry her brother nearly failed. Pharaoh is speaking:

'"You are the one who is offending me.[2] If I have no more than two children, is it right to have one of them marry the other? I will have Naneferkaptah marry the daughter of a general, [and I will have] Ahwere marry the son of another general, so that our family will increase." The time came, and they set the feast before Pharaoh. They came for me, and I was taken to the feast, [although my heart] was very sad, and I was not behaving as I had been the day before. Pharaoh said "Ahwere, was it you who had them come to me on this foolish errand, asking to marry [Naneferkaptah your] elder brother?" I said to him "Let me marry the son of a general, and let him too marry the daughter of another general, so that our family will increase." I laughed, and Pharaoh laughed [. . .] Pharaoh said "Steward, let Ahwere be taken to the house of Naneferkaptah tonight, and let absolutely everything splendid be taken with her." I was taken as a wife to the house of Naneferkaptah [. . .] Pharaoh had gifts of silver and of gold brought to me, and all the royal household had (gifts) brought to me. He slept with me that night, and he found me [. . . and he did not . . .] me ever again, and each of us loved the other. The time of my period came, and I did not have a period. It was reported to Pharaoh, and his heart was very glad. Pharaoh had many goods taken [to me . . .] and he had gifts of silver and gold and of cloth of royal-linen brought to me, which were very fine. The time of my giving birth came, and I gave birth to this boy, who is in front of you, whose name is Merib. He was inscribed in the register of the House of Life.'
(Naneferkaptah hears of a magical book written by the god Thoth, which is his for the taking if he can track down its place of concealment in the 'Sea of Koptos' and kill the serpent that guards it.) 'We went on board, and we journeyed, and we reached [Koptos . . .] the priests of Isis of Koptos and the chief priest of Isis. They came down to meet us, and they rushed to greet Naneferkaptah. Their womenfolk came down to meet me [. . .] of Isis and Harpokrates.' *(When Naneferkaptah has stolen the book, he returns to his patiently waiting wife.)* 'They rowed him by night just as by day, and he reached me [. . . as I was sitting(?)] by the sea of Koptos, without having drunk or eaten, and without having done anything at all, so I was in the state of someone who has reached the embalming house. I said to Naneferkaptah, [my elder brother,] "Let me see the book for which we have suffered these [. . .] torments". He handed me the book, and I read a formula from it, and I cast a spell on the sky, the earth, and the Underworld, and the mountains and the seas. I discovered everything that the birds in the sky and the fish in the waters and also the animals were saying. I read another formula, and I saw the sun as he rose in the sky

with his ennead,[3] and I saw the moon as he shone with all the stars in the sky, and their (true) natures. I saw the fish in the waters, although there were twenty-one cubits of water above them, even though I was no scribe, I would say, compared to Naneferkaptah my elder brother, who was a fine scribe and a very learned man.'

[1] Translation by W. John Tait.
[2] Possibly just 'You do me an injustice', or perhaps 'You are harming me (making a disastrous suggestion)'?
[3] The first nine deities of Heliopolis: the sun-god himself, Atum, Shu and Tefnut, Geb and Nut, and Osiris, Seth, Isis and Nephthys.

IV   Sickness, death and burial

Against the ever-present threat of sickness and death, charms and prayers offered as efficacious assistance as did the medical practitioner. Relatives and friends provided what help and support they could, hoping for recovery so long as life endured; and in the event of death, arranging for an appropriate funeral and some permanent reminder of the deceased in accordance with Egyptian or Greek tradition. The Egyptian practice of mummification was popular even among the Graeco-Egyptian élite. The family would send the corpse to be mummified, sometimes locally, sometimes at a religious centre such as in Ptolemaic Memphis, where guilds of undertakers, called 'Men of Anoubis', plied their trade on humans and sacred animals alike.[1] Burial did not always follow immediately, and the mummy might be kept for some years accessible to the remaining members of the family (cf. **228, 5.165(b)**), before burial in the necropolis outside the village or *metropolis*. Following Egyptian traditions, the mummy might be accompanied by magical texts designed to assist the dead person's passage to a blissful after-life.[2] The elaborateness and craftsmanship of the grave monument, whether in Greek, Egyptian, or mixed style, are indications of a family's disposable wealth (**272–6; Plates 35, 42–3, 45–7**).

[1] Thompson (1988), 155–89.
[2] Forman and Quirke (1996); see **Plate 44**.

264.   Christian prayer amulet to restore a woman's health

Magica varia (Pap.Brux. xxv) 2
Provenance unknown, seventh century AD

This charm, written on a small, rectangular piece of parchment, was to be worn by the woman desiring relief (cf. **266**).

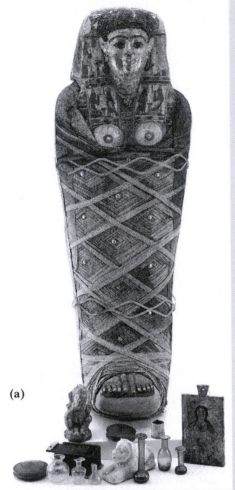

(a)

42 Mummy with grave goods and painted plaque
Royal Scottish Museum, Edinburgh, inv. 1911 210.3
Hawara, second century AD

This mummy was found covered with a cloth, on which were placed the items shown here **(a)**, including small glass jars, figures of a lion and of Harpokrates, and a wooden box with a sliding lid.[1] But most remarkable is the plaque found placed by the girl's head: one side depicts a woman seated in the posture of childbirth (cf. **6.222**), while the other shows a bearded man seated in front of a bookshelf, and holding a large pair of scissors **(b)**. Bowman (1996) plate 65, p. 111, suggests that he may be a tailor, but the identification as a learned doctor, or

(b)

obstetrician, would fit better with the other side.[2] The mummy mask represents a mature woman, but CAT scanning shows the body inside the wrappings to belong to a girl aged five to seven, too young to have died in childbirth. Such discrepancies between the outward appearance of a mummy and the body it contains are not unparalleled (Filer, 1997).

[1] See Petrie (1911), plate xiv; but the grave goods are hardly toys, as he describes them.
[2] Walker and Bierbrier (1997) cat. 61; catt. 60–73 give detailed descriptions of all items in the burial.

(a)   (b)

(c)

43   Wall-paintings in a woman's tomb

(Details from) Tomb 21 (after Gabra, 1941, plates XIII–XV)
Tuna el-Gebel, second century AD

This tomb, discovered in 1935 in the necropolis of Hermopolis, consists of four vaulted chambers, the two main ones decorated with funerary scenes in Egyptian style. Sometimes the deceased woman is shown in profile, wearing Egyptian dress **(b)**; in other scenes, such as her purification by Thoth and Horos **(a)**, she is depicted in Greek style, wearing a short-sleeved tunic and mantle. In both cases, her black skeletal shadow stands behind her. To the left of the door to the second chamber, Isis and Nephthys, seated, make a gesture of adoration to the solar disc which they hold up **(c)** (cf. **2.33**). See Gabra (1941), 39–50, Dunand and Lichtenberg (1995), 3255.

†Lord Jesus Christ, you who calmed the winds and the seas – for all things obey you with trembling – even now Lord, come for mercy and good will upon your servant So.ro., for her health, for her self-restraint, for her advantage, my Lord God, in accordance with your mercy through the

44   Judgement scene, Book of the Dead
Brussels Museum inv. E8388
Thebes, Ptolemaic period

Book of the Dead of the musician of Amon-Re, Senmonthis daughter of Esyris (Nes-Hor).
In funerary texts, as in magic, the mother's name is often preferred to that of the father as the
means of identification. Esyris, like her daughter Senmonthis, was also a musician. Female
priestesses acted in the choir, singing and playing their sistrum; the determinative after the
Egyptian word 'musician' shows a female figure holding a sistrum.

   The judgement scene is read from the (bottom) right: the deceased is flanked on each side
by a goddess Maat, symbolising truth, order and justice. The balance, operated by the gods
Horos and Anoubis, is in equilibrium, showing that her heart is as light as the Maat-feather,
and without any sin; the result is recorded by Thoth, the ibis-headed god of writing. She
therefore need not fear the terrible monster, seated on its pedestal, ready to devour the
unjust. On the left, the judge Osiris, king of the hereafter, sitting on his throne, welcomes
Senmonthis to his realm. Between Osiris and the monster are the four sons of Horos,
secondary divinities who take charge of the mummified intestines of the deceased. Above is a
gallery of forty-two judges (in two rows), assisting Osiris in his judgement.

intercessions of your holy martyr George. Release her from the troubles that
envelope her through the intercession of . . . our Mistress, the all-glorious
Mother of God and ever virginal Mary. For you have been glorified and will
be glorified for ages of ages. Amen. ††††††

265. A doctor writes?

P.Oxy. LIX 4001
Oxyrhynchos, late fourth century AD

Eudaimon's letter ranges over many topics, including a report about clothing and items sent to him by his mother and grandmothers, as well as thanks for Kyra's recovery from illness. His interest in eye salve, cupping vessels,[1] and the letter's address, suggest that he is a doctor, as perhaps also are other family members.

To my lady mother and my lady grandmothers, together with Kyra, Eudaimon sends greetings. I made haste right now to address you, once I found a good opportunity, praying to the divine providence that you may receive my letter in good spirits and in good health. For Heraklammon came and upset us very much, because he says 'Kyra our sister was sick'. Now, however, we thank the divine providence that helps us everywhere and in everything that she is again healthy. Let her know that the linen garments of our sister Kyrilla have been cut (from the loom). If I find a friend going, I intend to send them and the purple hooded cloak and the shoes. We now have the materials from Helene the embroideress, and I found only 4 books[2] in the baggage, but you wrote, 'We have sent off 5'. In fact, we received all the other things, except only the container of animal fat. As a result, let our brother Theodoros be eager to search . . . and to know about it . . . He furnished in place of the container of animal fat, a jar of eye salve. Also be eager to send me the folding bronze case,[3] so that I may make other materials, but not the same ones, and the heater in the same way, and the cupping vessels, so that I may make a . . .
(*In the left margin*) Also send three pounds of eye salve mixed from all . . . astringent substances and . . . so that I may get other attractive things . . .
(*Address on the back*) Send to the doctor's office. From Eudaimon.

[1] An essential item among doctors' instruments, used to draw blood to the surface of the skin.
[2] Or, '4 documents'.
[3] The meaning of the word *deltarion* is not totally clear; we follow Andorlini (1996), 8 and note 5; cf. Fischer (1997).

266. Spell against the ascent of the uterus

PGM VII 260–71
Provenance unknown, third century AD

The first columns of this long papyrus roll, two metres in length, contain numbered verses, copied at random from Homer's *Iliad* and *Odyssey*, arranged in groups of six: a method of divination similar to that involving the *Predictions of Astrampsychos* (**218**,

247; cf. **267**). The text then turns to magical spells and medicinal aids, including the following spell, designed to prevent the uterus from rising within a woman's body.

Views of the female body endorsed by the earliest writers in the Greek medical tradition, the Hippocratics of the fifth and fourth centuries BC, lie closer to popular notions than do the more sophisticated medical writers of later centuries, such as Herophilos, Soranos and Galen. The Hippocratics thought that the womb moved upward in the woman's body whenever it became hot and dry from overwork, or lack of irrigating male seed, searching for cool and moist places in an effort to restore its equilibrium.[1] As the womb tried to force its way toward the crowded places at the centre of a woman's trunk, it wreaked havoc with her physical and mental well-being, causing her to faint or become speechless. Her suffering was like an epileptic fit, sudden and devastating. The sickness was called 'uterine suffocation'; the term 'hysteria' was not used in antiquity. Foul odours at the nose and sweet smells at the vagina were prescribed, to lure the uterus back to its seat. Although Hippocratics assigned mechanical causes for uterine ascent, their odour therapies look to the popular view of the uterus as a sentient being in its own right, attracted by pleasant smells and repelled by unpleasant ones. Despite Herophilos' dissections (**222** introd.) which demonstrated that a woman's uterus was anchored in place by ligaments and thus unable to roam at will about the body, less sophisticated medical writers continued to claim that the uterus ascended; Muscio, a Latin translator of Soranos' gynaecological works in the fifth or sixth century AD, claimed that it rose 'as far as her chest'.

Spells were also popularly employed in the attempt to control this rambunctious organ; in this example, the woman was to wear the charm, written on a strip of tin, set in a cloth wrapper, on her body (cf. **264**).

Against ascent of the womb. 'I conjure you, womb – by him who set up his power over the Abyss, before there was heaven or earth or sea or light or darkness, by him who created the angels, of whom, first of all, Amichamchou and Chouchao Cheroei Oueiacho Odou Proseionges, and by him who sits over the cherubim, raising up the throne that is his own – that you sit back down in your seat and neither lean toward the right part of the ribs nor toward the left part of the ribs, that you not bite into the heart like a dog, but stand firm and remain in your own place,[2] gnawing on nothing, as long as I conjure you by the one who in the beginning made the heaven and the earth and all the things in it. Alleluia. Amen.'

Write this on a small strip of tin and wrap it in seven colours.

[1] King (1994); Hanson (1991a), 81–7; Aubert (1989), 424.
[2] A magic gemstone bears the inscription: 'Set the womb of this woman back into its own place, you who raise up the orb of the sun': Bonner (1950), 81–2.

267. Verses from Homer's Iliad to cure illnesses

PGM XXIIa 2–26
Hermopolis, fourth–fifth century AD

Another (prescription) for a bloody flow:[1]

'. . . *the wrath of Apollo, the lord who strikes from afar*'.   (*Iliad* I 75)
This charm, spoken to the blood, heals a bloody flow. If the patient gets well
and is ungrateful, take a pan of coals, put (the amulet on it?) and set it over
the smoke. Add a root, and also write this verse:
'. . . *for this reason he who strikes from afar sent griefs and still will send them*'.
                                                                             (*Iliad* I 96)
Write this for pain in the breasts and womb:
'. . . (*whom*) *the daughter of Zeus nurtured, but the grain-bearing fields bore*'.
                                                                             (*Iliad* II 548)
If this charm is carried together with a magnetic stone, or is also spoken, it
makes a woman unable to take up the man's seed:[2]
'. . . *you ought not to have been born, and to have perished without marrying*'.
                                                                             (*Iliad* III 40)
   Write this on a clean sheet of papyrus and tie it with the hairs of a mule.
Write this verse for a patient with elephantiasis and have the patient carry
it:
'. . . *as when some woman colours ivory with purple dye*'.   (*Iliad* IV 141)

Greetings, Helios, greetings, Helios, greetings, god over heaven, with your
name of the omnipotent one! From the seventh heaven give to me unwa-
vering favour before every human race and before all women – especially
before this woman. Make me handsome at her side as Iao, rich as Sabaoth,
beloved as Lailam, tall as Barbaras, honoured as Michael, famous as Gabriel,
and I will give you thanks.

[1] The patient is masculine in Greek, although 'bloody flows' were often a gynaecological
   problem; the Gospels tell of a woman with a '12–year flow', cured by touching Christ's
   garment (Matthew 10:20–2; Mark 5:25–9; Luke 8:43–8).
[2] Another contraceptive recipe from an early papyrus roll of medicaments called for a potion
   made from oak-gall, pomegranate seeds, flakes of alum (Mertens-Pack[3] 2418 = *P.Ryl.* III
   531, third–second century BC). For oak-gall and pomegranate as potentially effective
   contraceptives, see Riddle (1992), 94–5.

268.   Eirene sends condolences

P.Oxy. 1115
Oxyrhynchos, *c.* 28 October, second century AD

Two other letters from Eirene are preserved, both written on November 26 or 27;
if from the same year as **268**, they were written only about twenty-nine days later.[1]
Even though one of the later letters is also directed to Taonnophris and Philon,
other concerns now seem more pressing in Eirene's mind, since she makes no
further reference to the deceased (cf. **258** introd.). White (1986), 184–5, notes the
similarities between Eirene's letter and more formal, or literary, letters of consolation, such as Proclus 21.

Eirene to Taonnophris and Philon, be of good cheer. I was so grieved and I wept over the man who has died as much as I did for Didymas, and I carried out all the things that were fitting, along with all my household, Epaphroditos and Thermouthion, and Philion and Apollonios, and Plantas. But, even so, there is nothing a person can do toward things of this magnitude. At any rate, bring comfort to one another. Farewell. Hathyr 1.

(*Address on the back*) To Taonnophris and Philon.

---

[1] *P.Oxy.* I 116, and I 187 descr., ed. L. E. Winkworth, 'A Request for Purgatives: *P.Oxy.* I 187', *ZPE* 91 (1992), 85–7.

269. Notification of death submitted by the widow Tapapeis

SB XIV 11587
Philadelphia, 28 June (?) A D 47

In the Roman period, notifications of death were submitted to the village scribe and the royal scribe in the *metropolis* by close kin of a deceased man of taxable status (sometimes, as here, by the widow; more usually a brother or father), in order to secure the transfer of the tax payer's name from the rolls of those liable for capitation taxes to a list of the dead.[1] According to other tax records of Philadelphia, Abeis was forty-nine years old in the year he died; one son, Horos, named after his grandfather, appears on the tax rolls with Abeis. If he had other living children, they must have been either girls, or sons under fourteen years old.

Tapapeis, about four years younger than her husband, might face many years of widowhood; most widows did not remarry.[2] Several women in the archives of **Chapter 3** were either certainly or probably widows.[3] Adult children might offer the widow a degree of solace, as grown sons and daughters cared for their mother's physical and emotional well-being in recompense for her labours on their behalf during infancy (**Arch. J**). A family's wealth and social prominence also make a widow's life more pleasant. Tapapeis is apparently not so lucky on either count, since her eldest surviving son Horos is only fourteen years old, while her husband Abeis has been in default on his capitation taxes for the last three or four years.

To . . .[4] from Tapapeis, daughter of Pasis, with her guardian, her kinsman Adrastos, son of Diogenes. My husband Abeis, son of Horos, who pays poll tax at the village of Philadelphia, died in the month Epeiph of the present seventh year of Tiberius Claudius Caesar Augustus Germanicus Emperor. I therefore request that his name be entered among those who have died.

Tapapeis, aged about 45, with a scar on her right foot. Adrastos, aged about 50, with a scar on the third finger of his right hand.

(*2nd hand*) Tapapeis, the aforementioned, with her guardian Adrastos, the aforementioned, I swear by Tiberius Claudius Caesar Augustus Germanicus Emperor that . . . all the things written above are true. If I swear truthfully may good happen to me, but if I perjure, the opposite.

(*3rd hand ?*) Epeiph (?) 4 (?) . . .

[1] This notification was found with the papers of Nemesion the tax-collector (see **259**).

[2] Bagnall and Frier (1994), 123–7, and Hanson (1999). On widowhood generally, see Krause (1994).

[3] Tryphon's mother Thamounis (**D**); Apollonios' mother Eudaimonis (**E**); Taesion (**G**); Tasoucharion (**H**); Satornila (**J**); see also **224, 233, 234; 3.69, 74; 5.162, 177, 210, 217**.

[4] This copy was addressed to the village scribe; another copy, *SB* XIV 11586, was submitted to the royal scribe.

270. Lucretia Octavia rewarded for nursing her husband in his final illness

P.Diog. 10
Ptolemais Euergetis, 3 June AD 211

Lucretia Octavia belongs to a large and prominent family, which held both Antinoite and Roman citizenship.[1] Lucius Ignatius Rufinus may have been Lucretia Octavia's first husband, and the silence of the will on the subject of children suggests that the marriage was childless. Rufinus was already ill when he drew up his will early in March of 210, but lingered on for more than a year thereafter. His will, written in Latin (except for the subscription), conformed with Roman law;[2] the surviving document is a copy of the official will which was deposited in government archives after it was opened and read to Rufinus' heirs. Rufinus designated his brother as his sole heir, but reserved a small plot of land and a half share of a house with its furnishings for Lucretia Octavia.

Lucretia also inherited from her father Marcus Lucretius Minor (cf. Hobson, 1983, 219f.). When she died in AD 224 Lucretia Octavia had three minor sons, each from a different father. One son was under the legal guardianship of his father, apparently Lucretia Octavia's third husband, who survived her (she perhaps died while giving birth to another child of his). Lucretia Octavia's brother Marcus Lucretius Diogenes petitioned the strategos to appoint him guardian of her other two sons (*P.Diog.* 18); one child was said to be 'fatherless' (*apator*), while the father of the other was dead (the boy's name makes it unlikely that he was a posthumous child of Lucretia's first marriage to Rufinus). Thus, in the thirteen years since the death of Rufinus, Octavia Lucretia apparently had two subsequent husbands, as well as an unformalised liaison.

(*Latin*) Copy of the will. Lucius Ignatius Rufinus, Antinoite, has made his will. Lucius Ignatius Nemesianus, my brother, is to inherit all my property. All others are to be excluded, and he is to take possession of the inheritance from me within the one hundredth day from the time he knows that he is my heir and is able to inherit in good faith. I give and delegate to Lucretia Octavia, my wife, who has laboured much during the course of my illness, 5½ iugera[3] of land in wheat in the place of Potamon, adjacent to the property of Serenus, and half of my house called . . . neighbouring (the house of) Antonius Didumianus, veteran. In case anything is sold to pay a debt, or for any other reason, the expense will be born by my heir. And if I have any possession in my house, I want this to be my wife's. I want my body to be buried by my brother and heir, mentioned above.

In the village of Philadelphia of the Arsinoite nome, Herakleides division, 5 days before the Nones of March (=3 *March*), in the consulship of Faustinus and Rufus, year 19[4] of the Emperors Caesars Lucius Septimius Severus and Marcus Aurelius Antoninus and Publius Septimius Geta, Augusti, in the month Phamenoth, on the 7th day.

(*Greek*) Copy of the subscription: I, Lucius Ignatius Rufinus, have made my testament as stipulated above.

(*Latin*) Opened and read in the Forum of Augustus in the *metropolis* of the Arsinoite nome, 3 days before the Nones of June (=*3 June*), in the consulship of Quintianus and Bassus, in the same year, in the month Pauni, on the 9th day, with a majority of the witnesses present, who affixed their signatures:

> I, Lucius Valerius Lucretianus, have acknowledged (the document).
> I, Marcus L . . . nus, have acknowledged (the document).
> I, Flavius Diogenes, have acknowledged (the document).
> I, Arrius Niger, have acknowledged (the document).
> Marcus Aurelius Anoubion.
> Lucius A . . . Cottarus.

[1] The family's papers are collected in *P.Diog.*, with a family tree extending over five generations (p. 18). In **4.148**, Lucretia Octavia's sister-in-law Isidora (second wife of Marcus Lucretius Diogenes) divides her property.

[2] Other Roman wills are **4.139, 146**. Champlin (1991) discusses the family concerns expressed in Roman wills.

[3] A Roman unit of area; one iugerum = 0.252 hectare.

[4] A scribal error for 'year 18', compounded below by writing 'in the consulship of Quintianus and Bassus, in the same year': Quintianus and Bassus were consuls at Rome in AD 211 (= year 19, the year of Rufinus' death), the year following Faustinus and Rufus.

271. Preparations for a burial

P.Haun. II 17
Arsinoite nome (?), second century AD

Horion writes this letter about obtaining the materials necessary for mummification at the request of the deceased man's mother and sister.

. . . my father and my brother-in-law Sarapion. But still, with a view toward the thing that has happened to me, please buy good quality linen, as much as eighty drachmas worth, or more, for the burial of the man who has died – at any rate, you know the length needed. In the same manner I rolled up in this letter samples of spices for a mummy. In addition, buy carpenter's glue, two pounds (in weight). The dead man's mother and his sister, because of what has happened to them, have not been able to write anything to you, but they urged me to write to you concerning the above matters. Your family wishes you well, and they salute you. I pray that you are well, dearest one. And a half pound of safflower seeds for dyeing the linen.

(*Address on the back*) . . . to . . . dear one from Horion.

272. Grave monument of Tathotis

(Extracts from) Vienna inscription 5857 (ed. G. Vittmann, 'Die Autobiographie der Tathotis', *SAK* 22, 1995, 283–323) Saqqara, Ptolemaic period (second century BC?)

The funerary text of Tathotis, daughter of Tamounis, wife of Tjaanhuremou, and mother of Benaty, is inscribed in eight lines of hieroglyphs on a wide, low slab of limestone; a third of the first line is incised and the rest is written in ink. The deceased addresses visitors to the necropolis, describing her life, the careers of her husband and son, and her own magnificent burial. At the end Tathotis herself is addressed and promised a blissful afterlife. Translated here are the opening and the description of Tathotis' life and burial. Her ideal life is presented as accomplishments – resolving marital disputes, providing for widows, and so on – that are a woman's equivalents of a man's ethical achievements as a public official. This is not an easy text, written in the classical Egyptian language in the expanded sign repertory of the Graeco-Roman period. Our translation builds upon that of Vittmann and is indebted to the suggestions of John Baines.

The lady of the house of the eyes-of-the-king of Upper Egypt, the royal scribe who reckons everything and overseer of the granary, Tjaanhuremou, justified,[1] mother of the ears-of-the-king of Lower Egypt, the lector priest and chief, the royal scribe Benaty, Tathotis, justified, born of the lady of the house Tamounis.

She says: 'Everyone who comes in and out of the necropolis of the Ba of Ba's,[2] the sacred district of the Greatest of the Great, the great staircase of the Followers of Horos, the great necropolis of the primeval ones, the tomb of the Kings of Upper and Lower Egypt, the western horizon of the one who fashioned the sky[3] – may he rest in it as Atum. A good event happened to me. I was interred there by the survivors who bury as a pious duty(?). Read out the writing, hear what I did when I was upon earth, rejoice, hear my good fortune, and listen to my praises.

Sekhmet the Perfect One favoured me and I was fashioned beautifully and begotten excellently by the Potter (*Khnum*). I went upon the path of Hathor, and it was her majesty that pervaded my body. My heart was ordered to do what she loves and I was found to be in favour. If I sent women back to the houses of their husbands, they trusted me and they were not cast out again. I raised children and buried venerable ones. The sons of the favoured heeded me. I drove away red carnelian (*anger*) and brought turquoise (*calm*). I protected widows in their need.

The Mistress of Women (*Hathor*) distinguished me among ladies, she promoted me among noblewomen. She made great my sweetness in the heart of the royal scribe, he who reckons everything for the Perfect God.[4] She honoured me with a son, she distinguished me with a daughter. She furnished my house with my dependants and she caused me to be with him (my husband) until the time of laying down his seal (of office).[5] There was no other woman in his heart except for me. The one who came forth from me (*my son*) was one who accompanied His Majesty, who occupied his (father's) office when his (father's) body was buried. He anointed him with oil, with the work of Shesmu, and provided him with the best of the products of Tait.[6] (*Her husband's burial and her son's successful career at the royal court are omitted here.*)

The Golden One (*Hathor*), who made my estate great by assigning gifts, made me fortunate at the moment when my time had come and my hour was completed. I became cool (*was buried*) then in the Horizon of the Two Lands.[7] All Memphis attended behind me until I reached my heaven in the necropolis. My spirit was made effective by the god's fathers,[8] the priests and chiefs of the temple of Ptah, while the great lector priests led the ritual as *sem*-priest of Sokar. The rites and prescriptions were read out at the precise moment, the divine ceremonies at their times, every procedure without fault. I was treated perfectly by the keeper of secrets, the great one[9] of the west (necropolis) of Apis–Osiris, and the companions of the Iyt-temple[10] who are allotted successively(?) to the hours in their months of service. Upper Egypt sailed downstream and Lower Egypt sailed upstream, with every office-holder performing obeisance(?). Oil was prepared for me in all its proper ways by the attendants of the temples. All the hourly priests performed their work for me in executing the (prescribed) list of the *tmmt*-ritual. My(?) name was enhanced as one who is concealed (?) in the West, in the sacred land of Rosetau.'[11]

[1] Deceased.

[2] The identity of this deity and of the 'Greatest of the Great' is uncertain; perhaps Ptah or Osiris.

[3] This eulogistic description of the necropolis to which visitors are to come is typical of its period. A semi-mythological word for 'people' is used.

[4] I.e. 'she caused my husband to love me'.

[5] Probably Tjaanhuremou's death rather than his 'retirement'.

[6] Shesmu was the god of funerary oils and Tait the goddess of weaving.

[7] A term for the Memphite necropolis.

[8] A priestly title.

[9] Title of an embalming priest.

[10] A legendary temple in Letopolis, north of Memphis.

[11] A traditional designation of the Memphite necropolis.

273. Monument to Lysandre, a daughter who died before marriage

I.Métr. 83
Karanis, Roman period

Lysandre's parents Philonike and Eudemos had her gravestone adorned with this poem, written in elegiac couplets; its refinement underscores the wealth and devotion to Greek culture of some inhabitants of Karanis during the Roman period.[1]

What profit is there to labour for children, or why to honour them
 above all else, if we shall have for our judge not Zeus, but Hades?
My father took care of me for twice ten years, but I did not attain
4 to the marriage bed of the wedding chamber,
Nor did my body pass under the bridal curtain, nor did the girls my
 age make the doors of cedar resound throughout the wedding
 night.
My virginal life has perished. Woe for that Fate,
8 alas, who cast her bitter threads on me!
The breasts of my mother nourished me with their milk to no
 purpose at all, and to those breasts I cannot repay the favour of
 nourishment for their old age.[2]
I wish I would have left my father a child when I died, so that he
12 would not forever have an unforgettable grief through
 remembrance of me.
Weep for Lysandre, companions of my same age, the girl
 whom Philonike and Eudemos bore in vain.
You who approach my tomb, I implore you very much,
16 weep for my youth, lost prematurely and without marriage.

[1] Compare the elegies in Greek verse anthologies, e.g. *Anthologia Palatina* VII 261, 187, 568 (*The Greek Anthology* II, Loeb Classical Library).
[2] The Greek child's obligation to care for parents in their old age, *gerotrophia*, remains a potent ideal; see also **Ch. 3 Arch. J** introd., note 2.

274. Funeral monument of the young wife Thermion

I.Métr. 46
Alexandria, first century A D (?)

Thermion's husband Simalos set up a funerary monument for his wife, carved with a verse inscription expressing his grief over her death. Simalos begins with a parting greeting to Thermion and then imagines his dead wife cursing those responsible for her premature and painful death. He closes with his own, shorter song.

Best Thermion, farewell!

'Lords of the Underworld spirits below,
and holy Persephone, daughter of Demeter,
4   receive this wreckage of a miserable stranger, me,
Thermion, born from her father Lysanias,
and the noble wife of Simalos.
If anyone ever led the horrifying
8   Furies against my innards or my life,
never again, everlasting gods,
send that one any fate other than one such as I possessed.
I dwell below, because of a wasting illness of three months,
12   leaving the fruit of life which the omnipotent earth
grants to mortals, deprived of this
and of both my children, lords, and my husband,
whose heart was one with mine and (with whom) life was sweet.
16   I, poor wretch, deprived of all these,
as I was enduring such great calamities, I sent forth prayers
for my enemies and their children, that they go, root and branch,
to the great chamber of Hades and the gates of darkness.
20   But for my children (I pray that) they have a joyous life,
indestructible, and my husband too, and up to a ripe old age, (and) –
if, in fact, a word of prayer is worth anything in Hades –
that my enemies, against whom I utter my imprecations, receive them
    to the full!'
24   Now I, in my turn, give out a song of the Muses,
a joyous and sad song of my marriage with you,
Thermion, my wife, and I proclaim these words:
I shall raise up all the children you bore me
28   in a manner worthy of my love for you, wife,
and Lysas, your earlier child, I shall hold fast in the same manner
as my own children, setting forth my gratitude to you,
because you had a way of behaving that was blameless during your
    life.

(*Added opposite line 29*) (Year) 7, Pauni 26.

275. Epitaph for the young bride Sarapous

Hooper (1961), no. 58
Terenouthis, *c.* 5 October, Roman period

Sarapous' grave monument (see **Plate 45**) was excavated in the necropolis of
Terenouthis (Kom Abou Billou), located on the edge of the western desert about
forty miles north-west of modern Cairo, which has produced hundreds of grave

45 Grave monument for Sarapous
Kelsey Museum 21069
Terenouthis (Kom Abou Billou), Roman period

This limestone stela (35.8 x 24.6 cm) was incised with shallow strokes. Sarapous wears a full-length Ionic *chiton*, with a short cloak on top, girded under her breasts. She stands with arms outspread and palms raised, the gesture of prayer and supplication (*orans*) common to pagan and early Christian art (cf. Dunand, 1987). To either side of Sarapous is the seated jackal, one of the most frequent animals in the funerary imagery of Graeco-Roman Egypt, recalling Anoubis, Egyptian god of the dead. The text beneath is translated in **6.275**.

markers from the Roman period; see Bingen (1987), and (1996) for discussion of the date, and references to further bibliography.

> Sarapous, daughter of Euanthes, dying before her time, childless,
> Loving her husband, loving her brother,[1] loving her friends,
> About 14 years of age. (Year) 6, Phaophi 8.

[1] Or, 'her sister'.

276. Epitaph for two women and a young girl

SEG XX 554
Terenouthis, 7 or 8 November, AD 156 or 179

This text was inscribed upon a more elaborate and deeply carved, and therefore more expensive, monument than **275** (see **Plate 46**). Artemis, Isidora and Karpime were among at least thirty other casualties killed on the same day, Hathyr 11 of year 20, the majority of them women and children; most of the menfolk seem to have been elsewhere or escaped. See Bingen (1987) and (1996).

> Artemis, 47 years of age. Isidora, dying before her time, 8 years of age.
> Karpime, loving her children, 50 years of age. (Year) 20, Hathyr 11.

46 Grave monument for two women and a girl
Kelsey Museum 21180
Terenouthis (Kom Abou Billou), A D 156 or 179

On this deeply carved limestone monument (28.7 x 42.2 cm), architectural elements frame the funerary scene. Two women, dressed in the Ionic *chiton*, their curled hair descending to their shoulders, recline on the funerary couch with decorated pillows and mattress. On the frame of the couch to the left is a libation cup; above it, a jackal. Left of the couch on a raised platform stands the young girl in the dress, hairstyle, and pose conventional in this necropolis (cf. **Plate 45**). The text below the couch is translated in **6.276**.

277. Epitaph of Aline

I.Fay. I 59
Hawara, A D 24 (?)

This epitaph was discovered beside the head of the mummy of a young woman (**Plate 47**). Since the mummy belongs to the early first century A D, 'year 10' may refer to the reign of Tiberius.

Aline alias Tenos, daughter of Herodes, worthy (woman), many salutations. Year 10, 35 years old, Mesore 6th.

(a)

47 Mummy portrait of Aline and her children
Ägyptisches Museum, Berlin, inv.
11411, 11412, 11413
Hawara, early first century A D (?)

These three portraits, painted directly on the linen shrouds surrounding the bodies, come from a burial group which includes two other mummies, of a man and a girl, both with masks rather than portraits. The adult woman's hairstyle suggests an early first-century A D date ((a); cf. **Plate 34**); if the grave stela of Aline found with the burial (**6.277**) refers to this woman, her death may have occurred in A D 24 (year 10 of Tiberius). Her white tunic is decorated with vertical purple stripes (*clavi*), and she wears ball earrings and a necklace painted in gold leaf over stucco. Both the children's mummy wrappings are decorated with buttons in gilded stucco. The little girl's portrait (**b**) shows her wearing jewellery, although the body is that of a four or five-year-old. The little boy (**c**) was scarcely more than a toddler, aged between thirty months and three years at his death. See Germer, Kiskewitz and Lüning (1993); and for colour plates, Doxiadis (1995), 64–5.

(b)   (c)

278. Letter about transport of a mummy

W.Chr. 499
Thebes, *c.* 8 September, second–third century AD

Senpamonthes to her brother Pamonthes, greetings. I have sent to you the body of my mother Senyris, mummified and having a label about the neck, through the agency of Gales, whose father is Hierax, in his own boat, with the freight charge having been paid by me in full. The appearance of the mummy is as follows: the linen on the outside is pink coloured, and her name has been written (on the linen) over her belly. I pray that you, brother, are well. Year 3, 11 Thoth.

279. Mummy labels

Mummies were often identified, particularly if they needed to be transported, by inscribed wooden labels, or by writing directly on the shroud (see **Plate 48**), or both (cf. **278**).[1] The texts are always brief; Greek examples normally give the deceased's name and age at death, and occasionally its destination, while Demotic texts also usually include a short prayer to Osiris. They are difficult to date precisely, since the emperor's name is usually omitted even when a regnal year is recorded. While most published examples seem to derive from the Roman period, Ptolemaic examples are known, normally written in Demotic. The following Greek and bilingual examples are all of Roman date.

(a) Greek mummy label

P.Coll.Youtie II 104
Panopolis (?), second–fourth century AD

Tekysis, daughter of Psapsoumis, lived 22 years.

(b) Bilingual mummy label

SB I 1626 = CEML 902
Panopolite nome, *c.* AD 200

Artemidora must have been buried in a family tomb: labels also survive for her brother Horos (CEML 864), and sisters Thaminis (CEML 912), Artemidora junior (CEML 887), Onnophris (CEML 412), Isidora (CEML 472) and Senpsansnos (ed. M. Chauveau and H. Cuvigny, *CRIPEL* 9, 1987, 78–80); see Chauveau (1987), 132–3.

48   Fragment of Herais' funerary shroud
Pap. Lugd.Bat. XIX 34 (= P.Leid.inv. V29)
Panopolis(?), second century A D

Herais' mummy was identified by this inscription painted onto her linen shroud: 'Herais lived
7 years' (cf. **6.278–9**).

(*Greek*) Artemidora, daughter of Peteminis and Trompahbeithis[2] her
mother, lived for three years, for she died on the day of her birthday, but
(her name) will always be remembered.
(*Demotic*) Her soul is praised before Osiris–Sokar the great god, lord of
Jedou and Abydos, ruler of the Underworld, Artemi, justified (= *deceased*)
daughter of Petemin, her mother being Tronpahbeit, without being demol-
ished, without perishing, for ever and ever.

(c) Bilingual mummy label

Pap.Lugd.Bat. XIX 40A
Panopolis, second–third century A D

The wooden tag has four lines of Greek on one side, four lines of Demotic on the
other.

(*Greek*) Senpsennesis, daughter of Apollonios and Senharemephis her
mother.
(*Demotic*)[3] Her soul will serve Osiris–Sokaris, the great god, Lord of Abydos:
Senpsennesis, son[4] of Apollonios (and) her mother Senharemephis.

[1] See Quaegebeur (1978a); Walker and Bierbrier (1997), nos. 235–41 illustrate further examples.
[2] The first 'h' represents a Demotic sign inserted into the Greek name.
[3] Translated by Jan Quaegebeur.
[4] A scribal error for 'daughter'; Senpsennesis is a woman's name.

V   Weaklings or viragos? The ambiguities of womanhood

The notion of women's mental and moral inferiority to men was deeply imprinted in Greek and Roman culture, appearing in a range of writings from literature to medicine or law. Yet the texts from Graeco-Roman Egypt collected in this volume which explicitly invoke women's weakness or frailty (the ground on which the legal requirement of male guardians for adult women was justified) must be set against the vastly more plentiful documentation of their capability in undertaking responsible and active roles.[1] Although these responsibilities were often extensions of the family and household duties thought appropriate to women even within the restrictive norms of classical Athens, nonetheless they offered women in Egypt more diverse opportunities and greater visibility in society beyond the confines of the household than had been available to women in the earlier city-states.[2]

Many women undoubtedly faced impediments in protecting their interests outside the household, especially through their relative lack of basic education, which made male involvement in a woman's legal acts sometimes desirable even when not required by law (**233**; **4.144–5**). Inferior bodily strength may also have discouraged women from using direct action to attain their ends, although the papyri provide examples of women's participation in physical assaults (**254**; **3.89, 107**). But women's power to persuade and manipulate the sympathies of officials could actually be enhanced by emphasising and exaggerating their weakness and frailty.[3]

When invoking the power of the supernatural, to which both sexes turned through prayers and charms, religious rituals and magic spells, in the attempt to assert an otherwise elusive control over their future, women were on roughly equal terms with men, although the diviners and other experts in this field were normally male.[4] Indeed, women's access to supernatural power induced fear and suspicion in men, reflected in the promise Thais' husband extracted from her in her marriage agreement not to drug his food and drink (**255**). A woman acting outside male control, far from being weak, might easily become a potent threat to men.

A further element in this ambiguous perception of women lay in the unique physical functions of the mature female body: menstruation, pregnancy, childbirth, and lactation. Menstruation was likened to the Nile flood in heralding the fecundity of new life, growth and nourishment.[5] The menses also underscored women's unique ability to bleed and not die; yet their prodigality in wasting this blood whenever no child was being nourished in the womb justified giving females lesser rations. No general taboo existed against menstruating women; neutral and more positive references (especially **263**) can be found alongside the few cases of localised taboos connected with specific Egyptian and Greek cults.[6]

The special 'place of women' which existed in some communities of the Pharaonic period, apparently a communal menstrual space for the women of an entire town, was replaced in the Graeco-Roman period by space for individual households located under the stairs of multi-storey homes. Clauses referring to such spaces are found in Demotic agreements from Ptolemaic Thebes relating to the division or sale of houses: 'You/your women shall menstruate in the "women's space".'[7] This practice appears to continue into Byzantine and even early Islamic periods, implicitly attested in Coptic house divisions from seventh–eighth century AD Jeme, which ceded the stairs to the woman in cases where property is split between a man and a woman, but left it held in common in houses divided between two women. The preoccupation with the body evident in late antique Christian literature brings more explicit, but generally negative, attitudes towards menstruation. Female saints who cease to menstruate because of ascetic deprivation are praised, while healers such as the bishop Pisentius flee the touch of women with menstrual problems (a contrast with Christ's attitude in the Gospels; see **267** note 1).[8]

Women's greatest potential for exercising power over men was through the manipulation of sexual desire. A man might long for his partner to love him with a 'prostitute's love' (**283**), but the woman whose sexual passions and potency allow her to achieve ascendancy over a man, conquering his intellect and devouring his body, was an object of both fascination and fear. While the aggressive woman was by no means ignored in earlier literature, Graeco-Roman Egypt provides some notable examples (**288–9**).

[1] On the *kyrios* in classical Greek cities, see Schaps (1979), 48–60; on the *tutela mulierum* in Roman law, see **4.140**, and Dixon (1988), 41–67. On the theme of 'woman's weakness', see Beaucamp (1994), cf. **4.133** and note 3 below.

[2] Cf. van Bremen (1996), who sees élite women's public position in the Hellenistic and Roman cities of the Greek East as stemming from their roles within the family. Note that classical Greek city-states also attempted to circumscribe the behaviour of male citizens.

[3] Women's petitions to officials which invoke the theme of weakness: **2.5, 3.73, 5.177.**

[4] English translations of magical texts can be found in: Gager (1992) (Greek, including material from outside Egypt); Betz (1992) (Greek and Demotic); Meyer and Smith (1994) (Coptic). Gager (pp. 80–1, 244–5) and Winkler (1990), 71–98, stress the empowerment that magical practices brought to the individual.

[5] Montserrat (1996), 61–3, citing Ritner (1984), 209–13; cf. Hippokrates, *Superfetation* 30, *Barren Women* 218.

[6] For a full discussion of the Egyptian evidence for menstruation to the Ptolemaic period, see Wilfong (forthcoming(b)). The inclusion of menstruating women in hieroglyphic temple inscriptions and papyri listing things the gods abominate is concentrated in the Athribite and Kynopolite nomes; cf **2.40** from the Greek city of Ptolemais. The story about the Alexandrian women called *kerykinai* ('heralds'), who collected images of female pollution and threw them into the sea (Damascius fr. 103–4 Zintzen), more probably concerns amuletic remembrances of menarche than 'disposable' menstrual protection as suggested by Rea (1989); cf. **2.54** note 1.

[7] E.g. P.Louvre 2424, ed. Zauzich (1968), no.11.2 (267 BC).

[8] Coptic evidence about menstruation is discussed in Wilfong (forthcoming(a)), chapter 3.

280.   Demotic spell to bring on menstruation

O. Stras. D 1338[1]
Thebes, Roman period

This Demotic spell commands the physical world to halt its normal course until a woman's menses flow, appealing to the authority of Isis and Amun. Although copied onto an ostrakon, it has not been personalised with the name of a specific woman.

> Spell for causing blood to descend from the body of a woman.
> 'O heaven, do not create wind; O sea, do not create waves,
> while the compulsion is before the great noble god who rejoices over order.
> O heaven, do not . . . Seek after what I have said today,
> after what I have said as magic with the voice of Isis the great, the god's mother,
> as she seeks her brother (*Osiris*) in Kush, saying: "Come to me,
> O Gods of the South, North, East, and West, at the voice of Amun, the great god
> of Thebes. Come to me O Great Ennead, Little
> Ennead. Do not conceal yourself from me today. Perform this which I say to you.
> (By) the compulsion of the one who is on this Barque of Millions (*Seth or Re*), which the face of
> women . . . worship, the compulsion of Ptah-Tenen
> the Father of the Gods, the Great Daimon, the Abyss who is beneath the earth,
> the compulsion of the two sisters Isis and Nephthys, these two Goddesses.
> Move, move together with Renenet the Great Daimon, (by) the compulsion of
> every God and Goddess of Upper and Lower Egypt. Let
> (this woman) . . ."'

[1] Edited by Spiegelberg (1911), 34–7; the translation here follows closely the improved translation of Ritner (1995), p. 3343.

281.   Demotic papyrus with recipes for intercourse

Erichsen (1954)
Abusir el-Melek, late Ptolemaic–early Roman period

Enough sense can be made of this text, despite the seriously abraded surface of the papyrus, to show its unique character. It is a list of prescriptions, introduced by the word *phr.t*, 'prescription', or *k.t*, 'another (one)', for application to a woman's eyes, vulva and vagina, and to a man's penis. The mixture of medicine and magic in the prescriptions has parallels in the London–Leiden magical Demotic papyrus (P.BM 10070+P.Leiden I 383; see **282**), but there they form part of a general magical handbook, whereas this text apparently has a more specialised gynaecological focus.

. . . in a single linen bag. One should put it in her eye every day, one should do . . . palm . . . one should anoint her vulva and her vagina with it. Another one. A *lbs* fish, which . . . anoint her vulva with it, and one should sprinkle the door of her house with them . . . her husband. Roots of dum-palm, roots of red *htt*, roots of . . . manner once. You should spit their sap (*juice?*) in her face with your mouth. Prescription to [have ? a] child . . . You should anoint her vulva with it, you should make her cleanse herself with the milk of a [black?] cow . . . (*three fragmentary lines*)
(*line 10*) cowsmilk. You shall not have intercourse with her, do not place your phallus into her vulva . . . honey. Anoint her vulva with it. Prescription . . . words to be pronounced [by the one who] has had intercourse with her . . . to cook . . . from the hand of a woman . . . a single . . . of linen . . . you shall throw it in her vulva . . . all things . . . a woman. You shall not have intercourse with her . . . water. One should anoint her with honey . . . royal linen. They should put her on the . . . every phallus which had intercourse with her . . .

282. A Demotic charm to make a woman fall madly in love with you

P.BM 10070+P.Leiden I 383 (ed. Griffith and Thompson, 1904–9), verso col. XXXII 1–13
Provenance unknown, third century A D

This charm derives from an extensive papyrus roll of magic prescriptions, some thirty-three columns long, mostly written in Demotic, with three short sections in Greek.

To make (a woman) mad after a man: you should bring a live shrew mouse,[1] remove its bile and put it in one place; and remove its heart and put it in another place. You should take its whole body. You should pound it very much while it is dry; you should take a little of what is pounded with a little blood of your second finger and the little finger of your left hand; you should put it in a cup of wine; you should make the woman drink it. She is mad after you.

If you put its bile into a cup of wine, she dies instantly. Or put it in meat or some food.

If you put its heart in a ring of gold and put it on your hand, it gives you great praise, love, and awe.

[1] For other instructions about the use of the shrew mouse in attracting a woman, see earlier in the same handbook, PDM xiv 376–87 in Betz (1992), 217–8.

283. Love charm that attracts a woman to a man

PGM xxxvi 134–60
Provenance unknown, fourth century AD

Like the previous Demotic example, this magic book belonged to a professional, because the spells do not name individuals, but refer instead to 'this woman, whom that woman bore' and 'this man, whom that woman bore'. To make a spell effective for the customer, the seller copied it from the handbook and customised it, replacing 'this woman' and 'this man' with the names of the parties to be affected, as in **285–6, 2.48**.

A wondrous spell of attraction than which nothing is greater. Take myrrh and frankincense, the male variety, and cast them into a drinking cup, along with a measure of vinegar. At the third hour of the night (*about 9 pm*) put the mixture into the hinges of your door and repeat the spell seven times. This is the spell to be spoken.
    'Rise up, divinities in the darkness, and jump up onto the bricks and, after smearing mud on your faces, beat your breasts. For, because of this woman, whom that mother bore, the unlawful eggs are being burnt as a sacrifice – fire, fire, lawlessness, lawlessness. For Isis shouted out a great cry, and the world became confused; she tosses on her holy bed, and its bonds and those of the spirit world are dashed in pieces, because of the hatred and impiety of this woman whom that mother bore. You, then, Isis and Osiris and the (divinities) of the Underworld ABLAMGOUN CHOTHO ABRASAX, and the divinities who are under the earth, rise up, all you who are from the depths, and make this woman, whom that mother bore, sleepless, make her fly through the air, starving, thirsting, unable to sleep – make her love me, this man, whom that mother bore, with a gut-wrenching love, so that she glues her female womb to my male prick. If she wants to sleep, make up her bed with thorny coverlets of leather and prickles on her temples, so that she consents to a prostitute's love, because I adjure you who have been assigned your places under the fire – MASKELLI MASKELLO PHNOUKENTABAOTH PREOBAZAGRA RHEXICHTHON HIPPICHTHON PYRIPEGANAX. You have been tied down, woman, by the cords of the sacred palm tree, so that you may love this man completely, and nothing will release you, not a barking dog, nor a braying donkey; not a priest of Cybele, nor an exorcizer; not crashing of a cymbal, nor trill of a flute – but there is no preventive all-cure charm from heaven, but let her be overcome in her spirit.'

49   Uterine amulet
Hanson (1995)
Provenance unknown, Roman period

The fashion for wearing uterine amulets made of haematite (bloodstone, the stone that bleeds) flourished in Roman Egypt (cf. **6.284**). The obverse shows a uterus with a lock at the uterine mouth, to ensure that the organ opens and closes as required. Encircling the uterus is the snake that feeds upon its tail, the ouroboros, an image of protection and containment. The reverse contains the magical formula ORORIOU|TH IAEO IAO S|ABAOTH IAO. See further Hanson (1995); Ritner (1984).

284.   Charm to ensure a woman's faithfulness

PGM xxxvi 283–94
Provenance unknown, fourth century A D

The following spell, labelled 'a key for her womb' (*physikleidion*), comes from the same large roll as **283**. Uterine amulets from Roman Egypt frequently picture a uterus with a lock at the uterine mouth (**Plate 49**),[1] an indication that popular magic shared with the medical writers of the *Hippocratic Corpus* the desire to ensure that a woman's womb opened and closed at the appropriate times: opening to release menstrual blood and to receive the man's seed in order to initiate a pregnancy, and closing again after she has taken up the man's seed, retaining both the seed and the menses as nourishment for the developing foetus. The womb, tightly closed and locked after conception, also prevents a subsequent and additional pregnancy, or 'superfetation'. At birth the womb opens once more, for the baby to make its exit and stride into this world.[2] Some uterine amulets with locks also claim to cure menorrhagia, the 'female flux', or 'bloody flow' frequently mentioned by medical writers (cf. **267**).

Key to her womb. Take the egg of a crow and juice from the plant 'crow's-foot' and bile from a stinging eel; grind these with honey, and say this spell, whenever you are grinding and whenever you anoint your genitals (with it).
    This is the spell to be recited: 'I say to you, womb of this woman, open and receive the seed of this man and the unconquerable seed of the Iarphe

Arphe'. Write this. 'Let her love me for all her time, as Isis loved Osiris, and let her remain pure for me, as Penelope remained for Odysseus. But you, womb, be remembering of me for all the time of my life, because I am Akarnachthas.'

Say these words as you grind and as you are anointing your penis, and thus be together with her whom you desire, and only you will she love, and never will she sleep with anyone else, but only with you alone.

[1] See Aubert (1989), Ritner (1984). Bonner (1950), 79–94, remains useful especially for its many illustrations of magic gemstones. On the relation between the more formal gynaecology of the medical writers and popular magic, see also Hanson (1989b), (1990) and (1995).

[2] Writers in the *Hippocratic Corpus* seem ignorant of uterine contractions until the latest stratum of gynaecological treatises: Hanson (1991a), 87–96.

285.   Charm to bind Capitolina's lover Nilos to her

PGM XV 1–21
Provenance unknown, third century AD

I will bind you, Nilos alias Agathos Daimon, whom Demetria bore, with great evils. Nor shall I discover from the gods a pure way out for you! On the contrary, you are going to love me, Capitolina, whom Peperous bore, with a divine passion, and you will be for me in everything a follower, as long as I wish, in order that you may do for me what I want and nothing for anyone else; that you may obey only me, Capitolina; that you might forget your parents, your children, and your friends. Oh divinities, I summon you by my oath, all you who dwell in this place: ALUEAEL ...LIONO SOUAPHALO LYBALOLYBE OIKALLISSAMAEO LYBALALONE LYLOEU LUOTHNOIS ODISSASON ALELADA. I, Capitolina, possess the power, and you, Nilos, will give back the favours, when we meet. They are releasing all those drowned in the Nile,[1] the unmarried dead, and those carried away by the wind. I shall insert this pledge (into its box) in order that you might carry out all the things written on this slip of papyrus, for this is why I am summoning you, my divinities, by the violence that constrains you and the compulsion. Bring all things to completion for me and leap in and snatch up the mind of Nilos, to whom belong these magic articles, so that he may love me, Capitolina, and that Nilos, whom Demetria bore, may ever be with me at every hour of every day. I summon you divinities by the bitter necessities that bind you and by those carried away by the wind: IO IOE PHTHOUTH EIO PHRE. The greatest divinity IAO SABAO. BARBARE THIOTH[2] LAILAMPS OSORNOPHRI EMPHERA, the only begotten god in the heaven who shakes the depths, sending out the waves and the wind. Thrust forth the spirits of these divinities, wherever the box is, so that they, male or female, small or large, may carry out for me the things on the little slip, and may bind Nilos alias Agathos Daimon, whom Demetria bore, to me, Capitolina, whom Peperous bore, for the rest of his life. May Nilos love me with everlasting love – now, now, quickly, quickly.

[1] Cf. **2.26**.
[2] Mistakenly omitted from *PGM*.

286. Love spell to attract the woman Gorgonia to the woman Sophia

Suppl.Mag. I no. 42.1–25
Hermopolis Magna, third–fourth century A D (?)

This spell, written on both sides of an oval lead tablet, is typically garbled and syncretistic in its use of *nomina sacra* (cf. **283, 285; 2.48**), and in its intent to rouse a corpse to persecute the loved one. The setting in the bath-house has parallels – they were often supposed to be haunted, and their furnaces were notorious for causing fires. This text is unusual in adjuring the corpse–demon to take the form of a woman bath-attendant (which may imply that by this period male servants were not used in women's baths, cf. **4.130**), and in being a spell by a woman to attract another woman; see also e.g. *PGM* XXXII 1–19 (trans. Betz, 1992, 266). Since the text is, as is normal, very repetitive, only the beginning is given here; for a full translation see *Suppl.Mag.* I, from which this is adapted.

Seat of the hateful dark, prison(?)-mouth dog,[1] coiled with snakes, with three heads that move, traveller in the bowels of the earth, come, driver of spirits,[2] together with the Erinyes,[3] running wild with their sharp whips, holy snakes, Maenads,[4] dread maidens, come in response to my angry spells, before I persuade this (corpse) by force, by transforming him(??) make him a fire-breathing demon, listen and make everything be done quickly, not opposing me in any way, for you are the rulers of the earth, ALALACHOS, ALLECH, HARMACHIMENEUS, MAGIMENEUS, ATHINEMBES, ASTAZ-ABATHOS, ARTAZABATHOS, OKOUM, PHLOM, LONCHACHINACH-ANA, THOU, ZAEL AND LYKAEL AND ELIAM AND ELENEA AND SOCHSOCHAM, SOMOCHAM, SOZOCHAM, OUZACHAM, BAUZACHAM, OUEDDOUCH, by means of this corpse–demon set on fire the heart, the liver, the spirit of Gorgonia, whom Nilogenia bore, with desire and love for Sophia, whom Isara bore. Compel Gorgonia, whom Nilogenia bore, to be thrown, for Sophia, whom Isara bore, into the bath-house, and you become a bath-woman, burn, inflame, set on fire her soul, her heart, her liver, her spirit, with desire for Sophia, whom Isara bore, drive Gorgonia, whom Nilogenia bore, drive her, torture her body night and day, force her to be an outcast from every place and every house, loving Sophia, whom

Isara bore, she, given away[5] like a slave-girl, handing herself and all
her possessions over to her, because this is the will and command of the
great god, IARTANA, OUOUSIOU, IPSENTHAN CHOCHAIN CHOU (?),
EOCH, AEEIOUO,[6] IARTANA, OUSIOUSIOU, IPSOENPEUTHADEI,
ANNOUCHEO, AEEIOUO, blessed lord of the immortals, holding the
sceptre of Tartaros,[7] and of terrible, fearsome, hateful and life-draining
Lethe,[8] the harsh hairs(??) of Kerberos tremble at you, you crack(??) the
loud(?) whips of the Erinyes, the pleasant-sounding streams, the bed of
Persephone[9] delights your mind whenever you go to your longed for mar-
riage-bed, whether you are immortal Serapis, at whom the universe trem-
bles, whether you be Osiris, star(??) of the land of Egypt, your messenger(?)
is the wise boy and all < . . . ?>, yours is Anoubis, the pious herald of the
dead, come here, carry out my intentions, because I summon you by this
secret pact(?) . . .

[1] Kerberos, guard-dog of the entrance to the Greek Underworld.
[2] Probably Mercury.
[3] The Furies.
[4] The female followers of Dionysos.
[5] Greek *ekdote*, with connotations also of marriage; see **4.126** introd.
[6] The seven vowels of the Greek alphabet in order.
[7] The Greek Underworld, also called Hades (as is its ruler, to whom this section is addressed).
[8] The river of Hades.
[9] Wife of Hades; the Egyptian equivalents are Osiris (or Serapis) and Isis.

287. Demotic curses against a woman

O.Wien D 70 ed. K.-Th. Zauzich, *Enchoria* 18 (1991), 135–51
Provenance unknown, *c.* 50 BC to AD 50

The writer's words were painted with a brush pen on a very large ostrakon. This
message is, up to now, unique among Demotic texts, and the editor suggested that
the curses derive from the complaints of a rejected lover. The following translation
of this very difficult text is provisional.
    For references to further examples of invective against women in Demotic and
Greek literature, see H.-J. Thissen, 'Tadel der Frauen', *Enchoria* 14 (1986), 159–60.

Copy of the words of invective for Ms. Hawk[1]
    Are you a spirit that . . ., a raging fire, a misfortune for those who love a
woman? . . . Are you a burning woman, an abominable fire, a scorching
woman? The lamb is in her name, but the witch is in her behaviour! The
. . . which is overwhelmed with filth, which is weighted down with
repulsiveness. You should bathe yourself in blood, you should wash yourself
with urine. One should set a wheel-crown (?) on your head, a suit of armour
out of stinging nettles (?) on your body, a cloak of . . . One will let you

climb on the neck of the old sow. One will pull you out of . . . for the witches are being inspected today.[2] Go! No one will find enough water in the sea, you sow, for washing off your face. On the day of your birth already 9 snake-charmers were standing by. Already then when you were welcoming the evil omen against you, the day was at hand whose name nobody mentions.[3] Girl, your distress will destroy you. Your ending will finish you off. Somebody will toss out your flesh into . . . which smells bad. Somebody will throw your head, half long-haired and half bald on top, on your miserable face, your arms like tree branches, your legs like straw, hanging from your torso, your covering of an apron hangs down from your rump, your . . . in the size of a reed down from your body.

[1] Apparently a woman's name, meaning 'Hawk'; it is also possible that the text intended 'a female servant'.

[2] The following line was squeezed in subsequently.

[3] Probably the day of her death.

288. Setna Khaemwese succumbs to desire for Tabubu

(Excerpt from) P.Cairo 30646 (Spiegelberg 1906–8)[1]
First century BC

In this episode from the first Setna story (see **263**), Setna is led to ever more extreme lengths in his desire for the beautiful Tabubu, drawing up a maintenance document for her and pledging all his possessions (cf. **4.119**), disinheriting his sons by getting them to endorse the document, and finally having them killed. But on the point of fulfilling his desire, Setna awakes from his dream in a fevered state, sexually aroused and stark naked. Pharaoh arrives, and Setna is ashamed at his nakedness, but Pharaoh gives him clothes and reassures him that his children are safe.

However, one day Setna was strolling upon the sacred way of Ptah, and he saw a woman who was very beautiful – no woman had ever existed who looked quite so beautiful. She had on her much gold jewellery, and several women servants were walking behind her, and two bodyguards were assigned to her. The moment that Setna saw her, he did not know where on earth he was. Setna summoned his servant boy, and said 'Hurry over to that woman and find out about her.' The servant boy hurried over to the woman, and he accosted the servant girl who was walking behind her. He asked her 'What kind of woman is she?' She told him 'She is Tabubu, the daughter of the prophet of Bastet Mistress of Ankhtawy. She has come here to pray to Ptah the Great God.'

The boy returned to Setna, and recounted to him absolutely everything that she had told him. Setna said to the boy 'Go and say to the girl "Setna Khaemwese, the son of Pharaoh Usermare, has sent me to say 'I will give you ten pieces of gold: spend an hour with me. Or if you have (any thought of) an accusation of rape, I will deal with that for you! I will have you taken to a hideaway, and no one on earth will find you out."" The boy went back over to Tabubu, and he summoned her servant girl. He spoke with her, and she was aghast, as though what he had said was foul-mouthed. Tabubu said to the boy 'Stop dealing with this wretched girl. Come and [talk] with me.' The boy ran over to Tabubu, and he told her 'I will give you ten pieces of gold: spend an hour with Setna Khaemwese, the son of Pharaoh Usermare. If you have (any thought of) an accusation of rape, he will deal with that for you too! He will have you taken to a hideaway, and no one on earth will find you out.' Tabubu said 'Go and tell Setna "I am pure. I am not a nobody. If you want to have your way with me, you should come to Boubastos to my house. Everything is ready in it. You can have your way with me without anyone on earth finding me out, and I will not have demeaned myself [like] a whore, either."'

The boy returned to Setna, and recounted to him absolutely everything that she had told him. He said 'That is fine!' Everyone who was accompanying Setna was shocked. Setna had a boat fetched, and he went on board it. He hurried to Boubastos and came to the west of the town. He found a house that was very imposing, with a wall round it, and with a garden to the north, and a bench at the entrance. Setna asked 'This house, whose house is it?', and he was told 'It is the house of Tabubu.' Setna went inside the wall, and he looked around the garden-house. It was reported to Tabubu, and she came down. She took Setna by the hand, and she said to him 'By the good fortune of the house of the prophet of Bastet Mistress of Ankhtawy, which you have reached, I shall be very glad: come along up with me!' Setna walked up the stairway of the house with Tabubu, and he found the top storey elegant and decorated, with its floor decorated with genuine lapis and genuine turquoise. There was a great deal of furniture in it, which was covered with royal linen, and there were numerous gold cups on the sideboard. A gold cup was filled with wine, and she handed it to Setna. She said 'Please will you have something to eat.' He said to her 'I could not manage anything.' Incense was put on the brazier, and perfume was brought for him like the royal supplies. Setna celebrated with Tabubu, and he had never seen anyone like her.

Then Setna said to Tabubu 'Let us finish what we came here for.' She said to him 'You will reach your goal. I am pure. I am not a nobody. If you want to have your way with me, you will make for me a maintenance document and a payment document for absolutely all your possessions.' He said to her 'Let the schoolmaster be fetched', and he was fetched at once. He had a maintenance document and a payment document made for her for absolutely all his possessions. A moment later, it was announced to Setna 'Your children are below.' He said 'Let them be fetched up.' Tabubu got up, and she put on a dress of royal linen. Setna could see her whole body in it, and his desire grew even greater that it had been before. Setna said [to] Tabubu 'Let me finish what I came here for.' She said to him 'You will reach your goal. I am pure. I am not a nobody. If you want to have your way with me, you will make your children endorse my document. Do not let them dispute with my children over your possessions.' He had his children fetched, and he made them sign the document. Setna said to Tabubu 'Let me finish what I came here for.' She said to him 'You will reach your goal. I am pure. I am not a nobody. If you want to have your way with me, you will have your children killed. Do not let them dispute with my children over your possessions.' Setna said 'Let the execution you have got into your mind be done to them', and he had his children killed before him. She had them thrown down from the window to the dogs and the cats, and they ate their flesh, while he could hear them as he was drinking with Tabubu. Setna said to Tabubu 'Let me finish what I came here for. I have done for you absolutely everything that you have said.' She said to him 'Come along to this room.' Setna went to the room, and he lay down upon a bed of ivory and ebony, and his desire got its reward: Tabubu lay down beside Setna. He put out his hand to touch her, and she opened her mouth in a great scream, and Setna awoke . . .

[1] Translation by W. John Tait.

289.   Herodas, *Mime* 5: A mistress tortures her slave lover

P.Lond.Lit. 96
Composed at Alexandria (?), third century BC (?)

No biographical information survives about Herodas, and even the proper spelling of his name, Herodas or Herondas, is subject to debate. Evidence from his poetry suggests connections with Alexandria and the poets who frequented the Museum in the first half of the third century BC (**262**). His work survives mostly through papyrus copies which circulated in Egypt during the early Roman period.[1]

Herodas' poetic habits have much in common with the other poets of the Museum under Ptolemy II and Ptolemy III, in drawing on older Greek literary forms, while also changing these irrevocably. Herodas conflated the form and dialect of iambic lampoons, as written in archaic Ionia by Archilochos and Hipponax, with the mime, a type of drama that featured characters drawn from everyday life and settings that were sordid or risqué. In *Mime* 6, for example, two women, Koritto and Metro, discuss dildoes and how a particularly fine example was being passed around their circle of friends; see Lefkowitz and Fant (1992), no. 228. Bitinna, the main character of *Mime* 5, had a sexual relationship with her slave Gastron, but the affair has turned sour for her, since she suspects him of infidelity. Although Gastron protests his innocence and begs for mercy, Bitinna orders a flogging and then tattooing – until her slave Kydilla intercedes on Gastron's behalf and Bitinna forgives him – for this time.

The motif of a sex-crazed mistress recurs in a mime that probably was played in Oxyrhynchos in the second century AD. Here, too, the mistress suspects her slave lover of being unfaithful: 'Sir, did I command you to dig a trench, or to plough, or to shoulder rocks? Now that all the fieldwork is done, this cunt seems too hard for you who have been raised with womenfolk. You crazy one, what base act are you contemplating and boasting about – and this with the filly Apollonia? Grab him, slaves, and drag him off to his fate; now bring her out also, gagged as she is . . .'[2]

> BITINNA: You tell me, Gastron, is this so over-satisfied so that you
>   are no longer happy with the fact I move my legs for you, but you
>   go off after Menon's Amphytaia?
> GASTRON: Who me? Amphytaia? The woman you're talking about –
>   have I seen her?
> BITINNA: You dredge up excuses the whole day.
> GASTRON: Bitinna, I'm your slave. Use me as you want and do not
>   drink my blood night and day.
> BITINNA: What a big tongue you have got yourself. Kydilla, where is
>   Pyrries? Call him to me.
> PYRRIES: What is it?
> 10 BITINNA: Tie up this fellow – but do you still stand there? Take the
>   rope off the bucket and be quick. I swear, if, by torturing you, I do
>   not make you an example for the whole countryside, then don't
>   consider me to be a woman! Isn't he quite a Phrygian?[3] I am to
>   blame for this, yes I am, Gastron, because I considered you to be
>   one of the men. Still, if I made a mistake then, I swear you won't
>   find Bitinna a fool any longer, as you suppose. Come on, Pyrries,
>   take off his cloak and bind him tightly.
> GASTRON: No, no, Bitinna, I am a suppliant at your knees.
> 20 BITINNA: I tell you, take off your cloak. It is necessary for you to
>   know that you are my slave and that I paid three minas for you.
>   Damn that day which led you here. Pyrries, you are going to cry
>   with pain, because I see you doing just about everything rather
>   than tying him up. Bind his elbows together and once you have
>   them tied, saw them off.
> GASTRON: Bitinna, forgive my mistake. I am a man and I did
>   something wrong. If you ever catch me again doing things you
>   don't like, then tattoo me.[4]
> 30 BITINNA: Do not play around with me, but do it to Amphytaia, the
>   girl you take a roll with, and me . . ., a thing to wipe your boots
>   on.
> PYRRIES: He is well tied up for you.
> BITINNA: Watch out that he doesn't slip out and escape. Lead him to

the executioner's place, to Hermon, and command him to pound
into his back a thousand times and another thousand into his belly.

GASTRON: Are you going to kill me, Bitinna, without first checking
whether these are truths or lies?

BITINNA: Just a minute ago you said with your very own tongue –
'Bitinna, forgive my mistake.'

GASTRON: I was hoping to quench your anger.

40 BITINNA: Are you standing there just watching, and not leading him
off where I told you to? Lambaste him, Kydilla, on his beak, the
rascal. You, too, on my behalf, Drechon, go along where he leads.
(Kydilla), my slave, please give a rag to this abominable wretch so
that he hides his unmentionable tail. Then he will not be seen
naked throughout the marketplace. Pyrries, I am speaking to you
again, so you will tell Hermon to strike one thousand here and one
50 thousand there. Did you hear me? If you disobey any of what I am
telling you, you too will pay both principal and interest. Get
moving and do not lead him by Mikkale's, but on the straight path.
But it is a good thing, I just remembered – run, my slave girl, run
and call them back before they are far off.

KYDILLA: Pyrries, you poor old deaf thing, she is calling you. My
goodness, anyone will suspect that he is tearing a grave robber apart
– and not a fellow slave. Pyrries, do you see how violently you are
60 dragging him off to his tortures? My goodness, Kydilla is going to
see you with her own two eyes within five days at Antidoros' place,
rubbing on your ankles because of those items from Achaia[5] you
recently set aside.

BITINNA: You, then, bring him back here again, but keep him tied
up, just as he was, and fetch Kosis the tattooer – he is to come with
his needles and his black ink. You must be thoroughly spotted!
String him up and blindfold him, just like Daos' penalty.[6]

KYDILLA: My goodness, Ma'am, but now forgive him – thus may
70 Batyllis live and may you see her entering a husband's house and
may you pick up her children in your arms. I beg you. (He has
only made) this one mistake . . .

BITINNA: Kydilla, do not make me annoyed in any way, or I shall
run out of the house. Am I to forgive this man, seven times over a
slave? What woman, when she met me, would not spit into my
face with good reason? No, by our Lady Tyrant – but because he
does not know himself, although he is a man, he will know very
soon, once he has the label on his forehead.

80 KYDILLA: But it is the twentieth day (of the month) and the
Gerenian festival is on the fifth (day from today) –

BITINNA: All right, now I forgive you. But you owe the favour to
her whom I love no less than Batyllis, because I brought her up

under my very own care. When we have poured our libations to
the dead, you shall then spend a honeyless festival after festival.

1 *Mimes* 1–7 are preserved in full on papyrus; *Mimes* 8–9 are known only in papyrus frag-
ments, *Mimes* 10–13 only from quotations in later authors; all are translated into English by
Cunningham (1993). A date of *c.* AD 100 was assigned to the papyrus *P.Lond.Lit.* 96 by P.
J. Parsons, *Classical Review* 31 (1981), 110; cf. *New Docs.* 3 (1983), 59–60, no. 19.

2 *P.Oxy.* III 413 (lines 117–22), reprinted in Cunningham (1987), Appendix 7; translated in
full in *Sel.Pap.* III, no. 77.

3 Phrygians are legendary for cowardice in Greek literature.

4 Tattoos were a mark of disgrace, since they were set on animals (cf. **5.187**) and slaves to
mark them as the master's property.

5 The context suggests that 'ankle fetters' are meant, but why they are 'from Achaia' is
unclear.

6 Daos is a name frequently given to slaves in New Comedy.

List and concordance of texts

The first reference cited gives the edition translated (except in the case of well-known literary texts, where no edition is given). The alternative editions and translations given in brackets are not an exhaustive list, but are intended to direct readers to other useful or common editions. For abbreviations, see List of Abbreviations; for works cited by author and date, see Bibliography.

A.   List of Texts

1   Plutarch, *Life of Pyrrhus* 4.4
2   *Syll.*³ 434–5 (excerpt); (= *IG* II² 687; *Staatsv.* III 476; trans. Austin, 1981, no. 49; Burstein, 1985, no. 56)
3   Theokritos, *Idyll* 15, lines 106–11
4   *P.Lond.* VII 2046
5   *P.Enteux.* 13
6   *OGIS* I 56 (excerpts); (trans. Austin, 1981, no.222 (excl. ll.46–73); Bagnall and Derow, 1981, no.136)
7   Polybius, XV.27.1–2; 29.8–30.1; 33.7–12 (excerpts)
8   Pausanias, *Guide to Greece* I.8.6–9.3
9   *P.Tebt.* III 720 (*BL* IX 358)
10   *P. Lille* I 22 (= Clarysse and Hauben, 1991, no. 4)
11   *BGU* XIV 2438 (excerpts)
12   *I.Fay.* III 205
13   Plutarch, *Life of M. Antonius* 26–7 (excerpts)
14   Plutarch, *Life of M. Antonius* 85
15   Galen, *De compositione medicamentorum secundum locos* (XII.403–4 Kühn)
16   *SB* I 982 (= *IGRR* I 1109)
17   *P.Oxy.* II 244
18   *P.Oxy.* III 502 (beginning)
19   *BGU* II 362 (excerpt); (full trans. Johnson, 1936, no. 404; excerpts *Sel.Pap.* II 340 and 404)
20   *P.Cair.Masp.* III 67283
21   *PSI Congr.XVII* 14
22   *P.Mich.inv.* 4394a (ed. W. Clarysse and P. J. Sijpesteijn, *Archiv* 41, 1995, 56–61)
23   *P.Zen.Pestman* 50 (= *PSI* IV 328; *Sel.Pap.* II 411; trans. Bagnall and Derow, 1981, no. 139)
24   Diodorus Siculus, I.27.1–2
25   *P.Oxy.* XI 1380 (excerpts)
26   *I.Métr.* 87
27   **(a)** *BGU* V 1210.§84
     (b) Oliver (1989) no. 232 (= P.Col. VI 123.25–7 revised)

28 P.Lille dem. 31 (ed. de Cenival, 1977, 21–4)
29 *P.Enteux.* 21
30 P.BN+P.Louvre dem. 2412 (ed. M. Pezin, *BIFAO* 87, 1987, 269–73)
31 G. Wagner, *ZPE* 106 (1995), 123–5
32 *P.Lond.dem.* IV 6.9 (end)
33 *UPZ* I 18
34 *P.Cairo dem.* 30602 + *UPZ* I 130 (beginning)
35 *P.Mert.* II 73 (re-ed. M. Vandoni, *Aegyptus* 47, 1967, 243–6; *BL* VI 78–9)
36 *P.Oxy.* XXXVI 2782
37 *UPZ* I 1 (= *PGM* XL 1–18; trans. Betz, 1992, p. 280)
38 *P.Freib.* IV 73 (with W. Clarysse, *Enchoria* 16, 1988, 7–8)
39 BM Stele 147.6–12 (Reymond, 1981, no. 20) (trans. Lichtheim, 1980, 59–65, with further refs.)
40 *SEG* XLII 1131 (= *SB* I 3451; *LSCG* Supp. no. 119)
41 *P.Oxy.* II 242
42 *I.Alex.* 69 (= *SB* I 436)
43 *OGIS* II 675 (= *SB* V 8905; *IGRR* I 1287)
44 *P.Oxy.* XII 1449. 7–16 (= *Sel.Pap.* II 405.7–16)
45 O.Max. inv. 279+467 (ed. A. Bülow-Jacobsen et al., *BIFAO* 94, 1994, 32–3)
46 *P.Oxy.* I 112 (= *Sel.Pap.* I 176; *W.Chr.* 488)
47 *P.Oxy.* VIII 1149 (= *Sel.Pap.* I 194)
48 *SEG* XXVI 1717; (= S. Kambitsis, *BIFAO* 76, 1976, 213–23; *Supp.Mag.* I 47; trans. *New Docs.* I, 1981, no. 8; Gager, 1992, no. 28)
49 *P.Bon.* I 9
50 *SB* I 4665
51 Clement of Alexandria, *Miscellanies (Stromata)* IV.viii.58.2–60.1
52 *P.Mich.* III 158
53 Eusebius, *History of the Church* VI.41.1–7
54 Socrates, *History of the Church* VII.15
55 The Martyrdom of Paese and Thekla (excerpt; ed. Reymond and Barns, 1973, pp. 34–5)
56 *SB* XIV 11532
57 The Gospel of Thomas: Nag Hammadi Codex II 99.18–26 (ed. Layton, 1989, p. 92)
58 *P.Lips.* 43
59 *P.Oxy.* LXIII 4365
60 *Historia Monachorum in Aegypto* V.1–6 (excerpts)
61 *P.Oxy.* XLIV 3203 (trans. *New Docs.* I, 1981, no. 82)
62 *P.Lond.* V 1731.1–20
63 *P.Wisc.* II 64
64 *P.Oxy.* XVI 1954
65 Palladius, *Lausiac History* XVII.6–9
66 *P.Oxy.* VIII 1151
67 *P.Lond.* VI 1926 (trans. *New Docs.* 4, 1987, no. 123)
68 *IGA* V 48 (trans. *New Docs.* 3, 1983, no. 89)
69 *SB* XX 14303 ii.21–iii.58 (= *P.Corn.* 16)
70 *C.Pap.Lat.* 156 (= *W.Chr.* 212; *Jur. Pap.* 4; cf. *P.Mich.* III, pp. 152–4)
71 *P.Mich.* III 169 (= *C.Pap.Lat.* 162; trans. Lewis and Reinhold, 1990, II 482 §149)

119 P.Mich.inv. 4526 (ed. E. Lüddeckens, *Ägyptische Eheverträge*; Äg.Abh. I, 1960, 148–53)

120 *P.Tor.Botti* 16 (corr. Zauzich, *Enchoria* 2, 1972, 88)

121 **(a)** U. Kaplony-Heckel, *Die demotischen Tempeleide* (Äg.Abh. VI, 1963), no. 6
        (b) U. Kaplony-Heckel, *Die demotischen Tempeleide* (Äg.Abh. VI, 1963), no. 1

122 *P.Enteux.* 22 (*BL* VII 46)

123 *P.Eleph.* 1 (*BL* II 2.52, V 27, VI 35); (= *Sel.Pap.* I 1; *M.Chr.* 283; *Jur.Pap.* 18; *Pap. Primer* (4th edn), no. 25; *New Primer* no. 1)

124 *P.Cair.Zen.* I 59003 (= *Sel.Pap.* I 31; *C.Pap.Jud.* I 1; Scholl, 1990, no. 1)

125 *SB* XVI 12720.1–20

126 *P.Giss.* 2 (*BL* I 168, II.2 61, VII 59); (= Scholl, 1990, no. 55)

127 *BGU* IV 1103 (*BL* I 97); (= *Sel.Pap.* I 6)

128 *BGU* VIII 1848

129 *BGU* IV 1104

130 *P.Enteux.* 82 (= *Sel.Pap.* II 269)

131 *BGU* V 1210 (excerpts) (*BL* II.2 25–6, III 18, IV 7, VI 15, VII 19, VIII 43); (excerpts also in *Jur.Pap.* 93, *Sel.Pap.* II 206, *Pap. Primer* (4th edn), no. 54)

132 *P.Oxy.* II 267 (*BL* VI 96, VII 129, VIII 234); (= *M.Chr.* 281)

133 *P.Oxy.* II 261 (*BL* VIII 234); (= *Sel.Pap.* I 60; *M.Chr.* 346)

134 *P.Oxy.* XXXVIII 2843 (*BL* VII 153, VIII 262)

135 *P.Fam.Tebt.* 20

136 *P.Mich.* VII 434 (= *C.Pap.Lat.* 208–9; *Ch.L.A.* IV 249; *FIRA* III App.17)

137 *P.Heid.* III 237 (*BL* V 43, IX 103)

138 *P.Oxy.* II 237 cols. VI 4–VIII 7 (VII 19–29 in *Sel.Pap.* II 258)

139 *BGU* I 326 (*BL* I 435, II.2 15, III 11, VIII 23–4); (= *Sel.Pap.* I 85; *New Primer* no. 50; *FIRA* III 50; *M.Chr.* 316; *Jur.Pap.* 25)

140 **(a)** *P.Oxy.* IV 720 (*BL* I 327, III 132, VI 98, VII 130, VIII 237); (= *C.Pap.Lat.* 205; *M.Chr.* 324; *Jur.Pap.* 133; *FIRA* III 24; *Ch.L.A.* IV 269)
        (b) *P.Oxy.* XII 1466 (*BL* VII 139); (= *C.Pap.Lat.* 204)

141 *P.Coll.Youtie* II 67

142 *P.Oxy.* XII 1467 (*BL* VIII 246); (= *Sel.Pap.* II 305; *New Primer* no. 65; *Jur.Pap.* 14; *FIRA* III 27; trans. *New Docs.* 2, 1982, pp. 29–30)

143 *P.Oxy.* IX 1205 (*BL* V 78, VI 101, VIII 242); (= *C.Pap.Jud.* III 473)

144 *P.Oxy.Hels.* 26 (*BL* VIII 274); (trans. *New Docs.* 4, 1987, no. 24)

145 *P.Lips.* 29 (=*M.Chr.* 318)

146 *P.Princ.* II 38 (*BL* III 149)

147 *SB* VIII 9642(1) (*BL* VII 213–4, VIII 353)

148 *P.Diog.* 11–12

149 *P.Oxy.* VI 899 (*BL* I 328, III 133, IV 60, VI 99, VII 132, VIII 238); (= *W.Chr.* 361; *C.Pap.Jud.* II 418e)

150 *P.Oxy.* XXXVI 2780 (*BL* VII 153, VIII 262)

151 *PSI* I 76 (cf. Keenan, 1978)

152 *P.Oxy.* I 129 (= *Sel.Pap.* I 9; *M.Chr.* 296; *FIRA* III 21)

153 *P.Oxy.* VI 903 (*BL* III 133)

154 *P.Oxy.* L 3581

155 *P.Cair.Masp.* III 67310 + *P.Lond.* V 1711

156 *P.Lond.* V 1712

157 *CPR* IV 23

158 KRU 67.13–46
159 Balogh and Kahle, *Aegyptus* 33 (1953), 331–40
160 Till, *Bulletin de la Société d'Archéologie Copte* 4 (1938), 71–8
161 *Ep* 270
162 *P.Mich.* I 29 (=White, 1986, no. 20)
163 (a) P.Berl.dem. 3142 (ed. Grunert, 1981)
        (b) P.Berl.dem. 3144 (ed. Grunert, 1981)
164 *P.Mich.* III 182
165 (a) *Pap.Lugd.Bat.* XIX 2 (= *P.Tor.Botti* 28)
        (b) *Pap.Lugd.Bat.* XIX 3 (= *PSI* IX 1021)
166 *Sel.Pap.* I 27 (= *P.Grenf.* II 23a)
167 *SB* VIII 9790
168 *P.Mich.* V 266
169 *P.Fay.* 91 (= *Sel.Pap.* I 17; Montevecchi, *Contratti di Lavoro* no.6)
170 *P.Köln* II 100 (*BL* VIII 156); (= *SB* X 10500; *SB* X 10756; partly trans. Lefkowitz and Fant 1992, no. 202)
171 *P.Turner* 24
172 *P.Oxy.* XXXIII 2680
173 (a) *P.Oxy.* VI 932
        (b) *P.Oxy.* XXXVI 2789
174 *P.Oxy.* XLII 3048
175 *SB* VIII 9912 (*BL* VI 161); (= *P.Chept.* 11)
176 *P.Cair.Isid.* 64 (= *SB* VI 9168)
177 *P.Oxy.* I 71 col.2 lines 1–16 (*BL* I 314)
178 *P.Col.* VII 176
179 (a) *P.Charite* 7
        (b) *P.Charite* 8
180 (a) *P.Oxy.* XLVIII 3403
        (b) *P.Oxy.* XLVIII 3406
181 *P.Lond.* III 1007 b and c, pp. 264–5 (*BL* I 297, III 95, VII 88)
182 *SB* XIV 11376 (= *P.Hib.* I 89)
183 *BGU* VI 1273.1–40 (*BL* IX 26); (= *Sel.Pap.* I 65)
184 *Pap.Lugd.Bat.* XIX 6 (*BL* VIII 202); (= *BGU* III 995)
185 *P.Mich.* V 253
186 *P.Grenf.* II 45a (*BL* III 75, IX 96)
187 *M.Chr.* 260 (= *BGU* I 87)
188 *P.Tebt.* II 389 (= *M.Chr.* 173)
189 *P.Oxy.* LV 3798 (*BL* IX 204)
190 (a) *OMH* 72
        (b) *OMH* 50
        (c) *OMH* 93
191 *P.Oxy.* I 114 (*BL* I 316, II.2 93, IX 176); (= *Sel.Pap.* I 131)
192 *SB* XVI 12607
193 *P.Charite* 34
194 *BGU* II 405 (*BL* I 44, II.2 17); (= *Sel.Pap.* I 56)
195 *P.Ryl.* IV 662
196 *P.Oxy.* XVI 1957
197 *P.Cair.Masp.* I 67110 (*BL* VII 34)

198 *SB* IV 7358 (re-ed. H. C. Youtie, *ZPE* 13, 1974, 235–7)
199 *P.Köln* II 102 (= *SB* XII 11239)
200 *P.Mich.* I 16
201 **(a)** *PSI* IV 341 (= *Pap. Primer* (4th edn), no. 75)
     (b) *PSI* VI 599 (with p. xviii, *BL* VIII 399)
202 *P.Cair.Zen.* II 59295
203 *BGU* X 1942 (= *SB* X 10209; Scholl, 1990, no. 210)
204 *Stud.Pal.* XXII 40 (*BL* II.2 167, III 238, V 145, VI 196, VIII 481)
205 *P.Oxy.* XXXI 2593
206 *P.Oxy.* XXXI 2599
207 *PSI* IV 406 (= Scholl, 1990, no. 42)
208 *BGU* IV 1024 col.VI (*BL* I 88–9, VII 17, IX 25)
209 *P.Lond.* VII 1976 (= *New Primer* no. 4)
210 *P.Oxy.* XXII 2342 (*BL* IV 65–6, VII 148)
211 *P.Aberd.* 30 (*BL* III 211)
212 *P.Kellis* 8
213 *BGU* IV 1058 (*BL* VIII 39–40); (= *M.Chr.* 170; *C.Pap.Gr.* I 4)
214 *P.Oxy.* I 91 (= *Sel.Pap.* I 79; *C.Pap.Gr.* I 35 and plate 30 in that vol.)
215 *CPR* XVIII 1
216 *P.Corn.* 9 (= *Sel.Pap.* I 20; *Pap. Primer* (4th edn) no. 47; *New Primer* no. 52)
217 *P.Coll.Youtie* II 83
218 *Predictions of Astrampsychos* (excerpts; ed. Browne, 1983)
219 *P.Oxy.* XLVI 3312 (*BL* VIII 269); (trans. *New Docs.* 3, 1983, no. 1)
220 *SB* V 7572 (*BL* III 189; IX 247); (= *New Primer* no. 40)
221 *PSI* VIII 895 (re-ed. Manfredi, 1993)
222 Soranos, *Gynaecology* II 6
223 *PGM* CXXIIIa 48–50 (trans. Betz, 1992, p. 319)
224 *P.Gen.* II 103 (*BL* VIII 136)
225 *P.Münch.* III 57
226 *P.Mil.* II 84 (*BL* VI 77)
227 *SB* XVI 12606
228 *P.Fouad* I 75 (*BL* IV 32; VII 57)
229 *P.Mich.* V 228
230 *P.Oxy.* IV 744 (*BL* I 328, II.2 97, III 132, VII 130, VIII 237, IX 181); (= *Sel.Pap.* I 105)
231 *P.Mich.* III 202 (= *New Primer* no. 26)
232 *P.Oxy.* XXXVI 2791
233 *P.Lips.* 28 (= *M.Chr.* 363; *New Primer* no. 76)
234 *P.Oxy.* XVI 1895 (= *Sel.Pap.* I 11)
235 *KRU* 86.17–32
236 *P.Giss.* 80 (= *Sel.Pap.* I 116; trans. Lefkowitz and Fant, 1992, no. 215)
237 *P.Giss.* 85 (*BL* III 68); (trans. Lefkowitz and Fant, 1992, no. 215)
238 Bilingual schoolbook (excerpts), ed. Dionisotti (1982), 98–100
239 *P.Rain.Unterricht* (*MPER* NS XV) 7
240 *P.Tebt.* II 278, col. I 1–12
241 *P.Leid.Inst.* 5
242 *MPER* NS XVIII 269 I, folios IIa–IIIa, lines 55–83
243 *P.Oxy.* XLIV 3160 ii.12–25
244 *I.Memnon* 28 (= *SB* V 8210 with *BL* III 200, V 102)

245 *I.Memnon* 29 (= SB v 8211)

246 *SB* XVIII 13867

247 *Predictions of Astrampsychos* (excerpts; ed. Browne, 1983)

248 P.Berl. 13538 (end) (ed. Zauzich, 1978)

249 **(a)** Botti (1955); (corr. Pestman, in Veenhof, 1983, p.194)
     (b) *W.Chr.* 122
     (c) *P.Oxy.* IX 1213

250 **(a)** *P.Fuad I Univ.* 7 (*BL* III 61)
     (b) *P.Oxy.* III 524
     (c) *P.Fay.* 132 (= *W.Chr.* 485)
     (d) *P.Oxy.* XII 1579
     (e) *P.Oxy.* XII 1487 (= *Sel.Pap.* I 174)

251 *P.Oxy.* XLVI 3313 (trans. *New Docs.* 3, 1983, no. 2)

252 *P.Mich.* II 121 recto IV i (*BL* VI 80)

253 *P.Coll.Youtie* II 96

254 *P.Ryl.* II 124

255 *PSI* I 64 (*BL* I 390, IV 87, IX 311)

256 *SB* XVIII 14043

257 *BGU* IV 1105 (*BL* II.2 23)

258 *P.Oxy.* LIX 4004

259 *SB* XIV 11585

260 *P.Haun.* II 13 (trans. *New Docs.* 6, 1992, no. 2)

261 **(a)** Clement of Alexandria, *Paidagogos* III ii.4.2–5.4
     (b) Clement of Alexandria, *Paidagogos* II xi.116–17.1

262 Theokritos, *Idyll* 15, lines 1–99 (partly trans. Lefkowitz and Fant, 1992, no. 229)

263 P.Cairo 30646 (excerpt), (Spiegelberg 1906–8) (trans. Lichtheim, 1980, pp. 127–31)

264 *Magica varia* (Pap.Brux. XXV) 2

265 *P.Oxy.* LIX 4001

266 *PGM* VII 260–71 (= *P.Lond.* I 121, pp. 85–115; trans. Betz, 1992, pp. 123–4)

267 *PGM* XXIIa 2–26 (trans. Betz, 1992, p. 260)

268 *P.Oxy.* I 115

269 *SB* XIV 11587

270 *P.Diog.* 10

271 *P.Haun.* II 17

272 Vienna stela 5857 (excerpts) (ed. G. Vittmann, *SAK* 22, 1995, 283–323)

273 *I.Métr.* 83 (= SB III 6706)

274 *I.Métr.* 46

275 Hooper (1961) no. 58

276 *SEG* XX 554 (= Hooper, 1961, no. 171)

277 *I.Fay.* I 59

278 *W.Chr.* 499 (= *Pap.Lugd.-Bat.* XIX, pp. 230–1; photo: Walker and Bierbrier, 1997, cat. 250)

279 **(a)** *P.Coll.Youtie* II 104
     (b) *SB* I 1626 (= CEML 902)
     (c) *Pap.Lugd.Bat.* XIX 40A

280 O. Stras. D 1338 (ed. Spiegelberg, 1911, 34–7; cf. Ritner, 1995, p. 3343)

281 Erichsen (1954)

282 P.BM 10070 + P.Leiden I 383 verso col. XXXII 1–13 (ed. Griffith and Thompson, 1904–9) (= PDM XIV 1206–18, trans. J. H. Johnson in Betz, 1992, p. 250)

283 *PGM* XXXVI 134–60 (= *P.Oslo* I I; trans. Betz, 1992, pp. 272–3)
284 *PGM* XXXVI 283–94 (= *P.Oslo* I I; trans. Betz, 1992, p. 276)
285 *PGM* XV I–21 (trans. Betz, 1992, p. 251)
286 *Suppl.Mag.* I no. 42.1–25 (= *PSI* I 28)
287 O.Wien D 70 (ed. K.-Th. Zauzich, *Enchoria* 18, 1991, 135–51)
288 P.Cairo 30646 (excerpt), (Spiegelberg 1906–8) (trans. Lichtheim 1980, pp. 133–6)
289 Herodas, *Mime* 5 (= *P.Lond.Lit.* 96; Pack[2] 485)

B. Concordance

(i) Papyri, Ostraka, etc

(a) Greek and Latin

BGU I 87	**187**
BGU I 326	**139**
BGU II 362 (excerpt)	**19**
BGU II 405	**194**
BGU III 995	**184**
BGU IV 1024 col.VI	**208**
BGU IV 1058	**213**
BGU IV 1103	**127**
BGU IV 1104	**129**
BGU IV 1105	**257**
BGU V 1210 (excerpts)	**131**
BGU V 1210 §84	**27(a)**
BGU VI 1273.1–40	**183**
BGU VIII 1848	**128**
BGU X 1942	**203**
BGU XIV 2438 (excerpts)	**11**
C.Pap.Jud. I I	**124**
C.Pap.Jud. II 418e	**149**
C.Pap.Jud. II 436	**93**
C.Pap.Jud. II 437	**92**
C.Pap.Jud. II 442	**94**
C.Pap.Jud. III 473	**143**
C.Pap.Lat. 156	**70**
C.Pap.Lat. 162	**71**
C.Pap.Lat. 204	**140(b)**
C.Pap.Lat. 205	**140(a)**
C.Pap.Lat. 208–9	**136**
CPR XVIII I	**215**
Jur. Pap. 4	**70**
Jur.Pap. 14	**142**
Jur.Pap. 18	**123**
Jur.Pap. 25	**139**
Jur.Pap. 93 (excerpts)	**131**
Jur.Pap. 133	**140(a)**

Magica varia (Pap.Brux. XXV) 2	**264**
M.Chr. 18	**87**
M.Chr. 79	**91**
M.Chr. 117	**88**
M.Chr. 170	**213**
M.Chr. 173	**188**
M.Chr. 260	**187**
M.Chr. 281	**132**
M.Chr. 283	**123**
M.Chr. 296	**152**
M.Chr. 302	**86**
M.Chr. 316	**139**
M.Chr. 318	**145**
M.Chr. 324	**140(a)**
M.Chr. 346	**133**
M.Chr. 363	**233**
MPER NS XVIII 269 I fols. IIa–IIIa, lines 55–83	**242**
O.Max. inv. 279+467 (ed. *BIFAO* 94, 1994, 32–3)	**45**
P.Aberd. 30	**211**
P.Bon. I 9	**49**
P.Brem. 63	**94**
P.Cair.Isid. 64	**176**
P.Cair.Masp. I 67110	**197**
P.Cair.Masp. III 67283	**20**
P.Cair.Masp. III 67310 + *P.Lond.* V 1711	**155**
P.Cair.Zen. I 59003	**124**
P.Cair.Zen. I 59028	**77**
P.Cair.Zen. II 59295	**202**
P.Charite 7	**179(a)**
P.Charite 8	**179(b)**
P.Charite 34	**193**
P.Chept. 11	**175**
P.Col. VI 123.25–7 (revised)	**27(b)**

Bibliography

Adam, S. (1983), 'La femme enceinte dans les papyrus', *Anagennesis* 3.1, 9–19.

Adams, B. (1964), *Paramone und verwandte Texte: Studien zur Dienstvertrag im Rechte der Papyri* (Berlin).

Alston, R. (1995), *Soldier and Society in Roman Egypt: a Social History* (London–New York).

Andorlini, I. (1996), 'Il papiro di Strasburgo inv.G 90 e l'oftalmologia di Aezio', in A. Garzya and J. Jouanna (eds.), *Storia e ecdotica dei testi medici greci* (Naples), 7–15.

Andrews, C. A. R. (1990), *Ancient Egyptian Jewellery* (London).

Arjava, A. (1996), *Women and Law in Late Antiquity* (Oxford).

Arjava, A. (1997), 'The guardianship of women in Roman Egypt', *Akten des 21. Internationalen Papyrologenkongresses* (Stuttgart–Berlin), 25–30.

Aubert, J.-J. (1989), 'Aspects of ancient uterine magic', *Greek, Roman, and Byzantine Studies* 30, 421–49.

Austin, M. M. (1981), *The Hellenistic World from Alexander to the Roman Conquest. A Selection of Ancient Sources in Translation* (Cambridge).

Bagnall, R. S. (1980), 'Theadelphian archives: a review article', *BASP* 17, 97–104.

Bagnall, R. S. (1985), *Currency and Inflation in Fourth Century Egypt* (BASP Supplement 5; Atlanta).

Bagnall, R. S. (1991a), 'A trick a day to keep the tax man at bay: the prostitute tax in Roman Egypt', *BASP* 28, 5–12.

Bagnall, R. S. (1991b), 'Notes on Egyptian census declarations, II', *BASP* 28, 13–32.

Bagnall, R. S. (1993a), *Egypt in Late Antiquity* (Princeton).

Bagnall, R. S. (1993b), 'An Arsinoite metropolitan landowning family in the fourth century' in M. Capasso, *Papiri documentari greci* (Papyrologica Lupiensia II; Galatina), 97–101.

Bagnall, R. S. (1995), *Reading Papyri, Writing Ancient History* (London–New York).

Bagnall, R. S. and Derow, P. (1981), *Greek Historical Documents: The Hellenistic Period* (Society of Biblical Literature Sources for Biblical Study 16; Chico, CA).

Bagnall, R. S. and Frier, B.W. (1994), *The Demography of Roman Egypt* (Cambridge).

Bagnall, R. S. and Worp, K. A. (1978), *The Chronological Systems of Byzantine Egypt* (Stud.Amst. VIII; Amsterdam).

Bailey, D. M. (1991), *Excavations at El-Ashmunein IV: Hermopolis Magna: Buildings of the Roman Period* (London).

Bailey, D. M. (1996), ed., *Archaeological Research in Roman Egypt* (JRA Supp. Series, 19; Ann Arbor).

Barsby, J. (1973), ed., *Ovid: Amores, Book One* (Oxford).

Barton, T. (1994), *Ancient Astrology* (London–New York).

Beaucamp, J. (1985), 'La référence au veuvage dans les papyrus byzantins', *Pallas* 32, 149–57.

Beaucamp, J. (1992), *Le statut de la femme à Byzance (4ᵉ-7ᵉ siècle) II: Les pratiques sociales* (Paris).

Beaucamp, J. (1994), 'Discours et normes: la faiblesse féminine dans les textes pro-tobyzantines', *Cahiers du Centre G. Glotz* 5, 199–220.

Bell, H. I. (1950), 'A happy family', in S. Morenz, ed., *Aus Antike und Orient: Festschrift Wilhelm Schubart zum 75 Geburtstag* (Leipzig), 38–47.

Berger, A. (1953), *Encyclopedic Dictionary of Roman Law* (Transactions of the American Philosophical Society 43.2; Philadelphia).

Bergman, J. (1968), *Ich bin Isis. Studien zum memphitischen Hintergrund der griechischen Isisaretalogien* (Acta Universitatis Upsaliensis. Historia religionum 3; Uppsala).

Betz, H. D. (1992), ed., *The Greek Magical Papyri in Translation, Including the Demotic Spells* I (2nd edn; Chicago–London).

Bevan, E. R. (1927), *A History of Egypt under the Ptolemaic Dynasty* (London; reissued Chicago, 1968).

Bianchi, R. (1988), ed., *Cleopatra's Egypt. Age of the Ptolemies* (New York).

Bierbrier, M. L. (1997), ed., *Portraits and Masks: Burial Customs in Roman Egypt* (London).

Bing, P. and Cohen, R. (1991), *Games of Venus* (New York–London).

Bingen, J. (1987), 'La série Kappa des stèles de Térénouthis', in C. Saerens, R. De Smet and H. Melaerts (eds.), *Studia Varia Bruxellensia* I (Leuven), 3–14.

Bingen, J. (1996), 'Une nouvelle stèle de la "série Kappa" de Térénouthis', *Chronique d'Egypte* 71 (1996), 331–4.

Birley, A. R. (1988), *The African Emperor: Septimius Severus* (London).

Biscottini, M. V. (1966), 'L'archivio di Tryphon, tessitore di Oxyrhynchos', *Aegyptus* 46, 60–90 and 186–292.

Boak, A. E. R. and Peterson, E. E. (1931), *Karanis: Topographical and Architectural Report of Excavations during the Seasons 1924–28* (University of Michigan Studies, Humanistic series 25; Ann Arbor).

Bogaert, R. (1994), *Trapezitica Aegyptiaca. Recueil de recherches sur la banque en Egypte gréco-romaine* (Pap.Flor. xxv; Florence).

Bonner, C. (1950), *Studies in Magical Amulets, Chiefly Graeco-Egyptian* (Ann Arbor).

Borg, B. (1996), *Mumienporträts: Chronologie und kultureller Kontext* (Mainz).

Botti, G. (1955), 'Biglietti per l'oraculo di Soknebtynis in caratteri demotici', *Studi in memoria di I. Rosellini* II (Pisa), p. 13.

Bowersock, G. W. (1984), 'The miracle of Memnon', *BASP* 21, 21–32.

Bowman, A. K. (1985), 'Landholding in the Hermopolite nome in the fourth century AD', *JRS* 75, 137–63.

Bowman, A. K. (1992), 'Public buildings in Roman Egypt', *JRA* 5, 495–503.

Bowman, A. K. (1996), *Egypt after the Pharaohs, 332 BC–AD 642* (2nd edn; London).

Bowman, A. K., Champlin, E., and Lintott, A. (1996), eds., *Cambridge Ancient History* vol. x: *The Augustan Empire, 43 BC–AD 69* (2nd edn; Cambridge).

Bowman, A. K. and Rathbone, D. W. (1992), 'Cities and administration in Roman Egypt', *JRS* 82, 107–27.

Bradley, K. R. (1980), 'Sexual regulations in wet-nursing contracts from Roman Egypt', *Klio* 62, 321–5.

Breccia, E. (1922), *Alexandrea ad Aegyptum: A Guide to the Ancient and Modern Town, and to its Graeco-Roman Remains* (Bergamo).

Bremen, R. van (1996), *The Limits of Participation. Women and Civic Life in the Greek East in the Hellenistic and Roman Periods* (Amsterdam).

Bresciani, E. et al. (1978), 'Una rilettura dei Pap. dem. Bologna 3173 e 3171', *Egitto e Vicino Oriente* 1, 95–104.

Brown, P. (1988), *The Body and Society: Men, Women and Sexual Renunciation in Early Christianity* (New York).

Browne, G. M. (1970), 'The composition of the *Sortes Astrampsychi*', *Bulletin of the Institute of Classical Studies* (London) 17, 95–100.

Browne, G. M. (1974), *The papyri of the Sortes Astrampsychi* (Beiträge zur klassischen Philologie 58; Meisenheim am Glan).

Browne, G. M. (1983), ed., *Sortes Astrampsychi* (Leipzig).

Bruhn, J.-A. (1993), *Coins and Costume in Late Antiquity* (Dumbarton Oaks Byzantine Collection, Publication 9; Washington).

Brunt, P. A. (1987), *Italian Manpower 225 B.C.–A.D. 14* (amended edn; Oxford).

Burkhalter, F. (1990a), 'Archives locales et archives centrales en Egypte romaine', *Chiron* 20, 191–216.

Burkhalter, F. (1990b), 'Les statuettes de bronze d'Aphrodite en Egypte romaine d'après les documents papyrologiques', *Revue Archéologique* 1, 51–60.

Burstein, S. M. (1985), *The Hellenistic Age from the Battle of Ipsos to the Death of Kleopatra VII* (Translated Documents of Greece and Rome 3; Cambridge).

Cameron, A. (1978), 'The Theotokos in sixth-century Constantinople', *Journal of Theological Studies* 29, 79–108.

Cameron, A. and Long, J. (1993), *Barbarians and Politics at the Court of Arcadius* (Berkeley–Los Angeles–London).

Capel, A. K. and Markoe, G. E. (1996), eds., *Mistress of the House, Mistress of Heaven: Women in Ancient Egypt* (New York).

Casarico, L. (1982), 'Donne ginnasiarco', *ZPE* 48, 117–23.

Cenival, F. de (1972), *Les associations religieuses en Egypte d'après les documents démotiques* (Paris).

Cenival, F. de (1977), 'Deux papyrus inédits de Lille', *Enchoria* 7, 1–49.

Champlin, E. J. (1991), *Final Judgements: Duty and Emotion in Roman Wills, 200 BC–AD 250* (Berkeley-Los Angeles).

Chassinat, E. (1939), *Le mammisi d'Edfou* (MIFAO XVI; Cairo).

Chauveau, M. (1987), 'Les étiquettes de momies démotiques et bilingues du Musée du Louvre' (unpublished dissertation; Paris).

Clark, G. (1993), *Women in Late Antiquity: Pagan and Christian Lifestyles* (Oxford).

Clarysse, W. (1985), 'Greeks and Egyptians in the Ptolemaic army and administration', *Aegyptus* 65, 57–66.

Clarysse, W. (1986), 'Le mariage et le testament de Dryton en 150 avant J.-C.', *Chronique d'Egypte* 61, 99–103.

Clarysse, W. (1992), 'Some Greeks in Egypt', in J. H. Johnson ed. (1992), 51–6.

Clarysse, W. (1993), 'Egyptian scribes writing Greek', *Chronique d'Egypte* 68, 186–201.

Clarysse, W. and Hauben, H. (1991), 'Ten granary receipts from Pyrrheia', *ZPE* 89, 47–68.

Clarysse, W. and Sijpesteijn, P. J. (1995), 'A letter from a dancer of Boubastis', *Archiv* 41, 56–61.

Clarysse W. and Van der Veken, G. (1983), *The Eponymous Priests of Ptolemaic Egypt* (Pap.Lugd.Bat. XXIV; Leiden).

Clarysse, W. and Vandorpe, K. (1995), *Zénon, un homme d'affaires grec à l'ombre des pyramides* (Leuven).

Clarysse, W. and Vandorpe, K. (1998), 'The Ptolemaic apomoira', in H. Melaerts, (ed.), *Le culte du souverain dans L'Egypte ptolémaïque au IIIe siècle avant notre ère* (Studia Hellenistica 34; Leuven), 5–42.

Cockle, W. E. H. (1987), ed., Euripides, *Hypsipyle: Text and Annotation Based on a Re-examination of the Papyri* (Rome).

Copley, F. O. (1956), *Exclusus Amator: a study in Latin Love Poetry* (Baltimore).

Corcoran, L. H. (1995), *Portrait Mummies from Roman Egypt (I–IV Centuries A.D.)*, *with a Catalog of Portrait Mummies in Egyptian Museums* (The Oriental Institute of the University of Chicago Studies in Ancient Oriental Civilization, 56; Chicago).

Cotton, H. (1995), 'The archive of Salome Komaïse daughter of Levi: another archive from the "Cave of Letters"', *ZPE* 105, 171–208.

Crawford [Thompson], D. J. (1976), 'Imperial estates', in M. I. Finley (ed.), *Studies in Roman Property* (Cambridge) 35–70, 173–80.

Cribiore, R. (1996), *Writing, Teachers and Students in Graeco-Roman Egypt* (Am.Stud.Pap. XXXVI; Atlanta).

Crossan, J. D. (1992), *The Historical Jesus: the Life of a Mediterranean Jewish Peasant* (San Francisco).

Cunningham, I. C. (1987), *Herodas* (Leipzig).

Cunningham, I. C. (1993), in Theophrastus, *Characters*; Herodas, *Mimes*; *Cercidas and the Choliambic Poets* (Loeb Classical Library 225; Cambridge, MA–London), 197–317.

De Moor, A. (1993), *Koptisch Textiel uit Vlaamse privé-verzamelingen / Coptic Textiles from Flemish private collections* (Zottegem).

Debut, J. (1986), 'Les documents scolaires', *ZPE* 63, 251–78.

Dickie, M. W. (1993), 'Malice, envy and inquisitiveness in Catullus 5 and 7', *Papers of the Leeds International Latin Seminar* 7, 9–26.

Dionisotti, A. C. (1982), 'From Ausonius' schooldays: a schoolbook and its relatives', *JRS* 72, 83–125.

Dixon, S. (1988), *The Roman Mother* (London).

Doxiadis, E. (1995), *The Mysterious Fayum Portraits: Faces from Ancient Egypt* (London).

Drower, M. S. (1985), *Flinders Petrie: A Life in Archaeology* (London).

Dunand, F. (1978), 'Le statut des "hiereiai" en Egypte romaine', in *Hommages à Maarten J. Vermaseren* I (Leiden), 352–74.

Dunand, F. (1980), 'Fête, tradition, propagande. Les cérémonies en l'honneur de Bérénice, fille de Ptolémée III, en 238 a.C.', *Institut français d'archéologie orientale du Caire: Livre du Centenaire, 1880–1980* (MIFAO 104; Cairo), 287–301.

Dunand, F. (1987), 'Gestes symboliques', *CRIPEL* 9, 81–7.

Dunand, F. (1991), *Dieux et hommes en Egypte, 3000 av. J.-C. – 395 apr. J.-C.* (Paris).

Dunand, F. and Lichtenberg, R. (1995), 'Pratiques et croyances funéraires en Egypte romaine', *Aufstieg und Niedergang der römischen Welt* II 18.5 (Berlin–New York), 3216–315.

Dzielska, M. (1995), *Hypatia of Alexandria* (Cambridge, MA–London).

Effenberger, A. (1975), *Koptische Kunst. Ägypten in spätantiker, byzantinischer und frühislamischer Zeit* (Vienna).

Eitrem, S. and Amundsen, L. (1951), 'Three private letters from the Oslo Collection', *Aegyptus* 31, 177–83.

Elm, S. (1994), *'Virgins of God'. The Making of Asceticism in Late Antiquity* (Oxford).

Erichsen, W. (1954), 'Aus einem demotischen Papyrus über Frauenkrankheiten', *Mitt. Inst. Orientforschung* 2, 363–77.

Evans Grubbs, J. (1995), *Law and Family in Late Antiquity: The Emperor Constantine's Marriage Legislation* (Oxford).

Evans Grubbs, J. and Hanson, A. E. (forthcoming), 'Birthing: notes on *P.Oxy.* II 321, *O.Florida* 14, and *P.Gen.* II 103', *ZPE*.

Falivene, M. R. (1991), 'Government, management and literacy: aspects of Ptolemaic administration in the early Hellenistic period', *Ancient Society* 22, 203–27.

Fantham, E., et al. (1994), *Women in the Classical World* (New York–Oxford).

Faraone C., and Obbink, D. (1991), *Magika Hiera. Ancient Greek Magic and Ritual* (New York).

Farid, F. (1977), 'Paniskos: Christian or Pagan?', *Museum Philologum Londiniense* 2, 109–17.

Farid, F. (1979), 'Sarapis–Proskynema in the light of *SB* III 6263', in J. Bingen and G. Nachtergael (eds.), *Actes du XV Congrès international de papyrologie* IV (Brussels) 141–47.

Filer, J. (1997), 'If the face fits: a comparison of mummies and their accompanying portraits using computerised axial tomography', in Bierbrier ed., (1997) 121–6.

Fischer, K.-D. (1997), 'Was ist das δελτάριον in P.Oxy. LIX 4001?', in I. Andorlini (ed.), 'Specimina' *per il* Corpus *dei Papiri Greci di Medicina* (Florence), 109–13.

Fischler, S. (1994), 'Social stereotypes and historical analysis: the case of the Imperial women at Rome', in L. Archer, S. Fischler, M. Wyke (eds.), *Women in Ancient Societies: 'An Illusion of the Night'* (Basingstoke–London), 115–33.

Forman, W. and Quirke, S. (1996), *Hieroglyphs and the Afterlife in Ancient Egypt* (London).

Fraser, P. M. (1972), *Ptolemaic Alexandria* (3 vols.) (Oxford).

Frier, B. (1994), 'Natural fertility and family limitation in Roman marriage', *Classical Philology* 89, 318–33.

Gabra, S. (1941), *Rapport sur les fouilles d'Hermoupolis Ouest (Touna el-Gebel)* (Cairo).

Gager, J. G. (1992), ed., *Curse Tablets and Binding Spells from the Ancient World* (Oxford).

Gagos, T., Koenen, L. and McNellen, B. E. (1992), 'A first century archive from Oxyrhynchos: Oxyrhynchite loan contracts and Egyptian marriage', in J. H. Johnson ed. (1992), 181–205.

Gagos, T. and van Minnen, P. (1994), *Settling a Dispute: Towards a Legal Anthropology of Late Antique Egypt* (Ann Arbor).

Gallazzi, C. (1990), 'La "Cantina dei Papiri" di Tebtynis e ciò che essa conteneva', *ZPE* 80, 283–8.

Gallazzi, C. (1994), 'Tebtunis: piecing together 3,000 years of history', *Egyptian Archaeology* 5, 27–9.

Gallazzi, C. and Hadji-Minaglou, G. (1989), 'Fouilles anciennes et nouvelles sur le site de Tebtunis', *BIFAO* 89, 179–202.

Gardner, J. F. (1984), 'A family and an inheritance: the problems of the widow Petronilla', *Liverpool Classical Monthly* 9.9, 132–3.

Gardner, J. F. (1986), *Women in Roman Law and Society* (London–Sydney).

Gascou, J. (1985), 'Les grandes domaines, la cité et l'état en Egypte byzantine', *Travaux et mémoires* 9, 1–90.

Gazda, E. K. (1983), *Karanis: an Egyptian Town in Roman Times* (Ann Arbor).

Geraci, G. (1981), 'L'ὁ πρὸς τῆι συντάξει: note sull'amministrazione militare nell'Egitto tolemaico', *Proceedings of the XVI International Congress of Papyrology* (Am.Stud.Pap. xxiii; Chico, CA), 267–76.

Germer, R., Kischkewitz, H. and Lüning, M. (1993), 'Das Grab der Aline und die Untersuchung der darin gefundenen Kindermumien', *Antike Welt* 24, 186–96.

Gilliam, J. F. (1978), 'Some Roman elements in Roman Egypt', *Illinois Classical Studies* 3, 115–23 (reprinted in *Roman Army Papers*, 1986, 409–17).

Ginouvès, R. (1962), ΒΑΛΑΝΕΥΤΙΚΗ: *Recherches sur le bain dans l'antiquité grecque* (Paris).

Glare, P. (forthcoming), *Temples in Roman Egypt* (Cambridge).

Goldman, N. (1996), 'Isis revealed: cult and costume in Italy', in Bailey ed. (1996), 246–58.

Goudriaan, K. (1988), *Ethnicity in Ptolemaic Egypt* (Amsterdam).

Grassi, T. (1973), *Musica, mimica e danze secondi i documenti papiracei grecoegizi* (revised edn; Milan).

Grether, G. (1946), 'Livia and the Roman imperial cult', *AJP* 67, 222–52.

Griffith, F. Ll. and Thompson, H. (1904–9), *The Demotic Magical Papyrus of London and Leiden*, 3 vols. (Oxford).

Griffiths, J. G. (1970), *Plutarch's De Iside et Osiride* (Cambridge).

Grunert, S. (1981), *Thebanische Kaufverträge des 3. und 2. Jahrhunderts v.u.Z.* (Berlin).

Guéraud, O. and Jouguet, P. (1938), *Un livre d'écolier du IIIe siècle avant J.-C.* (Cairo).

Guimet, E. (1912), *Portraits d'Antinoe* (Paris).

Haensch, R. (1992), 'Das Statthalterarchiv', *ZSS(RA)* 109, 209–317.

Haensch, R. (1994), 'Die Bearbeitungsweisen von Petitionen in der Provinz Aegyptus', *ZPE* 100, 487–545.

Häge, G. (1968), *Ehegüterrechtliche Verhältnisse in den griechischen Papyri Ägyptens bis Diokletian* (Cologne).

Hamer, M. (1993), *Signs of Cleopatra: History, Politics, Representation* (London).

Hanson, A. E. (1984), 'Caligulan month-names at Philadelphia and related matters', *Atti del XVII Congresso internazionale di papirologia* iii (Naples), 1107–18.

Hanson, A. E. (1987), 'The eighth months' child and the etiquette of birth', *Bulletin of the History of Medicine* 61, 589–602.

Hanson, A. E. (1989a), 'Village officials at Philadelphia: A model of romanization in the Julio-Claudian period', in L. Criscuolo and G. Geraci (eds.), *Egitto e storia antica dall' ellenismo all'età araba: bilancio di un confronto* (Bologna), 429–40.

Hanson, A. E. (1989b), 'Diseases of women in the (Hippocratic) Epidemics', in G. Baader and R. Winau (eds.), *Die Hippokratischen Epidemien: Theorie-Praxis-Tradition* (*Sudhoffs Archiv*, Beiheft 27; Stuttgart), 38–51.

Hanson, A. E. (1990), 'The medical writers' woman', in D. M. Halperin, J. J. Winkler, F. L. Zeitlin (eds.), *Before Sexuality: The Construction of Erotic Experience in the Ancient Greek World* (Princeton), 309–38.

Hanson, A. E. (1991a), 'Continuity and change: three case studies in Hippocratic gynecological therapy and theory', in S. B. Pomeroy (ed.), *Women's History and Ancient History* (Chapel Hill–London), 73–110.

Hanson, A. E. (1991b), 'Ancient illiteracy', in *Literacy in the Roman world* (*JRA* Supp. 3; Ann Arbor), 159–98.

Hanson, A. E. (1992), 'Egyptians, Greeks, Romans, *Arabes*, and *Ioudaioi*, in the first century A.D. tax archive from Philadelphia: P.Mich. inv. 880 recto and *P.Princ.* III 152 revised', in J. H. Johnson ed. (1992), 133–45.

Hanson, A. E. (1994a), 'Obstetrics in the *Hippocratic Corpus* and Soranus', *Forum* 4, 93–110.

Hanson, A. E. (1994b), 'A division of labor: roles for men in Greek and Roman births', *Thamyris* 1, 157–202.

Hanson, A. E. (1995), 'Uterine amulets and Greek uterine medicine', *Medicina nei Secoli arte e scienza* (*Journal of History of Medicine*) 7, 281–99.

Hanson, A. E. (1998), 'Talking Recipes in the Hippocratic Corpus', in M. Wyke (ed.), *Parchments of Gender: Deciphering the Body in Antiquity* (Oxford).

Hanson, A. E. (1999), 'Widows too young in their widowhood', in D. Kleiner and S. B. Matheson (eds.), *I, Claudia* II (University of Texas Press, 1999).

Hanson, A. E. and Green, M. H. (1994), 'Soranus: *Methodicorum princeps*', *Aufstieg und Niedergang der römischen Welt* II 37.2 (Berlin–New York), 968–1075.

Harper, G. M. (1928), 'A study in the commercial relations between Egypt and Syria in the third century before Christ', *AJP* 49, 1–35.

Harris, W. V. (1989), *Ancient Literacy* (Cambridge, MA).

Hauben, H. (1980), 'Le transport fluvial en Egypte ptolémaique. Les bateaux du roi et de la reine', *Actes du XVe Congrès International de Papyrologie* IV (Pap. Brux. XIX; Brussels), 68–77.

Hauben, H. (1989), 'Aspects du culte des souverains à l'époque des Lagides', in L. Criscuolo and G. Geraci (eds.), *Egitto e storia antica dall' ellenismo all'età araba: bilancio di un confronto* (Bologna), 441–67.

Hauben, H.(1993), 'Femmes propriétaires et locataires de navires en Egypte ptolémaïque', *Journal of Juristic Papyrology* 22, 61–74.

Hazzard, R. A. (1992), 'Did Ptolemy I get his surname from the Rhodians in 304?', *ZPE* 93, 52–6.

Heinen, H. (1989), 'Onomastisches zu Eiras, Kammerzofe Kleopatras VII', *ZPE* 79, 243–7.

Hengstl, J. (1972), *Private Arbeitsverhältnisse freier Personen in den hellenistischen Papyri bis Diokletian* (Bonn).

Herrmann, J. (1957), 'Vertragsinhalt und Rechtsnatur der διδασκαλικαί', *Journal of Juristic Papyrology* 11, 119–39.

Heyob, S. K. (1975), *The Cult of Isis among Women in the Graeco-Roman World* (EPRO 51; Leiden).

Hobson, D. W. (1983), 'Women as property owners in Roman Egypt', *TAPA* 113, 311–21.

Hobson, D. W. (1984), 'The role of women in the economic life of Roman Egypt: a case study from first century Tebtynis', *Echos du monde classique / Classical Views* 28 (n.s. 3), 373–90.

Hobson, D. W. (1985), 'House and household in Roman Egypt', in N. Lewis (ed.), *Yale Classical Studies* 28 (= *Papyrology*), 211–29.

Hobson, D. W. (1989), 'Naming practices in Roman Egypt', *BASP* 26, 157–74.

Holum, K.G. (1982), *Theodosian Empresses: Women and Imperial Dominion in Late Antiquity* (Berkeley–Los Angeles–London).

Hooft, P. van't, et al. (1994), *Pharaonic and Early Medieval Egyptian Textiles* (Leiden).

Hooper, F. A. (1961), *Funerary Stelae from Kom Abou Billou* (Kelsey Museum of Archaeology Studies 1; Ann Arbor).

Hopkins, K. (1978), *Conquerors and Slaves* (Cambridge).

Hopkins, K. (1980), 'Brother–sister marriage in Roman Egypt', *Comparative Studies in Society and History* 22, 303–54.

Howgego, C. J. (1992), 'The supply and use of money in the Roman world 200 B C to A D 300', *JRS* 82, 1–31.

Husselman, E. M. (1961), 'Pawnbrokers' accounts from Roman Egypt', *TAPA* 92, 251–66.

Husselman, E. M. (1979), *Karanis Excavations of the University of Michigan in Egypt, 1928–1935: Topography and Architecture* (Kelsey Museum of Archaeology Studies 5; Ann Arbor).

Husson, G. (1983), *OIKIA: Le vocabulaire de la maison privée en Egypte d'après les papyrus grecs* (Paris).

Iversen, E. (1939), 'Papyrus Carlsberg No. VIII: with some remarks on the Egyptian origin of some popular birth prognoses', *Historisk-filologiske Meddelelser udgivet af det Kgl. Danske Videnskabernes Selskab* 26.5, 1–31.

Johansen, F. (1994), *Catalogue: Roman Portraits, Ny Carlsberg Glyptotek* vol 1 (Copenhagen).

Johnson, A. C. (1936), *Roman Egypt to the Reign of Diocletian* (= T. Frank, ed., *Economic Survey of Ancient Rome* II), (Baltimore).

Johnson, A. C. (1950), 'Egypt in the third century', *Journal of Juristic Papyrology* 4, 151–8.

Johnson, B. (1981), *Pottery from Karanis: Excavations of the University of Michigan* (Ann Arbor).

Johnson, J. H. (1992), ed., *Life in a Multi-cultural Society: Egypt from Kambyses to Constantine and Beyond* (Chicago).

Judge, E. A. (1981), 'Fourth-century monasticism in the papyri', *Proceedings of the XVI International Congress of Papyrology* (Am.Stud.Pap. XXIII; Chico, CA), 613–20.

Just, R. (1989), *Women in Athenian Law and Life* (London).

Kaster, R. A. (1988), *Guardians of Language: The Grammarian and Society in Late Antiquity* (Berkeley–Los Angeles–London).

Keddie, N. R. and Baron, B. (1991) eds., *Women in Middle Eastern History: Shifting Boundaries in Sex and Gender* (New Haven–London).

Keenan, J. G. (1978), 'The case of Flavia Christodote: observations on PSI 1 76', *ZPE* 29, 191–209.

Keenan, J. G. (1980), 'Aurelius Phoibammon, son of Triadelphus, a Byzantine Egyptian land entrepreneur', *BASP* 17, 145–54.

Keenan, J. G. (1984), 'Aurelius Apollos and the Aphrodite village élite', *Atti del XVII Congresso Internazionale di Papirologia* III (Naples), 957–63.

Keenan, J. G. (1989), 'Roman criminal law in a Berlin papyrus codex', *Archiv* 35, 15–23.

Keenan, J. G. (1994), 'The will of Gaius Longinus Castor', *BASP* 31, 101–7.

Kehoe, D. P. (1992), *Management and Investment on Estates in Roman Egypt during the Early Empire* (Pap.Texte Abh. XL; Bonn).

Kendrick, A. F. (1920), *Catalogue of Textiles from the Burying-Grounds in Egypt* vol. I, *Graeco-Roman Period* (London).

King, D. (1996), 'Roman and Byzantine dress in Egypt', *Costume (Journal of the Costume Society)* 30, 1–15.

King, H. (1994), 'Once upon a text', in S. L. Gilman et al. (eds.), *Hysteria Beyond Freud* (Berkeley), 5–90.

Koenen, L. (1970), 'Kleopatra III als Priesterin des Alexanderkultes', *ZPE* 5, 61–84.

Koenen, L. (1993), 'The Ptolemaic king as a religious figure', in A. W. Bulloch et al. (eds.), *Images and Ideologies: Self-definition in the Hellenistic World*, (Berkeley–Los Angeles–London), 25–115.

Kokkinos, N. (1992), *Antonia Augusta* (London–New York).

Krause, J.-U. (1994), *Verwitwung und Wiederverheiratung* (= *Witwen und Waisen im römischen Reich* I) (Stuttgart).

Kuehn, C. A. (1993), 'A new papyrus of a Dioscorian poem and marriage contract', *ZPE* 99, 103–15.

La Riche, W. (1996), *Alexandria: the Sunken City* (London).

Layton, B. et al. (1989), *Nag Hammadi Codex II, 2–7, together with XIII.2, Brit. Lib. Or. 4926(1), and P.Oxy. 1, 654, 655* vol. I (Leiden).

Lefkowitz, M. R. and Fant, M. B. (1992), *Women's Life in Greece and Rome* (2nd edn., Baltimore–London).

Lesko, B. S. (1989), ed., *Women's Earliest Records: from Ancient Egypt and Western Asia* (Atlanta, Georgia).

Lewis, N. (1974), *Papyrus in Classical Antiquity* (Oxford).

Lewis, N. (1983), *Life in Egypt under Roman Rule* (Oxford).

Lewis, N. (1986), *Greeks in Ptolemaic Egypt* (Oxford).

Lewis, N. (1990), 'Women in public offices', *BASP* 27, 38–40.

Lewis, N. (1993), 'The demise of the Demotic document: when and why', *JEA* 79, 276–81.

Lewis, N. (1997), *The Compulsory Services of Roman Egypt* (2nd edn, Pap. Flor. XXVIII; Florence).

Lewis, N. and Reinhold, M. (1990), *Roman Civilization* I (Republic) – II (Empire), (3rd edn, New York).

Lichtheim, M. (1980), *Ancient Egyptian Literature: A Book of Readings* Vol. III: *The Late Period* (Berkeley–Los Angeles–London).

Lightfoot-Klein, H. (1989), *Prisoners of Ritual: An Odyssey into Female Genital Circumcision in Africa* (New York–London).

Lloyd, A. B. (1976), *Herodotus, Book II, Commentary* 1–98 (Leiden).

MacCoull, L. S. B. (1986), 'Coptic Documentary Papyri as a Historical Source for Egyptian Christianity', in B. Pearson and J. Goehring (eds.), *The Roots of Egyptian Christianity* (Philadelphia), 42–50.

MacCoull, L. S. B. (1988), *Dioscorus of Aphrodito. His Work and his World* (Berkeley).

MacCurdy, G. (1932), *Hellenistic Queens* (Baltimore).

Manfredi, M. (1993), 'Affetti familiari (*PSI* VIII 895)', in M. Bandini and F. G. Pericoli (eds.), *Scritti in memoria di Dino Pieraccioni* (Florence), 255–61.

Masciadri, M. M. and Montevecchi, O. (1982), 'Contratti di baliatico e vendite fiduciarie a Tebtynis', *Aegyptus* 62, 148–61.

Masciadri, M. M. and Montevecchi, O. (1984), *I contratti di baliatico* (*CPGr* I; Milan).

McCredie, J. R. et al. (1992), *Samothrace, 7. The Rotunda of Arsinoe* (Princeton).

Merkelbach, R. (1995), *Isis Regina–Zeus Sarapis: Die griechisch-ägyptische Religion nach den Quellen dargestellt* (Stuttgart–Leipzig).

Messeri Savorelli, G. (1990), 'Frammenti del primo testamento di Dryton?', in M. Capasso et al. (eds.), *Miscellanea Papyrologica in occasione del bicentenario dell'edizione della Charta Borgiana* (Pap.Flor. XIX; Florence), 429–36.

Meyer, B. (1992), 'Les femmes et les bains publics dans l'Egypte grecque, romaine et byzantine', in *Proceedings of the XIXth International Congress of Papyrology* II (Cairo), 51–60.

Meyer, M. and Smith, R. (1994), *Ancient Christian Magic: Coptic Texts of Ritual Power* (San Francisco).

Minnen, P. van (1994a), 'House-to-house enquiries: an interdisciplinary approach to Roman Karanis', *ZPE* 100, 227–51.

Minnen, P. van (1994b), 'The Roots of Egyptian Christianity', *Archiv* 40, 71–85.

Modrzejewski, J. M. (1974), 'A propos de la tutelle dative des femmes dans l'Egypte romaine', *Akten des XIII. Internationalen Papyrologenkongresses* (Munich), 263–92 (= Modrzejewski, 1990, ch. 3).

Modrzejewski, J. M. (1979), 'Régime foncier et statut sociale dans l'Egypte ptolémaïque', in *Terre et paysans dépendants dans les sociétés antiques (Colloque Besançon, mai 1974)* (Paris), 163–88.

Modrzejewski, J. M. (1981), 'La structure juridique du mariage grec', in E. Bresciani (ed.), *Scritti in onore di Orsolina Montevecchi* (Bologna), 231–68.

Modzrejewski, J. M. (1988), '"La loi des Egyptiens": le droit grec dans l'Egypte romaine', *Proceedings of the XVIII International Congress of Papyrology* (Athens), 383–99 (= Modrzejewski, 1990, ch. 9).

Modrzejewski, J. M. (1990), *Droit impérial et traditions locales dans l'Egypte romaine* (Aldershot).

Montevecchi, O. (1950), *I contratti di lavoro e di servizio nell'Egitto greco, romano e bizantino* (Milan).

Montevecchi, O. (1979), 'Πόσων μηνῶν ἔστιν', *ZPE* 34, 113–17.

Montevecchi, O. (1981), 'Una donna *prostatis* del figlio minorenne in un papiro del II^a', *Aegyptus* 61, 103–5.

Montserrat, D. (1993), 'The representation of young males in "Fayum portraits"', *JEA* 79, 215–25.

Montserrat, D. (1996), *Sex and Society in Graeco-Roman Egypt* (London–New York).

Moorhead, J. (1994), *Justinian* (London).

Morris, R. B. (1978), 'The economy of Oxyrhynchus', *BASP* 15, 263–73.

Most, G. W. (1981), 'Callimachus and Herophilus', *Hermes* 109, 188–96.

Naber, J. C. (1930), 'Ad papyrum Graecum lepidi argumenti (BGU 1105)', *Aegyptus* 11, 179–84.

Naldini, M. (1968), *Il cristianesimo in Egitto* (Florence).

Nielsen, B. E. (1994), 'A woman of property: Techosous alias Eudaimonis', *BASP* 31, 129–36.

Nowicka, M. (1970), 'A propos de tours – PURGOI dans les papyrus grecs', *Archeologia* 21, 53–61.

Nutton, V. (1993), 'Galen and Egypt', in J. Kollesch and D. Nickel (eds.), *Galen und das hellenistische Erbe* (Stuttgart), 11–31.

Oates, J. F. (1963), 'The status designation Πέρσης τῆς Ἐπιγονῆς', *Yale Classical Studies* 18, 1–129.

Oliver, J. H. (1989), *Greek Constitutions* (Philadelphia).

Orrieux, C. (1983), *Les papyrus de Zénon. L'horizon d'un grec en Egypte au IIIᵉ siècle avant J.C.* (Paris).

Orrieux, C. (1985), *Zénon de Caunos, parépidèmos, et le destin grec* (Paris).

Parássoglou, G. M. (1978), *Imperial Estates in Roman Egypt* (Am.Stud.Pap. XVIII; Las Palmas).

Parca, M. G. (1991), *Ptocheia or Odysseus in Disguise at Troy (P.Köln VI 245)* (Am.Stud.Pap. XXXI; Atlanta).

Parlasca, K. (1966), *Mumienporträts und verwandte Denkmäler* (Wiesbaden).

Parlasca, K. (1969), *Repertorio d'arte dell'Egitto greco-romano* (ed. A. Adriani) ser. B vol. I (Palermo).

Pelling, C. (1996), in A. K. Bowman, E. Champlin and A. Lintott (eds.), *Cambridge Ancient History* vol. X: *The Augustan Empire, 43 BC–AD 69* (2nd edn; Cambridge), ch. 1.

Perdrizet, P. (1911), *Bronzes grecs d'Egypte de la Collection Fouquet* (Paris).

Pestman, P. W. (1961), *Marriage and Matrimonial Property in Ancient Egypt: a Contribution to Establishing the Legal Position of the Woman* (Pap.Lugd.Bat. IX; Leiden).

Pestman, P. W. (1978), 'The land "The Point" in the domain of Pestenemenophis', *Textes grecs, démotiques, et bilingues* (Pap.Lugd.Bat. XIX; Leiden), 193–205 (Appendix A).

Pestman, P. W. (1981a), ed., *A Guide to the Zenon Archive* (Pap.Lugd.Bat. XXI; Leiden), 2 vols.

Pestman, P. W. (1981b), 'Nahomsesis, una donna d'affari di Pathyris; L'archivio bilingue di Pelaias, figlio di Eunus', in E. Bresciani (ed.), *Scritti in onore di Orsolina Montevecchi* (Bologna), 295–315.

Pestman, P. W. (1983), 'Some aspects of Egyptian law in Graeco-Roman Egypt: title-deeds and ὑπάλλαγμα', in *Egypt and the Hellenistic World* (Studia Hellenistica XXVII; Louvain), 281–302.

Pestman, P. W. (1985a), 'Fûreter dans les papiers de Totoês: archives familiales grecques-démotiques de Turin', in *Textes et études de papyrologie grecque, démotique, et copte* (Pap.Lugd.Bat. XXIII; Leiden), 144–8.

Pestman, P. W. (1985b), 'Lo scriba privato Amenothes, figlio di Panas (tre documenti provenienti dall' archivio di Totoes', in *Textes et études de papyrologie grecque, démotique, et copte* (Pap.Lugd.Bat. XXIII; Leiden), 167–97.

Pestman, P. W. (1995a), 'Appearance and reality in written contracts: evidence from bilingual family archives', in M. J. Geller and H. Maehler (eds.), *Legal Documents of the Hellenistic World* (London), 79–87.

Pestman, P. W. (1995b), 'Haronnophris and Chaonnophris: two indigenous pharaohs in Ptolemaic Egypt (205–186 BC)', in S. P. Vleeming (ed.), *Hundred-Gated Thebes: Acts of a Colloquium on Thebes and the Theban area in the Graeco-Roman Period* (Pap.Lugd.Bat. xxvii; Leiden), 101–37.

Petrie, W. M. F. (1889), *Hawara, Biahmu, and Arsinoe* (London).

Petrie, W. M. F. (1911), *Roman Portraits and Memphis (IV)* (London).

Pomeroy, S. B. (1977), '*Technikai kai mousikai*: the education of women in the fourth century and in the Hellenistic period', *American Journal of Ancient History* 2, 51–68.

Pomeroy, S. B. (1986), 'Copronyms and the exposure of infants in Egypt', in W. V. Harris and R. S. Bagnall (eds), *Studies in Roman Law in Memory of A. Arthur Schiller* (Leiden), 147–62.

Pomeroy, S. B. (1988), 'Women in Roman Egypt', *Aufstieg und Niedergang der römischen Welt* II 10.1 (Berlin-New York), 708–23.

Pomeroy, S. B. (1990), *Women in Hellenistic Egypt: from Alexander to Cleopatra* (revised edn; Detroit).

Pomeroy, S. B. (1994), *Xenophon, Oeconomicus: A Social and Historical Commentary* (Oxford).

Préaux, C. (1939), *L'économie royale des lagides* (Brussels).

Préaux, C. (1959), 'Le statut de la femme à l'époque hellénistique, principalement en Egypte', *Recueils de la Société Jean Bodin XI: La Femme* (Brussels), 127–75.

Purcell, N. (1986), 'Livia and the womanhood of Rome', *Proc. Camb. Philol. Soc.* n.s. 32, 77–105.

Quaegebeur, J. (1978a), 'Mummy labels: an orientation', in *Textes grecs, démotiques et bilingues* (Pap.Lugd.Bat. xix; Leiden), 232–59 (Appendix F).

Quaegebeur, J. (1978b), 'Reines ptolémaïques et traditions égyptiennes', in H. Maehler and V. M. Strocka (eds.), *Das ptolemäische Ägypten* (Mainz), 245–62.

Quaegebeur, J. (1988), 'Cleopatra VII and the cults of the Ptolemaic queens', in R. Bianchi (ed.), *Cleopatra's Egypt: Age of the Ptolemies* (New York), 41–54.

Quaegebeur, J., Clarysse W. and Van Maele, B. (1985), 'Athena, Neith and Thoeris in Greek documents', *ZPE* 60, 217–32.

Rathbone, D. W. (1983), 'The weight and measurement of Egyptian grains', *ZPE* 53, 265–78.

Rathbone, D. W. (1990), 'Villages, land and population in Graeco-Roman Egypt', *Proc. Camb. Philol. Soc.* ns 36, 103–42.

Rathbone, D. W. (1991), *Economic Rationalism and Rural Society in Third-century AD Egypt: the Heroninos Archive and the Appianus Estate* (Cambridge).

Rathbone, D. W. (1996), 'Monetisation, not price-inflation, in third-century AD Egypt?', in C. E. King and D. G. Wigg (eds.), *Coin Finds and Coin Use in the Roman World: the Thirteenth Oxford Symposium on Coinage and Monetary History* (Studien zu Fundmünzen der Antike X; Berlin), 321–39.

Ray, J. D. (1976), *The Archive of Hor* (London).

Ray, J. D. (1987), 'Phrases in dream-texts', in S. P. Vleeming (ed.), *Aspects of Demotic Lexicography* (Leuven), 85–93.

Ray, J. D. (1994), 'Hatshepsut, the female pharaoh', *History Today* 44.5 (May), 23–9.

Rea, J. R. (1985), review of M. Drew-Bear, *Le Nome Hermopolite, sites et toponymes* in *JEA* 71 (Reviews Supplement), 68–70.

Rea, J. (1989), 'On κηρυκίνη: P.Heid. IV 334, P.Köln VI 279, and CPR I 232', *ZPE* 79, 201–6.

Reymond, E. A. E. (1981), ed., *From the Records of a Priestly Family from Memphis* I (Äg. Abh. XXXVIII; Wiesbaden).

Reymond, E. A. E. and Barns, J. W. B. (1973), *Four Martyrdoms from the Pierpont Morgan Coptic Codices* (Oxford).

Riccobono, S. (1950), *Il Gnomon dell'Idios Logos* (Palermo).

Riddle, J. M. (1992), *Contraception and Abortion from the Ancient World to the Renaissance* (Cambridge).

Ritner, R. K. (1984), 'A Uterine amulet in the Oriental Institute collection', *Journal of Near Eastern Studies* 43, 209–21.

Ritner, R. K. (1995), 'Egyptian magical practice under the Roman Empire', *Aufstieg und Niedergang der römischen Welt* II 18.5 (Berlin–New York), 3333–79.

Robins, G. (1993), *Women in Ancient Egypt* (London).

Root, M. C. (1979), *Faces of Immortality: Egyptian Mummy Masks, Painted Portraits and Canopic Jars in the Kelsey Museum of Archaeology* (Ann Arbor).

Rostovtzeff, M. (1922), *A Large Estate in Egypt in the Third Century B.C.* (Madison, WI).

Rousseau, P. (1985), *Pachomius: the Making of a Community in Fourth-Century Egypt* (Berkeley–Los Angeles).

Rowlandson, J. L. (1981), 'Sales of land in their social context', in *Proceedings of the XVI International Congress of Papyrology* (Am.Stud.Pap. XXIII; Chico, CA), 371–8.

Rowlandson, J. L. (1995), 'Beyond the polis: women and economic opportunity in early Ptolemaic Egypt', in A. Powell (ed.), *The Greek World* (London), 301–22.

Rowlandson, J. L. (1996), *Landowners and Tenants in Roman Egypt: the Social Relations of Agriculture in the Oxyrhynchite Nome* (Oxford).

Saller, R. P. (1994), *Patriarchy, Property and Death in the Roman Family* (Cambridge).

Samuel, A. E. (1965), 'The role of *paramone* clauses in ancient documents', *Journal of Juristic Papyrology* 15, 221–311.

Samuel, A. E. (1989), *The Shifting Sands of History: Interpretations of Ptolemaic Egypt* (Lanham, MD).

Sanders, H. A. (1933), 'A Bilingual Request for Appointment of a Guardian', *Aegyptus* 13, 169–75.

Sandy, D. B. (1989), *The Production and Use of Vegetable Oils in Ptolemaic Egypt* (BASP Supp. VI; Atlanta, GA).

Sauneron, S. (1959), *Les songes et leur interprétation* (Paris).

Schaps, D. (1979), *The Economic Rights of Women in Ancient Greece* (Edinburgh).

Scheidel, W. (1995), 'Incest revisited: three notes on the demography of sibling marriage in Roman Egypt', *BASP* 32, 143–55.

Scheidel, W. (1996), *Measuring Sex, Age and Death in the Roman Empire: Explorations in Ancient Demography* (JRA Supp. 21, Ann Arbor).

Schneemelcher, W. (1991), ed., *New Testament Apocrypha* II, English translation, R. McL. Wilson (Cambridge–Louisville).

Schneider, H. D. (1982), *Beelden van Behnasa: Egyptische kunst uit de Romeinse Keizertijd 1e-3e eeuw na Chr.* (Zutphen).

Scholl, R. (1983), *Sklaverei in den Zenonpapyri. Eine Untersuchung zu den Sklaventermini, zum Sklavenerwerb und zur Sklavenflucht* (Trier).

Scholl, R. (1990), *Corpus der ptolemäischen Sklaventexte*, 3 vols. (Stuttgart).

Schwartz, J. (1962), 'En marge du dossier d'Apollonios le stratège', *Chronique d'Egypte* 37, 348–58.

Schwartz, J. and Wild, M. (1950), *Fouilles Franco-Suisses I: Qasr Qarun/Dionysias (1948)* (Cairo).

Scott, J. W. (1986), 'Gender: a useful category of historical analysis', *American Historical Review* 91.4, 1053–75.

Sealey, R. (1986), *Women and Law in Classical Greece* (Chapel Hill–London).

Sebesta, J. L. and Bonfante, L. (1994), *The World of Roman Costume* (Madison).

Sethe, K. (1913), 'Sarapis und die sogenannten κάτοχοι des Sarapis', *Abhandlungen Göttingen* II 14.5 (Berlin).

Shaw, B. (1992), 'Brother–sister marriage in Graeco-Roman Egypt', *Man* 27, 267–99.

Sijpesteijn, P. J. (1976), 'A happy family?', *ZPE* 21, 169–81.

Solmsen, F. (1979), *Isis Among the Greeks and Romans* (Cambridge, MA).

Speidel, M. P. (1985), 'Furlough in the Roman army', in N. Lewis (ed.), *Yale Classical Studies* 28 (= *Papyrology*), 283–93.

Spiegelberg, W. (1906–8), *Die demotischen Papyrus* (Catalogue général des antiquités égyptiennes du Musée du Caire) (Strassburg), vols. I p. 88 and II plates 44–7.

Spiegelberg, W. (1911), 'Aus der Strassburger Sammlung demotischer Ostraka', *ZÄS* 49, 34–41.

Staden, H. von (1989), *Herophilus: the Art of Medicine in Early Alexandria* (Cambridge).

Stead, M. (1981), 'The high priest of Alexandria and all Egypt', in *Proceedings of the XVI International Congress of Papyrology* (Am. Stud. Pap. XXIII: Chico, CA), 411–18.

Storch, A. and Heichelheim, F. (1931), 'Zum Traumglauben und Traumverständnis der Antike', *Zentralblatt für Psychotherapie* 4, 559–69.

Tait, W. J. (1992), 'Demotic literature and Egyptian society', in J. H. Johnson ed. (1992), 303–10.

Tait, W. J. (1994), 'Egyptian fiction in Demotic and Greek', in J. R. Morgan and R. Stoneman (eds.), *Greek Fiction: the Greek Novel in Context* (London), 203–22.

Tait, W. J. (1996), 'Demotic literature: forms and genres', in A. Loprieno (ed.), *Ancient Egyptian Literature: History and Forms* (Leiden), 175–87.

Temkin, O. (1991), trans., *Soranus' Gynecology* (pb reprint of the 1956 edn; Baltimore).

Thomas, J. D. (1976), 'The date of the revolt of L. Domitius Domitianus', *ZPE* 22, 253–86.

Thompson, D. B. (1973), *Ptolemaic Oinochoai and Portraits in Faience. Aspects of the Ruler Cult* (Oxford).

Thompson, D. J. (1983), 'Nile grain transport under the Ptolemies', in P. Garnsey et al. (eds.), *Trade in the Ancient Economy* (London), 64–75, 190–92.

Thompson, D. J. (1987), 'Ptolemaios and "The Lighthouse": Greek culture in the Memphite Serapeum', *Proc. Camb. Philol. Soc.* n.s. 33, 105–21.

Thompson, D. J. (1988), *Memphis under the Ptolemies* (Princeton).

Thompson, D. J. (1994), 'Literacy and power in Ptolemaic Egypt', in A. K. Bowman and G. Woolf (eds.), *Literacy and Power in the Ancient World* (Cambridge), 67–83.

Till, W. C. (1948), 'Die koptischen Eheverträge', in *Die Österreichische National-bibliothek: Festschrift für Josef Beck* (Vienna), 627–38.

Till, W. C. (1954), *Erbrechtliche Untersuchungen auf Grund der koptischen Urkunden* (Vienna).

Tran Tam Tinh, V. (1973), *Isis Lactans. Corpus des monuments gréco-romains d'Isis allaitant Harpocrate* (EPRO 37; Leiden).

Turner, E. G. (1980), *Greek Papyri* (2nd edn; Oxford).

Turner, E. G. (1982), 'The Graeco-Roman Branch', in T. G. H. James (ed.), *Excavating in Egypt: the Egypt Exploration Society, 1882–1982* (London), ch. 9.

Turner, E. G. (1984), 'Ptolemaic Egypt' in F. W. Walbank (ed.), *Cambridge Ancient History*, VII.1 (2nd edn; Cambridge), ch. 5.

Turton, G. (1974), *The Syrian Princesses. The Women who Ruled Rome A.D. 193–235* (London).

Tyldesley, J. (1994), *Daughters of Isis: Women of Ancient Egypt* (Harmondsworth).

Vandoni, M. (1964), *Feste pubbliche e private nei documenti greci* (Milan).

Vandoni, M. (1974), *I documenti di Trifone* (Milan).

Vandoni, M. (1975), 'Dall'archivio del tessitore Trifone', *Proceedings of the XIV International Congress of Papyrologists* (London), 331–6.

Veenhof, K. R. (1983), ed., *Schrijvend Verleden* (Leiden).

Vogelsang-Eastwood, G. (1994), *De Kleren van de Farao* (Amsterdam).

Wagner, G. and Quaegebeur, J. (1973), 'Une dédicace grecque au dieu égyptien Mestasytmis de la part de son synode', *BIFAO* 73, 41–60.

Walker, S. and Bierbrier, M. (1997), *Ancient Faces: Mummy Portraits from Roman Egypt*.

Walther, W. (1981), *Woman in Islam* (Leipzig).

Watson, A. (1966), 'The identity of Sarapio, Socrates, Longus and Nilus in the will of C. Longinus Castor', *The Irish Jurist* 1, 313–15.

Weingärtner, D. G. (1969), *Die Ägyptenreise des Germanicus* (Pap.Texte Abh. XI; Bonn).

Westermann, W. L. (1932), 'Entertainment in the villages of Graeco-Roman Egypt', *JEA* 18, 16–27.

Westermann, W. L. (1948), 'The *paramone* as a general service contract', *Journal of Juristic Papyrology* 2, 9–50.

White, J. L. (1986), *Light from Ancient Letters* (Philadelphia).

Whitehorne, J. E. G. (1984), 'Tryphon's second marriage (*P.Oxy.* II 267)', in *Atti del XVII congresso internazionale di papirologia* III (Naples), 1267–74.

Whitehorne, J. E. G. (1994), *Cleopatras* (London).

Wilcken, U. (1906), 'Zu den Genfer Papyri', *Archiv* III, 369–75.

Wilfong, T. G. (forthcoming(a)), *The Women of Jême: Gender and Society in a Coptic Town in Early Islamic Egypt* (Ann Arbor).

Wilfong, T. G. (forthcoming(b)), 'Synchronous menstruation and the "Place of Women" in Ancient Egypt: Hieratic Ostracon Oriental Institute Museum 13512', in E. Teeter and J. Larson (eds.), *Gold of Praise: Studies on Ancient Egypt in Honor of Edward F. Wente* (Chicago).

Will, E. (1979–82), *Histoire politique du monde hellénistique (323–30 av. J.-C.)* vols. I–II (2nd edn; Nancy).

Winkler, J. J. (1990), *The Constraints of Desire: the Anthropology of Sex and Gender in Ancient Greece* (New York).

Winter, J. G. (1933), *Life and Letters in the Papyri* (Ann Arbor).

Winter, E. (1977), 'Das Kalabscha-Tor in Berlin', *Jahrbuch Preußischer Kulturbesitz* 14, 59–71.

Wipszycka, E. (1965), *L'industrie textile dans l'Egypte romaine* (Wroclaw–Warsaw–Krakow).

Wipszycka, E. (1972), *Les ressources et les activités des églises en Egypte du IVe au VIIIe siècle* (Pap.Brux. x; Brussels).

Witt, R.E. (1971), *Isis in the Graeco-Roman World* (London).

Wolff, H. J. (1979), 'Neue Juristische Urkunden v: Eine neue Quelle zum Eindringen römischen Rechts in Ägypten', *ZSS(RA)* 96, 258–68.

Wyke, M. (1992), 'Augustan Cleopatras: female power and poetic authority', in A. Powell (ed.), *Roman Poetry and Propaganda in the Age of Augustus* (London), 98–140.

Youtie, H. C. (1971), 'Βραδέως γράφων: Between literacy and illiteracy', *Greek, Roman, and Byzantine Studies* 12, 161–76 (= *Scriptiunculae* II, Amsterdam 1973, 629–51).

Youtie, H. C. (1975a), '"Ἀπάτορες": Law vs. Custom in Roman Egypt', *Le Monde Grec . . . Hommages à Claire Préaux* (Brussels) 723–40 (= *Script. Post.* I, Bonn 1981, 17–34).

Youtie, H. C. (1975b), 'Questions to a Christian Oracle', *ZPE* 18, 253–7 (= *Script. Post.* I, Bonn 1981, 225–9).

Youtie, H. C. (1976), 'Paniskos and his wife's name', *ZPE* 21, 193–8 (= *Script. Post.* I, Bonn 1981, 307–10).

Zauzich, K.-Th. (1968), *Die ägyptische Schreibertradition in Aufbau, Sprache und Schrift der demotischen Kaufverträge aus ptolemäischer Zeit*, vol. I (Äg. Abh. XIX; Wiesbaden).

Zauzich, K.-Th. (1978), *Demotische Papyri aus den staatlichen Museen zu Berlin* I: *Papyri von der Insel Elephantine* (Berlin).

Zauzich, K.-Th. (1983), 'Demotische Texte römischer Zeit', in G. Grimm, H. Heinen, E. Winter (eds.), *Das römisch-byzantinische Ägypten, Akten des internationalen Symposions 26–30 September 1978 in Trier* (Aegypt.Trev. II; Trier), 77–80.

Index